Understanding Research in
Personal Relationships

Understanding Research in Personal Relationships

A Text with Readings

William Dragon and Steve Duck

SAGE Publications
London ● Thousand Oaks ● New Delhi

Editorial Arrangement and Chapter 1 © William Dragon and
Steve Duck 2005

First published 2005

SAGE Publications Ltd
1 Oliver's Yard
55 City Road
London EC1Y 1SP

SAGE Publications Inc.
2455 Teller Road
Thousand Oaks, California 91320

SAGE Publications India Pvt Ltd
B-42, Panchsheel Enclave
Post Box 4109
New Delhi 110 017

British Library Cataloguing in Publication data

A catalogue record for this book is available
from the British Library

ISBN 0 7619 4221 1
ISBN 0 7619 4222 X (pbk)

Library of Congress Control Number available

Typeset by C&M Digitals (P) Ltd., Chennai, India
Printed in Great Britain by Cromwell Press Ltd, Trowbridge, Wiltshire

To Deidre, Will and Amanda – with love
WD

To Joanna, Ben and Gabriel – with love
SD

Contents

Acknowledgements

The editors and the publisher wish to thank the following for permission to use copyright material and extracts:

Chapter Two: ATTRACTION
Donn Byrne (1997) An overview (and underview) of research and theory within the attraction paradigm. *Journal of Social and Personal Relationships, 14* (3), 417–431 © 1997 Sage Publications.

Susan Sprecher & Steve Duck (1994) Sweet Talk: The importance of perceived communication for romantic and friendship attraction experienced during a get-acquainted date. *Personality and Social Psychology Bulletin, 20* (4), 391–400 © 1994 Society for Personality and Social Psychology, Inc.

Chapter Three: LOVE
Clyde Hendrick, Susan Hendrick, Franklin H. Foote & Michelle J. Slapion-Foote (1984) Do men And women love differently? *Journal of Social and Personal Relationships, 1*, 177–95 © 1984, SAGE Publications.

Nancy K. Grote & Irene H. Frieze (1998) 'Remembrance of things past': Perceptions of marital love from its beginnings to the present. *Journal of Social and Personal Relationships 15* (1), 91–109 © 1998, SAGE Publications.

Susan S. Hendrick & Clyde Hendrick (2002) Linking romantic love with sex: Development of the perceptions of love and sex scale. *Journal of Social and Personal Relationships, 19* (3), 361–78 © 2002, SAGE Publications.

Chapter Four: SEXUALITY
Susan Sprecher, Kathleen McKinney, & Terri L. Orbuch (1987) Has the double standard disappeared? An experimental test. *Social Psychology Quarterly, 50* (1), 24–31 © 1987, American Sociological Association.

Robin R. Milhausen & Edward S. Herold (1999) Does the sexual double standard still exist? Perceptions of university women. *Journal of Sex Research, 36* (4), 361–368 © 1999, Society for the Scientific Study of Sexuality.

Chapter Five: RELATIONSHIP DEVELOPMENT
Leslie A. Baxter (1992) Root metaphors in accounts of developing romantic relationships. *Journal of Social and Personal Relationships, 9*, 253–275 1992, SAGE Publications.

Dan Weigel & Colleen Murray (2000) The paradox of stability and change in relationships: What does chaos theory offer for the study of romantic relationships? *Journal of Social and Personal Relationships*, *17* (3), 425–449 © 2000, SAGE Publications.

Chapter Six: SOCIAL POWER
Susan Sprecher (1985) Sex differences in bases of power in dating relationships. *Sex Roles*, *12*, 449–462 © 1985, Plenum Publishing Corporation.

Toni Falbo, & Letitia Anne Peplau (1980) Power strategies in intimate relationships. *Journal of Personality and Social Psychology, 38,* 618–628 © 1980, The American Psychological Association.

Chapter Seven: RELATIONAL MAINTENANCE
Kathryn Dindia & Leslie A. Baxter (1987) Strategies for maintaining and repairing marital relationships. *Journal of Social and Personal Relationships 4*, 143–158 © 1987, SAGE Publications.

Jill Gilbertson, Kathryn Dindia & Mike Allen (1997) Relational continuity constructional units and the maintenance of relationships. *Journal of Social Personal Relationships*, *15* (6), 774–790 © 1998, SAGE Publications.

Marianne Dainton (2000) Maintenance behaviors, expectations for maintenance, and satisfaction: Linking comparison levels to relational maintenance strategies. *Journal of Social and Personal Relationships*, *17* (6), 827–842 © 2000, SAGE Publications.

Chapter Eight: JEALOUSY
Gregory L. White (1980) Inducing jealousy: A power perspective. *Personality and Social Psychology Bulletin*, *6* (2), 222–227 © 1980, Society for Personality and Social Psychology, Inc.

Bram P. Buunk, Alois Angleitner, Viktor Oubaid & David M. Buss (1996) Sex differences in jealousy in evolutionary and cultural perspective: Tests from the Netherlands, Germany, and the United States. *Psychological Science*, *7* (6), 359–363 © 1996, American Psychological Society,

Chapter Nine: CONFLICT IN RELATIONSHIPS
Linda K. Acitelli, Elizabeth Douvan & Joseph Veroff (1993) Perceptions of conflict in the first year of marriage: How important are similarity and understanding? *Journal of Social and Personal Relationships*, *10*, 5–19 © 1993, SAGE Publications.

David L. Vogel & Benjamin R. Karney (2002) Demands and withdrawal in newlyweds: Elaborating on the social structure hypothesis. *Journal of Social and Personal Relationships*, *19*, 685–701 © 2002, SAGE Publications.

Chapter Ten: RELATIONSHIP DISTURBANCE
Leslie A. Baxter (1984) Trajectories of relationship disengagement. *Journal of Social and Personal Relationships*, *1*, 29–48 © 1984, SAGE Publications.

Sandra Metts, William R. Cupach & Richard A. Bejlovec (1989) 'I love you too much to ever start liking you': Redefining romantic relationships. *Journal of Social and Personal Relationships*, *6*, 259–274 © 1989, SAGE Publications.

Duck, S.W. (1982) A topography of relationship disengagement and dissolution. In S.W. Duck (Ed.) *Personal relationships 4: Dissolving personal relationships* Figure 2 from Duck (1982) © Academic Press.

Chapter Eleven: LONELINESS
Brian H. Spitzberg and Daniel J. Canary (1985) Loneliness and relationally competent communication. *Journal of Social and Personal Relationships*, *2*, 387–402 © 1985, SAGE Publications.

Lars Tornstam (1992) Loneliness in marriage. *Journal of Social and Personal Relationships*, *9*, 197–217 © 1992, SAGE Publications.

Chapter Twelve: THE IMPORTANCE OF SOCIAL NETWORKS
Robert M. Milardo & Barry Wellman (1992) The personal is social. *Journal of Social and Personal Relationships*, *9*, 339–342 © 1992, SAGE Publications.

Robert M. Milardo (1992) Comparative methods for delineating social networks. *Journal of Social and Personal Relationships*, *9*, 447–461 © 1992, Sage Publications.

Graham Allan (1998) Friendship, sociology and social structure. *Journal of Social and Personal Relationships*, *15*, 5, 685–702 © 1998, SAGE Publications.

Chapter Thirteen: CYBER RELATIONSHIPS
Malcolm R. Parks & Kory Floyd (1996) Making friends in cyberspace. *Journal of Communication*, *46*, 1, 80–97 © 1998, SAGE Publications.

Malcolm R. Parks & Lynne D. Roberts (1998) 'Making MOOsic': the development of personal relationships on line and a comparison to their off-line counterparts. *Journal of Social and Personal Relationships*, *15*, 4, 517–537 © 1998, SAGE Publications.

1 Reading Research on Relationships

Anyone wanting to read a book on relationships already brings a lot of expertise from the many relationships seen in life – for example, with caregivers, perhaps siblings, and friendships. You may have been in romances, some of which did and some of which did not work out as you planned. We all know a lot about relationships from these common experiences; in particular we know that they are good when they work and bad when they do not.

Nevertheless, we may not know *why* they work or what can prevent them going wrong. How do relationships start? What makes them develop? How can they go wrong? What about sex? And loneliness? And enemies? And alliances? Is it true that similarity is essential for relationships or do opposites attract?

In addressing some of these matters we can look inside ourselves for things that appear to be true from our own experience. Alternatively, we can ask other people and compare notes, or we can interrogate "common sense" or our cultural belief system as enshrined in magazine quizzes, for example ("Ten ways to improve your friendships", "Does he really care? Twelve key signs", "Divorce the easy way: pitfalls to avoid", "15 tips for livening up your sex life", "Six sophisticated options for a fab first date"). We've all read them, or at least we have friends of cousins of ours who have told us about them!

The trouble is that our own intuitions, our friends' advice, and the comments in magazines might be wrong. After all, the "experts" in magazines merely fifty years ago were just famous people who were willing to let everyone know their opinions. More recently the experts have been people with some credentials, like good therapists or famously insightful observers who have written books. Nowadays the advice in magazines tends to rely on the ideas of people with PhDs and some of them even do research that is of high quality. But why should we believe *them*?

The ultimate answer to questions like these will be found through research that strips away the personal opinions of gurus and common sense and finds out what is actually true in the population at large. Anyone can do research. You set out with a question and you look into it. You then come up with an answer that is based on research. The more carefully you do the research the more confident you might be of the value of your answer.

The problem is that research – good research, that is – is not only challenging to do but quite rare; common sense opinions are much more frequently the basis for beliefs about relationships. There are huge numbers of ways to do research badly and for you to become confident in the answers that you rely upon, you must be sure that the research was asking the right questions, was well done, informative, conducted in a sensible and reasonable way, and was interpreted correctly.

As you learn to read and understand research and to comprehend what it tells you and what it does not, you, as a reader interested in questions about relationships, need to know how to avoid being misled by glib research. You need to understand what questions to ask about a research report, study design, interpretation of a set of results, and so on, so that you can confidently trust the conclusions that are offered for you.

One goal of this book, then, is to show you some of the ways in which that set of critical reading skills can be acquired as part of your learning about the nature of relationships. As we introduce new topics in the study of relationships, we will also show you how the research was done on that topic and we will teach you some ways to examine that research critically and carefully. We will also show you how the research developed across time, starting with a classic report and moving along to more recent work. Thus we focus on fostering readers' critical skills in such areas as recognizing themes from different theoretical positions, noting how research develops, and observing the "course corrections" that are made in ideas during the evolution of scientific inquiry.

The skills that you will acquire as you are led through this material by our editorial comments will therefore not be restricted to only a greater understanding of the topics that have been researched but will develop your detailed understanding of how to *evaluate* such research. This skill should be generalizable: you will learn not only how to do specific critical assessment of the papers that we have selected for you here, but also the broader skills that will be useful when you read other papers and reports in the future, whether about relationships or any other topics. You will develop the ability to comment on reports that you see in the media, or to add wise observations to comments made by friends and colleagues about relationship issues. You might even be able to apply your expertise in the workplace later on, as you think about ways to solve relationship problems at work!

Start with an interesting question

The thing that guides all of your research is a question that interests you. The first step in any research then depends on you being able to identify and formulate a sensible question in a way that can be researched. The question "Does similarity make relationships work?", for example, is an interesting question, but it is so broad and general that you cannot really begin to study it until you have decided what sort of similarity you mean and how you are going to measure it. Not only that, but you also have to decide what you mean by "work": how will you base your decisions about whether similarity is effective, what will you compare its effects with, and how much "better" does it have to work before you will conclude that it is "what makes relationships work"? And what kind of relationships anyway? Marriage? Friendship? Child–parent relationships? Work relationships? Customer–business relationships? What? And how many studies are you going to do before you decide you have gathered enough evidence to answer the question? On what sorts of people should you try your question? Does age or sex of the people matter? Might only some sorts of similarity work for only some ages of people in only some kinds of relationships …?

Don't worry! These sorts of thoughts come to mind pretty easily as soon as you start to look further into any general question that you want to research. As soon as some of these things come to your mind you have already begun researching, because a very large part of any research is simply thinking carefully about the central question and the terms within the question. And another encouraging thing is that you are not alone in coming to grips with this.

Next step: the history

If you want to know the answer to some question – let's say, the question of whether opposites attract – it may just happen that you are the first person ever in the history of the world to ask it. More likely someone else thought of it first. (Sorry! That's life.) In that case, to save yourself all the trouble of doing a lot of experiments and research yourself, you should always start by finding out what previous thinkers have suggested and what other researchers have done. You might find some good ideas there or you might find that you have a better idea than they had and that you can develop their research more thoroughly as a result. It is always worth finding out first, though, so research begins with a germ of an idea, an interesting question, and then a search through the archives of previous research.

One thing that you will learn from this book, then, is how the development of research occurs as a result of examination of previous research activity by other scholars and its later refinements by researchers. One researcher might start the ball rolling by asking the simple question "Do opposites attract?" and would then be faced with the first issue that researchers must deal with: "How can I make that question researchable?" In technical terms, this is the issue of **operationalizing** a key concept. A researcher could do a study on this particular question by looking at whether, for example, a short person tends to partner a tall one. In this case we would say that the researcher had **operationalized** the notion of oppositeness (or complementarity) through the construct of "comparisons of height" and that is not the only way to operationalize oppositeness or complementarity. Someone may come along later and say it is not height that matters so much as "personality", and they do a study on whether a dominant person tends to partner a submissive one. They operationalize the construct of complementarity through the assessment of matching of personality. Someone may then come along later and say it is not personality, in terms of broad traits like dominance, that matters in determining whether opposites attract but rather it is a matter of whether the two people have complementary styles in solving arguments. So that person goes off and does a study on that. By observing and learning about such reactions to and developments from previous research we reach a clearer understanding, at least in the ideal case, of the broad question that we sought to understand. We also observe that the operationalization of the key construct can be different in different studies, making comparison between them more complicated, and this is one of the first things that an intelligent consumer of research looks at: the operationalization of the key constructs.

As you read the coming chapters, then, think carefully about, take notes, and reserve for class discussion, the matter of how the researchers operationalized the key constructs. Careful attention to this issue in itself makes you a more subtle reader of research and will significantly enhance your understanding of what a piece of research tells you, if anything. Also, as you read, you need to be evaluating how the researchers have done their review of the topic. The first part of a journal article is the review of the history of the topic, a place where the authors establish the warrant for their own work by explaining why people find this topic interesting, what they have done about it, and what questions remain to be understood. As you read this part of an article, you need to be thinking generally about whether the position sounds persuasive, interesting, insightful, enlightening, leading to something you want to know the answer to, and so forth. Do not assume that this review is the only way that the topic can be reviewed. What might the authors have left out? Do they have some sort of axe to grind? Does it feel as if they have represented the other research well? (In many cases you will not really know, but you can take a guess.) Above all, do not be afraid to register and note your criticisms of their arguments if you have any.

After you have formed an idea about how the key constructs have been operationalized, you probably have a reasonable idea of what to study and how it can be investigated. At this point, then, comes the Big Issue: is it all a matter of specific prediction of what will be found in the research or just "take it as it comes and see whatever you get"? Is it "I wonder if it will rain tomorrow. Let's see." or is it more specified, such as "Tomorrow we will have showers and thunderstorms"?

Sometimes we might just be interested in finding something out that we simply do not know, for example whether people who go out for a pizza have better dates than people who go out to the movies, but we aren't really sure which way it will turn out because there are no solidly based theoretical reasons for assuming that one rather than the other causes better dates. In that case we pose a general **Research Question** (**RQ**): Do pizzas make dates go better than movies dates? Whatever our research finds, it should add something to our general understanding: we didn't know anything about the relative effects of pizzas and movies before the research, but after it we'll know some basic facts.

On other occasions we might have a reason for believing that things will turn out a particular way, and this idea might be solidly based on theory. For example, we might think that couples who talk about their conflictive issues by listening carefully to one another and reflecting back the other person's remarks might have a better chance of solving their conflicts than do people who do not listen to one another (Acitelli et al., 1997). In this case we state a **hypothesis** and it is **directional**, that is to say, it specifically predicts the way that we expect things to work out: couples who listen will be more satisfied than couples who do not listen. If things do not come out exactly that way, then our research will have shown that the theory on which we based our hypothesis is not supported by our research.

Most of the research that you will read in the rest of this book will be the second approach. There has been enough previous research on key questions in relationships that we know the basic facts and figures – the pieces of the jigsaw – and we are now trying to understand how the pieces fit together exactly. Therefore, most of the research articles will present a clear hypothesis and will report the results of testing it. Once in a while the studies add a new question and state it as RQ because the authors of the paper do not know what to expect or predict, but most of the time the reports are designed specifically to test the value of theoretical assumptions and so will state the hypothesis clearly and test it directly.

Whether the test is a good one is, of course, something you will be learning to assess. Again in reading research you should not feel shy about critique. Even published research can have oversights or omissions that can be spotted if you read thoughtfully.

Some basic issues in design and analysis

Given the above, the next thing that you (as an intelligent consumer of research) need to think about is at another level of expertise. You need to assess the quality of the design and execution of the study that was intended to test the hypothesis that was stated. So how do you go about doing that?

Usually any study of events in the world presents us with a combination of two things that seem to be relevant to one another. For example, we see people dressing up and going to parties and we later see them coming out in pairs that are different from the groupings that went in. We might also observe that people kiss more in public at night than in the daytime, especially on the way out of parties. Having observed the combination of events we then need to decide whether one element *causes* the other. Do parties cause kissing? Do parties cause people to pair up differently from the groupings that went into them? Does similarity cause attraction? Do pizzas cause dates to be enjoyable?

We all want to know what causes things to happen and unfortunately we cannot always tell that merely from observing that two things usually happen together. For example, from the observation that people on first dates often go to the movies we cannot assume that movies cause people to go on first dates. On the other hand, from the fact that people go red when they are embarrassed, we might deduce a workable hypothesis that embarrassment somehow causes redness and we might then devote some research to find out how that causal linkage works exactly.

When a researcher can show that two things go together but does a study that cannot help us to say which causes which, then we talk of a **correlational study**, or a **correlational relationship**. For example, if we find that similarity and liking go together we can only say that they are correlated, until we can definitely show that similarity causes liking, instead of liking causing similarity (which is actually quite a reasonable idea: the more you like someone, the more you might try to be like them). [But see Chapter 2 for a clever way in which one researcher was able to determine the direction of causality in this relationship.] What is "the **direction of causality**"? This means the way in which the relationship between the two things works, e.g., that we can say that A causes B and not the other way about. The search for **causal relationships** as distinct from correlational relationships is what lies at the heart of research. We all want to be able to say that Thing One causes Thing Two to behave in the way that it does.

We have been writing about "things" causing other "things" to happen and it is time that we introduced the more formal term "**variables**". Research in relationships is about variables; that is to say, it is about things that occur in the real world in many different strengths and forms, such as attraction, height, physical beauty, satisfaction, love, and so on. When a scientist finds a variable and can relate its behavior to another variable then you see bliss. A scientist likes to be able to say "Variable A causes Variable B to act in a specific way". Many of the studies that are reported in the rest of this book are devoted to assessing the effects of a given variable on another variable, for instance the effects of conflict on happiness or the effects of social skill on loneliness. In that simple statement you have two sorts of variables. In research the **independent variable** is Variable A, the variable that has an effect, whereas Variable B is the **dependent variable**, the variable that is affected by the other one.

OK, so you now have the idea that research is about the effects of an **independent variable** on a **dependent variable** and that we are, by and large, looking for **causal relationships**. [Not all research is like this, as we shall see, but we will introduce different methods as we go along, rather than do it all here.] So what is next? Well, you have to test the idea on real people. Very often researchers pick on a group of people who happen to be around, and who look like reasonable specimens of the parts of the human race that are relevant to the testing of the hypothesis. Such a convenient group of people chosen for study is usually known as a **convenience sample**. There are many cases where that set of people is a fair choice (for example, if you want to find out how people respond to witnessing an accident, you have to use the people who saw it happen) but in cases where the researcher wants to say something that is true of "all Americans" or "all humans" or "all men" or "all conservatives", it is necessary that the sample is a reasonable representation of the whole group that the researcher wants to understand. Obviously the most accurate way of finding the answer would be to ask all Americans, all humans, all men ... the relevant question but that would not be practical, so researchers just pick on a small sample of people they can actually work with. Thus the **sample** – the group of people who are to be used for the study – has to be **representative** and they will be representative if they are not systematically picked with some special feature (not all of them should be redheads, or left-handed, or dwarfs) since those features are not representative of all people at large. Researchers usually take a lot of trouble to ensure that their sample is **randomly selected**, meaning that they take steps to ensure that no particular biases are systematically built into the sample: it is not mostly left-handers or all sports-players or 90% Republicans or only 18-year-olds, if such features would fail to represent the broad group of people you seek to understand. If you want to understand what makes marriages successful, then you would not want a sample that consisted of unmarried 18-year-olds; if you want to understand how first dates work well, you probably would not want to have a sample that consisted only of parents of 10-year-old children, if you want to understand "romance" then your sample should not just consist of heterosexuals ... and so on; you get the picture.

Having decided on the kind of sample to be used, another issue for investigators is to decide on a **between-subjects design** or a **within-subjects design**. In a within-subjects design, each subject (that is, each individual in the sample) is exposed to two or more experimental conditions during the experiment. For example, the subject might go on a date to a pizza parlor and then go on another date to a movie, rating both experiences so that the researcher can compare everyone's reactions. Since the same person experiences both conditions of the experiment, this sort of design controls for initial differences between the subjects, since each subject is, as it were, his or her own comparison group. There are, however, some problems with a within-subjects design, such as the effects of the *order* in which experimental conditions are experienced; the person might be tired of dating after the first condition (pizza date) and so might be less interested in the movie date anyway, for instance. Can you think of other problems with this sort of design?

The second sort of design – **between-subjects design** – assigns different subjects to different conditions and so the data of different subjects in the different conditions are ultimately what is compared. In such a design the effects of order (or of experience or learning or fatigue – did you get all of those limitations of the within-subjects design?) are eliminated. However, there is a cost, namely that the groups might actually have started out different from one another independently of the conditions experienced in the experiment. Therefore, each design has its limitations that must be dealt with and you should learn to bear them in mind as you read the reports in the rest of the chapters.

We'll illustrate these things more fully as the chapters progress – that, after all, is one purpose of this book – and we have already oriented you broadly to some of the main concepts that will be elaborated as you learn more. One final set of things that we will fill out in more detail, but which you need to understand broadly, before you launch yourself at the research wholesale, concerns the ways in which researchers make decisions about the meaning of their results.

Yes, this stage is about statistics, but do not fear. Statistics are really all about *logic* and so they simply do the same sort of things that we have been talking about already: they give you ways to understand the underlying logic of findings from research and they give you logical ways to make decisions about the meanings of those results. Researchers look for several things in the logic of their statistics and we'll introduce two here: **variance** and **probability**.

When you collect lots of data it tends not to be all the same, whether it is people's shoe sizes, political preferences, or annual income. In short the data varies or contains **variance**. Some subjects will rate the pizza date 7 out of 10 on a 10-point scale, some will rate it 3/10 on that scale, some 10/10, and so on. That variance in scores and ratings is what you work with at this stage of research. The researcher's job is to work out what bits of the variance come about by chance or "error" and how much because of something more interesting. How much of the differences in rating of the pizza date came from the fact that subjects didn't really care or rushed the questionnaire, or couldn't find a meaningful difference between a 3/10 and a 4/10 on the scale – a sort of "what the heck" response. If people didn't find the task meaningful then their scores will vary unsystematically, by chance, as a result of "error". If the differences are meaningful, then the variance will be systematically representative of that fact. People who rated the event 3/10 *really* didn't enjoy it as much as those who rated it 5/10.

Researchers approach this matter of variance with two goals in mind; first to be able to explain the variance in a way consistent with their hypotheses – which basically tells us that researchers really do have a good handle on what makes the data turn out the way it did. Second, they want to be able to explain – or pin down – as much of the variance as they can. If they can explain a higher proportion of the variance using their hypothesis than they can by using some other hypothesis then they go home smiling.

This raises the second topic we will introduce here: **probability**. How do you know that your hypothesis works better than another hypothesis, or better than chance? To make these judgments, the statistical tests are held up against **probability**. In short, researchers ask themselves: how likely is it that the results I got would happen just by pure coincidence? This is the point where researchers talk about (statistical) "significance". A significant result is one that happens *very* rarely just by chance. For example, if a study works with an independent variable and comes up with a result in the dependent variable that you would expect to come across only five times in a 100 by pure chance, then you might be persuaded that the study must have shown that the independent variable really does affect the dependent variable. Logic says that if you alter something and you have the predicted effect that would otherwise only happen extremely rarely, then you have shown that the alteration of the Independent Variable had the predicted effect on the Dependent Variable. In the reports that you read in the rest of this book, such a result will tend to be represented by a report that "the results were significant at the **p < .05 level**". What this means is that the results would have happened less than five in 100 times by pure chance (the results have a chance probability of less than .05, which is 5/100). So when you see a report of the form "$p < .05$" (or $p < .01$ or $p < .001$) it is a shorthand way of saying "this result would happen only five times out of 100 (or 1/100 or 1/1000) by pure chance". In the research that you will read, such a result is regarded as sufficient grounds for believing that the independent variable really does affect the dependent variable, and that the research has shown this to be the case. For this reason, researchers will talk of a result of $p < .05$ as "significant", meaning that it meets the established minimum criterion for demonstrating a relationship. Note that this does not mean the researchers have "proven" that their explanation is correct; there is still a risk that their result may be due to chance alone. It is safer to say that the hypothesis was supported or confirmed and not to say anything at all about "proof". [Watch out for this one when you read newspaper reports about scientific research!]

Note that $p < .05$ is an absolute criterion for significance as accepted in the social sciences. Thus a result either does or does not reach criterion. You can't have a result that nearly makes it; just like in tennis the ball is in or the ball is out; "nearly in" is the same as "out". Unfortunately you will find, even in the papers reprinted in this book, some cases where the researcher falls victim to the strong tendency for all humans to believe that we are right, and so when our results don't quite make it to the criterion, many weaker souls will try to observe that "there is a trend towards significance". However, the $p < .05$ criterion is not a correlation coefficient but a black-and-white in-or-out criterion. When you read papers that say they found a trend, become very skeptical. The researchers are publicly violating their own profession's rules for assessing results, so make sure you write that down in your critiques of such articles.

Although this has been only a brief introduction, it provides enough of a grounding that you can now begin to read some research and not be out of your depth, even though the papers you will read were written for professional researchers. As we go along, you will find that you are getting the hang of it and can understand why the authors say some of the things that they do. But do not let your guard down! They might be saying things that you can criticize on various grounds and you should not hold back.

One more word about the editing of this book. In the last several decades there have been many studies of the influence of sex and gender on relational life and several of the chapters here will present evidence about this. We have been very careful to use the word "sex" when we are talking about the distinction between men and women, biological males and biological females, boys and girls. We use the word "gender" to refer to social roles or to the products of socialization that result in people having masculine or feminine traits.

Masculine traits are most often found in men, feminine traits most often found in women, but there is no necessary consequence here.

Why does this comment matter? Many earlier researchers tended to write about gender when they really measured only sex. Several studies report "gender differences" when the writers never studied that at all; they just used a question about the subjects' sex (men or women) and then reported the results as if they were about gender. This is a serious and misleading error. It would be like measuring a car's speed and assuming that the result told us about the comfortableness of the ride. The two might be connected but you cannot infer one straightforwardly from the other.

Accordingly in all articles here that make this mistake, we have edited all instances of the words to be consistent with the above. If the writers assessed only sex then that is what their article now says; we have changed it from the original. If they properly assessed gender then that is what the article reports and we have left the original as it stood.

Do not be shy about making notes as you read this material. We'll guide you through it and focus you on some key points that occur to us, but as you become increasingly expert in this critique, you should always be confident in your own thoughts and reactions. As your judgments become more sophisticated, so also will your critiques about whether the research is good or could be improved, and you may even go on to think of ways to advance it in the future.

How to use this book

Now let's start to look at some of the questions that researchers have asked about relationships and the ways in which they have tackled them. We will introduce new details that will help you to assess their research as we go along. In addition, each chapter will tackle a different question about relationships and so will magnify your grasp of the sorts of research that are done on a particular topic. Each chapter will introduce more terms and more approaches to research so that, in parallel with learning about new relationship questions, you will also learn more about the techniques and skills that you need to evaluate that research.

We hope it is obvious from the above that the book has a number of pedagogical purposes and will introduce you to two things specifically: topics in relationship research (as many as we can fit in, but not exhaustively!) and also, in the course of doing that, make you more sophisticated readers of research by introducing you to different techniques in research with the pros and cons of using them. This parallel development – different substantive topics in relationship research; research techniques – is intended to make you more critical readers and to increase your learning about the topics as well as your critical abilities in understanding whether the writers are justified in drawing any conclusions that they draw.

The book is composed in such a way that we will raise issues for you to consider about a particular topic (such as jealousy or love or conflict) and we will then steer you to think about those issues as you read the primary research articles that were done about the topics. Our pedagogical goal is to foster your abilities to select the right questions to ask as you read these articles, and then at the end of the articles we will take you back to those issues and see if you agreed with us about what was right and wrong with the article, which questions it settled and which ones still remain. As you go through the book you will get better at this and the task will correspondingly get a little more challenging each time as your learning grows and as you can begin to raise the bar that you can jump, as it were.

In parallel with this growth in your education about the topics themselves and in your critical skills in approaching the topics, we will also challenge you to think about the methods that were used in the various studies, gradually increasing the sophistication of the level at which you understand the methods of research. In each chapter we will raise methodological issues and discuss them with you; we will then move along to the next study that dealt with a topic in a different or more advanced way. To help you along the way, key topics and terms are defined and described in full during the text and are printed in **bold type** throughout the book. A quick reminder about the meaning of these terms can be found in the Glossary at the end of the book. In this way your learning about critique of research will develop another strand.

Finally we will round out each chapter by drawing the threads of the articles together and helping you to see which questions remain to be looked at by future research. By such a means we intend to emphasize the continuing development of research and the importance of critical evaluation of even the most recent work, since that is what researchers do themselves.

By giving the book this basic structure we are able to teach a number of things at once and by selecting articles that offer a wide range of theories and methods we can help educate you about the methodological and theoretical styles and issues that make up the complex array of research that is done. Each chapter assumes the terms and methods that were described in the preceding chapters and so a further sort of progression in your understanding and ability to "consume" research is provided by this structure.

Research can be exciting; reading research can be exciting; the structure of this book and of each of the chapters within it is intended to help you to learn why we believe that research on relationships is so important and how a critical understanding of it can help you to greater insight about your own relationships.

2   Attraction

One of the earliest enterprises undertaken by the first researchers into human relationships was an attempt to understand the things that create initial attraction – the first response that indicates a positive overall attitude to another person and starts the growth of liking and perhaps intimacy. Obviously this is one of the primary activities of relating and we all know the importance of a strong "first impression". Earliest studies focused on the physical characteristics that made someone attractive (Perrin, 1921), but after many years, the focus turned to the psychological characteristics that could lay the foundation for liking and relating (Newcomb, 1956). It is not by any means a new idea that friends tend to be similar psychologically or that we are drawn to similar others more than to dissimilar others. Aristotle is the first writer credited with the observation in Western culture, so the idea goes back at least 2500 years in the human mind. It turns out to be a rather difficult notion to test, however, especially in the laboratory where **causal direction** can be established. Of course we could always measure groups of friends for psychological similarities, but that will not tell us whether the chicken of similarity comes before the egg of friendship or vice versa. In short, such real-life groups would at best provide us with **correlational data** even though we really want to know which causes which. **Correlations** are represented in reports most often with the **r-score**, a statistic that reports the amount of correlation between two variables, thus indicating the strength of their connection and the degree to which they behave in the same way. The r-score can range from −1 to +1, with a negative score representing opposition between the two variables and a positive score indicating that they tend to behave in the same way. Even a score of +1, however, does not show that the behavior of one variable *causes* the behavior of the other; it merely indicates that they are identical in their activity. Thus the researcher can never be certain, using correlational data, which variable causes which to behave in the way that they work and some form of causal method needs to be used instead.

An innovative suggestion was offered by Schachter (1951) and by Smith (1957) and was developed extensively by Donn Byrne (1961, 1971, 1997b), whose name became most closely associated with the idea, even infamously. The technique became known as the Bogus Stranger technique and involves manufacturing similarity between people and then exploring the effects of this similarity on their ratings of liking. We will let Byrne (1997b) describe the technique and its underpinnings in the article reprinted below, but you can no doubt see already that "manufacturing similarity" is going to be the crux of the whole thing and that it is a difficult problem to solve. Having solved it, however, Byrne is able to make the "similarity" into an **independent variable (IV)** so that the resulting levels of attraction and liking become **dependent variables (DV)** in a truly causal design and it is then going to be possible to say how much similarity causes how much liking.

Byrne (1997b, below) presents a very strong – and witty – rendition of the path of the development of his research, in the course of which he addresses some of the critiques that have been leveled at his paradigm. Note that he reports studies that were conducted specifically to address some of the critiques made of his earlier work and that he set out to test the predictions of critics relative to his own predictions from his theory. This is a reasonable way for a scholar to attend to critiques; criticism, debate and discussion of ideas are supposed to be a part of the way in which research and theory develop. Note also that Byrne addresses some of the critiques on logical grounds rather than empirical ones, but also uses empirical tests, so that he brings two guns to his defense: logic and empiricism. As part of his review, Byrne represents the views of critics in ways that suit his own purposes, of course, and although Byrne does this quite fairly in the present article, the critical reader needs to be thinking about problems with the paradigm that might not have been mentioned. Also reflect carefully on the ways in which criticisms are set up, reported and addressed. Consider whether the evidence in favor of a critique is presented as strongly as the evidence for rebuttal. In such a review the author has control over the topics that are introduced, the manner in which a critique is presented, and the overall judgment about the state of things both before and after the critique. Take care to assess these things thoughtfully; always be aware that if you have criticisms of a method or paradigm they could be ones that the author chose not to present or deal with. Why might that be? In some cases the author may have presented new evidence about the paradigm that answers or undermines your critique in such a way that your objection to some feature of the previous methods is now no longer valid. In other cases, the author may not credit your critique or may not have thought of it or ways to answer it. Evaluate for yourself what you think is the most likely option there.

Byrne's theoretical interpretation is built on **classical conditioning** theory, something originally developed by Pavlov in his work on dogs. Pavlov built his work on the dog's **unconditioned response** (i.e., salivation) to food (an **unconditioned stimulus**). This response exists in the natural world and does not have to be trained (or "conditioned"): show a dog food and it starts to salivate. Pavlov found that he could introduce a **conditioned stimulus** (in this case the sound of a bell) to which a dog did not normally respond by salivating in the natural world and, by pairing the sound of the bell with the introduction of food, Pavlov could eventually condition the dog to salivate to the sound of the bell alone. This type of salivation to the sound of the bell was labeled a **conditioned response**. Byrne, who will describe this process in the article below in order to explain why we like people who are similar in attitudes, applied the same idea to attitude similarity from a stranger. He argues that humans are naturally wired to respond affectively (emotionally) to attitude statements (so the natural response – affect – is an **unconditioned response** to an **unconditioned stimulus** – attitude statements). He goes on to claim that when a stranger is associated with attitude statements then the stranger can come to evoke affect (i.e., the stranger serves as a **conditioned stimulus** to produce the **conditioned response** of affect/emotion). When the conditioned response is positive then we label the feeling as "liking" and when the conditioned response is negative, we label the feeling "dislike". [Note that "**affect**" with an "a" means emotion and "**effect**" with an "e" means either, as a verb, to cause or, as a noun, a consequence.] Byrne talks in the article about **controlling for the effects** of [a variable]. This is a reference to the scientific method of taking a situation and holding everything constant except one thing, the thing you are interested in testing. In this case, then, the experimenter controls for the effects of the variable in which he or she has no interest, controlling (that is, holding constant) any effects that those variables are known to have in order that the relevant variable in the study can be studied working on its own.

Since Byrne's is a review paper, it does not take the standard format for an empirical article. Instead the author gives a programmatic overview of his work, beginning with his earliest experiences and his subsequent ways of developing his research towards his major goal. After you have read this article, write down a list of your evaluations and compare them with ours afterwards.

An Overview (and Underview) of Research and Theory within the Attraction Paradigm

Donn Byrne

Over the years, I have frequently sought to describe how a body of research can grow and develop without necessarily encroaching on or being encroached on by the independent efforts of others to investigate the same or similar phenomena. We have offered such analogies as playing in one's own sandbox (Byrne, 1978) and laying out one's own yellow brick road through an opaque forest teeming with lions and tigers and bears (Clore & Byrne, 1974). More recently, while teaching a graduate attraction seminar, I happened upon a magazine ad for Erector Sets depicting a small boy engaged in a construction project, gazing thoughtfully into space. It was a mildly epiphanic moment – the small boy was myself, and the construction process seemed to be an appropriate analogy for building a coherent conceptual model with consistent, connecting operations (Byrne, 1997a). You may be as uninspired by the blinding clarity of this insight as were my students, but at least keep it in mind as we examine the attraction paradigm, past and present.

Planning decades of research in advance?

Even in those blissful days when research funds flowed from what we hoped would be Washington's dedication to a never-ending fountain of truth, there was one aspect of the grant application process that seemed absolutely meaningless to me. The expectation that an investigator should be able to lay out a two-year or three-year research plan simply made no sense; I can describe what has been done, but not what will be done. My applications squeaked by because I pretended to describe 'future research' that had already been conducted but not yet published along with a few unexciting and largely fictional proposals that seldom led anywhere. (If this confession means that I must return the money, I'm only kidding.) In the early stages of most subfields of social psychology and for an individual who is unsure about what he will do this afternoon, there is little to be gained by designing a multi-year plan.

In the early stages of a paradigm, the ideas for any given investigation originate in a wide variety of unexpected sources – personal experiences and concerns (Byrne, 1997a), a student's insight in a seminar (Byrne et al., 1969b), my mother's criticism of presidential candidate George McGovern as being too 'wishy-washy' (Allgeier et al., 1979), or a student's vague interests that can be shaped, Skinner-like, into theoretical relevance (Byrne & Rhamey, 1965). In time (as a paradigm matures) research can be planful and purposeful; examples include hypotheses derived from theory (Smeaton et al., 1989) and the necessity to explain data that seem to be inconsistent with one's existing model (Byrne & Lamberth, 1971).

So, how did the attraction paradigm come to be? For any such endeavor to succeed, two interrelated factors are required: An investigator must be committed to *operational* and *conceptual* consistency (Byrne, 1971). In many scientific fields, that statement would seem banal, obvious, and perhaps insulting; in much of social psychology, that same statement is an almost heretical admission of non-creativity.

The first factor, *operational consistency*, involves a simple, though often ignored rule. When progressing from one study to the next, an investigator should keep constant all operations except the single new element being studied. Francis Bacon alluded to such matters – at the beginning of the 17th century – as a necessity in order to avoid confounding the effects of two or more variables. Oddly enough, our graduate students seem to be taught about confounds within experiments much better than about confounds between experiments.

The second factor, *conceptual consistency*, refers to the need to incorporate any and all relevant findings into one's theoretical framework. Thus, findings should be interrelated not only empirically, but also conceptually. The reason that a given investigator selects a given theoretical approach is not clear, but it seems likely that we each rely in part on untestable meta-theoretical assumptions and in part on more explicit formulations such as learning theory, genetic determination, or cognitive consistency. Whatever the origins of a conceptual formulation, and however much it is elaborated and altered over time, logical consistency is cyclical. Otherwise, science would resemble a child's game in which the rules change from moment to moment to suit the individual player. Sometimes, of course, a finding does not fit the model, and the options include a re-evaluation of the procedures and operations and, if necessary, a modification and expansion of the theoretical structure in order to take account of the anomaly. A more radical option, and a truly desperate last resort, is to conclude that there is a basic flaw in one's conceptual model. To date, I have resisted the latter option.

A general point to remember is that the first factor is of little value without a coherent theoretical framework while the second factor is of little value without a coherent empirical framework. Together, they provide the crucial components of scientific activity.

Now we consider what all this has to do with attraction research.

From a general interest in attraction to experimentation on a specific problem

As discussed elsewhere (Byrne, 1997a), the source of my abiding interest in attraction most likely began in childhood as the result of living in a peripatetic family whose frequent relocations took me to school after school where making (or not making) new friends presented an annual crisis. Though my first empirical research involved propinquity and acquaintanceship (Byrne & Buehler, 1955), my "real" attraction research had its implicit beginning when I read Ted Newcomb's (1956) APA presidential address in which he touched on such matters as attraction and reinforcement. Specifically, he suggested that attraction between persons is a function of the extent to which reciprocal rewards are present in the interaction. For me, that was truly an "aha!" experience; I read his article while studying for my qualifying exams in Clinical Psychology even though its content had absolutely nothing to do with my chosen field. No matter – it made eminent sense and seemed both accurate and important. I ruminated about it many times over the next couple of years. Later, with a doctoral degree and a growing disinterest in clinical, I woke up early one hot Austin morning to the mockingbirds' trill, following one of the many legendary parties enjoyed by the Texas department. In addition to a headache, I had a realization (Byrne, 1979). Essentially, I decided I must follow Newcomb's lead with an investigation of the effect of attitude similarity on attraction. The specific topic was suggested by many observations of my father's evaluations of other people that were based on whether their views did or did not coincide with his own. That is, I had concluded long before that attitudes were among the determinants of attraction. Newcomb's paper easily convinced me that attitude similarity must involve reinforcement. These two beliefs led me to design an experiment to test the more accessible of the two. I might add that I heard the voice of James Earl Jones saying, "Build a paradigm, and they will come". The truth is, I had not yet learned about paradigms, very few decided to come to this particular cornfield, and all I heard was the mockingbirds.

Selecting the operations and procedures needed to investigate the effect of attitude similarity–dissimilarity on attraction

I eventually discovered that other psychologists had previously studied the similarity-attraction effect in an experimental setting:

Schachter (1951) manipulated agreement in order to determine the relative amount of communication directed at group members with deviant vs. non-deviant opinions, and Smith (1957, 1958) manipulated value similarity to determine its effect on acceptance and perceived similarity in the context of Heider's (1958) interpersonal theory; my blissful ignorance of this work afforded me the opportunity to create my own operations and procedures (Byrne, 1961). Only in retrospect is it now possible to identify this simple experiment as Landmark 1. I inadvertently initiated a new paradigm rather than working within an existing one.

A great deal of thought went into planning the research details because attraction appeared to be a central aspect of human behavior. I did not know at the time that this methodology would guide the experimental details of hundreds of future investigations (Griffitt & Byrne, 1970). The primary constraint was financial; as a new PhD, I had no grant money and no doctoral students. The department could afford to pay for paper and duplication but little else, so the independent and dependent variables had to remain within the technological boundaries set by the ditto machine.

The independent variable was attitude similarity, and the identification of appropriate attitude topics was provided by undergraduates in my classes who listed topics which they at one time or other discussed with friends and acquaintances; these issues were transformed into 26 7-point attitude items (agree–disagree, for–against, favor option A vs. option B, etc.). The importance of these 26 issues was rated by other students, and the issues were perceived by them to range from relatively important (integration, God, and premarital sex) to relatively unimportant (western movies, music, and political affiliation).

The experimental procedure involved administering the attitude scales to students in class and later presenting the same students with what was purported to be a scale filled out by a same-sex fellow student in another class at the university (with the name and

Byrne, Table I *Mean evaluative responses as a function of percentage of similar attitudes expressed by a stranger*

| | Attitudinal condition | | |
| | Similarity | | |
Evaluation	0%	50%	100%
Attraction	4.41	7.20	13.00
Intelligence	3.06	3.93	5.63
Knowledge	2.65	3.56	4.65
Morality	3.47	4.33	5.76
Adjustment	2.71	3.50	6.00

Note: Based on data reported in Byrne (1961). The attraction scale ranges from 2 (least positive) to 14 (most positive), while the four other scales range from 1 (least positive) to 7.

other identifying data about this stranger seemingly scissored out of the scale, imitating the military censors who cut passages out of my brother's letters from the Aleutian Islands during World War II). The ostensible purpose of the study was to determine just how much students could learn about one another from the limited information provided by an attitude scale. Besides being affordable, this method of presenting a bogus fellow student's attitudinal responses controlled many other variables that could have (and we now know *do* have) an influence on attraction such as physical attractiveness, age, height, ethnicity, educational background, non-verbal behavior, etc. The scales of the "other students" were prepared on my kitchen table with several different pens and pencils of various colors, making check marks and *x*s, writing large and small, left-handed and right-handed. In a **between-subjects design**, four experimental groups were created: some students were given a stranger who agreed with them on all 26 topics, others a stranger who disagreed on all 26 topics, still others a stranger agreeing on the 13 most important and disagreeing on the 13 least important topics, or agreeing on the 13 least important and disagreeing on the 13 most important topics. The limiting parameters (100% and 0%) and the inclusion of an intermediate degree of agreement (50%) were lucky happenstances, but of considerable value.

The **dependent variable** – attraction – consisted of two 7-point evaluative items borrowed from sociometric research (Lindzey & Byrne, 1968): how much one *likes* the other person and the degree to which one would *enjoy working with* that person. These items were preceded on the Interpersonal Judgment Scale by four additional items designed to support the cover story, by asking for perceptions of the stranger's intelligence, knowledge of current events, morality, and adjustment.

The highly significant results were based on several fortuitous aspects of the experiment: attitudinal stimuli actually do exert a powerful effect on interpersonal evaluations, the experimenter's false assertion that another student had filled out the bogus scale turned out to be believable, and the response measure was perceived as straightforward and unambiguous. Though the original data were not presented in the same way, Table 1 provides clues as to why this research might catch one's attention.

Observe that the evaluations of strangers appear to be affected by degree of similarity, and statistical analysis confirms this impression. The effect of topic importance was, to my surprise, much weaker than had been assumed, suggesting the unexpected possibility that attitudinal content does not matter greatly in this context. Thus, the two intermediate (50% similarity) groups could reasonably be collapsed into one. The progression of attraction means across the three conditions suggests that no similarity, intermediate similarity, and total similarity represent three points along a stimulus continuum. That observation may seem obvious now, but at the time, it was closer to "hmm ... I wonder".

Stumbling across the linear function

With the powerful rewards provided by statistical significance plus a publication in an APA journal, the probability of continuing to pan for scientific gold in this particular creek bed greatly increased. As should be expected, however, alternative explanations can be proffered even for the apparently clear-cut findings of a simple experiment. Almost immediately, a valid criticism was raised. Many of the attitudinal positions (pro-God, anti-integration, pro-westerns, pro-rock music, etc.) were perceived to be the overwhelming consensus of Texas undergraduates. A quick check of these subjects' attitudinal responses verified this hypothesis of attitude homogeneity. So, rather than manipulating attitude similarity–dissimilarity as I intended, perhaps I had unintentionally varied normality–deviancy.

The test of this possibility became Landmark 2 (Byrne, 1962). The seven attitude items eliciting the most diverse responses were selected from the original 26. At that time and place, student opinion was evenly divide about such topics as racial integration in public schools, smoking, and the goal of making money. Presumably, if normality–deviancy were the crucial independent variable rather than similarity–dissimilarity, agreement–disagreement on these seven controversial topics would *not* affect attraction. If, in contrast, similarity–dissimilarity continued to affect attraction under these conditions, it might be useful to explore the effect of several degrees of intermediate similarity beyond 50%. So, the procedures of the first study were repeated using the 7-item attitude scale, and this time the

between-subjects design involved eight groups in which strangers expressed either seven similar and no dissimilar attitudes, six similar and one dissimilar attitude, etc., continuing to no similar and seven dissimilar attitudes. The findings were unambiguous in that the similarity–dissimilarity manipulation had the hypothesized effect on attraction, ruling out the alternative normal–deviant interpretation. Also, the eight attraction means were neatly ordered in terms of the stranger's similarity (with only one minor and nonsignificant inversion).

You may have noticed that this second experiment, to my embarrassment, incorporated the common methodological weakness described earlier. Because I did not know then what I know now, in moving from the initial 26-attitude experiment to the 7-attitude experiment, not only were the topics chosen on the basis of yielding diverse opinions (the new variable being investigated) but the total number of attitude topics was changed from 26 to 7 (a second, confounding, new variable). Had there been a failure to replicate the original findings, the explanation could have been either the absence of normal–deviant topics or the reduced scale length, and additional research would have been needed to provide clarification. Thanks to blind luck, the similarity effect *was* replicated, and we also had tentative evidence that the number of attitudes (at least between 7 and 26) was irrelevant.

For the next few years, we spent a lot of time fooling around with attitude similarity in the context of such variables as racial prejudice (Byrne & Wong, 1962), real and assumed similarity of spouses (Byrne & Blaylock, 1963), and dispositional mediators of the similarity-attraction relationship (Byrne, 1965) along with research unrelated to attraction. Such activity kept us off the streets, provided tenure for me and degrees for students, and convincingly demonstrated that consistent operations are a prerequisite for consistent findings. Something, however, was lacking. Our research seemed to be moving "horizontally" rather than "vertically".

A breakthrough occurred when we decided to identify the stimulus in the attitude studies more precisely by pursuing a seemingly arcane question. Specifically, we wanted to determine whether the attitude–attraction effect was determined by the relative number of similar vs. dissimilar attitudes expressed by a stranger, the total number of similar attitudes communicated by that individual, or some combination of the two. This was obviously not theory-driven research in that each of the three possible outcomes was compatible with reinforcement affect theory. In any event, Landmark 3 in this paradigm (Byrne & Nelson, 1965) was an experiment involving four levels of relative similarity (the proportion of similar attitudes was either .33, .50, .67, or 1.00) and three levels varying the number of similar attitudes (4, 8, or 16). In order to create each of the resulting 12 conditions, it was necessary to use attitude scales varying in length from 4 to 48 items. We found that proportion had a highly significant effect on attraction, but neither the number of similar attitudes nor the interaction between proportion and number was significant.

An immediate implication of this finding was that all of our data (representing almost 800 research participants) from previous experiments could be combined (despite the utilization of attitude scales of varying content and varying length) permitting us to plot the functional relationship between proportion of similar attitudes and attraction. My colleagues in learning research were plotting functions, so I wanted attraction research to resemble what the big boys and girls do. The result was the now notorious *linear function*: $Y = 5.44X + 6.62$, in which Y is attraction, X is proportion of similar attitudes, 5.44 is the empirically derived slope, and 6.62 is the empirically derived Y-intercept. That was so aesthetically pleasing that I would have been glad to erect a plaque with the linear function chiseled on it just outside of Mezes Hall, near the statue of Governor Hogg (father of Miss Ima – true trivia), but I settled for an inscribed tie clasp kindly given to me by my students.

Why was this stuff important? It took me a while to articulate a satisfactory answer. Back when I was only an eighth grader at

Washington Junior High in Bakersfield, Spence (1944) published a most impressive and still extremely relevant paper about theory construction in psychology. I was unaware of it until more than two decades had passed, but let me quote two brief passages that strongly influenced how I came to interpret attraction research:

> In some areas of knowledge, for example present day physics, theories serve primarily to bring into functional connection with one another empirical laws, which prior to their formulation had been isolated realms of knowledge. The physicist is able to isolate, experimentally, elementary situations, i.e., situations in which there are a limited number of variables, and thus finds it possible to infer or discover descriptive, low-order laws. Theory comes into play for the physicist when he attempts to formulate more abstract principles which will bring these low-order laws into relationship with one another ... (pp. 47–8)

> Without the generalizations which theories aim to provide we would never be in a position to predict behavior, for knowledge of particular events does not provide us with a basis for prediction when the situation differs in the least degree. The higher the level of abstraction that can be obtained the greater will be both the understanding and the actual control achieved. (p. 62)

Eureka! Science begins with simple, isolated, controllable situations in which it is possible to establish lawful relationships; then, the progression is from simple to complex, specific to general. I finally understood what I was doing.

"Low-order laws" may be common in science, including other fields of psychology, but they have not been all that common in social psychology. Perhaps the non-normative nature of our research strategy had something to do with the apparent irritation expressed over the years by various colleagues in response to experiments in 'elementary situations', the easily replicable similarity effect, and the lawful mathematical function (Aronson & Worchel, 1966; Rosenbaum, 1986; Sunnafrank, 1992). Graduate students often ask why this work continues to evoke attack, but I honestly do not know why annoyance persists. Indifference maybe, but not annoyance. Leaving aside emotions, the original proportion–attraction formula was about as low-order as you can get, but that of course was only the beginning.

The utility of a law is ultimately defined by its generality. Thus, if this linear function were found to apply only to paper-and-pencil attitude presentations in the context of a spurious cover story given to Texas undergraduates who indicated attraction by making check marks on two 7-point scales, its value in the great scheme of things would be slim to none. To determine whether we were dealing with something more wide-reaching than that, it was essential to conduct a great many experiments that provided overwhelming evidence as to the generality of the relationship – to diverse attitudes (Byrne & Nelson, 1964) as well as other kinds of similarity (Byrne et al., 1966a, 1967) presented in various stimulus modes and contexts (Byrne & Clore, 1966) to quite different populations (Byrne & Griffitt, 1966; Byrne et al., 1969a, 1971) in which attraction was measured in a variety of ways (Byrne et al., 1971). We also extended the findings to relatively complex "real-life" settings such as computer dates (Byrne et al., 1970) and short-term residents of fall-out shelters (Griffitt & Veitch, 1974). Had we not conducted such research, the issue of generality would have been raised (and validly so) as a major limitation of this research. Had generality been lacking, I'm willing to bet that multiple cries of "I told you so!" would have rung out across the fruited plains. Nevertheless, when generality became so obvious that we could describe the relationship as "ubiquitous", some colleagues concluded that we were unimaginatively studying the same thing over and over. As one anonymous reviewer put it, "Surely, before we read more of Byrne's work he should tell us what to do with it" (Byrne, 1971: 278) – a tempting invitation indeed. Tongue-in-cheek, I confided to one such critic that my next major project involved determining the effect on attraction of Tuesday vs. Wednesday. Perhaps he is still waiting for that imaginary article to appear, so that he can be appalled.

In defense of the critics, let me state candidly that there is a good reason for the lack of excitement generated by the search for the low-level generality of a low-order law. To find that changes in content, stimulus mode, population, and response measures do not change the predictable relationship between similarity and attraction is actually not very exciting. OK, it's dull. What's good enough for Vice President Gore is good enough for psychological research. If the goal of behavioral science is prediction rather than excitement, however, these investigations were necessary. Analogously, when trying to build a multi-storied elevator with an Erector Set, work on the base also fails to raise one's pulse rate, but if you skip that step, the exciting generator is likely to wobble and fall.

There is, however, a bit more to the attraction paradigm than the seeming ubiquity of the effect of similarity on attraction. Empirical consistency and generality are nice, and they renew one's faith in the predictability of human behavior, but theoretical consistency and generality constitute the big enchilada. With an encompassing theoretical framework, it should be possible to account for a great many quite different phenomena. If so, we must redefine attitude similarity as simply one representative of a much broader class of stimulus events and attraction as simply one representative of a much broader class of response events. Watch out! This is where conceptualizations based on simple, limited experiments can metamorphose into far-reaching explanations of almost everything.

Donn tries to explain it all: from classical conditioning to the behavior sequence

According to Newcomb, interpersonal rewards constitute an essential element in determining attraction. In our work, therefore, similar attitudes were assumed to act as rewards and dissimilar attitudes as punishments because they satisfied or failed to satisfy the effectance motive (Byrne & Clore, 1967; Byrne et al., 1966b). We tossed in the assumption that positive affect is elicited by rewards and negative affect by punishments. It was further assumed that positive affect resulted in a positive evaluative response and negative affect in a negative evaluative response. At its simplest level, the previous statement means that people like feeling good and dislike feeling bad.

To apply such constructs to attraction, it was necessary to incorporate associational learning. In brief, our early attraction experiments were conceptualized as employing attitude statements (**unconditioned stimuli**) to elicit affective responses (**unconditioned responses**) that were associated temporally and spatially with a stranger (**classical conditioning**) who became the **conditioned stimulus** for implicit affective responses (**conditioned responses**) which determined implicit evaluative responses that, in turn, were reflected in overt evaluative responses such as attraction.

An additional aspect of this process was the fact that subjects were presented with a mixed array of similar and dissimilar attitudes eliciting both positive and negative affective responses. These units of affect were assumed to be combined in some kind of internal calculus that resulted in a single evaluative response. It was proposed that the formula for the linear function simply reflects how people may be wired to combine varying numbers of positive and negative events to reach an evaluation – don't blame me.

Among the many implications of this model is the prediction that quite different types of stimulus events (attitudes, personal evaluations, physical appearance, race, etc. along with pre-existing mood, room temperature, background music, etc.) would be expected to elicit affective responses that vary not only in valence but also in magnitude. Just as in the simple situation in which magnitude is more or less constant, the affective responses must be combined, yielding an evaluative response expressed as attraction.

In Landmark 4, Byrne & Rhamey (1965) investigated the relative effects on attraction of attitude similarity and personal evaluations, yielding a more general conceptualization of stimulus events and a revised and more general combinatorial formula:

$$Y = m \left[\frac{\sum (P \times M)}{\sum (P \times M) + \sum (N \times M)} \right] + k$$

in which Y represents any evaluative response, P and N represent units of positive and negative affect (each of which is multiplied by its magnitude, M, and then summed); m and k are the empirically derived constants indicating the slope and Y-intercept of the linear function. In a leap along the dimension from low to high abstraction, we were now describing evaluation as a linear function of proportion of weighted positive affect. Attitude similarity and attraction thus represented only a specific example of this more general conceptualization.

As a depiction of behavior, the model specifies that any stimulus that elicits an affective response or that is associated with an affective response is evaluated on the basis of the relative number and the relative strength of positive and negative units of affect. Any evaluation-relevant behavior such as attraction, physical proximity, dating, marriage, purchasing, judging, voting, etc. is determined by the effects of two mediators: implicit affective responses and implicit evaluative responses.

Further, affect, evaluation, and reinforcement are conceptualized as three interactive constructs. A great many non-obvious predictions follow from this triangular hypothesis. For example: (I) Any variable that is found to have an effect on evaluative responses should elicit affect (e.g., Clore & Gormly, 1974) and serve a reinforcement function in a learning paradigm (e.g., Golightly & Byrne, 1964); (II) Any variable that is found to elicit affective responses should have an effect on evaluative responses (e.g., Fisher & Byrne, 1975; Griffitt, 1970) and serve a reinforcement function in a learning paradigm (e.g., Griffitt & Kaiser, 1978); and (III) Any variable that serves a reinforcement function in a learning paradigm should have an effect on evaluative responses and elicit affective responses (e.g., McDonald, 1962).

Despite my infatuation with this model, it was not sufficiently inclusive to deal with complex aspects of human interactions. As was noted from time to time, people think as well as feel. As a result, cognitive variables can modify and even override emotional considerations. Perhaps the simplest illustration is going to the dentist; despite negative affect, we periodically make appointments (however reluctantly), enter the dental office, sit in the designated chair, undergo varying degrees of discomfort and pain, and then pay money to the individual who did this to us. Rather than basing our actions on affect, such behavior is determined by what we know and believe about dental hygiene, our expectations about the long-term negative consequences of avoiding this very unpleasant task, and our ability to imagine what it is like to undergo root canal surgery or wear dentures. Further, some activities (e.g., love, sex, aggression) seem to be partially influenced by the extent to which the individual is physiologically aroused, as indicated by a rapid heartbeat, the production of adrenalin, vasoconstriction or vasodilatation, and the presence of moisture on the epidermis. The probability of approach vs. avoidance-evaluative behavior, then, is based on positive and negative factors of varying magnitude associated with six mediators: affect, evaluation, cognition, expectancy, fantasy, and arousal. Some of these constructs may be redundant, additional ones have to be added in the future, and the way in which the elements interact must be determined with greater precision than has so far been done. In other words, this model, labeled the *behavior sequence*, represents a work in progress (Byrne, 1982; Byrne & Kelley, 1981; Byrne & Schulte, 1990).

For the record, the need for this kind of expansion of the affect-evaluation model

was first made clear to me when I heard Elaine Hatfield outline a theory of passionate love at a symposium in New London, Connecticut (Hatfield, 1971). A second impetus was provided by research attempting to predict contraceptive behavior (Byrne & Fisher, 1983), coercive sexuality (Hogben et al., 1996) and interpersonal relationships (Smith et al., 1993).

Empirical landmarks are easier to label than theoretical ones. Because conceptual formulations develop and expand, they must change over time, as can be traced through Byrne & Clore (1970), Byrne (1971), Clore & Byrne (1974) and Byrne (1992).

Work in progress: adult attachment patterns as mediators in the behavior sequence

Our empirical efforts have previously been concentrated on the affect-evaluation portion of the behavior sequence. Currently, our group has begun exploring the role of infant attachment patterns as first described by Bowlby (1969), then developed by Ainsworth et al. (1978), and extended to adult interpersonal behavior by, among others, Shaver & Hazan (1994). With attachment concepts, the remaining portions of the behavior sequence become essential.

At the moment, we are pursuing the formulations of Bartholomew and her associates (Bartholomew, 1990; Bartholomew & Horowitz, 1991; Griffin & Bartholomew, 1994a, 1994b). Briefly, two underlying positive–negative dimensions (based on early experiences with one's primary caregiver) are proposed: perceptions of self and perceptions of other people. That is, people differ in assessing their self-worth and also in assessing the trustworthiness of others.

These two dimensions were hypothesized to be orthogonal, and recent work at Albany by Stephanie McGowan and Lisa Daniels confirms their independence. When considered simultaneously, the dimensions yield four quadrants into which individuals can be categorized with respect to perceptions of self and others. (1) Those on the positive end of each dimension, a *secure* attachment pattern, have a positive self-image and expect other people to be trustworthy and supportive. Such individuals have good interpersonal skills, deal well with others, and easily establish and maintain positive relationships; (2) Those on the negative end of each dimension, a *fearful* attachment pattern, perceive themselves in negative terms and expect the worst of others. Their interpersonal skills are inadequate, other people pose a threat, and relationships are avoided; (3) Those who perceive themselves negatively but are positive about others have a *preoccupied* (or *clingy*) attachment pattern; they get involved in relationships but feel they are unworthy so are anxious and ambivalent about interacting with a partner; and (4) Those who have a positive opinion of themselves but distrust other people, a *dismissing* attachment pattern, are hesitant to become involved in relationships, but

when they do they feel that they deserve better because they are suspicious about the motives and intentions of the partner.

Those involved in attachment research are well aware of the lack of conceptual and empirical consistency in that there is disagreement about whether there are three basic attachment patterns or four along with disagreement about the choice of instruments with which to measure such patterns. Our first step, therefore, is simply to assume there are four patterns and then to do our best to create, borrow, and adapt measuring techniques that we can use thereafter in a consistent fashion. We will be able to test a variety of hypotheses dealing with individual differences in attachment as predictors of interpersonal behavior.

With respect to planning ahead, I can more or less tentatively articulate what we will be doing next. As to the specifics of what will happen after that, however, I don't have a clue. Well, maybe a bit of a clue. Stay tuned.

Have you written down your list of evaluative reactions to this paper?

Byrne's paper demonstrates that intellectually demanding reports need not be dry. His paper also shows how criticism can be used as a valuable stimulus to further research and is not always best taken defensively. Even hostile critique can, in professional scholarly hands, lead to theoretical and empirical growth. Note also his important but often overlooked observation that every theorist probably relies "in part on untestable meta-theoretical assumptions". This gently points out that theorists often build personal assumptions and theories into their formal theory: those who have always believed that humans are basically complex *animals* will doubtless favor a biological approach to explaining human experience; those who see humans as essentially rational, will develop theories of the *logic* lying beneath human behavior, and so on. Such basic assumptions are barely testable because they are essentially root beliefs about human nature, which are beyond test, except tests of faith. Byrne also supposes that an individual theorist's personal experience might shape his or her sets of interests, beliefs and personal assumptions about behavior.

As is clear from Byrne's own report, his work has been subject to considerable – even violent – criticism from the beginning. Much of the early critiques focused on the artificiality of the situation, the fact that the manipulation of attitudes was deceptive, or the unlikelihood of the transfer of findings from the laboratory to the outside world. You may have written these down as points in your own evaluative list. Byrne attempted to answer these critiques in a number of ways, first by pointing out that any experimental manipulation is done for the purposes of testing something under controlled conditions and not for the purpose of reflecting the complexity of real-life processes: indeed, the very reason that we use laboratory techniques is precisely to *control* (or eliminate from the experiment) any influences felt to be irrelevant to the central process that we want to understand, or else to strip it down into component parts and then understand the relative influence of each part, bit by bit. Byrne's other answer was to try out his paradigm in real-world contexts, and he lists some of them in the paper. The attitude-similarity reinforcement effect worked with people seeking bank loans, defendants in jury trials, and on first dates, all of which situations were all the more successful, the greater the attitude similarity between the people involved. These criticisms have therefore been adequately dealt with.

Critiques from communication studies were focused on the fact that the Bogus Stranger technique short-circuits important processes of communication in the acquaintance process (Bochner, 1984; Duck, 1976). In real life we do not hand some-one our attitudes on a report sheet; rather the person has to communicate with us and we with them in order to find out what each of us believes and whether we are in fact similar in attitudes about given topics. There are also important social norms that cover the amount, style, and timing of revelation of attitudes: for example, we would be unlikely to discuss our attitudes to parenthood on a first date. Also people are not always entirely honest in first encounters because we are all aware of the importance of first impressions and so we do a lot of **face management** – that is to say, we make sure that we emphasize an appearance or "face" that we are nice people rather than openly and honestly declaring all our deeply held attitudes about controversial topics. Thus the means, timing and style of communication about atti-tudes could be quite different in real-life encounters from the way that they are represented in the standard attraction paradigm. This observation does nothing to undermine Byrne's contention about the relevance and importance of the reinforcing effects of attitude similarity, but it complexifies the process in real life by which atti-tude similarity might exert its pulling power. In real life we need to do considerable detective work to find out another person's attitudes, but we also extrapolate from what we observe to broader schemes of attitudes that we have not yet seen: for example, from the fact that someone believes in capital punishment, we might also deduce that the person is against gun control, votes Republican, and supports President Bush. We can later check out whether we are right, but the revelation of one attitude can be used by observers to generalize to other, unseen, attitudes.

A further issue with the Attraction Paradigm is that *sequences* of interactions are not represented in the approach. The Attraction Paradigm is not uniquely reproach-able for this fact, but nonetheless the limitation does apply. In real life, people who are getting acquainted do meet more than once and the ways in which the second meeting fulfils or undercuts the expectations generated in the first meeting can make a difference to subsequent development (or not) of the potential relationship.

The following paper by Sprecher and Duck (1993) explores this issue by looking at the ways in which perceived communication plays a role in the future develop-ment of dating. One of its main points is to stress the role of communication in the consolidation of the acquaintance process. The authors considered subjects' percep-tions of communication quality as a function of similarity but they also make some points about the importance of communication for future development of the acquaintance process.

The study uses a number of different analytic techniques, starting with a paired *t*-test. The *t*-test, of which the paired *t*-test is one form, essentially measures the amount of difference that is found between the means of scores derived from two samples and it evaluates that difference in terms of the general amount of **variance** found in the population as a whole. In the paired **t-test** the "two samples" are data from two separate groups that are, in theory, "matched" in some way (for example we might measure men's and women's performance on the same test). In other forms of the *t*-test the "two samples" are scores from the same person under two separate sets of conditions (for example, drunk and sober). The *t*-score essentially tells an investigator whether the difference between the "two samples" (men–women; drunk–sober) is greater than the difference that he or she should expect to find in view of the general amount of variation that is found in the world as whole. If the difference is greater than would be expected by chance (i.e., if the probability of finding that specific degree of difference between two samples is less than five in 100, $p < .05$) then the two samples of scores are declared to be really different – and the difference is attributed to whatever was done to create (in an experiment) or used as (in a naturalistic study) a point of difference between them – say, the difference between "people after a shot of alcohol" and "people after a shot of water" or between "women" and "men".

Another analytic technique used in this study involves tests of **correlational relationship.** In a correlational test, the basic idea is to find the amount of correspondence between one set of scores (A) and another set of scores (B). In other words this test is about similarity rather than about difference, as the *t*-test is. For example, we might be interested to see how much correspondence there is between "Drowsiness" (A) and "Time spent listening to political speeches" (B) or whether "Altitude of flight" (A) is correlated with "Time since take off" (B). The results of such analysis are reported as "*r*-scores" and the present study reports intra-couple *r*-scores on test items: i.e., it reports how much the two members of the couple corresponded in their scores on a test.

The difference between the two sorts of test (*t*-test and *r*-score) is one discussed above: a *t*-test is based on the assumption of **direction of causality** (i.e., that the difference between men's and women's scores is caused by their sex) whereas the *r*-score simply indicates that there is an *association* between two sets of scores without being able to make any judgment about what caused it.

Another technique mentioned here is **stepwise regression**. Broadly speaking, this technique looks at the overall results and tries to see if a better explanation of them is provided by temporarily ignoring one of the variables or "controlling for" its effects. By systematically taking the effects of each relevant variable out of the whole equation you can discover if any of them is, as it were, masking the true effects of some other variable. The intention is to find the best explanation for the variance (see Chapter 1 for a reminder about this).

A final element of the paper is concerned with **factor scores**. **Factor analysis** takes the different scores that people produce to different items on a test and looks for underlying patterns that can be attributed to specific factors. For example if you score highly on "I like to punch people", "I am often angry", "I take offence easily", "If someone insults me then I usually hit them", then an investigator might find that all of these scores are explained by the same underlying factor, say, Belligerence. Researchers talk of the **factor loadings** of an item. These loadings are a statistical indication of the extent to which a particular item ("I like to punch people", say) is a good fit with the underlying factor of Belligerence. The higher the loading, the greater the parallelism between the item and factor as a whole. Researchers look for the smallest number of factors that will explain the data, say a three-factor solution or a four-factor solution. In those cases, three or four underlying factors can be used satisfactorily to explain all the subscales of a particular measure.

As you read the paper by Sprecher and Duck, therefore, you should look out for uses of different techniques of statistical analysis used to answer different questions, such as degree of difference or degree of correspondence. Also be aware of the emphasis of the paper on communication but note that the paper does not measure it as it occurs, only as people report it having happened. This could be an important limitation of the paper.

Some terms that come up in the paper are "Field of eligibles/desirables/availables" and "Semantic Differential Scale". The **field of availables** is all those people who are available as a possible date or romantic partner (i.e., irrespective of age or any-thing else, all those people who are "out there" as potential partners). The **field of eligibles** is all those people whom a person regards as eligible as a partner (by reason of age, social class, religion, or whatever other criteria the person regards as neces-sary to be met before any kind of partnership would be sought). The **field of desir-ables** is those people whom the person actually desires as a partner. You can see that each of these fields is a successively smaller set.

The **Semantic Differential Scale** (Osgood et al., 1957) is a means of measuring the underlying meaning of a topic, idea or object to a person. It consists of a number of bi-polar scales (such as good–bad, pleasant–unpleasant, etc.) on which the person can rate a topic, so that the underlying meaning of the topic to the person can be worked out and even drawn in a diagram. Finally, the study also reports the "**Cronbach's alpha**" scores, which are basically measures of consistency and agreement between the different subscales of an overall measure. The higher the Cronbach's alpha, the more the subscales can be relied upon as measuring the same central underlying construct.

Sweet Talk: The Importance of Perceived Communication for Romantic and Friendship Attraction Experienced During a Get-Acquainted Date

Susan Sprecher and Steve Duck

Boy meets girl, girl meets boy, and the two have their first extended interaction (e.g., a first date). What factors determine how attracted they will be to each other, how much they will desire to see each other again, and whether they actually will see each other again? Although an enormous amount of research has been conducted on factors affecting initial attraction, questions still remain. First, the role of talk and other dynamic interaction variables has been neglected in the study of attraction, whereas individual attributes have been overemphasized. Second, little research differentiates types of attraction and tests whether the predictors of one type of attraction (e.g., romantic) are the same as predictors of another type (e.g., friendship). Third, most studies focus either on initial attraction responses – often to a bogus stranger – or on developed relationships that already have an extended life, and so they do not look at the "consolidation" of relationships (e.g., from first meeting to second meeting).

In the present research, data are presented from a "get-acquainted date" study that considers the importance of communication as a determinant of romantic (dating) and friendship attraction and of desire for and actual further interaction. The impact of communication is considered relative to the social psychological variables of partner's physical attractiveness and similarity (Feingold, 1990, 1991). We treat all three variables as social judgments that emerge during the course of the interaction. Our assumption is that attraction for another after a first interaction is influenced not by the static physical characteristics or cognitive structures imported to the interaction but by the quality of the communication and the judgments of the other that are constituted in this communication. Consistent with our assumption, research has shown that perceptions of similarity and of the other's physical attractiveness are more important predictors of initial attraction than are actual similarity and objective physical attractiveness, respectively (e.g., Curran & Lippold, 1975; Walster [Hatfield], Aronson, Abrahams, & Rottmann, 1966).

Relationship scholars have recognized the importance of talk or communication in the initiation and development of relationships, particularly recently (e.g., Baxter & Dindia, 1990; Douglas, 1987; Duck, 1985; Tolhuizen, 1989). However, most of this work has been laboratory-based and has not explored the role of communication in the ongoing process of attraction and in the consolidation of relationships across time. We propose direct attention to this vehicle of negotiation and relational consolidation processes. Duck and Pond (1989) have theoretically connected the essence of talk with the essence of relating and have urged researchers to attend to relationship partners' talk and to the way in which such talk is recalled. These authors argue that the recall of talk is essentially the recall of relationships, because the ways talk is recalled reflect the relationship partners' perceptions of the emotional interior of the relationship, "significant" events of an interaction, and their own vision of its status. There are, therefore, theoretical reasons to pay closer attention to the nature of talk in relationship initiation, just as to its role in the full enlivening of that relationship in its later stages.

The role of communication in the early interactions of the attraction process has not been totally ignored in earlier research, either by social psychologists or by communication scholars. For example, Insko and Wilson (1977) reported that pairs of strangers who actually communicated with each other liked each other more and rated each other more positively than pairs of strangers who only observed each other interacting with a third person and did not interact together. Sunnafrank and Miller (1981) and Sunnafrank (1984) found that the opportunity to communicate with a stranger moderates, and in most cases overwhelms, the effect of preexisting attitude similarity on attraction in an initial encounter. These previous studies, however, examined only the opportunity to interact or did not measure the quality of the interaction. Furthermore, the studies were conducted in the laboratory, not in naturalistic dating.

In one recent study, however, interaction was considered in the natural context of the first date. Robins (1989) considered the factors that predict women's attraction to a partner and desire to continue a relationship after a first date. The major independent variables were perceived attitudinal and demographic similarity and perception of positive and negative interaction events occurring on the first date (measured by the occurrence or nonoccurrence of several events in the relationship). Of these factors, positive interaction events and attitude similarity were found to be predictive of the women's attraction for their partner on a first date (men were not studied). Robins' study, however, has limited applicability to the role of quality communication in the attraction process because Robins measured "interaction events" rather than the quality of the communication.

What do we mean by quality communication? We are not referring solely or even primarily to self-disclosure, which has been argued by some to be the major vehicle of relationship growth and intimacy (e.g., Derlega & Winstead, 1986; Reis & Shaver, 1988) but, in fact, makes up only a small portion of all talk that occurs in real-life relationships and interactions (e.g., Dindia, Fitzpatrick, & Kenny, 1989; Duck, Rutt, Hurst, & Strejc, 1991). Instead, we are referring to how personal, smooth, efficient, important, and satisfying (among other dimensions) the communication is *perceived* to be. This is not the same as studying communication in the behavioral ways employed by other investigators (e.g., Planalp & Benson, 1992; Sillars, 1991) but is based on the logical assumption that persons' evaluations of the communication are important in determining relationship satisfaction, as Gottman (1979) has shown. Duck (1991) also argued for a theoretical analysis of the formation of such evaluations in their own right and independently of their correlation with behavioral indexes of communication quality. In this study, therefore, a portion of the Iowa Communication Record (see Duck et al., 1991) is used to measure several such dimensions of perception of relational communication, in the same manner as the Rochester Interaction Record (Wheeler & Nezlek, 1977) assesses perceptions of social interaction. For purposes of comparison with the social psychological literature on self-disclosure,

however, we also include assessments of the level of self-disclosure.

The first purpose of this study is to describe the overall impressions formed by the dating partners in their first interactions and to assess the degrees of agreement/similarity within couples and between women and men. The second and the major purpose of the study is to examine the relationship of (a) the quality and other aspects of the communication during the date to (b) the expressed attraction and outcome of the date. We hypothesize that the quality of the communication on a first date will be positively related to the degree of attraction experienced and the desire to see the other again. We are also interested in examining the importance of quality communication as a predictor of attraction relative to perceived self-disclosure, similarity, and partner's physical attractiveness. We examine these issues separately for men and women because previous research suggests that we will find physical attractiveness to be more important to men than to women (e.g., Feingold, 1990) and similarity and quality communication to be more important to women than to men (e.g., Feingold, 1991). Furthermore, although predictors of romantic attraction have not generally been compared with predictors of friendship attraction within the same study (for an exception, see Aron, Dutton, Aron, & Iverson, 1989), a comparison across studies and our own intuitions suggest that physical attractiveness will be a more important predictor of romantic attraction than of friendship attraction. Quality communication and perceived similarity should be important predictors of both types of attraction, although they may be overwhelmed by physical attractiveness in the prediction of romantic attraction.

Method

Subjects were 166 students (83 men and 83 women) from a midwestern university who participated in all the phases of this "get-acquainted date" study. Subjects were recruited in one of two ways, either through volunteer procedures in class or through the agency of friends.

Random matches. Sixty-eight men and women (forming 34 heterosexual pairs) were volunteers obtained from several introductory sociology classes who expressed on a brief questionnaire that they would be interested in participating in the get-acquainted date study. From the pool of interested students, men and women were assigned to each other for the get-acquainted date study. Assignment was random, with the exceptions that the two partners should not be obtained from the same university course, they should be the same age or the man should be older, and, if possible, they should be of the same race. These last criteria provided correspondence to the practicalities of the "field of eligibles" in the real world, where dating partners are typically of the same race and are close in age. Earlier get-acquainted date studies took the same approach (e.g., Walster [Hatfield] et al., 1966).

Friend-arranged matches. The remaining 98 subjects (49 heterosexual pairs) were obtained through the intermediation of acquaintances, as research has suggested that many real-life romantic relationships begin with an introduction from a friend (e.g., Sprecher & McKinney, 1987). Working for class credit in an upper-division relationship course, pairs of student acquaintances matched unacquainted opposite-sex members of their respective social networks. The students were allowed to exchange information about their respective friends to form the best match possible. These pairings, then, should not be considered random but, rather, are somewhat representative of the nonrandom matches that naturally occur in the real world of date selection.

Procedure. All subjects completed a questionnaire before the date, met their assigned partner in a public location for a date lasting approximately 1 hr, and completed a questionnaire after the date. The procedure differed slightly, however, for the two groups of subjects and so will be described separately below.

Procedure for the random matches. Once a research assistant identified a match from the volunteer forms, she called the two potential partners to make sure they were still interested in participating and to find a time that was convenient for both of them to go on the date. (If a student was no longer interested in participating, another volunteer was selected as a replacement.) After one or more phone calls to each of the partners, the time and place of the date were arranged, and each member of the couple was also scheduled to come into a research office to complete the predate questionnaire. The two partners were always scheduled to come at different times. When the subjects arrived to complete the predate questionnaire, they were also given a letter that described the study and the postdate questionnaire with a campus envelope addressed to the investigator, a faculty member on campus. Subjects were directed to complete the postdate questionnaire within a 24-hr period after the date and to send it back through campus mail to the investigator (some subjects had to be called and reminded to complete the questionnaire).

Procedure for friend-arranged matches. Students, working in pairs for an optional course requirement, were given oral and written instructions on how to arrange the get-acquainted dates and collect the questionnaires before and after the date from their respondents. After the research pair matched a man and a woman from their respective networks and made the arrangements for the date, each member of the pair met his or her friend to deliver the letter of introduction to the study and have the friend complete the predate questionnaire. At this time the subject was also given the postdate questionnaire and a campus envelope. The subject was given the option of either sending both questionnaires back through campus mail or returning the questionnaire in sealed envelopes through the student in the class.

Measurement

Quality of talk. To measure the quality of the communication on the first date, a portion of the Iowa Communication Record (ICR) (see Duck et al., 1991) was included in the postdate questionnaire. First, subjects were asked to judge the communication on the date on the following 4-point **semantic differential scales**: relaxed versus strained, personal versus impersonal, attentive versus poor listening, informal versus formal, in-depth versus superficial, smooth versus difficult, open versus guarded, great deal of understanding versus great deal of misunderstanding, free of communication breakdowns versus laden with communication breakdowns, free of conflict versus laden with conflict. Four other questions from the ICR were also included: "Indicate the extent to which you think the talk was interesting" (1 = interesting, 9 = boring); "Indicate the extent to which you were satisfied with the interaction" (1 = satisfied, 9 = not satisfied); "How valuable was this conversation to you for your life right now?" (1 = extremely important to 9 = not important at all), "How valuable was this conversation for your future?" (1 = extremely important to 9 = not important at all). Items were subsequently recoded so that the higher number [indicated the more positive adjective].

With the total sample, a **factor analysis** was conducted on the 14 items included from the original ICR. The results from this factor analysis were very similar to the factor analysis results obtained by Duck et al. (1991) using a wider range of questions, including some on dimensions (factors) not assessed here. Two factors emerged, which were labeled (a) Communication Quality and (b) Depth and Value of Communication. For each factor, the factor scale score was represented by the mean of the items loading on that factor. The first factor explained 55.6% of the variance. The following 10 ICR items loaded (all > .60) on this factor for the total sample: relaxed/strained, attentive/poor listening, informal/formal, smooth/difficult, open/guarded, great deal of understanding/ great deal of misunderstanding, free of communication breakdowns/laden with communication breakdowns, free of conflict/laden with conflict, extent to which the talk was interesting, and extent of satisfaction

with the interaction. Loading on Factor 2 (all > .60), which explained 10.2% of the variance, were the other four ICR items: personal/impersonal, in-depth/superficial, how valuable conversation was right now, and how valuable conversation was for the future. **Cronbach's coefficient alpha** was .93 for Communication Quality and .85 for Depth and Value of Communication.

The postdate questionnaire also assessed the extent of personal information revealed in the interaction (i.e., self-disclosure): "How much personal information did your partner disclose?" and "How much personal information did you disclose?" (1 = a lot, to 9 = not much, but later recoded so that the higher number indicated greater disclosure).

Perception of partner's physical attractiveness. In the postdate questionnaire, subjects were asked how physically attractive their dating partner was (1 = not at all to 7 = extremely). Also included was the option "not sure" (this option was chosen by none of the males and only one of the females).

Perceived similarity. Two items assessed the degree of similarity. One question was "Based on your talk, how much did you find that you had in common?" (1 = a lot, to 9 = not much, but later recoded so that the higher number indicated greater similarity). Second, in a section that asked the subjects to judge the characteristics of the partner, subjects were asked to indicate the extent to which the other person "has your same interests and values". Subjects responded on a 1 (*not at all*) to 7 (*extremely*) response scale or checked the option "not sure". These two items were correlated .78 ($p < .001$) for both men and women. A two-item index of perceived similarity was created from these two items.

Attraction. Three questions were asked that are the dependent variables in this study:

(1) How attracted were you to this person as a possible dating partner?
(2) How attracted were you to this person as a possible friend?
(3) How much would you like to see the person again?

Subjects responded to each item on a 1 (*not at all*) to 7 (*extremely*) response scale.

The follow-up interview

At the end of the predate questionnaire, subjects were told that they might be contacted later to see whether they had had any further contact with their date and that, for this to be accomplished, they had to provide identifying information (name, telephone number, etc.). Not all subjects provided the identifying information. Furthermore, not all those who provided the information could subsequently be located. During one semester, the data were collected near the end of the term, and as a result, follow-up contact could not be conducted until the following semester, when some of the participants had moved and could not be traced. Follow-up data were available for 113 (57 men and 56 women) of the 166 participants (68%). For 71 of the original 83 couples, follow-up data were obtained from at least one member. The major purpose of this telephone follow-up interview was to see whether any further dating or contact had occurred between the partners. One of the questions asked in the follow-up interview was "Did you ever go on a second date or get together again as friends?" (1 = yes; 2 = no).

Results

Subjects' evaluations of the first date

The first purpose of this study was to provide a description of the impressions that opposite-sex strangers made of their interaction and of each other after interacting in the date-like situation.

Quality of the communication and other impressions. The subjects judged the quality of the communication on the first date to be high (average response was above 7 on a 9-point response scale) and the depth and value of the communication to be moderate (average response was around 5 on a 9-point response scale). The difference in the ratings on the two factor scores was significant for both men and women, as indicated by paired *t*-tests (t = 13.14, $p < .001$, for males; and $t = 15.13$, $p < .001$, for females). We found no sex differences on either of the communication factor scores or on any of the individual communication items constituting the factor scores. Furthermore, the partners agreed at least somewhat in their assessment of the communication in the interaction, especially in regard to its quality (how relaxed, informal, smooth, etc., the interaction was). The intracouple correlations were .45 ($p < .001$) for Communication Quality and .24 ($p < .05$) for Depth and Value of Communication.

Subjects reported a moderate amount of personal disclosure and perceived that their partner had disclosed more than they had, as indicated by a **paired-samples *t*-test** (t = 2.05, $p < .05$, for males, and $t = 2.91$, $p < .01$, for females). Men and women did not differ significantly in their assessment of the level of self-disclosure in the relationship, either for self or for the partner. There was no actual reciprocity in self-disclosure ($r = .04$, n.s., between Partner A's own disclosure and Partner B's own disclosure), but there was perceived reciprocity (the **correlation** between one partner's perception of own disclosure and perception of other's disclosure was .43 for men and .67 for women, both *ps* < .001).

Attraction and desire to see other again. On all three dependent measures [i.e., measures of the **dependent variable**] of liking, subjects scored, on the average, at the midpoint or higher on the 1 (not at all) to 7 (extremely) response scales. Both men and women were more attracted to the other person as a possible friend than as a possible dating partner ($t = 6.54$, $p < .001$, for males, and $t = 9.49$, $p < .001$, for females). On only one of the three dependent variables was a significant sex difference found. Women were more attracted to their partner as a friend than men were ($t = 2.17$, $p < .05$).

Although many subjects experienced attraction, attraction was not mutual. Intracouple correlations for the separate dependent measures were nonsignificant. Furthermore, the measure of desire to continue the relationship was not significantly correlated between partners.

The role of communication in the attraction process

The **correlations** between the two ICR factor scale scores, Communication Quality, and Depth and Value of Communication, and the three dependent measures were all positive and significant.

Correlations between the two self-disclosure items and the dependent measures are also positive and significant but are generally not as large as those found for the ICR factors. However, to further examine the importance of the quality of the communication relative to self-disclosure, we conducted a **stepwise regression** that included communication quality and the two self-disclosure items as the independent variables (these results are not tabled). This **stepwise regression** was conducted for each dependent variable and for men and women separately. For men, communication quality emerged as the primary or only significant predictor for each of the dependent measures. The **variance** explained by communication quality was .19 for romantic attraction, .20 for friendship attraction, and .27 for desire to see the other again. For women, communication quality was the major predictor of friendship attraction (explaining 46% of the variance) and the desire to see the other again (explaining 41% of the variance) but was not a significant predictor of dating or romantic attraction (for this variable, it was own self- disclosure that was the primary predictor, explaining 21% of the variance).

Next, we used stepwise regression to examine whether quality of communication is a significant predictor of attraction while controlling for perceived similarity and perceptions of the other's physical attractiveness. We also included method of recruitment of subjects (random matches vs. matches by an agency of acquaintances) as a control variable

in the models. The independent variables (which are all perceptions) are positively intercorrelated.

In none of the analyses for the stepwise regression did the method of recruitment significantly predict attraction. The relative importance of the three primary variables– quality communication, perceived physical attractiveness, and perceived similarity– was found to depend on both sex of subject and type of attraction measure. Below we describe the results for each of the dependent variables.

Romantic (dating) attraction. For both men and women, perceived physical attractiveness of the partner was the most important predictor of dating attraction. Similarity was the second most important predictor for both sexes. Quality communication did not emerge as a significant predictor of romantic attraction in the multivariate analyses for either sex.

Friendship attraction. For men, perceived similarity and perceived physical attractiveness (in that order) were the significant predictors of attraction to the other as a friend. For women, quality communication was the most important predictor of how attracted they were to the other as a friend, and perceived similarity was the second most important predictor.

Desire to see other again. For men, perceived similarity and physical attractiveness were significant predictors of desire to see the other again. For women, the most important predictors of desire to see the other again were quality communication and perceived physical attractiveness.

Analyses from the follow-up

On the basis of the data from the 113 respondents contacted on follow-up (i.e., at least one member of 71 of the original 83 pairs), it was determined that 10 couples had some type of further contact and 60 did not (1 couple disagreed and so was deleted from this analysis). The couples who saw each other again differed (on grouped *t*-tests) from those who did not in the following ways: Males were more likely to perceive their partner as physically attractive, $t(68) = 5.46$, $p < .001$, and similar to themselves, $t(68) = 3.71$, $p < .01$, and were more likely to evaluate the communication as of higher quality, $t(67) = 4.23$, $p < .001$. Only one difference emerged on the scores for females. Females who saw their partner again rated him as more similar to themselves than females who did not see their partner again, $t(66) = 2.80$, $p < .05$.

Discussion

In the present study, which was a get-acquainted date study modeled loosely after the "Coke date" or "computer date" studies conducted in the 1960s (e.g., Byrne, Ervin, & Lamberth, 1970; Walster [Hatfield] et al., 1966), we were interested primarily in examining whether the quality of the communication on the first date is related to the partners' attraction for each other and desire to see each other again. By simultaneously comparing the effects of communication factors and other traditionally measured factors, we hoped to add to the understanding of the relative effects of these variables. All the same, this study on its own does not answer every question about the direction of causality, and we therefore draw substantially on the authority of other literature that has taken the effects singly and tested the direction of causality.

Before we discuss the results for our main hypothesis, we will highlight some of the interesting descriptive information concerning the evaluation of the communication in the interaction and the attitudes about the partner.

Perceptions of the first date

The communication in the get-acquainted ("first date") exercise was judged by the participants, who were strangers to each other before the interaction, to be of high quality and to be moderate in value. The subjects also reported that a moderate amount of personal information was disclosed during the interaction. These descriptive results suggest that interactions between previously unacquainted individuals can be quite pleasant and have the potential to create friendship and romantic pairings.

Indeed, many of the subjects did experience attraction for their partner. Furthermore, the subjects were more attracted to the other as a friend than as a dating partner. This finding is discriminative, in that subjects evidently made distinctions between different types of attraction, and it therefore argues that the results should be explained not in terms of blanket effects of social desirability but rather by some other influence. For example, most people have only one dating partner at a time but several friends, and this is one possible reason that subjects expressed more friendship attraction than dating attraction as they interacted with someone they were meeting for the first time. Although the subjects expressed attraction for their partner, very few couples actually did see each other again, and there are several possible reasons for this. For instance, (a) the attraction responses of the partners were not correlated (i.e., often one partner was attracted and the other was not); (b) the matches were somewhat random; (c) the couples may have defined the interaction more as a one-shot scientific study than as a way to meet someone who could potentially enter their lives; and (d) unions may have been less likely to develop between these people if they had no other opportunities to run into each other (e.g., in class).

Because men and women can sometimes experience relationships in different ways, we examined possible sex differences in evaluations of this first date. The men and women were very similar in reacting to the interaction. Men and women did not significantly differ in judgments of the quality and value of the communication, and they were similar in their self-disclosure ratings (i.e., men and women reported disclosing a similar amount of personal information). Furthermore, in their reports concerning partner's disclosure, no sex differences were found. These findings are consistent with research that shows very few sex differences in level of self-disclosure in dating (e.g., Rubin, Hill, Peplau, & Dunkel-Schetter, 1980) but are not consistent with the findings from a laboratory study by Derlega, Winstead, Wong, and Hunter (1985). Derlega et al. found that males disclosed more intimately than females to an opposite-sex partner in a get-acquainted exercise. In their study, however, men and women self-disclosed through written notes in the laboratory. The results of our more naturalistic study suggest that men and women feel that they disclose to an equal degree in initial dating situations. The only difference found between men and women in the attraction measures was that the females, as a group, expressed more friendship attraction for their partner than the males. This finding may demonstrate women's overall greater interest in friendship.

We also examined the extent of agreement and reciprocity between the partners in their evaluation of the first date. The partners agreed moderately in their judgments of the quality of the communication and agreed slightly in their judgments of the value of the communication and the degree of similarity in the couple. Although the partners broadly agreed in their evaluations of the quality of the communication, they did not experience reciprocity or mutuality in attraction. That the partners did not experience reciprocal attraction is not surprising, given that the partners were not matched on any dimension (e.g., interests, physical attractiveness) that might increase mutuality in attraction. Walster [Hatfield] et al. (1966), who randomly matched subjects for a date, also did not find any similarity in the dating partners' attraction for each other (the correlation was near zero).

Interestingly, both men and women judged the partner's self-disclosure to be more personal than their own. This may be an example of an actor–observer difference. The actor (the subject) knows how much he

or she discloses in many other situations and in many types of relationships but knows only what the other (the partner) has disclosed in this situation and so may rate it as more personal than the actor's own.

Predictors of attraction

As we turned to look at how communication affects attraction, we began by examining the ... relationships between the communication variables and the attraction variables. Each of the communication variables, including the two self-disclosure items, had significant and positive correlations with the attraction measures. The correlations (overall) were higher for the ICR factor scores than for the self-disclosure items (as traditionally measured), and stepwise regression results further confirmed the greater importance of quality communication in predicting attraction. Many previous assessments of self-disclosure have confounded the actual delivery of a self-disclosive message with other elements of communication quality, such as warmth, openness, and personalness. The present results suggest that the unconfounding of these efforts is important and that communication quality rather than self-disclosure is more responsible for increased attraction. Of course, it should also be remembered that the present design does not alone answer the chicken–egg question of whether communication quality causes attraction or attraction inflates impressions of communication quality. Considerable amounts of previous research demonstrate that the causal directions are indeed convoluted (e.g., Conville, 1988; Cupach & Comstock, 1990), but Gottman (1979) and Wampler and Sprenkle (1980) have clearly shown that improvements in the quality of communication lead to improvements in the quality of relationships (see also Montgomery, 1988).

We were also interested in comparing the quality of the communication with two other documented predictors of attraction, perceived similarity and perceived physical attractiveness. These results demonstrate the importance of perceived physical attractiveness and similarity as predictors of attraction. These variables have been emphasized in previous social psychological literature on determinants of initial attraction. In this study, they were the strongest predictors of romantic attraction for both men and women (of course, causal direction also cannot be determined between these variables and attraction). These results also demonstrate the importance of quality communication, although its effect depended on both sex and the particular attraction measure. Quality communication was never a major predictor of attraction for men but was the primary predictor of women's attraction to the other as a friend and the desire to see the other again.

Thus we found communication quality to be more important to women than to men and more important in friendship attraction than in romantic attraction (at least for women). These findings confirm our expectations. We did not, however, find similarity to be a more important antecedent of attraction for women than for men. Our finding is inconsistent with a recent conclusion reached by Feingold (1991), who conducted a meta-analytic study and found that similarity was more important to women than to men. However, most of the studies reviewed by Feingold looked at similarity as objectively measured (e.g., the degree to which two partners scored similarly on an attitude scale) rather than as perceived by the subjects.

Whereas quality communication was a more important predictor of attraction for women than for men, the results of the follow-up suggest that men's scores on communication quality and the other variables may be, to a greater degree than women's scores, determinants of whether the couple

has any further contact. The number of couples who had any further contact is too small, however, to make much of these data. If we could have confidence in these results, however, the finding is not surprising in light of the fact that it is still often the male who is assertive in the early stages of the relationship (e.g., he does the asking out).

Conclusions

We began this article by arguing that the role of talk or communication is crucial to examine in the initial attraction process. We conclude by proposing that the quality of communication may be even more important to both men and women than suggested by these results. For example, quality communication may serve as a context in which similarity is discovered and in which desirable characteristics of the other become more salient. The least that can be claimed for these results is that communication variables matter more than has been credited by those evaluating the total package of factors that affect dating progress. Our results indicate that, among a mix of other influential variables (those usually studied in social psychological accounts of romance and relational development), communication quality is at least a considerable factor, particularly for women. If these results do nothing else, they should convince readers that including specific and direct assessments of talk is important in the future elucidation of the dynamics of relationship initiation. In future research on the role of communication in the attraction process, both perceived quality of communication and behavioral measures of communication could be assessed.

One interesting thing to note here is that the authors used a method of determining direction of causality in their results by reference to the results of other studies. Since some of the authors' own results were correlational (and so the direction of causality could not be ascertained), they make reference in the Discussion section to the findings of other scholars who had already determined the direction of causality between the variables concerned, thus permitting the present authors to make a causal argument about their own findings. Do you see any dangers in this process or does it strike you as a valid method of deduction when faced with findings that are not "directional"?

The authors of the paper were also concerned about two things: about the extension of a first date to a second date, and also about the role of communication in acquaintance. Are you satisfied that they measured communication adequately? The authors asked participants to recall the quality of conversation that they had experienced and perceptions may be different between people. However, those *perceptions* may be the influence that affects subsequent feelings of attraction. The authors also noted that in previous research there has been confusion between delivery of *content* of self-disclosure, on the one hand, and the *quality of communication* on the other, especially in terms of its warmth or personalness, for example. What do you make of that?

Remember also that subjects were relatively youthful and were going on first dates, so the findings about the importance of perceived physical attractiveness could be heightened by these things in a way that would not generalize to other (later) dates or to, say, internet dating or the dating habits of older divorcees. Or it might; we don't know. What do you think? How could you find out?

The authors also note that the study shows that it is possible to distinguish different types of attraction (romantic or friendship attraction). Remember that Byrne's attraction paradigm used measures of liking and measures of "desire to work with another person" as the measures of attraction in the Interpersonal Judgment Scale. How many types of attraction could there be and how could it matter if they can be differentiated? For instance consider whether these different types of attraction could be important in evaluating men's and women's attraction, whether to other men or to other women.

Think about these issues in preparation for the following chapter, which is about love.

3   Love

Love, as we have all heard, is a many splendored thing, and that idea (that love has many aspects and different elements) has appealed to researchers. All the same, love appears, on the face of it, to be an elusive concept that one cannot really study soundly. In fact, researchers have devised a number of methods for assessing the concept and its accouterments. For example, love can be studied as composed of a mixture of six separate types identified first by Lee (1973). This approach is represented by the research of Hendrick et al. in the first article.

It might seem very odd that scientists would attempt to measure love, but … . Well, that's what we do! This chapter presents some of the research that has been devoted to the measurement of love and to understanding its relationship to marital satisfaction and sex. Some of the research reported here has been very carefully devoted to the development of good ways of measuring its core and its components. We have chosen to edit out quite a lot of the technical details about scale construction in order to focus on the ways in which scientific research has advanced our understanding of the ways in which love "works". The development of such scales to measure such things as love is nevertheless one of the important ways in which the science of relationships has achieved credibility and the best ways to measure some elusively personal emotions. Those readers who wish to pursue these details should consult the original sources reprinted here.

These papers do not exhaust (nor fully represent) the sorts of work that have been done on love, but they do show how one strand of such work can be developed. You need to know that such research has recently been criticized for, for example, not attending to the moral basis on which love is encouraged by some religions (Cere, 2001: http://www.thepublicinterest.com/archives/2001spring/article2.html). Others criticize it for misrepresenting love and they prefer to use a prototype approach (Fehr, 1993) that looks at the features of love experiences that are common and prototypical. Also some researchers have noted that love is a complex set of feelings, behaviors, attitudes, emotions and attachments, some of the latter being based on childhood experiences and amounting to a personality type. We might ask ourselves whether, when we love someone, whether we really do definitely feel a complex of things or just an overwhelming sense of pleasure, undifferentiated. Do we need to ask what is primary? "Where is fancy bred? or in the heart or in the head?"

The first paper included here was a pioneering attempt to develop a measure of the components of love in order to see if men and women experience love differently. The other two papers use this classic paper as a basis for investigating the relationship between types of love and marital satisfaction, on the one hand, and types of love and attitudes to sex, on the other. Hendrick et al. (1984) was a pioneering effort to understand the components of the experience of love in the two sexes. You will see that the authors wanted to discover whether men and women experienced love differently and they found some interesting ways in which "difference" turns out to be found. The other two papers develop the theory and technique to apply them to specific other questions about love.

The study uses **Likert scales**. These kinds of scales are common in research in the social sciences and are 1 to N (usually 1–7 or 1–5) report scales where a person is presented with a range of possible answers (for example, Very much agree, Agree, Unsure, Disagree, Very much disagree). Other examples would be "always, sometimes, rarely, never". The scales are usually *numbered* rather than given as words (or the words may be translated into numbers so that 1 would be assigned to "Very much agree" and 5 would be assigned to "Very much disagree", in the example above). These scales are much used in relationship research because they help to separate out components of a person's overall attitude to some specific aspect of the relationship that interests the researcher. They offer social scientists a way to establish the frequency and intensity of certain forms of emotion or experience relative to other related items. Think as you read this paper of the reasonableness of such measures. Do we really think in terms of such scales? Remember how often, and perhaps without recognizing our debt to Likert, we say things like "How do you rate this on a scale from one to ten?". Are such scales valuable and realistic ways of establishing the occurrences of social behaviors or emotions or communication styles?

Variants of **Cluster analysis** techniques are also used in some of these papers, an important set of techniques used in the social sciences for discovering the ways in which things "go together". It really works rather like this. Suppose I emptied out all my loose change. I could collect/cluster all the dimes together, all the quarters together, all the dollar bills together and all the five-dollar bills … and so on. These clusters would be derived from the fact that the things put into each cluster are similar on some criterion (they are worth the same as the other coins or notes in their cluster). Grouping things that are the same is the first step of a cluster analysis. Next, one wants to find "higher order" clusters that can connect together some of the first-round clusters. In the above example, I could create a cluster of silver coins, a cluster of copper coins, a cluster of bank notes … Now I could create another even higher cluster of "coins worth less than a dollar bill" which would include the copper coin cluster, the silver coin cluster … Finally I would find that the data set called My Loose Change is a supercluster made up of two higher order clusters (a) "Banknotes" and (b) "Coins worth less than a dollar bill" (with its sub-clusters of "copper coins", "silver coins", …). In the studies reported below, some of the authors want to look at the ways in which different measures and elements of love cluster together, and in the final paper the authors are looking at two clusters of data, one on love and one on sex, and they are asking the "Super-cluster Question": are Love and Sex separate things or do they make one Super-cluster of attitudes? In technical language, initially each variable is considered as a separate object and similarity between variables is established statistically to determine a mathematical distance between clusters. The program starts arbitrarily with a first variable and forms clusters by joining variables with the smallest maximum distance. This procedure continues until one cluster containing all of the items is formed, if possible, but failing that, the goal is to find the smallest number of clusters that will meaningfully include all of the original data.

Principal components analysis and **factor analysis** are, to all intents and purposes here, variations on this basic idea and we will come to them later. In these cases, however, the purpose is not necessarily to link clusters in a hierarchical tree with a super-cluster at the top; it is to find those things that go together into classes that are separable from other classes found in the data, so that following the earlier example, things in my pocket could be factored into loose change, keys, memorabilia, Swiss Army knife gadgets, … all separate classes of data but not hierarchically related to one another.

Another set of techniques that will come up here and in later chapters is based on **Analysis of Variance**, usually shortened to **ANOVA**. The function of this analytic technique is like it says on the can: It is a way of analyzing the variance (see Chapter 1) in a way that tells the researcher which sources are the most influential and important in the whole mix of variance generated by the study. We look for the effects of chance ("error") and the effects of all the main variables in the study. For example, when men and women behave significantly differently on a variable (say attitudes to physical attractiveness – see Chapter 4) we would talk of a **main effect** of sex on attitudes to physical attractiveness. When a variable has an effect only in the presence of another variable (for example, if men and women differ in their attention to physical attractiveness only on first dates but not on later ones) then we'd talk about an **interaction effect** between sex and timing of date, because the dependent variable is affected by the *combined*, interactive effect of the two independent variables.

Before you read these papers, think about these questions:

What is love? Can it be measured and if so how should it be assessed best (using words, actions, nonverbal cues)? Is love one thing or a composite of others, and if so, what are they? And specifically for the first paper, make some predictions about the ways in which men's and women's experiences of love might be different. What are your guesses?

Do Men and Women Love Differently?

Clyde Hendrick, Susan Hendrick, Franklin H. Foote and Michelle J. Slapion-Foote

During the past decade [1974–84], love has progressed from a not quite reputable area for scientific study to a domain of increasing sophistication. Theories of love are numerous (e.g., Cook & Wilson, 1979; Kelley, 1983) and increasing attention is paid to problems of measurement. Initial notions of love as a global construct are being replaced by multidimensional constructs that promise greater yields in precision of knowledge. The present study sought to advance this trend by detailed analysis of one multi-dimensional theory, the "colors of love" proposed by John Alan Lee (1973, 1977).

Lee developed a typology of love styles that formed a closed circle. Through a complex interview procedure and data reduction techniques, Lee identified three primary types of love styles; Eros (romantic love), Ludus (game-playing love), Storge (friendship love), and three main secondary styles, Mania (possessive, dependent love), Pragma (logical, "shopping list" love), and Agape (all giving, selfless love). These different styles are equally valid but different ways of loving, according to Lee.

Lasswell & Lasswell (1976) recognized the value of Lee's typology for everyday life as well as for clinical practice. They developed a 50-item true–false scale to measure the six love styles. Each subject was given a score on each of the six subscales by simply counting the number of "true" responses for a given scale. Thus each subject could be profiled on all six subscales …

The present research was undertaken in the conviction that Lee's work represented an important conceptual advance in the study of love. If so, it is important to have a valid easily administered instrument to measure the constructs. Because Lasswell & Lasswell (1976) reported that they had done extensive validation work, we used their 50 items, plus four new ones, including two from a dissertation supervised by the first author (Fuller, 1982, unpub.). Instead of using the true–false format, subjects rated the items on a five-point scale. We believed the resulting scale would better lend itself to analyses than the original scale.

In addition to the scaling interests, we were also concerned with sex differences in love attitudes. A great many studies show sex differences in sexual attitudes but there is little work on attitudes toward love. Rubin, Peplau & Hill (1981) presented suggestive data from the Boston Couples Study indicating that men fall in love more easily than women. Further, women are more cautious about entering relationships and engage in more "comparative shopping". Such behaviors suggest that different attitudinal orientations toward love may

exist between the sexes. Hatkoff & Lasswell (1979), in a study that differed from the present one in sample heterogeneity, instrument format, and types of data analysis, found that a larger percentage of males than females scored high on the ludic and erotic subscales, but females tended to be slightly more manic, storgic and pragmatic. These data suggest that strong mean differences may exist between the sexes on an item-by-item basis in love attitudes. If true, it might well be that the factor structure of love attitudes is somewhat different for males and females.

In summary, the present study intended to assess the structure of the scale developed by the Lasswells to measure Lee's typology and to study attitudes toward love as a function of subjects' sex. This study was part of a larger study that measured sexual attitudes, but only the love attitude data will be considered in the current report.

Method

A questionnaire entitled "Attitudes About Love and Sex" was developed that included an explanation about the study of attitudes, a brief section of background questions, a section entitled "Love Attitudes Scale" that contained the 54 love items and a section entitled "Sexual Attitudes Scale" that contained 102 items written by the first two authors. The scale was constructed to use machine-scored answer sheets. The items in the attitude sections were rated on a five-point basis: A = strongly agree (1), B = moderately agree (2), C = neutral (3), D = moderately disagree (4), E = strongly disagree (5). The letters were transformed to the corresponding numbers for data analyses.

Sample characteristics

The scale was administered during the Spring and Fall semesters of 1982 to 835 introductory psychology and sociology students attending the University of Miami.

A few students did not complete all of the attitude items, so the effective sample consisted of 813 students, 374 males and 439 females. Because large numbers of students take introductory psychology, the sample was reasonably representative of the student population, which includes White non-Hispanic, Hispanic, Black, and Asian students. The mean age of the sample was 19.2 years, reflecting a mixture of freshmen and sophomores.

Two questions related specifically to love. One question asked "How many times have you been in love?". Results were: none = 11.4 percent, once = 37.0 percent, twice = 29.1 percent, three or more times = 19.9 percent, and 2.6 percent of the students failed to respond. Males and females did not differ. A second item asked "Are you in love now?" The responses were: no = 45.7 percent, yes = 51.4 percent, no response = 2.9 percent. There was a significant sex effect for this item (2 = 24.9, df = 1, *p* < .0001). For the males, 56.7 percent were not in love while 43.4 percent were in love; for the females 38.9 percent were not while 61.1 percent were in love.

Students who had never been in love were asked to respond in terms of what their "responses would most likely be" in a love relationship. Students not in love at the present time were given no special instructions.

The present scale consisted of the Lasswells' original scale (Lasswell & Lobsenz, 1980, p. 60), converted from a true–false to a Likert format. Two additional items were added to the Eros subscale and two to the Storge subscale so that they would conform to the length of the other subscales.

Results

The 54 items from the Love Attitudes Scale were subjected to three types of analyses; ANOVAs to study sex and religious differences, **factor analysis** to study structure of the scale and a **cluster analysis** as a second approach to the issue of structure.

There were no major findings regarding the religious differences, so they will not be considered further.

Sex differences

The items, means and significance level are shown in Table 1. The items are grouped conceptually in terms of the six love styles, as defined by the Lasswells' research. Items 51, 52, 53 and 54 were generated from Fuller's (1982) dissertation and by the current authors, and items 1–50 were from the Lasswells' scale. A two-tailed probability of .05 or less was used to assess significance.

(1) *Eros*. There were significant differences between males and females on four of the nine items. Males responded more erotically on three of these items, agreeing more than females that they kissed soon after meeting, that they were first attracted by physical appearance and that physical attraction is one of the best aspects of being in love. However, males disagreed more than females that they enjoyed having similar material possessions as the lover (Item 41). Both sexes tended to slightly disagree with the item and it may reflect romantic behavior from another era. On balance, the results suggest that males are somewhat more erotic in orientation than females.

(2) *Ludus*. There were significant sex differences on four of the eight items and males were more ludic on three of these comparisons; on keeping love secrets (Item 15), getting over love affairs easily (Item 27) and implied sexual acts with others (Item 34). However, females agreed relatively more that it is okay to keep one's lover slightly uncertain (Item 6). On balance, the results show a tendency toward more ludic responses by males.

(3) *Storge*. Eight of the ten items showed significant sex effects. Females scored in a more storgic direction on all eight comparisons. Thus, love came slowly and quietly (Item 2), required caring first (Item 5), was best when based on friendship (Item 21), etc., relatively more for females than for males.

Hendrick et al., Table 1   *Means for males and females for the six love styles*

Items	M	F	p
Eros			
1. I believe that 'love at first sight' is possible.	2.42	2.58	–
7. The first time we kissed or rubbed cheeks, I felt a definite genital response (lubrication, erection).	2.47	2.50	–
17. We kissed each other soon after we met because we both wanted to.	2.14	2.31	< .05
20. Usually the first thing that attracts my attention to a person is his/her pleasing physical appearance.	1.71	1.97	< .05
23. At the first touch of his/her hand, I knew that love was a real possibility.	2.82	2.73	–
35. Before I ever fell in love, I had a pretty clear physical picture of what my true love would be like.	3.23	3.05	–
41. I like the idea of having the same kinds of clothes, hats, plants, bicycles, cars etc., as my lover does.	3.62	3.28	< .05
52. Strong physical attraction is one of the best aspects of being in love.	2.38	2.61	< .05
54. I am delighted with the appearance of my lover.	1.68	1.65	–
Ludus			
6. It's always a good idea to keep your lover a little uncertain about how committed you are to him/her.	3.31	2.95	< .05
14. Part of the fun of being in love is testing one's skill at keeping it going and getting what one wants from it at the same time.	2.69	2.70	–
15. As far as my lover goes, what he/she doesn't know about me won't hurt him/her.	3.10	3.36	< .05
26. I have at least once had to plan carefully to keep two of my lovers from finding out about each other.	3.23	3.38	–
27. I can get over love affairs pretty easily and quickly.	3.24	3.62	< .05
33. I enjoy flirting with attractive people.	2.00	2.04	–
34. My lover would get upset if he/she knew of some of the things I've done with other people.	2.73	3.11	< .05
46. It would be fun to see whether I can get someone to go out with me even if I didn't want to get involved with that person.	2.74	2.79	–
Storge			
2. I did not realize that I was in love until I actually had been for some time.	2.75	2.59	< .05
5. You can't love unless you have first had caring for a while.	2.61	2.25	< .05
8. I still have good friendships with almost everyone with whom I have ever been involved in a love relationship.	2.45	2.52	–
21. The best kind of love grows out of a long friendship.	2.68	2.41	< .05
29. The best part of love is living together, building a home together and rearing children together.	2.47	2.30	< .05
32. Kissing, cuddling and sex shouldn't be rushed into, they will happen naturally when one's intimacy has grown enough.	1.99	1.51	< .05
37. It is hard to say exactly when we fell in love.	2.47	2.31	< .05
50. The best love relationships are the ones that last the longest.	2.77	2.91	–
51. Love is really a deep friendship, not a mysterious, mystical emotion.	2.73	2.49	< .05

Hendrick et al., Table 1   (Continued)

Items	M	F	p
53. The most satisfying love relationships are those that develop between good friends.	2.74	2.59	< .05
Pragma			
4. From a practical point of view, I must consider what a person is going to become before I commit myself to him/her.	2.92	2.60	< .05
9. It makes good sense to plan your life carefully before choosing a lover.	2.66	2.57	< .05
16. It is best to love someone with a similar background.	2.84	2.59	< .05
28. A main consideration in choosing a lover is how he/she reflects on my family.	3.19	2.90	< .05
31. A main consideration in choosing a partner is whether or not he/she will be a good parent.	2.79	2.50	< .05
38. I couldn't truly love anyone I would not be willing to marry.	2.94	2.75	–
42. I wouldn't date anyone that I wouldn't want to fall in love with.	3.93	3.68	< .05
47. A main consideration in choosing a partner is how he/she will reflect on one's career.	3.07	2.89	< .05
49. Before getting very involved with anyone, I try to figure out how compatible his/her hereditary background is with mine in case we ever have children.	3.67	3.45	< .05
Mania			
3. When things aren't going right with us, my stomach gets upset.	3.12	2.53	< .05
10. When my love affairs break up, I get so depressed that I have even thought of suicide.	4.31	4.21	–
11. Sometimes I get so excited about being in love that I can't sleep.	2.55	2.42	–
18. When my lover doesn't pay attention to me, I feel sick all over.	2.99	2.74	< .05
22. When I am in love, I have trouble concentrating on anything else.	2.86	2.72	–
25. I cannot relax if I suspect that he/she is with someone else.	2.29	2.19	–
39. Even though I don't want to be jealous, I can't help it when my lover pays attention to someone else.	2.11	2.15	–
43. At least once when I thought a love affair was all over, I saw him/her again and the old feelings came surging back.	2.20	1.86	< .05
45. If my lover ignores me for a while, I sometimes do really stupid things to try to get his/her attention back.	3.03	2.78	< .05
Agape			
12. I try to use my own strength to help my lover through difficult times, even when he/she is behaving foolishly.	1.88	1.70	< .05
13. I would rather suffer myself than let my lover suffer.	2.29	2.35	–
19. I cannot be happy unless I place my lover's happiness before my own.	3.06	3.16	–
24. When I break up with someone, I go out of my way to see that he/she is OK.	2.80	2.84	–

(Continued)

Hendrick et al., Table 1   (Continued)

Items	M	F	p
30. I am usually willing to sacrifice my own wishes to let my lover achieve his/hers.	2.79	2.68	–
36. If my lover had a baby by someone else, I would want to raise it, love it and care for it as if it were my own.	3.57	3.29	< .05
40. I would rather break up with my lover than stand in his/her way.	2.53	2.42	–
44. Whatever I own is my lover's to use as he/she chooses.	2.33	2.30	–
48. When my lover doesn't see or call me for a while, I assume he/she has a good reason.	2.44	2.53	–

Note: The higher the score, the greater the disagreement with the item: 1 = strongly agree, 2 = moderately agree, 3 = neutral, 4 = moderately disagree, 5 = strongly disagree.

(4) *Pragma*. Seven of the nine items showed significant sex effects. In every case, females scored in a more pragmatic direction. These items show shopping-list practicality such as concern for what a person is going to become (Item 4), similarity of background (Item 16), reflection of lover on family (Item 28), etc. It should be noted that on an absolute basis, both sexes were somewhat ambivalent because responses tended toward the scale mid-point. However, on items with a tendency toward disagreement (e.g., Item 49), females disagreed less than males.

(5) *Mania*. Four of the nine items showed significant sex effects. Females subscribed more to items such as upset stomach over love problems (Item 3), feeling sick all over (Item 18), surge of old feeling on seeing an old lover (Item 43), and doing stupid things to get attention (Item 45). On balance, the results suggest more manic love attitudes for females than for males.

(6) *Agape*. There were sex differences on only two items. Females were more likely to help a lover through difficult times (Item 12) and to disagree less that they would raise a lover's baby by someone else (Item 36).

In summary, the data indicated that females were more storgic (love as friendship) and pragmatic in their conceptions of love than males. There was also a tendency for females to be more manic, although this effect may simply reflect the tendency of females to report more physical symptoms than do males (e.g., Mechanic, 1978). Males tended to be more game-playing (ludic) and erotic than females, although these two tendencies were not as pronounced as the females' pragmatic, friendship orientation. Finally, charitable agapic love seemed not to show real sex differences.

Factor analysis of the love attitudes scale

A **principal components factor analysis** ... was performed ... for the 54 items of the Love Attitudes Scale, separately for each sex. Conceptually, we were somewhat uncertain what to expect from the factor analyses. The Lasswells wrote six sets of items to measure the six love styles. Ideally, these six sets of items would load on six [distinct] factors. However, ... Lee (1973) viewed Eros, Ludus and Storge as independent primary factors. However, Pragma, Mania and Agape were viewed as mixtures of pairs of the primaries. Mania was conceived as a mixture of Eros and Ludus, Pragma as a mixture of Ludus and Storge, and Agape as a mixture of Eros and Storge. It seemed entirely possible that the items measuring the secondary styles might split and load on their respective pairs of primary factors. It was an issue to be decided empirically.

...

The first three factors ... clearly represented Pragma, Mania and Agape, respectively. These are the three secondary love attitude mixtures in Lee's conceptual theme.

...

Factor 1 – Pragma. The Lasswells' Pragma scale originally included nine items, all but one of which (Item 38, "I couldn't truly love anyone I would not be willing to marry") loaded on the first factor for males and for females (Item 42 appeared only for females). In addition, the male factor included two Storge items and the female factor included one Storge and one Eros item. The Storge items are congruent with Pragma items since Pragma is ostensibly a mixture of Storge and Ludus. This scale reflects the "shopping list" quality of Pragma with such items as "A main consideration in choosing a lover is how he or she reflects on my family" (Item 28).

Factor 2 – Mania. The Lasswells' Mania scale originally contained nine items, all of which loaded on the second factor (Item 43 appeared for females only). In addition, one Eros item loaded on the female factor. This was the most sharply defined factor in the scale and reflects the possessive, demanding, almost hysterical quality of manic love in such items as "When my lover doesn't pay attention to me, I feel sick all over" (Item 18).

Factor 3 – Agape. The Lasswells' Agape scale was originally defined by nine items. Males loaded on five of these items and females on six items. In addition, males showed modest loadings on two Storge and one Eros item, and females on one Storge and two Eros items. Perhaps the latter result is just a hint of the mixture of Eros and Storge primaries from which Agape is theoretically supposed to be formed. Although several ostensibly Agape items did not load on the factor, it nevertheless clearly seems to represent the Agape construct that is exemplified by such items as "I would rather suffer myself than let my lover suffer" (Item 13).

The results for the first three factors provided an elegant confirmation of three of Lee's love constructs and the Lasswells' scales that measured the constructs. Unfortunately, the remainder of the factor analyses did not show such clear results ... There was a match between males and females on four of the factors [but] males and females did not match on two factors each and these data are presented separately for each sex in the bottom panel ...

A Ludus factor emerged fairly clearly for both sexes (males, F4; females, F7) ... The ludic items that loaded on the factor seemed to reflect the secretive, non-disclosing aspect of the ludic style: the ostensibly ludic items that did not load on the factor seemed to reflect skill and playfulness. Conceptually, playfulness should be an aspect of Ludus; however only manipulative secrecy was suggested by the factor.

The remaining three factors on which there was a male–female match tended to be mixtures of two of Lee's conceptual love styles, and one of these was bipolar in nature. Specifically, the factors emerged as mixtures of Storge/Agape, Eros/Ludus and bipolar Storge/Eros ...

The Storge/Agape factor appeared fairly strongly (males, F5; females, F6). The mixing of Storge and Agape items is theoretically consistent since Agape is ostensibly a mixture of Storge and Eros. The Storge items that loaded on this factor seemed to reflect the storgic emphasis on friendship as a basis for love, while the Agape items appeared to reflect attitudes which are as appropriate to a friendship as to a romantic love relationship. The agapic items were definitely more on the commonsense side of Agape than on the more ethereal, self-sacrificing side. It should be noted that females were more storgic than agapic relative to males. Indeed, only the commonality of Item 48 to both sexes justifies the mixed label for females.

The Eros/Ludus factor emerged quite clearly for both sexes (males, F6; females, F5). The Eros items portrayed the strong sensual basis of erotic love, while the Ludus items were concerned with the superficial pleasures of love. In total, this factor seemed to represent a surface attraction factor based on sensuality and on here-and-now interaction. Females loaded more heavily than males on the ludic items, so perhaps for them the factor is really Eros/Eros.

The bipolar Storge/Eros factor appeared conceptually strong (males, F8; females, F9). The Storge items seemed to reflect a temporal aspect of love, the gradual progression of friendship into love. The Eros items that had negative loadings reflected a parallel, if philosophically opposite, temporal aspect of love, the rapid progression from initial encounter to love. Thus, the bipolar Storge/Eros factor juxtaposed the "evolutionary" and "revolutionary" viewpoints of loving, with Storge items showing friendship ripening gradually into caring and then love while negative Eros loadings reflected the opposite of touching, kissing and loving almost at first sight.

[T]wo male factors and two female factors … did not match. Male Factor 7 appeared to be a rather weak Eros factor. The male mixed factor (F4) is a disparate factor, although it has a sensual instrumental quality. The female splinter Mania factor (F4) included several different types of items and may be viewed as a sort of "possessiveness" factor. The goal seemed to be keeping oneself secure and unthreatened in the relationship while keeping one's partner a bit off-balance. The final female factor (F8) appeared as a splinter Agape factor, reflecting an unselfish, caring quality.

Although the final two male and two female factors discussed could not be matched, each individual factor offered some measure of conceptual meaningfulness and each factor accounted for a substantial portion of the male and female variances, respectively.

Most of the items loaded on one or more factors [see **factor loading** in the glossary]. For males, only items 36, 38 and 52 did not load on a factor. For females, only items 14 and 41 failed to load on a factor. However, for males, six items (21, 23, 24, 29, 43, 53) loaded on two factors. Seven items (12, 25, 29, 39, 42, 48, 50) loaded on two factors for females and one item (52) loaded on three factors.

Cluster analysis of the Love Attitudes Scale

The nature of the results of the factor analysis suggested that further probing of item structure was desirable. Since the Lasswells reported use of cluster analysis, we decided to explore item structure in this way as well.

The first run combined both sexes, as apparently did the Lasswell data … The optimal solution was three major clusters. Each of these three clusters included one of Lee's three secondary love styles (Mania, Pragma, Agape) and the two primary styles associated with the respective secondary style. Thus, the first major cluster contained Mania (eight items), Ludus (six items), and Eros (four items). Within this cluster, there were distinct sub-clusters of Mania and Ludus but not Eros items.

The second major cluster contained Agape (all nine items), Storge (seven items), Eros (three items) and one stray Mania item (Item 43). Within the cluster, there were distinct sub-clusters of Agape and Storge but not Eros items.

The third major cluster contained Pragma (all nine items), Storge (three items), Ludus (two items) and two odd Eros items (Items 35 and 41). Within the cluster, there was a distinct sub-cluster of Pragma items and a two-item Ludus cluster.

Thus, among the six love attitude styles, only Eros was not represented by its own cluster, although Eros was strongly represented on the first cluster. However, the distribution of Eros items suggests that Eros may be a theme that pervades the other styles of love. This conclusion seems consistent with the results of the factor analysis … In general, however, the results of the clustering provide strong support for Lee's theory, especially the notion that secondary love styles are mixtures of two primaries. The major puzzle was why the three secondary styles emerged so strongly (on both factor and cluster analyses), while the primaries tended to remain as less well-defined background factors.

Because of our interest in sex differences in love styles, the same clustering routine was applied to the item correlations separately for males and females. Unfortunately, little useful information emerged. For males, a large cluster emerged that contained items from four of the love styles. Two minor clusters also emerged that contained mostly Ludus items and mostly Agape items, respectively. For females, one large cluster and two minor clusters also emerged. The large cluster included items from four of the love styles and the small clusters contained mostly Mania items and mostly Storge items, respectively. It was unclear why well-defined clusters emerged for both sexes combined, but not for each sex separately.

Discussion

The two primary goals of the present study were to investigate sex differences in attitudes toward love and to assess the validity of Lee's (1973) typology of love styles using the Lasswells' (1976) love attitudes scale.

Lee's typology

Factor analyses performed separately for males and females resulted in seven fairly clear factors on which the sexes matched. In addition, two other small factors were unique for each sex. The first three factors were the most clearly defined and included Pragma (F1 practical love), Mania (F2 hysterical love), and Agape (F3 selfless love). These factors reflected the secondary love styles within Lee's typology.

Ludus, one of Lee's primary styles, also emerged clearly as a factor. Three other factors were composites. Storge/Agape, a primary–secondary composite, seemed to emphasize friendship. In contrast, both Eros/Ludus and Storge/Eros were composites of two of Lee's primaries. Eros/Ludus was best described as "superficial attraction".

Storge/Eros reflected, in bipolar fashion, gradual versus rapid progression in love. It should be noted that in these four factors, each primary appeared twice and only one secondary factor, Agape, appeared. Thus, the primaries were well represented, even though they did not tend to appear as independent constructs. The composite factors included pairings of love styles that were congruent with Lee's theory, e.g., Eros with Ludus, Storge with Eros.

...

Sex differences in attitudes

Perhaps the most interesting data to emerge in the present study were the differences between females and males in attitudes toward love. Males and females differed on approximately half the total scale items (except for Agape items, which showed almost no sex differences), with females revealing themselves to be more manic, storgic and pragmatic than males, while males appeared more ludic and erotic. These results supported previous love attitude research (Hatkoff & Lasswell, 1979) and were what one would predict from the volumes of sociological research on male–female differences in attitudes toward sex (e.g., Ferrell, Tolone & Walsh, 1977; Laner, Laner & Palmer, 1978; Luckey & Nass, 1969; Medora & Woodward, 1982; Mercer & Kohn, 1979). Women's sexual attitudes have historically been more conservative than men's with regard to such issues as premarital coitus, living together before marriage and extramarital sex. The double standard continues to exist in sex attitudes (Ferrell et al., 1977) and appears to exist in love attitudes as well.

The female emphasis on pragmatic, storgic love in the present study appears to reflect greater female conservatism. Traditionally, women have been socialized to marry both a love partner and a potential provider. Though more women than ever before are in the work force and provide for themselves and their families, their attitudes apparently still lag behind their behavior. Looking for a potential provider would require careful consideration (Storge) and perhaps a shopping list of attributes (Pragma). One might assume that younger women would be free from such stereotypical thinking, but the data from this young sample did not bear this out. Women's tendency to report more manic attitudes may merely reflect a greater willingness to report symptoms, or it may accurately represent a female tendency in love relationships. The traditional female role has included dependency and emotional expressivity, both of which are underlying themes of manic love.

Males were found to be more ludic and erotic than females. The instrumental quality that is Ludus' trademark is consistent with sex attitude research that shows males to be more liberal and less commitment-oriented in their attitudes than are females. The popular media stereotype exaggerates male ludic qualities with an emphasis on male-fostered one-night-stands and superficial sexuality. However, the Boston Couples Study data indicate that once involved in a relationship, males are less likely than females to initiate a breakup (Rubin et al., 1981). Thus we must remember that our generalizations are just that. To some extent, traditional males have been socialized to seek sensuality (Eros) in an instrumental way (Ludus) while their female counterparts have been socialized differently. It would be quite surprising, given these considerations, if there were no sex differences in love attitudes.

Although the present study examined subjects' love attitudes without considering the length of time that a subject might have been in love, future research would do well to consider the length of a relationship, its stage of development, the level of commitment and so on. In their study of romanticism and love in a heterogeneous sample (dating, cohabiting and married couples), Cunningham & Antill (1981) found very complex linkages between type of relationship, previous relationship experiences and love and romanticism. Thus, future research in this area requires a multivariate approach and hopefully an increasing reliance on longitudinal studies.

Although this study is twenty years old, and it is possible that men's and women's attitudes have changed with the generations, more recent research has nevertheless tended to confirm the basic pattern reported here. It does appear that women and men love differently, at least insofar as relatively unattached, relatively young, men and women are concerned. An interesting question that arises, then, is "What happens when a man and a woman get married and are necessarily involved in the negotiation of any differences in the love styles that they bring to the marriage?" Also does young love drop out as people age, such that the love styles of older folks follow different patterns and pathways? The next article explores some of these and other questions, using the same basic framework as the previous paper.

The authors discuss here the differences between a **retrospective longitudinal study** and a **cross-sectional** one. In a **retrospective study**, one population is studied looking back over a period of time, in this case, say a population of 40-year-olds would look back over the 20 years as they aged from 20 years old to 40 years old and they would report differences in love attitudes as they remember them changing and being changed by events (for example, the birth of children). This is usually accomplished by means of asking them to reminisce or recall specific events that are of interest to the researcher. In a **cross-sectional study**, the researcher picks different populations to represent the groups that the researcher wishes to compare. In this case the researcher would select a sample of 20-year-olds and a sample of 40-year-olds and compare their answers, making the assumption that any differences found in the data are due to the effects of age. Each design has its strengths and weaknesses: a retrospective technique is typically criticized for running the risk of having subjects falsely remember their feelings such a long time ago, so that any reports they give are either systematically biased or unsystematically biased toward the person's current opinion. A cross-sectional design is usually criticized on the grounds that any differences found between groups cannot be firmly attributed to age differences, as opposed to generational differences, different experiences of the historical period that they are in, and so forth. The strength of each technique is that it attempts to make some assessment of change in relationships as a result of time.

The authors also use a statistic to determine **goodness-of-fit**. This is a technique that is used to test whether a sample of data came from a population with a specific hypothesized distribution or in other words how well the data fit a particular hypothesis about how it should really look in an ideal world. The general procedure consists in statistically measuring the distance between the hypothesis and the data and then calculating the probability of obtaining data which have a still larger value than the value observed, assuming the hypothesis is true. In the case below, the authors have several different models of the possible ways in which love relates to marital satisfaction and they test these various models against the data looking for the one that fits best, using this technique.

The study further reports a **factor analysis**. Factor analysis takes the scores that people produce to different items on a test and looks for underlying patterns that can be attributed to specific factors. For example if you score highly on "I like to punch people", "I am often angry", "I take offence easily", "If someone insults me then I usually hit them", then an investigator might find that all of these scores are explained by the same underlying factor, say, Belligerence. Factor analysis attempts to represent the connections between variables as closely as possible with the fewest number of factors. A good factor analysis is one that makes sense! The procedure is largely intuitive, with the investigator working on until a solution is found to make intuitive sense and also to cover the data in the best way statistically. Researchers talk of the **factor loadings** of an item. These loadings are a statistical indication of the extent to which a particular item ("I like to punch people", say) is a good fit with the underlying factor of Belligerence. The higher the loading, the greater the parallelism between the item and factor as a whole. Researchers look for the smallest number of factors that will explain the data, say a three-factor solution or a four-factor solution. In those cases, three or four underlying factors can be used satisfactorily to explain all the subscales of a particular measure. Two special kinds of factor analysis are **exploratory and confirmatory factor analysis.** In the first case the researcher has no particular assumptions about how things will fall out and is simply exploring the data to see what pops out in a way that makes sense. In the second case, confirmatory factor analysis, the investigator has working ideas about the structure of the data and sets out to confirm that these hypotheses are good representations.

'Remembrance of Things Past': Perceptions of Marital Love From its Beginnings to the Present

Nancy K. Grote and Irene H. Frieze

[O]ur research addresses a number of questions pertaining to the retrospective and current perceptions of love of middle-aged men and women, who have been married an average of 18 years. The bulk of previous studies on love has been conducted with undergraduate samples of young adults in non-marital romantic relationships. Instead, this study investigates important questions about love in ongoing, relatively satisfying marriages.

How do married men and women remember their early love for their current spouse at the beginning of the relationship and how do they currently perceive their marital love? What implications do changes in perceptions of love have for the current affective quality of the marriage? To answer these questions we obtained a sample of 581 college-educated, married men and women who ranged in age from 45 to 47 years old, and asked them questions about their perceptions of love at two relationship stages – currently in the marriage and retrospectively, at the beginning of their love relationship when they were 26 years old, on average. Our study's **"retrospective longitudinal"** design has advantages over **cross-sectional studies** of love relationships inasmuch as age, birth cohort, educational level and relationship status are held constant and are not confounded in the data. Although there are disadvantages of retrospective reporting, such as the likelihood of distortion and forgetting, we are interested less in the objective reality of remembered perceptions of love

than in the subjective and salient meaning that they hold for our respondents in terms of their marital relationships.

To measure love in our study, we chose Lee's (1977) six types of love – Eros, Ludus, Storge, Pragma, Mania and Agape, because we thought they provided a more comprehensive picture of the quality of loving than other measures of love. Existing scales of these love perceptions were revised to be more appropriate for marital love. After the revi-.. sion, we decided to exclude the measures of Pragma and Mania from the study because of their weak psychometric properties. The following review thus pertains exclusively to Eros, Storge, Ludus, and Agape.

A classic study in the marriage literature, *The Significant Americans* (Cuber & Harroff, 1965), revealed how affluent, mostly college-educated married people from 35 to 55 years of age felt about premarital sex, extra-marital affairs and married love from its inception to its current state. This study is atypical in taking a retrospective longitudinal approach to understanding marital love. Equally, changes in love have been examined cross-sectionally by comparing the strength of types of love across a number of separate samples of subjects each at a different relationship stage of casually dating, exclusively dating, engaged and married. In some of these studies, the effects of relational stage on love are confounded with the effects of relationship length (e.g., Frazier & Esterly, 1990; Morrow et al., 1995). Similar to Cuber & Harroff we looked at how retrospective perceptions of love at the beginning of the love relationship compared with current perceptions of marital love. Further, in our retrospective longitudinal approach we controlled for the effects of marriage length in analyses pertaining to love and relationship stage. In the following review of four types of love – Eros, Ludus, Friendship-Based Love and Agape – the cited studies examine changes in love either longitudinally or cross-sectionally across relationship stages, whereas our study focuses on changes in perceptions of love, based on retrospective and current data.

Eros or erotic love may be defined as a self-confident, sensual type of loving based on attraction to the physical image of the beloved (Lee, 1977) and the enjoyment of sexual intimacy (Grote & Frieze, 1994) ... Therefore what the literature has shown about relationship stage and passionate love or sexual intimacy may also be relevant for Eros.

Most researchers have agreed with Berscheid & Walster (1974) that passionate or romantic love is of brief duration. Estimates on the life of passion have given it at most 2 to 3 years (Tennov, 1979). Sternberg (1986) has reasoned that the surge of passion, similar to the high of an addiction, may decrease over time due to a habituation effect whereby one eventually reaches a more or less stable, low level of arousal toward one's beloved. Alternatively, the intensity of passion may diminish, once uncertainty in the relationship abates, commitment rises, and realism about the partner sets in ... [B]ased on the overall evidence, we predict that our subjects' retrospective perceptions of erotic love will be significantly higher at the beginning of the love relationship than currently in the marriage when commitment is presumably greater.

A striking contrast to the image of passion or Eros fading as love relationships become more committed has been the picture of the sturdy growth of companionate love as relationships progress to marriage (Hatfield & Walster, 1978). This type of love is similar in conception to Storge (Hendrick & Hendrick, 1986; Lee, 1977) or Friendship-Based Love

(Grote & Frieze, 1994), the latter defined as a comfortable, affectionate, love for a likable partner, based on companionship, enjoyment of common interests and mutual activities and shared laughter. Furthermore, other kinds of love found in the literature – conjugal love (Munro & Adams, 1978) and intimacy (Acker & Davis, 1992), seem to bear some relation to Friendship-Based Love.

Certainly, it makes sense that Friendship-Based Love (FBL) would become greater as the relationship moves from the beginning, less committed stage to the current marital stage. For example, compared with dating undergraduates, married adults (Driscoll et al., 1972) and engaged men (Knox & Sporakowski, 1968) showed greater conjugal love ... [H]owever, not all evidence suggests that FBL should increase across relationship stages. For college-educated adults, there was no change in the level of conjugal love from the single to the married stage, perhaps because this level was quite high to begin with (Munro & Adams, 1978). Nevertheless, consistent with much of the earlier evidence, we predict that the current perception of FBL in the marriage will be higher than it was thought to have been at the beginning of the love relationship.

Ludus is a non-committal, pursuing and distancing love game played with a variety of partners (Lee, 1977). Not surprisingly, ludic love has been found to be negatively associated with relationship continuity for dating undergraduates (Hendrick et al., 1988) ... [A]s lovers become more serious and committed to the relationship, and particularly once they are engaged or married, it is likely that ludic love would diminish. Indeed, marital norms, probably more than dating norms, emphasize that one be committed to the relationship and not stray from the fold (Hansen, 1987). Consequently, we expect that the perceived strength of Ludus will be weaker in current marriages than at the beginning of the relationship.

Agape is dutiful, selfless caring for the well being of the partner without regard to self-interest or the expectation of reciprocation.

As an intimate relationship becomes more serious and committed, it is likely that one would perceive the well being of the partner to be of increasing concern ... Indeed, one cross-sectional study has shown that married people tend to be more altruistically other-oriented (similar to agapic love) toward their partners than the non-married (Grauerholz, 1988). We therefore predict that the current perception of agapic love in the marriage will be higher than it was remembered to have been at the beginning of the relationship.

Although changes in perceptions of love are the central focus of our study, we are also interested in sex associations with love. In our previous work with the same sample of married adults, we found that men and women did not differ currently in the strength of Eros or Ludus, whereas women showed more Friendship-Based Love and men more Agape. With respect to beginning perceptions of love, we expect that men will recall that they were more ludic than will women and that women will recollect that they were more expressive of Friendship-Based Love than will men. These predictions are consistent with sex differences in love attitudes previously reported for dating undergraduates (Hendrick & Hendrick, 1986; 1988; 1990; Hendrick et al., 1988).

Recently, a number of researchers have recognized the importance of relationship awareness (Acitelli, 1988) or relationship thinking (Cate et al., 1995) as they contribute to the quality of an intimate relationship. The work of Cate and his colleagues has been guided by a social cognitive model of relationship thinking which is predicated on the notion that long-term memories pertaining to the relationship influence how people process current incoming information and how they currently think about and evaluate their intimate relationships. In this model, one dimension of relationship thinking is "positive affect thinking", which is measured by a scale containing both retrospective and current descriptive items. Cate et al. (1995) found that positive affect thinking significantly related to relationship

satisfaction. Similarly, we think that one's personal history of past love experiences with one's spouse is often brought to bear on one's current feelings toward the spouse and that the nature of this type of social cognitive comparison influences one's marital quality. Further, we are interested not only in the positive, but also in the negative effects of perceived past ways of loving on the marriage. Thus we think it plausible that differences between one's remembrance of early love with one's current spouse and one's current experience of marital love with the same partner will have significant meaning for the affective quality of the marriage ...

For example, we expect that were erotic love perceived to have been stronger at the beginning of the relationship than currently this difference might relate to less sexual and marital satisfaction. The same prediction could be made for Friendship-Based Love and for Agape with respect to marital satisfaction. By contrast, if at the beginning ludic love had been perceived to be stronger than current Ludus, this change might predict more satisfaction in the marriage and less extra-marital activity. Further, we expect that a decrease in perceived FBL will relate to less reliance on the spouse for help or comfort as well as less respect for, spending less time with, and feeling less close to the spouse. In addition, because of the selflessness and significant other-focus of agapic love, we predict that a decrease in perceived Agape will relate to less concern for the welfare of the spouse, helping the spouse less and rating the spouse as less important than friends ...

In brief, the study is intended to contribute to the love literature in the following ways: the effects of age, birth cohort, educational level, relationship status and relationship length are not confounded in the results; a large sample of middle-aged, married adults in relatively lengthy marriages is used, instead of young adult college students in short-term dating relationships; relationship stage (beginning and current) and sex associations with four different perceptions of love are examined; and the associations between changes in love perceptions and marital satisfaction as well as other relationship characteristics are tested for each sex. In sum, we make the following predictions:

1. Relationship stage and love perceptions: the perceived strength of Eros and Ludus will be weaker and the perceived strength of Friendship-Based Love and Agape greater in the current marital relationship than they were thought to have been at the beginning of the love relationship.

2. Sex and beginning love perceptions: men will recall stronger Ludus than will women, whereas women will recollect stronger Friendship-Based Love (FBL) than will men.

3. A decrease in perceived current Eros, FBL and Agape, relative to perceived beginning Eros, FBL and Agape, will relate to less marital satisfaction. A decrease in perceived current Ludus, relative to perceived beginning Ludus, will be associated with greater marital satisfaction.

4. A decrease in perceived current Eros, relative to perceived beginning Eros, will positively predict less sexual satisfaction; a decrease in perceived current Ludus, relative to perceived beginning Ludus, will predict less non-monogamy in the marriage; a decrease in perceived current Friendship-Based Love, relative to perceived beginning FBL, will predict less relying on the spouse for help or comfort, spending less time with the spouse, respecting the spouse less and feeling less close to the spouse; a decrease in perceived current Agape, relative to perceived beginning Agape, will predict helping the spouse less, feeling less concern for the welfare of the spouse and rating the spouse less important than friends.

Method

In late 1990 and early 1991, a total of 1268 subjects received a mailed 25th college reunion questionnaire. This population had graduated in 1966 from a men's or women's college in the northeastern United States. The questionnaire was answered anonymously ... More information on the procedure may be found in Grote & Frieze (1994).

The sample consisted of mostly white, college-educated, men ($n = 340$) and women ($n = 254$), married an average (mean) of 18 years. Length of marriage ranged from 1 to 28 years. The men and women were not married to each other ...

Relationship Stage: Regarding the experience of love, subjects were directed to describe how they thought they felt at the beginning of the love relationship with their current spouse and how they currently felt in the marriage with the same partner. Everyone received the two sets of instructions in the same order. The subjects reported a mean age of 26 years (ranging from 12 to 46 years) when their love relationships began ...

Love Perceptions Scales: In order to assess adequately the experience of love in a sample of middle-aged, married adults, we thought it necessary to use a measure of love attitudes that was relevant and meaningful to them. Although the Love Attitudes Scale (LAS) of Hendrick & Hendrick (1986; 1990) had sound psychometric properties, we conjectured that subjects married an average of 18 years might have difficulty identifying with some of the LAS scale items. We thus decided to revise the Hendricks' LAS (1990), which had been derived originally from the theoretical work of Lee (1976) and the love scales of Lasswell & Lasswell (1977) as described in Grote (1993).

We performed **confirmatory** rather than **exploratory factor analyses** on the love data for several reasons. First, we had hypothesized that certain love statement items would strongly load on particular latent factors (love perceptions), and we wanted to test these predictions. Second, we expected that the love factors would be intercorrelated, and we wanted the analyses to take these intercorrelations into account. Third, we wanted to assess the **goodness-of-fit** of various models of the data. Thus, we used Bentler's (1989) EQS program to conduct these analyses.

Initial confirmatory factor analyses utilized the scale items for all six beginning and current love perceptions or latent factors–Eros, Ludus, Friendship-Based Love (FBL), Pragma, Mania and Agape. Ultimately, the Pragma and Mania scales were dropped from the analyses of both beginning and current love perceptions as their psychometric properties were revealed to be problematic ...

...

The final measure of love perceptions consisted of a 21-item scale for beginning retrospective love perceptions (Eros, Ludus, Friendship-Based Love and Agape) and a 22-item scale for current corresponding love perceptions. The scoring of the love scale items (1 = "strongly disagree", 5 = "strongly agree") was changed from the Hendrick & Hendrick (1990) scoring system (1 = "strongly agree"; 5 = "strongly disagree") because to us it made sense to equate the relative strength of a love perception with a high or low value ...

Changes in Love Perceptions: To assess changes in beginning (retrospective) and current perceptions of Eros, Ludus, Friendship-Based Love and Agape, we created difference scores, subtracting the value of each beginning love perception from the value of each corresponding current love perception. Changes in love perceptions ranged from –4 (decrease) to +4 (increase).

Marital Satisfaction: The Relationship Assessment Scale (RAS) developed by S. Hendrick (1988) was used to evaluate the degree of satisfaction in the marriage ... The alpha coefficients for this scale were high – .91 for men and .89 for women. Items were rated on a 5-point **Likert scale**.

Other Relationship Characteristics: Sexual satisfaction was assessed on a 1 (low) to 5 (high) scale by two items indicating satisfaction with sexual activity and frequency. The **alpha coefficient** was .89. Non-monogamy of self in the relationship was measured by asking, "Have you had sexual relations with others than your spouse since you have been together?" A categorical non-monogamy variable indicated: 1 = "No" or "No, but I think about it"; 2 = "Yes, currently" or "Yes, in the past and currently". Each of five variables – "spending time with spouse", "respecting

spouse", "feeling close to spouse", "helping spouse" and "feeling concern for the welfare of spouse" was rated on a 1 (not at all) to 4 (very much) scale. "Importance of spouse relative to friends" was assessed by a difference score (importance of spouse minus importance of friends), which ranged from – 3 (friends more important) to 3 (spouse more important).

Results

A one-way **MANOVA** tested sex differences in age, length of marriage, number of children living in the home, marital satisfaction and additional relationship characteristics. The results showed that men and women differed on five out of a possible 13 comparisons: ... women (45.76 years on average) were slightly younger than men (45.90 mean years of age) ..., had been married almost 20 years, 2 years longer than men, ... and had fewer children in the home (1.4 on average) than men (1.7 on average) ... In addition, women expressed more sexual satisfaction than men, ... and were less likely than men to rate their spouse more important than friends ... Because men and women differed on length of marriage and length of marriage was significantly related to several love perceptions, this variable was included as a covariate [*i.e., something that behaves similarly to another variable and can, to all intents and purposes, be taken with it in analyses. Eds*] in all of the multivariate analyses testing predictions related to sex and relationship-stage effects on love perceptions ...

The intercorrelations among beginning and current love perceptions and length of marriage, separately for men and women ... revealed moderate to high consistency between all of the beginning and current love perceptions. The intercorrelation between current Eros and current FBL was high; but in previous analyses with the same sample of adults these love perceptions were also empirically distinguishable from each other (Grote & Frieze, 1994). The few statistically significant correlations between length of marriage and love perceptions were mostly low. For both men (r = .14) and women (r = .28), the greater the perceived strength of beginning Agape, the longer the marriage. Additionally for women, the perceived strength of current agapic love positively predicted marriage length (r = .15). Finally, the longer that men were married, the less erotic love they currently reported (r = – .14) ...

We expected that the perceived strength of Eros and Ludus would be weaker and that of FBL and Agape stronger in the current marital relationship than they were thought to have been at the beginning of the love relationship. First, we tested for significant sex by relationship-stage interaction effects on love perceptions ... It appeared that the perceived strength of men's agapic love was greater currently than it was thought to have been at the beginning stage, whereas the level of women's Agape perceptions remained the same ...

To ... identify specific relationship-stage effects on love perceptions for men and women, we conducted separate-sex **repeated measures MANCOVAs** [*i.e., Multivariate Analysis of Covariance, or analyses of several related variables at once, some of which had been assessed more than once. In a repeated measures design, subjects complete the same measure at least twice. Here they filled out scales for "20 years ago" and for "now". Eds*]. Again, length of marriage was the covariate and significantly related to the love perceptions ... For men, out of four possible relationship-stage changes in love perceptions, there were three significant effects ... As predicted, the perceived strength of erotic love was currently lower than it was thought to have been at the beginning ($F(1, 331)$ = 45.4, p < .001), as was the perceived strength of current ludic love ($F(1, 331)$ = 290.3, p < .001). The perceived strength of current agapic love was higher than that of beginning Agape ($F(1, 298)$ = 50.3, p < .001). Interestingly, the perceived strength of Friendship-Based Love remained the same across relationship stages ... Further, there were two out of four possible significant changes in love perceptions. Similar to the

men, women reported that the perceived strength of their erotic love ($F(1, 248)$ = 13.0, p < .001) and ludic love ($F(1, 248)$ = 189.5, p < .001) was weaker currently than it was thought to have been at the beginning. Perceptions of FBL and Agape did not change across stages.

Finally, we found some significant sex associations with beginning love perceptions ... With respect to beginning love perceptions, ... three out of four possible sex differences were found: ... Men were higher than women on perceived beginning Ludus ($F(1,579)$ = 5.1, p < .05) and women were higher than men on perceived beginning Friendship-Based Love ($F(1, 579)$ = 9.2, p < .01). We also found that men reported stronger perceived beginning agapic love ($F(1,579)$ = 6.5, p < .01) than women. [W]omen were currently stronger than men on perceived FBL, whereas men were currently stronger than women on perceived Agape.

To consider the possibility that the pattern of findings for sex and relationship stage might be different, recently married adults were excluded from the sample and we redid all the analyses including only those adults married 5 years or more ... The only exception to this pattern was that men's reconstructions of beginning Eros was significantly higher than women's.

We expected [and found] that changes in love perceptions would significantly relate to marital satisfaction ... Decreases in perceived erotic, friendship-based and agapic love, and an increase in perceived ludic love were significantly associated with less marital satisfaction for men and women. In addition, we tested whether a change in each of these love perceptions still predicted marital satisfaction when current levels of each type of love were controlled in the analyses ... [C]hanges in women's perceived Friendship-Based Love or FBL (beta = .12, p < .01) and women's perceived Agape (beta = .29, p < .0001) still related to marital satisfaction after the effects of current FBL and Agape had been accounted for ...

Next, we thought that changes in love perceptions would significantly predict certain relationship characteristics. This set of predictions was again supported for the most part ... [A] decrease in perceived erotic love related to less sexual satisfaction for men and women. This relation was stronger than those between the other change variables and sexual satisfaction (as determined by the test for difference between dependent correlations). Moreover, ... a decrease in perceived Eros negatively predicted less sexual satisfaction for men ... and women ...

With respect to ludic love, a decrease in perceived Ludus significantly related to less non-monogamy of self in the marriage for men and women ... more so than the other change variables (again tests for differences in independent correlations were used). Further, this decrease in perceived Ludus negatively predicted less non-monogamy for men, ... even when the effect of current Ludus was controlled in the analysis ...

... [A] decrease in perceived Friendship-Based Love was significantly associated with less reliance on the spouse for help and comfort, as well as spending less time with spouse, respecting the spouse less, and feeling less close to the spouse ... [A] decrease in perceived FBL predicted relying on spouse for women marginally, ... respecting the spouse for men, ... spending less time with the spouse for men ... and feeling less close to the spouse for men, ... and women ...

Finally, a decrease in perceived agapic love was significantly related to helping the spouse less, feeling less concern for the welfare of the spouse, and rating the spouse less important than friends ... After accounting for the effects of current Agape ... a decrease in women's perceived Agape predicted feeling less concern for the welfare of the spouse ... and rating spouse less important than friends for men ... and women ...

Discussion

In the present study, middle-aged men and women were asked to give their current perceptions of marital love and to recall their love at the beginning of the relationship with their spouse, usually before marriage when the majority of them were young adults. Retrospective perceptions of beginning love do not take the place of actual data collected [at the time]; rather they represent what the individual remembers thinking, feeling or behaving at the beginning of the love relationship. As Cuber & Harroff (1965) point out, these remembrances are often fraught with distortions; yet they are important because they constitute reality for these married adults and are the bases for present feelings and future paths of interaction. Accordingly, we found that recollections of love at the beginning of the relationship in conjunction with current appraisals of marital love have meaning for the affective quality of the marriage.

A brief comparison of the ordering of sample means for beginning and current love perceptions reveals that their relative perceived strength was similar at both stages: perceptions of Friendship-Based Love, Eros and Agape were the strongest and perceptions of Ludus the weakest. With respect to relationship stage and love perceptions, most of the study predictions were confirmed. The strength of erotic love was perceived to be lower currently than it was thought to have been at the beginning of the relationship ... [C]urrent Eros was still moderately strong for these married adults, a phenomenon suggesting that these marriages are not as a whole the "devitalized" or "passive-congenial" relationships that Cuber & Harroff (1965) described in their retrospective study of marital quality. The perceived strength of ludic love, which was quite low at both stages, showed a significant decrease from beginning to current. Although this finding is derived from our retrospective longitudinal approach, it is nevertheless consistent with data from earlier longitudinal studies ... (Hendrick et al., 1988; ... Rusbult, 1983; ... Johnson & Rusbult, 1989).

Unexpectedly, we found no change in the perceived strength of FBL across relationship stages. On second glance, it is not surprising that the level of FBL was thought to have been strong in beginning love relationships that ultimately led to marriage. Similarly, in a cross-sectional study, Munro & Adams (1978) reported that for college-educated adults, compared to those with a high school education, conjugal love (similar to FBL) started out high before marriage and stayed at the same level across three family life stages – no children, children present and children out of the home ...

Finally, ... the perceived strength of Agape was greater currently than it was thought to have been at the beginning; this significant effect occurred only for men, however. Previous evidence has demonstrated that the degree of relative emotional dependency on the partner, more than sex, may account for the level of Agape in an intimate relationship (Frazier & Esterly, 1990; Grauerholz, 1988). It is possible, therefore, that men showed a greater change from the beginning to the current, in the strength of perceived agapic love for their spouse, because they had become more emotionally dependent on their spouse relative to their friends. Similarly, perhaps women's Agape stayed the same across stages because they were no more emotionally dependent on their spouse currently relative to their friends than they were at the beginning of the love relationship ...

What implications do these changes in love perceptions have for the current affective quality of the marriage? Quite a few, we found. Decreases in perceived erotic, friendship-based and agapic love, as well as an increase in perceived ludic love from beginning to current, were significantly related to less marital satisfaction for men and women. Further, the contributions made by changes in perceptions of FBL and Agape to marital satisfaction were still significant for women, even when the effects of current levels of FBL and Agape were accounted for in the analyses. Similarly, a decrease in perceived erotic love significantly related to less sexual satisfaction for men and women, not only more than the other changes in love perception variables, but also controlling for current Eros ... Again, controlling for current

FBL, we observed that a decrease in men's perceived FBL was significantly related to respecting the spouse less and spending less time with the spouse and that a decrease in men's and women's perceived FBL was connected to feeling less close to the spouse. Finally, controlling for the effect of current agapic love, we found that a perceived decrease in Agape predicted men feeling less concern for the spouse and women rating the spouse less important than friends. Overall, despite some differences, the patterns of associations between perceived changes in love and aspects of marital quality were more similar for men and women than distinct ...

Our study was not set up to test the causal directions implicit in this set of associations. Even though we suggest that how one thinks about one's past relationship history might shape one's present feelings toward and activities with the spouse, it is also clear that this process is not one-way, but reciprocally interactive. Undergoing a difficult and disappointing period in one's marriage may likewise influence the quality and content of what is remembered at the beginning of the love relationship. For example, under marital strain one might be motivated to recall times at the beginning of the relationship when the partner seemed more thoughtful or romantic; this recollection, in turn, might weaken one's current marital or sexual satisfaction with the spouse. On the other hand, one possibility consistent with previous work on mood-congruent recall (Bower, 1981) is that during marital distress one might be more inclined to remember an inconsiderate act on the part of the partner early in the relationship; this recollection consequently might soften one's current feelings of disappointment – at least the relationship isn't getting any worse. Alternatively, this realization might make one reassess the viability or desirability of staying in the marriage.

Although the issue of sex differences in love perceptions was not the central focus of this study, we found some significant sex effects. At the beginning of the love relationship, the pattern of retrospective love perceptions was fairly consistent with the configuration previously reported for undergraduate young adults (Hendrick & Hendrick, 1988; Morrow et al., 1995) – men thought that they were more ludic in love than women did, whereas women recalled friendship-based love more than men did. Further, men perceived that they were stronger in beginning Agape than did women ... Although apparently counter to the stereotype of the self-sacrificing female in heterosexual intimate relationships (Bernard, 1981), our finding on the relative perceived strength of men's beginning Agape, may not be as inconsistent as it first seems. Bernard was talking about self-denying behavior on the part of women vis-à-vis their partners, whereas Agape refers to a general love attitude toward the partner which may or may not translate into specific actions. Note ... that men's current agapic love showed relatively low correlations with the activities of helping the spouse or spending time with the spouse ...

Sex differences in current perceptions of marital love were similar to those at the beginning, except for the convergence in Ludus for men and women. In light of the influence of the sexual revolution on this cohort of women, perhaps those women who were more ludic in their marriages did not experience the constraint of the sex-based double standard regarding marital non-monogamy. In general, inasmuch as the associations between sex and beginning and current love perceptions were mostly modest, they should not be unduly exaggerated, as Wright (1988) has pointed out. Moreover, other subject variables that correlate with sex, such as relative emotional dependency should be considered in future research on this issue.

An important limitation of the study is the possible lack of generalizability of the findings procured from this white, highly educated, professional, affluent married sample to other groups of married adults ... The advantage of using our kind of sample is to learn how love operates under optimal conditions, for people who have considerable economic resources, whose marriages, though not without problems, are mostly very satisfying ...

The data gathered through the use of our retrospective longitudinal design are a present and subjective reconstruction of past love experiences at the beginning of the relationship. This retrospective approach cannot replace data gathered prospectively, nor does it warrant conclusions about a clear cause and effect relation between past and present love perceptions. However, ... such a design is able to control for cohort effects that plague cross-sectional studies, and attrition effects that affect longitudinal research ... Most importantly, however, we emphasize that retrospective perceptions of love are not intended to give an objective representation of how individuals actually felt at the beginning of the relationship. In fact, these reconstructions could be a number of things: idealizations, mood-congruent recollections or even social representations of how people are expected to feel at the beginning of a love relationship. As mentioned earlier, any remembrance of past love is colored by the [present] marital situation and thus continually subject to cognitive revision. Nevertheless, this type of recollection signifies the present meaning a person's earlier love history has for him or her. This meaning has implications, we found, for the current affective quality of the marriage ...

You will have noticed that the authors are extremely careful to note the benefits and disadvantages of the longitudinal retrospective technique that they employed. You might want to reflect on the previous and later chapters here to consider whether this sort of issue arises in those other places too. When you need to review the issues that arise in relation to retrospective and cross-sectional approaches to data, then this chapter would be a good one to revisit.

In the above study, the authors developed some interesting further information about the nature of Love Styles and their intertwining with biological sex in the experience of long-term heterosexual marriage. They found some consistent sex differences in the experience of love that fit well with those outlined in the first paper by Hendrick et al. For example, the strength of agapic love was higher currently than it was thought to have been at the beginning for men. Men and women differed in love experiences to a greater extent at the beginning of the relationship than currently. Most importantly, changes in perceptions of love appear to have meaningful implications for the current affective quality of the marriage for both men and women.

Through these studies we get a sense of the development of work on Love Styles and a clearer understanding of the ways in which styles of loving are correlated with other aspects of life and relational experience throughout life. One particularly interesting thing is the indication that Love Styles change in particular ways over the life of marriage and as a function of sex. This raises some interesting questions about the persistence of Love Style and its relation not only to biological sex but to sexual experience also. The next paper makes an attempt to connect Love Styles with other indications of relational activity, namely sexual activity. The authors present a compelling case for looking at love and sex in the same study, a relatively new idea from a strongly theoretical viewpoint. If love and sexuality are connected – perhaps for evolutionary reasons – then it should be possible to find different ways in which particular love styles relate to sexual choices.

This paper, by Hendrick and Hendrick, offers us a different theoretical approach to the link between love and sex, via evolutionary theory, and builds on the earlier paper on love types and linking them to sexual attitudes. In their research, Hendrick and Hendrick devoted a lot of effort to the creation and development of scales to measure important but elusive concepts. One of their early papers was the one that began this chapter. The original of the paper presented here is extremely careful and thorough in this scale development work, but we have omitted some of it here for pedagogical reasons. We also want to focus readers on the substantive findings of the research. Interested readers can of course consult the original for these omitted details.

Linking Romantic Love with Sex: Development of the Perceptions of Love and Sex Scale

Susan S. Hendrick and Clyde Hendrick

Although love and sex have been linked in poetry, drama, and literature throughout the centuries, philosophers and social scientists have had differing views of how (or even whether) the two are intrinsically connected. Aron and Aron (1991) localized scholarly work on the relation between love and sex on a unidimensional continuum, anchoring "love is really sex" at one end and "sex is really love" at the other end. Approaches to sexuality that ignore love or consider it as a result of sexuality fit under the "love is really sex" end of the continuum; approaches that either separate love and sex or that see them as heavily overlapping fit at the midpoint of the continuum; and approaches that ignore sexuality or consider it as a minor part of love fit under the "sex is really love" end of the continuum ... To move beyond a continuum approach to love and sex ... requires a meta-concept of an underlying motive for both love and sexuality ...

Evolutionary psychology

Within the parental investment model (Trivers, 1972), reproductive fitness (i.e., evolutionary success in passing on one's genes) is a non-conscious process that has shaped somewhat different romantic strategies for women and men: Men "maximize their (reproductive) fitness by impregnating as many women as possible, whereas women maximize their fitness by investing heavily in each of the relatively few infants they may produce" (S. Hendrick & Hendrick, 1995, p. 57). The evolutionary psychology approach has understandably emphasized sex as the mechanism for reproduction and has been much less concerned with love's contribution. The importance of love and affection to sexuality was implicit in findings by Laumann and his colleagues (Laumann, Gagnon, Michael, & Michaels, 1994) in their large-scale study of sexual behavior in the United States. In their research, the respondents expressing greatest emotional satisfaction and physical pleasure in their relationships were those who were partnered and in a monogamous relationship. Buss (1999) was much more explicit when he acknowledged romantic love's historical and cross-cultural significance and its potential utility in bonding women and men and achieving greater certainty of paternity (for men) and greater confidence in a man's

resource commitment (for women). Mellen, an anthropologist, noted that the sexual drive guaranteed enough pregnancies and births, but only bonding between parents (cemented by love) could guarantee infant survival. "This is why most of us today have strong tendencies to love as well as to make love" (Mellen, 1981, p. 141).

Sex differences in sex and love

Emphasis on the parental investment model has focused heavily on sex differences in reproductive strategies (e.g., men copulating more widely, women focusing on each potential offspring) that may lead to differences in sexual strategies (e.g., men more sexually permissive than women) and differences in love strategies (e.g., women more practical and friendship-oriented in love than men). And such differences do indeed exist (e.g., S. Hendrick & Hendrick, 1995); however, men and women are also similar on many love and sex attitudes, and in the patterns of relationships between love and sex measures (and between love and sex measures and related variables such as relationship satisfaction). For example, in studying sexual desire, a somewhat different construct from love or sex but related to both, Regan and Berscheid (1996) found both sex similarities and sex differences. They found that the sexes did not differ in their beliefs about the state of sexual desire; however, more women than men defined the goals of sexual desire, as love, intimacy, or commitment, whereas more men than women viewed the goal of desire as sexual activity. Overall, women adopted a more relational or person-centered orientation to sexuality, and men adopted a more recreational or body-centered orientation (e.g., Delamater, 1989). These findings were generally consistent with the literature reviewed by Sprecher and McKinney (1993), who noted that people believe that sex is most acceptable within a loving relationship, that intimate partners (especially women) are motivated to have sex to express love, that the amount of love experienced for a dating partner is positively correlated with the level of sexual intimacy, and that feelings of love between partners may affect their desire for frequent sex. Such findings suggest strong links between love and sex ...

Basis for the current research

If one accepts the assumption that sex and love are linked in the service of evolution, then studying the two constructs in tandem – rather than separately, as they have so often been considered – is theoretically compelling. Although scholars have occasionally hypothesized about such links, they have seldom studied them. One major gap in the research has been a lack of focus on laypersons' views about the links between love and sex in their own relationships. One exception was a study by Weis, Slosnerick, Cate, and Sollie (1986), who developed a scale to assess cognitive associations among sex, love, and marriage (SLM). Their eight-item SLM scale dealt with such issues as love and sex, casual sex, and infidelity, within the framework of marriage.

Our primary goal for the research was to assess laypersons' current conceptions of how love and sex are linked in their relationships, and from such qualitative conceptions develop a quantitative measure assessing love/sex attitudes simultaneously. We intended to assess all types of romantic, partnered relationships and thus did not wish to restrict our focus to love and sex in marriage. [Eds: much of this element of the study has been omitted here and interested readers should consult the original full paper.] A second goal of the research was to examine sex similarities and differences on the new love/sex measure, within the framework of an evolutionary psychology perspective. We conducted a series of studies to explore persons' perceptions of how sex and love might be related in their romantic relationships. Two broad types of findings were expected.

1. We expected that people would be able to link love with sex in their relationships,

and we expected to find several different themes in people's qualitative responses, including both the "sex is really love" and "love is really sex" perspectives (Aron & Aron, 1991) ... [W]e anticipated finding the occurrence of more themes emphasizing love than themes emphasizing sex. We also expected to find that love themes would relate more strongly to love variables than to sex variables in existing measures and that sex themes would relate more strongly to sex variables than to love variables in existing measures.

2. We expected to find both sex similarities and differences in quantitative linkages between sex and love. Based on work in evolutionary psychology and our own previous research, the following general prediction was made. Women will be more endorsing of the themes emphasizing love, whereas men will be more endorsing of the themes emphasizing sex.

[Eds: a Pilot Study was conducted to assess themes in reports connecting love and sex, and resulted in 27 themes that referred to relationship-specific beliefs rather than to general beliefs about love and sex. A full study (Study I in the original paper) was conducted to test the measurement properties of the scales and this resulted in "some intriguing data" that nevertheless led the authors to revise the scales somewhat. The paper continued to deal with the new scales and eventually reports data from combined samples of two studies reported in the original paper. We have edited out much of the technical work that the authors performed in order to ensure that their scales were good and proper ways to measure the things that they wanted to access. This allows us to focus on substantive findings that resulted from this research. Full details of the research are, of course, given in the original article.]

Sample. The final combined sample consisted of 376 participants, 78% women, and 22% men ... Only participants who reported being in a current romantic relationship and who provided complete data were included in the sample. (Scaling analyses that also included persons not in a current romantic relationship [e.g., **confirmatory factor**

analyses] were consistent with analyses reported below, but ANOVAs indicated substantial differences between persons currently in a relationship and persons not currently in a relationship. Thus, the latter were dropped from consideration for all further analyses.)

Procedure. A lengthy relationship-oriented questionnaire was administered to groups of undergraduate students who volunteered to complete the questionnaire as part of their course requirement in an introductory psychology course.

Instruments. Measures ... included demographics, the Love Attitudes Scale: Short Form (**alphas** ranged from .67 for Ludus to .87 for Agape), the Sexual Attitudes Scale (alphas ranged from .75 for Sexual Practices to .91 for Permissiveness), and items assessing sexual desire, emotional satisfaction, and physical pleasure. New measures used with the combined sample included the following scales.

Relationship Assessment Scale: This 7-item **Likert scale** (Hendrick, 1988; Hendrick, Dicke, & Hendrick, 1998) is a single factor scale measuring general relationship satisfaction (alpha = .86). Commitment: This 4-item Likert scale adapted from Lund (1985) assesses commitment to a relationship (alpha = .88). *Self-Disclosure Index*: This Likert scale contains 10 items and measures self-disclosure to a target person, in this study the romantic partner (Miller, Berg, & Archer, 1983) (alpha = .89). *Romantic Beliefs Scale (RBS)*: This scale is a 15-item, 4-factor Likert measure (Sprecher & Metts, 1989). It has four subscales: Love Finds a Way (alpha = .75), One and Only (alpha = .71), Idealization (alpha = .68), and Love at First Sight (alpha = .54). [*Eds: the original paper discusses the ways in which the scales were developed and tested scientifically. We have omitted these important details here.*] ...

Sex comparisons

A ... purpose of this research was to explore sex differences and similarities in linking love and sex. We had predicted that women would

be more endorsing of scales emphasizing love, and men would be more endorsing of scales emphasizing sex ... Although there were few sex differences for love attitudes, sexual attitudes, and relationship variables, those that did occur were consistent with previous research. Men were more endorsing of agapic love and sexual permissiveness than were women, whereas, women were more endorsing of pragmatic love and self-disclosure than were men. Contrary to predictions, however, women and men did not differ on any subscales of the Perceptions of Love and Sex Scale. The lack of mean differences did not indicate that correlation patterns would be similar for the sexes, however, so correlations among the measures were computed for women and men separately. When these correlations (80 pairs in all) were compared, men and women differed on only three, fewer than would be expected by chance. It was concluded, therefore, that women and men in the combined sample, who were currently in a romantic relationship, were very similar both in their levels of endorsement of the subscales of the Perceptions of Love and Sex Scale and in their correlations between the subscales of the Perceptions of Love and Sex Scale and the other measures.

General discussion

...

Consistency with evolutionary theory

One of our initial purposes in this research was to determine whether women and men would differ in their perceptions of the links between love and sex and, if they did differ, whether such differences would be consistent with evolutionary theory. We predicted that women would be more endorsing of themes (subscales) emphasizing love, and that men would be more endorsing of themes (subscales) emphasizing sex. In fact, women and men did not differ on any of the subscales ... Perhaps evolutionary theory would expect that persons already in a relationship would be less likely to exhibit sex differences in relational strategies. However, the social structural perspective can also speak to this lack of sex differences. Perhaps as Eagly and Wood (1999) have proposed, particular sex differences will lessen "to the extent that women and men are similarly placed in the social structure" (p. 417). Placement in partnered romantic relationships may represent similar placement in the social structure, at least to some degree.

People's views about love and sex

As we noted in the introduction, the current research was exploratory and was guided by the over-arching assumption that, for heuristic purposes, some scholars may conceptualize love and sex as existing at two ends of a continuum; however, lay people more typically link the two phenomena when considering romantic relationships. We also expected that, to whatever degree one phenomenon or theme was given primacy over the other, more love themes than sexuality themes would emerge. Such was the case.

The final four subscales were Love is Most Important (love is the primary entity); Sex Demonstrates Love (sex is important but in some ways subsumed by love); Love Comes Before Sex (love comes first); and Sex is Declining (sex is no longer as much a part of the relationship). Participants may provide a perspective not only on social scientists' propositions regarding the love–sex continuum, but also on more philosophical/ metaphysical questions regarding human destiny. If the human task is to promote genetic fitness, then perhaps sex subsumes love. If the task is to promote communion among humans (Baumeister & Leary, 1995), then perhaps love subsumes sex. This particular research speaks to love's primacy, though within the linking of love with sex. Interestingly, the primacy of love notwithstanding, sex – or rather its decline – was extremely important and was a strong negative predictor of commitment. The power of negative events to have more shaping power than positive events in relationships is underscored by Gottman's (1994) prescription of a ratio of five positive events to one negative event as necessary to maintain a good relationship. Love may be essential, but so may be a quality of non-eroding sexuality.

The present research has limitations, particularly in sampling. Asking questions about love and sexuality of persons of differing ages, life and relationship stages, family constellations, and racial and ethnic backgrounds is essential to a fuller understanding of these issues. In addition, culture is a major generalizability limitation in the current research. Nevertheless, some exploratory research employing the original open-ended question with married participants (Najera, 2000) revealed a number of themes, some of them almost identical to those expressed in the Perceptions of Love and Sex Scale subscales. Thus, we believe that our measure is appropriate for older and married respondents.

We also believe that the measure can be used in several ways in future research. For example, it could be employed in research assessing how partners experience love and sexuality during major life transitions such as the birth of the first child or a serious illness of one of the partners. The scale would also be appropriate for research on infidelity in relationships. The measure could be useful in therapy settings, where the Sex is Declining subscale might be used to differentiate more distressed from less distressed couples seeking therapy.

In the final analysis, however, perhaps the most important point to be taken from this research is that people appear to link love and sexuality in their romantic relationships. And such links are measurable. Thus the measure developed in the current research can aid our understanding of intimate relationships and the intertwining of love and sex within them. ...

This approach is quite noticeably a modern one, given that children did not survive in earlier times, so some of the above questions are quite particular to the present day where the survival of children is assumed as normal. Furthermore in previous times, marriage was not based on personal choice but often on political factors to do with family needs for political alliances, or on pragmatic necessity (you were the only person of one sex of marriageable age in the community so you married the other one). In such circumstances, many of the Pragma items would have been immaterial 200 years ago and the whole notion of Pragma is essentially founded in the belief that free choice of mates is normally exercised.

The above analysis also focuses specifically on "legitimate" sex and love relationships yet the assumptions that link love to sex might be thought of differently if one were to conduct research on extra-marital affairs. For example, VanderVoort and Duck (2004) have discussed the differences in forms of relationship between love and sex in extra-marital affairs, and there is also some discussion (Duck & VanderVoort, 2002) about the differences between sexual relationships judged legitimate (marriage, dating) and those judged unconventional but tolerated (marriage of "convenience"), disapproved (consensual sado-masochism), scandalous (love between doctor and patient) and utterly forbidden (sexual love between adult and child or between brother and sister).

Finally one issue that may change or have already changed the attitudinal links between sex and love is contraception. Many of the concerns that previously affected the link have been allayed by the modern reliability of contraception and many attitudes about relationships have likewise been modified. When sexual activity is driven as much by thoughts of pure pleasure as it is by intentions to conceive or fears of conception, then the nature of the relationship between love and sex changes in some interesting ways that you might like to discuss in class.

4 Sexuality

We will next present some research findings in sexuality: specifically, we will focus on the Sexual Double Standard and two theoretical positions that may already be familiar to you. Although these two positions are at times painted as incompatible, a delicate interrelationship can sometimes be discerned by their explanations for a narrow effect (i.e., the Sexual Double Standard).

The authors of the lead article in this chapter (Sprecher, McKinney, & Orbuch, 1987) present an excellent historical and methodological background for our discussion of the sexual double standard between men and women. In its most orthodox form, women are evaluated harshly if they engage in any sexual activity before marriage; while in the conditional form, women are not judged more harshly than men if they are sexually active within the context of a committed relationship. Sprecher et al. consider the changing nature of sexual norms and the recent reports of the disappearance of the double standard with some skepticism. Instead, they argue that the conditional double standard still exists but is not expressed overtly and that some recent research reports that use survey techniques are too clumsy and reactive to accurately assess its presence. Instead Sprecher et al. employ a person perception technique using a completely **between-subjects** experimental design with each subject **randomly assigned** to only one experimental condition in the experiment. This design addresses the problems identified by the authors in previous research very nicely, but you may want to consider the relative advantages and disadvantages of survey and experimental techniques as you read this article.

The second article in this chapter (Milhausen & Herold, 1999) attempts to resolve the debate between **Social Learning Theory** and Evolutionary Theory with regard to the sexual double standard. However, Milhausen and Herold encounter a methodological challenge when attempting to measure attitudes toward sexuality given that participants' personal beliefs may be at odds with their knowledge of societal expectations. In other words people might answer in **socially desirable** ways when asked questions about their sexual attitudes, which is to say that they might lie in order to make themselves look good!

You are already familiar with a statistical procedure called **factor analysis** from the articles you read in Chapters 2 and 3. If you need a refresher on it then you may want to glance back at these pages before starting your reading in this chapter. Also, as you evaluate the results presented by these researchers in this chapter on the sexual double standard it may be useful for you to consider what evidence is presented that differentiates an orthodox double standard from a conditional double standard. Finally, how subtle is the double standard that is identified by the researchers and could the nature of their samples have contributed to the reported strength of their effect?

Has the Double Standard Disappeared? An Experimental Test

Susan Sprecher, Kathleen McKinney, and Terri L. Orbuch

According to a double standard of premarital sexual behavior, sexual intercourse before marriage is judged to be more acceptable for males than for females (Reiss, 1960). In general, research conducted in the 1950s and 1960s indicated that the double standard was prevalent (e.g., Ehrmann, 1959), particularly in its transitional or conditional form (Kaats & Davis, 1970). According to the transitional or conditional double standard, males are allowed more freedom than females to engage in premarital sex, but females are permitted to be sexually active as long as they are in affectionate relationships (Walsh et al., 1983). This is a more egalitarian double standard than the orthodox double standard, which condemns premarital sexual intercourse for women regardless of the circumstances.

Research conducted more recently indicates that there has been a continued waning of even the conditional double standard and an emergence of a single, egalitarian premarital sexual standard. The sexual standard most frequently endorsed is what Reiss (1967) termed "permissiveness with affection." Men and women believe that premarital intercourse is acceptable for both sexes within a relationship characterized by affection and some commitment. Those who adhere to a more permissive standard (e.g., "permissiveness without affection") also tend to apply it equally to men and women. Most of this recent research consists of survey studies using small, nonprobability [not randomly selected] samples of college students (e.g., Ferrell et al., 1977), although in one study (Delamater & MacCorquodale, 1979) a large

probability sample of both students and nonstudents was interviewed.

Although the common proclamation is that the double standard no longer exists (Delamater & MacCorquodale, 1979), another possibility to consider is that it has taken a more subtle form. More specifically, the results indicating that the double standard has disappeared may be an artifact of the specific scales used in **survey research** to assess premarital sexual standards, in combination with the influence of prevalent societal norms. Typically, the respondents are first asked if it is acceptable for a man to engage in premarital intercourse (or another sexual behavior), and then the same question is asked in reference to a woman (see, for example, the Reiss, 1960, Premarital Permissiveness scale). The purpose of cross-sex *comparisons is probably fairly transparent to the respondents, which can cause them to try to appear more consistent and egalitarian than they actually are.* [Emphasis added by Eds.] Although the same scales were used during a previous time, when evidence was found for a double standard, societal norms have changed. *Egalitarianism is now a prominent norm in our society.* [Emphasis added by Eds.]

If there is a single sexual standard, it should be evidenced in a methodology that is characterized by less direct and obtrusive measures of sexual standards. The person perception experiment affords the opportunity to assess sexual standards more unobtrusively. Subjects can be asked to form impressions of a hypothetical person after receiving information about his/her sexual behavior. Sex of the stimulus person can be experimentally manipulated so that subjects are randomly assigned to evaluate either a male or a female, but not both. This **between-subjects random assignment** of sex helps to assure that when subjects react to a particular sex, their responses are not influenced by how they did or will respond to the other sex [*as they would in a within-subjects design or survey – added by Eds*].

There is another advantage of using a person perception experiment for examining the possible existence of the double standard. The person perception experiment examines the actual consequences or effects of a double standard in the form of perceptions or evaluations that are made of others who have certain sexual histories. This methodology can more directly address the question of whether there is greater condemnation of sexually active women than of men, particularly if the sexual activity occurs in casual relationships. This was proposed several years ago by Reiss (1960), but has never been adequately tested. A double standard is evidenced if women are more negatively evaluated than men for engaging in the same sexual behavior under the same conditions.

Recently, a few such person perception experiments have been conducted. Although these studies vary somewhat in their design and the dependent variables measured, they all indicate nonsupport for a double standard. That is, in these studies, a female stimulus person has not been judged significantly more negatively, overall, than a male stimulus person for the same sexual behavior (e.g., Garcia, 1983).

Perhaps the reason that more support for the double standard was not found by Garcia (1983) and Istvan and Griffitt (1980) is because only the degree of sexual behavior was manipulated, and not the context in which the sexual activity occurs. That is, information was presented about the sexual experience of the stimulus person, but no information was presented about the conditions under which the sexual activity occurred. If the double standard still exists, however, it is most likely to be in a conditional or

transitional form, with differences in standards for men and women minimal for affectionate, committed relationships, but more pronounced for casual relationships. Subjects in these experiments may have assumed that a female stimulus person had her sexual experiences in (a) close relationship(s), and thus did not judge her more negatively than a man.

In two other recent person perception experiments (Jacoby & Williams, 1985; Mark & Miller, 1986), the emotional context of the sexual activity was considered, but in ways that were confounded with other variables. In the Jacoby and Williams (1985) study, the emotional context of sexual activity was manipulated by presenting information concerning the total number of sexual partners, number of partners for whom affection was felt, and the number of partners for whom love was felt. Such a manipulation requires the subjects to do calculations and it's questionable whether they actually did. Mark and Miller (1986) manipulated the emotional context of sexuality, but in combination with the degree of sexual activity. A person was presented as either a virgin, as having sexual experiences in committed relationships, as having sexual experiences in casual relationships, or no information was presented. Although the experiment was thoughtfully designed, it also does not allow for (or at least it did not present) a direct test of the interaction between sex of stimulus person and the emotional context of sexual activity. This is the particular test that is needed, however, to examine the degree of the transitional double standard.

Description of this research

Because the previous person perception experiments have not adequately tested for the possible existence of the transitional double standard, this study was designed to do so. Sex of a stimulus person and the emotional context of his/her sexual activity are independently manipulated for the purpose of examining the significance of the interaction between them. If a transitional or conditional double standard is operating, a female will be evaluated more negatively if sex occurs in a casual than in a more serious relationship, whereas evaluations of a male will be less affected by the emotional context of the sexual activity.

Because the focus of this research is specifically on the effect of the context of the sexual experience in interaction with sex, sexual activity is not varied. For all subjects, information about the first sexual intercourse experience of a hypothetical person is presented. The focus is on the first coitus because of its significance in our society (Cams, 1973). The stimulus person is presented as having his/her first sexual intercourse in either a casual or a steady relationship.

In this study, sex of subject and sex of the stimulus person will not be confounded, as it was in some of the previous research (e.g., Istvan & Griffitt, 1980; Jacoby & Williams, 1985). In these previous studies, male and female subjects judged only those of the opposite sex. Consequently, the effects they found for sex (for example, as presented by Jacoby & Williams, 1985), are difficult to interpret because they could be due to sex of subject, sex of target, or an interaction between the two. In our research, each subject is randomly assigned to judge either a male or a female, which allows for the separation of the effects of sex of stimulus person and sex of subject.

The effect of another characteristic of the stimulus person, in addition to sex, will also be considered in this study. This is the age at which the sexual activity occurs. Surprisingly, previous research on sexual standards has not considered how the strength or nature of the double standard, and acceptability of sexual activity more generally, might depend on the age of the targets for whom standards are assessed. However, because the age at first coitus is decreasing (Zelnik & Kanter, 1980), and the age at marriage is increasing (Glick, 1979), the period of premarital sexual activity is now potentially longer than it has ever been. The sexual behavior that is considered to be acceptable for a single adult may not be the same as that for a single teenager. We hypothesize that the double standard will be more pronounced in the judgments of teenagers than of young adults. This can be considered another type of a conditional double standard, with age rather than quality of the relationship as the conditional factor. As norms change and people become more accepting of the premarital sexual behavior of women, this acceptance will likely come more quickly for the sexual activity of females who have reached adulthood than of females who are still teenagers.

The subjects in this study are asked their impressions of the hypothetical person on a wide range of personality characteristics. This will allow us to examine more specifically the extent of the effect of the double standard. The two hypotheses that will be tested in this person perception experiment are the following:

(1) Evaluations of a female will be more negative if she has first coitus in a casual rather than a steady relationship, whereas the evaluations of a male will be less affected by the type of relationship in which sexual activity occurs.

(2) Evaluations of a female will be more negative if she has first coitus as a teenager rather than as a young adult, whereas the evaluations of a male will be less affected by age at first coitus.

Method

The subjects were 233 males and 320 females attending one of two universities during the spring of 1985. Of the total 553 subjects, 371 (67%) were from the University of Wisconsin-Madison, and 182 (33%) were from Oklahoma State University. A majority of the subjects were white and middle class. The mean age was approximately 21 years. All four undergraduate class levels were represented: 10% were freshmen, 31% were sophomores, 26% were juniors and 31% were seniors (1% were graduate students, and .5% were special students).

The research was conducted during class time in several introductory and upper division sociology courses. The subjects were given a questionnaire that contained instructions, manipulations, and dependent measures, and was titled "Accuracy of Person Perception Based on Limited Information About a Person's Sexual Behavior." In the written instructions, the subjects were told that they would be reading through a page of a questionnaire completed by a high school or college "student" from another research study and then would be asked to estimate the student's personality and attitudes from the information presented. As part of the cover story, the subjects were told that the impressions they formed of the student would eventually be compared with information actually provided by him/her.

The page from the bogus survey contained questions about the person's first intercourse experience and was designed to look authentic. It was typed in a different typeface than the rest of the questionnaire and copied on a different color of paper. To make it appear as if the page was taken from a larger questionnaire, the title on top of the page was "Section III: Your First Sexual Intercourse Experience" and the page number was "7". The answers to the questions were handwritten.

All of the manipulations were contained within this page, primarily through responses to a set of questions. At the top was the student's sex, which was either male or female. The age of the student at first coitus was manipulated by indicating either 16 or 21 in answer to the question, "At what age did you have your first sexual intercourse experience?" (The same age was given to the next question, which asked the age of the partner at the time of the experience). The stage of the relationship in which first intercourse occurred was presented as either a steady dating relationship that had lasted almost a year or a casual dating relationship

that had lasted one week. Each subject was randomly assigned to one of 24 versions of the "page." Several additional questions about the sexual experience were also included on the page in order to make it appear more realistic. The answers to these additional questions were identical for all subjects. For example, "no" was the response to the question "Did you tell your friends about this experience?" and "a friend's apartment" was the answer to the question "Where did you have the sexual intercourse experience?"

After examining the page ostensibly completed by a student in another study, the subjects were asked to indicate their impressions of him or her. Specifically, the subjects were asked to rate the "student" on 23 personality characteristics using seven-point bipolar scales. These personality characteristics included, for example, dominant–submissive, popular–unpopular, sexually inexperienced–sexually experienced, cold–warm, and intelligent–unintelligent. [*Eds: This study cleverly embeds its key questions beneath other materials so that the participants will not find the key issues too transparently obvious. You should look for this sort of technique when critiquing articles and if different techniques are used you should consider their impact on the subject's potential awareness of the experimental hypothesis of the research.*]

Results

Description of subscales that are the dependent variables

The 23 adjective pairs referring to personality characteristics were **factor analyzed** for the purpose of developing subscales to serve as dependent variables in the analysis. Four factors emerged from this analysis. Based on the factor loadings, each of the adjective pairs was assigned to one of the four factor scales. To be assigned to a particular factor scale, the item had to **load on the factor** .50 or above. One personality item (career-oriented, not career-oriented) did not meet this criterion and thus was eliminated from the analyses.

The first factor scale contains seven adjective pairs related to Sexual and Other Values, and is described by such adjectives as sexually experienced, sexually liberal and liberal in sex-roles. The second scale contains eight adjectives which refer to Maturity and Intelligence – for example, wise, responsible, careful and intelligent. Four adjectives which refer to a Positive Personality make up the third scale and these include the adjectives likeable, moral and warm. The last scale contains three adjectives that refer to dominance–dominant, active and masculine. **Cronbach's alpha**, a measure of internal consistency, was .92 for the Sexual and Other Values scale, .87 for the Maturity and Intelligence scale, .70 for the Positive Personality scale and .60 for the Dominance scale. The mean scores on these scales were the **dependent variables** in the analyses.

Overview of the analysis

To examine whether a double standard is manifested in the evaluations the subjects formed of the stimulus person, the mean responses to the factor scales were subjected to an **ANOVA**. The factors to be considered, singly and in interaction with each other are: sex of the stimulus person (male or female), age of the stimulus person (16 or 21), relationship type (casual or steady) and sex of subject (male or female).

With a total of 48 cells, the number of subjects in the cells ranged from 6 to 17, with a mean of 11 subjects per cell. There was an unequal number of subjects per cell because there were more female than male subjects, and because the number of questionnaires planned for each class was often more than the number of students attending on that particular day. The focus of this research, however, is on examining the effects of two-way interactions (for example, between sex of stimulus person and stage of the relationship at first coitus), and the number of

subjects per cell for these interactions range from 110 to 160.

Main effects

Before the results are presented that are germane to our hypothesis that the evaluations of the stimulus person will reflect a conditional double standard, the **main effects** will be considered. Significant main effects were found for all of the manipulated independent variables:

Sex of stimulus person. Females received a significantly higher score on the Sexual and Other Values scale, and significantly lower scores on the Maturity and Intelligence, Positive Personality and Dominance scales than did males.

Age of stimulus person. Younger stimulus persons received significantly higher scores on the Sexual and Other Values and Dominance scales, and significantly lower scores on the Maturity and Intelligence and Positive Personality scales.

Stage of the relationship. Males and females who had first coitus in a casual relationship received significantly higher scores on the Sexual and Other Values and Dominance scales and significantly lower scores on the Maturity and Intelligence and Positive Personality scales.

These results indicate that there are differences in evaluations based on these characteristics (i.e., sex, age, stage of relationship) for people who have engaged in first coitus under the conditions presented. They do not, however, indicate whether these same differences would be found if information had not been presented about the individual's sexuality.

Interactions

Next, the results are presented for the interactions between sex of the stimulus person and each of the two conditional factors considered in this study-stage of the relationship in which the sexual activity occurs and age of the stimulus person at first coitus. The analyses indicated that there were no significant higher-order interactions of these variables with sex of subject, which means that male and female subjects did not significantly differ in their perceptions. Thus, the results presented below apply to both male and female subjects.

Stage of the relationship at first coitus. The interaction between sex of stimulus person and stage of the relationship in which first coitus occurs was significant for two of the four scales: the Positive Personality scale and the Dominance scale. The pattern of means and post-hoc comparisons among the cells indicated that both male and female stimulus persons were perceived to have a less positive personality if they had first coitus in a casual relationship than in a close relationship ($p < .001$). The difference between the two conditions, however, was somewhat greater for the female than for the male stimulus person.

On the Dominance scale, the male stimulus person was perceived to be more assertive if first coitus occurred in a casual relationship rather than in a close relationship ($p < .001$). Whereas the opposite pattern of means was found for the female ($p = $ n.s.). Because the characteristics contained in the Dominance scale (e.g., active, dominant) are considered to be desirable traits in our society (Broverman et al., 1972), this finding also demonstrates a double standard.

Age at first coitus. The interaction between sex and age of the stimulus person at first coitus was significant for three of the four scales: Maturity and Intelligence, Positive Personality, and Dominance. As predicted, a female was perceived less favorably by the subjects on the dimensions of Maturity and Intelligence and Positive Personality if she had first coitus at age 16 rather than age 21 ($p < .001$). On the other hand, a male received approximately the same score on the Positive Personality scale, regardless of whether he had first coitus at age 16 or 21 ($p = $ n.s.). Furthermore, although he was

perceived more negatively on the Maturity and Intelligence scale if he was age 16 at first coitus rather than age 21 ($p < .05$), the difference was not as large as it was for the female stimulus person. A slightly different pattern was found for the Dominance scale. A male having first coitus at age 16 was perceived to be more dominant than a male having first coitus at age 21 ($p < .001$), whereas there was basically no difference in how a 16 versus 21 year old female stimulus person was perceived ($p = $ n.s.). These results, particularly for the Positive Personality scale, suggest that the double standard exists to a greater degree if standards are assessed for teenagers (i.e., age 16) than for young adults (i.e., age 21).

In sum, the results provide evidence for a conditional double standard. Although having first coitus in a noncommitted relationship or at a young age generally has a negative effect on how both a male and a female are evaluated on many personality dimensions, the negative effect is greater for the female.

Discussion

Overall, this research indicates the existence of a conditional double standard. In the person perception experiment conducted, both a male and a female stimulus person received negative evaluations (especially on general personality characteristics) if first coitus occurred in a casual relationship or at the age of 16, but evaluations of a female were more negative than those of a male under these conditions. Furthermore, the male was perceived to be more dominant when he had first coitus in a casual relationship (rather than in a close relationship), or at age 16 (rather than at age 21), whereas the female was not. Although some might argue that a double standard is demonstrated only if females are more negatively evaluated while males are more positively evaluated for having sex in a casual rather than a close relationship (or age 16 rather than age 21), we consider the difference in the degree of the negative evaluations for males versus females to also demonstrate a double standard, albeit a more subtle one.

These findings contradict some recent survey research. For example, Delamater and MacCorquodale (1979, p. 227) concluded, "Our results indicate that in the sense of accepting premarital coitus for men but not for women, the double standard has disappeared." The person perception paradigm employed in this study is different from the survey methodology in several ways, which could account for the different results.

First, measuring the double standard via a person perception experiment reduces the possibility of a social desirability bias. Because a norm of egalitarianism is pervasive, the more transparent measures typical of survey studies may elicit egalitarian responses that do not completely reflect what the individuals honestly believe. In contrast, the person perception experiment disguises, in several ways, the purpose of assessing the double standard. Subjects are randomly assigned to give responses to one sex and not both, a cover story is presented that encourages honest responses, and the actual measures taken (first impressions of a specific person) are less subject to being biased by **socially desirable responses**.

Another difference between this experiment and the previous survey research is in how the double standard is **operationalized**. As stated by Delamater and MacCorquodale,

their survey research focuses on whether the double standard has disappeared in the broad sense in which the sexual activity occurs and the age of the individual. The data imply that an appropriate (positively or less negatively evaluated) sexual script for women involves delaying first intercourse until they are in a more serious relationship and have reached the age of young adulthood. Norms about the relational context of sexual activity and the age at first coitus seem to be much less stringent in scripts for men.

Part of these **sexual scripts** may involve making different attributions for sexual behavior. This may be especially true for attributions about women's sexual behavior since their scripts appear to be more constrained by contextual features. When a woman's sexual behavior matches the sexual script appropriate for her sex, such behavior may be more likely to be perceived as the result of external/contextual factors, and as appropriate. On the other hand, when her behavior violates the script, it may be seen as the result of negative, internal dispositions; that is, she is seen as a "bad girl." In this latter situation, observers may make more negative evaluations about her. Differential attributions as an intervening variable between knowledge of sexual behavior and its context, and perceptions of the target person must be directly assessed in future studies.

Further research examining the double standard and other premarital sexual standards should be continued – through person perception experiments, as well as survey studies.

This article takes a decidedly pro-**social learning approach** to explaining the sexual double standard. The authors argue that people in a particular society learn that different sexual scripts apply to men and women. The data support the argument that people use different scripts when interpreting the behavior of teenage men and women. Further, through the application of these scripts, women are more harshly evaluated when participating in the same behaviors as males of the same age. Sprecher et al. refer to differential application as a "conditional" double standard since it does not apply to older women.

The authors' use of an experimental design rather than a survey reduces the likelihood of participants expressing an egalitarian **social desirability** bias (i.e., answering in a way that makes them look good rather than being otherwise honest: their answers are ones that are socially preferred, even "politically correct"). Therefore, they have successfully demonstrated a double standard when others had argued it no longer existed. However, the subtle and conditional nature of the double standard may be an artifact of their sample's demographics and their results may underestimate the strength and pervasiveness of the double standard in college students. For example, the authors argue that the bias is subtle and in response to a perceived social norm of egalitarianism. However, their sample was made of students enrolled in lower and upper division sociology courses. Perhaps people who enroll in these courses (especially majors in upper division courses) hold a stronger sense of egalitarianism than students enrolled in other courses (e.g., business, physics, mathematics). In addition, the sample was primarily Caucasian and one must wonder if different variations of sexual scripts are learned and used in different subcultures in a given society. Rather than negate the effect reported by the authors, it is possible that a broader examination of the population will produce a stronger form of double standard.

Does the sexual double standard still exist more than a decade after Sprecher et al. reported support for a conditional version of this bias? The final article in this chapter is by Milhausen and Herold and it attempts to answer this question by building on the method of Sprecher et al. (1987). However, Milhausen and Herold's approach differs from the first article in this chapter in several significant ways. First, Milhausen and Herold seek to measure attitudes of women toward the double standard. For example, the researchers ask the participants whether they believe others in society hold a double standard and whether they personally believe in a double standard. This is a departure because the person perception paradigm used by Sprecher et al. assessed actual behavior. Milhausen and Herold (1999) used a sample that contained only women, but more significantly they used a survey rather than an experimental design (both changes from Sprecher et al., 1987).

Milhausen and Herold predict that women will have more negative attitudes toward sex and will endorse a double standard by judging sexually active women more harshly than men. This prediction is assessed through the use of multiple questions, both open and closed ended. Therefore it would be valuable to consider the consistency of participants' responses with regard to the predictions across the full range of questions included in the survey.

As in past chapters we encourage you to think critically about statistical and methodological issues while reading an article, considering the choices and compromises that an author makes to address her or his question of interest. For example, Sprecher et al. (1987) avoid some methodological issues by using an experimental design rather than a survey. As you read this last article in the chapter you may find it useful to consider why Milhausen and Herold chose to go back to a survey technique. Was this decision influenced by the type of research question being asked or perhaps the constraints of data collection? In addition, you may want to consider the choice of samples and procedures used to collect the data while completing the article. How would these decisions affect the external and internal validity of this study?

Does the Sexual Double Standard Still Exist? Perceptions of University Women

Robin R. Milhausen and Edward S. Herold

The sexual double standard has been the focus of considerable research since the 1960s. Ira Reiss (1960), the pioneer researcher, defined the orthodox double standard as prohibiting premarital sexual intercourse for women but allowing it for men. This standard evolved into the conditional double standard in which women were permitted to engage in sexual relations only within a committed love relationship, whereas men were permitted to have as many sexual partners as they wanted without condition. In studying the double standard, researchers have generally focused on one of three main issues: sexual behavior, evaluations of men and women who engage in certain sexual behaviors, and personal preferences regarding the sexual background of hypothetical partners.

Research on the sexual behavior of men and women suggests that the double standard still influences both sexes. Men have reported sexual intercourse at earlier ages (Weinberg, Lottes, & Shaver, 1995) and a greater number of lifetime sexual partners than have women (Laumann, Gagnon, Michael, & Michaels, 1994). Evolutionary psychology has been used to explain the sex differences in sexual behaviors. According to this perspective, sex differences have developed through human evolution because they are related to reproductive capacities (Weiderman, 1993). Because men have greater reproductive capacities, it is considered beneficial for them to inseminate as many females as possible to maximize the survival of their offspring (e.g., Oliver & Shibley Hyde, 1993).

Social learning theory has also been used to explain the double standard. According to social learning theory, women are punished for behaving in sexually permissive ways by being stigmatized or isolated, whereas men are rewarded by achieving popularity or admiration for the identical behaviors (e.g., Sprecher, Regan, McKinney, Maxwell, & Wazienski, 1997). Under the rubric of social learning theory, **sexual script theory** has emerged to explain patterns of sexual behavior. In following traditional scripts, men are socialized to desire and engage in frequent casual sexual activity with multiple partners, whereas women are encouraged to limit their sexual experiences to encounters within committed, monogamous relationships (Sprecher et al., 1997).

Despite the considerable differences in men's and women's reported sexual behaviors, research specifically focused on attitudes regarding the double standard has resulted in conflicting findings. These differences may be explained by the different criteria used to measure the double standard, with one group of researchers having focused on evaluations of sexual behaviors and the other group focused on partner preferences.

One approach has involved asking participants to rate certain sexual behaviors of hypothetical men and women. Spreadbury (1982) found that women were more likely to label other women's sexual behaviors as promiscuous than men's sexual behaviors, indicating that women supported the sexual double standard. Sprecher, McKinney, and Orbuch (1987) gave subjects information about a hypothetical target's first sexual experience, and asked them to rate the target in terms of various personality characteristics. Although both male and female profiles were given negative personality evaluations if their first intercourse experience happened at a young age and in an uncommitted relationship, evaluations of females were slightly more negative.

The other approach to the double standard has measured partner preferences rather than behavioral evaluation. Researchers using this approach generally have reported a single standard of preferences for both men and women. O'Sullivan (1995) found that among men and women, highly experienced targets were perceived to be less desirable as a dating partner and as a spouse. Sprecher et al. (1997) found men and women both preferred potential marriage or dating partners to have no sexual experience rather than either moderate or extensive sexual experience. However, Oliver and Sedikides (1992) found that when it came to casual dating relationships, men were more likely than women to prefer partners who were more sexually experienced.

These findings have been interpreted in two different ways. Oliver and Sedikides (1992) concluded that men who prefer sexually permissive women for dating partners while preferring less experienced women for more committed relationships may be endorsing the double standard, in that they are willing to date "bad girls" so as to have sex with them, whereas they would not consider these same women as marriage partners. Nevertheless, these men are at least accepting of sexually experienced women for some relationships. On the other hand, Sprecher, McKinney, and Orbuch (1991) suggested that because most women are not willing to accept men with high levels of sexual experience for any type of relationship, these results indicate a reverse double standard in which men are allowed less sexual freedom than women in dating relationships.

Researchers, in measuring the double standard, have typically relied upon ratings of hypothetical targets or profiles as their primary methodology (e.g., Sprecher et al., 1991). Checklists or profiles are highly artificial, and cannot include all characteristics that are taken into account when evaluating real people in the real world. As Oliver and Sedikides (1992) have noted, sexual behavior is not judged in a vacuum. Yet, most profile studies (with the exception of Sprecher et al., 1997) have not considered the importance of sexual permissiveness in relation to other characteristics, such as personality characteristics or physical attractiveness. For example, women may prefer a man who has had few sexual partners, yet may choose to date a highly experienced man if he has other desirable characteristics.

In rating hypothetical targets in terms of desirability as dating or marital partners, usually men and women have only been asked to rate opposite sex profiles (e.g., Oliver & Sedikides, 1992). Thus, most researchers have focused only on between-sex differences when studying the double standard. Only a few (e.g., O'Sullivan, 1995) have addressed within-sex differences. Consequently, the effects found for sex are difficult to interpret, because they could be a result of sex of subject, sex of target, or an interaction between the two (Sprecher et al., 1987).

In our study we have attempted to address some of these limitations. As suggested by Sprecher et al. (1997), we measured preferences for ideal relationship partners in addition to tolerable levels of sexual experience for a dating partner. Measures of actual previous behavioral choices regarding partner selection were also included. To counter social desirability effects, following Sprecher's (1989) research design, we used a **between-subjects design** in which one half of the sample evaluated male behavior and the other half evaluated female behavior. We also analyzed within-sex differences. Most importantly, as suggested by Sprecher et al. (1997) we included some open-ended questions to better understand participants' perceptions of the sexual double standard, their perceptions of both men and women with many sexual partners, and the motivations behind their partner preferences and choices.

The main objective of this research was to study the attitudes and behaviors of university women regarding the sexual double standard. In particular, we wanted to determine if women's perceptions of the double standard would be similar to or different from their own personal acceptance or rejection of the double standard. We purposely focused on women because previous research has indicated that women generally are the ones who decide how far sexual behavior will proceed in a relationship (McCormick, 1994). Given that women are seen as the "gatekeepers" of sexual behavior, we believed that it was more critical to understand women's attitudes toward the double standard than men's. In addition, women have been found to be more judgmental of other people's sexual behavior than have men (Spreadbury, 1982).

Based on previous literature, we developed two hypotheses:

(1) Women will endorse a sexual double standard in which women are judged more harshly for having many sexual partners than are men.

(2) The more sexual partners women have had, the more accepting they will be of men who have had many sexual partners.

Methods

The participants who volunteered to take part in this study were a **convenience sample** of 174 unmarried female undergraduate students enrolled in a first year course on Couple and Family Relations at a Canadian university. Nine of the women indicated they were lesbian or bisexual and they were not included in the analysis, thus reducing the sample to 165. The women ranged in age from 18 to 25 ($M = 19.6$; $SD = 1.2$). Thirty-nine percent had not dated in the last four weeks and 44% were involved in a steady relationship with one partner only. The women's number of previous past sexual partners ranged from 0 to 11 ($M = 1.69$; $SD = 1.93$). One third (32%) had not experienced sexual intercourse, 27% had one sexual partner, 25% had two or three partners, and 16% had four or more partners.

Number of partners. Number of previous sexual partners was measured by the open-ended question "With how many partners have you had sexual intercourse?"

Perceived sex differences in sexual interest. Two of the underlying tenets of the double standard are that women enjoy sex less than men and are less interested in sex. Two items measured perceived sex differences in sexual interest: (a) "Women can enjoy sex as much as men do," and (b) "Women are not as interested in sex as men are." Responses ranged from (5) *Strongly agree* to (1) *Strongly disagree*. Item b was **reverse coded** for the analysis [*Eds: that is to say, scores were mathematically adjusted so that a 5 was treated as a 1, 4 as 2 and so on so that both scales a and b had the positive score of 5 meaning the same thing, "Strongly agree", with an affirmative, rather than with a negative, statement.*]

Importance of sex. Another belief underlying the double standard is that most women do not consider sex to be important. How important the women considered sex to be was measured by "How important is sex to you?" Responses for this item were: (a) *Very important*, (b) *Somewhat important*, (c) *Of little importance*, and (d) *Not important*. Responses were reverse coded for the analysis.

Perceptions of a societal double standard. Two items measured women's beliefs about societal norms regarding the sexual double standard: (a) "Women who have had many sex partners are judged more harshly than men who have had many partners", and (b) "Is there a double standard for sexual behavior (a standard in which it is more acceptable for a man to have had more sexual partners than a woman)?" Respondents were asked to explain their answer. Responses included: (a) *Definitely yes*, (b) *Probably yes*, (c) *Probably not*, and (d) *Definitely not*. To determine if the women believed there was a difference between the sexes regarding enforcement of the double standard, they were asked "Who judges women who have had sex with many partners more harshly?" Responses were (a) *Women*, (b) *Men*, and (c) *men and women judge equally harshly*.

Personal endorsement of the sexual double standard. In testing our first hypothesis, women's endorsement of the sexual double standard was measured by administering two versions of the same question, with one half of the subjects receiving the version for a male friend and the other half receiving the version for a female friend: "You have a very close male friend (female friend) who is looking for a casual date. He (she) has met someone whom he (she) likes and finds attractive. You know that this woman (man) has had intercourse with more than 10 different men (women). You would discourage him (her) from dating her (him)." Response choices ranged from (5) *Strongly agree* to (1) *Strongly disagree*. This **between-subjects design** followed procedures outlined by Sprecher (1989).

We also used a second indicator of the women's endorsement of the double standard by including an item asking for labels the women would use to describe others with high levels of sexual experience. In tandem with the previous question, the students were given one of two versions of an open-ended question which asked them to list words specifically describing either a man or a woman who has had many partners: "What words would you use to describe a man (woman) who has had many sexual partners?"

Preference for men with many or few partners. According to the double standard, men who have had many sexual partners are admired and preferred by women. Therefore, it was assumed that if the women did not prefer men with a history of many partners that they would be rejecting the double standard. Two different types of items were used to measure women's preferences for dating men who have had many or few sexual partners. The first item was "I would prefer not to date someone who has had intercourse with more than__partners". The second item was "You meet a good-looking, charming man who really appeals to you. You are very physically attracted to him. You have heard that he has had sex with about 10 women over the last four years. You are certain that he is not infected with a sexually transmitted disease. You would go out with him." The first item was solely focused on number of partners without taking into account any other characteristics. The other item was purposely constructed so that positive personality characteristics were associated with men who had many partners. This was done to determine to what extent women were willing to accept highly experienced men if they had other desirable characteristics.

The women were also asked about their actual behaviors regarding partner choice: "Have you dated someone in the past who has had more sexual partners than you would have liked?" Responses were *yes/no*. Women who answered yes were asked "If yes, were you bothered by this (a) *A lot*, (b) *Somewhat*, (c) *A little*, and (d) *Not at all*."

To obtain insight regarding motivations for dating or not dating men with many partners, women were asked two open-ended questions about men with many partners. So as not to bias the responses, the participants were asked to give both positive and negative characteristics of men who had many partners: (a) "What is it about a man who has had many sexual partners that might make him a more desirable dating partner?" and (b) "What is it about a man who has had many sexual partners that might make him a less desirable dating partner?"

Procedure

The research was conducted during regular class time. The researchers stated that the study was focused on the sexual attitudes of unmarried, heterosexual women. Students were given a questionnaire that included an information sheet and a separate consent form. A questionnaire was given to everyone in the class so that all of the students would have the opportunity to view it, even if they did not fit the criteria or did not wish to hand in a completed survey. Students were informed that the questionnaire was to be completed on a voluntary basis, and that they were not obligated to hand it in. They were encouraged to sit apart from one another and, when finished, they placed their questionnaires into boxes at the front of the classroom to ensure anonymity.

Coding of open-ended questions

Categories for the open-ended questions were developed by the researchers after they had reviewed all of the written comments made by the respondents. The responses were coded using these categories by two independent raters who were graduate students. The percentage agreement between the two raters was obtained for each of the questions, resulting in inter-rater reliability ratings ranging from .80 to .97.

It should be noted that for each question many of the respondents listed two or more words or phrases, with some of the words belonging in one category and others belonging in another category. Because of this, the total percentage for each category was more than 100%.

Results

Perceived sex differences in sexual interest. Ninety-nine percent of the women strongly agreed or agreed that women can enjoy sex as much as men do. Sixty-nine percent strongly disagreed or disagreed with the statement that women are not as interested in sex as men are.

Importance of sex. When asked how important sex was to them 17% of the women reported *very important*, 59% reported *somewhat important*, 17% reported *of little importance*, and 7% reported that sex was *not important* to them.

Perceptions of a societal sexual double standard. The women were in almost unanimous agreement that the double standard is a pervasive influence in society. Ninety-five percent indicated that they definitely or probably believed a double standard exists (a standard in which it is more acceptable for a man to have more sexual partners than a woman). Ninety-three percent indicated that they definitely or probably agreed that women who have many sex partners are judged more harshly than men who have many sex partners. The women's comments were coded under four main categories: (a) Women Penalized, (b) Men Rewarded, (c) Women Not Focused on Sex, and (d) Men Focused on Sex. The **inter-rater reliability** for the coding of these categories was .86.

Within the first category, labeled Women Penalized, 49% of the respondents indicated that women were harshly labeled and penalized for having many sexual partners. Comments included (e.g., "women have to be careful not to ruin their reputations"). In the second category, Men Rewarded, 48% of the respondents indicated that men were encouraged to have, and rewarded for having, many partners (e.g., "guys are admired by peers"). The women reported that men who had many partners were often seen as "studs," "cool," "successful," and "popular." For the third category, labeled Women Not Focused on Sex, 10% indicated that women were supposed to be less interested in sex (e.g., "Culturally speaking, women have been restricted into thinking that their sexual needs are not as important as men's and that [sex] is disgusting"). Finally, in the fourth category, named Men are Sexually Focused, 9% of the women stated that it is natural for males to be more interested in sex: "Naturally, men seem to have a stronger (less controllable) sex drive, and act upon it."

Seven percent of the respondents made comments suggesting that the double standard was disappearing. However, there were differing opinions about why this was happening, with some believing that both men and women were judged harshly for having many partners, and others believing that neither men nor women were judged harshly for this.

The women clearly believed that there are two distinct standards for the sexual behavior of men and women. Interestingly, almost one half of the women (46%) believed that it is women themselves who are the harshest judges of women's sexual behavior. Whereas 42% believed men and women were equally harsh judges, only 12% believed that men were the harshest judges of women's sexual behavior.

Personal endorsement of the sexual double standard. To provide insight into whether the women themselves supported the double standard, the students were asked to list words they use to describe either a man or a woman who has had many partners. Almost all of the words listed for both highly experienced men and women were negative, indicating the women judged men just as harshly as they judged women. Contrary to the double standard, the vast majority of women listed only negative words to describe a highly experienced man. The negative words were coded under the main categories of (a) Sexual Predator, (b) Promiscuous, and (c) Sexually Focused. The coding inter-rater reliability was .80.

Forty-six percent of the sample used words which indicated that the man who had many partners was seen as a Sexual Predator. The term "player" was the most common of all the words the women selected. A player was defined as a man who uses women for his own pleasures without regard for their feelings. Other words used were "manipulative," "arrogant," and "insensitive." Forty-two percent of the sample listed terms which came under the second category of Promiscuous (e.g., "slut"). Finally, 10% of the women described the male as Sexually Focused and not wanting a committed relationship: "Sex is impersonal to him – not much of an emotional intimate thing." This man was also considered a risk for infidelity.

Five percent listed words indicating that the highly experienced male had psychological problems such as "low self-esteem" and "confused." Seven percent said they did not want to make a judgment without knowing

more about the person. One quarter of the women (24%) listed positive attributes, with "experienced" being the most common term.

The women also gave mainly negative labels for women who had many partners. The negative labels were coded under the categories of (a) Promiscuous, (b) Psychologically Damaged, and (c) Sexually Focused. The inter-rater coding reliability was .81. Most of the women (59%) used words which fell into Promiscuous (e.g., "slut"). Twelve percent of the sample used terms suggesting a highly experienced woman was Psychologically Damaged (e.g., "insecure"). Finally, 8% of the women responded with words or phrases belonging to the category Sexually Focused. The respondents felt that these women were uncommitted and focused on sex rather than the relationship. Seven percent commented that experienced women were at greater risk of STD/HIV infection. Seven percent also reported they did not want to make a judgment without knowing more about the person.

Although most of the respondents used negative labels, 29% used positive words to describe women who had many partners. These words included "experienced," "independent," "free to make her own choices," "unashamed," "outgoing," "fun," "sexy," "open-minded," and "in touch with her own desires."

Preference for men with many or few partners. When asked to state the upper limit for the number of partners they would prefer their dating partners to have had, almost all (95%) were willing to accept a partner who had experienced intercourse with at least one partner. The majority of the women preferred a man who had not had too many partners. Only 9.5% of the women stated that they would be willing to accept a man who had more than 10 partners as a dating partner. The median number of acceptable partners was a maximum of four.

When given more information about a potential dating partner, one half (52%) of the women agreed that they would date an attractive and appealing man who had had sex with about 10 women over the past four years, assuming he was not infected with an STD. One quarter (26%) of the women indicated they would not go out with this man, and 22% were undecided. About one third (36%) of the women reported having dated someone in the past who had more sexual partners than they would have liked. Of these women, 25% were bothered a lot by this, 52% were bothered somewhat, and 23% were bothered only a little.

In summary, most women indicated preferring a man who has not had too many sexual partners. Yet, many indicated a willingness to date such a man if he had other appealing characteristics. The finding that one third admitted dating someone who previously had more partners than they would have preferred reinforces the fact that women take other characteristics besides number of partners into account.

Women were asked in two separate items what it was about a man who had many past sexual partners that could make him either a more desirable or a less desirable dating partner. Most women listed several negative attributes that they associated with a highly experienced man. Their responses were coded into four categories: (a) Casual Attitudes Toward Sex and Relationships, (b) Risk of Disease, (c) High Sexual Expectations, and (d) Sexual Predator. The inter-rater coding reliability was .97.

Sixty-three percent of the respondents listed words which fit into the Casual Attitudes Toward Sex and Relationships category. These women believed that highly experienced men would have casual attitudes toward sex and relationships (e.g., "I am just another notch on his belt"). Within the category Risk for Disease, 55% of the women listed words expressing their concern about the greater risk of experienced men having an STD or HIV. In the category of High Sexual Expectations, 19% cited these concerns: "He would expect sex right away," and "I would worry about not living up to other partners." Finally, under the Sexual Predator category, 15% of the respondents indicated concerns about

exploitation (e.g., "takes advantage of women," "is dangerous").

When women were asked to specifically indicate what might make a highly experienced man a more desirable dating partner, 11% stated that there was nothing desirable about this type of man, and another 5% did not make any response. However, 84% of the women listed at least one positive attribute. These attributes were classified into the three categories of (a) Sexually Confident, (b) Appealing Personality and Appearance, and (c) Exciting Sexual Partner. The inter-rater coding reliability was .96.

Of those who listed desirable characteristics, the great majority by far (74%) reported words belonging in the Sexually Confident category. These women focused on sexual confidence and expertise (e.g., "He knows how to satisfy a woman").

It should be noted, however, that although the women listed sexual experience as a positive attribute, some prefaced their comments with the qualification that sexual expertise was not that important to them.

Fourteen percent of the women gave characteristics falling under the category of Appealing Personality and Appearance. These included "popular," "attractive," and "others have found him desirable." The fact that other women might find the experienced man appealing definitely made him more desirable among some of the respondents. Finally, 12% reported that a sexually experienced man as an Exciting Sexual Partner would be "sexually adventurous," and "willing to try new things."

Hypothesis One: Women's personal endorsement of the sexual double standard. We hypothesized that women would endorse a double standard which judges women more harshly than men for having many sexual partners. To test this, one half of the women were given the item asking if they would discourage a male friend from dating a female who had 10 previous partners, whereas the other half were asked whether they would discourage a female friend from dating a male who had 10 previous partners. Surprisingly, women were more likely to discourage a female friend from dating a highly experienced male than a male friend from dating a highly experienced female. The mean score for the male friend condition was 3.17 ($SD = .96$) and the mean score for the female friend condition was 3.57 ($SD = 3.57$), $t(1, 163) = 2.75$, $p = .007$, effect size = .21. The effect size indicates that while there is a significant sex difference in the direction opposite to that which we predicted, the magnitude of the difference is modest. Thus, the hypothesis that women would personally endorse the double standard (one which judges women more harshly than men) was rejected. Instead, these findings suggest a reverse double standard which is harsher toward men than women.

Hypothesis Two: The more sexual partners women have had, the more accepting they will be of men who have had many partners. Hypothesis Two was supported in that women who had more sexual partners were less likely to judge highly experienced men negatively. A higher number of past sexual partners was correlated with a willingness to date an attractive, charming man who had sex with 10 women over the last four years ($r = .33$, $p < .01$) and accepting a dating partner with a higher number of partners ($r = .51$, $p < .01$). The magnitude of the correlations indicates that the number of partners a woman has had is a strong predictor of their acceptance of men with many partners.

Discussion

Although the women overwhelmingly perceived a societal double standard in which they felt women's behavior was judged more harshly than that of men, the students did not personally support the double standard. Furthermore, by asserting that sex is important to them, these women have rejected one of the fundamental tenets underlying the double standard.

Traditionally, another indicator of support for the sexual double standard has been the words used to describe men and women with many sexual partners. In this study, contrary to the double standard, the women gave mostly negative labels to both men and women who were highly sexually experienced. Interestingly, some of the words that have traditionally been used to describe the behavior of women were also used by this sample to describe men who had many partners, in particular the word "slut." This choice of words is an indication of a shift toward a more negative evaluation of men who have many partners. Men were also commonly categorized as being sexual predators. The term "player," a relatively new term not yet reported in the literature, was often used to label highly experienced men as being manipulative and exploitative.

It should be noted that the question asking for words to describe a man or a woman who has many sexual partners was preceded by the question which asked if the participants believed there was a double standard in which it was more acceptable for a man to have had more sexual partners than a woman. Given that almost all of the respondents agreed with this statement, we might have expected that the respondents would have been predisposed to offer substantially fewer negative labels attached to the men than to the women. That this did not happen indicates that our female respondents were clearly making a distinction between their perceptions of societal norms and their own feelings regarding the double standard.

The respondents believed that other women, as opposed to men, were likely the more severe judges of women's sexual behavior. Considering it has been assumed that the double standard is the product of a patriarchal culture in which men seek to limit the sexuality of women, it is interesting that a substantial portion of women would feel that women are more likely than men to control other women's sexuality.

In a direct test of the double standard, the students were asked whether or not they would discourage either a female or a male friend from dating someone who had had intercourse with more than 10 partners. Contrary to our hypothesis, the women did not personally endorse the double standard. In fact, they were more likely to discourage a female friend from dating a highly experienced male than to discourage a male friend from dating a highly experienced female. These findings again suggest that women today may be judging highly experienced men more negatively than experienced women (a reverse double standard). This might be explained by the traditional script: Men are seen as strong and capable of self-preservation, whereas women are seen as potential victims who need to be defended. O'Sullivan (1995) noted that a highly experienced male might be seen as someone who is more likely to ignore signs of resistance during a sexual encounter.

Most researchers have not made a distinction between women's preferences for level of sexual experience in a potential mate and the level of experience they are willing to tolerate given other positive attributes. Our findings suggest that many women are willing to make exceptions and date experienced men if they possess other positive qualities. The distinction between tolerable levels of sexual experience and preferred levels of sexual experience in a potential partner can perhaps explain discrepant past findings regarding the sexual double standard. Clearly, for many women personality characteristics can exert a more powerful influence over partner preferences than the level of sexual experience (Sprecher et al., 1997). Nevertheless, there are some women who will reject men who have had many previous sexual partners as potential dating partners regardless of what other positive characteristics they might possess.

As predicted in our second hypothesis, women who had more sexual partners were more likely to accept a dating partner who had more sexual experience. Because sexually experienced women are more attracted to sexually experienced men, the probability of these men having even more sexual partners in the future is heightened. As indicated in the open-ended question which asked the women to list positive aspects of an experienced man, several of the women indicated

that this man could be appealing because he might have greater sexual expertise, and thus be better able to sexually satisfy his partner.

If the double standard does not, in fact, exist in society, how can we account for such different levels of sexual behavior in men and women? Perhaps men are aware of the negative stigma attached to having many partners, yet they care less than women about being judged or gaining bad reputations. Alternatively, men may believe that their male peers are supportive of sexual conquests and, consequently, they may be less concerned with how they are evaluated by women. Research is needed to determine which explanation is more accurate.

Our study has provided useful methodological contributions toward enhancing research on the double standard. The use of different types of measurement to study the double standard highlights the fact that the type of question asked can shape the responses that are obtained. For example, this study points to a clear perception of the double standard at a societal level, although its existence is not supported through women's own beliefs and values. Including open-ended items in the questionnaire was important, as these items provided a richer context for understanding women's perceptions of the double standard. Our study also addressed both real and ideal partner preferences, a distinction which is often ignored in checklist studies. Finally, in our study, unlike in much of the previous research, participants evaluated the behavior of both men and women instead of only an opposite-sex partner.

Despite these contributions, there are some weaknesses in this study. For example, in designing diverse measures of the double standard, single-item measures were used rather than standardized scales.

The major weakness is the use of a **convenience sample** of young university women from a single class. It is important to note the limited sexual experience of this sample, as 32% had not had sexual intercourse and 27% had experienced sexual intercourse with only one person. Given the nature of our sample, the findings cannot be generalized to the larger society. To obtain a more complete understanding of the double standard, it is important that men be surveyed, as well as other groups of women who are older and not enrolled in a university.

The item asking who judges women who have had many sexual partners more harshly might be criticized for not taking into account the fact that some people may not judge these women harshly. Nevertheless, research findings, including those in this study, have determined that most people do judge others who have had many partners in a negative light, and that women are more likely to do so than men (Spreadbury, 1982).

The item which asked women if they would go out with a man who had 10 partners suggested that they would be certain he was not infected with an STD. Of course, in real life it is unrealistic to make such an assumption. However, it has been found that many people assume they can differentiate between people who are likely to have an STD and those who do not, and believe that by being more selective in their partner choices they are reducing the risk of infection (Herold & Mewhinney, 1993).

In conclusion, the finding that most of the women did not personally support the double standard appears to offer more support for learning theory rather than for evolutionary theory in explaining the double standard. For evolutionary theory to be supported, presumably most women would be accepting of the double standard and have a more positive view of men who have had many partners. How would evolutionary theory account for the fact that women differ in their acceptance of men's having many partners depending upon their own level of sexual experience?

Obviously more research is needed, with diverse samples including both men and women before we can make more definitive conclusions about which theoretical approach appears to be more valid. We hope that the use of different measurement strategies illustrated in this study will encourage other researchers to adopt more creative approaches in their measurement and analysis of the complexities of the sexual double standard.

Given the wealth of questions asked of participants, it is challenging to track the pattern of support or disconfirmation of the overall hypothesis that a double standard still exists. However, there are several key findings reported by the authors that help clarify the results. First, women report a belief that society holds a double standard. Second, although they believed others hold such a standard, the women participating in this study did not appear to personally endorse a double standard. Third, women reported seeing no difference between men and women in the interest in or enjoyment of sex; however, this is a bit of a straw man argument and may not actually bear on assessing the validity of a double standard. Fourth, about half the women believed that women were harsher than men in their assessment of the sexual activity of other women. Finally, a number of women demonstrated a type of "reverse double standard" derogating men who had more than the median number of sexual partners. Taken together these results suggest a schism in the thought processes of the participants permitting them to simultaneously believe that "others hold a double standard, but I do not". While it is possible that the women in this study hold beliefs that are not representative of larger society as the authors suggest, this leaves us with conditional support for a double standard since only a small portion of a population attend a four-year college or university course. Why might college-educated women not hold a double standard (and in fact employ a reverse double standard for men) while a double standard remains prevalent in non-college women and men in general? It may be the case that younger and more educated people hold more egalitarian attitudes toward sexuality than the general population. Other possible alternatives may come to light by examining the methods employed in the study to collect the data.

As mentioned earlier, the sample was college-aged women. However, they were taking a class on "Couple and Family Relations". While these women may have been more enlightened that the general population due to life experiences before entering college, one wonders whether a **self-selection bias** for enrolling in this course might make the sample more homogeneous on matters of sexual egalitarianism. In addition, since it is unclear when in the semester the study was completed and how much course content was covered before the data collection, the class content may have impacted the participants' attitudes toward sexuality and relationships leading to a more egalitarian stance than the general population (and possibly than the general college population as well). A second issue concerning data collection may also have produced a more egalitarian attitude among the women and the reported schism between themselves and society. The survey used in the study was quite long and although each question was different in content and approach, together they repeatedly addressed presence of a double standard. Therefore, it is possible that the cumulative impact of repeated questioning on the same general topic sensitized the participants so they were more likely to provide the researchers with **socially desirable responses** and potentially ones that were consistent with course content presented before the data collection. In addition, the **potentially reactive nature** of the survey may have been augmented by the data collection procedure since it was done during regular class time, in the location where such topics may have been presented, and possibly in the presence of the professors who may have expounded course content related to the research question. Such a situation places the participants in a position of selecting a subject role to play and it is possible that participants in this situation chose to give answers that were consistent with either the course content or the anticipated attitudes of the researcher/instructors. Given the nature of the survey and the data collection setting, it is possible that the participants were able to guess the researchers' hypotheses.

Although the methodological issues raised above may not have had an impact on the present study, it is always useful to consider issues of sampling and reactivity whenever doing a critical reading of research reports. It may also be useful to outline what steps you might take to change an article's procedures to reduce the possibility of sampling error or reactivity. How would you alter the procedures used in this study and still address the same research question?

5 Relationship Development

What is it that develops when a relationship develops? Although this question is rather shocking in some ways, because we all assume that we know the answer ("intimacy" of course, fathead!), it is actually not that simple and researchers have spent the last twenty years or so trying to figure out where "common sense" went wrong. Our most likely idea is that "something" gets deeper or stronger or that we move along a pathway of intimacy toward the ultimate destination of a closeness that is written in the stars and in Hollywood movies. But is that right?

Consider the alternative that is also present in common sense, at least as represented by the dating agencies. As far as these are concerned, people get along and become intimate simply because they start out as Right for each other. The process of getting to know someone else is simply the uncovering of those pre-existing magnetic forces that made them Right in the first place. In short nothing at all develops. We start out Right for each other and we simply discover that fact in more detail and with greater certainty. Thus dating agencies take our attitudinal pulse, work out our likes and dislikes and then declare that there is someone else out there who matches up with these preferences of ours and is the perfect partner. Nothing changes as we get to know one another; we simply know more about what was there already.

Perhaps now you are beginning to wonder. Don't we sometimes get to know someone who seems Right and then find that we simply cannot get along or cannot work out a form of relationship that is right for us both? But if we are Right for someone else why cannot we work out relational behaviors and roles that make the Rightness work properly? So is there something behavioral about relationships that has to be worked out even with a Right partner?

All right let's start again. What happens is that relationships go through stages and at each stage we have to discover that we are (still) Right for each other. That's it. But are there really stages in relationships or do we perhaps just like to think there are or perhaps find it easier to act as if there are? Is "being engaged" that different from being married, except for the existence of a marriage licence?

The papers that we will read here are developments of two basic ideas, first that the ways in which we think about relationships are largely metaphorical and that we can talk about the "growth" of relationships or the burning fires of love or being head over heels in love with someone or working out our relationship but that is only because people like using metaphors to describe things that are really hard to understand – one of which things is "the development of relationships". We don't actually catch fire when we fall in love and we do not water our relationships to make them grow, but we can say that we burn hot with passion or can essentially liken a relationship to a plant that needs tending and water, because we have some idea of what those things are like. Those metaphors help us to describe our feelings in meaningful ways. The second idea in the papers here is that perhaps relationships do not develop systematically at all. Perhaps what happens is that life is more chaotic than that and we don't really understand what is going on. In that case it makes a certain sense for us to try to *impose* some sort of order on chaotic events by using descriptions that we and other people can relate to. In short we take a chaotic experience and make an order out of it just by using language that makes sense of it for us.

Yes of course you find this odd right now but let's look at the papers and see how you feel afterwards. The first paper points out some of the metaphors that we freely use to describe relationships and their change. The idea here is that the metaphors that we choose are actually helpful in making relationships understandable but that we have several choices about the sorts of metaphor that we can pick. The paper puts more flesh on this idea by uncovering some of the many "root metaphors" that underlie our descriptions of relationships (such as "working at relationships", or the "journey of discovery" that takes place when we get to know someone).

Baxter's paper reinforces the point that adoption of any metaphor is adoption not just of some flowery language but adoption of a *way of thinking* (Lakoff, 1986). Such "thoughtways" have the effect of directing and constraining – as well as assisting and expanding – our thinking about a relevant topic. The paper introduces some key aspects of metaphorical analysis, including the distinction between **tenor** and **vehicle** in metaphor, and the notion of **experiential Gestalt**. An experiential Gestalt (from the German for "pattern") refers to a wholeness of a sensation or experience that is difficult to pick apart and analyze in its parts. For example, "love" can involve a whole set of experiences that change our ways of feeling and yet are hard to analyze and separate, as we saw in Chapter 3. We experience instead a general experiential Gestalt of being in love, when we feel good, but sometimes sad, and know that the other person is the source of this general sense of pleasure and fulfillment, and occasionally also of sadness. All the same, it is sometimes hard to work out why the person makes us feel that way. "I don't know; it's just that, like, I feel *great* when we're together". Because we may feel stupid being made so inarticulate by our feelings, we might tend to use metaphor to get us out of our difficulty. "I'm head over heels in love" is a more vivid and instructive way to convey the sense of elation and loss of control that goes with being in love. Metaphors involve a **tenor** and a **vehicle:** when we suffer the slings and arrows of outrageous fortune or *fall* in love, the tenor is the thing cited (slings, arrows, falling) and the vehicle is the associated metaphorical image (slings and arrows are *weapons of assault*; falling occurs when we *lose control* of ourselves). Note that metaphors can be explicit in language, for example, "You are talking *crap*", or else they can be so far hidden that their implicitness disguises the fact that they are metaphors at all (Hi *Honey*, I'm home!). As Baxter uncovers, there are several hidden threads to the metaphors that we tend to use about relationships, mostly to do with work, journeys of discovery or irresistible forces. These basic underlying organizing threads that provide specific frameworks for metaphors Baxter calls **root metaphors**.

The study uses a **Stratified Random Sample,** that is to say, a sample that is selected randomly with the exception that the investigator makes sure that a particularly desired feature is present in the sample. If you randomly select subjects from a population then it is possible, but not very likely, that you would end up with 50 men and 50 women in it. If you want to make sure that you have equal numbers of men and women (say 50 of each) then you carry out the sampling entirely randomly until one group, say the women, reaches a total of 50 and from that point on you sample randomly only men (i.e. you sample men, randomly, rather than the whole population randomly) until you end up with 50 men as well. The result is a stratified random sample, stratified, in this case, by sex.

In analyzing the data the paper uses **cluster analysis,** which was introduced in Chapter 3 (have a look there if you need a refresher) *but* in this case the paper represents the results in a **dendrogram.** A **dendrogram** (Greek: "Written as a tree") depicts the relationships between the clusters created during the cluster analysis as the branches of a tree. Take a quick look at the diagram on page 95 to see how this looks. The study also uses **Cohen's kappa** as a measure of the agreement between coders. This technique essentially assesses the extent to which coders of the same data reach the same conclusions about the manner in which it should be classified. A high kappa indicates good solid agreement between different coders.

Root Metaphors in Accounts of Developing Romantic Relationships

Leslie A. Baxter

The last two decades have witnessed a burgeoning of research activity devoted to understanding the process of personal relationship development. Researchers have generated a rich domain of metaphoric imagery to describe this process (Duck, 1984b; 1987). Ironically, researchers have paid only limited systematic attention to the underlying metaphors used by relationship parties in describing their own developing relationship experiences. Yet, metaphors constitute a vivid and powerful lens by which to make sense of the human experience (Lakoff & Johnson, 1980). The current study, grounded in both qualitative and quantitative methods, seeks to describe the root metaphors (Pepper, 1942) used by heterosexual romantic parties in accounts about their developing relationships.

This study builds upon a growing body of social scientific work in the analysis of relationship accounts. A relationship account is a story-like explanation of past actions and events, an organized narrative of sense-making by which the account-giver organizes the meaning of his or her relationship (Harvey et al., 1989). To date, most research on relationship accounts has been guided by one of three analytic approaches: attributional, cognitive and interpretive. The *attributional approach* is illustrated by the work of Harvey and his colleagues (Harvey et al., 1989) in understanding a person's causal explanations of his or her failed relationship or by the work by Surra and her colleagues (Surra, 1990) in identifying parties' perceptions of the causal determinants of changes in their relationship. Researchers with a *cognitive orientation* have an interest in determining the memory structure forms, or schemas, by which people store their knowledge of relationship processes. Honeycutt et al. (1989), for example, have presented evidence in support of MOPs, or memory organization packets, in which relationship participants store knowledge of the interaction events, and their order of sequencing, which typify the prototypical romantic relationship growth process. Researchers with an *interpretive orientation* have an interest in describing the semantic themes around which informant discourse centers. Owen (1984), for example, observed seven themes that emerged in the discourse of relationship parties: commitment, involvement, work, uniqueness, manipulation, respect and fragility.

The root metaphor provides a holistic, gestalt unit by which to capture parties' relationship accounting, in contrast to the narrower and more specialized units of analysis reflected in attributional, cognitive and interpretive approaches. **Root metaphors**, also called conceptual archetypes (Black, 1962), conceptual metaphors (Lakoff & Johnson, 1980) or main metaphors (Koch & Deetz, 1981), capture fundamental **experiential gestalts** of the form "A is B" with "A" referred to as the **tenor** and "B" referred to as the **vehicle**. Tenors and vehicles can be expressed explicitly through the grammatical construction "A is B" but they typically are latent rather than manifest in discourse (Lakoff & Johnson, 1980). Root metaphors may provide a particularly efficient way for relationship parties to account for their developing relationships. According to a number of scholars (e.g. Fainsilber & Ortony, 1987), metaphors enable the expression of what is difficult to express at a literal level. In addition, metaphors afford a compactness and vividness of expression difficult to match through other linguistic forms. Given the emotional,

cognitive and behavioral complexity which characterizes developing relationships, the systematic study of metaphors may afford insights to researchers which have not been detected through more specialized analytic units such as attributions and MOPs.

However, metaphors likely serve as more than efficient poetic expressions. A number of scholars, representing a diverse range of disciplines, have argued that metaphors play an important role in the ways in which humans *make sense* of their world (Black, 1962; Ortony, 1979). According to Lakoff & Johnson (1980: 3), the fact that our conceptual systems are fundamentally metaphorical in nature implies that "the way we think, what we experience, and what we do everyday is very much a matter of metaphor". In short, metaphors not only serve as poetic devices by which to represent social reality but, in addition, they serve as organizing frameworks by which to shape people's constructions of social reality. The root metaphors with which relationship parties recount their relational stories may constitute perceptual lenses which frame developing relationships in specific and limiting ways for the relationship parties, drawing attention to some features to the neglect of other features. The study of root metaphors of developing relationships may shed insight into holistic logics of relating which parties use to guide their performance in, and sense-making of, personal relationships.

Long an analytic mainstay in rhetorical and literary studies, metaphor analysis has increasingly been used in the social sciences as scholars have recognized the centrality of metaphor to the human experience ... Although Owen (1985) has provided a persuasive argument for the heuristic value of metaphor analysis in understanding personal relationships, research has been limited ... Some relationships researchers have presented parties with researcher-defined metaphors in order to solicit respondent perceptions of which metaphors best fit their relationships, while other scholars have posited logical typologies of metaphoric images (e.g., McCall, 1982).

However, given the focus of the current study on informant-generated metaphor usage, only metaphor research grounded in the "native's point of view" is discussed here. Only four published studies could be identified which have direct bearing on the current study. Perhaps the most comprehensive metaphor analysis related to personal relationships is Kovecses's (1988) study of the metaphors contained in approximately 300 conventionalized English expressions about love. Kovecses identified approximately three dozen metaphoric images in these conventionalized expressions, including, among others: love as a journey (e.g., "We're at a crossroads"); love as a force (e.g., "There were sparks"); love as a nutrient (e.g., "I can't live without him"); love as unity (e.g., "We were made for each other"); love as heat (e.g., "She set my heart on fire"); love as fluid in a container (e.g., "She was filled with love for him"); love as a hidden object (e.g., "He found love"); love as an opponent (e.g., "She was overcome by love"); love as valuable commodity (e.g., "I gave her all my love"); love as sport (e.g., "He fell for her hook, line and sinker"); love as game (e.g., "She plays hard to get"); love as living organism (e.g., "My love for her will never die"); love as disease (e.g., "He's love-sick"); and love as machine (e.g., "Something went wrong"). Although Kovecses's study is more comprehensive than the other three, it is limited to conventionalized linguistic expressions and ignores metaphoric expression in interpersonal contexts. Conventionalized expressions, each of which typically carries but a single metaphor, do not inform us about possible interrelationships among metaphors in interpersonal usage. Relationship parties may construct and describe the development of their romantic relationship through single metaphoric images, but it seems just as reasonable to expect that they experience the process as a fabric of mixed metaphorical gestalts. Only careful analysis of metaphoric entailments and co-occurrences in metaphoric expressions can address the question of how root metaphors relate to one another in the broader

pattern of relational accounting. Further, the emotion of love is but one component of a complex system of affective, cognitive and behavioral characteristics of developing relationships.

Two studies have employed the case study method, each analyzing the language used by two female respondents in describing their respective personal relationships. As a secondary aspect of their interpretive case study research which focused more broadly on the semantic themes of "communication" evident in the discourse of two female informants, Katriel & Philipsen (1981) suggested three metaphorical images which the two informants associated with personal relationships in general: relationship as machine, relationship as investment and relationship as organism. Owen's (1990) case study analysis of two female respondents' descriptions of their relationships yielded the metaphorical images of relationship as journey, relationship as container, relationship as family and relationship as fairytale. Although these two studies present varied metaphors, their case study method does not address questions of typicality and generalizability of the identified metaphorical images (Owen, 1990).

The fourth study of direct relevance to the current investigation is Quinn's (1987) interpretive study of metaphors contained in open-ended interviews with eleven married couples about the institution of marriage. Her respondents described marriage as a manufactured product, i.e., something which required work, craftsmanship, durable materials, good components that have been put together well, and an overall sound structure or design. Marriage was also conceived as an ongoing journey, in which partners arrived at a destination by following a path after starts and stops, detours and side trips. Marriage as a durable bond was also evident in references such as being cemented or tied together. Finally, marriage was described as an investment in which the spouses invested time and effort in order to reap mutual benefits. Quinn's study affords a detailed description of her sample's understanding of the marital relationship, but the root metaphors of marriage may not generalize to all personal relationship types. All personal relationships doubtless share certain features in common, but sufficient research has accumulated to document the necessity of understanding each specific type of personal relationship for its unique characteristics. The current study focuses on the heterosexual romantic relationship.

These four studies share several features in common. From a content perspective, the metaphors of journey, machine manufactured product, and investment commodity each emerged in three of the four studies. The prevalence of these metaphoric images may suggest broader American cultural themes, which romantic partners rely upon in making sense of their own idiosyncratic relational experiences. However, when considered as a set, these studies are limited with respect to the scope of discourse examined (conventionalized expressions), the scope of the phenomenon examined (generic relationships, marriage or the single emotion of love) and/or sample size (case studies based on two respondents). The current study, based on an analysis of 106 romantic relationship accounts, seeks to build upon these four studies. The issues addressed in the current study flow from the following two research questions:

RQ1: What are the root metaphors employed by parties in accounts of their developing romantic relationships?

RQ2: What is the pattern of co-occurrences among root metaphors in relationship accounts?

Method

Participants were 106 undergraduates at a private university who were selected through a **stratified random sampling** of all enrolled undergraduate students. The stratification variable was sex to ensure a corpus of relationship accounts lacking a sex

sampling bias. A research team was created and consisted of twelve trained undergraduates who were selected by the primary investigator based on their performance in a research methods class and the researcher's perception of their interpersonal skills. The members of the research team underwent approximately 5 weeks' training on the research project before actual data collection. If a student's name was selected through the sampling procedures, a member of the research team contacted the person to determine eligibility and willingness to be interviewed. Prospective participants were not eligible for inclusion in the study unless they were currently in a heterosexual romantic relationship of at least 1 month's duration. The mean relationship duration for the 53 males and 53 females in the study was 20.2 months, and the median length was 16 months. No sex difference was found in relationship length ($t(104) = 1.16; p > .05$). Interviewing was done by members of the research team ... After an initial introduction by the interviewer which reminded the respondent that every relationship was different with no right or wrong answers, the respondent was given a piece of paper upon which to record and label the history of the relationship from first meeting to the present. Consistent with the conception of an account as a story-like narrative, respondents were asked to imagine that their relationship was a book and that they were constructing a "table of contents" of the book's chapters. Respondents were asked to divide their relationship into an appropriate number of chapters and to title each chapter in a way that captured the essence of that chapter. Respondents identified from 2 to 11 chapters for their relationship "books", with a mean of 5.61 chapters and a median of 5 chapters. Once a respondent had completed writing the "table of contents", the interviewer asked the respondent to elaborate verbally on each listed "chapter" by providing an expanded description of what the chapter was all about. This elaboration was solicited through a single, unstructured question ("Can you describe for me what this chapter was like?"). The respondent was allowed to say as much or as little as he or she felt necessary to describe the chapter with no additional prompts or probes by the interviewer; when the description of a given chapter was completed, the interviewer moved on to the next listed chapter title and asked for a description of what that chapter was about. The data for the current study consist of the written "table of contents" chapter titles and the audiotaped elaborations provided by the respondent for each chapter. Part one of the interview took approximately 30 minutes to complete.

The researcher employed the semantic sorting procedure described by Koch & Deetz (1981) for locating root metaphors. Written transcripts of the portions of the 106 taped interviews of relevance to the current study were given careful readings by the researcher on multiple occasions in order to minimize the number of overlooked latent or manifest metaphors embedded in the discourse. Each instance of manifest or latent metaphoric expression was recorded on a 3×5 inch card. Instances of mixed metaphors within the same grammatical sentence were double coded. For example, one informant stated that "We experienced a lot of potholes along the way that took time and effort to get over but, looking back, I guess we really moved fast from the time we first met to get to this chapter." Reference to the "potholes along the way", "moving fast" and "get(ting) to" led to the categorization of this discourse as a journey metaphor. However, reference to "potholes" and "time and effort" led to its double-coding as a work metaphor. The discourse that surrounded the expression was also recorded in order to assist in the identification of entailments. Once metaphoric expressions had been recorded, the researcher sorted the instances into clusters based on apparent similarities in vehicles and entailments. Each cluster composed one root metaphor. Researcher judgments of root metaphors were checked for reliability by asking a second independent coder to identify metaphors from a 25 percent random sample of

the discourse data. Absolute coder agreement was 80 percent and Cohen's (1960) **kappa** was .76.

Results

A total of 472 metaphoric expressions were identified in the discourse, with a mean of 4.45 total metaphoric expressions per interview and a mean breadth of 3.03 different root metaphors mentioned at least once per interview. The interpretive semantic sorting procedure reduced this corpus of expressions to seven root metaphors, plus a miscellaneous category that accounted for 3 percent of the total expressions. The first three root metaphors (work, journey of discovery and uncontrollable force) dominated the data, collectively accounting for 63 percent of all expressions. The remaining four root metaphors (danger, organism, exchange and game) were less salient than the first three, but nonetheless offered vivid imagery of developing relationships. Males and females did not differ in the total number of metaphoric expressions they employed ($t(104) = 1.33$; NS) or in the number of different root metaphors evidenced in their discourse ($t(104) = .82$; NS). In addition, males and females did not differ in the type of root metaphor employed ...

Relationship development as work. The root metaphor that appeared with greatest frequency in the data was labeled relationship development as work. Approximately 60.4 percent of the respondents referenced this root metaphor at least once in their discourse, accounting for 24.8 percent of all metaphorical expressions. Three interrelated entailments were evident for the root metaphor of work. Effortfulness, common to all of the kinds of work, was perhaps the most salient characteristic of this root metaphor. For parties having this experiential gestalt, the presence of struggle and effort was a natural and expected part of relationship development rather than evidence of a doomed or failed relationship;

the absence of effortful work suggested that the relationship was failing or insufficiently serious. A second, and related, entailment evident in the respondent discourse was an orientation toward outcomes or products. The activity of relational work was to be appreciated not for its own sake but rather for the achievement of a desired outcome, a smoothly functioning relationship. Progress toward the outcome or product provided the standard for evaluation of whether or not the relationship was developing successfully. The specific kinds of work mentioned by respondents suggested a third entailment of relationship development – the assembly of parts. In relationships, the "parts" which needed to be assembled were the respective relationship parties, including their needs, goals, habits and schedules.

The work metaphor was expressed through a variety of kinds of metaphoric work. Typical is the following excerpt from a female respondent's account of a chapter in her 44-month romantic relationship: "In between these two chapters, [my partner] went on an overseas program for a term ... So we got back to school and it was hard getting into the groove of being together when we were used to being by ourselves. That caused some problems but we worked through that ... by arguing it out basically. Neither of us likes to argue, but we both know that it's a bad thing not to argue. You can't expect a relationship to last very long if you don't talk about the problems that always crop up. So we've gotten to where we can argue more now. This is when we first started to really see that." From the perspective of this root metaphor, problems inevitably occur in relationships and must be worked through. The particular problem identified in this chapter was difficulty in co-coordinating interdependence, caused by a temporary geographic separation of the parties. The developing relationship was effortful and necessitated work, particularly in the form of arguing. The respondent and, presumably, her partner were willing to engage in the unpleasant task of arguing in order to ensure the outcome of a long-lasting relationship.

A different kind of metaphoric work is captured in this account excerpt from a male respondent reporting on his 14-month relationship. Entitled 'The Big Test', this particular chapter compared his developing relationship to the work of exam preparation: "Well, after that first "Wow!" sensation when you first meet somebody, then comes the Big Test. If you pass the test then you know you have a serious relationship ... It's a series of trying to reach agreement on goals or outlooks on a whole bunch of little stuff and not so little stuff ... It's kinda like taking a test. You get what you deserve – if you put in your time and study a lot, chances are the grade will be OK but it doesn't come without work, at least for me." To this respondent, the assembly of parts involved the meshing and coordination of goals between the relationship parties. Inevitable problems arise, which the parties must overcome through effort which is conceived as a "test" of the seriousness of their relationship.

Relationship development as a journey of discovery. The second most common root metaphor to emerge in respondent discourse was the vision of their developing relationship as a journey or adventure of discovery. The expressions that clustered in this root metaphor accounted for 20.3 percent of all metaphoric expressions and appeared in 57.5 percent of the interviews. The root metaphor of a journey of discovery emphasized change and discovery. From this **experiential gestalt**, the successful relationship was one which was moving and never stagnant. Movement was directed toward perpetual discovery, whether learning new things about one's partner, oneself or the relationship. Whereas the work root metaphor emphasized effort in order to achieve the outcome of a well assembled and smooth-running relational machine, the journey of discovery root metaphor emphasized that the relationship was a process of discovery to be appreciated in the moment for its benefits of enrichment. Representative of the root metaphor is the following excerpt from a male respondent who was describing a particularly frustrating period in his 20-month relationship with his girlfriend: "This was a kind of holding pattern for our relationship ... We knew each other so well at that point – we had logged so many hours of time together that we just kinda put on this automatic pilot. We were getting tired of each other ... Neither one of us was getting any excitement out of the relationship." The source of this respondent's frustration was that the relationship's momentum had ceased; the parties were no longer discovering new things about one another and excitement had ended. The relationship was overly routinized as the parties continued to enact their metaphorical joint air trip.

A similar theme is evident in this female's account of her 22-month relationship with her boyfriend. In a chapter titled "The Beginning of the Relationship", the respondent explained why she decided to get involved with her boyfriend: "Well, he's from Mexico, and I really liked the fact that he was from a different culture. It provided that Mystery Factor, so that we could keep that Wow-this-is-really-neat-about-you-or-different-about-us feeling. You get bogged down in a rut otherwise. Ya gotta keep finding the new in relationships, keep rediscovering. It's a bummer if a relationship gets old and you find yourself doing the same things and going to the same places and saying the same things. You're just going in circles then." This respondent was attracted to her boyfriend because she thought that their cultural difference increased the probability that they would be able to sustain the quality of relationship "newness", i.e. ongoing discovery.

Relationship development as an uncontrollable force. The third root metaphor presented a vision of the developing relationship as some natural or psychological force over which the relationship parties had no control. A total of 17.8 percent of all metaphoric expressions displayed this root metaphor and 53.8 percent of all respondents evidenced the root metaphor at least once in their discourse. The respondent discourse included many types of uncontrollable forces, from powerful river currents that swept the parties along, to darkness in which the parties were powerless to see what was going on, to drug addictions which the parties were powerless to overcome. Two central entailments described the root metaphor of uncontrollable force. First, the relationship parties attributed to the relationship a causal force independent of their own individual actions. This **experiential gestalt** presented the relationship as the actor and the individual parties as the objects of that action. Second, the relationship was granted not only independent causal force but force sufficiently powerful to render the relationship parties helpless to control the process and the outcome.

This root metaphor is captured in a male respondent's explanation of a chapter in which his school grades suffered because of his metaphoric addiction to his 16-month relationship: "The relationship just engulfed us totally ... Nothing was as important as our being together ... I skipped classes and slept through classes because of time spent with her. I shirked responsibility to school and obligations to other friends and family. My Mom and family were basically slapping me telling me to wake up and become a responsible person and realize that there were other things going on besides my relationship with my girlfriend. It didn't do any good. It was like I was drugged or something. I knew that my grades were going downhill, but I just couldn't help it." Powerlessness to affect the relationship also manifested itself in a passive or laissez faire stance, as revealed in this excerpt from a female respondent's account of her 8-month relationship. Elaborating on a chapter titled "What's Next?" this respondent said: "Well, this chapter is right now. With graduation and stuff the issue is what's next for us. We're just going to wait and see what happens to 'us'. We always kinda ... take things as they come. Some things are just meant to be and others aren't." In both of these examples, the relationship parties perceived that they were helpless objects affected by relational forces beyond their control.

Additional root metaphors. Images of relationship development as danger were evident in 9.3 percent of all expressions and in 34 percent of the interview texts. Expressions that involved this root metaphor indicated that developing relationships were scary and frightening experiences filled with the risk of being tied down, burned and otherwise hurt. As a consequence of this danger, relationship parties should enter relationships cautiously with their defenses ready. In essence, the self was at risk through loss of autonomy or through rejection by the other. From the **experiential gestalt** of danger, relationship parties should be on the alert in order to prevent sacrifice of self's independence or esteem. Representative of the root metaphor is this elaboration of an early chapter entitled "Don't Play With Matches" in a male's account of his 20-month relationship: "We got to know each other really slowly. But that's OK with me. At first. I'm always real cautious … I have my guard up all the time, because I don't want to get burned."

Relationship development as economic exchange accounted for 8.7 percent of all metaphoric expressions and was present at least once in 30.2 percent of respondent interviews. Respondents who articulated this **experiential gestalt** processed relationship development in cost–benefit terms, seeking to maximize gain to self with the realization that the other party was engaged in the same enterprise. Thus, negotiation, bargaining and compromise are typical relational actions in this gestalt. Typical is this excerpt from a male respondent's account of a chapter from his year-long relationship: "It's basically a trade-type deal. I get sex and she gets to go around calling us 'boyfriend–girlfriend'". The same theme of bargaining is evident in this female's account of her 10-month relationship: "We make compromises, that's what our relationship is all about. In this chapter, which took place over the Christmas holidays, we split everything in half. You know, Christmas Eve with one set of parents, Christmas Day with the other parents. Stuff like that." Relationship development as a living organism was evidenced in 8 percent of the metaphoric expressions and appeared

in 27.4 percent of the respondent interviews. Interviewees expressed an image of their relationship as a living, growing organism that experienced birth, infancy, growth into maturity through a natural progression of stages, degeneration and renewal, threats to its survival and the risk of death. This root metaphor was similar to the root metaphor of uncontrollable force in according the relationship autonomous status as a player in the developmental dynamic. However, unlike the uncontrollable force root metaphor, the relationship was not perceived as a force so powerful that it rendered the parties helpless. Instead, the parties acted with the relationship organism, giving it life, nurturing it through its infancy and during its other times of need in order for it to grow. Relationships, in turn, matured to become a source of influence and support for the relationship parties. Representative of this root metaphor is the following excerpt from a male respondent's account of his 2-year relationship. In elaborating on a chapter titled "Stumble", the respondent was elaborating on the presence of a romantic rival. Metaphorically, the relationship is cast as a runner who falters but recovers with even greater strength: "It [the presence of the rival] made our relationship falter. But it didn't die out. It didn't even fall down. It just stumbled a little bit. And in looking back, our bond was even stronger because of this little stumble it had."

The last root metaphor, *relationship development as a game*, was evident in 8 percent of the metaphoric expressions and appeared in 27.4 percent of the respondent interviews. The metaphoric games ranged from organized sporting games (e.g., "She moved from on deck to the batter's box"), to the chase of the hunt (e.g., "I called this chapter "Cat and Mouse" because we alternated being the pursuer and the pursued"), to "head games" in which the parties scammed one another with deceptive actions in order to win one another over. When games were explicit and being played fairly they were sources of fun, amusement and challenge. By contrast, the connotation was typically negative if one was not being treated fairly by the partner.

Co-occurrences among root metaphors

Respondent discourse was characterized by multiple metaphors in which more than one root metaphor was featured. To analyze the pattern of co-occurrences in the discourse data, a **hierarchical cluster analysis** was used. Input data for the cluster analysis consisted of a matrix of similarities for metaphor pairs which was derived in two steps. First, all transcripts were dummy coded (0, 1) to represent the absence or presence, respectively, of at least one instance of each root metaphor type. Second, a matrix of pair similarity was derived from this information ...

The cluster analysis indicated that the root metaphors of force and danger were first to merge into a single cluster, ... followed by the emergence of the work–exchange cluster ... and then the journey–organism cluster ... Although the game root metaphor ultimately merged with the work–exchange cluster, the combination occurred only [at a reduced level]. Given the amalgamation pattern in cluster mergers, the four-cluster solution was accepted as the best summary of the co-occurrences in metaphoric expression (Aldendenfer & Blashfield, 1984). Figure 1 presents the summary dendrogram that emerged from the cluster analysis procedure.

The entailments of the seven root metaphors suggest a logical coherence to the cluster analytic findings. The root metaphors of uncontrollable force and danger appear to fit together because of the greater risks involved when one is not in control of the relationship. If relationship parties perceived that they were in control of their relationship's development, they could easily prevent sacrifice of autonomy or damage to self-esteem. However, because these respondents framed relationship development as a force beyond their control, the process is a dangerous one plagued with risks. The entailments associated with its constituent metaphors also help to explain the coherence of the work–exchange cluster. The effortfulness of relationship development constitutes an inherent cost of involvement which is offset by the product – a smooth-running relationship. Because each party is actively seeking to maximize his or her reward/cost ratio, the parties must engage in bargaining and compromise, both of which are effortful activities. Last, the root metaphors of journey and organism contain common themes of ongoing change

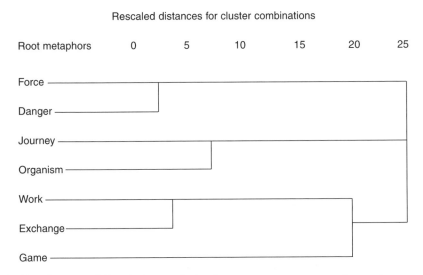

Rescaled distances for cluster combinations

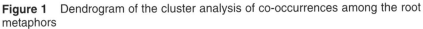

Figure 1   Dendrogram of the cluster analysis of co-occurrences among the root metaphors

Baxter, Table A   *Summary of the major elements of the folk-logics of developing romantic relationships*

Element	Work–exchange	Journey–organism	Force–danger	Game
Fundamental Premise	**Relational development is**			
	an inherently effortful process of coordinating the parties' individual wants and needs	an ever changing process of growth for the parties and their relationship	a risky undertaking in which the parties can be hurt and over which they have limited control	the enactment of scripted episodes in which parties can win or lose
Locus of change	**Relationship change is determined by:**			
	hard work by the parties in coordinating their individual wants and needs	the very act of being in a relationship which by definition, is a dynamic and growing thing	inherent features of the relationship over which the parties exert no control	how well games are enacted and the choices made by the parties over which game to play
Diagnostic Criteria	**Relational success is evidenced by:**			
	Smooth coordination of the two individuals	ever present momentum and discovery	a relational destiny in which parties are not hurt	a party winning at his or her games
	Relational 'warning signals' are:			
	loss of smooth coordination	loss of momentum	powerlessness to stop damage to one or both parties	breaking the rules of a game or lack of agreement on which game is being played
Guidelines for performance	**Relationship parties should:**			
	work hard and be willing to compromise	appreciate the moment and strive for spontaneity and flexibility	proceed with caution and hope for the best	choose to play games useful for their purposes and become skilled in order to win

and relationships-as-becoming, thereby explaining the emergence of the journey–organism cluster. The ongoing journey of discovery in relationship development is what allows growth and maturity, both for the individuals and for the relationship as a metaphorical living organism.

The four main clusters of metaphoric imagery suggest fundamental folk-logics of relationship development which parties use in making sense of their developing romantic relationships. Each of these organizing logics draws attention to certain features of the relational dynamic while ignoring other features. Each organizing logic entails an implicit theory of how relationships change. Criteria by which to assess relational outcomes are also implied in the various organizing logics. The organizing logics also constitute implicit guidelines for relationship parties in how they should conduct their relational lives. Table A provides a summary of the central [elements] of each organizing logic.

The question "What is at the heart of relationship development?" evokes very different answers depending on the particular folk-logic. From the logic of work–exchange, the heart of relationship development is the hard work necessary in managing the inevitable coordination problems which occur between the relationship parties. From the journey–organism logic, the heart of relationship development lies in fluidity and ongoing growth. According to the folk-logic of force–danger, relationship development is a risky chance, and whether one emerges happy or hurt is determined by forces over which the parties have little say. Last, the game folk-logic locates the heart of relationship development in the mix of which scripted enactments are selected for "play" and who "wins" each round.

Discussion

...

The root metaphors identified in this study show a partial resemblance to those found in previous research. Some of the emergent root metaphors appear to be straightforward replications of previous research, a finding which suggests that romantic partners access some broader cultural themes in making sense of their idiosyncratic relational experiences. In particular, the work, exchange and organism metaphors appear to mirror, respectively, the machine/manufactured product, investment/commodity and organism imagery found in many of the metaphor studies that hold direct relevance to this study. However, other emergent root metaphors in this study are not as prevalent in previous research. With the exception of Kovecses's (1988) work, the danger, game and force metaphors of the current study bear little resemblance to metaphors found by previous relationship researchers. The absence of these metaphors in some of the previous research might be attributable to the current study's focus on romantic relationships. This relationship type has been characterized more than other types of personal relationships by its semantic themes of fragility and manipulation

(Owen, 1984), themes which would imply danger and risk, "gamesmanship" and perhaps the ultimate inability of the parties to control their relationship's destiny. Although a journey metaphor was identified in this study it is both like and unlike the journey metaphor labeled by previous researchers. Consistent with previous work (e.g., Lakoff, 1986) the journey metaphor suggests movement through a variety of paths or routes. However, this study's journey metaphor is unlike previous versions of the image in its de-emphasis of a particular destination or outcome, instead substituting a fluid process-oriented outcome of perpetual discovery. Whereas the journey metaphor from previous research implies an ultimate target goal for which the parties are aiming, the metaphoric imagery in the current study suggests that relationships may not have predetermined destinations at all. At best, relationships may be characterized by transitory goals which are ever changing in response to ongoing discoveries the parties make about themselves, one another and their relationship.

Interestingly, three of the four fundamental folk-logics derived from the combinations of root metaphors bear resemblance to the basic approaches to relationship development which Duck (1984b; 1987) has identified among relationships researchers. The Mechanical Model, which Duck (1984b: 510) describes as "engines where partners get into gear and mesh together" is a direct equivalent of the work–exchange folk-logic. Duck's Route, Horticultural and Cellular Models, taken collectively, are similar to the journey–organism folk-logic, albeit with a stronger emphasis on a pre-planned destination. The predetermined quality of Duck's Film Model resembles the uncontrollable force entailment of the force–danger organizing logic.

Duck (1984b; 1987) painted his portrait of different underlying researcher conceptions of the relationship development process in order to draw attention to the fact that personal relationship research was implicitly driven by fundamentally different assumptive sets rather than a unitary set of assumptions with interchangeable vocabularies and terms. The findings of this study underscore Duck's point but do so from the native's point of view to complement Duck's analysis of researchers' assumptions. Put simply, relationship development is not a unitary dynamic. Abandonment of a unitary conception of relationship development holds many implications for subsequent research. Most importantly, scholars should realize that any single organizing logic can capture only partially the relationship development process. Conceiving of relationship development through a single assumptive logic privileges only some variables and issues to the neglect of others. The research agenda should become that of determining the boundary conditions under which each underlying logic holds validity. At least two possibilities merit serious research attention. One distinct possibility is that the different folk-logics identified in this study may all hold relevance for a given relationship but at different developmental points in the relationship's history. That is, relationship development may not be a matter of changes in degree as one developmental logic plays itself out, but rather a process that entails qualitatively different logics at different developmental points ...

As you reflect on this paper, there are a number of points to which we would draw your attention. First there may be a problem with the fact that participants were included on the basis of a minimum relationship length of one month. That is not a terribly long time for a relationship to develop. However there are several answers to this criticism: the most obvious is that this was a minimum requirement and there were many people in the study whose relationship exceeded that considerably (the mean relationship length was 20 months, remember). Second, even if the minimum length of relationship was one month, quite a bit of development can take place in that time and also people may be able to recall the sorts of things that have happened to them in previous relationships that would still make a study of metaphors informative, using such subjects.

A more serious issue for you to consider and discuss in class is this: the author uses the term "folk-logic" in the paper quite a lot and also talks of the "native perspective". In fact we are not seeing logic at all as that term is normally understood; we are seeing a clustering of terms in a way that makes sense, but that sense might not be "logical" in the normally accepted meaning of the term. Indeed one of the most interesting aspects of this study is its demonstration of the preference of "natives" for *images* over logic. Since images and metaphors carry entailments and restrictions on thinking (as was noted at the start of this chapter), the claim that the use of metaphors is "logical", even if described somewhat dismissively as "folk-logical", is misleading and something for you to evaluate carefully in your discussions.

Other issues to consider in discussion are these: Is relationship development a process of applying different metaphors, or different elements of a metaphor, to a process that is basically disorderly so that we may understand it better? Or is there an underlying order that the metaphors really pick out for us? In short, is the process of relationship development one of growth of emotions or growth of understanding?

If we talk about relationship growth as a growth of understanding are we under-estimating the role of emotions, and if we talk of relationship growth as the inten-sification of emotions are we underestimating the importance of a growth of understanding of our partner, ourselves and the formation of "the relationship"?

So far our thinking about relationships has assumed that, whether we impose order on them or they are themselves orderly underneath, relationships are sus-ceptible to an analysis based on order. Recent developments in other areas of the social sciences have focused instead on the underlying chaos of much that occurs and the next paper offers a timely incorporation of the Chaos Theory approach to relationships, noting that there are many ways in which relationships are simply unpredictable and not subject to the laws of logic that we normally seek as bases for our interpretation of them. Chaos Theory exposes some of these unpredictabil-ities and, the authors suggest, helps us to understand relationship activity more fully.

There are many terms introduced here, such as **phase shifts**, and **hysteresis** which sound off-putting but are very well explained by the authors themselves as the paper progresses (one means essentially that organisms change and move along from one form of action to another: think of the ways in which insects move from eggs to larvae to pupae to nymphs and yet remain "the same" insect. These are what are denoted by "phase shifts". Hysteresis refers to the fact that a cause can occur some way from its effects and there is a delay in the occurrence of the effect of a cause. Simply put, it can sometimes take time for the effects of a given cause to be felt, something all too obvious to politicians attempting to "kick start" an ailing economy, where the effects of a policy change may not show themselves for several months at least).

One term not explained here is **measurement error**. You can probably work out for yourself what it means: whenever you take data readings of anything, whether it be human behavior or the positions of the planets, there are risks that the wrong numbers will be recorded or the incorrect data written down or the wrong things measured. Thus some of the variation that you get when you measure human behavior could be nothing to do with an underlying variety of the things you are observing; instead it is merely an *appearance* of variety that is solely created by mea-surement errors of the kind noted above. In order to be sure that the data are "true" an investigator has to be sure that measurement errors have been minimized and accounted for.

Note that in keeping with the paper that we have just read, this next paper starts off using Chaos Theory as a sort of metaphor rather than as a direct application, although it moves on later to using it specifically to explain relationship phenomena. The essential argument is that relationships are not orderly developments and that there can be enormous and disproportionate effects of small events (e.g., a chance remark in a conversation can end a relationship unexpectedly). As you read the paper, jot down some examples of instances in your life where these principles could be observed. At the end of the paper we want you to be in a position to reflect carefully on whether this paper offers us an exciting new way to think about rela-tionships or is not really applicable (or perhaps something in between these two positions).

The Paradox of Stability and Change in Relationships: What Does Chaos Theory Offer for the Study of Romantic Relationships?

Dan Weigel and Colleen Murray

For years, researchers of romantic relationships have struggled to find the patterns of stability in the jumbled river of relational change. The hope has been that if researchers could only find the true underlying cause and effects in relationship development, they could predict relationship trajectories. Relationship development would be completely predictable given the right parameters. Consequently, linear stage models that included a beginning, middle, and end to a relationship largely influenced early models of relationship development. For example, Duck (1982), Wood (1982), and Knapp (1984) proposed various stage models involving coming together and coming apart in generally sequential phases.

More recently, however, these researchers and others have suggested that relationships do not always follow patterns of linear change. Some relationships end only to be reborn in a new form. Others begin and end so often that it is difficult to even identify any stable sequence. More recent conceptions of relationships tend to minimize their linear stage nature. Baxter and Montgomery (1997), for example, contend that relationships are continually being driven by internal tensions that must be managed moment by moment. Management of these tensions does not occur in a linear manner. In fact, Baxter and Montgomery see relationship change as "an indeterminate process with no clear end states and no necessary paths of change" (p. 341). Likewise, Duck and Wood (1995) argue for an approach that focuses on

the daily management of conflicting stresses rather than linear stages.

In addition to questions of linearity, in the studies of relationship development there are always the outliers – the renegade couples who do not fit neatly into the expected patterns. These renegades often are explained away as **measurement error** and ignored. However, it is often from studying these nonconformists that important implications for the fuller understanding of behavior emerge (Duke, 1994). Attempts to explain both the conformist and nonconformist couples, as well as the linear and nonlinear changes, are where chaos theory may be useful.

Although chaos theory has its origins in the physical and biological sciences, in recent years it has gained popularity in the social sciences as an approach for studying social systems. Chaos theory has been popularized through its exotic terminology – **butterfly effects**, cascading events, bifurcations, and attractor states [explained below]. Yet the concepts are finding their way into the social sciences to explain processes such as social change (Nowak & Vallacher, 1998), neuropsychology (Barton, 1994), family development (Ward, 1995), psychotherapy and assessment (Heiby, 1995), and marital stability (Gottman, Swanson, & Murray, 1999). Chaos theory touches on many key issues of interest to relational and marital studies scholars: How do relationships change? Why do they change? What things influence the changes? How do we predict the outcomes of change? The focus on attempting to understand change is at the heart of chaos theory. The application of chaos theory is sometimes difficult because much of the argument of the theory has been developed through complex mathematical formulae that may initially overwhelm some social scientists who do not have a grounding in advanced mathematics. But the concepts of chaos theory may be useful to the study of relationships (Ward, 1995). Therefore, the key question becomes: Does chaos theory offer fresh insights into the study of relationships?

This article assesses the relevance of chaos theory in understanding development and change in romantic relationships. First, several key elements of chaos theory are described in light of relationship development. Methodological approaches and issues are then explored. Finally, several implications of chaos theory for understanding relationships are discussed.

Before launching into a description of chaos theory, we first need to understand three broad types of change – deterministic, random, and stochastic. **Deterministic change** occurs when one can accurately predict the long-term outcomes of change given the initial conditions of the system and the fact that specific changes in the initial conditions cause specific results (Kincanon & Powel, 1995). For example, one can accurately predict the trajectory and final outcome of a pool ball given the initial force of striking, the angle of roll, friction of the pool table, air resistance, and so forth. Deterministic change is completely predictable. Kincanon and Powel (1995) see a reliance on deterministic change as the basis for all scientific study before the 20th century. In contrast, **random change** lacks all predictability and gives completely different results, no matter how much we know about the initial conditions. Random change is completely unpredictable. Kincanon and Powel (1995) give the example of how the lottery system is random in that knowing the numbers that were picked in last week's

lottery is of no help in predicting this week's numbers.

Finally, **stochastic change** falls somewhere in-between deterministic and random change. While it may be possible to make some predictions about stochastic change in the short-term, long-term prediction becomes more difficult. Unlike linear systems, small changes in the initial conditions of chaotic systems can give completely different long-term results (Kincanon & Powel, 1995). Stochastic change can appear in systems that are recursive (i.e., where output from one point in time becomes input into the next [such as a dating relationship, where results of one date can affect the likelihood of a further date]), thus allowing the system to react to sudden or unexpected change. At times, "chaotic" systems, more commonly called "nonlinear dynamic systems", may have elements of all three types of change. They may be deterministic (even though nonlinear), with a well-defined order of transitions, or stochastic, such that the transitions between states are probabilistic (Nowak & Vallacher, 1998). Even elements of randomness may enter the system on occasion. Because relationships are recursive systems, there is a dynamic imbalance, not between individuals but between the order and disorder within the system. To try to better understand nonlinear dynamic systems, we explore some key concepts of chaos theory in the next section and apply the concepts to romantic relationships.

Chaos theory and romantic relationships: nonlinear dynamic systems

A key focus of chaos theory is understanding linear systems and nonlinear dynamic systems. Some systems are linear, where specific changes in one variable can be expressed as a direct proportion of changes in the other variable. Take, for example, a thermostat and the temperature of a room. By raising the thermostat 1° from 70° to 71°, the temperature in the room will average 1° warmer. Raise the temperature 5° to 75° and the room will average 5° warmer. In other words, specific causes lead to predictable results. Much of the research on relationships is designed to identify key variables and elements that will allow us to predict linear changes and states in relationships. If we know the conditions of a relationship at point A, we can predict its condition 1 month later at point B, and another month later at point C, and so on. Conceivably, we would be able to predict the relationship's condition months and years later. Viewing relational growth in a linear fashion is to think of relationships as moving "in a unidirectional manner from states of less to more on several key dimensions" (Baxter & Montgomery, 1997, p. 341).

Many systems, however, are anything but linear. A nonlinear dynamic system is one that evolves over time. The state of the system at one point in time determines the state of the system at the next moment (Nowak & Vallacher, 1998). Furthermore, a nonlinear dynamic system has the ability to change from one pattern to another in a seemingly sudden manner. The weather is a good example of a nonlinear dynamic system. When viewed over a long span, the weather shows a pattern of regularity coinciding with the seasons. However, specific weather changes are essentially unpredictable beyond the scale of a day or two (Lorenz, 1979). Weather patterns never quite repeat themselves, and even the most complete information is not enough to specify the subsequent behavior of the weather system. In nonlinear dynamic systems, small causes may produce disproportionately large effects, or none at all. Even the smallest perturbation, such as the rise in water temperature in the ocean, can be amplified into dramatic differences in global weather, "rendering it virtually unpredictable beyond a few days" (Thelen & Ulrich, 1991, p. 25). Prediction of future states of nonlinear dynamic systems based on current states is extremely difficult.

A key question, therefore, is: Are romantic relationships linear systems or nonlinear dynamic systems? If relationships were simple, linear systems, they would develop along an orderly trajectory. Partners would meet, spend time together, fall progressively deeper in love, marry, and "live happily ever after." Such a linear pattern in relationships is far from the rule, however. The majority of budding romantic relationships do not even make it to engagement and marriage (Lloyd, Cate, & Henton, 1984) and those that do follow anything but a smooth path. In a recent study, Surra and Hughes (1997) found that more than half (54%) of the couples in their study exhibited unpredictable and nonlinear relational trajectories involving a large number of turning points. Partners identified events such as new rivals, unresolved differences, meeting the partner's family, and job changes as turning points that greatly changed the nature and progress of the relationship. Similar findings by Baxter and Bullis (1986) indicated that college students reported a mean of 9.2 relationship turning points during courtship. Nonstudent couples reported a mean of 8.6 turning points in their premarital relationships (Bullis, Clark, & Stine, 1993). Therefore, it appears that, for many couples, relationship development is not easily described by a simple, predictable linear progression.

Nonlinear dynamic systems can produce quite unpredictable changes, where small initial differences result in disproportionately large consequences (Ward, 1995). The nonlinearity of nonlinear dynamic systems is reflected in what is called "sensitivity to initial conditions." This means that, depending on the initial conditions of the system, the outcomes can diverge dramatically over the long-term (Barton, 1994). Kincanon and Powel (1995) provide an example of the importance of initial conditions by looking at two water molecules in a river. The two molecules may start out next to each other with velocities that are close and they will stay together in the river for some time. Eventually, however, the molecules will be far apart in the river and their futures will look completely different. The small difference in the initial conditions for the two molecules leads to futures that are substantially different.

A study by Heaton and Call (1995) on the survival rates of marriages helps illustrate the importance of initial conditions in relationships. By examining age at marriage in over 10,000 couples, the likelihood of a marriage surviving 5 years for those people marrying between 27 and 29 years of age was 87.4%. For those couples marrying just a few years younger (23–26 years old), the chances of the marriages surviving to 5 years were almost identical at 87.1%. By 10 years the survival rates of the two groups were beginning to diverge, with a rate of 80.4% for the 27–29-year-olds and 77.5% for the 23–26-year-olds. The divergence continued at 15 years where the survival rate for the 27–29-year-olds was 76.7%, while the survival rate for 23–26-year-olds was 70.1%. Finally, at 20 years, the marital survival rate of 27–29-year-olds was 74.3% and 67.2% for 23–26-year-olds. The seemingly inconsequential initial difference of a few years of age at marriage between the two groups resulted in a cumulative difference over the course of the marriage. The two groups were virtually identical at 5 years, but followed different trajectories as their survival rates grew further apart. If the marriages were linear, the initial minor differences would have created similar minor differences after 20 years. However, in nonlinear dynamic systems, even small differences in initial conditions can cause the systems to assume divergent paths.

An additional reason that the behavior of a nonlinear dynamic system cannot be predicted in long time spans is that we never know the initial data with infinite accuracy. As Nowak and Lewenstein (1994) point out, our knowledge always contains some rounding errors, or uncertainty. Given a nonlinear dynamic system, and given that all estimates of initial conditions contain at least small errors, even small errors in estimating and measuring initial values might be amplified into large errors of prediction later

on. For example, assuming we could develop an agreed-upon measure of relationship quality, our measurement of the quality of a specific romantic relationship would still contain some errors in measurement and uncertainty. These errors will become magnified over time so that the gap between the relationship's actual trajectory in quality and where we would have predicted grows as time passes. Therefore, precise long-term prediction of nonlinear dynamic systems will be impossible, even though the actual system and laws governing its evolution may be understood (Baker & Gollub, 1990).

Based on the concept of initial conditions, seemingly insignificant changes that occur at one point in time can result in significant differences in behavior patterns later. This is sometimes referred to as the "**butterfly effect**" in which a butterfly flapping its wings over the Amazon might produce a storm next month in Texas (Kauffman, 1991). Because of the nonlinearity of global weather, even the smallest perturbation – metaphorically, the beating of the wings of a single butterfly – can be amplified into dramatic differences in global weather. The concept of a **butterfly effect** might explain how seemingly insignificant events, such as a careless comment during an argument or the chance meeting with an old boyfriend, may become devastating for a couple. The careless comment or chance meeting may cause a ripple of other events that can drastically alter the course of the relationship.

The opposite also may be true. In a stable nonlinear dynamic system, a disturbance can be absorbed into the details of the system without disturbing the overall stability, while in a linear system it creates irreversible change (Nowak & Vallacher, 1998). What would seem to be major causes entered into the system may create only minor changes. Roloff and Colvin (1994) illustrate how in some relationships seemingly serious relational transgressions can be dealt with and absorbed without causing the relationship to end. Transgressions can include behaviors like severe conflict, abuse and violence, sexual infidelity, and criminal behavior. In a linear system, such transgressions would create significant change and likely destroy the relationship. Some relationships, however, persist and absorb such transgressions by using behaviors such as the reformulation of relational understandings and rules, minimization of the transgression, justification, prevention of further transgressions, and the use of retribution (Roloff & Colvin, 1994).

The ability of nonlinear dynamic systems to resist change in spite of mounting or decreasing pressure is called **hysteresis**. Tesser and Achee (1994) provide an example of hysteresis centered on perceptions of love and overt displays of love. If perceptions and behavioral displays of love start out low in a relationship, there is a tendency for the behavioral displays to remain low even though perceptions of love may have increased substantially. Only when a threshold is passed does the display of love increase dramatically. The opposite also occurs. When perceptions and behavioral displays of love both start out high, then displays tend to remain high even when perceptions of love have decreased substantially. When a threshold is fallen below, displays of love will decrease suddenly. Hysteresis helps explain why, in nonlinear dynamic systems, a perturbation can create either significant change or no change at all. This is what makes predicting the outcomes of change in nonlinear dynamic systems difficult under the rules of traditional science.

The occurrence of hysteresis points out the importance of thresholds, called **control parameters**, in understanding nonlinear dynamic systems. All systems, even those in a steady state, exhibit some degree of variability in behavior. When the amount of variability increases in a system, it becomes less stable. Thelen and Ulrich (1991) state that at a critical value of the "control parameter", the variability in the system becomes amplified and the system is free to explore other patterns and seek new stable states. Control parameters act as catalysts for system change; the parameters do not control the system in the sense of a command or a prescription, but

operate more as thresholds. When a certain level of the control parameter is crossed, the system can be thrown into nonlinear change. In this way, Gottman's ratio of 5 to 1 in terms of negativity/positivity in marital communication serves as a control parameter. For example, in a series of studies, Gottman (1994) found that what creates potentially fatal problems in some marriages is the level of negativity and positivity in couples' communication. Whenever the amount of negative communication in a marriage exceeds the positive at a ratio greater than 5 to 1, the couple is at risk for potentially destructive communication and marital difficulties. Whenever the threshold ratio of negativity to positivity is crossed, it can propel the relationships down a negative cascade.

Phase shifts

As Duck (1994b) points out, most relationships have periods of calm and stability. Studies that capture couples in such a steady state would likely find representative linear characteristics. However, all relationships also experience periods of instability and change (Duck, 1994a,b). Dynamic systems undergoing extreme instability tend to break apart and lose much of their order and pattern (Young, 1991), and can lead to what are called **phase shifts** (Gleick, 1987). A phase shift is the process through which the system changes from one state to another qualitatively different state in a seemingly sudden or discontinuous manner (Thelen & Ulrich, 1991). For example, a simple pot of water progresses through several phases as it changes from room temperature to boiling. At room temperature, the molecules in the pot bump around randomly, and, as long as the temperature does not change, the overall behavior of the molecules stays the same. When the pot is placed on the stove with the burner on, the bottom layer of water gets warmer and less dense and tries to rise, but the cooler temperature of the top layer prevents the warm water from rising. As the bottom layer becomes hotter, however, a critical point is reached at which the warmer water begins to rise through the cooler upper layer and suddenly forms itself into a new stable and ordered pattern of rolls. With further warming, this pattern also becomes unstable and the pot boils with another, seemingly chaotic, pattern that eventually produces steam. In a nonlinear dynamic system, phase shifts occur when the system experiences internal or external pressure and the current steady state is unable to assimilate the pressure.

In relationships, phase shifts frequently occur at times of transition in which relationships often take on new meanings and functions (Trickett & Buchanan, 1997). With each transition, a nonlinear dynamic system is faced with bifurcation. One transitional point that may initiate a phase shift in the marital relationship is the transition to parenting. The transition to parenting involves the appropriation of the parenting role and the negotiation of a new marital reality after the birth of the first child (Stamp, 1994). Roles, responsibilities, power, time, and space in the marital relationship all have to be renegotiated and redefined (Veroff, Young, & Coon, 1997). Johnson and Huston (1998) found that spouses realign their role preferences and expectations after the birth of the first child. For some couples, this is a task that creates only minimal discomfort; for others, it is a change that creates tremendous turmoil and crisis. The trajectory the relationship takes following the transition can take any number of directions. For example, Belsky and Kelly (1994) report that nearly half of married couples experience a change in the marital relationship during the transition to parenting. Some couples experience accelerated decline in marital quality, others experience minor declines, while still others even experience some improvement in their marital relationship. Clearly, a number of marriages experience a shift in the marital system following the transition to parenting.

The point at which the previously stable phase becomes unstable and the system shifts to another phase is called a **bifurcation point**. A bifurcation point marks changes in a pattern of behavior (Nowak & Lewenstein, 1994). Thus, when a dynamic system is pushed further and further from its steady state by internal and external pressures, it may reach a threshold beyond which it cannot recover. At this point, two or more new steady states become available and the system moves to one of those states. Ward (1995) likens the process of bifurcation to a decision tree. The initial condition begins with the trunk. With each bifurcation, the tree branches out. Under stable conditions, the system may follow one branch over another, and change will appear smooth. If, however, there is sufficient pressure upon the system, it may shift suddenly to another branch, producing disjointed change. "Although the route a system has taken to reach its present state is evident, this position cannot be predicted from a knowledge of its starting point" (Ward, 1995, p. 631). An impending phase shift is sometimes evident as the system will exhibit increased fluctuations as it approaches the bifurcation point (Baron, Amazeen, & Beck, 1994).

Baron et al. (1994) used Levinger's (1980) ABCDE model of relationship development to model a bifurcation point. The ABCDE model purports that one trajectory that relationships can take is from Attraction to Building a relationship to Continuance to Divergence to Exit. Levinger treated continuance as a bifurcation point, which can lead to one of three qualitatively different states: growing satisfying continuation, placid static continuation, or unstable conflictual continuation. Both placid and unstable continuation will lead to relationship deterioration. In Baron et al.'s modeling of this potential bifurcation point, the route a given couple takes depends upon the dynamic interaction of the mutuality of emotional investment, level of intimacy, frequency of interaction, and affect intensity. By generalizing this approach, it becomes easier to see relationship development as a series of bifurcations and phase shifts.

Once a phase shift occurs, the system cannot go back to the previous state. As indicated earlier, nonlinear dynamic relationships are marked by significant turning points. Turning points trigger a reinterpretation of what the relationship means to the participants (Graham, 1997). Turning points are often dramatic episodes in the couple's life that either move the relationship forward or cause it to drift backward (Yerby, Buerkel-Rothfuss, & Bochner, 1995). For example, when a person first says "I love you" the relationship is changed drastically. The relationship cannot be turned back. The system is faced with the choice of bifurcations. The couple can escalate the relationship or run away as fast as is humanly possible. Baxter and Bullis (1986) identified a number of relationship turning points, such as first becoming sexually intimate, providing assistance in times of crisis, or surviving a major fight. As stated by Yerby et al. (1995), "turning points are experienced either as break*throughs*, after which the relationship soars to higher levels of commitment, or as break*downs*, after which the relationship falls apart" (p. 101). Turning points illustrate relationship growth as phase shifts that are accompanied by "positive or negative explosions of relational commitment" (Baxter & Bullis, 1986, p. 486).

Attractors

Relationships require a certain degree of stability to survive. If couples were experiencing continual phase shifts, there would be little energy left for doing anything else but renegotiating the relationship. Stability does not mean a lack of movement, tension, or dynamics; rather, stability can be seen as a regular pattern of behavior. In chaos theory terms, patterns of stability are called **attractors**. Gleick (1987) defines an attractor as a point or pattern around which, or toward which, phenomena seem to be drawn. For instance, the attractor for a bowl of water sitting peacefully on a table is one of calmness.

We could create a perturbance in the water by dropping a small stone into the bowl. Ripples would immediately rush to the sides of the bowl and back to the middle. Gradually, the ripples would calm and the bowl of water would be drawn back to its attractor state of calmness. Just as the ripples of a pool will return to calm after being perturbed by the rock, a relationship will return to its preferred pattern, or attractor, following a disturbance. An attractor is often displayed mathematically and graphically in the chaos literature. For example, if one were to graph the movement of a pendulum, it would be a gradual spiral into a point as the pendulum comes to rest. In his attempts to predict weather, Lorenz (1979) mathematically plotted a pattern that loosely resembles a figure of eight. A similar plotting of dialectic tensions in relationships may provide an intriguing scheme for studying attractors in relationships. In her conceptualization of relational dialectics, Baxter (1994) proposes three primary dialectic contradictions underlying relationships: autonomy–connection, predictability–novelty, and openness–closedness. At any given time in each dialectic, one pole is dominant over another. For example, at one period the relationship may move toward autonomy, but it would eventually come back to connection. Relationship development is a continual pull between the two poles of the dialectic. Each of the three dialectics operates concurrently. Thus, the relationship is being continually pulled between autonomy–connection, predictability–novelty, and openness–closedness.

By taking just two of the dialectics, autonomy–connection and predictability–novelty, and assuming that we could measure the relationship regularly over time on these two dialectics, we could plot a pattern of where the couple [has balanced] the two dialectics at a particular time (Figure 1). With our first measurement, we might find that the couple was high on autonomy and high on [predictability]. With the second measurement, we might notice that the couple had moved to high on connectedness, while remaining high on predictability. At the third time, we might discover that the couple has changed back to high on autonomy, but is now high on novelty. By this point, we might have a strong suspicion that this relationship is unstable. With the fourth measurement, we could discover that the couple was now balancing high on both connectedness and novelty. At the fifth time, we might find that the couple is again high on autonomy and predictability. At this point, we would probably throw up our hands in frustration. However, if we had plotted the progression of the measurements, we would see that the couple's struggles with dialectic contradictions had corresponded roughly to a figure of eight pattern, similar to the one Lorenz found by plotting changes in weather (Figure 1). If we could get past our exasperation and continue sampling the couple for dozens more times, we might find that the figure of eight pattern regularly repeats itself. What we would discover is the pattern, the attractor, which is underlying the present couple's relationship. Of course, other patterns might be possible, an oval or even a star, for example. Whatever the pattern, the main point is that the relationship will follow that pattern as it manages the dialectics. The pattern it displays illustrates the attractor guiding the relationship. If Baxter's third dialectical contradiction were added, we could then plot a three-dimensional representation of the attractor.

Duke (1994) identifies a key characteristic of attractors in that they represent a pattern of behavior that is never exactly regular or predictable, but falls into an identifiable configuration over time. In the case of the dialectic tensions, if we only sampled our relationship at a few points in time it may seem substantially different each time, but, in fact, may not be; or it may appear stable because we only measured at T1 and T5. Rather, measurement may merely represent varying points within the overall pattern of the same attractor. We might find that the figure of eight pattern repeats itself regularly, even though the exact location of the score

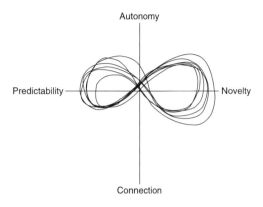

Weigel and Murray, Figure 1
A hypothetical plotting of relationship dialectics

in each quadrant of the graph would change slightly. Attractors do not specify exactly how behavior will occur, but in what range we should expect to find it. An attractor in relationships can be conceived of as the behavioral pattern that underlies the period of stability. Perhaps nothing can create as much turmoil in a marital relationship as a separation and divorce. Divorce implies relationship dissolution and most would see it as the official termination of the relationship. But Masheter (1997) has studied patterns of post-divorce relationships and found that the divorce was not the actual end of most relationships. In most cases, the relationship continues on after the divorce, particularly those divorces involving children. In fact, Masheter (1997) contends that many divorced couples have a relatively healthy relationship. Post-divorce relationships involve renegotiating a new reality (attractor) following the chaos of the divorce. Graham (1997) found five patterns in post-divorce relationships: (i) gradual relational progress, characterized by slow and steady progress toward a fully functioning post-divorce relationship; (ii) disrupted progress, referring to a pattern of initially-high hopes for the relationship, interrupted by a significant emotionally charged event(s), and then a steady recovery; (iii) sustained adjustment, described as a relatively high-quality relationship that was maintained since the time of divorce; (iv) disjointed erratic cycle, characterized by considerable change and fluctuation, highs, and lows; and (v) eventual deterioration, starting with high hopes, but a rather immediate and continued decline in the relationship. Out of the disorder of the divorce, these patterns of strange attractors emerged, some linear and some nonlinear. Graham captures the essence of phase shifts and new attractors when she says that we need to recognize that "relationships sometimes dissolve in one form only to be reborn in another, which is an important step in the way we conceptualize and think about relationships" (p. 351).

Attractors not only provide patterns to which systems are drawn following a phase shift, but also provide boundaries or limits to the behavior of the system. Applying this idea of attractors as setting boundaries to relationships, behaviors will fluctuate, but within limits. One case in which 436 attractors may define and limit behavior in the system is the relationship rules couples develop. As stated by Shimonoff (1980), rules "may function to regulate, interpret, evaluate, justify, correct, predict, and explain behavior" (p. 83). Rules do not govern behavior, directly; rather, they serve as guidelines for how individuals should or ought to behave in certain circumstances (Honeycutt, Woods, & Fontenot, 1993). Following a phase shift or transition, couples will need to adapt previous rules, discard ones that are no longer useful, and establish new rules for behavior which is now accepted and which is not. Couples may even have rules to govern the shift to new strange attractors. Rules may not only provide a pattern of stability to the relationship, but also define the limits of behavior.

Self-organization

Complex nonlinear dynamic systems are composed of many heterogeneous sub-elements that change over time (Nowak & Vallacher, 1998). A developing organism, for example, contains sub-elements such as cells, enzymes, chemicals, neural systems and reproductive systems. A developing relationship also contains numerous sub-elements, such as interaction patterns, rituals, rules, expectations, tensions, individual competence, and so forth. These sub-elements change over time and are free to act either as individual elements or to combine in an almost infinite number of ways (Nowak & Vallacher, 1998). Under certain conditions, these elements show coherence and the elements cooperate to produce form and flow that has pattern and complexity. The form into which the components assemble can be thought of as a preferred state of the system – the attractor. The relational system settles into that pattern and returns to it when perturbed. Under other conditions, the relational system components may reassemble into other stable attractors. The interesting thing about nonlinear dynamic systems is that their structure emerges out of an interaction within the system's parts, and between the system and its environment (Ward, 1995). In chaos theory terms, this occurrence is called self-organization, or the ability of the system to continuously reorganize itself. For instance, Thelen and Ulrich (1991) point out that, during development, what begins as a single cell is prompted by both internal and environmental stimuli to form organs and eventually to develop the cognitive abilities of a human being, who in turn relates to other individuals to form social networks. Self-organization is neither hardwired in terms of predetermined characteristics and developmental trajectories, nor at the total mercy of environmental forces. The new state is neither completely determined by internal relational dynamics nor driven by external environmental context forces (Thelen & Ulrich, 1991). In terms of romantic relationships, the couple does not willfully direct what the relationship will become (though some may try); rather, the relationship emerges from the interaction among basic internal elements, such as attitudes, desires, expectations, histories, and communication patterns, and is further shaped by the environment. Therefore, following the principle of self-organization, the essence of relationship development is not predetermined, but emerges from the ongoing dynamics of the system itself.

It may be possible to see the concept of self-organization in the process of how couples adapt to a major crisis, such as infidelity, disabling illness, or loss of a job (McCubbin, McCubbin, & Thompson, 1993). In attempting to adapt to the crisis, the couple will draw upon internal and external resources, coping strategies, and perceptions. When the crisis occurs, it can throw the relational system into disequilibrium, and, if strong enough, can initiate a phase shift. Gradually, by drawing upon these internal and external resources, the relational system either returns to a state of equilibrium or self-organizes a new relational state (i.e., new attractor). McCubbin et al. (1993) believe that the new state may be either stronger and more resilient than the previous state (bonadaptation) or weaker and less resilient (maladaptation). The key to understanding the self-organization principle is that the relational system reorganizes itself out of apparent disorder.

Following a phase shift, couples need to develop or adapt new rules, rituals, and routines to reinforce the new relationship organization. Many of the old patterns that were useful may no longer be useful. Communication is the process through which self-organization may occur in relational systems (Ward, 1995). During periods of stability, Duck (1994a) believes that couples use routine communication to maintain the status quo. When thrown into a phase shift, couples use more strategic communication to self-organize a new steady state. Wynne (1984) proposes a hierarchy of interaction skills necessary to respond to changing needs in the system. When experiencing change, couples need to reconfirm attachments and caring for one another, create shared meaning and a sense of mutual understanding, engage in joint problem solving, establish new mutual relationship patterns, and reinforce emotional

sharing and intimacy. As relationships change, new behavior prompts accommodation by the partners. For example, new communication patterns may be established when a spouse suffers an accident or debilitating illness (Wood, 1995). Following the phase shift created by the serious illness, the couple self-organizes a new communication pattern and steady state. What may have been an egalitarian communication pattern will likely become more established as the ill spouse becomes less independent.

The existence of chaotic relationships and scale of observation

At this point in the examination of chaos theory, an odd question arises. Given the amount of nonlinear, unpredictable change in relationships, why is it that, over the course of 2, 10 or 20 years, many relationships appear stable? One reason for this has to do with the scale of observation. Duke (1994) believes that there can be rapid changes over short periods, but over long periods there will tend to be trends that do not change. Depending on the scale from which one observes phenomena, "the very same object or event may appear at the very same moment in time as being anywhere from unchanging to unstable" (Duke, 1994, p. 278). Coming to understand the giant Red Spot on Jupiter is an example of the importance of scale. From a far distance the Red Spot looks stable and orderly on the face of Jupiter. Yet, the fly-by of Voyager in 1978 revealed that the Red Spot was a huge system of turbulent gaseous flow. Similar conclusions can be drawn about the development of organisms. Thelen (1990) demonstrates that over the life span, the ontogenetic trajectories [i.e., developmental pathways] of all members of a species are globally similar. Yet the individual pathways are highly variant; no two individual life spans are the same.

If one examines the minute-by-minute, day-to-day interactions of couples, behavior might appear almost random. But over the course of a few weeks, regular patterns would begin to emerge. Over the course of a year or two, these patterns would appear almost intractable. Even substantial phase shifts might be masked from the broader scale of a year. For example, if we gathered data on instances of negative and positive affect toward one's partner over several days, we might see patterns of high variability as couples experience arguments, intimacy, violated expectations, and reminiscences. These patterns of affectivity might be so variable as to appear almost random. However, during the same time frame, if we were to measure a more global dimension, such as relationship satisfaction, we might see only minor swings in satisfaction. Stepping back still another step, if we were to measure a spouse's commitment to remaining in the relationship, we might find no variance whatsoever. Hence, nonlinear dynamic systems like romantic relationships exhibit both linear and nonlinear characteristics depending on the scale of observation and the status of their present steady states.

The time frame of observation can also influence the appearance of stability and chaos. Erwin (1996) contends that if social systems are studied over time, a number of nonlinear patterns emerge: systems in which things flow smoothly at most times, with occasional periods of rapid fluctuation and divergence; systems in which things are usually not smooth and multiple interfering cycles frequently interrupt the system; and nondescript systems in which patterns cannot be discerned. Furthermore, Gragnani, Rinaldi, and Feichtinger (1997) studied the cyclical dynamics in relationships and found that unstable relationships seemed to follow two patterns: (i) ones in which the intensity of the chaotic periods declined over time, and (ii) ones in which the period of time between chaotic episodes increased over time so that they appeared to be stable relationships.

Long-term relationships, such as those described by Robinson and Blanton (1993), may appear stable over the life span of the relationship, yet, looking back, during a given day or week of those relationships, we might have seen nonlinear, chaotic, and unpredictable behavior. Thelen (1990) sees this possibility of chaos theory conceptually accounting for the occurrence of both differences in individual relationships and global similarities across relationships as one of the strengths of the chaos perspective. The localized variability illustrates the differences in individual relationships; the broad stable patterns illustrate the global similarities across relationships.

Herein lies the paradox of nonlinear dynamic systems. They can appear highly stable or highly variable, depending on the scale and time frame of observation. From one viewpoint a given relationship may look smooth and stable, yet from another perspective the same relationship may appear dangerously volatile ...

Although we have chosen to end the excerpt of the article here, the authors then go on to give several detailed ideas for the specific study of relationships using the above principles. They emphasize the importance of long-term analysis of nonlinear dynamic systems "not to isolate momentary changes, but to discover the patterns of change over some time scale. Consequently, research into relationship processes from a chaos theory perspective involves close observation and analysis of interaction over time. Once patterns have been identified, it is possible to formulate and test hypotheses about chaotic principles." The clear intention of such recommendations for research is the emphasis on the fact that research is exploring dynamic processes and so should use a method that can expose *dynamics* rather than "one-off" activity.

The various implications for relationship studies offered by the authors include the way in which Chaos Theory helps describe several processes within relationships and relationship development by providing a framework for understanding the jerky, discontinuous, and occasionally inactive periods of nonlinearity in relationship life. "The idea of the butterfly effect and sensitivity to initial conditions underscores why even the seemingly smallest events can create such turmoil for couples. Similarly, chaos theory may explain why relationship transitions can be difficult for some couples and not others. Even the concept of self-organization seems relevant to how couples reconfigure their relationship following transitions and changes. As such, chaos theory highlights relationships as a process rather than as a state, and may provide explanations for some of the noise that often plagues the study of relational development."

The authors also note that Chaos Theory "impacts the way we look at predictability since it is a feature of nonlinear dynamic systems that the same cause might have a whole range of possible outcomes. Predictability is possible during periods of stability, but decreased predictability occurs during periods of instability and phase shifts (Gottman, 1991) … If romantic relationships are nonlinear dynamic systems, we may never be able to fully predict future outcomes and trajectories. It may be that there will always be those outlier couples, couples undergoing phase shifts, which do not fit the linear expectations. Yet, we may be able to identify a general pattern in which the relationship might regularly be found. Chaos theory, through its focus on emergence, allows for the joining of determinism and indeterminism, causal and stochastic methods, and the interweaving of causality and randomness (Goldstein, 1996)."

A further important contribution of Chaos Theory is that "by viewing relationships as dynamic systems, variability within and among relationships becomes the norm, rather than the deviant … Chaos theory … informs us that variability in relationship development is normal rather than abnormal (Nowak & Vallacher, 1998). The variability found using linear and causal approaches might not be due solely to **measurement error**, but to the possibility that relational variability is truer than relational constants. Thus, rather than being consumed with cause and effect, the role of relationship scholars may better be served to create theories that make social dynamics and relationship patterns intelligible to scientists and the public."

Finally, Chaos Theory helps us to see nonlinear dynamic processes not as problematic, whereby the "variability and unpredictability doom our research efforts … but in fact we may be able to exploit the 'inherent noisiness of relationships in a principled way to open doors on the dynamics of change and to explore the limits of predictability' (Thelen, 1990: 37) … If … we view variability as not only the inevitable consequence of relationship development but the very substance from which change is sculpted, we begin to look at the local vacillations as well as the global patterns."

The authors are duly cautious also about their suggestions, noting that the complex mathematical techniques involved in Chaos Theory are not familiar territory for most social scientists and there is a risk of the misuse or wild application of specific mathematical terms that could end up confusing everyone. For example the fact that relationships are nonlinear dynamic systems does not mean they are chaotic in the everyday sense of the term. Chaos Theory by contrast invites us to look at the underlying systematic patterns that underpin apparent randomness, as we have seen above. However, the approach is certainly a novel one and may have opened up some interesting trains of thought for you about the way that relationships work.

One important element of the article is its emphasis on the value of making observations of relationships across long periods of time. This of course is not always a practical suggestion but there have been many attempts recently to develop techniques for measuring relationship activity for long periods, some of which you will read as this book progresses. Many such techniques rely on the gathering of diary data from relationship partners who keep records of their interactions with one another over periods of time ranging from several hours to several months (Wheeler & Nezlek, 1977; Duck et al., 1991).

As you come to the end of this chapter then, you should be thinking about the ways in which relationships develop over time, even over the time of one extended interaction such as a first date. How does the discussion of relationship development parallel or mimic or directly challenge the study of attraction that we looked at in Chapter 2? Is development of relationships steered by early encounters? Does the development of relationships depend on daily management of relational activity or on other things such as whether people are Right for each other? Where does Love fit in (see Chapter 3)? How far does relationship development depend on such things as trust and the belief that your partner will be an honest broker who will act fairly and in your own interests as far as possible? The next chapter will tell us.

6 Social Power

The **bases of power** have been widely discussed in the context of continuing or long-term relationship such as marriage. However, it is reasonable to assume that the foundation for the power relationship within the dyad was established earlier in the relationship, when the couple was dating (Sprecher, 1985). The two articles you will read in this chapter examine power within this early phase of courtship. Generally, these and other studies have applied models of power sharing based on long-term heterosexual relationships. These are adapted to some degree by each set of authors; however, these changes should prompt several questions in you. For example, can a single model capture the shifting nature of power sharing throughout the lifespan of a long-term relationship? How might these models need to change to fit dating couples?

In the first article presented in this chapter, Sprecher (1985) clearly outlines the rationale for examining power reciprocity in dating couples rather than solely concentrating on married couples as in previous research studies. Of particular note is her emphasis on expanding the pool of power attributes to those traditionally controlled by women (e.g., affection, companionship, expressiveness). Previous studies had concentrated on male-controlled resources such as economic status and wealth. In addition, her assessment of both absolute control as well as "perceived" control of resources is critical in an analysis of the power dynamic in relationships. Finally, we introduce you to the concepts of **resource-based dependency** in relationships and the **principle of least interest** with the wielding of power in this article.

A major focus of this paper is the sex differences in the possession and use of different resources. Before you begin reading, it would be useful to consider which sex might be more likely to control and use different resources (e.g., socioeconomic, affective, sex, services, expressive, intelligence, companionship, and physical appearance). It would also be useful to consider whether control of these resources actually produces a feeling of power in the individual wielding the power. A second question to consider with regard to power is that most models of power in relationships have been based on traditional heterosexual relationships. Is there any reason these principles cannot be applied directly to gay male and lesbian relationships?

Sex Differences in Bases of Power in Dating Relationships

Susan Sprecher

While a great deal of research has explored power in intimate relations, almost all of the research has been of marital or family power. Virtually unexplored is the operation of power in dating relationships. However, because dating is a critical stage from which later marriages and families are formed, a theoretical understanding of power in intimate relationships must incorporate power as it is manifested in the dating stage of a relationship. The purpose in the present study is to examine bases of power for dating relationships, and to see how these differ for men and women.

As pointed out in a recent review of family power (McDonald, 1980), power is *both* a behavioral and a perceptual phenomenon. The importance of perceptions of power in a social relationship cannot be overestimated. Viewing the balance of power in the relationship from the perspective of the participants suggests that there may really be two power relations in a heterosexual dyad – a "hers" and a "his." Bernard (1972), for example, has suggested that wives and husbands objectively and subjectively experience two different marriages – e.g., that no such entity as a "real" marriage common to both spouses exists. This distinction between each partner's perception of the relationship would apply to all relationships, including dating relationships.

Because each partner experiences a slightly different relationship, there will not always be agreement between the man and woman on how power is distributed in the relationship. Although "real" power may be thought of as a property of the relationship (McDonald, 1980), the process through which power

arises depends on individual definitions of the power relation. As several theorists have argued, it is the individual's perception of the power distribution that determines how she/he behaves in the relationship (e.g., McDonald, 1977). Reflecting this importance of power as a perceptual phenomenon, the focus in this study will be on power *as perceived* by each partner in the dating relationship.

Several theorists have argued that the dyadic property of power resides in one partner's dependence on the other (e.g., Thibaut & Kelley, 1959). Dependence can arise from exchange both within the dyad and within the larger network in which the dyad is located. As defined by Cook and Emerson (1978), dependence is a joint function of the relative value of resources provided by each partner and the availability of similar resources outside the relationship. The more powerful (less dependent) person is one for whom (a) the value of resources potentially provided to her/his partner is greater than the value of resources potentially obtained from her/his partner, and/or (b) there are alternative exchange relations through which she/he may obtain at least the same value of resources the partner has to offer.

Studies of marital power have dealt with both parts of this dependence function. Several studies report that the greater the socioeconomic resources of one partner relative to the other, the more powerful is that partner (for a review, see McDonald, 1980). The effects on power of alternative exchange relations have usually been assessed by examining the relationship between an individual's control of socioeconomic resources and her/his power (e.g., Blood & Wolfe, 1960). It is assumed that the greater absolute resources controlled by an individual, the more likely she/he can find alternative relationships that would be as rewarding or more so than the present relationship.

There are several limitations of previous research on power. The first major limitation of studies examining bases of power is that a relatively narrow range of resources has been used. In studies examining the relationship between resources and power, resources have primarily been operationalized in terms of socioeconomic indicators. Safilios-Rothschild (1970, 1977) has suggested that the focus on socioeconomic resources represents a male bias in research on power. Stereotypically feminine resources such as love have not been included in these studies, despite their importance in intimate relationships. Safilios-Rothschild identifies five such categories of feminine resources that are exchanged in intimate heterosexual relationships: affection, expression, companionship, sex, and services. In studies of power it is important to examine this wider range of resources.

A second major limitation of past research is that resources *controlled* in an intimate relationship (for example, the level of education or income of each partner) have been examined rather than resources actually *contributed* to the relationship. However, it is less clear whether contributions of resources, and especially of particular types of resources, will be positively related to having power in the relationship. In fact, a social psychological theory of bargaining (Michener & Suchner, 1972) states that power involves the capacity to influence the behavior of the other in order to acquire needed and desirable resources: "Social power involves both the *capacity to influence* the behavior of the other, which enables a person to obtain valued outcomes, and the *capacity to resist* the influence of the other, which permits him to deny others the outcomes they want from him" (p. 239). According to this theory, then, contributions of resources should be negatively related to power.

A third limitation of past research is that no studies have directly assessed the availability of attractive alternatives to the present relationship. Having access to desirable alternative relationships entails both being desirable (e.g., having valuable resources to potentially offer someone) *and* having alternative others in the environment.

As pointed out in the introduction, most of the research on power in intimate relationships concerns marital power. Few studies have examined exchange and power in dating relationships. In one early classic study (the "Rating and Dating" complex), Waller (1937) illustrated that the courtship process could be best described as bargaining behavior. He found that young men and women try to advance themselves by dating the most desirable partner. Desirable personal resources controlled by unmarried women included such things as sorority membership, physical attractiveness, and being a good dancer. Personal resources found desirable in men included possession of a car, money for social activities, and fraternity membership. Waller found that if relationships of unequal status occur, the partner with higher status (more desirable resources) may "exploit" the other. In general terms, exploitation may be thought of as the exercise of power. He also found that the person who is least involved in the relationship can usually exercise more power. Waller (1937) wrote, "That person is most able to dictate the condition of the association whose interest in the continuation of the affair is least." In a more recent study of dating couples, perceived power was directly assessed and related to other aspects of the relationship. Based upon an interview study of 231 dating couples, Peplau (1979) found that the partner who was least involved in the dating relationship tended to be more powerful. Peplau also found that a very important factor related to the balance of power in the dating relationship was the educational and career goals of women. The higher the educational goals of a woman, the more powerful she was perceived to be. In this study, bases of power in dating relationships are further explored.

What about sex differences in power? In general, it has been reported that husbands are more powerful than wives (e.g., Bernard, 1972). This sex difference in power has also been reported for dating couples (Peplau, 1979). Resource and social exchange theorists have tended to view the sex power differential (male having more power than the female) as the "natural" and equitable result of the differential resources possessed by men and women and/or the differential alternative exchange relations available to men and women. As indicated above, most of the empirical research on marital power has used socioeconomic indicators to represent personal resources. Since men are more likely to be employed and generally have greater earnings than women, their greater power has been attributed to the operation of an equitable exchange process.

Although women have fewer opportunities than men to acquire income and status in the existing sex-stratification system, there are other ways in which women may acquire power. Evidence suggests that women who do not have access to socioeconomic resources may gain power by controlling love and sex in the relationship. As long as her partner is very much in love with her, the woman may gain power by controlling the reciprocation of the partner's love. In a cross-cultural study, Safilios-Rothschild (1977) found that women who thought their husbands were the partner more in love perceived that they themselves had power to make important decisions more often than those women who perceived themselves to be the partner more in love. While this general trend was also found for men, the difference was not significant. In addition, it has also been found that women who have little direct access to money and prestige may use sex as a resource to gain power in the relationship (Safilios-Rothschild, 1977). It is possible, then, that socioeconomic resources may be an important basis of power for males, while controlling the reciprocation of love may be an important basis

of power for females. Such sex differences will be explored in this study.

Method

Fifty dating couples participated in an interview study on relationships. Volunteers were sought from a sorority and fraternity at the University of Wisconsin. It was required that their partner, who also was often a Greek [fraternal organization] member, participate in the study. Because the respondents were volunteers, they may not be representative of all young dating couples. The analyses reported here, therefore, must be considered somewhat exploratory, providing preliminary evidence upon which future studies of more representative samples may be based. The majority of the respondents were undergraduate students ranging in age from 18 to 22. In general, the couples had been going together for at least six months and were dating exclusively at the time of the study. None of the couples were cohabiting.

The questionnaire was self-administered, and was completed by each individual separately from her/his partner. All respondents were guaranteed that the information would be kept strictly confidential. The questionnaire, which took approximately 45 to 60 min to complete, examined several aspects of the relationship.

Power. Responses to three items were summed to form an index of Perceived power in the relationship. The three items were: 1. In your relationship, who has the most power? Responses ranged on a 7-point scale from "My partner has much more power than I do" to "I have much more power than my partner"; 2. In your relationship, who do you think has more of a say about what the two of you do together? Responses ranged on a 5-point scale from "My partner has much more of a say" to "I have much more of a say"; 3. In your relationship, who makes the most sacrifices? Responses ranged on a 5-point scale from "I make many more sacrifices than my partner does" to "My partner makes many more sacrifices than I do."

Responses to the three items were scaled such that the higher the number, the greater the perceived power. **Alpha coefficients** of scale reliability for males and females were .58 and .68, respectively, which were considered satisfactory for a scale of three items.

Contribution of Resources. To measure resources contributed in the relationship, respondents were given a list of eight resources and asked to describe their own contributions to the relationship and their partner's contributions. The list of resources was a modified version of those identified by Safilios-Rothschild (1977) as being resources potentially exchanged in the intimate relationship. They include: (1) socioeconomic, (2) affective, (3) expressive, (4) physical appearance, (5) intellectual, (6) companionship, (7) sex, and (8) service resources. The response scale provided to describe the contributions ranged from (+4) = extremely positive to (–4) = extremely negative. Using the evaluative descriptors allows the respondents to answer with respect to both the amount they contribute and how they value the contributions.

Relative Involvement. Because of the importance of the exchange of love in the relationship, a more specific question was asked about who loved more in the relationship. Responses ranged on a seven-point scale from "Partner loves much more" to "I love much more."

Access to Alternatives. Access to alternatives was measured directly by asking the respondents how easy or difficult it would be to find a new dating partner – given what they had to offer and how many "eligibles" were available: 1. If you found yourself unattached again, for whatever reason, and wanted to find a new partner, how easy/difficult would that be given the number of "eligibles" you are aware of? 2. How easy/difficult would it be to find a new partner, given what you feel you have to offer? Responses ranged from (1) = very difficult to (4) = very easy. Responses to the

two items were summed to form the index of "access to alternatives."

Results

In spite of the fact that today most men and women subscribe to an egalitarian philosophy, the evidence reviewed suggests that males perceive themselves as having more power than do females. However, a sex difference was not found in this sample of dating couples. There was *no* significant difference between men and women daters in how powerful they perceived themselves to be in the relationship. The overall power index score for males was 10.84 (*SD* = 2.24); for females it was 10.76 (*SD* = 2.36). The scores were slightly in the direction of perceiving oneself as being powerful in the relationship.

1. Relative Contributions of Resources. Based upon resource theory it was expected that the more resources an individual contributed to the relationship relative to what her/his partner contributed, the more power the individual would perceive her/himself as having. Relative contributions were calculated by subtracting perception of partner's contributions from own contributions. The more positive (or less negative) this difference, the more powerful the individual was expected to perceive her/himself to be.

There was *no* positive correlation between relative contributions and perceived power for either males or females. In fact, there was a significant *negative* correlation between contributions of resources and perceived power for females. The more females perceived themselves as contributing relative to their partner, the *less* powerful they felt.

I also explored the association between relative contributions of specific types of resources and power perceptions. For males, only contributions of affective resources seemed to be significantly correlated with feeling powerful – and it was a negative correlation. The more affective resources males perceived they contributed relative to their partner, the less powerful they perceived themselves to be. For females, there were four significant negative correlations between relative contributions of specific resources and perceiving the self as powerful: affection, expressiveness, physical attractiveness, and services. Another way of phrasing this is that the less females contributed of these resources, the more powerful they perceived themselves to be. Thus, resource theory was not supported either overall, or for any specific resource, for either males or females.

In general, the more affective resources (i.e., love, affection) that males or females contributed *relative* to what their partners contributed, the less powerful they perceived themselves to be. This tendency, as we had expected, was stronger for females than for males. This relationship was also found when we examined the item asking *who loves more in the relationship*. The more women perceived they loved relative to their partner, the less power they perceived themselves as having ($r = -.45; p < .001$). For males, on the other hand, there was no significant correlation between relative involvement and perceived power.

2. Absolute Contributions of Resources and Access to Alternatives. Based upon social exchange theory, it was expected that the greater the absolute contributions to the relationship, the more powerful the individual would perceive her/himself to be. This was based on the assumption that the more the individual has to contribute to the relationship, the more she/he is probably also desirable to available alternative dates.

For absolute contributions, the correlation with power was found to be positive and significant for males ($r = -.27; p < .05$). For females, on the other hand, the correlation was negative (but not significant). In general, then, the more males perceived they contributed to the relationship, the more power they perceived they had. Conversely, the more females contributed, the less power they perceived they had.

It was also explored more specifically how absolute contributions of particular types of resources were associated with being

powerful. For males, the greater absolute contributions of five categories of resources were positively correlated with power: affection, physical attractiveness, intelligence, companionship, and sex. For females, on the other hand, there were *no* categories of resources for which absolute contributions were positively associated with feeling powerful. Instead, there were two types of resources that were negatively correlated with having power: physical attractiveness and services. It is interesting to note that the relation between absolute contributions of physical attractiveness and being powerful was the opposite for males and females – significantly positive for males and significantly negative for females.

By examining absolute contributions of resources it was assumed that the more resources an individual has to contribute, the more potential others she/he would be able to attract – and this potential serves as a **basis of power**. In addition, "access to alternatives" was directly assessed by summing the items asking how easy it would be to find a new partner given: (1) the number of "eligibles" available, and (2) what the individual has to offer. The relationship was significantly positive for males ($r = .28; p < .05$). The easier it was perceived to develop alternative relationships, the more power the male perceived he had. However, the correlation was negative (but not significant) for females. Having access to alternatives did not seem to affect the perceived power of females.

Summary and discussion

No evidence was found that contributing more resources than one's partner was positively related to feeling powerful in the relationship. In fact, there seemed to be a general tendency for both men and women to perceive themselves as having less power the greater their relative contributions. Surprisingly, this was true even for socioeconomic resources, the type of resource examined in past studies.

This negative relationship between contributing more resources than one's dating partner and feeling powerful in the relationship suggests the importance of distinguishing between resources *contributed* and resources *controlled*. In general, past studies testing resource theory have used resources that were controlled by the individual (i.e., an income, an education). In such studies, resource theory was supported. In this study, however, resources contributed were measured, and no support was found for resource theory. The relationship between resources and power may depend, then, on whether resources controlled or resources contributed are examined. As suggested by the bargaining theory by Michener and Suchner (1972), being powerful may involve convincing the partner to contribute desirable resources, but being able to resist contributing in return the desirable resources one controls.

While no support was found for resource theory, it was found that the higher the absolute level of resources men perceived themselves as contributing to the relationship, the more powerful they perceived themselves to be. Presumably, this power is based on their ability to use resources to attract alternative dating partners who can provide desirable rewards. For females, the relationship between absolute contributions of resources and perceived power was actually negative, but not significant. In addition, the easier men thought it would be to find a new dating partner, the greater their perceived power. The relationship was negative (nonsignificant) for females. These combined results suggest that males and females differ in the degree to which factors outside the relationship are a **basis of power** within the relationship. Males may be more likely than females to derive power within the relationship from their standing in a wider social network. Males have the upper hand in the initiating of dating relationships – and thus are in a better position to use the

ability to attract alternative dating partners as a basis of bargaining power in the relationship. If females are dissatisfied with their present relationship they often have to passively wait for someone to show an interest in them; dissatisfied men, on the other hand, can more actively seek alternative others.

Absolute and relative contributions of specific types of resources seemed to be related differently for males and females to perceived power. In general, there was a tendency for stereotypically female characteristics (i.e., physical attractiveness, sexual favors, personal services) to be negatively correlated with perceived power for women, perhaps because those women who contribute high levels of such resources have developed less assertive (powerful) feelings about themselves. These resources, however, tended to be positively correlated with perceived power for men.

Physical appearance was, for example, a type of resource for which there was a sex difference in how contributions were associated with perceived power. The higher the level of physical appearance the men perceived they contributed to the relationship (e.g., the more physically attractive they perceived themselves to be), the more likely they were to feel powerful. This is what can be expected considering that physical attractiveness is a characteristic of the self that often determines one's market value in attracting alternative dating partners (Walster, Aronson, Abrahams, & Rottman, 1966). However, the more women perceived they contributed in physical appearance, the less powerful they perceived themselves as being. There was also a negative correlation for women between relative contributions of physical attractiveness and being powerful. Perhaps physically attractive and physically unattractive women are treated in different ways that lead unattractive women to be more assertive than attractive women. In a recent study of undergraduate men and women (Reis, Wheeler, Spiegel, Kernis, Nezlek, & Perri, 1982), it was found that although attractive men scored higher than unattractive men on a scale to measure assertiveness, unattractive women scored higher than attractive women.

Males and females also differed in how sexual and affective contributions were related to power. In general, the higher the absolute level of contributions of sex, the more powerful males perceived themselves to be. This relationship, however, was negative (but nonsignificant) for females. That the ability to perform sexually may be more of a basis of power for males than for females is consistent with sexual stereotypes. Similarly, the more affection men contributed, the more power they perceived they had. For women, on the other hand, the more absolute contributions of affection, the less power they perceived themselves as having.

For both males and females, the more affective resources contributed relative to the partner, the less power they perceived themselves as having. This finding is consistent with the principle of least interest (Waller, 1937) and recent empirical research (Peplau, 1979). This relationship was stronger for females than for males, as we had predicted. For women, it was found that the less they loved relative to the partner, the more power they perceived themselves as having. For males, this relationship was not significant. Thus, for women an important basis of power appears to be the control of the reciprocation of love in the relationship.

Women probably have traditionally had to become skilled at controlling their emotions in their heterosexual relationships in order to acquire any bargaining power. Indeed, evidence has been found that men are more romantic than women. For example, men are more likely than women to endorse such beliefs as "To be truly in love is to be in love forever" and "A person should marry whomever he loves regardless of social position," and to have other similar romantic attitudes. It has also been found that men are the first to fall in love (e.g., Coombs & Kendell, 1966) and the last to fall out of love (Rubin, Peplau, & Hill, 1981). Thus the evidence suggests that men may value and need the love from a woman more than women value and need the love from men. Often unable to have access to other desirable resources (money, status), women have had to use the control of love as a means to gain some power in the relationship.

While love may be treated as a "resource" that is contributed to the relationship, there is an alternative way of understanding love as it relates to the exchange of resources in the relationship. Love may act as a barometer to indicate how much the individual needs the partner. In general, dependence is often equated with romantic love (Reik, 1944); furthermore, dependency often arises because the other person is providing the desirable resources one needs. Those who perceive themselves as loving more in the relationship may feel less powerful in the relationship because of their greater need for the other. Women's sense of power in the relationship may be especially dependent on how much she feels she needs (or loves) the partner. In general, then, it appears that the bases of power may differ for males and females. Females seem more likely to gain power if they control the reciprocation of their partner's love. For males, on the other hand, the ability to attract alternative other dating partners seems to be an important basis of power. In addition, while past research and cultural stereotypes would suggest that males are more powerful than females, I did not find a significant difference between males and females in perceived power.

The results for this study suggest that further research should examine more clearly how contributions vs. control of resources may be related to power. In addition, these findings demonstrate the importance of expanding the range of resources considered to include both stereotypically "male" and "female" resources as potential bases for power in intimate relationships.

Although it is surprising men and women in the sample felt equally powerful in their relationships, one wonders whether this was due to sharing each power source equally or did each sex exert control of complementary power sources. The results suggest males control more resources and more traditionally masculine ones while women control fewer overall resources and those are traditionally feminine resources (e.g., love, sex). However, more interesting in the analysis was the clear support of the **principle of least interest**, operationally defined here as "the partner that contributes the least resources (but controls the resource) has more power". So, it is not simply control that is important in the wielding of power, but the judicious allocation of resources. A final tantalizing piece of data concerns traditionally feminine resources. Generally, males as well as females who contributed traditionally feminine resources held less power in their relationships.

Have you considered the application of these principles to all relationships regardless of the stage of courtship or sexual orientation of the partners? What did you decide? Are traditional sources of power available to young as well as older individuals? Are traditional resources likely to be coveted by people in nontraditional relationships? Finally, although Sprecher did not present an analysis of the reciprocity of power within the data couples, what would you expect to find if you had conducted the analysis?

One important question in all of this concerns power and sexual orientation. Did you conclude there would be differences between lesbian, gay male and heterosexual couples? Were you able to generate any specific predictions? Did they conform to traditional heterosexual sex roles or did you predict they would reverse for lesbian and gay male couples? The second article you will read in this chapter by Falbo and Peplau (1980) directly attacks this question. However, the authors of this article **operationally define** power in relationships using different criteria from Sprecher (1985). Rather than concentrating on the control and allocation of resources, they examine the persuasive techniques used in relationships (what the authors refer to as power "strategies"). You may want to consider this difference as you read the article and reflect on whether this change of focus between the articles is unimportant to the overall research question. Also, note the care taken to make the demographic characteristics of the heterosexual and homosexual participants as equal as possible to rule out potentially confounding variables.

Finally, Falbo and Peplau use an advanced statistical procedure called **Multidimensional Scaling (MDS)** that you probably are not familiar with at this point in your studies. Briefly, this statistical method captures the way people organize items or events and tries to describe the organization using the fewest number of dimensions. The data collection procedure is simple (but the statistical analysis is not): subjects are asked to say how different or similar the items are in a set of things. For example, if the question involved a set of 20 universities, people might be asked, "Is The University of Iowa more similar to The University of Minnesota or to Cornell University?" Participants would complete an exhaustive list of comparisons and the statistical analysis would reveal the participants' underlying organization using the fewest number of factors or dimensions as possible (e.g., two). In this article, judges rated the similarity of thirteen power strategies. An example of one comparison might be the following. Is "I ask him to do what I want" more similar to "I try to persuade him my way is right" or to "I pout or threaten to cry if I don't get my way." As you read this article you may want to consider whether or not power strategies can be organized on as few as two dimensions.

Power Strategies in Intimate Relationships

Toni Falbo and Letitia Anne Peplau

Research on power in intimate relationships (Safilios-Rothschild, 1970) has generally focused on decision making and the balance of power within couples. The present study differs from previous investigations in that it attempts to uncover the dimensions underlying the power strategies used in intimate relationships. In addition, this research investigates some of the associations between sex, egalitarianism, sexual orientation, and power strategies used in intimate relationships.

Recently, Falbo (1977) introduced a two dimensional model of general power strategies. This model was derived from open-ended essays written on the topic "how I get my way" (Goodchilds, Quadrado, & Raven, 1975). One potentially important factor omitted from consideration in the original model was the possible effect of the target of influence on the individual's choice of a power strategy. Although most subjects did not specify a target when writing open-ended essays, those who did indicated that their power strategies varied depending on the target. For example, one young man wrote:

> "This depends on who I am trying to get it from or with. With my parents, I tell them I want something, then play it cool and eventually get it. With friends, I will fight verbally although not physically for it. With girlfriends, I simply turn the other way, walk off, or whatever the situation demands."

The first goal of this study is to generate a model of power strategies in intimate relationships and to examine the similarity between this new model and the Falbo (1977) two dimensional model of general power strategies.

A second goal of this research is to investigate the impact of sex and egalitarianism on power strategies used in intimate relationships. Traditional sex roles dictate that men and women should exert influence in different ways, and the literature suggests that men and women sometimes use sex-typed power tactics in dating relationships (Peplau, 1979).

Sex differences in power strategies have been found within married couples (e.g., Kipnis, 1976) and mixed-sex pairs of college students in laboratory studies (Johnson, 1978). Although sex role socialization may be one explanation for sex differences in the use of power strategies, power differences between the sexes may also account for these sex differences. Henley (1975) has noted that sex differences in such interpersonal behaviors as touching, self-disclosure, and verbal interruptions often mirror differences between the behavior of high and low power individuals. Thus it may be that men's greater power in relationships is the basis for sex differences in power strategies used in intimate relationships. Since present day love relationships vary considerably in the extent to which partners prefer equal power, it is possible to examine the associations between equality and power strategy use. It seems likely that values about power and perceptions of relative power within a relationship affect the choice of power strategies, and this finding may help explain sex differences in power strategy use. This research investigates these possibilities.

To broaden the scope of the model and to examine differences in power strategy use as a function of sexual orientation, both homosexual and heterosexual men and women were included in this study. Homosexual relationships provide an opportunity to examine how men and women exercise power when sex role constraints may not be operative. Whether same-sex couples use strategies more typical of their sex or whether homosexual couples have a different means of influencing each other than heterosexual couples do is unclear. Since little is known about the nature of homosexual relationships (Morin, 1977), it is not possible to make precise predictions about possible similarities or differences between the use of strategies by heterosexuals and homosexuals. To the extent that all men and women in the culture are socialized to adopt sex-typed strategies of influence (cf. Gagnon & Simon, 1973), one might expect sex differences in power strategies rather than differences based on sexual orientation. But to the extent that homosexuals have views about power in relationships that differ from views of heterosexuals (Mannion, 1976), one might expect the power strategies of homosexuals to differ from those of heterosexuals.

Method

Data collection and analysis took five steps. First, volunteers were recruited to complete a questionnaire on their romantic/sexual relationships. One item in the questionnaire asked the participants to write an essay on the strategies used with their intimate partner. Second, a code was developed to categorize the strategies found in the power essays. Third, experts generated the data necessary to produce the dimensional model. Fourth, these data underwent **multidimensional scaling (MDS) analysis**. Fifth, to examine the associations between characteristics of the individuals, their relationships, and power strategy use, a series of regression analyses was performed so that relevant variables could be projected as vectors into the MDS configuration.

As part of a larger study of intimate relationships, 434 participants were recruited during 1976 and 1977. Homosexual women were recruited for a study of "lesbian relationships" by advertisements placed in a university newspaper, a feminist student publication, and leaflets distributed at a university campus. Homosexual men were recruited for a study of "gay men's relationships" by advertisements placed in a university newspaper, leaflets distributed at a university campus, and through a university gay students association. Heterosexual men and women were recruited at the same university through classes taught in several academic departments. A total of 127 lesbians, 151 gay men, 90 heterosexual women, and 66 heterosexual men participated in this research by completing a lengthy questionnaire concerning their background, attitudes, and romantic/sexual relationships. Participants who were currently in a romantic relationship answered questions about the partner and their relationship. Participants who were not currently in a relationship answered comparable questions concerning their most recent past romantic relationship.

For the analyses reported here, it was important to have comparable samples of homosexual and heterosexual women and men. To achieve this objective, subsamples of 50 lesbians, 50 gay men, 50 heterosexual women, and 50 heterosexual men were selected from the larger sample. In each subgroup, half the respondents were currently in a relationship, and half were not. To increase comparability, all the individuals in these groups were unmarried white university students with a low proportion of missing data in their responses to the questionnaire. Because the lesbians were slightly older and reported having longer relationships than gay men, it was decided to select a heterosexual sample that reflected these small differences. That is, heterosexual women were selected to be as similar as possible to lesbians in their mean age and duration of relationship; heterosexual men were selected so that their mean age and relationship durations were similar to those of the gay men. There were no significant differences in relationship duration within sex between heterosexuals and homosexuals.

However, homosexuals were still significantly older, $F(1, 191) = 3.79$, $p < .05$, than heterosexuals (M difference = .85 years). Overall, women in this sample differed from men in being significantly older, $F(1, 191) = 13.53$, $p < .001$ (M difference = 2.65 years) and in describing relationships that lasted longer, $F(1, 191) = 13.08$, $p < .001$ (M difference = 8.20 months). Nonetheless, these differences are quite small relative to those found in previous research comparing heterosexuals and homosexuals (e.g., Saghir & Robins, 1973).

The questionnaire. Participants spent approximately 1 hour completing an anonymous questionnaire, either in a small group setting or individually. Slightly different versions of the lengthy questionnaire were administered to lesbians, gay men, and heterosexuals. The first part of the questionnaire concerned participants' backgrounds, including questions about age, race, marital status, and whether or not the person was currently in a romantic/sexual relationship. Also included were several measures of personal attitudes. Pertinent to this study were measures concerning the individual's preferences for power and independence in a love relationship. Two items assessed the importance given (on a 9-point scale) to "having more influence than my partner in our joint decision-making" and "having an egalitarian (equal-power) relationship." A five-item personal autonomy scale (Peplau et al., 1978) assessed the importance that individuals gave to having friends and interests outside their intimate relationship and to enjoying the relationship now rather than insisting on a future commitment.

The second part of the questionnaire focused on a specific romantic/sexual relationship. Individuals described their current relationships or, if they were not in a relationship at present, their most recent past relationship. Throughout the questionnaire, the symbol (___) was used to refer to this specific intimate partner. Of particular relevance for this article are questions pertaining to power. To assess participants' power

strategies, they were asked to write an open-ended essay describing "how I get (___) to do what I want" or, for past relationships, "how I got (___) to do what I wanted." Students also indicated their personal assessment of the overall balance of power (Peplau, 1979) in the relationship on a 5-point scale ranging from "I have much more say" to "we have exactly equal say" to "(___) has much more say." In addition, students indicated how long the relationship had lasted and rated their personal satisfaction (on a 9-point scale) with the relationship.

All essays ($N = 434$) were read by six coders, who divided responses into discrete power strategies. Strategies were defined as acts presented by the essay writers as instrumental in getting their way. To develop a coding scheme for the power strategies used in intimate relationships, raters attempted to apply two earlier coding schemes (Falbo, 1977; French & Raven, 1959). Each of the individual categories from these earlier schemes was used. If fewer than five instances of any of these categories could be found, the category was not retained in the final list of power strategy categories. Using this criterion, seven power categories were included from previous coding schemes. Two of the six bases of power proposed by French and Raven were used, although considerably altered in meaning. That is, *reward power*, as described by French and Raven, was recast here as *positive affect*. French and Raven's *coercive power* was reflected in the strategy here called *negative affect*. Five of the categories used by Falbo (1977) were also used: *reasoning, bargaining, hinting, persuasion,* and *persistence.*

Strategies that did not fit into the previous coding schemes were examined to find common themes. Strategies were grouped together into a category if the coders could agree that they shared a common meaning and that there were at least five instances of each. For example, "I grow silent and cold," "I leave and go into another room," and "I clam up" were grouped together into the category called *withdrawal. Six* categories were created this way. They were: *withdrawal, laissez-faire, telling, asking, stating importance,* and *talking.* The categories of withdrawal and stating importance represent subsets of the broader categories *negative affect* and *telling,* respectively.

The net result of this procedure was the development of a set of 13 power strategy categories that accounted for 98% of the strategies that occurred in the total sample of essays. Of the 200 participants in the subsample, 83% reported using at least 1 power category. The amount of agreement between coders in their use of the power categories was computed by the formula provided by Winter (1973). All agreement scores were above .80.

Nine experts in the field of power and intimate relationships provided the data necessary for the MDS analysis. They did this by making ratings of similarity. The experts received a description of the study, definitions of the strategies, instructions about the rating task, and a matrix on which to record ratings. The experts rated the similarity between each power strategy and every other strategy on a 10-point scale ranging from 0 to 9, and these ratings were analyzed using an MDS procedure. To aid in interpreting the MDS dimensions, seven of the experts subsequently rated each strategy on several attributes including: direct/indirect, unilateral/interactive, active/passive, and good/ bad. Only seven experts did these ratings, because two of the nine original experts were already familiar with the MDS results and this knowledge might have influenced their attribute ratings. Attribute ratings were made on 7-point **semantic differential scales** [Eds: *a semantic differential scale is a bipolar scale anchored on either end by opposing adjectives. For example, imagine a bipolar scale that is a horizontal line made up of seven dashed lines and on one end sits the word "active" and on the other end is the word "passive." (Active: _ _ _ _ _ _ _ : Passive). Participants place a mark along the scale that best represents their evaluation. This format can be repeated for additional comparisons (e.g.,*

direct/indirect) and the ratings for each scale can analyzed individually and as a summed score.]

[*A large section of the methods section has been edited out at this point, Eds.*]

Results

[A large piece of the results section has been edited out at this point, Eds.]

Sex *and sexual orientation.* To test for sex differences, the proportion of women (vs. men) reporting each strategy was examined. This analysis was done separately for the two sexual orientation groups, only heterosexuals had a statistically significant relationship ($R^2 = .77$) with the configuration. This (% *heterosexual women*) indicates that the strategies reported by heterosexual men and women differ in that men are more likely to report using bilateral and direct strategies, whereas women are more likely to report using unilateral and indirect strategies. A similar finding indicates that lesbians and gay men did not differ significantly from each other in the types of strategies they reported using.

To test the idea that homosexuality per se is associated with the use of strategies in intimate relationships that differ from those used by heterosexuals, a **multiple optimal regression** analysis was performed on the proportion of homosexuals (vs. heterosexuals) reporting each strategy. The results were not significant ($R^2 = .46$), meaning that homosexuals did not differ significantly from heterosexuals in the types of strategies they reported using in intimate relationships.

Egalitarianism. Other analyses examined personal preferences concerning power in intimate relationships. Two oppositely worded items concerned the importance to the person of having equal power and of having greater influence than the partner. People who gave great importance to equality of power between intimate partners ($R^2 = .76$) were more likely to report using unilateral strategies; people who deemphasized the importance of equal power were more likely to report using bilateral strategies. In similar fashion, people who gave little importance to having more influence than their partner $(R^2 = .60)$ used such unilateral strategies as laissez-faire and withdrawal, whereas people who preferred having relatively greater personal influence used such bilateral strategies as bargaining, persuasion, and reasoning.

The perceived balance of power was also significantly related to the strategy configuration $(R^2 = .71)$. Individuals who reported having relatively greater power than their partner in their relationship were likely to report using bilateral power strategies.

Other characteristics. Measures of autonomy and independence indicate that people who prefer intimate relationships in which the partners are relatively independent are more likely to report using unilateral strategies; people who deemphasize personal autonomy are more likely to report using bilateral strategies. In addition, the measures of personal satisfaction with the relationship are significantly associated with the use of direct power strategies. Individuals who are satisfied with their relationships are likely to use such direct tactics as asking, whereas less satisfied individuals are likely to use more indirect strategies, such as hinting.

Three variables were considered to determine whether the model derived here could account for the range of participants' ages and relationship durations in the sample, as well as to determine if the model could account equally well for power strategies in an ongoing versus ended relationship. These three variables underwent **multiple regression analysis** yielding the following results: age $R^2 = .42$, duration $R^2 = .44$, and currentness $R^2 = .35$. These results did not reach significance. These findings mean that none of these characteristics significantly differentiated participants in terms of their power strategy use in intimate relationships. This suggests that the initial age and duration differences between sex and sexual orientation groups do not significantly alter the

relationships among sex, sexual orientation, and power strategy use.

Other analyses. To clarify the sex, egalitarianism, and sexual orientation results, five two-way **analyses of variance** were conducted. In these, the two **independent variables** were sex and sexual orientation, and the **dependent variables** were the participants' scores on the variables measuring preferences for and perceptions of having more influence, preferences for having equal influence, satisfaction, and autonomy.

No significant differences were found among the four groups in their satisfaction with their intimate relationships. But differences were found in participants' preferences for personal autonomy and egalitarianism in relationships, and in their perceptions of the actual balance of power in relationships. In general, these results lend credence to the notion that sex differences in power strategy use may reflect sex differences in preferences and perceptions of power.

Specifically, our results indicate that women placed greater value on autonomy than did men, $F(1, 194) = 12.20$, $p < .001$, by showing greater preference for combining an intimate relationship with independent friends and activities. Women showed a greater preference than men did for having equal power in a relationship, $F(1, 194) = 31.78$, $p < .001$, and they deemphasized the importance of having greater power than their partner, $F(1, 194) = 10.20$, $p < .002$. Consistent with this sex difference in power preferences, women were also more likely to report that their relationship had an egalitarian (versus one-sided) balance of power, $F(1, 194) = 3.91$, $p < .05$.

Two significant differences associated with sexual orientation were also found. Heterosexuals scored higher than homosexuals on preference for having relatively greater personal power, $F(1, 194) = 6.14$, $p < .01$, and for perceptions of actually having somewhat greater power than their partner, $F(1, 194) = 8.39$, $p < .004$. Homosexuals and heterosexuals did not differ in the importance given to having equal power in a relationship, nor in their preference for personal autonomy. Finally, no interaction effects were found for sex and sexual orientation in any of the five dependent variables.

Discussion

The study generated a two-dimensional model of power strategies in intimate relationships. According to this model, the two dimensions along which power strategies vary are labeled *directness* and *bilaterality*. The directness dimension includes strategies from "hinting" (indirect) to "asking the target about a desired goal" (direct) and is most strongly associated with satisfaction in the relationship; greater satisfaction is related to the use of direct strategies. The bilaterality dimension runs from strategies such as "persuasion" (bilateral end) to strategies "doing what you want anyway" (unilateral end) and is most strongly related to preferences for personal independence in intimate relationships. A stronger preference for independence is related to the use of unilateral strategies. Further, the two-dimensional model presented here accounts equally well for current and past relationships and for the range of ages and relationship durations represented in this sample.

A major goal of the present study was to identify associations between sex, sexual orientation, egalitarianism, and power strategy use in intimate relationships. Only among heterosexuals did the sex of the participants have a significant impact on the power strategies reportedly used in intimate relationships. Male heterosexuals were more likely to report using bilateral and direct strategies. In contrast, female heterosexuals were more likely to report using unilateral and indirect strategies.

Note further that sex differences among heterosexuals parallel the experts' good/bad ratings. This suggests that strategies used by male heterosexuals would be regarded as better than those used by female heterosexuals. Rather than simply indicating a bias, the experts' good/bad assessment of the strategies is supported by the additional finding that the use of primarily direct, but also bilateral, strategies is associated with greater satisfaction in the relationship.

The sex differences found among heterosexuals do not entirely fit into the results and conclusions of previous research (e.g., Johnson, 1978) that women are more likely than men to use indirect strategies. The finding here that women are also more likely to use unilateral strategies is new and perhaps the results can be best explained in terms of power differences between heterosexual men and women. It is argued here that because men expect compliance to their influence attempts, they use bilateral and direct strategies. Conversely, because women anticipate noncompliance, they are more likely than men to report in their essays the use of unilateral strategies. Unilateral strategies do not require the partner's cooperation. Support for this interpretation comes from the fact that men in this sample were more likely than women to perceive themselves as having greater power than their intimate partner. Thus men perceived themselves to be influencing their partner from a position of relative strength, whereas women perceived themselves to be influencing their partner from a weaker or subordinate position. Note that bilateral and direct strategies are used not only by men but also by people who prefer and perceive themselves as having greater power than their partner.

Homosexuality was not associated with a distinctive pattern of power use in intimate relationships, nor was there an interaction of sex and sexual orientation in strategy use. Counter to the stereotype that homosexuals engage in cross-sex behavior, lesbians did not resemble heterosexual men in power use, nor did gay men show a pattern similar to that of heterosexual women. Overall, lesbians did not differ significantly from gay men in the types of strategies they reported using.

Sex differences play a large role in the use of power strategies in this article, much in the same way they do for resource control and allocations (Sprecher, 1985), they follow traditional sex roles. In this article males use power strategies that are direct and bilateral (stronger) while females use indirect and unilateral strategies (weaker). Although these results conform to what might be predicted from simple adherence to traditional sex roles, it is more interesting to note the lack of any effect of sexual orientation on the use of power strategies. If power strategies (and allocation of resources) are predicated on the reciprocity inherent in each sex adhering to a complementary sex role, why would individuals of the same sex employ the same power strategy? In other words, why would a complementary pattern not develop in same-sex relationships? Additionally, is reciprocity in power-sharing strategies related to relationship satisfaction? Finally, both articles evaluate power strategies in dating couples. Do these power strategies evolve as the romantic couple deepens and lengthens their relationship? And, of course, do the results from the 1980s still hold for couples dating today?

7   Relational Maintenance

In our enthusiasm to explain the initiation and development of relationships, researchers initially overlooked one of the more perplexing aspects of relationships, namely the ways in which they are held together after they start. Obviously relationships do not continually develop, or else sixty-year marriages would be centers of Nirvana that would overwhelm the participants with a surfeit of ecstasy. In fact our common experience is that relationships stabilize at a level of commitment, satisfaction, and depth that is maintained more or less consistently once that level is achieved. Once at that level, feelings for a partner can survive aging, the onset of chronic illness, or loss of sexual function; indeed, these negative events can affect commitment and a sense of loyalty in a *positive* direction.

How, then, are relationships maintained? There are two basic answers to this question. Either relationships stay together unless they are brought to an end; or else relationships fall apart unless they are held together. Some approaches (for example, Exchange-based and Interdependence Theories, see Chapter 6) assume that if the balance of exchange is satisfactorily sustained (that is, if the benefits and costs are about equally matched), then the relationship will continue until Doomsday. We'll call this approach the Inactive Maintenance Approach. Other approaches assume that active maintenance is required and that the relationship will crumble without it. We'll refer to these as Active Preventive Maintenance Approaches. Within the Active Preventive Maintenance Approaches are two basic forms. The issue, as we shall see, is whether such maintenance is conscious and strategic or unconscious and routine. In the former case researchers assume that some form of dedicated strategic activity is required by both parties to water and nourish the relationship. In the latter case, researchers argue that maintenance is systematic but unconscious and that daily routines of behavior themselves maintain the relationship. Although these two positions (strategic versus routine) can be reconciled (e.g., "there is some strategy and some routine enactment involved in maintaining relationships"), we will explore these positions in this chapter, starting with the earliest research – which focused on deliberative strategy – and moving on to more recent work that has emphasized the unconscious and non-deliberate means by which relationships are maintained, and also tests Interdependence Theories against this idea (i.e., the recent work tests the Inactive versus the Active Preventive positions).

One of the first pieces of research to explore relationships was the work of Dindia and Baxter (1987) who examined the strategies of maintenance for relationships. As you read this paper, which is reproduced below, a classic piece of work in the field, you should note the analytic styles and empirical techniques that are used to open up a new area for study. The authors go out and ask real people **open-ended questions** about how they do something and then record and try to make sense of the list of responses, breaking them down into categories and groups, and then looking for underlying structure in those groups and categories. **Open-ended questions** are such questions as "How do you maintain a relationship?", "How did you feel then?","What was going through your mind at that point?". Such questions do not have predetermined answers and are distinct from **closed-ended questions,** with answers such as "Yes", "No", "Five", or "I did". Examples of **closed-ended questions** are "Do you maintain a relationship by giving people gifts?", "Did you feel angry?", "Did you think of calling your mother?". Also the questions were asked in **counterbalanced order:** this means that half of the subjects were asked question A and then question B, whereas the other half was asked in the order B – A. This procedure is intended to balance or control for any effects of the order in which questions are asked.

Exploratory research about a new topic is necessarily a mixture of intelligent guess-work by the researchers and then confirmation of those guesses by statistical means. Obviously the researchers need to confirm that they are reading the data "correctly" and so one big issue in such work is the question of **inter-rater reliability,** a means of establishing the degree of agreement about structure and categories as they appear to different people who look at the data. Keep an eye out for places where it is necessary to verify that reasonable people would "see" the same things in the data. The different readings of the data by different people were assessed and compared by a statistical technique that establishes the extent to which different individual coders agreed about the coding of particular items in the subject participants' open-ended reports. There is rarely 100 percent agreement about such things, especially if there are a lot of data to be coded. The statistical method does the work of establishing how much item-by-item or overall agreement there was between judges. In the case of the paper below, the result was 82 percent agreement, which is well above the degree accepted by most tests of agreement, which are typically set arbitrarily at 70 percent. It is generally agreed that if raters agree 70 percent of the time that some theme is presenting in the data, then the investigators are justified in taking that as a true reading of what the data say.

The study reports the use of **standard values** and **Z-values**. These are solutions to one of the frequent problems in research, namely that values found in a particular study may not in themselves tell us very much. If you score 68 on a midterm, is that good or bad? Standardized scores help us to make comparisons. The raw score of 68 doesn't have much meaning until you know how the score relates to the average ("the Mean"). For example, you need to know whether the score is above or below the mean and how far above or below the mean, but that still doesn't help unless you know the spread of scores from other people. Also if you are trying to compare scores from two different tests, one where you scored 68 and one where you scored 75, you cannot tell if you did better on the test where you scored higher unless you know the range and the mean of both tests. Each test is different, so being 7 points above the mean on one test may be *better* than being 15 points above the mean on another test. It is only when we know how many *standard* units each score is above or below the mean that we can compare the two performances. The computation of standard values allows us to make comparisons of raw scores that come from very different sources and it is done essentially by comparing the distribution of scores on each test to a theoretical "normal" distribution. Then you are able to say that one score was, say, 1.90 standard units above the theoretical normal average while the other was 1.87 units above that average. Hence you can decide which test showed the better performance. A common way to make such comparisons is to calculate *Z*-scores, which range from below the mean to above the mean. A *Z*-score tells how many "standard units" (known as "standard deviations") someone is above or below the mean. Someone scoring the minus number of standard units below the mean (say, −1.4) is exactly as far below the average as is someone who scores the positive number (in this case +1.4) *above* the mean. Someone who is in that position would have done as well or better than only 8 percent (i.e. 100–92) of the students who took the test. Someone who is +1.4 standard deviations above the mean would have done as well as or better than 92 percent (i.e., 100–8) of the students who took the test.

When reading the study also try to consider what it leaves out. In particular reflect on the thousand tiny ways in which relationships are thought of as being continuous. For example, we do not wake up each day and look at our sleeping partner wondering whether we are still in a relationship. The fact that we felt "related" last night is enough to give us confidence that we are still related. Why is that?

Strategies for Maintaining and Repairing Marital Relationships

Kathryn Dindia and Leslie A. Baxter

exchange theory

Relationship maintenance and repair do not happen of their own accord. Some theorists assume that relationships are naturally predisposed to decay in the absence of continuing investment of exchange (e.g. Levinger, 1983). Others (e.g. Altman et al., 1981) argue that relationships are in a constant state of flux that precludes steady state maintenance without concerted relationship effort. The high rate of divorce and premarital couple break-up documents the fact that too few relational partners cope effectively with their relationship maintenance and repair. Because relationship maintenance and repair necessitate proactive relational work by the partners and because many couples appear to lack efficacy in their attempts at maintenance and repair, research needs to examine what it is that partners are doing in their everyday relational management.

The existing maintenance/repair literature can be criticized for its inadequate empirical grounding. Most of the relationship repair literature ignores the actions taken by relationship parties and studies instead a variety of professional intervention techniques and programmes (Duck, 1984a). The domain of work that addresses the strategies available to the relationship parties is quite limited. Although Davis (1973) presented an intriguing menu of strategic actions available to relationship parties seeking preventive or corrective stabilization, he failed to verify his observations empirically. Ayres (1983) attempted empirical documentation, but he developed his pool of strategy items from a limited pilot group consisting of himself and fourteen students and confined his analysis to hypothetical relationship scenarios. Further, Ayres did not include the marital relationship among his hypothetical relationship scenarios. Yet this long-term relationship is probably the most relevant for studying maintenance and repair strategies. The paucity of relevant research leads to the first research question: RQ1: What are the strategies that marital partners use to maintain and repair their relationship?

Although existing research knowledge is limited in the maintenance/repair area, several additional issues relevant to relationship maintenance and repair seem ripe for exploration. First, it seems useful to enquire whether maintenance and repair should be distinguished from one another. Conceptually, repair of a relationship implies that something has gone awry that needs correcting. By contrast, relationship maintenance involves an effort to continue the present relational state without anything necessarily having gone wrong. Because repair and maintenance conceptually involve different relational exigencies, it is reasonable to enquire whether their enactments feature different social strategies by the relationship parties. Existing research and theory shed little insight on this issue. As Duck (1984a: 164) has observed, the relationships literature is characterized by a "confounding single-mindedness". Theorists presume that relationship repair, stabilization, intervention, enhancement, improvement and maintenance compose a unitary rather than a complex set of relational exigencies, each of which may involve unique coping strategies or techniques. Strategies that are employed to stabilize the continuation of a relationship should logically be related to the sources of relational instability to which they are responsive (Ayres, 1983). Whether maintenance and repair are distinguishable at the level of strategy use is the focus of the second research question: RQ2: What are the strategies that marital partners use to maintain versus to repair their relationship?

In contrast to the first two research questions that focus at the descriptive level only, it seems useful to enquire whether the size and type of strategy repertoire is correlated with a variety of variables that seem intuitively relevant to relationship maintenance/repair.

Relationship satisfaction, perhaps the most frequently studied aspect of close relationships, is one of these relevant variables. Among the plethora of variables that researchers have correlated with relationship satisfaction, process phenomena have clearly been under-represented in favour of antecedent psychological and sociological variables (Spanier & Lewis, 1980). Thus, existing work does not provide a definitive indication of how relational partners can maintain satisfying relationships. Although open communication is popularly regarded as necessary for a successful relationship (e.g. Katriel & Philipsen, 1981), research is far from consistent on the effects of open disclosure in relationships (Bochner, 1982). It might be reasonable to expect that the partners with the largest maintenance and repair strategy repertoires would have an increased probability of experiencing satisfying relationships. However, the presence of a strategy repertoire does not assure a partner's ability to select a situationally appropriate strategy nor a partner's ability to enact the strategy once selected. Yet the latter abilities are necessary for satisfaction (Spitzberg & Cupach, 1984a). The third research question explores the possible relationship between satisfaction and the quantity and type of strategies generated by respondents: RQ3: To what extent is relational satisfaction related to reported maintenance and repair strategies?

Participation in a marital enrichment programme is an additional variable that seems intuitively relevant to relationship maintenance and repair. Since the early 1960s, a variety of marital enrichment programmes has gained popularity. Although these programmes differ in their specifics, they share a common goal of helping "healthy" couples realize their potential through improved communication (Markman et al., 1982). Unfortunately, evaluation research on the effects of marital enrichment programmes is problematic. In addition to the methodological flaws that characterize this evaluation work (Markman et al., 1982), research on the long-term effects of couple participation is limited (e.g. Markman et al., 1982). The longitudinal research that does exist focuses for the most part on partner perceptions of the participation instead of more objective indicators of long-term effect (Lester & Doherty, 1983). If couples who have participated in marital enrichment programmes display larger strategy repertoires for maintenance and repair, the long-term benefits of such participation would gain tentative empirical support. On the other hand, programme participants may experience only short-lived effects of their enrichment experience with no internalized changes manifested in larger maintenance and repair strategy repertoires. This discussion is summarized in the study's fourth research question: RQ4: Do maintenance and repair strategies vary as a function of participation in a marital enrichment programme?

It also seems intuitively reasonable that relationship length might relate to maintenance and repair strategy repertoires. The longer a person is married, the more opportunities he or she has had to develop an elaborate repertoire of maintenance and repair strategies. But such opportunity may not be realized. The general drift toward decline in marital quality with increasing years of marriage perhaps suggests that maintenance and repair repertoires atrophy with time. Apart from repertoire size, marriages of different lengths may present unique exigencies to marital partners that are manifested in different maintenance and repair strategies. What maintains a five-year marriage may not be effective in maintaining the twenty-five-year marriage. Length of marriage is addressed in the study's fifth research question: RQ5: Do maintenance and repair strategies vary as a function of length of marriage?

The final variable included in this study is sex. Substantial sex role research suggests that male–female differences are likely to generalize to maintenance and repair. First, because females are socialized more than males to value their relationships, to monitor their relationships more closely (Baxter & Wilmot, 1985) and to display a more pragmatic stance in relationship functioning (Baxter, 1986; Hendrick et al., 1984), they may be more aware than males of the need for proactive relational work and more motivated to invest energy to maintain the relationship. Secondly, because females appear to anchor their relationships in disclosive communication in contrast to the greater activity-orientation characteristic of males (Baxter & Wilmot, 1985), it seems reasonable to expect corresponding differences in the maintenance and repair strategies of males and females. This discussion is summarized in the study's single research hypothesis: H1: The maintenance and repair strategy repertoires of females will be larger, more communication-oriented, and less activity-oriented than the strategy repertoires of males.

Methods

Respondents consisted of 100 marital partners (fifty couples). Specifically, students enrolled in comunication courses were instructed to locate a married couple from their personal network who would be willing to participate in the study. The student handed each couple partner a separate questionnaire and made certain that the partners responded independently of one another. The student then collected both questionnaires from the couple and returned them to the researchers, assuring the respondents of their anonymity.

Descriptive statistics were computed for the sample based on respondent answers to background questions. The mean age of respondents was thirty-eight ($SD = 13.6$). Husbands reported a mean of fifteen years ($SD = 2.4$) of education compared to fourteen years ($SD = 2$) reported by wives. Couples were married a mean of fourteen years ($SD = 13.3$) with a mean of 2.1 children ($SD = 2.9$). The modal income for husbands was more than $25,000, whereas the modal income for wives was less than $5,000. Seventy-six percent of husbands worked outside the home full-time, compared to

42 percent of wives. Thirty percent of wives neither worked outside the home nor went to school. Forty-eight percent of the sample were Catholic and 28 percent were Protestant. Ninety-two percent of the sample were Caucasian.

Respondents completed the Locke–Wallace Marital Adjustment Scale (Locke & Wallace, 1959) as a measure of marital satisfaction (mean score for the sample was 114.0 with $SD = 23.4$). In addition, they answered a series of background questions from which sample demographics, length of marriage, and previous participation in a marital enrichment programme were determined. Last, respondents were presented, in **counter-balanced order**, the following questions to solicit maintenance and repair strategies, respectively:

> We are trying to determine what spouses do when they are trying to maintain their relationship in a healthy state. This usually happens when one or both spouses think that relationship is good the way it is and he and/or she wants to prevent the relationship from going downhill. What do you do, or have you done in the past, when you are trying to keep your relationship from going downhill?

> We are trying to determine what spouses do when they are trying to repair their relationship. This usually happens when one or both spouses think that their relationship is not as good as it used to be, that their relationship has gone downhill, and he and/or she wants to restore the relationship to its previous healthy state. What do you do, or have you done in the past, when you are trying to bring your relationship back to what it was in the past?

Respondents were allowed to list a maximum of ten maintenance strategies and ten repair strategies.

The strategy typology employed in data coding was derived through a combination of deductive and inductive methods. The rich insights of Davis (1973) were used as the deductive basis for the typology development. The strategy types discussed by Davis were supplemented with additional types that the authors inductively derived in re-analysing the 652 strategies that composed the raw data

in a pilot questionnaire study with married couples (Dindia & Emery, 1982). The authors independently read all of the pilot data, deriving additional category types to supplement Davis' list. Then the authors met to discuss their supplementary categories, reaching consensus on the additional categories to be added to Davis' list and how the categories related to one another. The resulting product was a coding typology that consists of 49 coding categories that are clustered into twelve superordinate types (see Table 1 for a summary listing).

The first major category, changing the external environment, is drawn from Davis' (1973) discussion. Consistent with Davis' discussion, the coding typology distinguishes two variations within this superordinate type. Seeking or creating a barren/hostile environment (IA) assumes that the parties will be driven closer when they face adverse external conditions. The creation of a mutual enemy, for example, illustrates this strategy. The reverse logic is true in strategy IB, seeking or creating a fertile/benign environment. The assumption is that a supportive environment, e.g. a romantic candle-lit setting, will be conducive to relational intimacy.

The second major category consists of communication-related strategies (IIA–E) that emerged from the pilot study data and were not addressed by Davis (1973). Five variations of the general communication strategy were identified: (1) general references to communication or a quantitative increase in communication with the partner; (2) references to symbolic contact with the partner, e.g. a ritualistic phone call at noon to enquire "how things are going"; (3) references to general openness and honesty in communication with the partner; (4) references to talk about the day, typically enacted when the parties met after separation during the daytime; and (5) references to shared feelings with the partner, distinctly affective in nature.

The third major category, metacommunication, flows from Davis' analysis and was verified in the pilot data. Three specific

Dindia & Baxter, Table 1   *Frequency of reported strategies*

Strategy type	Maintenance	Repair
I. Changing external environment (0.50)	**1**	**1**
A. Barren/hostile	0	0
B. Fertile/benign	1	1
II. Communication strategies (0.88)	**53**	**30**
A. Talk	36	26
B. Symbolic contact	1	0
C. Openness/honesty	7	3
D. Talk about the day	3	0
E. Share feelings	6	1
III. Metacommunication (0.75)	**21**	**47**
A. Talk about problem	14	39
B. Interim progress reports	5	5
C. Time-out	2	3
IV. Avoid metacommunication (0.71)	**6**	**3**
V. Anti-social strategies (0.67)	**1**	**5**
A. Argument	0	1
B. Ultimatums	0	3
C. Equilibrium tests	0	0
1. Insolence	0	0
2. Sullen	0	0
3. Hypercritical	0	0
4. Obstinate	0	0
D. Extreme tests		
1. Imply relationship has no future	0	0
2. Break contact	1	1
3. Be cold	0	0
4. Refuse self-disclosure	0	0
5. Refuse favors	0	0
6. Threaten exclusiveness/common space/future	0	0
VI. Prosocial strategies (0.84)	**77**	**51**
A. Maintain equilibrium		
1. Nice	11	3
2. Cheerful	4	7
3. Refrain from criticism	8	2
4. Give in	7	14
B. Opposites		
1. Imply relationship has future	1	3
2. Maintain contact	0	0
3. Be warm	34	14
4. Provide favors	12	8
5. Assure exclusiveness	0	0
VII. Ceremonies (0.93)	**58**	**39**
A. Commemorative		
1. Origin celebrations	2	0
2. Reminisce	0	5
B. Ceremonies re. end of relationship	1	0
C. Piacular	2	1
D. Communion/celebration	10	7
E. Reassurance rituals		
1. Expressions of affection	32	13
2. Compliments	5	3
3. Gifts	6	10

(Continued)

Dindia & Baxter, Table 1   (Continued)

Strategy type	Maintenance	Repair
VIII. Anti-rituals/spontaneity (0.96)	**12**	**1**
IX. Togetherness (0.86)	**63**	**26**
A. Time together	23	16
B. Shared activity	24	8
C. Spend time with network	16	2
X. Seeking/allowing autonomy (0.81)	**7**	**5**
XI. Seeking outside help (0.85)	**19**	**10**
A. Seek outside help	8	8
B. Joint use of prayer/religion	7	0
C. Individual use of prayer/religion	4	2
XII. Other and uncodable (0.70)	**50**	**38**

Note: Numbers in parentheses indicate percentage agreement for category.

types of metacommunicative strategies were coded (IIIA–C). The first and most apparent form of metacommunication is "talk about the problem", and/or suggestions for improvement. An interim progress report refers to periodic relationship talks by the partners in which they assess how well they are meeting their explicit and implicit relationship rules. The third metacommunicative strategy, the "time-out", refers to an explicit decision by a party to pause temporarily before discussing the specific relational problem.

The fourth major category also comes from Davis and refers to the absence of metacommunication as the party conspicuously opts to avoid the problem or a potentially volatile issue by keeping quiet and "letting it pass".

The fifth superordinate category of antisocial strategies was drawn from Davis' (1973) discussion. This major category is organized hierarchically with several levels of finer-grained distinctions. Collectively, these strategies are coercive attempts to change the relational partner in some way. The first minor category, arguments and "Talking-to's", is in contrast to the "working-through" tone of the three metacommunicative strategies discussed above. This strategy includes references to verbal and/or physical fights in which blame is cast. The second antisocial strategy includes ultimata and threats that are delivered by the party to his or her marital partner, e.g. threatening to boycott visits to the partner's relatives.

Strategy VC contains a variety of substrategies that collectively are referred to as negative equilibrium tests by Davis (1973). Insolence (rude or impolite behavior), sullenness (e.g. the "silent treatment", pouting, sulkiness), hyper-critical behavior (general nagging or criticism of the other's actions), and obstinacy (stubbornness and refusal to compromise) were grouped as negative equilibrium tests.

The fourth and final subcategory of the antisocial category represents extreme tests of equilibrium that were identified by Davis (1973). These extreme equilibrium tests differ from the previous category in their intensity of stress to the equilibrium or stability of the relationship. Indicating a lack of a future with the partner, as in a threat of divorce or break-up, is the first extreme equilibrium test. Breaking contact with the other party, e.g., moving out for a week or walking out of the house, is a second extreme equilibrium test. Breaking contact is not to be confused with the "time-out" strategy mentioned above in which the party takes a temporary time out before engaging the other in a relationship talk. Breaking contact is also not to be confused with the milder negative actions of insolence or sullenness. Acting cold toward the other, as if he or she is a non-person, is the next extreme equilibrium test. In contrast to the milder actions of insolence and sullenness, acting cold denies the other's personhood and thus constitutes a more extreme challenge to the equilibrium of the relationship. The refusal of self-disclosure implies an explicit refusal to disclose, rather than the mere absence of openness. Similarly, the refusal to engage in favour-doing suggests the explicit refusal to enact a favour rather than the mere absence of volunteered favour-doing. Last, an exclusivity threat involves an action such as flirting with a third party in which the partner hints at disloyalty or infidelity.

Major category VI refers to prosocial strategies which, for the most part, represent the counterparts of strategies described above as antisocial. These strategies were added because of their presence in the pilot data and their natural oppositeness to Davis' equilibrium tests. The first broad prosocial minor category, maintaining equilibrium, mirrors the antisocial negative equilibrium tests discussed above (VC 1–4). Being nice, courteous and polite are the reverse of the antisocial action of insolence. Cheerfulness, pleasantness and friendliness are counter to the antisocial strategy of sullenness. Refraining from criticism and corrective advice contrast with the antisocial strategy of hyper-criticism. Last, actions in which a party gives in, appeases, or compromises through sacrifice, are opposite to the antisocial strategy of obstinacy.

The second subcategory in the superordinate category of prosocial strategies captures the opposites of the extreme tests of equilibrium summarized above (VD 1–6). Indicating a future together, e.g., bringing up the topic of a new home purchase or the desirability of children, mirrors the antisocial strategy of indicating lack of a future. A prosocial strategy that mirrors breaking contact is maintaining contact. Being warm, the counterpart of acting cold, goes beyond the basic politeness or respect one would offer virtually anyone and thus is not to be mistaken with the milder prosocial strategy VI A 1. The "being warm" strategy involves a treatment of the other as an intimate. The opposite of refusing self-disclosure involves increased communication with the other, several variations of which have already been presented in the communication-related major category II.

Favour-doing, e.g., the preparation of a special meal or helping the partner out in a time of need, constitutes the counterpart of refusing favours. Last, verbal and nonverbal assurances of one's exclusivity constitute the opposite of the antisocial strategy of threatening exclusivity presented above.

The seventh major category includes a variety of strategies, all of which share a ceremonial or ritualistic quality (Davis, 1973). Commemorative celebrations, e.g., anniversaries or birthdays, ritualistically honor origins of one kind or another. Reminiscence refers to occasions in which the parties recall past pleasurable times. Ending ceremonies involve a ritualistic assessment of "What would you do if I weren't here?" and make the other more appreciative of the relationship. Another ritual identified by Davis (1973) is the piacular ceremony that expiates guilt, e.g. the ritualistic making-up after an argument. Communion rituals involve a common meal, e.g., dining at a favorite restaurant. Reassurance rituals represent a strategy with several variations. The other can be assured of his or her partner's affection and devotion through expressions of that affection (e.g., nonverbally, a kiss, or verbally, "I love you"), through compliment-giving, or through gift-giving.

The eighth major category was present only in the pilot study data and was not discussed by Davis (1973). It represents the opposite of ceremony and ritual: actions designed to introduce novelty or stimulation into the relationship. Actions such as bringing home a surprise or doing something new and different together illustrate the desire to change the predictable and routine.

The ninth major category was present only in the pilot data and was not discussed by Davis (1973). Togetherness is a general strategy that could take one of three strategic forms. First, spending more time together with little regard as to how that time is spent. Secondly, spending time together enacting specific activities. Thirdly, spending time together by jointly visiting with other social network members.

The tenth major category was also present only in the pilot data and was not discussed by Davis (1973). Individual autonomy is the opposite of togetherness. This strategy refers to spending time alone as a coping strategy. This strategy captures all references to taking or giving "space" or autonomy of action. Such strategies are responsive to the perception that the other party or oneself is being smothered by the relationship. Unlike breaking contact, the intent of such autonomy seeking/granting actions is not to coerce the other party into changing his or her attitudes or actions.

The eleventh major category of strategies clusters all actions that involve seeking outside assistance. These various strategies were derived inductively from the pilot study data. Reference to seeking outside assistance such as professional counselling, advice from a relative, and so forth, comprises substrategy XIA. Substrategy XIB refers to the couple's joint use of their religion as a source of assistance, e.g., conversations with the family minister. Substrategy XIC includes individual uses of religion, e.g., praying for guidance about the relationship.

The twelfth category type captures miscellaneous and uncodable strategies that were reported.

The authors independently coded all the strategies generated on respondent questionnaires using the 49-category typology. Overall percentage agreement in coding decisions into the eleven major categories (the basis for data analysis) was 82 percent.

The percentage agreement for each of the eleven major categories is indicated in Table 1. All coding discrepancies were resolved through joint review and discussion by the authors. Reliability was deemed adequate for all the categories except changing the external environment and antisocial strategies which were subsequently dropped from the data analysis.

The effect of the independent variables on number of strategies was examined through the use of **analysis of covariance ANCOVA** with **repeated measures** (sex and enrichment programme participation were the between-subjects factors and maintenance/ repair was the within-subjects factor). The SPSS-X and BMDP analysis of **covariance**

with **repeated measures** programmes do not allow two covariates in the same analysis. Consequently, two separate analyses were conducted, one for marital satisfaction and the other for length of marriage as the covariates.

Hierarchical log-linear logit models were fitted to the data to test the effect of the **independent variables** on types of strategies reported. The categorical variables were maintenance/repair, sex, and enrichment programme participation. The covariates were marital satisfaction and length of marriage. Although the coding scheme identifies 49 subcategories of maintenance/repair strategies, these substrategies were combined into their superordinate types for the log-linear analysis. Two superordinate categories, changing the external environment and antisocial strategies, were not included in the data analysis because of their infrequent occurrence and low reliability.

Results

Table 1 provides a summary of the frequencies with which the 658 reported strategies were distributed across the superordinate strategy types and across substrategies within a given superordinate type. The hierarchical model fitting procedure provides a test of the **best fitting model** to the data. The results of this procedure indicated that the best fitting model for the data was strategy, strategy by maintenance/repair and strategy by enrichment programme participation ($L^2 = 44.93$, $p = .475$; $\chi^2 = 40.25$, $p = .673$, $df = 50$; power of χ^2 for this sample greater than .995 for a medium effect size). A complete set of results for all possible tested logit models is available from the first author [*sic*]. The **main effect** of strategy in the best fitting logit model indicates that the strategy categories are not equiprobable. The **standardized values** for the parameter estimates of the strategy types were examined to specify the nature of this main effect. *z* **values** having absolute values greater than 1.96 indicated deviation of the strategy from the overall effect at the .05 level. Only one superordinate strategy type, prosocial strategies, was reported more frequently than expected ($z = 3.14$). By contrast, five superordinate strategy types occurred less frequently than expected: avoid metacommunication ($z = 5.04$); seeking/allowing autonomy ($z = 5.13$); anti-ritual/spontaneity strategies ($z = 4.23$); and seeking outside help ($z = 3.17$).

The results of the **log-linear analysis** indicated that the effect of maintenance/repair on type of strategy was significant. The standardized values for the **parameter estimates** for the effect of maintenance/repair on strategy type were examined to specify the nature of the effect. Metacommunication occurred more frequently when the goal was repairing the relationship than when the goal was maintaining the relationship ($z = -3.20$). Anti-ritual/spontaneity strategies occurred more frequently when the goal was maintaining the relationship than when the goal was repairing the relationship ($z = 2.13$).

The results of the **analysis of covariance** indicated a significant **main effect** for maintenance versus repair ($F(1,95) = 7.81$; $p = .01$). The mean number of maintenance strategies was 3.67 compared with a mean of 2.64 repair strategies.

The results indicated no relationship between maintenance/repair strategies and marital satisfaction. The analysis of covariance with repeated measures indicated that the effect of marital satisfaction on the number of strategies was not significant ($F(1,95) = .85$). The results of the log-linear analysis indicated that the effect of marital satisfaction on strategy type also was not significant given that satisfaction did not emerge in the best-fitting logit model.

The results with regard to previous participation in a marital enrichment programme were mixed. The analysis of covariance with repeated measures indicated that previous participation in a marital enrichment programme had no effect on the number of strategies ($F(1,95) = 1.05$). As indicated above, the results of the best-fitting model indicated

that attending a marital enrichment programme had a significant effect on strategy type. The standardized values for the parameter estimates for the interaction of enrichment programme participation and strategy type were examined. Spouses who had been involved in a marital enrichment programme sometime during the course of their marriage reported more strategies in which they sought help outside the marriage ($z = 3.74$). There was a nonsignificant tendency ($z = 1.92$) for couples who had attended a marital enrichment programme to report that they sought and allowed autonomy more than spouses who had not attended such a programme.

The results concerning length of marriage were mixed, as well. The analysis of covariance with repeated measures revealed a significant main effect of length of marriage on the number of strategies ($F(1,95) = 10.24$; $p = .01$). The negative regression coefficient ($-.05046$) indicates that the longer the spouse is married, the fewer strategies he or she listed to maintain/repair the marriage. The best fitting log-linear logit model indicated that length of relationship did not have a significant effect on types of strategies reported.

Neither the analysis of covariance on number of strategies ($F(1,95) = 2.15$) nor the log-linear analysis on type of strategy indicated a significant effect for sex. Because strategy type was analysed as a ten-category variable, it is possible that the effect of sex on overall strategy type would not be significant but the effect of sex on a particular strategy category might be significant. Specifically this may be true for communication-related and activity-oriented strategies if H1 is valid. The log-linear model for the main effect of strategy and the interaction of sex and strategy type is the appropriate model to test the effect of sex on specific strategy types. The standardized values for the parameter estimates for the interaction of sex and strategy type were examined, indicating that the only superordinate strategy in which males and females differed at the .05 level was seeking outside help ($z = -2.35$). Females were more likely to seek external assistance. No significant differences were found for general communication strategies ($z = -.46$), metacommunication ($z = -.57$), and avoidance of metacommunication ($z = .97$). Similarly, no difference emerged for the activity-oriented strategy type of togetherness ($z = -.30$).

Discussion

The results of this study support Davis' (1973) claim that relationship partners have a rich repertoire of strategies available to them in maintaining and repairing their relationships. However, the results of this study support an extension of the types of strategies discussed in previous research. In particular, our respondents reported using several general communication strategies, various types of prosocial strategies, strategies of anti-ritualizing and spontaneity, togetherness strategies, autonomy seeking/granting strategies, and seeking outside assistance, none of which was reported by Davis (1973) or Ayres (1983).

Not all strategy types were equally likely to be reported. The greater-than-chance reporting of prosocial strategies and the less-than-chance reporting of metacommunication avoidance and antisocial strategies may be a social desirability artifact of the self-report questionnaire. However, social desirability is less reasonable as an explanation for why autonomy enhancement, anti-ritualizing, outside assistance, and changing the external environment strategies were reported less frequently than chance would predict. Marital partners appear not to avail themselves of the full range of potential maintenance/ repair strategies, relying instead on a relatively narrow band of strategies that are either communication-oriented (the general communication strategies, metacommunication, prosocial "warmness" and ceremonial expressions of affection) or activity-oriented (the togetherness strategies). The use of communication-oriented strategies confirms

the folk belief in talk as an "elixir" in relationships (Katriel & Philipsen, 1981). Despite the claim by some theorists (e.g., Hays, 1985) that relationships that become close shift from quantity of interaction to quality indicators, the togetherness strategies suggest that a minimum threshold of time together is perceived as necessary in relationships. However, the absence of a significant relationship between strategy choice and satisfaction suggests that belief in communication and togetherness may be a cultural folk myth, not actuality.

Only limited support was found for distinguishing maintenance from repair. Marital partners did report more strategies to maintain their relationship than to repair it. Further, anti-ritualizing was more salient and metacommunication was less salient when the goal was relationship maintenance as opposed to relationship repair. However, in general, there was substantial overlap in maintenance and repair strategies. The implications of this redundancy need further research. It may be that marital partners have an insufficiently developed repertoire of strategies available to them for repairing their relationship and by default simply call up their maintenance strategies. Alternatively, the exigencies of repair and maintenance may share enough in common to warrant the use of the same strategies. The latter analysis gains credence in the finding that relationship satisfaction was unrelated to strategy choice for maintenance and repair.

Previous participation in a marital enrichment programme did not affect the number of strategies reported, although a difference was found for the types of strategies that were reported with participants in a marital enrichment programme seeking outside help more than non-participants. This finding may be a method artifact, however, because this superordinate category included participating in a marital enrichment programme as one form of outside assistance. Existing evaluation research (Giblin et al., 1985) suggests a general decline in the effects of marital enrichment programmes over time.

Therefore, the absence of a real difference between the enrichment programme participants and non-participants is not too surprising. Nonetheless, the absence of a difference raises the question of how effective marital enrichment programmes are in the long-run.

Length of relationship appears to relate negatively to the number of strategies reported. Partners married for longer periods of time rely on fewer maintenance and repair strategies. However, no systematic differences emerged in the types of strategies employed by partners from marriages of different duration. To the extent that a smaller strategy repertoire signals non-responsiveness, it may imply marital stress at some future point. Alternatively, the partners from longer marriages may actually use as many strategies as their counterparts from shorter marriages and may simply fail to report all of their repertoire because the strategies have become so habituated that they are no longer salient. The latter alternative gains credence in the absence of an association between satisfaction and number of strategies reported.

The hypothesized sex differences in number and type of maintenance/repair strategies failed to gain support in the study. The sexes may employ the same basic repertoire of strategies but differ instead on the frequency with which they employ each strategy type. Alternatively, males and females may *perceive* themselves as equivalent in their strategic work but actually differ in their behavior.

We should briefly acknowledge some limitations of this study as a guide for future work. Self-report data need to be offset with data collection procedures that are closer to the actual processes of maintenance/repair, e.g. diary records or observational data of role-playing or actual interaction. The sample used in this study disproportionately represented couples who are white, middle-class, religiously affiliated, and whose marriages are relatively long-lived. A broader demographic sample would be desirable. Subsequent work should also compare the maintenance/repair strategies of married couples, divorced couples and premarital couples. The marital enrichment participation variable needs to be approached in more complex ways. Approximately fifteen different types of programmes currently exist (Giblin et al., 1985) and the effects of each type of enrichment programme need to be examined separately. Last, our organization of the forty-nine strategies into fewer superordinate types needs verification among marital partners themselves.

The maintenance/repair area is rich with possibilities, all of which need investigation to complete our understanding of relationship functioning to include not just initiation and termination processes but maintenance and repair. Parties in long-term relationships devote substantial time to maintenance/repair work, yet researchers' knowledge of the relative use and effectiveness of different strategies is presently limited and in need of expansion.

From this groundbreaking study we learn that couples do report active strategies to maintain and repair relationships. The strategies themselves overlap, but there is a difference between maintenance and repair, with more strategies used in maintenance than in repair. The number of strategies was negatively correlated with length of relationship, meaning that there are fewer strategies used by people who have longer relationships. The study therefore establishes some key facts about maintenance but leaves open a number of questions about its enactment in real life. Is it a phase in the development of all relationships or is it a behavior that occurs daily in most satisfactory relationships? Does the existence of strategies of maintenance suggest that strategies are all there is? Or can relationships be maintained by means other than calculated and conscious efforts? What about the fact that relational partners spend a great deal of time apart without imagining that because their partner is, say, at work, the relationship is in trouble? Surely, we have some sense of the continuity of relationships (i.e., relationship maintenance) that is independent of specific strategic activity.

Sigman (1991) suggested that there are processes that bridge those gaps. This proposal is an antidote to the views that suggest that relationships are dependent on active behavior and derive most of their existence from face-to-face interaction. Gilbertson et al. (1998), below, tested that idea. Note the ways in which the decade between this and the Dindia and Baxter (1987) study casts up changes in the basic themes of the research current at the time. In particular it is important to attend to the authors' claims that maintenance of relationships can be done by routine means instead of only strategically. The paper introduces a sophisticated way of looking at **RCCUs (Relational Continuity Constructional Units)** and divides them into **prospective units** (those activities or statements that imply that there is a future to the relationship), **introspective units** (those items that recall the relationship to partners without actual co-presence physically; that is to say that the two partners do not have to be in one another's company at the time the thoughts about them occur, but the thoughts themselves sustain the relationship), and **retrospective units**, which derive from shared history or stories, photographs of the relationship in progress, and other physical or narrative evidence that the relationship has a past. As you read this article below, think about the ways in which the data were gathered, and how this opened up the possibility of studying not only strategies but also routine maintenance.

The study further reports a **factor analysis** which was described in Chapter 4.

Like Dindia and Baxter, the Gilbertson study uses a measure of **inter-rater agreement**. The study also reports "**Reliability**" in terms of "alpha = .94". What this means is that the scores on the relevant scales (Norton's QMI) were consistent with each other 94 percent of the time. That is to say, 94 percent of the time a reporter said the same sort of thing on each question of the measure, which can therefore be taken as a good indication that the measure assesses what it claims to assess, namely in this case the quality of their marriage. The paper also uses **multiple regression** and **t-tests,** which we have previously described.

Relational Continuity Constructional Units and the Maintenance of Relationships

Jill Gilbertson, Kathryn Dindia and Mike Allen

While research on the relational maintenance stage of social and personal relationships has grown in the past decade, relationship maintenance remains largely understudied. Indeed, Duck (1994a) calls relationship maintenance the 'vast unstudied void in relational research' (p. 45). The relationship maintenance phase of relationships constitutes, in large part, the majority of the time spent in relationships; generally long-term relationship partners spend more time maintaining their relationship than they spend initiating or terminating it (Duck, 1988). In addition, relational maintenance is a difficult stage of relationships. The high turnover of relationships, especially the high divorce rate, attests to the difficulty involved in maintaining satisfying and lasting relationships. Therefore, research that contributes to the understanding of relational maintenance is theoretically and practically important.

Existing research on relational maintenance focuses primarily on typologies of relational maintenance strategies (e.g., Dindia & Baxter, 1987; Stafford & Canary, 1991). In addition to these typologies, which largely focus on strategic maintenance behaviors, some researchers (Bruess & Pearson, 1995; Dainton, 1995; Dainton & Stafford, 1993) have turned their attention to routine maintenance behaviors. Dainton & Stafford (1993) differentiate the two by defining strategic behavior as conscious and intentional behavior enacted by partners to maintain the relationship, whereas routine maintenance behavior occurs at a lower level of consciousness and is not intentionally used to maintain the relationship. Duck (1988) argued for the need to look at routine behaviors, stating, "there are many other instances where the little things of life keep us together" (p. 99). For example, people probably do not think of asking a partner how his or her day went or telling their partner how their day went as strategies to "maintain" their relationship. However, these acts may nonetheless function to maintain the relationship.

Dainton (1995) compared couples' use of strategic and routine maintenance behaviors. Dainton developed a typology of interaction types based on a daily interaction log completed by subjects. The typology included seven categories of interaction: instrumental, leisure, mealtime, affection, conversations, conflict and network. Dainton had subjects rate how much thought each interaction required and how typical it was for the relationship. Dainton then combined these scores to come up with an index of routineness. Dainton discovered that the majority of interactions that couples engage in is routine, rather than strategic. The category of affection was rated by subjects to be the most routine and the most important to the relationship.

Similar to routine maintenance, behaviors are the rituals that function to maintain relationships. Bruess & Pearson (1995) focused on the types and uses of interpersonal rituals in marriages. They developed a typology of seven ritual types: Couple Time Rituals, Idiosyncratic/Symbolic Rituals, Daily Routines and Tasks, Intimacy Expressions, Communication Rituals, Spiritual Rituals and Patterns/Habits/Mannerisms. Bruess & Pearson (1995) studied the functions of these rituals. They found that marital rituals, such as communication rituals and performing everyday tasks together, served to bond and maintain the relationship. Overall, it is clear that couples engage in both strategic and routine behaviors that function to maintain the relationship.

A major distinction between the present study on relational maintenance behaviors and previous research on relational maintenance behaviors is that the present study is guided by Sigman's (1991) theoretical perspective on relational maintenance, whereas, previous research on relational maintenance behaviors is atheoretical (see Dindia, 1994; Dindia & Canary, 1993). Sigman noted that relationships are more than discrete moments of face-to-face interaction. As stated by Sigman (1991), "relationships are 'larger' than the physical presence or interactional accessibility of the participants" (p. 108). Thus, according to Sigman, relationships are continuous despite discontinuous periods of physical and interactional co-presence. Couples manage the discontinuous aspects of social relationships by using **Relational Continuity Constructional Units (RCCUs)**. RCCUs are behaviors that relational partners engage in before, during, or after an absence that function to construct the continuity of the relationship during periods of absence.

RCCUs are divided by Sigman into three types: (i) prospective units, (ii) introspective units, and (iii) retrospective units. **Prospective units** are those behaviors that relationship partners perform before physical separation. Prospective units "define the meaning and duration of the impending separation and of the likely return" (Sigman, 1991, p. 112). Behaviors in this category include farewells, agenda establishments (projections of future interactions) such as "I'll see you at the office tomorrow morning", and the use of "tokens" and "spoors". The offering of a token, such as a wedding or engagement ring, symbolizes the continuity of the relationship. Spoors are objects left behind (such as a toothbrush in one's lover's bathroom), which indicate the previous physical presence of a person. Tokens and spoors provide a sense of continuity and of likelihood of return (Sigman, 1991).

Introspective units occur during times of relational non-co-presence. Introspective units constitute the relationship's continuity during periods of absence. The wearing of wedding bands is an example of an introspective unit. Affiliative artifacts, such as team jackets, wedding bands and photographs of the relationship partner all signal the existence of the relationship even though the partner is not present. Another type of an introspective unit is the mediated contact between relationship partners. Greeting cards, notes, phone calls and electronic mail messages allow the partners to remain connected even when face-to-face interaction is not possible.

Retrospective units occur after the period of relational non-co-presence has ended. Greetings and conversations that allow the partners to "catch-up" on what happened to each other during the period of absence are examples of retrospective units. Vangelisti & Banski (1993) note that "by discussing the experiences they had while they were separated during the day, relational partners may

be engaging in an activity that defines their togetherness" (p. 150). In other words, debriefing conversations serve to maintain the continuity of relationships. Vangelisti & Banski found that the amount of time relationship partners reported spending in debriefing conversations was positively related to relational satisfaction.

There is considerable overlap between Sigman's concept of RCCUs and the relational maintenance behaviors discussed by other researchers. Sigman defines RCCUs as behaviors that function to construct the continuity of relationships (i.e., maintain relationships). However, Sigman does not explicitly define RCCUs as either strategic or routine maintenance behaviors. We would argue that RCCUs may be strategic or routine maintenance behaviors. Couples may routinely (without thinking about maintaining the relationship or intending to maintain the relationship) kiss each other goodbye or say "I love you" and this behavior may function to maintain the relationship. Alternatively, an individual may kiss his/her partner goodbye or say "I love you" as a conscious and intentional strategy to maintain the relationship. In reality, the difference between strategic and routine maintenance behaviors may not be dichotomous. Some relational maintenance behaviors may start out as strategic but become routine over time. Some behaviors may be strategic for some partners/couples and routine for others, or be perceived as strategic by some partners/couples but not by others. Finally, strategic/routine may not be characteristic of maintenance behaviors but of their uses on particular occasions. RCCUs may be produced routinely but they may also be used in a strategic manner on occasion.

Previous research indicates that there is a negative relationship between the amount of time partners spend apart and marital satisfaction (Kilbourne et al., 1990: e.g., Kingston & Nock, 1987; White, 1983); the more time couples spend apart, the more dissatisfied they are with their relationship. Similarly, the more time couples spend together (relational co-presence), the more satisfied they are with their relationship. Thus, the following hypothesis was tested: **H1**: There is a positive relationship between relational co-presence (or time spent together) and marital satisfaction.

But all couples have to spend some time apart and some more than others. Sigman's theory is important because it provides an understanding of why time apart negatively impacts relationships (because it disrupts the continuity of relationships) and how relationships can be maintained despite periods of absence (with behaviors that construct the continuity of the relationship before, during and after periods of absence). Specifically, Sigman (1991) suggests that it is necessary for relational partners to maintain the continuity of their relationship through periods of non-co-presence with RCCUs. Thus, we hypothesized that couples' enactment of RCCUs allows them to maintain relational satisfaction, and, in particular, that couples' enactment of RCCUs allows them to maintain relational satisfaction regardless of how much time they spend apart. Thus, the following hypotheses were tested: **H2**: there is a positive relationship between RCCUs and relational satisfaction; and **H3**: there is a positive relationship between RCCUs and relational satisfaction when the level of co-presence is held constant.

Method

Questionnaires were distributed to 108 married and cohabiting couples. Sixty-six couples returned their questionnaires, resulting in a return rate of 61 percent. Of those questionnaires returned, 10 were deemed unsuitable for use because they were incomplete or the partners failed to follow the instructions for reporting amount of time spent together. **Convenience sampling** was used to recruit participants in this study. Participants (a student and his or her partner) were recruited from undergraduate communication courses in a large, public, urban Midwestern university. To measure the types and frequencies of RCCUs, a list of RCCUs was generated using Sigman's (1991) discussion of RCCUs as a guideline. Questions regarding RCCUs were divided into three sections that corresponded to Sigman's categories of prospective, introspective and retrospective units. Prospective units included items performed before the absence such as "Tell your partner what you will be doing during the time you are apart" and "Kiss your partner good-bye". Introspective units included items performed during the absence such as "Telephone them while you are apart", "Leave notes for them", and "Display pictures of your partner". Retrospective units included items performed after the absence such as "Greet your partner" and "Discuss how your day went". Additional RCCUs were added based on the results of a pilot study involving 50 undergraduate students who were currently involved in a romantic relationship. Respondents in the pilot study completed a preliminary version of the RCCU questionnaire used here. Specifically, they responded to the list of RCCUs generated from Sigman's essay and an open-ended question asking them to list any other behaviors they performed to sustain their relationship before, during, or after an absence, and to report the percentage of time they performed this behavior before, during, or after an absence. The primary researcher coded the open-ended responses using an inductive coding procedure. Based on this analysis, several additional RCCUs, such as, "leaving messages on the answering machine for each other", were added to the list of RCCUs used in the main study.

To measure the frequency of RCCUs, participants were asked to report the percentage of time they performed this behavior before, during, or after an absence. This was clarified by informing participants, that if, for example, they perform the RCCU every time they are apart, they should put 100 percent, if they perform the RCCU about half of the time they are apart, they should put 50 percent, if they never perform this RCCU, they should put 0 percent. Participants were informed that they should list the percentage they felt most accurately described how frequently they performed the RCCU before, during, or after an absence. Respondents estimated a percentage on their own (from 0–100 for each RCCU), i.e. they were not provided with a series of percentages (e.g., 0–20, 21–40, 41–60), and asked to select the one that most closely approximated their behavior. There was no time frame given for this question; that is, participants were asked to list the percentage of time they perform this behavior before, during, or after an absence in general, as opposed to a given day or week. Table 1 lists all the RCCUs.

Following the list of RCCUs was an open-ended question asking subjects to list any other behaviors they performed to sustain their relationship before, during, or after an absence, and to report the percentage of time they performed this behavior before, during, or after an absence. The primary researcher and an undergraduate communication major coded the open-ended responses using an inductive coding procedure. To create the coding categories, the primary researcher examined 25 percent of the returned questionnaires to determine if there were patterns in the responses to the open-ended questions. Based on this examination, a list of additional categories was created. The undergraduate communication student was then trained in the use of this coding scheme. The primary researcher and the undergraduate student then coded all the responses independently. Afterwards, any disagreements in coding were resolved by discussion.

Overall intercoder reliability for these open-ended responses was 83 percent agreement. Two prospective units were coded: eating together ($n = 9$), and engaging in sexual activity ($n = 12$). Two introspective units were coded: thinking/daydreaming about partner ($n = 7$), and performing tasks to show love/concern for partner ($n = 6$). Six retrospective units were coded: eating together ($n = 15$), engaging in sexual activity ($n = 12$), doing chores/household tasks

together ($n = 12$), talking with each other ($n = 17$), cuddling ($n = 6$), and relaxing together ($n = 10$). The category of talk was deemed qualitatively different from discussing how your day went. Respondents seemed to indicate that they had more in-depth conversations that were different from debriefing conversations, or "discussing how their day went". The category of relaxing together included responses such as "hang out together", and "watch TV together". Because of the small number of participants listing these RCCUs and the resulting lack of variability for these items, they were not included in any of the analyses reported in this paper. However, they will be discussed at the end of this paper under issues for future research.

In this study a stylized time journal was used to help subjects accurately record the amount of time they spent with their partner. This journal consisted of a timetable with days of the week listed in columns and times of the day (e.g., 8:00–9:00, 9:00–10:00, 10:00–11:00) listed in rows. For each day and time slot on the table, subjects listed what they were doing; subjects were instructed to choose from a list of seven activities to fill out the timetable. The activities they chose from were: "work" (which included commuting time), "school" (which included commuting time), "study", "sleep", "meeting", which was used to designate regularly scheduled (daily or weekly) activities done outside of the home and without the relationship partner, "special" which was used to designate activities not happening on a daily or weekly schedule, but which were done outside the home without the relationship partner, and "partner", which was used to designate time spent with their relationship partner. Subjects were instructed to leave the space blank for any time periods when they were doing an activity that did not fit into the preceding categories. To improve the accuracy of the table, instructions were added telling the subjects to draw a horizontal line through a slot in the table to indicate if an activity began or ended on the half-hour. The number of hours of partner time the subjects reported during the week served as the operational definition of co-presence. A follow-up question completed at the end of the week asked respondents to indicate how typical the week was on a scale from 1 to 5 with 1 being "very atypical" and 5 being "very typical" to ascertain whether the amount of time spent together during the week of the study was similar to the amount of time the couple typically spends together per week. Participants were also asked their level of satisfaction with the amount of time spent with their partner. Participants completed Norton's Quality Marriage Index (QMI) (Norton, 1983) to measure the amount of relational satisfaction.

Results

Reliability of Norton's QMI was alpha = .94. Agreement between partners' reports of co-presence was $r(56) = .85$. Because partners' reports of co-presence were highly reliable, a couple co-presence score was calculated using the mean of partners' scores. Partners reported spending an average of 31.21 hours a week together (11.41 SD) with a range from 6 to 56.5 hours. The mean rating of typicality for the amount of relational co-presence for the week the log was completed was 3.55 (with a standard deviation of .948). Therefore, it is reasonable to assert that the amount of time spent together during the week of the study is generalizable to the amount of time the couples typically spend together.

Subjects reported using a wide variety of RCCUs. Table 1 reports the mean percentage of time before, during, or after an absence that subjects reported using each RCCU. Overall, subjects reported using prospective and retrospective units a majority of the time. Retrospective units, in particular, were used for a large percentage of the time: subjects reported using all of these RCCUs at

least 80 percent of the time following an absence. There was more variability in the percentage of time subjects reported using the various introspective units during an absence.

Participants' responses to the **closed-ended questions** eliciting RCCUs were factor analyzed using confirmatory factor analysis. The **confirmatory factor analysis** (CFA) was conducted using theorems developed by Hunter (1980) and was consistent with the process described by Levine and McCroskey (1990). A successful CFA analysis requires that: (i) each factor generates sufficient reliability, (ii) each item **loads** highest on the relevant **factor**, (iii) each factor possesses internal consistency, and (iv) the items demonstrate parallelism in the inter-factor correlation matrix. Reliability is calculated using **Cronbach's alpha** for each factor. The test of internal consistency is a χ^2 test that compares the expected correlations generated by multiplying the factor loadings of the same factor to the actual correlation generated by the data. Theoretically, the comparison should generate a non-significant χ^2 if the model fits. The test for parallelism generates a χ^2 test comparison of the actual correlation matrix to an expected matrix as well. The expected correlation is the triple product of the actual correlations of each item on its own factor multiplied by the correlation between the factors.

The results of the CFA confirmed a three-factor solution corresponding to the three types of RCCUs, with all the prospective units loading on the first factor, which was labeled prospective units, all the introspective units loading on the second factor, which was labeled introspective units, and three of the four retrospective units loading on the third factor, which was labeled retrospective units. Items loading on the third factor, retrospective units, included things done immediately upon being reunited after an absence (e.g., "greet your partner", "say hello", "kiss/hug partner your partner hello", "ask how their day went") and could be represented as greetings. The item "discuss

Gilbertson et al., Table 1   Enactment of RCCUs

Prospective units	Average percentage of the time RCCU is enacted before, during, or after an absence (+ SD)
Tell your partner what you will be doing during the time you are apart	84.34 (21.21)
Tell your partner when you expect to return home	87.79 (21.06)
Tell your partner good-bye	94.19 (13.09)
Kiss your partner good-bye	83.71 (25.22)
Tell your partner you love them	74.70 (30.78)
Make plans to do something with your partner once you are back together	59.95 (28.79)
Attempt to spend time together before you have to be apart	67.20 (29.32)
Introspective units	
Telephone them when you are apart	59.60 (32.59)
Leave a message for them on the answering machine	36.50 (37.09)
E-mail them when you are apart	3.28 (14.90)
Leave notes for them	32.69 (28.87)
Wear something which reminds you of your partner, for example, jewelry or clothing	32.36 (40.75)
Bring you partner's name into the conversation when you are talking to others	55.05 (29.92)
Buy your partner flowers	11.59 (20.64)
Buy your partner a gift	23.52 (27.00)
Do something nice for your partner while they're gone	49.64 (29.08)
Meet them for lunch	23.75 (29.08)
Display pictures of your partner	39.23 (43.22)
Retrospective units	
Greet your partner (say hi)	95.35 (17.43)
Kiss and/or hug your partner hello	83.88 (28.52)
Ask how their day went	85.23 (23.23)
Discuss how your day went	80.19 (25.87)

Note: Total N = 112.

how your day went" did not load on this factor and may represent a separate type of retrospective unit that doesn't necessarily occur immediately upon reuniting (i.e. is not a greeting behavior). However, because it was one item, its reliability could not be assessed and it was dropped from further analysis.

The reliabilities for each factor were acceptable: prospective units ($\alpha = .86$), introspective units ($\alpha = .80$), retrospective units ($\alpha = .91$). Internal consistency was met by each of the factors (prospective units, $\chi^2 = 17.78$, *d.f.* = 20, *p* < .05; introspective units, $\chi^2 = 29.74$, *d.f.* = 54, *p* < .05; retrospective units, $\chi^2 = .03$, *d.f.* = 2, *p* < .05). This indicates that the internal structure of the correlations between items of the same factor is consistent with the hypothesized structure. Parallelism was demonstrated by the inter-factor correlation matrix ($\chi^2 = 155.11$, *d.f.* = 130, *p* < .05).

Hypothesis 1 proposed that relational co-presence (or time spent together) is positively related to relational satisfaction. Co-presence was operationally defined as the number of hours during the week of "partner" time (i.e. co-presence) that the partners reported. Correlations were conducted between the amount of co-presence and female and male partner satisfaction. The relationship between co-presence and satisfaction was significant for women ($r(56) = .41$, *p* < .05) and men ($r(56) = .30$, *p* < .05). Thus, similar to past research, the more time spent together the greater the satisfaction for women and men. Similarly, the more time spent apart (relational non-co-presence) the lower the satisfaction for women and men.

Hypothesis 2 proposed that there is a positive relationship between RCCUs and relational satisfaction. **Correlations** were run between the percentage of time before, during, or after an absence that relational partners enact prospective, introspective and retrospective RCCUs and female and male relational satisfaction. The percentage of time before/during/after an absence that women report enacting RCCUs was correlated with female relational satisfaction. This was true of the prospective, introspective and retrospective units ($r(56) = .60$, .29, .53, respectively, $p < .05$). Significant correlations were found between female prospective and retrospective units and male relational satisfaction ($r(56) = .35$, .32, respectively, $p < .05$). The percentage of time that men enacted RCCUs before/during/after an absence was not significantly correlated with male or female satisfaction. Thus, in general, women's use of RCCUs was related to both female and male relational satisfaction, whereas, men's use of RCCUs was not related to female or male relational satisfaction.

Hypothesis 3 proposed that there is a positive relationship between RCCUs and relational satisfaction when co-presence is held constant. Two multiple regressions with male and female satisfaction as the dependent variables, and co-presence and male and female prospective, introspective and retrospective RCCUs as the independent variables, were run. The results of the **stepwise multiple regression** indicated that the best equation predicting female relational satisfaction is the equation with female and male prospective RCCUs and co-presence ($R = .69$, $F = 15.52$, $p < .01$). The partial correlation coefficients indicate that female prospective RCCUs (partial $r = .60$, $F = 29.35$, $p < .01$), male prospective RCCUs (partial $r = .32$, $F = 5.89$, $p < .05$) and co-presence (partial $r = .29$, $F = 4.63$, $p < .05$) are significant predictors of female relational satisfaction when the linear effects of the other independent variables have been removed from both the independent variable and relational satisfaction. Thus, female and male prospective RCCUs are positively related to female relational satisfaction when co-presence is held constant.

The results of the multiple regression equation with co-presence, and male and female prospective, introspective and retrospective RCCUs as the **independent variables**, and male relational satisfaction as the **dependent variable**, indicate that male relational satisfaction is best predicted by the equation including female prospective RCCUs ($R = .35$, $F = 7.58$, $p < .01$). The only significant predictor of male relational satisfaction, when the linear effects of the other independent variables have been removed from both the independent variable and relational satisfaction, is female prospective RCCUs. Thus, female prospective RCCUs are positively related to male relational satisfaction when co-presence is held constant.

Discussion

The results of this study provide support for Sigman's (1991) theoretical perspective on the continuity construction of relationships. Study participants reported using a variety of RCCUs before, during and after an absence. Generally, prospective and retrospective units were used a larger percentage of the time than introspective units. This may be explained by the nature of introspective units. Whereas prospective and retrospective units are generally activities that anyone can do on a regular basis with very little effort (e.g. tell your partner you love them, tell them what you are going to do that day, greet them when they come home, ask what they did that day) several of the introspective units may be more difficult or even impossible for some couples to accomplish regularly. For example, many people may not have access to the technology needed to email their partner, telephone them, or even to leave a message for them on an answering machine. Another introspective unit, meeting the partner for lunch, may not be possible for some couples because of scheduling issues. An additional explanation is that some of the introspective units, such as buying flowers or gifts for your partner, may be thought of as special, rather than routine behaviors, and therefore not enacted regularly.

Hypothesis 1 predicted that there is a positive relationship between relational co-presence and relational satisfaction: the more time couples are together, the more satisfied they are with their relationship. As predicted, there was a positive relationship between the amount of time spent together and both female and male relational satisfaction. Another way to state this is that the more time couples spent apart, the less satisfied they were with their relationship.

Hypothesis 2 predicted that there is a positive relationship between RCCUs and relational satisfaction. The results of the study were that female prospective, introspective, and retrospective RCCUs were positively related to female relational satisfaction. Female prospective and retrospective RCCUs also were correlated with male relational satisfaction. Thus, when women use more RCCUs both they and their partner are more satisfied with their relationship. Men's RCCUs were not correlated with female or male relational satisfaction.

Hypothesis 3 predicted that RCCUs are positively related to relational satisfaction when the effect of co-presence is held constant. Specifically, we tested whether the partial correlations between the various types of RCCUs and relational satisfaction were significant. Multiple regressions were computed using co-presence and prospective, introspective and retrospective RCCUs as the independent variables, and male and female relational satisfaction as the dependent variables. The best fitting equation of female relational satisfaction was the equation with female and male prospective, units and co-presence as the independent variables. Thus, female and male prospective RCCUs and co-presence predict female relational satisfaction. The partial correlation coefficients indicated that female and male prospective RCCUs are significant predictors of female relational satisfaction when the effect of co-presence is held constant. The best fitting equation of male relational satisfaction was the equation with female prospective RCCUs as the independent variable.

Thus, it appears that for women, what they and their male partners do to construct the continuity of their relationship before an absence (saying good-bye, kissing your partner good-bye, telling your partner you love him/her, telling your partner when you will be home, etc.) affects relational satisfaction. For men, what their female partners do to construct the continuity of the relationship before an absence, affects relational satisfaction. Thus, it appears that prospective RCCUs, in particular, female prospective RCCUs, construct the continuity of a relationship during periods of absence.

It has been argued that women are expected to be "relationship specialists" (Wood, 1997) and that both men and women tend to assume that women are responsible for maintaining relationships and are better at it than men. While we were not initially interested in nor did we hypothesize sex differences in RCCUs, as a follow-up test of the "relationship specialist" hypothesis we conducted a post hoc analysis of whether women perform more RCCUs than men. The results of three **paired t-tests** between male and female partners' prospective, introspective and retrospective RCCUs were all non-significant ($t = -1.41$, -1.44 and $-.97$, respectively). These results indicate that women do not perform more RCCUs than men. However, the results of the tests of Hypotheses 2 and 3 indicate that what women do to construct the continuity of their relationship has more of an impact on both women's and men's relational satisfaction than men's RCCUs. Thus, the results of this study provide mixed support for the 'relationship specialist' hypothesis.

As previously stated, only the **partial correlations** between female and male prospective RCCUs and relational satisfaction were significant. The partial correlations between female and male introspective and retrospective RCCUs and male and female relational satisfaction were not significant. It may be that what a couple does before an absence simply matters more to relational satisfaction than what is done during or after an absence. Alternatively, there may be a rival hypothesis for why introspective and retrospective RCCUs were not related to relational satisfaction.

Regarding introspective RCCUs, it makes sense that an individual's use of some of the introspective RCCUs would not be related to her/his partner's relational satisfaction, because they are behaviors the partner may not be aware of. For example, an individual is unlikely to be aware that their partner is displaying their picture during an absence, or bringing their name up in conversations with others. Therefore, these introspective units would not be expected to play a part in the partner's satisfaction, but should play a role in self-satisfaction. However, a majority of introspective units are behaviors that the partner would be aware of (e.g., phoning and leaving notes for partner, meeting for lunch) and therefore should predict partner satisfaction. Although female introspective RCCUs were correlated with female satisfaction, this correlation disappeared when the effect of co-presence and other types of RCCUs were held constant.

With regard to retrospective RCCUs, it should be noted that retrospective RCCUs consisted entirely of greeting behaviors ("greet your partner, say hello", "kiss/hug your partner", "ask how their day went"). The **variance** shared between prospective, introspective and retrospective units was high, which indicates that individuals who perform one type of RCCU are also likely to perform the other types of RCCUs. Thus, individuals who said good-bye to their spouse before an absence are probably the same spouses who greeted their spouse after an absence and the variance accounted for by greetings (retrospective RCCUs) may be subsumed by the variance accounted for by good-byes (prospective RCCUs).

One issue that needs to be considered for future research is how to operationally define co-presence/non-co-presence. Sigman defines non-co-presence as times when the partners are "not available for face-to-face interaction" (p. 110). In this study, we defined co-presence as the number of hours individuals spent with their partner not including sleep time. We realize that one could argue that if partners are sleeping in the same bed or room, they are available for face-to-face interaction. Similarly, there may

be times when couples are technically together but unavailable for face-to-face interaction. An example of this is if one partner has an office at home and instructs the other partner not to interrupt him/her when she/he is working. Determining the amount of time a couple spends together is a complicated issue.

Another issue is the **operational definition** of RCCUs. Based on Sigman (1991) and the results of a pilot study, a list of prospective, introspective and retrospective units was created for this study. In addition, participants were asked to list any additional activities they did before, during, or after an absence to maintain the continuity of their relationship. Several additional RCCUs were generated from this procedure but could not be included in the analyses because of the small number of people who listed these behaviors and the resulting **lack of variability.** However, these behaviors may constitute important types of RCCUs that should be included in future research measuring RCCUs. It is impossible to determine from the results of this study if these additional types of RCCUs were mentioned by only a few of the study participants because they were employed only by these study participants or because there was no cue to remind participants of this behavior (as in the closed-ended questions). If these behaviors had been included in the checklist of RCCUs, we do not know whether more partners would have listed these RCCUs. Thus, future studies should use an expanded list of RCCUs, which includes those units generated by participants' responses to the open-ended questions in this study. Including these items in a checklist of RCCUs may prompt more subjects to report whether or not they use these units.

There is a second reason to include an expanded list of RCCUs in future research. The list of RCCUs used in this study was submitted to **confirmatory factor analysis** to determine whether there were three types of RCCUs as suggested by Sigman: **prospective, introspective** and **retrospective RCCUs.** The item "discuss how your day went", did not load on the retrospective RCCUs factor (which was composed of greetings behaviors, e.g., saying hello, kissing and hugging your partner, and asking how their day went) and was consequently dropped from the study. Debriefing conversations may represent a separate type of retrospective RCCU than greeting behaviors. Catching up on the events that occurred during an absence may be an important RCCU for the continuity of a relationship after periods of absence. Vangelisti & Banski (1993) found that the length of debriefing conversations was correlated with relational satisfaction. Thus, items measuring debriefing conversations should be included in future studies of RCCUs. Indeed, future research might profitably include some of the additional retrospective RCCUs generated from the open-ended questions used in this study, such as spending time and doing things together after an absence (eating, sex, doing household chores together, cuddling, etc.) and talking together after an absence (more than just talking about what happened during the absence). Perhaps these items would load with items measuring "catching up" as a separate dimension of retrospective RCCUs.

The results of this study offer partial support for Sigman's (1991) theory on the continuity construction of social relationships. Couples reported enacting RCCUs before, during and after an absence. RCCUs seem to play a role in constructing the continuity of a relationship across periods of absence. The use of prospective RCCUs (e.g., saying good-bye to your partner before you leave) predicted relational satisfaction when co-presence was statistically controlled. In particular, female and male prospective units predicted female relational satisfaction and female prospective RCCUs predicted male relational satisfaction when the amount of time spent together was held constant. However, it is not clear from the results of this study whether RCCUs cause relational satisfaction or vice versa. Nonetheless, it is clear that when the variance accounted for by co-presence is held constant, prospective RCCUs are positively related to relational satisfaction.

This research also has implications for relational maintenance theory, and research in general. This study supports the call for increased attention to routine maintenance behaviors. Many of the RCCUs, especially prospective and retrospective RCCUs, would seem to be routine behaviors. Greetings, good-byes, and so on, may not be enacted with the explicit goal of maintaining the relationship; however, these behaviors are related to relational satisfaction. Therefore, relational maintenance researchers should consider including these types of routine maintenance behaviors in their typologies of relational maintenance behaviors.

Note that the study concludes with several ideas for future research, suggesting that the definition of RCCUs still requires greater certainty and that the *factors* that show up in this study require more substantiation in the future. This means that the underlying principles proposed for this research appear to be observable as predicted, but it would be a good idea for other researchers to confirm that they are observable in other circumstances and with other subject populations than the ones used by the authors here.

The research that we have considered so far focuses on the strategic ways in which relationships are maintained, but the previous paper (Gilbertson et al.) has introduced the idea that relationships can be sustained by means of activities that are not conscious. The latter idea is one of the important developments of research on maintenance, which has recently taken up the notion that relationships can be maintained merely by the routine everyday behaviors that occur almost unnoticed in any relationship. Dainton (2000) has been a leader in this line of research, arguing that relationships are maintained by much that is just not noticed in everyday life.

As you read the next article, by Dainton, try to imagine the ways in which your own relationships might be routinely sustained. In particular note the comparison of Interdependence Theory assumptions (Inactive Maintenance) about relationships as compared to non-strategic or uncalculated ways in which maintenance occurs (Active Preventive Maintenance). Bear in mind that an assumption of Interdependence or Exchange Theories is based, loosely, on the claim that people calculate profits and losses in and from their interactions. Note also the theoretical approach that the author adopts in order to test exchange and interdependence theories as predictors of relationship maintenance. How does this economic model comport with your own personal experience of relationships? Is it realistic or does it seem overly mechanistic and based on capitalist principles that reduce relationships to shopping transactions? Interdependence Theory is one of the major theories in the social psychology of Human Relationships. How does it match up when tested against the realities of everyday life? Note that the paper starts out with a strategic approach (compare Dindia and Baxter, 1987, the one we started with here), but ends up showing that interdependence theory does not adequately explain all the ways in which relationships are maintained.

The study uses **Likert scales**. For a reminder on these refer to Chapter 3. Note also that, like Gilbertson et al., this paper uses measures of reliability to establish the degree to which different people agree about certain things measured in the study. Dainton focuses not on the frequency of use of maintenance behaviors but on their relevance to relationship satisfaction and this marks an important move in such research. Dainton also uses a **Bonferroni correction** for interpreting probability levels. This is one technique for adjusting significance levels when multiple tests are being run on the same data; the running of multiple tests increases the chance of getting "significant" results by pure chance and so cautious researchers lower the level of significance in order to correct for that risk of misinterpreting significance. The Bonferroni method is one technique for doing this.

Maintenance Behaviors, Expectations for Maintenance, and Satisfaction: Linking Comparison Levels to Relational Maintenance Strategies

Marianne Dainton

Social exchange theory has emerged as one of the primary explanatory mechanisms for the process of relational maintenance (Canary & Zelley, 2000). Two specific research programs have utilized social exchange concepts to study maintenance: Canary and Stafford (e.g., 1992) used equity theory, and Rusbult created the investment model (e.g.,

Rusbult, Drigotas, & Verette, 1994), which is grounded in interdependence theory. Both equity and interdependence theories suggest that the partner's use of maintenance strategies serves as a reward to individuals in relationships, and the theories would predict that the extent to which one's expectations for maintenance activities are fulfilled affects one's own relational satisfaction.

Interdependence theory contends that relational outcomes are dependent upon the rewards and costs that relational partners experience (Thibaut & Kelley, 1959). The theory suggests that outcomes are evaluated relative to expectations that individuals hold out for what they feel they deserve. These expectations are called the **comparison level (CL)**. Relational satisfaction, then, is calculated by the discrepancy between what an individual actually experiences and what he or she expects to experience. If outcomes meet or exceed the CL, the individual is satisfied; if outcomes fall below the CL, the individual is dissatisfied.

Interdependence theory further suggests that satisfaction alone cannot account for relational stability. Thibaut and Kelley (1959) argued that, in addition to satisfaction, relational stability can be determined through consideration of alternatives to the relationship (the **comparison level for alternatives, or CL_{alt}**). That is, if outcomes meet or exceed alternatives, the relationship will be stable. However, if outcomes fall below perceived alternatives to the relationship, the relationship will likely be unstable.

A fruitful avenue for speculation is that Stafford and Canary's (1991) maintenance strategies might serve as rewards to relational partners; as such, interdependence theory would predict that meeting or exceeding one's expectations for maintenance behaviors (CL) would increase satisfaction with the relationship. The assumption that relational maintenance behaviors are rewarding is not new. Canary and Stafford (1992) argued that maintenance behaviors serve as both outcomes and inputs in equity calculations – in short, maintenance behaviors engaged in by

the partner are rewards, but maintenance behaviors engaged in by the individual are costs. As further support, Guerrero, Eloy, and Wabnik (1993) determined that the maintenance behaviors developed by Stafford and Canary (1991) function as rewards in moving relationships from the stages of escalation, stability, and de-escalation. Accordingly, it makes sense to suggest that perceptions of the partner's use of maintenance behaviors are rewarding. The next section articulates more clearly the nature of relational maintenance behaviors.

Relational maintenance refers to behaviors enacted by relational partners to keep their relationship in a specified state or condition (Dindia & Canary, 1993). In an effort to identify those behaviors that function as relational maintenance, Stafford and Canary (1991) asked individuals in relationships what they did to maintain a satisfactory relationship. Factor analyzing the responses, they uncovered five maintenance techniques: positivity (behaving in a cheerful and optimistic manner), openness (self-disclosure and direct discussion of the relationship), assurances (messages stressing commitment to the partner and relationship), social networks (relying upon common friends and affiliations), and sharing tasks (equal responsibility for accomplishing tasks that face the couple).

All of the previous research focused on perceived use of maintenance activities rather than maintenance activities relative to expectations. If indeed relational maintenance behaviors function as rewards, then interdependence theory would predict that the more one's expectations for the partner's use of maintenance behaviors are met or exceeded, the greater one's satisfaction with the relationship.

[Eds: In the original paper, the author reports a preliminary study, Study 1, which we have edited out. The study assessed the perceived fulfillment expectations for the use of relational maintenance behaviors by one's partner and one's own relational satisfaction and looked at the individual's relational satisfaction as differentially predicted by the expectancy fulfillment of the partner's

use of the five maintenance behaviors. Results supported the hypothesis that there is a linear, positive relationship between perceived fulfillment of expectations for the use of relational maintenance behaviors by one's partner and one's own relational satisfaction. There was a positive, linear relationship between the extent to which an individual's expectations for his or her partner's use of maintenance behaviors were met and his or her own relational satisfaction. Moreover, expectancy fulfillment for the partner's use of maintenance behaviors accounted for a moderate amount of the variance in satisfaction.] ...

Previous research supports the notion that maintenance behaviors are rewarding to relational partners (e.g., Guerrero et al., 1993), but this does not mean that individuals actually hold expectations for their partner's use of such behavior. Furthermore, it does not clarify the nature of those expectations – it may be that individuals hold stronger expectations for certain maintenance behaviors than for others. Finally, it does not address the relationship between expectations and perceptions of maintenance behavior. Accordingly, in Study 2, the following research questions were tested:

RQ1: What are individuals' expectations for their partner's use of relational maintenance activities?

RQ2: To what extent are there differences in expectations for the partner's use of various maintenance activities?

RQ3: What is the relationship between people's expectations for their partner's use of maintenance behavior and perceptions of the frequency of that behavior?

Moreover, the results from Study 1 indicated that 38 % of the **variance** in relational satisfaction could be explained by expectancy fulfillment of two behaviors: assurances and positivity. Although these results indicate that expectancy fulfillment does predict a moderate amount of the variance in relational satisfaction, previous research utilizing frequency measures of maintenance activities alone has explained up to 56% of the variance in satisfaction (Dainton et al., 1994; Stafford & Canary, 1991). This raises the question of the relationship between people's expectations for, and, perceptions of, the frequency of their partner's use of maintenance behavior. More to the point, the question remains: Which matters more in maintaining a relationship, sheer frequency of particular behaviors or frequency relative to expectations, as interdependence theory would predict?

Counter to the claims of interdependence theory, for example, previous research has determined that outcomes alone might be better predictors of relational satisfaction than outcomes relative to expectations. Sternberg and Barnes (1985) found that actual feelings of love were superior to comparison levels of love in predicting satisfaction. Similarly, and more closely related to the present endeavor, Morrow and O'Sullivan (1998) found that absolute levels of romantic behaviors accounted for 60% of the variance in satisfaction, with CL discrepancies adding only an additional 6% to the variance. Michaels et al. (1984) found that outcomes alone were a stronger predictor of satisfaction than were outcomes relative to expectations, (in)equality, or (in)equity. Finally, Ruvolo and Veroff (1997) found that CL discrepancies for desired personality characteristics in the spouse did not predict satisfaction for husbands, although actual ratings of personality did. However, these authors found that CL discrepancies did predict satisfaction for wives. Combined, these studies suggest that interdependence theory explanations of satisfaction might not be as strong as competing explanations. Thus, the following research question is posed:

RQ4: What are the relative contributions of perception of partners' use of maintenance behaviors and maintenance expectancy fulfillment in predicting satisfaction?

Finally, interdependence theory suggests that reward values as well as expectations change over time (Rusbult, Onizuka, &

Lipkus, 1993; Thibaut & Kelley, 1959). In particular, Thibaut and Kelley (1959) argue that newly-weds might hold unrealistic expectations for marriage. Combined, these theoretical propositions suggest that individuals in relationships of longer duration might be more likely to meet (rather than experience outcomes lower than or exceeding) expectations, because (a) expectations have likely been modified due to experience (Murray, Holmes, & Griffin, 1996), and/or (b) relationships in which expectations are not met are more likely to be terminated (Rusbult et al., 1993). In contrast, Sabatelli and Cecil-Pigo (1985) found no significant correlation between marital length and MCLI scores (a measurement of comparison level). However, in that study, the MCLI was scored using a traditional Likert scale, wherein 1 = *outcomes much below expectations*, 4 = *meeting expectations*, and 7 = *outcomes much above expectations*. Accordingly, it is not surprising that a linear relationship between the MCLI and relational duration was not found, because, as argued earlier, relationships of longer duration are more likely to meet expectations rather than exceed them. Accordingly, using interdependence theory, the first hypothesis is offered:

H: The longer the relationship, the more likely an individual will report meeting (rather than exceeding or falling below) expectations.

Study 2: Method

Respondents included 283 individuals recruited by students in an undergraduate communication research class at a private, urban university in the Northeast US. As part of a class research project, each student was asked to distribute questionnaires to 12 individuals currently in a romantic relationship. Respondents were assured of complete confidentiality. Attached to the questionnaire was an envelope; after filling out the questionnaire, respondents sealed it

in the envelope and either returned it to the student (who gave the sealed envelope to the instructor) or mailed it directly to the course instructor. A 90.7% return rate was achieved.

Instrumentation. Because both expectations and perceived enactment of maintenance behaviors were of interest, respondents were asked to complete Stafford and Canary's (1991) measure of relational maintenance twice. The first time, respondents were instructed:

Everyone has slightly different expectations for relationships. The next set of questions is concerned with your expectations for what relationships should be like, regardless of what your current relationship is actually like. Think about your expectations, and indicate the extent to which you agree with the following statements.

Statements described the partner's use of each maintenance activity (e.g., "I expect my partner to ask how my day has gone"), and respondents were given a standard Likert scale wherein 1 = *strongly disagree* and 7 = *strongly agree*. Reliabilities, means, and standard deviations were as follows: expectations for positivity alpha = .85 ($M = 5.71$, $SD = .77$); expectations for openness alpha = .83 ($M = 5.84$, $SD = .87$); expectations for assurances alpha = .74 ($M = 6.05$, $SD = .86$); expectations for networks alpha = .79 ($M = 4.99$, $SD = 1.29$); and expectations for sharing tasks alpha = .75 ($M = 6.12$, $SD = .95$).

After completing this section, respondents were instructed:

Relationships often do not always meet all our expectations, even when they are happy. In the next section, please indicate the extent to which your partner has actually performed these behaviors in the last two weeks. Please do not report on things he or she once did but hasn't done lately – report only on what he or she has done recently.

Again, a standard Likert scale was used. Reliabilities, means, and standard deviations were as follows: positivity alpha = .88 ($M = 5.48$, $SD = .99$); openness alpha = .88 ($M = 5.07$, $SD = 1.44$); assurances alpha = .84 ($M = 5.86$, $SD = 1.32$); network alpha = .87 ($M = 5.12$, $SD = 1.74$); and sharing tasks alpha = .88 ($M = 5.47$, $SD = 1.46$).

In this study, expectancy fulfillment was **operationalized** by creating discrepancy scores. Specifically, an individual's report of the partner's use of maintenance behaviors was subtracted from his or her level of expectations for those behaviors. In keeping with the original/description of the Comparison Level articulated by Thibaut and Kelley (1959), signed discrepancy scores were used rather than absolute values, as it was presumed that outcomes could be less than, meet, or exceed expectations. Reliabilities, means, and standard deviations for discrepancies were as follows: discrepancy for assurances alpha = .75 ($M = -.21$, $SD = 1.45$); discrepancy for networks alpha = .77 ($M = .13$, $SD = 1.88$); discrepancy for openness alpha = .81 ($M = -.78$, $SD = 1.47$); discrepancy for positivity alpha = .83 ($M = -.24$, $SD = 1.11$); and discrepancy for tasks alpha = .78 ($M = -.65$, $SD = 1.58$).

Finally, satisfaction was … measured by Norton's (1983) Quality Marital Index (QMI). Alpha reliability for the scale was .96 ($M = 35.32$, $SD = 8.22$).

Results

The first two research questions asked about individuals' expectations for their partner's use of relational maintenance activities and the extent to which there might be variations in expectations for different maintenance activities. Results indicate that individuals expected all five maintenance activities to be performed by their partner, with mean scores ranging from 4.99 for networks to 6.12 for sharing tasks. In order to determine if there were significant differences in the expectations for these behaviors, a series of **paired *t*-tests** was performed. Using a **Bonferroni approach** to correct for multiple comparisons, p was set at .005. The partner's use of networks was expected less than all other maintenance activities, and the partner's use of tasks and assurances was expected more than other maintenance activities.

The third research question asked about the relationship between people's expectations for, and perceptions of, the frequency of their partner's use of maintenance behaviors. Two-tailed **Pearson correlations** indicated only small to moderate relationships between the two variables. The largest relationships were .27 between one's expectations for the partner's use of openness and the perception of his or her use of openness, and .26 between one's expectations for the partner's use of networks and his or her perceived use of networks.

The fourth research question sought to determine the relative contributions of the perception of the partner's use of maintenance behaviors and the discrepancy between expectations and perceived behavior in predicting satisfaction. Following Sternberg and Barnes' (1985) method, two **hierarchical regression equations** were computed. For the first equation, the discrepancy scores for the maintenance behaviors were entered as a block in the first step, and they accounted for 42% of the variance. In the second step, the actual maintenance scores were entered as a block. The actual maintenance behaviors accounted for an additional 21% of the variance. The order of entry was reversed in the second equation, and in this equation the actual behaviors contributed 61% of the variance, and the discrepancies added only 2% to the variance. Thus, both actual maintenance behaviors and discrepancies between expected and actual behaviors are important in predicting satisfaction. However, the actual behaviors contributed more to the discrepancies (.21) than the discrepancies added to the actual behaviors (.02). Moreover, the top two predictors according to standardized regression coefficients were the actual use of assurances ($P = .80$) and the actual use of openness ($\beta = -.31$), providing evidence that actual behaviors are relatively more important in predicting satisfaction than are discrepancies between actual and expected behaviors.

Finally, the hypothesis predicted that the longer the relationship, the more likely an individual will report meeting (rather than exceeding or falling below) expectations. In this case, the **absolute value** [i.e., the value without the plus or minus sign] of the discrepancy was used rather than the signed value, so that a score of zero reflected meeting expectations, and increasing scores reflected a greater deviation from expectations (whether above or below). Accordingly, a negative correlation would be expected. One-tailed Pearson correlations were calculated, and the hypothesis was not supported. Specifically, there was no significant correlation between relational length and the absolute discrepancy in assurances, networks, or tasks. There were two significant, positive correlations between relational length and the absolute discrepancies of openness ($r = .19$, $p < .01$) and positivity ($r = .13$, $p < .01$), indicating the opposite of the hypothesis – the longer an individual was in a relationship, the greater his or her discrepancy between what was expected and what he or she perceived as actually occurring.

To probe why the results did not support the hypothesis, separate correlations were calculated between relational length and (a) expectations for maintenance behaviors, (b) partners' perceived use of maintenance behaviors, and (c) signed discrepancies for maintenance behaviors. Specifically, results indicate that, in general, expectations stay the same over time – there was only one significant correlation, between relational length and expectations for the use of networks. However, perceived use of openness ($r = -.24$) and positivity ($r = -.14$) decreased with relational length, creating negative discrepancies between expectations and outcomes. The correlation between relational length and perceived actual use of tasks was positive (.17). Accordingly, it seems that rewards (partner's use of maintenance behaviors) stay the same or decrease over time, but expectations stay relatively the same.

General discussion

The goal of these studies was to use interdependence theory to understand relational maintenance. The results provide limited support for an interdependence theory explanation of maintenance. Significant findings and salient implications are highlighted, as well as limitations and areas of future research.

The first significant result was that, although expectancy fulfillment for the partner's use of maintenance behavior was positively associated with relational satisfaction, as interdependence theory would predict, and the extent to which one's expectations for assurances and positivity were exceeded accounted for a moderate amount of the variance in satisfaction, expectancy fulfillment was not as potent in predicting satisfaction as was the sheer frequency of use of maintenance behaviors. These results, combined with a host of other studies that have found that *outcomes alone* are stronger than *outcomes relative to comparison levels* in predicting satisfaction, shed doubt on the relative usefulness of the comparison level construct in predicting satisfaction (see Michaels et al., 1984; Morrow & O'Sullivan, 1998; Rusbult, Johnson, & Morrow, 1986; Ruvolo & Veroff, 1997; Sternberg & Barnes, 1985). Note that this does not discount the notion of expectations altogether; there is a large amount of research suggesting a link between outcomes relative to expectations and satisfaction. What is suggested here is that future research should include measures of outcomes in addition to measures of expectancy fulfillment when studying relational satisfaction.

A second significant result of these studies is also inconsistent with interdependence theory. Specifically, interdependence theory suggests that what is considered rewarding varies over time, and that expectations themselves change over time. Expectations are specifically proposed to change as a function of experience. The results reported in Study 2 regarding the links between relational length and expectations for maintenance suggest this might not be the case, at least not in terms of maintenance behavior. There was only one significant correlation between the two variables; individuals in relationships of longer duration were slightly more likely to expect their partner to use social networks in maintaining their relationship. Conceptually, this makes sense. It is likely that the networks of partners in long-term relationships are larger and more overlapping.

Although this slight increase in expectations for the use of networks makes sense, the lack of significant results as a whole indicates that expectations for maintenance behaviors do not change over time. Perhaps this is because respondents answered the question using ideals, which might not change as much as realistic expectations. Moreover, it looks as though there is little variation in expectations for maintenance ... At least when it comes to maintenance behavior, expectations seem consistent and stable.

Despite the fact that expectations do not seem to change as a whole, there is stronger evidence that perceptions of the partner's use of maintenance activities (i.e., rewards) might change over time. Specifically, there were three significant correlations between relational length and perceptions of the use of maintenance behavior: perceptions of the use of openness and positivity decreased with relational length, while perceptions of the use of tasks increased with relational length. To explain these findings, it may simply be that, over time, relationships require more "work," and that familiarity breeds more negative (rather than positive) interaction styles (Stafford & Dainton, 1994).

The implications of the results of these studies for interdependence theory should not entirely overshadow the implications of these studies for our understanding of relational maintenance. For example, the results of Study 2 indicate significant differences in expectations for relational maintenance activities, with expectations for the partner's use of sharing tasks and assurances being significantly higher than those for other maintenance activities. Interestingly, in Study 2, the perceived use of assurances was also the strongest predictor of satisfaction, which makes sense given individuals'

heightened expectations for this activity. Furthermore, in Study 1, which considered performance relative to expectations, assurances was also the strongest predictor. These results, together with the results from previous research (e.g., Dainton et al., 1994; Stafford & Canary, 1991), indicate that assurances are likely the most potent means for maintaining satisfactory relationships. Surprisingly, the use of tasks (which was the single most expected behavior) did not enter the equation for satisfaction. Accordingly, it may be that performing tasks is so strongly expected that using this strategy might not be a reward in and of itself, but that failure to perform tasks might be perceived as a cost.

Continuing with a discussion of the regression results in Study 2, openness was a **negative predictor** of relational satisfaction. This too is consistent with previous research (Dainton et al., 1994; Stafford & Canary, 1991). Stafford and Canary suggested that this may be because once the variance due to partner's positive and assuring disclosures is removed, remaining disclosures may be negative in nature. An alternative explanation is that the results may be due to the nature of the sample; perhaps the sample was disproportionately traditional or separate (Fitzpatrick, 1988) in their beliefs about communication, i.e., groups that do not value self-disclosure. For example, Kelley (1999) found that partners in different couple types hold different expectations for relational communication. If openness is not valued, it makes sense that neither the perceived use of openness nor meeting one's expectations for openness will be important for one's relational satisfaction. Indeed, Weigel and Ballard-Reisch (1999) found that the frequency of the use of openness in traditional couples was not associated with the partners' marital satisfaction. In contrast, it may be that, contrary to popular belief, self-disclosure simply is not important to maintaining a satisfactory relationship.

Finally, results indicated that expectations for maintenance behaviors and perceptions of the partner's use of such behaviors were only slightly to moderately related to each other. Correlations ranged from .16 between expectations for assurances and the perceived use of assurances to .27 for expectations of openness and perceived use of openness. These results are significant for several reasons. First, counter to Rusbult et al.'s (1986) argument that it is difficult for respondents to separate outcomes from their expectations, the results of this study indicate that the respondents were indeed able to differentiate between the two. Second, it indicates that the respondents may not be idealizing regarding their partner's use of maintenance behaviors, because respondents did not respond the same way for expectations and perceptions. Furthermore, the means for all but one of the discrepancy calculations were negatively signed, indicating that perceptions of actual behavior were lower than expectations for that behavior. Thus, despite Murray et al.'s (1996) finding that individuals' conceptions of their ideal partners tended to change in response to the qualities of their actual partners, the results of this study indicate that perceptions and expectations for the use of maintenance behaviors are distinct, with expectations remaining higher than perceptions of the behavior.

There were several limitations to the research reported. First, by using Stafford and Canary's (1991) typology of proactive/ constructive maintenance strategies, maintenance strategies that might not be as positively construed have been overlooked. It

may be that expectations for potentially negative maintenance behaviors vary more than expectations for proactive/constructive behaviors, making discrepancies more powerful in predicting satisfaction. Relatedly, by operationalizing the comparison level as perceptions of the partner's use of maintenance behavior relative to expectations for that behavior, in essence only rewards were considered to be outcomes rather than rewards minus costs, as Thibaut and Kelley (1959) proposed. Still, this operationalization is consistent with previous research (Morrow & O'Sullivan, 1998; Rusbult et al., 1993; Sternberg & Barnes, 1985). Finally, as noted earlier, the cross-sectional nature of the present studies precludes being able to determine if indeed expectations for and perceptions of maintenance strategies change over time.

The results ... suggest that Stafford and Canary's maintenance strategies can be used in operationalizing the comparison level; individuals in romantic relationships do hold expectations for their partner's use of maintenance behaviors; and the more an individual had his or her expectations for the partner's use of maintenance behaviors fulfilled, the more relational satisfaction was reported. However, outcomes alone (i.e., perceptions of the partner's use of maintenance behaviors) were stronger predictors of satisfaction than were outcomes relative to expectations, casting doubt on interdependence theory predictions.

This paper shows that Interdependence Theory does not work in important respects when it comes to explaining relationship maintenance. It also asserts that the underlying unnoticed daily patterns of behaviors in relationships are as powerful a glue for maintaining relationships as are other forms of strategy and technique. In effect it indicates that the conscious effort to maintain relationships is at best equal to, if not less important than, the unconscious sorts of activity that keep relationships going. Note that having found non-confirmatory results initially, Dainton conducted follow-up analysis to test the ideas further and test possible explanations for the non-significant results. Note also that Dainton's research was programmatic, that is to say that the researcher conducted one study (which we abridged) and then went on to conduct another related study on the basis of the results of the information gathered from the first one. The studies were directed towards the same goals but took different forms.

In addition to all these points, the paper raises a number of questions about future directions for the research that suggest that there is a prosaic and unnoticed element contributing to relational maintenance, namely the everyday behaviors that serve to sustain and enact the relationship beyond any conscious strategies that have previously been the object of research.

As you proceed with your relationships, consider carefully the extent to which they are maintained by conscious intervention and the extent to which they "just continue" by means of everyday conversations and activities that simply keep them in place.

8   Jealousy

Jealousy, typically seen as part of the dark side of personal relationships (Spitzberg & Cupach, 1998), may appear at virtually any stage of a relationship. The impact that jealousy has on each member of a partnership and on the quality of their relationship dictates the importance of this emotion in any discussion of relationships. As an emotion, there is both a physiological component as well as a cognitive component (Schachter & Singer, 1962) – i.e., there is an underlying physical change (such as a rush of adrenalin) and a cognitive interpretation of its meaning ("I feel jealous" or "I feel angry"). Perhaps this dual nature of jealousy has contributed to the debate over the underlying cause of jealousy. Is it a learned (cognitive) phenomenon as Social Learning Theory would predict, or an ever-present reproductive adaptation (physiological) as modern versions of evolutionary theory suggest (Buss, 1999)? In this chapter you will read two articles, each grounded in a different theoretical orientation. Buunk, Angleitner, Oubaid, and Buss (1996) take a decidedly pro-evolution stance in the interpretation of their data, while White's (1980) explanations suggest a social learning orientation. As you read these articles you may consider the strengths of each argument and how the neglected approach might be beneficial in the context of the data being explained. For example, rather than completely excluding one or the other explanation, perhaps Schachter's suggestion that emotion does not occur until the inputs from cognitive as well as physiological factors are integrated by the person could serve as a unifying position (Buunk may get closest to this ideal with the idea of an environmental "trigger").

Another issue to consider while reading the articles is how the authors define jealousy. Do they differentiate between jealous "thoughts" and "behaviors" that suggest jealousy, or do they ask subjects to report a global assessment of their experience of jealousy? A critical question might concern whether subjects use the same definition of jealousy when responding. For example, if two people say they would be jealous if their partner slept with another person, does "jealous" mean the same thing to both people and is their experience of jealousy at the same intensity level? Are there measurement instruments that would permit this level of analysis and are they worthwhile? A related question concerns the report of jealous thoughts by subjects. Would it be valuable to have people distinguish between thoughts of jealousy in the past with the same or a different partner, or with their present partner, or to consider a potential relationship at some future time? If so, how might this change our understanding of the studies presented in this chapter?

As discussed above, White takes a decidedly cognitive view with an emphasis on perceived power differences in relationships and the impact they have on the experience of jealousy. He proposes that females in romantic relationships with males have less power and would therefore be more likely to induce jealousy in their romantic partner in order to gain power or to lessen the perceived power difference. It is implied that power differences in relationships are situational/cultural and probably not dispositional/personality based. However, it is open to debate how influential long-term social reinforcements are in shaping the development of dispositions.

While reading this article you may consider the fact that only heterosexual couples were used in the study. Would the predictions about the role of power on the experience of jealousy also apply to gay male and lesbian relationships? A second point involves the amount of dependency one feels in a relationship and how likely that would be to induce jealousy. One method used to define dependency is the couple's courtship stage. White predicts that the greater the interdependence in the later stages of courtship the more frequent inducements of jealousy. The question to ask here is whether greater interdependence is associated with greater power discrepancies and therefore more jealousy inducements.

Inducing Jealousy: A Power Perspective

Gregory L. White

Romantic jealousy may be defined as a complex of thoughts, feelings, and actions which follow threats to self-esteem and/or threats to the existence or quality of a relationship, when those threats are perceived to be generated by the existence of a real or potential attraction between one's partner and a (perhaps imaginary) rival. The potential destructive force of these threats is well known, though not well understood (e.g., White, 1977). Why, then, would anyone deliberately induce jealousy in a romantic partner? What are the potential benefits from such attempts that outweigh the often volatile consequences of jealousy?

Inducing jealousy may be understood, in part, as a power tactic. Waller and Hill (1951) and Thibaut and Kelley (1959) point out that if one's partner has a relatively more available or attractive alternative relationship, then the partner is in a position of relative power. This is because the relatively less interested or less involved partner can directly or indirectly threaten to leave the relationship at greater harm to the more involved partner than to himself or herself. An "alternative" relationship can include family, work, hobbies, or being alone. When the alternative is a real or potential romantic partner, however, jealousy can easily develop (White, 1977).

If this analysis is correct, then a person relatively more involved in a romantic relationship (more dependent) may be able to gain greater outcomes (or control) by leading his or her partner to believe that an attractive alternative relationship is available. To reduce the threat to self or relationship, the threatened partner would have to act to increase the level of outcomes of the threatening partner. Unfortunately, this ploy may backfire if the threatened partner's outcomes drop below what he or she may want to stay in the relationship. One major source of diminished outcomes would be the cost to self-esteem in the face of a rival.

Of course, a variety of other motives for deliberate inducement may coexist with the desire for better outcomes or greater control. However, to the extent that [jealousy] inducement is a strategy to increase control, it is more likely to be used by those whose control is most weak, presumably those more involved than their partners.

In order to test this hypothesis, and in order to gain descriptive data concerning the motives and techniques used to induce jealousy, 300 people comprising 150 romantically involved couples taking part in a larger survey study were asked to give **open-ended responses** to questions asking if they had ever deliberately induced jealousy. They were asked to indicate why and how they had attempted to do so. In addition, each person rated his or her relative degree of involvement in the romantic relationship.

Method

A 35-page "Relationships Questionnaire" was constructed in order to investigate a variety of hypotheses concerning jealousy, including those outlined above. This questionnaire was administered to 150 romantically involved heterosexual couples who had responded to various advertisements in student newspapers and dormitories at the University of California, Los Angeles. Each respondent was paid $1.50 for participation [In 1980, this was worth something!!]. Partners took the questionnaire in isolation from each other.

Each person was asked: "Have you ever tried to get your partner jealous over your relationship with someone else on purpose? That is, have you ever intentionally tried to make your partner jealous? If yes, please outline your reasons. If yes, how did you try to make your partner jealous?" These questions were intended to assess the motives and techniques involved in inducing jealousy.

Based partly on the theoretical concerns outlined earlier and partly on the nature of the responses, a content analytic coding scheme was developed for use in categorizing the techniques and motives for inducing jealousy. The five motive categories were Increase Rewards, Bolster Self-Esteem, Test Relationships, Revenge, and Punishment. Coding rules and examples are:

(1) *Increase Rewards.* A specific reward or desired outcome of the inducement is mentioned. Examples are: "I wanted him to spend more time with me," "So that he would take me out more," and "Wanting more attention."

(2) *Bolster Self-Esteem.* This is a specific reference to need for approval for one's personality or behavior. Examples are: "Because I was feeling inadequate," "I was feeling low and needed to remind him that I'm special to him," "Insecure about myself."

(3) *Test Relationship.* This is a reference to a desire to increase closeness in the relationship or to test the strength of the relationship. Examples are "To see if he still cared," "To test his love," "To inspire possessiveness."

(4) *Revenge.* Person induces jealousy because partner has made him or her jealous. Examples are: "Out of anger because he was going out," "Because she was doing it to me."

(5) *Punishment.* A desire to hurt the partner is mentioned. Examples are: "I was angry at him … We were having a fight."

Five techniques were coded for inducing jealousy: talking about past relationships, talking about current relationships, flirting, dating or sexual contact with another, and lying about the existence of a rival.

Two independent raters, blind to the hypothesis of the study, rated all responses. The raters agreed on 89.1% of their ratings, averaged across all categories. The percentage of agreement ranged from 77.7% for the technique of talking about current relationships to induce jealousy to 95.8% for the revenge motive. In cases where the two raters disagreed, a third rater's judgment was used to generate a majority rule.

Results

There were 4 self-reported stages of courtship indicated by respondents: (1) casual dating, where one or both partners were dating others (21% of the sample), (2) serious or exclusive dating (50%), (3) cohabitation (13%), and (4) engagement or marriage (16%). Males were an average 22.3 years old, females were an average of 20.9 years old. Over 91% of respondents were enrolled in college. The model couple was a junior man and sophomore woman who had been dating for 18 months. Nonmarried couples had been dating from one month to 84 months, with median of 11.9 months courtship.

Each partner rated himself [or herself] as much more, more, equally, less, and much less involved than his [or her] partner. Responses were collapsed into more involved (19.7%), equally involved (49%), and less involved (31.3%). There were no sex differences in tendency to rate self at any level of involvement. There was little effect of dating stage on ratings or involvement, except that casual daters were more likely to rate themselves as less involved, and less likely to rate themselves as equally involved than respondents in the other three stages.

The correlation between partners' ratings of relative involvement is −.471, indicating that when one partner rated self as less involved, the other was likely to rate self as more involved. Of the 149 couples for which data are available, 61% agreed completely on their ratings of relative involvement. There was a slight bias for subjects of both sexes to rate self as equally involved when the partner had rated himself or herself as less involved.

In the sample, 73 subjects reported deliberately inducing jealousy. Females were more likely to report inducement than males, 31.3% to 17.3%, or $\chi^2(1)=7.88$, $p < .005$. There is no effect of involvement on male reports, $\chi^2(2) = 1.13$, ns, but level of involvement is related to female reports, $\chi^2(2) = 6.66$, $p < .036$. The more involved females were almost twice as likely to report

inducement than those females less or equally involved.

There was no effect of involvement on reports of the motives or techniques related to inducing jealousy. However, females tended to be categorized as having the Increase Rewards motive more than males, 38.3% to 15.4%, $\chi^2(1) = 3.37$, $p < .06$ [not significant]. Overall, the most frequently recorded motive was Test Relationship (39.7%), followed by Increase Rewards (30.1%), Revenge (9.7%), Bolster Self-Esteem (8.4%), and Punishment (1.4%). The most popular method of inducing jealousy was to discuss or exaggerate current attractions to others (51.4%), followed by flirting (27.8%), dating others (23.6%), outright fabrication of another attraction (13.9%), and talking about former girlfriends or boyfriends (11.1%).

Discussion

Women in this study were more likely to report inducement, especially so if they were in what could be considered a low-power position relative to the partner being more involved in the relationship. Though there was no evidence that level of involvement per se was related to the various motives for inducing jealousy, females were more likely to report inducing jealousy in order to gain a specific reward.

Why should females be more likely to induce jealousy than males, particularly the more involved females? The effect of relative involvement seems to rule out a simple response bias explanation – that females are more honest, have better memories for interpersonal strategies, or are more likely to exaggerate inducement as a way of helping the researcher collect data. Taking the finding as non-artifactual, one explanation is that jealousy inducement is an exercise of power consistent with both sex roles and the position of relative dependence.

Johnson (1976) reviews evidence that female exercise of power is stereotypically constrained to indirect and personal forms of power. Indirect power, or manipulation, occurs when the influencer attempts to disguise the manipulation attempt. Personal power is based on resources available in interpersonal relationships such as love, esteem-maintenance, the relationship itself. Inducing jealousy deliberately to gain control is both indirect and personal; the attempt is disguised, and the resources implied as shifting to rival are certainly personal. Males, on the other hand, are more free to exercise direct and concrete power. A more involved male may seek other methods to augment control in the relationship.

The suggestion that inducing jealousy can be viewed as a power tactic opens up the possibility that ordinary jealousy is related to the way in which power is shared in the couple. Previous discussions of jealousy have attributed it to high dependency characteristics of the jealous person, but as a function of personality rather than of the relationship (e.g., Berscheid & Fei, 1977). It seems plausible, however, that two people in a couple shape their power relationship in a way that is not wholly attributable to their personalities. For example, males may have relatively greater power because of their status in society (Gillispie, 1971). Consideration of the power struggle within the couple may provide as useful an insight into jealousy as consideration of individual psychology.

Although over twenty years old, this article clearly presents sex differences in the use of jealousy as an interpersonal tool in relationships. Females who report being more involved are also more likely to report inducing jealousy in their partner, and most often to test the strength of a relationship. The author explains the sex differences in light of perceived power inequities in relationships. In so doing he concentrates on the impact situational factors have on the experience and use of jealousy in relationships rather than relying on **distal causes** such as personality traits or evolutionary imperatives. The clarity of such **proximal explanations** is alluring and places the focus of experiences of jealousy on the dynamic interplay between both partners rather than residing in one or the other romantic partner.

It is tempting to generalize to relationships other than the heterosexual ones examined in this study. Similar predictions for inducing jealousy could be made for gay and lesbian couples based on perceived power differences and commitment. For example, if power and dependency are linked to income levels in gay male relationships as Harry (1984) suggests, then jealousy should be more frequently used by the more dependent member of the couple. Although a similar prediction could be made for lesbian couples, power and dependency may not be as closely linked to income levels (Blumstein & Schwartz, 1983).

One prediction that was not fully supported in the study was that greater inducements of jealousy would occur at more advanced levels of relationship development. Although the author reports little effect of relationship stage on jealousy inducements, this may be due to the fact that jealousy is induced at different times in a relationship for different reasons. For example, the most frequent motive reported for inducing jealousy was "testing the relationship." But this might be a more likely motive early in a relationship. In addition, motives such as "Increased Rewards" might also ebb and flow with the different stages of courtship producing an overall flat effect across relationship stages in this study.

The second article in this chapter takes a pro-evolutionary approach in assessing the experience of jealousy in romantic relationships. Rather than focus on inducing jealousy as in the previous article, these authors examine whether males and females experience the emotion of jealousy differently across three cultures. Central to their argument is that jealousy is a "basic human emotion" and thus the experience of males and females should be similar in very different cultures to support an evolutionary explanation of jealousy. Buunk et al. (1996) present a clear introduction to the theory of evolution and discuss the interplay between sexual and emotional infidelity, the uncertainty of male paternity and the distribution of resources in relationships. The results of this analysis lead them to predict that males will experience greater jealousy to potential threats of sexual infidelity than women in all cultures, while women will experience greater emotional jealousy to potential threats than men in all cultures. The dilemma presented to participants to test these predictions involves a forced choice scenario where they must indicate whether sexual or emotional infidelity would cause the most jealousy. The results are cast in terms of the percentage of participants selecting the sexual jealousy alternative. Therefore, a key issue to track while reading this article is whether men selected the sexual infidelity option significantly more often than women in each culture. A related issue involves the magnitude of the difference between men and women in each culture. Should we expect men to vary significantly across cultures in reports of sexual jealousy to support an evolutionary perspective? Should we expect women to be similar in their experience of sexual jealousy across cultures to support an evolutionary perspective? Finally, as a basic human emotion, would we assume a more physiological and less cognitive mediated explanation of jealousy?

Sex Differences in Jealousy in Evolutionary and Cultural Perspective: Tests from the Netherlands, Germany, and the United States

Bram P. Buunk, Alois Angleitner, Viktor Oubaid and David M. Buss

Social scientists have frequently observed that sexual jealousy can be a strikingly strong emotion. In his classic work on the natives of the Trobriand Islands, for example, Malinowski (1932) noted that "jealousy, with or without adequate reason, and adultery are the two factors in tribal life which put most strain on the marriage tie" (p. 97). The sociologist Davis (1948) noted that jealousy is a "fear and rage reaction fitted to protect, maintain, and prolong the intimate association of love" (p. 183). Despite the potentially powerful impact of sexual jealousy, emotion researchers have devoted relatively little attention to it.

According to most emotion researchers, jealousy is not a primary emotion. Instead, it is considered a derivative or blend of the more basic, central, primary emotions (e.g., Frank, 1988). As a consequence, it has been relatively ignored by mainstream emotion researchers, who focus their efforts on emotions deemed more basic, such as fear, disgust, and sadness.

Recently, however, jealousy has received increasing attention (e.g., Salovey, 1991). For example, cumulating evidence indicates that mate sexual jealousy is a major cause of wife battering and homicide across a large number of cultures (e.g., Daly & Wilson, 1988). The two times when a woman faces the greatest risk of harm from a husband or boyfriend are when he suspects her of a sexual infidelity and when the woman decides to terminate the relationship (Daly & Wilson, 1988). Given an emotion powerful enough to provoke violent and sometimes lethal reactions, sexual jealousy can hardly be considered to be a peripheral emotion from the perspectives of the magnitude of arousal, the coherence of events that trigger its activation, and the magnitude of impact on people's lives. Indeed, from these perspectives, a compelling case can be made for the primacy of sexual jealousy as a basic human emotion and for the urgency of understanding its nature and functioning.

Although in anthropological records, most acts of violent sexual jealousy are committed by men (Daly, Wilson, & Weghorst, 1982), studies in Western cultures find few sex differences in sexual jealousy (Salovey, 1991). When researchers have asked global questions such as "Do you consider yourself a jealous person?" or "How often do you get jealous?" men and women have typically responded identically (Bringle & Buunk, 1985). Moreover, research has thus far not convincingly shown that either sex responds more negatively than the other when confronted with the possibility of the partner's sexual involvement with someone else. When differences are found, women usually report more negative feelings than men in response to extradyadic involvement of the partner (e.g., Buunk, 1995).

Until recently, there was not a theory that could predict or explain sex differences in jealousy. Fifteen years ago, however, evolutionary psychologists predicted that, psychologically, the cues that trigger sexual jealousy should be weighted differently in men and women (e.g., Daly et al., 1982). The evolutionary rationale stems from an asymmetry between the sexes in a fundamental aspect of their reproductive biology: Fertilization occurs internally within the woman. This is not a biological law. There is nothing in evolutionary theory that dictates

that fertilization must occur internally within the woman. Although it is a widespread trait, occurring in all 220 species of primates, 4,000 species of mammals, and countless insect species, it is not universal. Fertilization occurs internally within the male in some species (females literally implant their eggs within the male), and it occurs external to both sexes in some species, notably certain fish (Trivers, 1985).

The fact that fertilization occurs internally within women, however, means that over human evolutionary history, men have faced a profound adaptive problem that has not been faced by women: uncertainty in their parenthood of children. Some cultures have sayings to describe this phenomenon, such as "mama's baby, papa's maybe." Studies using blood samples or DNA fingerprinting are rare, but estimates based on existing evidence suggest that approximately 9% to 13% of children today have putative fathers that are not their genetic fathers (Baker & Bellis, 1995). Paternity uncertainty, in short, is not just a hypothetical possibility. It is a reality and probably has been throughout human evolutionary history. From a man's perspective, in the evolutionary past, a sexual infidelity on the part of his mate would have been tremendously damaging in reproductive currencies because of compromises in paternity certainty. First, the man would risk losing the mating effort he expended, including time, energy, risk, and nuptial gifts devoted to attracting and courting the woman. Second, he would suffer mating opportunity costs lost through foregone chances to attract and court other women. Third, the man would risk losing the woman's parental effort because it might be channeled to a competitor's child and not his own. Fourth, and perhaps most important, if the man would invest in the child, he would risk investing resources in a genetic vehicle that did not contain his genes. Because of the large costs linked with compromises in paternity, evolutionary psychologists have predicted that men's sexual jealousy will be triggered centrally by cues to sexual infidelity.

Women have faced a different set of adaptive challenges. A mate's sexual infidelity does not jeopardize a woman's certainty in parenthood. The child is her own regardless of her mate's sexual philandering. Nonetheless, if her mate becomes interested in another woman, she risks losing his time, energy, resources, parental investment, protection, and commitment – all of which could get diverted to a rival woman and her children. Because the emotional involvement of a man with another woman is a reliable leading indicator of the potential diversion and loss of the man's investment, evolutionary researchers have proposed that cues to emotional infidelity would be central triggers of women's jealousy (Buss, Larsen, Westen, & Semmelroth, 1992).

The predicted sex differences have been found within the United States. In a series of forced-choice experiments, men indicated greater distress to a partner's sexual than emotional infidelity, whereas women indicated greater distress to a partner's emotional than sexual infidelity (Buss et al., 1992). These findings have been replicated by other researchers within the United States (Wiederman & Allgeier, 1993), and show up in measures of physiological distress as reflected by increased electromyographic activity, increased electrodermal response, and elevated heart rate (Buss et al., 1992). In addition, some earlier studies offered findings in line with the evolutionary perspective. Francis (1977), for example, found that among men, sexual involvement with a third person was the most mentioned situation in evoking jealousy, whereas among women, the partner spending time or talking with a third person turned out to be the most frequently mentioned triggers of jealousy.

Cross-cultural data, however, are crucial for testing this evolution-based hypothesis. First, because the sex-linked triggers are hypothesized to be species-typical characteristics of evolved human psychology, data from other cultures are required for adequate testing (e.g., Symons, 1979). Second, it is well documented that cultures differ tremendously in their attitudes toward aspects of sexuality such as premarital sex and extramarital affairs (e.g., Buss, 1989). For example, whereas over 75% of the U.S. population unequivocally disapproves of extramarital sex, the comparable percentage in the Netherlands is less than 45% (Buunk & van Driel, 1989). Furthermore, cultures differ in their emphasis on sexual equality (Frayser, 1985). Cultures that emphasize sexual equality and have particularly liberal attitudes about sexuality for both women and men should provide an especially rigorous challenge for testing the hypothesized sex differences in sexual jealousy. Thus, we sought to conduct parallel studies in three countries with different cultures – the Netherlands, Germany, and the United States. In particular, including the Netherlands seems appropriate because the Dutch appear to downplay sex differences and emphasize equality between the sexes more than people from virtually any other culture for which reliable data exist (Hofstede, 1994).

Study 1: The United States

After reporting age (mean = 18.6, *SD* = .92) and sex (*N*=115 men and 109 women), subjects at a large Midwestern university were presented with the following dilemmas, interspersed at different locations within a larger instrument:

> Please think of a serious or committed romantic relationship that you have had in the past, that you currently have, or that you would like to have. Imagine that you discover that the person with whom you've been seriously involved became interested in someone else. What would upset or distress you more (please circle only one):
>
> (A) Imagining your partner forming a deep emotional attachment to that person.
> (B) Imagining your partner enjoying passionate sexual intercourse with that other person.

Subjects completed additional questions, and then encountered the next dilemma, with the same instructional set, but followed by a different, but parallel, choice:

(A) Imagining your partner trying different sexual positions with that other person.
(B) Imagining your partner falling in love with that other person.

The first empirical probe, contrasting deep emotional attachment with passionate sexual intercourse, yielded a large and highly significant sex difference ($t = 6.96$, $p < .0001$), with the sexes differing by 43% in the responses to which infidelity scenario was more distressing. The contrast between a partner trying different sexual positions with someone else versus falling in love with that other person again was highly significant ($t = 5.45$, $p < .0001$). The sexes differed by 32% in their responses.

Study 2: Germany

A sample of 200 Germans from the city of Bielefeld participated in a parallel study. After reporting age (mean = 26.07, $SD = 3.67$) and sex ($N = 100$ men and 100 women), they responded to the same dilemmas as in the U.S. study [except they were translated into German]. The first empirical probe contrasted deep emotional attachment with passionate sexual intercourse. This probe yielded a significant sex difference ($t = 2.06$, $p < .02$).

The responses to the contrast between a partner trying different sexual positions with someone else versus falling in love with that other person show that the sex difference was again highly significant ($t = 4.03$, $p < .0001$).

A comparison between Germany and the United States reveals that the percentages of women endorsing the sexual infidelity scenario were almost identical for the two cultures, differing by only 2% for the first infidelity scenario and 4% for the second scenario. In sharp contrast, the men from the two cultures differed considerably. Fully 33% more of the American men than the German men expressed greater distress to sexual than to emotional infidelity in the first dilemma, and 14% more American than German men expressed greater distress to sexual than to emotional infidelity in the second dilemma. Although the problematic nature of translation makes absolute comparisons of this sort of interpretation questionable, the results do suggest that the smaller sex difference in the German sample than in the U.S. sample may be due to differences in men's responses, rather than to differences in women's responses.

Study 3: The Netherlands

A sample of 207 Dutch undergraduate students, 102 males and 105 females, participated in this study (mean age = 21.6, $SD = 2.73$). The same dilemmas were presented as in the U.S. and German studies [following translation]. For both probes, the same introduction was presented as in both other countries. The first probe, contrasting deep emotional attachment with passionate sexual intercourse, yielded a significant sex difference ($t = 3.41$, $p < .001$). This sex difference is larger than the sex difference found with the German sample, but smaller than the sex difference found with the American sample. The responses to the contrast between a partner trying different sexual positions with someone else versus falling in love with that other person showed a sex difference that again was significant ($t = 2.11$, $p < .04$).

A comparison of the responses from the three cultures is revealing. First, responding to the same probes, the sexes differed in the same ways in all three cultures, providing support for the evolutionary psychological hypothesis about sex linkage in the weighting given to the triggers of sexual jealousy. Second, the results suggest that these cultures differ in the magnitude of this sex difference. The difference between males and females is consistently large within the American sample, but ranges from small to medium within both European samples.

Discussion

This research makes two contributions to current knowledge about the nature of sex differences in jealousy. First, these studies provide the first systematic cross-cultural tests of the evolutionary psychological hypothesis that men and women differ in the weighting given to the triggers of sexual jealousy. Because the sexes have faced different adaptive problems caused by a mate's infidelity – compromised paternity confidence for men and the diversion of resources and investment for women – the sexes have been predicted to give different weighting to sexual acts of infidelity versus acts that signal emotional involvement and hence the potential diversion of resources over time.

The German and Dutch cultures provide especially rigorous tests of the hypothesis because these cultures have more relaxed attitudes about sexuality, including extramarital sex, than does the American culture; furthermore, these European cultures emphasize sexual equality, especially in the sexual domain, more than American culture does. The fact that the sex differences still emerged in these cultures provides support for the evolutionary psychological hypothesis. Even in the Netherlands, where values strongly de-emphasize sex differences (Hofstede, 1994), and where a majority feels extramarital sexual relationships are acceptable under certain circumstances (Buunk & van Driel, 1989), men still tend to become more upset than women over their partner showing purely sexual interest in a third person, and women tend to become more upset than men over their partner expressing a desire for romantic and emotional involvement with someone else.

The second contribution of the present research is demonstrating that the magnitude of this sex difference differs across cultures. The Dutch and German samples showed small to moderate sex differences, whereas the American sample showed a large sex difference that was consistent across the empirical probes. Although the direction of the sex difference in jealousy is consistent across cultures, culture clearly matters in determining the magnitude of this sex difference. Further research may be directed more at identifying cultural features that account for such differences.

Several limitations qualify these results. First, although the German sample was selected in part from the adult population, the samples from the United States and the Netherlands were students. Thus, the results may not be representative of the entire cultures of these countries, and the results of the three studies are not completely comparable. Second, the vagaries of translation render exact comparisons of absolute percentages problematic; such comparisons should be interpreted with caution. Third, given that the individual probes undoubtedly contain some unreliability of measurement, the findings may actually underestimate the magnitude of the sex difference within each culture. The findings thus may be regarded as lower-bound estimates of the magnitude.

Although some investigators (e.g., Hupka & Ryan, 1990) might interpret the cultural differences found in the present research as a disconfirmation of the evolutionary psychology framework, such an interpretation would be mistaken. Evolutionary hypotheses are sometimes misinterpreted as implying rigid, robot like, instinctual behavior that suggests that the individual is oblivious to the social environment. In fact, **evolutionary psychology** postulates psychological mechanisms that were designed to respond to the social environment. Clearly, the jealousy mechanisms examined in these studies are sensitive to sociocultural conditions, even though the particulars of these cultural conditions are not yet known.

One explanation for the cross-cultural differences is that in sexually more liberal cultures where men may distribute their mating effort over a number of women, and hence devote less investment toward any one woman, men are less sexually jealous of any particular woman. Another possibility is that women in more sexually liberal cultures secure investments from a larger number of men, and hence are less jealous of any one partner's emotional involvement with other women. Still another possibility is that women in more sexually egalitarian cultures are more self-reliant for resources, and this self-reliance alters the intensity of jealousy they experience about a partner's emotional involvement with another woman.

Future research could profitably examine these and other features of the different cultures to pinpoint more precisely the causal locus of the cultural effect. Future research could also examine other cultures, including, at the other extreme, those that are more sexually conservative (e.g., perhaps China and Indonesia in the East, or Ireland within Western Europe) or that emphasize greater sexual inequality (e.g., Iran), to test the suggestion that these cultures might reveal even larger sex differences than those found within the United States. Given the importance of sexual jealousy in spousal violence and homicide, such studies might take an especially high priority.

Taken together, these studies suggest a complex portrait of human sexual psychology – one that is sex-differentiated, but also sensitive to cultural context. Whereas **evolutionary psychology** has been critical in guiding us to pose questions about sex differences in the triggers of jealousy and guiding a cross-cultural search for their existence, a cultural perspective has been valuable in uncovering variation in the magnitudes of those sex differences. Combining evolutionary and cultural perspectives may provide the most valuable models for exploring the mysteries of the uniquely human sexual psychology.

The authors of this study have effectively demonstrated that men and women in different cultures respond similarly to the same basic question about sexual versus emotional jealousy. In each culture examined, men were more concerned about sexual infidelity than the women of that same culture. Buunk et al. (1996) argue that the size and consistent direction of the sex difference supports an evolutionary mechanism for jealousy. Although differences in effect sizes exist between cultures, this may be explained as the result of short-term evolutionary adaptation to individual cultural pressures.

Although Buunk et al. make a strong case for consistency across cultures; the stability appears to reside mostly in the responses of the women in their samples. In fact, men responded quite differently between cultures. Perhaps if the authors had conducted a statistical test on just the male data they would have found significant differences between cultures. This result would be more supportive of social learning explanation than the evolutionary one presented by the authors.

This article raises several statistical and methodological issues that are useful to discuss within the context of jealousy. One issue involves determining the correct analysis for data collected. As demonstrated above, a significance test of men across culture may have suggested different conclusions about the role of evolution and the experience of jealousy. In addition, when conducting cross-cultural research Matsumoto (1994) suggests that it is better to transform the raw data to reflect individual cultural influences before conducting statistical tests such as *t*-test or ANOVAs since one may report spurious findings. It is unclear whether such a transformation was used and whether the effects sizes might be smaller than those reported in the article after such a transformation was completed. There are also several methodological issues to consider within the context of jealousy. Can the responses of participants be treated as identical when is it unknown whether they are responding to a current, past, or imagined relationship as in Buunk et al., (1996)? Although this procedure is common practice, one wonders whether people respond differently to infidelity in a current relationship since it has greater saliency (cognitively and physiologically) than past or imagined relationships. Note that the previous article (White,

1980) used current couples and had them respond to questions concerning that relationship, thereby providing greater consistency and more certainty about the participants' responses when making comparisons. Finally, is it better to use a global assessment of jealousy or to separate possible types of jealous responses? Buunk et al., use a global measure of jealousy (which of these two situations would produce greater jealousy). Pfeiffer and Wong (1989) suggest that jealous reactions can be separated into thoughts, feelings, and behaviors and provide a scale to measure each subcategory. If people can evaluate these separate components, might they lead to more complex understanding of jealousy? Clearly White (1980) falls into this category since he had subjects evaluate their behavior as well as their cognitions related to episodes of jealousy. Alternatively, if as Nisbett and Ross (1980) argue, people have little ability to self-reflect, then perhaps a global measure is adequate in assessing jealousy.

Although Buunk et al. appropriately do not attempt to extend their findings to gay male and lesbian relationships, it nevertheless would be interesting to consider whether their model allows predictions of jealous reactions to potential sexual and emotional infidelities in homosexual couples. Recent data (Sheets & Wolfe, 2001) suggest this evolutionary theory is less well suited to explaining patterns of jealousy in gay male and lesbian relationships than other approaches.

We began this chapter with a brief discussion of the nature of emotion and two opposing theories of emotion and jealousy. The intent of this chapter was not to present a comprehensive evaluation of this topic and the varied positions on the nature of jealousy. Excellent full discussions can be found in Guerrero and Andersen (1998) and Buunk and Dijkstra (2000). Rather, this chapter was intended to offer you an opportunity to entertain both ends of the continuum and consider how a middle ground might be established.

9 Conflict in Relationships

"Love is the triumph of Imagination over Intelligence."

– Benjamin Franklin

It appears that in some situations we choose to perceive relationships as we expect them to be rather than how they actually exist (e.g., Hendrick & Hendrick, 1988). Our desire to see things as better, or worse, than they are in reality appears to affect how we experience conflict and satisfaction in our relationships. In this chapter you will read two articles addressing different aspects of the perception of conflict. First you will read Acitelli, Douvan and Veroff's (1993) study of newly married couples. Their examination will highlight the distinction between real and perceived understandings of behaviors during conflicts by each spouse. Of great interest here is the degree to which the couple share perceptions of how they acted during a recent dispute (either constructively or destructively). The second article in this chapter, by Vogel and Karney (2002), also examines the behavior of newly married couples but looks at the demand/withdrawal pattern indicative of distressed couples identified by Gottman (1979). This is a specific analysis of one destructive problem-solving strategy rather than an analysis of a combination of strategies (destructive and constructive) as in Acitelli et al.

It is difficult to have a discussion of conflict without also considering perceptions of well-being in relationships. Therefore, each article evaluates conflict and its effect on relationship satisfaction. In addition, the experience of conflict is enmeshed with power and sex issues. Further, each article's authors address this relationship and the role it plays in either causing or perpetuating conflict for couples. As in previous chapters, we encourage you to attend to research design and statistical issues while reading. The articles in this chapter use a variety of research designs (cross-sectional, longitudinal) and a variety of measurement approaches (self-report surveys, behavioral observations). Particularly noteworthy, however, is the care taken by Vogel and Karney (2002) in adjusting their statistical analysis using the **Bonferroni p adjustment** to avoid **capitalizing on chance** (i.e., making the p-value stricter and therefore making it more difficult to claim that one has a significant effect because repeated significance tests were performed on the same data set. Repeated tests on a data set will eventually produce a significant effect, but it will be due to chance not to your target variables). Do the other authors in this book modify their analyses against this error?

The quotation by Benjamin Franklin suggests perception may be more powerful than reality when it comes to love. The work of Acitelli, Douvan and Veroff (1993) suggests it may also be true for one predictable part of romantic relationships – conflict. The authors of this article present a cogent argument for the need to understand shared cognitions/perceptions in relationships. For their actual research design, however, the authors focus on the perceptions of spousal behavior in conflict situations. Acitelli et al. believe that when assessing conflict resolution behaviors, perceived similarity will be greater between marriage partners than actual similarity. Further, they predict that perceived, rather than actual similarity, will better predict martial well-being. Given that discussions of conflict and well-being in relationships often require us to consider power and sex, Acitelli et al. predict that *wives* (traditionally having less power in heterosexual relationships) would *more accurately* perceive their husbands (and their own) attitudes and behaviors in conflict situations since much research has shown a greater need for people of lower power/status to accurately monitor and predict the behavior of high-power individuals in their lives so they can respond effectively in most situations. If this is the case, then it is also possible that this increased accuracy on the part of wives may contribute to the overall well-being of the marriage.

Acitelli et al. used a longitudinal design where couples were followed for four years. Although this is not an extraordinarily lengthy time period in the study of couples, their research question focused on perceptions in the *early* stages of marriage. Given the potential volatility of these earlier stages of marriage, you may want to review the effect of subject attrition on the sample characteristics. Also, be cognizant of the potential problems with self-report measures of behavior we mentioned in Chapters 1 and 2 and how the authors of the study attempt to minimize these effects. Do they use the approach you predicted?

Perceptions of Conflict in the First Year of Marriage: How Important are Similarity and Understanding?

Linda K. Acitelli, Elizabeth Douvan and Joseph Veroff

As Berger and Kellner (1964) theorize, marriage is a process of constructing a shared reality or shared perceptions of a couple's experiences. Marital relationships provide a fitting backdrop for the study of partners' perceptions of self and other which may be the building blocks from which the spouses' shared reality is constructed (Laing et al., 1966). Whereas *person perception* involves one person's perception of another, *interpersonal perception* involves studying the relationship between partners' perceptions of one another (Sillars & Scott, 1983). According to Berger and Kellner (1964), partners' differences in perceptions decrease over time. Therefore, the early years of marriage are crucial to the formation of shared perceptions.

Interpersonal perceptions of spouse and other may be related in several ways. We focus on three: when both partners' self-perceptions are congruent, partners are said to be *similar*; when one person's perception of the self and perception of other are congruent, there is *perceived similarity* for that person; and when a partner's perception of the other corresponds with the other's self-perception, there is *understanding*. We refer to these as *perceptual congruence* variables. Even though researchers do not agree on use of terms, they do nevertheless agree that these perceptions and their interrelations can have important consequences for the partners' everyday interactions and their satisfaction with the relationship. We relate these perceptions of interaction to marital well-being.

The referents of perception in a marriage can be almost anything, ranging from the perceptions of the relationship to perceptions of spouses' food preferences. Each in their own way can be important to the study of marriage. However, we heed the advice of Sillars (1985) who warns that the consequences of perceptions of similarity and understanding may depend on the specific referent of these perceptions and the context within which these perceptions occur. In the present study, then, we are limiting the focus to particular referents in a particular context, namely spouses' behaviors in conflict situations. The conflict context is a major arena for marital communication and relationship negotiation. Though it is not the only setting in which couples create a shared reality, we would assert its critical role in that development. In conflict, discrepancies between partners' views are exposed, affect is aroused and differences are negotiated toward a shared view or at least a decision to allow the different views – the discrepancy – to stand (i.e., agreement to disagree). Indeed, unexposed differences may reinforce separate as opposed to shared

realities. In general, we expect that the relationship between perceptual congruence of conflict behaviors and marital well-being will be positive.

Furthermore, when looking at spouses' perceptions of each other during conflict, we expect that the importance of perceptual congruence may depend on whether the perceived behaviors are constructive or destructive to conflict resolution. Other studies (e.g., Crohan, 1992) have demonstrated that these different types of behaviors have different consequences for marital well-being. For example, it may be more important to a marriage for partners to agree not to insult one another – since insult is destructive to conflict resolution – than to agree to try to look at the conflict in a new light – which is constructive to conflict resolution. Thus, in delineating types of conflict responses, we are further specifying the referents of perception by distinguishing between behaviors that are constructive and those that are destructive.

This article focuses on the following hypotheses derived from findings reported in the literature on interpersonal perception in close personal relationships:

(1) Perceived similarity is greater than actual similarity (e.g., Sillars, 1985). Sillars has suggested that this reflects the fact that people use their own direct perspective as a reference for judging other people even when they have previous experience that could distinguish the other person's perspective.

(2) Understanding (i.e., accurate perception) of partners' behaviors will be greater for destructive than for constructive behaviors. Literature indicates more accurate recall of information that is more immediate, vivid, easily observed and negative in emotional tone (Sillars, 1985). For some spouses, destructive behaviors may also be unusual, and novelty has been shown to increase arousal (Berlyne, 1963).

We also pursue an analysis to determine the unique contributions of actual similarity, perceived similarity and understanding to marital well-being in the first year of marriage. In this data set, we are able to control for shared variance and compare the unique contribution of each of these perception variables.

(3) Perceived similarity will be more predictive of marital well-being than will actual similarity (Levinger & Breedlove, 1966). White (1985) and Bochner et al. (1982) warn that global measures of perception are multidimensional and may mask both issue-specific variance and variance that depends on the salience of the issue for the couple. In our work, we focus specifically on constructive or destructive behaviors during a disagreement. We explore the relationship of actual and perceived similarity to marital satisfaction separately for positive and negative behaviors.

(4) Wives' understanding of their husbands will contribute more to marital well-being than will husbands' understanding of their wives. In a review of several studies on interpersonal perception between intimates, Sillars and Scott (1983, p. 165) note that "the relationship between understanding and marital adjustment has been found to hold only when the wife is the respondent and the husband's perception is being predicted." Furthermore, Allen and Thompson (1984) found that husbands' understanding of their wives does not predict communication satisfaction for either spouse, but wives' understanding of their husbands predicts husbands' satisfaction. The authors attribute this difference to a power differential: the person with low power needs to be able to understand and predict the actions of the more powerful partner in order to salvage some modicum of control.

Method

Data were obtained from a 4-year longitudinal study of 373 newlywed couples conducted by Veroff et al. (1985) of the Institute for Social Research at the University of Michigan. The sample was drawn from listings of marriage licenses in Wayne County, Michigan, from April through June 1986. The sample was largely urban and was heterogeneous with regard to socioeconomic status and educational background. Respondents' average level of education was at least 1 year of post-secondary education. All respondents were in their first marriage and all wives were under 35 years of age (so that they would be in their childbearing years to be eligible for other research purposes of the larger project). At the time of the first interview, the mean age for husbands was 27 and the mean age for wives was 25, interviews were conducted between 5 and 8 months after their wedding and then again in their third year of marriage. In this study, we are reporting on results from the first-year interviews only. Spouses were interviewed separately in their homes for about an hour and a half on various aspects of married life.

In approximately 40 percent of the couples, at least one partner said he or she could not think of a recent disagreement or that they never disagreed or argued. This reduced the size of the group for this study to 236 couples. Furthermore, when spouses' reports were compared to see if they were reporting on the same disagreement, it was found that approximately 70 percent of this group were not referring to the same event. To see if it was necessary to reduce the sample further, we divided the couples into matched groups (partners who referred to the same disagreement) and unmatched groups (partners who referred to different disagreements). We performed several one-way ANOVAs testing whether or not these groups differed with regard to: their reports of behavior during conflict; the congruence of the partners' reports of conflict behavior; their marital well-being; and their communication about the relationship. Results indicated that these groups were not significantly different from one another in these respects. Thus, we decided to use the entire group of 236 and, like Crohan (1992), acknowledge that we were assessing perceptions of behavioral styles in conflictive situations rather than perceptions of behaviors occurring during one incident. Missing data further reduced the sample to 219.

Measures of conflict behaviors. In one section of the survey, "Differences and Disagreements," spouses were asked (separately) to think of the last time the couple had disagreed or argued about something in the past month or so. They were asked to report perceptions of self and spouse during the disagreement. Each question was asked twice, once for the respondent's own behavior and once for the respondent's perception of the spouse's behavior. For example, each spouse would indicate how true the following statements were: "I calmly discussed the situation" and "My wife/husband calmly discussed the situation;" or "I yelled or shouted at my wife/husband" and "My wife/husband yelled or shouted at me." Responses ranged from 1, very true, to 4, not at all true. The measures we utilize in this study were derived from twelve pairs of items. Six of the pairs are labeled constructive (i.e., calmly discussing the situation, listening to each other's point of view, finding out what the other is feeling, saying nice things, trying to compromise, suggesting a new way of looking at things) and six are labeled destructive (i.e., yelling/shouting, insulting or calling each other names, threatening, bringing the spouse's family into the argument, bringing up things that happened long ago, having to have the last word). Earlier studies on these data have shown that these items cluster together as separate factors (e.g., Crohan, 1992). Cronbach's alphas were computed separately for husbands' and wives' reports of constructive behaviors (husbands' alpha = .71; wives' alpha = .70) and destructive behaviors (husbands' alpha = .68; wives' alpha = .69)

and demonstrate reasonably adequate, but not high, internal consistency.

Measures of perceptual congruence. Indices of similarity, perceived similarity and understanding were obtained for 12 pairs of items. For example, comparing what the husband said he did on a particular item to what he said his wife did would yield a measure of husband's *perceived similarity*, indicating the degree to which he thought he and his wife did the same thing. Comparing what the husband said his wife did to what the wife said she did would yield a measure of *understanding*. We derived *actual similarity* of response by comparing the husband's self-reported behavior to the wife's self-reported behavior. Note that we refer to actual similarity of response to the items which does not imply that we have a direct measure of actual similarity of behavior.

Congruence measures (perceived similarity, actual similarity, understanding) ranged from 1, complete incongruence, to 5, complete congruence. For example, if both spouses responded "very true" to "I calmly discussed the situation," their actual similarity score for that item would be 5 because their responses were identical. On the other hand, if a wife endorsed "not at all true" (4) and her husband responded "very true" (1), their actual similarity score would be 1 because their responses were completely incongruent. Assigning scores to a matrix has a conceptual advantage over an absolute discrepancy score in that it distinguishes between responses that are *somewhat congruent* and *somewhat incongruent* as follows. The difference between very true (1) and somewhat true (2) is 1 and is the same as the difference between not very true (3) and not at all true (4), so the partners in each pair are *somewhat congruent* in that they both gave either a positive or negative response. The difference between somewhat true (2) and not very true (3) is also 1, but partners who gave these responses are *somewhat incongruent* because one spouse gave a positive response while the other spouse gave a negative response. Thus, couple scores that are somewhat congruent are assigned the number 4, and scores that are somewhat incongruent are assigned the number 3.

We obtained actual similarity, perceived similarity and understanding scores for each pair of items (e.g., "I calmly discussed the situation" and "My wife calmly discussed the situation"). Then we obtained averages for each of the three congruence measures on constructive and destructive items separately. These averages are the scores for perceived constructive similarity and perceived destructive similarity; actual constructive similarity and actual destructive similarity; and constructive understanding and destructive understanding.

Measure of marital well-being. Marital well-being was measured by averaging the standard scores of 6 items: (1) Taking things together, how would you describe your marriage? Would you say your marriage is very happy, a little happier than average, just about average or not too happy? (2) When you think about your marriage – what each of you puts into it and gets out of it – how happy do you feel? Would you say very happy, fairly happy, not too happy or not at all happy? (3) How certain would you say you are that the two of you will be married 5 years from now? Would you say very certain, fairly certain, not too certain or not at all certain? (4) How stable do you feel your marriage is? Would you say very stable, fairly stable, not too stable or not at all stable? (5) In the last few months how often have you considered leaving your wife/husband? Would you say often, sometimes, rarely or never? (6) All in all, how satisfied are you with your marriage? Would you say you are very satisfied, somewhat satisfied, somewhat dissatisfied or very dissatisfied? This 6-item measure of marital well-being was derived from previous factor analyses, has been demonstrated to be internally consistent (alpha = .83; Crohan & Veroff, 1989) and has considerable **construct validity** (see Hatchett et al., 1995). In the present study, the measure of marital well-being is not averaged into a couple score, but is rather reported separately for husbands and wives.

Results

Hypothesis 1: Perceived similarity is greater than actual similarity. **Pair-wise comparisons** between the means of actual similarity scores and perceived similarity scores supported the first hypothesis. [*Eds: When t-test comparisons are made between scores on two different measures from the same subjects they are called pairwise comparisons or matched sample t-tests. All participants in this experiment filled out both the perceived and actual similarity scales, so comparisons between these scores are considered pairwise comparisons. The logic behind this statistical test goes beyond this book but is similar to the reasoning used to account for the greater consistency in participants' scores in* **within-subjects designs** *where more than one rating or observation is used from the same person.*] Perceived similarity was significantly higher than actual similarity for both husbands and wives for both constructive and destructive behaviors. Wives' perceived constructive similarity ($M = 4.09$; $SD = .72$) was significantly greater than actual constructive similarity ($M = 3.59$; $SD = .68$; $t = -8.81$, $p < .001$). Husbands' perceived constructive similarity ($M = 4.27$; $SD = .68$) was significantly greater than actual constructive similarity ($M = 3.59$; $SD = .68$; $t = -12.38$, $p < .001$). Likewise, wives' perceived destructive similarity ($M = 4.15$; $SD = .72$) was significantly greater than actual destructive similarity ($M = 3.89$; $SD = .71$; $t = -5.97$, $p < .001$). Husbands' perceived destructive similarity ($M = 4.36$; $SD = .63$) was significantly greater than actual destructive similarity ($M = 3.89$; $SD = .71$; $t = -9.41$, $p < .001$).

Hypothesis 2: Understanding of partners' behaviors will be greater for destructive than for constructive behaviors. This hypothesis was also confirmed. Wives' understanding of husbands' destructive behaviors ($M = 4.04$; $SD = .69$) was significantly greater than wives' understanding of husbands' constructive behaviors ($M = 3.65$; $SD = .68$; $t = -6.77$, $p < .001$). Husbands' understanding of wives' destructive behaviors ($M = 3.93$; $SD = .66$)

was also significantly greater than husbands' understanding of wives' constructive behaviors ($M = 3.66$; $SD = .66$; $t = -4.63$, $p < .001$).

Hypothesis 3: Perceived similarity will be more predictive of marital well-being than will actual similarity. We performed simultaneous regression analyses of the contributions of actual similarity, perceived similarity, understanding and spouses' perceptions of their own behaviors to first-year marital well-being. There were four separate analyses – for husbands' well-being regressed on both constructive and destructive measures and wives' well-being regressed on both constructive and destructive measures. The hypothesis was confirmed for both husbands and wives with regard to the constructive items. Perceived similarity was at least marginally related to marital well-being in all four models. For the constructive items, wives' perceived similarity (beta = .20, $p < .01$) contributed significantly to their marital well being and to a greater degree than actual similarity (beta = $-.09$, NS). For husbands, perceived similarity contributed only marginally to their marital well-being (beta = .12, $p < .10$), but to a greater degree than actual similarity (beta = $-.03$, NS). The results with regard to the destructive items indicate that the contributions of perceived similarity and actual similarity to marital well-being are almost equal but in opposite directions, with actual similarity being negatively related to both spouses' marital well-being. For wives' destructive items, actual similarity was negatively and significantly related to marital well-being (beta = $-.19$, $p < .05$).

Hypothesis 4: Wives' understanding of their husbands will contribute more to marital well-being than will husbands' understanding of their wives. This hypothesis was partially supported. For both constructive and destructive items, wives' understanding of husbands explained more variance in both spouses' marital well-being than did husbands' understanding of wives. However, wives' understanding of husbands *significantly* predicted marital well-being for wives only. Wives' understanding of husbands appears to be a strong predictor of marital well-being for wives for both constructive

and destructive items. Wives' understanding of husbands was not a significant predictor of husbands' marital well-being. Husbands' understanding of wives was [not significantly] predictive of wives' marital well-being and only for the destructive items (beta = .14, $p < .10$).

Overall, the results indicate that the perceptual variables are much better predictors of marital well-being for destructive items than for constructive items. The percentage of variance accounted for by the constructive items for husbands and wives was 9 and 6, respectively, while the percentages for destructive items were 19 and 33. It also appears that the perceptual congruence variables are better predictors of marital well-being for wives than for husbands, while spouses' perceptions of their own behaviors were more predictive of husbands' well-being.

Discussion

Our results indicate that perceived similarity between spouses is greater than actual similarity of response within both contexts of constructive and destructive conflict behaviors. This finding is consistent with previous literature on assumed similarity in marriage (e.g., Levinger & Breedlove, 1966) and with more recent literature on the "false consensus effect" (Ross et al., 1977) where persons assume that others are more like themselves than the others report themselves to be. Explanations offered (e.g., McFarland & Miller, 1990) for the false consensus effect are that people overestimate commonness to assure themselves of the appropriateness or correctness of their own response, to protect their self-esteem and to consensually validate their own preferences. In addition, believing that their own qualities are positive, respondents may believe that the positive target group also possesses their characteristics. Results also support Sillars's (1985) contention that people use themselves more as the basis for making judgments about others than they actually use the others (or "targets" of perception).

Destructive behaviors were more accurately perceived (or understood) than were constructive behaviors. This result is consistent with the literature on social cognition and personal relationships that demonstrates that negative behaviors are more easily noticed and more accurately recalled (Gaelick et al., 1985). The constructive behaviors are not as vivid, or novel, and do not command as much attention. Some may even call them affectively neutral (Sillars, 1985). It is rather unfortunate that positive behaviors may go unnoticed by spouses.

Thus, we see that partners understand spouses' negative behaviors better than spouses' positive behaviors. This may also help explain the "negative reciprocity" cycle that Gottman (1979) and others have noted in distressed couples. Gottman found that, in distressed couples, positive behaviors elicited by one spouse were not as likely to be reciprocated as negative behaviors. We would speculate, then, that positive behaviors may be less easily interpreted and more often go unnoticed in comparison to negative behaviors. Negative behaviors are more clearly understood as negative and, thus, may be more likely to evoke a negative response.

Earlier work has revealed that the relationship between perceived similarity and marital satisfaction is stronger than the relationship between actual similarity and marital satisfaction. However, the earlier studies focused on partner attitudes and role expectations and did not require partners to report on behavioral interactions during conflict. Our study adds the behavioral dimension by requiring respondents to report perceptions of their interactions with each other, not just their attitudes or preferences or what they think their partners' attitudes or preferences are.

The relationship between perceived similarity and marital well-being was consistent across both types of conflict behaviors, although the causal direction is not clear, as it is not clear in other literature, and indeed literature on similarity in friendship suggests that there is a reciprocal causality between similarity and attraction. Newcomb (1961) found that some time after an initial acquaintance, friends' attraction preferences changed in favor of those with similar attitudes. Blankenship et al. (1984) demonstrated that partners' personality characteristics become more similar through interactions over time. Both studies show that some form of similarity both predates and follows the development of relationships. These findings are consistent with Berger and Kellner's (1964) postulation that, in marriage, partners' perceptual differences decrease over time. Note, however, that in our study, actual similarity of response was not as important as perceived similarity in predicting marital well-being.

For the most part, perceptual congruence variables contributed more to the marital well-being of wives than of husbands. The individuals' perceptions of their own constructive and destructive behaviors were more important to husbands' well-being. In other words, a wife's marital well-being is more closely linked to the relationship between partners' perceptions, while a husband's marital well-being is more clearly connected to the individual spouses' self-reports. Although not specifically parallel to our study, findings from other studies show that women's well-being is tied to relational variables such as relationship talk (Acitelli, 1992) and reciprocity of social support (Acitelli & Antonucci, 1990), and that women, compared to men, are relationship oriented in general (e.g., Gilligan, 1982). We would speculate that the relational and individual orientations of females and males are manifesting themselves in our data.

The finding that wives' understanding of their husbands predicted wives' marital well-being, while husbands' understanding of wives did not predict husbands' well-being is also consistent with earlier research (Sillars & Scott, 1983). Allen and Thompson (1984) point to differences in power between husbands and wives that make it more important for wives to understand husbands than for husbands to understand wives. The person in a position of greater power (the husband in this case) has no great need to understand the person in the position of lesser power (the wife). Wives' understanding of their husbands may give them a sense of control and some access to the resources of their husbands, perhaps also explaining why wives' understanding was related to wives' happiness, but not to husbands'. In addition, as traditional caretakers of relationships, women's understandings of their husbands should contribute to smooth relationship functioning.

Another intriguing result is that for destructive styles, actual similarity was negatively related to wives' marital well-being. We hypothesize that this result is related to Gottman's (1979) findings that distressed partners are more likely to reciprocate negative behaviors with each other while non-distressed couples do not get caught in the negative reciprocity cycle. Thus, when one partner is destructive while the other is not, wives are more likely to be happy than in a situation where partners are similar in destructive styles. Again, for wives, it is a matter of how the perceptions relate to one another, whereas for husbands, it is more a matter of the degree to which each spouse reports engaging in destructive behavior.

We also found that the destructive items predicted the degree of marital well-being better than the constructive items did. Related research (e.g., Gaelick et al., 1985) indicates that negative behaviors are more easily recalled and seem to have more impact on perceptions than positive or affectively neutral behaviors. In addition, Bradbury and Fincham (1987) show that dissatisfied spouses are more sensitive to their partners' negative behaviors than to other behaviors. Perhaps the unhappy spouses in our study noticed the presence of destructive behaviors more than happy spouses did. They may also have reciprocated such behavior, and also been affected by it enough to cause them further unhappiness. Although the causal direction is not clear, earlier research would suggest a bidirectional "vicious cycle."

Thus, we have evidence for the benefit of understanding a spouse's conflict style, particularly for women, and particularly with regard to destructive conflict styles. In a related study, Corsini (1956) demonstrated that the relationship between wives' understanding of husbands' personality characteristics and couples' satisfaction was due to the extent to which the husbands were typical (i.e., were like other husbands rather than unique) and the extent to which their wives saw them this way. One might suggest that our findings be interpreted in a similar fashion. However, Kenny (1991) has analyzed the data from the present study and found that a wife's marital well-being relates to her understanding of her husband's unique destructive style, not to her understanding of how typical he is as Corsini's work suggests. On the other hand, with regard to the constructive styles, marital well-being of both husbands and wives is related to understanding the extent to which one's spouse is typical, calling into question the meaning of understanding with regard to constructive styles.

An important finding in this study is that perceived similarity operates more strongly than actual similarity with regard to conflict management styles. As couples negotiate their shared reality in the first year of marriage, they evidently develop couple norms for how to fight which become part of the way they think about their lives. There are also some indications that the more they think they are congruent with regard to fighting, the better they feel about their marriage. Whether they are actually similar is another matter. In fact, there is evidence that actual similarity with regard to destructive conflict styles is associated with marital dissatisfaction for wives. These findings are extremely important in light of the distinction that Duck (1991) makes between similarity and shared meaning. He points out that "the importance of similarity is not its existence, but the *recognition* of its existence by the persons concerned" (Duck, 1991, p. 21). Our findings suggest that perceived similarity is more important than actual similarity in the early stages of a marriage. Perhaps, over time, spouses become more similar in line with their perceptions (see White, 1985), and perhaps those perceptions of similarity and the communication of those perceptions help make it so.

The authors of this article found support for most of their predictions. Couples did in fact have greater perceived than actual similarity in their conflict resolution behaviors. However, note that the authors define "actual" similarity as that which a researcher can locate. Consider the implications of such a view and the possible limitations that it entails. For example, what happens if the researchers disagree with the couple themselves? The authors note somewhat incongruously that this term does not imply that they have a direct measure of actual similarity, however.

The authors also found that wives were more accurate in their perceptions than their husbands, and their perceptions were better predictors of marital well-being than husbands' perceptions. These sex differences were attributed to the asymmetrical power of males and females in most societies and that females (in the lower power position) need to more accurately assess and predict male (higher power) attitudes and behaviors. Additionally, destructive behaviors were more accurately perceived by both husbands and wives. The authors argue that the saliency of negative behaviors may contribute to a negative reciprocity cycle (Gottman, 1979). However, are all destructive behaviors equally salient and would we expect similar patterns to emerge if each destructive technique were analyzed separately rather than a combination of several as in the present article? The next article in this chapter narrows their consideration of destructive behaviors to a single communication pattern – demand/withdrawal.

In the previous article Acitelli, Douvan and Veroff (1993) grouped several destructive problem-solving techniques (yelling/shouting, insulting or calling names, threatening, bringing the spouse's family into the argument, bringing up things in the past, having the last word) into a single category and conducted their analysis based on the combined effect of these behaviors. Although we would agree that these behaviors are all harmful (and that it is unlikely we would ever be able to construct an exhaustive list of destructive behaviors), other techniques could be added to more fully represent this class of behaviors. For example, Gottman (1979) suggests that distressed couples often display a demand/withdrawal communication pattern that hinders the ability of the couple to resolve conflicts effectively. Vogel and Karney (2002) examined this particular pattern in an observational study where couples were videotaped while discussing one problem selected by each spouse. Once again we must consider the role of power and sex, this time for the demand/withdrawal pattern. Would you expect the husband or wife to demand or withdraw in conflict situations? Would husbands (or wives) be more likely to demand when certain topics were discussed, or would the same demand/withdrawal pattern emerge regardless of topic? Finally, previous research has demonstrated the demand/withdrawal pattern in established couples. Would we expect it to be present even in newlyweds? If so, what implications would this have for explaining potential causes of distress later in marriage?

As noted above, Vogel and Karney (2002) are noteworthy in their description of the techniques they used to avoid experimental error and possible confounds in their experiment. Pay close attention to these efforts and to their use of the **Bonferroni *p* adjustment** to avoid capitalizing on chance due to repeated significance tests. The technique increases the critical value needed to claim significance with each additional significance test performed on a single data set. (So, for example, it raises the stakes from $p < .05$ – five chances in a hundred – to $p < .01$ – one chance in a hundred – as the standard for judging whether an observed result is "unlikely" to occur merely by chance.) Finally, the authors are very candid about the design limitations of their study. Their discussion of these issues models the forthright approach needed when evaluating the contribution of your own work to a larger set of empirical literature.

Demands and Withdrawal in Newlyweds: Elaborating on the Social Structure Hypothesis

David L. Vogel and Benjamin R. Karney

A central feature of a successful close relationship is the ability to resolve conflict (Canary, Cupach & Messman, 1995). Indeed, research confirms that the behaviors partners exchange during problem-solving interactions account for a variety of important relationship outcomes. In marital relationships, for example, the quality of couples' problem-solving behaviors accounts for cross-sectional and longitudinal variability in their satisfaction. Furthermore, observations of couples' interactions have been shown to predict whether or not a marriage will end in divorce (e.g., Gottman & Levenson, 1992). Accordingly, patterns of communication behaviors, and especially problem-solving behaviors, have become a central target for interventions aimed at alleviating or preventing marital distress (e.g., Baucom & Epstein, 1989).

One particularly relevant set of behaviors occurs when one partner exhibits demanding behavior (e.g., asking for changes in the relationship), while the other partner concurrently exhibits withdrawal behavior (e.g., attempting to avoid discussing the issue). This **demand/withdraw pattern**, although common in intimate relationships, is especially likely to be exhibited by distressed or less satisfied couples (e.g., Heavey, Christensen, & Malamuth, 1995). Furthermore, the demand/ withdraw pattern is also related to misunderstanding between partners and it appears to predict declines in relationship satisfaction over time (e.g., Smith, Vivian & O'Leary, 1991).

Whereas most specific behaviors that have been shown to have negative consequences

for relationships (e.g., blaming, stonewalling, name-calling) are demonstrated to similar degrees by men and women (e.g., Cupach & Canary, 1995), a distinguishing feature of the demand/withdraw pattern is that there appear to be reliable sex differences in the extent to which partners demand or withdraw during problem-solving discussions. Specifically, numerous studies have shown that, when interacting about an area of difficulty or attempting to resolve a problem, women are more likely to express demands and men are more likely to exhibit withdrawal (e.g., Vogel, Wester, & Heesacker, 1999). Initial attempts to account for this difference suggested that women and men bring differences in needs and desires (e.g., Christensen, 1988), biological dispositions (Gottman & Krokoff, 1989), or socialized problem-solving abilities (Tannen, 1995) to their communication style in a relationship. Christensen and colleagues (e.g., Christensen & Shenk, 1991), for example, demonstrated that women desire more closeness and men desire more autonomy within a relationship and that the desired level of closeness within a relationship affects the use of demand and withdraw behaviors. Those individuals who desired greater autonomy were more likely to withdraw, whereas those individuals who desired greater closeness were more likely to demand.

In contrast to this early research, however, more recent attempts to account for sex differences in demand/withdraw behaviors have focused less on qualities that may be intrinsic to men and women and more on the effects of the social structure within which men and women are embedded. Drawing from the large body of work investigating sex as a context-dependent phenomenon (e.g., Deaux & Lafrance, 1998), the social *structure hypothesis* suggests that the demand/withdraw pattern develops as a result of sex-based power and resource inequalities within contemporary life (e.g., Kluwer, Heesink, & Vliert, 2000). Such inequalities (e.g., men's control over household income, women's presumed responsibility for housework or childcare) lead to problem-solving discussions in which there is an asymmetrical dependence of one partner on the other for a successful outcome of the discussion (Sagrestano et al., 1998). In contrast to a focus on intrinsic sex differences, the social structure hypothesis suggests that differences in the communication styles of men and women reflect strategic responses to this unequal situation. Those individuals who need their partner's cooperation are more likely to employ demand behaviors during the discussion in order to try and elicit a change in the other. Those individuals who do not need their partner's cooperation are more likely to withdraw from the discussion in order to maintain the status quo. Thus, this perspective suggests that demand/withdraw patterns are most likely to occur in any situation "where one partner needs the other's cooperation for resolution of the conflict [whereas] the [other] partner can achieve satisfaction without the other" (Sagrestano et al., 1998, p. 293). In this view, women are more likely to be observed making demands and their husbands are more likely to be observed withdrawing simply because women happen to be in the subordinate role more often and men in the superior role.

Previous research comparing the two accounts of sex differences in demand/withdraw offers some support for the social structure hypothesis. For example, although wives tend to demand more than husbands and husbands tend to withdraw more than wives across previous studies of marital interaction, Christensen and colleagues have found that this difference emerges only during discussions of topics selected by wives. When couples are specifically requested to discuss a problem selected by the husband, the differences disappear. These results are consistent with the idea that the demand/withdraw pattern is not based on individual or sex-related characteristics, but on power differences present in the relationship (Sagrestano, 1992). The discussion of an issue in which the wife desires the most change is a place where asymmetry is likely to be the greatest and as such the wife is more likely to pressure for change and the husband is more likely to withdraw.

Despite the consistency of the research, support for the social structure explanation of the demand/withdraw pattern has nonetheless been limited in several ways. First, research on demand/withdraw has been conducted almost exclusively on well-established marriages. Thus, it is not clear whether the commonly observed sex differences in demand/withdraw behaviors are present early in the marriage, or whether they only emerge as the marriage develops. In support of the latter possibility, a number of researchers have observed that couples tend to adopt more traditional roles the longer they are married (e.g., Markman, Silvern, Clements, & Kraft-Hanak, 1993). Furthermore, inequity and communication difficulties may change over the course of the relationship (Markman & Kraft, 1989) as repeatedly unsuccessful resolutions of the same conflict can lead to communication patterns characterized by increased polarization and asymmetry (Heavey et al., 1993). Thus, the focus on established marriages leaves open the possibility that changes in a marriage over time give rise to the demand/withdraw pattern, rather than the pattern being a causal factor in the development of marital outcomes. In contrast, establishing the presence of sex differences in demand/withdraw among younger, relatively satisfied couples would support the idea that these differences are not a product of experience in the marriage, but arise from enduring factors that exist before the marriage, like sex or social structure. The first goal of the current study was to address this limitation by examining whether sex differences in demand/withdraw behaviors could be observed in a sample of newlywed couples.

A second limitation of the research is that associations between demand and withdraw behavior have generally been assumed rather than demonstrated. Thus, for example, studies have examined sex differences in the demand/withdraw pattern by creating a composite demand/withdraw score for each spouse, without first examining demand and withdraw behaviors separately. There are two problems with this approach. First, examining only the composite demand/withdraw score leaves the precise nature of any sex differences uncertain. For example, sex differences in a demand/withdraw composite score may arise from sex differences in demanding behaviors, withdrawal behaviors, or both. Second, creating a composite demand/withdraw score assumes that increased levels of demand in one partner are associated with increased levels of withdrawal in the other partner. As far as we are aware, there has been no observational research on marital interactions that has confirmed this assumption, leaving the meaning of the composite score in doubt. The second goal of the current study was to evaluate the association between demanding and withdrawing behaviors in early marriage, by examining both behaviors separately in a sample of newlywed couples.

A third limitation of research on the social structure hypothesis is that most operationalizations of power and social structure have been indirect. For example, to manipulate the power balance in a problem-solving discussion, most research on the social structure hypothesis has asked couples to discuss two topics, one chosen by the husband and one chosen by the wife. The assumption of this research has been that partners will each choose topics in which they are seeking change, but this may not necessarily be the case. Husbands, in particular, may choose topics for which they know their wives desire change, as a way of pre-empting or alleviating potential conflict. The fact that

research on the social structure hypothesis has obtained no sex differences at all for discussions of husbands' topics lends some support to this idea. Evaluating precisely how imbalances in the desire for change affect the nature of marital interactions requires that each partner's power during each topic be measured more directly. The third goal of this study was to elaborate on the role of power imbalances in the use of demand/ withdraw behaviors by directly assessing this aspect of power during newlyweds' problem-solving discussions.

Method

Newlywed couples were solicited by two methods. First, advertisements were placed in community newspapers and bridal shops offering up to $300 to couples willing to participate in a longitudinal study of marriage. Second, applications for marriage licenses were reviewed and couples eligible to participate on the basis of the information available on their applications were sent a letter of invitation. Couples responding to either method were interviewed further over the phone to determine whether they met the following criteria: this was the first marriage for each partner; the couple had been married less than three months; neither partner had children; each partner was at least 18 years of age and wives were less than 35 years of age (to allow that all couples were capable of conceiving children over the course of the study); each partner spoke English and had completed at least 10 years of education (to ensure comprehension of the questionnaires); and the couple had no immediate plans to move away from the area. The first 82 eligible couples that arrived for their scheduled interview composed the current sample. Analyses revealed no significant differences in age or years of education between couples recruited through the different types of solicitations.

On average, husbands were 25.1 ($SD = 3.3$) years old, and had completed 16.3 ($SD = 2.4$)

years of education. Forty percent were employed full time and 54% were full-time students. Wives averaged 23.7 (*SD* = 2.8) years old and had completed 16.3 (*SD* = 1.2) years of education. Thirty-nine percent were employed full time, and 50% were full-time students. Slightly over 70% of the sample was Christian (over 45% were Protestant) and 83% of husbands and 89% of wives were white. The mean combined income of couples was less than $20,000 per year.

Procedure

Eligible couples were scheduled to attend a 3-hour laboratory session. Before the session, they were mailed a packet of questionnaires to complete at home and bring with them to their appointment. This packet contained the dependent measures as well as a letter instructing the partners to complete all questionnaires independently of each other.

As part of the laboratory session, each spouse was first interviewed separately. At the end of the interview, each spouse identified an area of difficulty in the marriage, and verbally agreed to spend 10 minutes discussing the issue with his or her spouse. Spouses subsequently participated in two 10-minute videotaped discussions in which they were left alone to "work towards some resolution or agreement" for each topic. The order of the two interactions was determined through a coin flip. If both spouses chose the same topic, the spouse who lost the coin flip was asked to choose a second topic. Couples were paid $50 for participating in this phase of the study.

Measures

Marital satisfaction. As part of the packet of questionnaires that spouses completed at home, spouses reported on their satisfaction with the quality of the marriage. The most common measures used to assess marital satisfaction ask spouses to report their global sentiments towards the marriage, as well as

their level of agreement about specific problem areas (e.g., the Marital Adjustment Test; Locke & Wallace, 1959). As several authors (e.g., Fincham & Bradbury, 1987) have pointed out, however, the use of such omnibus measures can lead to inflated associations with other unrelated variables that also address problem-solving abilities. To ensure that these two ideas were not confounded in the current study, spouses were asked to indicate their satisfaction with the marriage using an instrument that exclusively assesses spouses' specific feelings about the marriage. This version of the **Semantic Differential** (SMD; Osgood, Suci & Tannenbaum, 1957) asks spouses to rate their perceptions of their relationship, using 15 pairs of opposing adjectives (e.g., *Bad–Good, Dissatisfied–Satisfied, Unpleasant–Pleasant*) and a 7-point **Likert scale**. Scores potentially range from 15 to 105. In the current sample, the internal consistency of this measure was .91 for husbands and .93 for wives.

Topic importance. Some authors have suggested that limiting the topics that spouses may select can diminish spouses' interest in the discussions they engage in during laboratory sessions (Klinetob & Smith, 1995). To avoid this potential problem, we adopted a nonrestrictive topic selection procedure, allowing each spouse to choose his or her own topic for the problem-solving discussions. Before each discussion, both spouses independently rated how important the topic of the upcoming discussion was to them on a 7-point Likert scale (from *Not at All Important* to *Extremely Important*).

Demand and withdrawal behaviors. To evaluate the extent to which couples engaged in the demand/withdraw pattern during their interactions, videotapes of the interactions were coded using a global rating system adapted from Klinetob and Smith (1995). This system is based on Christensen's (1987) original definitions of demand/withdraw, and requires observers to provide overall ratings of each spouse's behaviors after watching a complete 10-minute interaction. The system consists of two scales for each spouse, one measuring the degree of withdrawal and the other measuring the degree of demanding. The withdrawal scale asked coders to place the spouse's behavior on a 5-point scale from "involved" to "withdrawn." The demand scale asked coders to place the spouse's behavior on a 5-point scale from "no demand" to "demand." Research using this system has shown that these observational codes correlate with self-report measures of demand/withdraw patterns (see Klinetob & Smith, 1995) and are sensitive to variability in these behaviors even among less established relationships (e.g., Vogel, Wester, Heesacker, & Madon, 2003). Additionally, Holtzworth-Munroe, Smutzler, Bates, and Vogel (1995) found high correspondence between this coding system and the global coding system used by Christensen and colleagues (e.g., Christensen & Heavey, 1990).

Before ratings of demand and withdrawal behaviors were obtained, six independent raters (three male and three female undergraduate research assistants), who were blind to the research hypotheses, received approximately 30 hours of training from the first author in the use of the rating system. Training consisted of viewing and rating a series of videotapes from a separate study of couples interacting. Raters were instructed to consider frequency, intensity, and duration of the participants' verbal and nonverbal behaviors before making their ratings.

To ensure that **inter-rater reliability** remained acceptable throughout the coding process, each week two random subsets of three raters were assigned to observe 10 couples (12 couples the final week) with one set of three raters observing the husband's discussion topic and one set of three raters observing the wife's topic (i.e., all topics were coded by three independent raters) for a given couple. The mean of the three raters' scores was used in the final analyses. Because these ratings involved global judgments rated on a **continuous scale** [*How demanding was the spouse on a 5 point scale, Eds*] rather than a **categorical one** [*Demand was used, Yes or No, Eds*], the reliability of the coding was assessed through **Pearson correlations** [*Because it requires both variables*

to be continuous, Eds] between the raters across interactions (e.g., Tinsley & Weiss, 1975). At the end of training, the mean correlation between any subset of three raters was .81. The subsets of three raters continued to achieve acceptable reliability throughout the study with an overall correlation .84 for ratings of withdrawal behavior and .75 for ratings of demanding behavior.

Results

The newlyweds in this sample were generally satisfied (as expected, given that all were within six months of their marriage), were generally discussing problems of moderate importance, and were generally rated as engaging in low levels of demand and withdraw behavior. However, there was substantial variability on all of these variables, justifying further analyses. It is worth noting that, with one exception, none of the behaviors examined here were significantly associated with either spouse's marital satisfaction scores, the exception being that husbands were more demanding during discussions of wives' topics when wives were less satisfied ($r = -.28$, $p < .02$).

To evaluate whether the results of previous studies of social structure and demand/withdraw replicated among newlywed couples, we followed procedures used by Christensen and his colleagues to assess the conjunction of demand and withdraw within each interaction (e.g., Christensen & Heavey, 1990). Following their precedent, ratings of the wife's demanding behavior and the husband's withdrawal behavior were summed to generate a score indicating the degree of wife-demand/husband-withdraw in each interaction. Similarly, ratings of husband's demanding behavior and wife's withdrawal behavior were summed to generate a score indicating the degree of husband-demand/wife-withdraw in each interaction.

Differences in the extent to which couples demonstrated each kind of pattern across topics were evaluated using a 2×2 repeated-measures **analysis of variance (ANOVA)**. The first factor was sex (wife-demand/

husband-withdraw vs. husband-demand/ wife-withdraw) and the second factor was whose topic was being discussed (his topic vs. her topic). The order of the interactions (i.e., whose topic was discussed first) was entered as a between-subjects control variable in all analyses. Results indicated no significant main effect of sex, but a significant main effect of topic ($F(1, 80) = 7.7$, $p < .01$), quali- fied by a significant sex by topic interaction ($F(1, 80) = 4.9$, $p < .03$). To determine the nature of the interaction, **pair-wise compa- risons** of all four cell means were performed using a **Bonferroni adjusted *p*-value** of .0125 (.05/4). As the means suggest, couples demonstrated significantly more wife-demand/husband-withdraw ($M = 3.5$, $SD = 1.1$) than husband-demand/wife-with- draw ($M = 3.0$, $SD = 1.1$) during discussions of wives' topics ($t(81) = 3.44$, $p < .001$), but this difference was in the opposite direction and not significant during discussions of hus- bands' topics. These results replicate previous research demonstrating that the tendency for wives to demand and husbands to withdraw more than vice versa emerges during discus- sions of issues selected by wives, but disap- pears during discussions of issues selected by husbands (e.g., Christensen & Heavey, 1990). However, also as hypothesized, the effect size of the difference for these couples is smaller than has been found for more established couples. For example, among the longer-term couples in the Christensen and Heavey (1990) study, the **effect size** *r* was .52, whereas in the current study the effect size *r* was .13. [Eds: the size of an effect refers to the proportion of the variability in the dependent variable attributable to an independent or predic- tor variable. We will have more to say about effect size in a later chapter.]

Associations between demand and withdraw

Thus far, examining a summary score of ratings of demand and withdraw behav- ior demonstrated that the results of previous studies of established marriages repli- cate among newlywed couples, such that

wife-demand/husband-withdraw was more likely than husband-demand/wife-withdraw, but only during discussions of topics selected by wives. Examining demand and withdraw behaviors separately allowed us to extend this finding by specifying this difference more precisely.

Is one spouse's tendency to demand change associated with a greater tendency to with- draw in the other spouse? To address this question, we examined correlations between each spouse's demanding and withdrawing behavior during each interaction. Contrary to the assumptions of previous research, the correlations reveal that the tendency of one spouse to make demands was not signifi- cantly associated with the tendency of the other spouse to withdraw. Rather, during discussions of wives' topics, wives' tendency to make demands was associated with signif- icantly less withdrawal on the part of their husbands. This association did not reach significance for husbands' topics, nor were husbands' demands associated with their wives' withdrawal during either topic.

In contrast to the expected complemen- tarity between spouses' demand and withdraw behaviors, the more prevalent result within the correlations was similarity. Thus, during wives' topics, each spouse's tendency to with- draw was significantly positively correlated with the partner's withdrawal behavior and each spouse's tendency to demand was signif- icantly positively correlated with the partner's demanding behavior. During husbands' top- ics, the correlation between each spouse's tendency to withdraw was again significantly positive, but the correlation between their tendency to make demands did not reach significance. These results suggest that, when demand and withdraw behaviors do occur in newlywed couples, spouses tend to mirror each other's behavior rather than exhibiting complementary behavior.

Sex differences in demand and withdraw

The lack of the predicted association between demand and withdraw behaviors raises ques- tions about the sex differences observed in research and replicated here. If demand and withdraw behaviors are not associated, then differences in the way husbands and wives engage in the demand/ withdraw pattern may result from differences in demanding, differences in withdrawal, or both. To clarify the nature of the sex difference, we conducted Bonferroni corrected (.05/4 = .0125) paired sample *t*-tests comparing wives and husbands in their tendency to engage in each kind of behavior during each interaction. These analyses revealed that, during discussions of wives' topics, wives were significantly more demanding than husbands ($t(81) = -2.5$, $p < .01$), but husbands were not significantly more withdrawing than wives. Nor were any other sex differences statistically significant across the two discussions. Thus, the elevated levels of the wife-demand/husband-withdraw pattern identified earlier appear to reflect an increase in wives' use of demanding behaviors during discussions of their own issues, rather than any corresponding increase in husbands' tendency to withdraw.

Correlates of demand and withdraw: topic importance

One way to explain how these behaviors may arise in relatively satisfied couples is to examine correlates of demand and withdraw behaviors. To elaborate on the social structure hypothesis, the final set of analyses examined spouses' ratings of the importance of the topics they were discussing. The social structure explanation of demand/withdraw suggests that, regardless of sex, spouses ought to make more demands when discussing topics of greater importance to them, and to withdraw more when discussing topics of less importance to them. To address this idea directly, we examined the associations between each spouse's ratings of the importance of each topic and their behavior during discussions of that topic.

Paired sample *t*-tests revealed that, on average, husbands and wives did not rate their partner's topics as less important than

their own nor did they rate their partner's topics as less important than their partners did. In addition, both spouses' ratings of each topic were significantly positively correlated with each other (for husbands' topics, $r = .36$, $p < .01$, for wives' topics, $r = .33$, $p < .01$), although the correlations between each spouse's ratings of the two topics were not significant.

During discussions of husbands' topics, husbands were less likely to withdraw the more important they or their spouse rated the topic. No other behavior was significantly associated with ratings of the importance of husbands' topics. During discussions of wives' topics, husbands' ratings of topic importance were not significantly associated with either spouse's behaviors, but wives' ratings were associated with behavior. Specifically, consistent with the social structure predictions, the more that wives perceived the topic being discussed as important, the more they were rated as making demands and the less they were rated as withdrawing. In contrast to predictions, wives' ratings of importance were positively associated with husbands' demands, such that husbands were rated as making significantly more demands during discussions of topics their wives perceived to be important.

Discussion

When interacting to resolve a problem or area of disagreement, one sequence of behavior that appears to place couples at risk for negative outcomes is the demand/withdraw pattern, in which one partner demands a change, while the other partner withdraws and attempts to resist change (e.g., Heavey et al., 1995). Unlike other behaviors that have negative consequences for relationships, the demand/withdraw pattern has been linked to sex, such that women are more likely to report demanding, whereas men are more likely to report withdrawing (Christensen & Heavey, 1990). Observing this difference, some researchers have concluded that males and females have different languages for communicating in close relationships (Tannen, 1995). In contrast to this view, however, recent evidence suggests that sex differences in demand and withdraw behavior may result from power differences between males and females in the social structure (Sagrestano et al., 1998). The overarching goal of the current study was to elaborate on these explanations by examining observational data on demand and withdraw behaviors in newlywed couples.

The first specific aim of this study was to determine whether tests of the social structure hypothesis replicate among relatively satisfied couples in their first weeks of marriage. With respect to this goal, the current study found that, when the same procedures are used to calculate composite demand/withdraw scores, the results of research on the social structure hypothesis did replicate among newlyweds. That is, during discussions of problems selected by wives, the pattern of wife-demand/husband-withdraw was more likely than the pattern of husband-demand/wife-withdraw, but during discussions of topics selected by husbands both of these patterns were equally likely. Although the size of this effect was smaller among the newlyweds examined here, this is precisely the pattern of results observed by Christensen and Heavey (1990) among established marriages. Those authors interpreted this finding as support for the idea that sex differences in demand/withdraw behaviors arise from differences in the consequences of engaging in problem-solving discussions for men and women, rather than from intrinsic sex differences in the way men and women communicate. The current findings extend the support for this idea by demonstrating that the link between who desires the change and the presence of the sex difference is observable even among relatively satisfied newlyweds. Thus, as others have suggested (e.g., Vogel et al., 1999), the blueprint for marital communication may be established early or even before the marriage, and may simply be amplified as relationships develop.

The second aim of this study was to specify the nature of these differences by examining demand and withdraw behaviors separately. These analyses extended research on demand/withdraw in two ways. First, these data are the first that we are aware of to directly examine the correlations among observed demand and withdraw behaviors in marital interactions. In contrast to the assumption that one spouse's demands would be associated with the partner's withdrawal, these correlations revealed that each spouse's levels of each behavior tended to be positively correlated, such that spouses demanded more when their partner demanded and withdrew more when their partner withdrew. Thus, although the spouses in this study were demanding and withdrawing, there was no evidence for a demand/withdraw pattern per se in these interactions. How can this result be reconciled with the observation of clear patterns in more established relationships? One possibility is that the demand/withdraw pattern, rather than being a causal factor in the development of marital distress, may emerge only after marriages become distressed. Among the relatively satisfied couples studied here, both partners were equally invested in the problems under discussion. Over time, increased problems, stress, or unresolved conflicts may lead to greater power imbalances within the couple, which may ultimately lead to increased polarity in spouses' use of demand and withdraw behaviors. In support of this possibility, Noller, Feeney, Bonnell, and Callan (1994) reported that husbands and wives who were less satisfied as newlyweds were more likely to engage in demand/withdraw patterns after two years of marriage. Although this study did not examine the association between demand and withdraw directly, these findings are consistent with the idea that the association between demand and withdraw behaviors may emerge only as the quality of the relationship deteriorates (e.g., Heavey et al., 1995). A second possibility is that demand and withdraw behaviors are not strongly associated even among established relationships. This research is the first (that we know of) to directly examine the associations among demand and withdraw behaviors. Without similar analyses of the associations between these two variables within established or distressed relationships, it may be that conclusions about the existence of a clear demand/withdraw pattern have been premature.

As a second extension of the research, the independence of demand and withdrawal behaviors in these interactions suggested re-examining the sex differences in the demand/withdraw pattern. These analyses revealed that, during interactions in which sex differences emerge, wives were more likely to demand than husbands, but husbands were no more likely to withdraw than wives. This finding contrasts with results from studies of established marriages (e.g., Christensen & Heavey, 1990) that identified sex differences in both behaviors. Why should a tendency for wives to make more demands emerge earlier in the marriage than a tendency for men to withdraw? Even in the most satisfied relationships, societal inequalities are still likely to be present. Indeed, women continue to be responsible for more of housework than men (Kluwer et al., 2000), even during the initial stages of marriage. Furthermore, whereas most spouses today enter a relationship expecting equality, few couples actually achieve it. Thus, even early in the relationship, women may still be more likely than men to desire change, or at least to initiate negotiation to establish an egalitarian relationship. In the early stages of a relationship, husbands may be committed to resolving their wives' unmet needs, and so it makes sense there would be no sex differences in withdrawal even when wives are more demanding. Indeed, the fact that husbands and wives in the current sample perceived each other's topics to be as important as their own topics lends credence to this idea. Longitudinal research on the development of marital interaction patterns over time may [or may not] reveal that, as asymmetries in perceptions of importance emerge later in the marriage, sex differences in withdrawal may

[or may not] follow early sex differences in demand.

The final aim of this study was to examine whether observations of demand and withdrawal behavior are associated with a direct measure of each spouse's desire for change, namely the importance of each topic of discussion to each spouse. Results indicated that, regardless of who chose the topic, both spouses' behaviors were associated with how important they viewed the topic being discussed, such that spouses generally made more demands and were less likely to withdraw when the topic being discussed was perceived as more important. These results provide direct support for the social structure hypothesis, showing that behavior during a marital interaction is a function not of sex but of the investment of each spouse in the problem being discussed. The sex differences that were observed here and that have been observed more strongly in established marriages may therefore be seen as evidence that wives may be more likely to set the agenda for marital interactions, choosing topics that their husbands do not perceive as important. When husbands do perceive the topic being discussed as important, as was the case here, sex differences are greatly reduced.

Our confidence in the pattern of results here is enhanced by a number of strengths of this study. First, rather than relying on partners' self-reports of their behavior during conflict, the current analyses draw from observational coding of spouse's demand and withdrawal behavior. Thus, these data are free from possible bias due to self-presentation effects. Second, in contrast to research examining these issues among couples that vary widely in marital duration, the current data were drawn from a sample of newlywed couples. As a result, the current results are unlikely to be the result of uncontrolled factors like marital duration, the presence of children, or remarriage. Finally, the current study benefited from a direct assessment of each spouse's investment in the topics discussed, rather than relying on any implicit assessment of the power dynamics in the relationship.

Despite these strengths, the conclusions that can be drawn from these results are also limited in several ways. First, although the relatively homogeneous sample enhanced the **internal validity** of these results, generalizations to other populations should be made with caution. Research does allow us to suggest connections between these findings and those from less satisfied, more established marriages, but the possibility remains that the correlates and consequences of demand and withdraw behaviors may differ in couples who vary in ethnicity, or socio-economic status. Cross-cultural research, in particular, would strengthen claims about the role of social structure in intimate relationships, especially if sex differences vary across cultures that differ in levels of equality. Second, given the strictly cross-sectional nature of these data, any causal statements must be made with caution. In particular, any strong statements about the way demand and withdrawal behaviors may develop over time must await longitudinal tests of the patterns that appear to emerge early in marriage. Finally, whereas the size of the current sample compares favorably with other samples used to examine these issues, it is possible that a larger sample would have had more power to detect sex differences in the use of these behaviors.

The broader implications of sex differences in demand and withdrawal behaviors depend in large part on the source of these differences. If sex differences arise from intrinsic differences in the way that men and women communicate, then the negative outcomes associated with the demand/withdraw pattern might be prevented if husbands and wives were taught distinct sets of communication skills. The current findings, however, support an alternative view. Among relatively satisfied newlyweds, differences emerged only in rates of demanding, and only during discussions of topics chosen by wives. Furthermore, both spouses' behaviors were associated with their investment in the issues under discussion. These results are consistent with the idea that sex differences in demand and withdrawal behaviors may be a result of the different kinds of problems faced by males and females in close relationships, rather than from any intrinsic differences in their abilities. Severing the link between demand/withdrawal behaviors and negative outcomes may therefore require interventions that address those problems directly. Thus, the current findings speak to the potential benefits of considering not only the interactions between spouses, but also the context in which those interactions occur.

When composite scores of demand and withdrawal behaviors were used to sum across all interactions, a familiar pattern of wife-demand/husband-withdraw for wife-selected topics emerged. However, when individual exchanges were examined (demand followed by either a withdrawal or demand by the other spouse) a different pattern emerged with husbands and wives using the same strategy (i.e., demand → demand, withdraw → withdraw). The authors suggest the classic "wife-demand/husband-withdraw" pattern based on composite scores indicates that a template for harmful communication patterns may be established early in relationships, possibly during courtship. However, their unique analysis of individual behavioral exchanges reveals a "tit-for-tat" communication pattern in newlyweds and opens the possibility that the same pattern might be found in established or distressed couples if individual exchanges are the unit of measurement. The authors recognize that these results need to be replicated with additional samples and they also discuss the value of longitudinal designs in understanding the conflict strategies of couples in all stages of their relationships.

Vogel and Karney also found that although wives were more likely to identify problems, sex had less impact on the demand/withdraw pattern than the perceived importance of the topic for each spouse (spouses agreed that both lists of topics were equally important). One wonders if the pattern of demand/withdraw will change for these newlyweds as different situations emerge that alter the importance they attach to various topics of conversation. Perhaps they will demonstrate a decline in the "shared reality" demonstrated in this study and be replaced with the "shared perception" of similarity discussed by Acitelli et al., or a classic wife-demand/husband-withdraw pattern if relationship well-being declines – if of course the relevant variables to be studied legitimately can be operationalized in a way that does not beg the question; that is to say, if the means of measuring the variables does not prejudge the outcomes, as for example it would if the measure of conflict presupposes disagreement about perceptions. Finally, as Vogel and Karney suggest, a longitudinal design would address such issues across the stages of relationship development; but also a cross-cultural study would provide a more direct test of the social context hypothesis.

10 Relationship Disturbance

We have already looked at relationship initiation, development and maintenance, but as you can tell from the preceding chapters, we have moved now to the negative aspects of relational experience. In this chapter we deal with the things that happen when a relationship is disturbed or even breaks up. Is it just a matter of people deciding rationally and strategically that they are incompatible or is it a matter of emotional fluctuation and uncertainty? Is the experience the same for the breaker and the "breakee"?

In ways that reflect the progress of research on relational maintenance (Chapter 7), research on relationship dissolution began with the idea that break-up is strategic and controlled. Later research suggests a complex multi-layered experience in which strategic activity plays a part, but does not describe the whole. Recent research has also looked at what happens after a break up, since many romantic couples break up and either want to stay as "friends" or else have to continue to interact, willy-nilly, as a result of the fact that they have, say, property or children in common. Indeed, we will suggest (after Rollie & Duck, in press) that the topic has been mis-named: the study of the *dissolution* of relationships is based on a concluded activity where the outcome is already known. We'll suggest that it is more realistic for researchers to see this topic area as "relational disturbance" because partners do not necessarily know that it is anything else at the time when they are going through it. Research has typically represented "dissolution" as strategic, inevitable and goal-directed as we shall see, and we'd encourage you to reflect seriously on whether that idea captures the process at all well.

The first reading here (Baxter, 1984) is one of the earliest attempts to conduct an empirical exploration of the process of relationship break-up and it adopts a strategic focus. As with other exploratory work (cf. Chapter 7 and the Dindia & Baxter (1987) paper on relational maintenance) the technique is based on qualitative and **open-ended data**, which were then sifted into categories using a method known as **inductive analysis.** This technique, as you will recall, involves the researcher's close reading of the data and a preliminary sorting of it into groups so that tentative categories can be set up. Subsequently the validity and usefulness of these first tentative categories are tested against other elements of the data and adjusted as necessary until a category system remains that can satisfactorily incorporate and explain all the data. From this category system other work can be done on the data. In this case, as you will see, Baxter created a flow chart to explain how the categories are linked together to form parts of an overall process, and so produce a model of the process of relational disengagement. In theory, this model could apply to all types of falling out (when friends become enemies, for example), but the data were gathered, in this instance, from people who had been in a heterosexual romantic relationship.

The study introduces research on **retrospective accounts** where subject participants report on something that happened to them some time ago (cf. the Grote & Frieze paper in Chapter 3). This technique has been successfully used in a variety of research situations, especially those that involve the tracking of pathways of relationships over a period of time. Since it is difficult to access long past events in subject participants' lives, their memories are most often all we can get, especially when it comes to their feelings or emotional reactions. If the occurrence of events is what interests researchers then they usually make efforts to validate subject reports, but if the influence of feelings, experiences or memories is the topic of research this sort of method does not require such verification. Mere establishment of the person's own account of their feelings at the time is enough.

A critique of such methods, however, is that they produce data filtered through the hindsight of the reporters, who may want to massage their reports in order to make themselves look good. In the case of reports about relationship breakdown, this could lead to us getting a rosier and more one-sided view of the process than is justified. Also it is surprising just how often people disagree about things. Even partners in the same couple can give markedly different dates and reactions to the same event, a classic being data from Surra et al. (1988) where the two partners in a romantic couple differed by *more than a year* about the date on which they said the first sexual intercourse occurred.

In the following study by Baxter (1984), then, it is important to read the paper with these strengths and limitations in mind. The effects of feelings, memories, and beliefs may be more important in the reports of the break-up process than in some other relationship processes, but we do here have available only the views of one of the participants in the break-up.

Trajectories of Relationship Disengagement

Leslie A. Baxter

The break-up, or disengagement, of personal relationships is increasingly the focus of research attention. However, the vast majority of this work conceptualizes disengagement as an event rather than a process. As Duck (1982) recently noted, "the most important observation for research is that we must avoid the risk of seeing relationship dissolution as an event. On the contrary, it is a process, and an extended one with many facets" (p. 2). Certainly the limited amount of process-oriented disengagement research cannot be attributed to the absence of theoretical work on the process. [Three decades] ago, Altman & Taylor (1973) posited that the disengagement process was simply the relationship growth process in reverse, a view perpetuated in more recent theorizing (Knapp, 1978; Miller & Parks, 1982). However, some recent work has challenged the merit of this reversal hypothesis (Baxter & Philpott, 1982; Duck & Lea, 1982). Some theorists have advanced process views of disengagement which are not conceptually bound by the reversal hypothesis (Bradford, 1980). For the most part, these models focus on the emotional stages of marital break-up. Most recently, Duck (1982) has posited perhaps the most comprehensive model of the disengagement process, one which spans both psychological and social domains in its four phases of dissolution. During the first phase (the Intrapsychic) the person grapples in private with his or her dissatisfaction in the relationship. During the second (Dyadic) phase the person negotiates the dissolution with the partner. Phase three (the Social phase) involves the public presentation of the dissolution to social network ties. The final phase (labeled Grave-dressing) focuses on retrospection about, and recovery from, the break-up.

Given the psychological bent of most existing research in relationship dissolution, it is not surprising that this work is concentrated in the most psychologically oriented of Duck's four phases – the Intra-psychic (Edwards & Saunders, 1981) and the Grave-dressing (Thompson & Spanier, 1983). Further, the first and last phases of Duck's model are most amenable to an event conceptualization of disengagement. The interaction-based phases of Duck's model, the Dyadic phase and the Social phase, have received much less research attention.

The present study is part of the author's ongoing program of research focused on the Dyadic phase of Duck's model, that is, the process by which relationship parties negotiate their un-bonding. With the exception of a single study, however, this research program has not solicited information on the step-by-step sequencing of disengagement actions, focusing instead on two broad issues: (1) situational and individual difference variables which affect the initial disengagement action of the disengager (Baxter & Philpott, 1982) and (2) general interaction characteristics of disengaging relationships (Baxter & Wilmot, 1982). These two issues dominate in the disengagement work of other communication-oriented researchers as well (Wilmot & Carbaugh, 1983). In the single study that investigated action sequences, Baxter & Philpott (1980) asked respondents to complete hypothetical story-starts about relationships on the verge of break-up, generating step-by-step chronologies of what transpired in those relationships. We found that the disengagement process was more protracted in those stories in which the disengager initiated negotiation through avoidance strategies as opposed to open discussion between the relationship parties. Further, the stories revealed a cycling pattern between approach/avoidance strategies in instances where resolution was not accomplished in a single negotiated action. Although 75 percent of the study's respondents reported that they had either directly experienced a break-up similar to their fictionalized accounts or had indirectly witnessed other people experiencing such break-ups, the hypothetical nature of the task makes problematic the generalizability of the findings. Clearly, process-oriented data are needed relative to actual disengaging.

Existing theoretical work presents disengagement as a sequence of states more or less comparable from relationship to relationship, ignoring potential differences between relationships. As Kressel et al. (1980) have observed:

> Research on divorce, like that on acquaintanceship and courtship, has focused on the stages through which the relationship passes, with little attention to the patterned differences among individuals or couples. (p. 107)

Notable exceptions to this undifferentiated view are Davis (1973) and Kressel et al. (1980). At the theoretical level, Davis established the distinction between "fading away" and "sudden death" dissolutions. At the empirical level, Kressel and his colleagues noted four basic types of dissolution in their case studies of divorcing couples: (1) the enmeshed pattern, characterized by high levels of ambivalence, communication and conflict about the divorce decision; (2) the autistic pattern, characterized by high ambivalence about the divorce decision but the absence of explicit communication; (3) the direct-conflict pattern, frequented by open conflict and communication about the divorce decision at somewhat lower levels of intensity than with the enmeshed pattern; and (4) the disengaged conflict pattern, characterized by limited communication and conflict because the parties were no longer interested enough in one another to interact. Davis's "fading away" pattern appears to correspond to the fourth type observed by Kressel et al., and "sudden death" may parallel the direct-conflict pattern. However, the four types found by Kressel et al. are based on a small sample size of fourteen couples, and nine of these fourteen underwent mediation intervention efforts which may have produced "unnatural" dissolution processes. Empirical work is needed to examine dissolution patterns for relationships not subject to intervention by professionals.

The present study was designed to study the process of termination followed by relationships. Specifically, the research question was: What are the process characteristics by which relationship parties disengage their personal relationships?

Methods

Respondents were ninety-seven volunteers (sixty females, thirty-seven males) drawn from introductory communication courses with a mean age of 19.4 years and an age range of 18–29 years. All participating respondents had experienced the break-up of a heterosexual romantic relationship within twelve months before data collection. The terminated relationships ranged in length from one month to three years, with an average duration of 6.2 months.

Data collection procedures. Respondents provided retrospective accounts of their respective non-marital romantic relationship break-ups following the general procedure employed by Braiker & Kelley (1979). Each respondent was given a blank deck of $5'' \times 8''$ cards with oral and written instructions to record on the cards all of the important stages, periods or turning points in the dissolution of the relationship, commencing with the initial point at which the relationship first began to dissolve. Respondents were to record one stage/period/turning point per card, in the order in which they occurred, using as many cards as they perceived necessary. On each card respondents were asked to record two pieces of information: (1) a short phrase descriptor which captured the essence of that stage/period/turning point, and (2) a free-response paragraph which described all of the relevant details thought necessary for a more complete picture of the stage/period/turning point. On their last card respondents were asked to record general background information about themselves, their relationship partners and the relationship that dissolved. The free-response task required an average of about thirty minutes to complete, but participants ranged anywhere from fifteen minutes to over one hour in responding to the task.

Analysis procedures. Analysis had two parts: (1) development of a flow-chart model of the disengagement process; (2) coding of all process accounts in terms of the flow chart's distinctive features to discern the most frequent disengagement trajectories. Development of the flow chart resembled what Bulmer (1979) has labeled "analytic induction". In general terms "analytic induction" involves subjective sense-making of the data by the researcher through formulating categories for a given datum, "testing" these tentative categories in additional cases, revising the categories to fit these additional cases, "testing" the revised analytic categories on additional data cases and so forth until successive revisions produce a category set which captures the data as a whole. With specific reference to this study, the author derived elements of the flow chart inductively from a subset of the card decks and then analyzed the derived distinctive features against additional data cases, which in turn led to revision of the posited flow chart, which was again examined against additional data cases and so forth in a series of successive iterations. This process of analytic induction resulted in the flow chart of disengagement described in greater detail below. The author then applied this flow chart on a case-by-case basis to the process accounts in order to determine the most frequent disengagement trajectories; ninety-two of the ninety-seven accounts (95 percent) were successfully traced with the flow-chart model. In order to gauge the reliability of the author's case-by-case judgments, an independent coder assessed a 50 percent random sample of the accounts using the flow-chart model. Absolute agreement between the two sets of judgments was 83.6 percent, a level of agreement sufficiently high to warrant continued analysis with the author's set of judgments.

Results

The flow chart of disengagement Figure 1 details the flow chart which was constructed from the ninety-two codable accounts. Consistent with the symbol set employed by computer scientists, parallelograms ($\square$) indicate points of input or output, diamonds ($\diamond$) indicate decision points with "Yes" or "No" decision branches, and ellipses ($\bigcirc$) indicate entry or exit points for the model. Although it is complex, the flow chart captures the six critical features of the dissolution process by which the sampled relationships varied: (1) the gradual vs. sudden onset of relationship problems; (2) the unilateral vs. bilateral desire to exit the relationship; (3) the use of direct vs. indirect actions to accomplish the dissolution; (4) the rapid vs. protracted nature of the disengagement negotiation; (5) the presence vs. absence of relationship repair attempts; and (6) the final outcome of relationship termination vs.

relationship continuation (in transformed or restored form). These six features become apparent in progressing through the flow chart from the point of entry to the point of exit. This progression is verbally summarized in the following seven steps, which are also marked on the flow chart.

Step 1: the onset of relationship problems. The flow chart is entered at the point at which the relationship was retrospectively perceived to enter dissolution. Represented by the first parallelogram in the upper-left corner of Figure 1, two types of relationship "inputs" were evident in this set of accounts: "Incrementalism" and the "Critical Incident". Relationships characterized by Incrementalism involved the reported stockpiling of several relationship problems preceding the decision by at least one of the persons that the relationship should end. Relationships characterized by a Critical Incident involved a single reported relationship problem of major magnitude which erupted with little warning. The following excerpts from respondent accounts illustrate the Incrementalism and Critical Incident types, respectively:

> The first thing that upset me was that she didn't like my dog. I love my dog, and this bothered me. But we continued to see each other. Then I discovered that she had been married before. I started to wonder about how compatible we were, but we still continued as a couple. Then her former boyfriend started calling her up, which upset me because she didn't tell him about us. We argued a lot and things were tense between us then. I finally decided that I'd had it and wanted out.

> From a mutual friend, she found out that I had been seeing other people while she was away at school. She confronted me and it was all over.

In this data set twenty-three of the ninety-two accounts (25 percent) contained a critical incident.

Step 2: the decision to exit the relationship. Regardless of the type of relationship problem experienced, at least one of the parties formed a desire to dissolve the relationship, represented in an "input" factor in the model by the second parallelogram. At this juncture a crucial distinction emerged in the

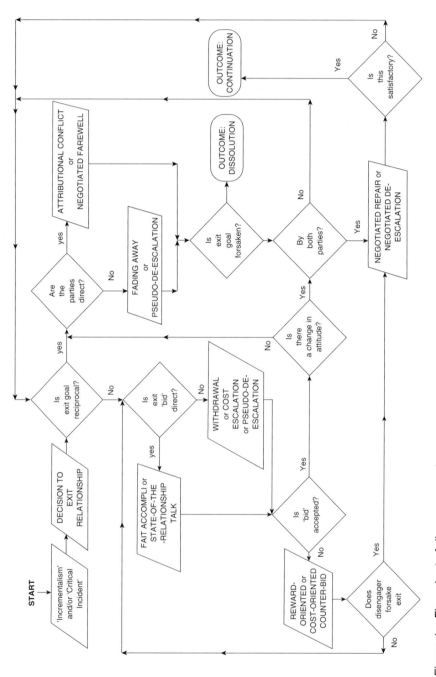

Baxter, Figure 1   Flow chart of disengagement

accounts between one-sided as opposed to two-sided resolutions to exit the relationship; the flow chart captures this juncture in the first diamond ("Is the exit goal reciprocal?"). In this data set 68 percent of the relationships were described as unilateral in the desire to terminate the relationship and 32 percent were described as bilateral desires to terminate; this distributional difference exceeds chance ($\chi^2 = 12.57$; df = 1; $p < .001$). In probability terms, then, there was a .68 likelihood that a relationship would follow the "No" branch at the first decision juncture in the flow chart and a .32 probability of following the "Yes" branch. Critical incidents were just as likely to precede unilateral as bilateral resolutions to exit.

For ease in following the flow-chart model, steps 3 through 5 below focus on unilateral terminations while steps 6 and 7 deal with bilateral terminations.

Step 3: initiating unilateral dissolution actions. Once a person unilaterally decided to exit a relationship, he or she faced the communicative task of informing or persuading the other party. Accounts varied on the degree of directness exhibited by the disengager in this communicative task or "bid" represented on the flow chart with a second decision juncture ("Is the exit 'bid' direct?").

Among unilateral resolutions to exit, 76 percent employed indirect, as opposed to direct, means of initially communicating with the partner, a difference significant beyond chance ($\chi^2 = 17.29$; df = 1; $p < .001$). This indirectness was manifested in three basic communicative actions whose frequency distribution significantly departed from chance ($\chi^2 = 24.50$; df = 2; $p < .001$): "Withdrawal" (66 percent of all indirect cases), "Pseudo-De-escalation" (22 percent) and "Cost Escalation" (12 percent). Withdrawal involved avoidance-based behaviors in which the disengager reduced the intimacy of contact and/or lessened the frequency of contact with the partner. Withdrawal is illustrated in this account excerpt:

I took a stand that related to too much homework for an excuse to avoid her. She then initiated

notes to me which contained certain things that both of us didn't like about the relationship. I never answered the notes, so she would call and try to get me to talk about the problems. I always kept the talks short and said I had to get off the phone.

Pseudo-De-escalation involved a false declaration to the other party that the disengager desired a transformed relationship of reduced closeness; the action is indirect because the desire to exit totally from the relationship is not made explicit. Pseudo-De-escalation is illustrated in this account excerpt:

I arranged to talk with her in a neutral location, the parking lot, outside of either car etc. What I said basically (hating the whole idea behind it) was "Let's go back to being just friends" (knowing full well I meant I wanted to salvage my ego, and hers, by saying indirectly the relationship was totally over).

Cost Escalation involved behavior towards the other party which increased his or her relational costs. Costs were escalated in many ways, but the following account excerpt illustrates the behavioral type:

I knew that if I told her that I did not want to continue the relationship it would really hurt her, so I thought I would be an "asshole" for a while to make her like me less and then I would tell her.

Although significantly less likely as a disengagement attempt, 24 percent of the unilateral resolutions to exit were initiated with Communicative directness. Basically two forms of directness were found in the accounts: Fait Accompli and "State-of-the-Relationship Talk". These represented 73 and 27 percent, respectively, of the direct cases, a difference beyond chance ($\chi^2 = 5.83$; *df* = 1; $p < .05$). Fait Accompli actions were characterized by an explicit declaration to the other party that the relationship was over with no opportunity for discussion or compromise. In contrast the State-of-the-Relationship Talk was characterized by an explicit statement of dissatisfaction and desire to exit in the context of a bilateral discussion of the relationship's problems. The following excerpts from respondent accounts illustrate the difference in tone that distinguishes these two forms of directness:

> On the phone, I told him I was tired of seeing him and that I was bored with him. I said I never wanted to see him again. [Fait Accompli]

> He brought up the issue of breaking up by saying that the fights we'd been having lately were due to our different needs. We had been together for over two years at this point, and he said we were both changing. We talked about it a long time, with me telling him that I would change to fit his needs. He said that he couldn't meet my needs and that this wasn't fair to me or to us in the long run. At the end of the talk, we both agreed to break up. [State-of-the-Relationship Talk]

Step 4: the initial reaction of the broken-up-with party. Regardless of whether the disengager was direct or indirect in communicating with the relationship partner, the model progresses to the decision juncture of whether the other party initially accepted the inevitability, if not the desirability, of the termination. Unilateral resolutions to disengage met significantly different initial acceptance rates from the other party depending on the directness of the disengager's bid. Unilateral disengagements initiated through indirectness had but a .22 likelihood of initial acceptance by the other party, in contrast to the 0.66 likelihood of initial acceptance when the disengager's actions were direct ($\chi^2 = 7.97$; df = 1; $p < .001$). Overall, 35 percent of the unilateral cases resulted in acceptance of the initial disengagement bid. Acceptance by the other party was greatest with Fait Accompli actions (.83 likelihood), probably because the other party perceived the futility of resistance. Acceptance was least likely if the disengager "eased into" the break-up by use of a Pseudo-De-escalation action (.09 likelihood); obviously such action perpetuated the other's hope that the relationship would eventually be restored.

However, despite these variations in acceptance, the modal reaction by the other party was resistance to the termination. This resistance manifested itself in two basic "counter-bid" responses by the other party:

reward-oriented or cost-oriented. Reward-oriented resistance attempted to alter the disengager's decision through the promise of, or enactment of, behavior which the disengager finds positive. Cost-oriented resistance, on the other hand, involved threatened or enacted sanctions against the disengager. The following account excerpts by disengagers typify these two types of resistance from the other party:

> At this point, I noticed that he was trying to get back at me. He talked about me to some of his friends (who were also my friends). They soon broke off from me and dropped a few things I had said, which were never meant to be repeated beyond my boyfriend. [Cost-Oriented]

> She was upset and tried a number of times to "rekindle the fire" by doing nice things for me, getting romantic, etc., but to no avail. [Reward-Oriented]

Step 5: ambivalence and repair scenarios. After an attempt by the disengager has met resistance from the partner, another decision juncture is reached in the flow-chart model: whether the disengager abandons his or her desire to exit the relationship. In those cases in which the exit goal was not abandoned and which thus cycled back through the model for additional negotiation, indirect action was the predominant form of the second disengagement bid. The likelihood of indirect action on the second disengagement attempt was equal regardless of the first attempt's degree of directness – about .75.

Only eight of the sixty-three unilateral resolutions to terminate led to a change of mind by the disengager following the initial attempt. However, the initial reaction of the other party was not statistically related to this change of mind. Half of the changes occurred when the partner had initially accepted the finality of the dissolution (that is, the decision at the flow-chart juncture "Is the 'bid' accepted?" was "Yes", and the outcome was "Yes" at the decision juncture "Is there a change in attitude?"), and the remaining half occurred after initial resistance from the partner.

Among the four cases in which the disengager experienced a change of mind after the other party had accepted the disengagement, half ultimately achieved a restoration ("Negotiated Repair") or transformation ("Negotiated De-escalation") which proved satisfactory, that is, a final outcome of continuation. The other two cases culminated in dissolution after cycling back through the flow chart for additional negotiation.

Among the four cases in which the disengager experienced a change of mind after initial resistance from the partner, only one case culminated in a satisfactory repair which led to the continuation of the relationship. The other three cases involved attempted repairs which proved unsatisfactory, cycling the parties back through the appropriate points of the flow chart for additional disengagement activity.

These eight instances of attitude change occurred following the initial disengagement bid. In relationships which required multiple "passes" through the flow chart in order to gain the acceptance of the other party, an additional eleven changes of attitude occurred, leading to repair attempts of which none were satisfactory. Thus at one stage or another of the dissolution process, nineteen of the sixty-three unilateral exits attempted a repair effort, or 30 percent. Although attempted repairs were more likely following direct actions (.40 likelihood) as opposed to indirect actions (.27 likelihood), the difference was not significant at the .05 level ($\chi^2 = .41$, $df = 1$).

Step 6: initiating bilateral dissolution action. A "Yes" outcome to the decision juncture "Is the exit goal reciprocal?" leads to a decision juncture about the directness employed by the disengaging parties ("Are the parties direct?"). Unlike the findings reported above for unilateral resolutions to exit, the bilateral situation displayed no bias beyond chance in favor of indirectness; 52 percent of disengagement bids were initiated indirectly and 48 percent involved direct communication between the two parties ($\chi^2 = .04$; $df = 1$). Parties in a bilateral dissolution displayed basically two types of indirect

action in negotiating their break-up: "Fading Away" and "Pseudo-De-escalation". Fading Away was characterized by implicit understanding that the relationship had ended. The following excerpt captures the flavor of Fading Away actions:

My lover was a married man who was visiting overnight on his way through Portland. We had a bad night, with a lot of unstated tension by both of us. On the way to the airport next day, we hardly spoke at all. When we did speak it wasn't concerning our relationship. We both knew that it was over and we would probably never see each other again (and that we were both relieved that it was over).

Pseudo-De-escalation is similar to that discussed above under the unilateral resolution to exit, but the deception is mutual rather than one-sided in this instance. The two relationship parties maintain the pretence of a continuing, if transformed, relationship, meanwhile intending total non-contact with one another. This bilateral Pseudo-De-escalation is illustrated in this account excerpt:

We communicated the desire to try and continue the relationship ("just friends") through letters and phone, but I said this just to make parting less painful, and he said it for the same reason. I know this because we ran into one another on vacation and had enough distance from the relationship to be more open about it.

Bilateral directness also took two forms: "Attributional Conflict" and "Negotiated Farewell". Although both parties may wish to exit the relationship, they may have very different views of what went wrong. Attributional Conflict captures a conflict, not over whether to exit, but on why the exit is necessary. Attributional Conflict is clearly evident in this account excerpt:

We had a most awful scene yelling and screaming at each other, and that's where the situation ended. We both wanted out, but were both angry with the other for causing the hurt. I wanted out because he was still seeing his former wife. He, of course, denied this, but said that he wanted out because I wasn't giving him enough breathing space – always accusing him of cheating when not with me.

Negotiated Farewell involves explicit communication between the parties which formally ends the relationship; however, unlike Attributional Conflict, this discussion is noticeably free of hostility and argument. The difference in tone is apparent in comparing the following account excerpt with the one above:

> Our relationship had been having a lot of problems, and we both experienced them. When we'd both had it, we went to dinner and had a good talk about what was going on. We realized that the best thing we had going for ourselves was our friendship and our communication, and both had been dying in the relationship. We decided to remain friends, but that romantic involvement just wasn't meant for us as a couple. (We're now great friends again; we just needed out of the strait-jacket relationship we had been in. Who knows? Maybe someday we'll both be ready for a romantic relationship with each other.)

Indirect disengagements largely involved Fading Away action (twelve of fifteen cases, or 80 percent) as opposed to Pseudo-De-escalation, a difference significant beyond chance ($\chi^2 = 5.40$; $df = 1$; $p < .05$). Direct disengagements were equally distributed among Attributional Conflict and Negotiated Farewell (each representing seven of fourteen cases).

Step 7: ambivalence and repair scenarios. Twelve of the twenty-nine reciprocal resolutions to exit (41 percent) involved a change of mind by both parties, leading to repair attempts. However, all but one of these attempted repairs proved unsatisfactory to at least one party and ultimately ended in termination of the relationship after cycling back into the model at the appropriate point. Repair attempts were more likely following indirect (.53 likelihood) as opposed to direct actions (.29 likelihood), but this difference was not significant ($\chi^2 = 1.85$; $df = 1$).

Based on this summary of the flow-chart model, one might be tempted to conclude that the flow chart is actually two separate flow diagrams, one for unilateral resolutions to terminate and the other for reciprocal resolutions to terminate. However, these two parts of the flow chart are linked for all unilateral dissolutions and for many unsuccessfully repaired bilateral dissolutions. Unilateral resolutions to exit which successfully gain the acceptance of the other party at some stage of the negotiation become bilateral at the point of acceptance by that person; as the flow chart suggests, acceptances not followed by a change of mind by either party feed into the bilateral part of the flow diagram for a capstone stage of Fading Away, Pseudo-De-escalation, Attributional Conflict or Negotiated Farewell. In addition many bilateral desires to exit which underwent repair ended in one-sided dissatisfaction with the repair attempt; as the flow chart demonstrates, such one-sided repair dissatisfactions feed back into the unilateral portion of the flow chart.

Trajectories of disengagement. The complexity of the flow-chart model suggests the large number of paths or trajectories which are possible for any given relationship dissolution once a decision to exit has been made by at least one relationship party. Variation among dissolutions, however, surrounds these basic distinctive features: (1) unilateral/bilateral exit resolution; (2) direct/indirect disengagement action; (3) single/multiple number of "passes" through the model; (4) attempted/unattempted repair action; and (5) termination/continuation outcome. If these five features were independent of one another and equally likely to appear, the number of trajectories would be 2^5 or thirty-two. However, these features are neither independent of one another nor equally likely to occur; thus a smaller number of trajectories captures the variation among dissolutions in these data.

The most frequent dissolution trajectory was unilateral and indirect, requiring multiple "passes" through the model, with no attempted repairs, and with an outcome of relationship termination. Twenty-eight, or 30 percent, of the ninety-two codable dissolutions matched this trajectory type which was labeled Persevering Indirectness.

Two trajectory types occupied a distant second place in overall frequency, each accounting for 11 percent of the codable dissolution cases. The first of these, labeled Ambivalent Indirectness, was characterized by unilateralness, indirectness, an attempted repair, multiple "passes" or disengagement attempts and relationship termination as the outcome. The second type of trajectory, labeled Swift Explicit Mutuality, featured bilateralness, directness, no attempted repairs, with a termination outcome achieved on the first disengagement attempt.

Nine percent of the dissolutions fit the Mutual Ambivalence trajectory, with bilateralness, indirectness, attempted repair, multiple disengagement attempts or "passes" through the model and termination as the final outcome.

Two trajectories each accounted for 8 percent of the dissolution cases: Swift Indirectness and Swift Implicit Mutuality. The Swift Indirectness trajectory was unilateral and indirect, with no attempted repair and a termination accomplished with the initial disengagement action. The Swift Implicit Mutuality trajectory had no attempted repairs, accomplishing termination through bilateral indirect disengagement action.

Two trajectories each accounted for 7 percent of the dissolution cases. The first of these, Ambivalent Directness, accomplished termination after initial unilateral directness was offset with a repair effort which proved unsuccessful and led to further disengagement action. The other trajectory, Swift Directness, involved unilateral directness which readily accomplished a termination. Although four other trajectories were evident in these cases, they collectively accounted for less than 9 percent of the dissolution cases.

Discussion

The five distinctive features of the flow chart which were used to discern trajectories were necessarily simplistic. Finer distinctions apparent in the flow-chart model were ignored for parsimony's sake. The directness/indirectness feature, for example, ignored the variety of ways in which this feature was manifested. The simple distinction between attempted and unattempted repairs ignored the placement of these repairs, that is, actions which preceded and followed the repair attempts. Despite this simplicity, however, the data support the argument by Kressel et al. (1980) that a differentiated approach to the disengagement process is necessary. A single set of stages or steps does not generalize to all, or even most, relationship dissolutions.

The eight trajectories identified in these break-up accounts display both similarities and differences with the works of Davis (1973) and Kressel et al. (1980). Swift Directness and Swift Explicit Mutuality appear similar to Davis's "sudden death". His "fading away" pattern bears some commonality with the Swift Indirectness and Swift Implicit Mutuality trajectories found in this data set, which in turn are similar to the disengaged-conflict pattern noted by Kressel et al. (1980). The enmeshed pattern noted by Kressel et al. (1980) bears some similarity to the trajectory of Ambivalent Directness. Their autistic pattern bears some similarity with Ambivalent Indirectness and Mutual Ambivalence. Last, their direct-conflict pattern shares some of the features of the Swift Explicit Mutuality and the Swift Directness trajectories. Despite elements of commonality, however, existing work in general fails to capture the complexity of the disengagement process reflected in the flow-chart model. In advancing a set of distinctive features associated with disengagement, the flow chart captures a larger array of possible paths to break-up than the two basic patterns identified by Davis (1973) or the four cited by Kressel et al. (1980). In fact the most frequent trajectory in these data, Persevering Indirectness, appears to lack a clear counterpart in existing work. At one level the tacit quality of Persevering Indirectness seems similar to "fading away" and the disengagement-conflict pattern. However, in these latter two patterns both parties seem coordinated in their acceptance of the break-up, quite unlike the situation in Persevering Indirectness. Quite discrepant from popular images of "break-up" in which the parties engage in confrontational combat, Persevering Indirectness captures a gradual wearing down of the other party's resistance.

The direct and indirect disengagement actions included in the flow-chart model display similarity with existing work in disengagement strategies. Directness/indirectness has consistently emerged in this body of work as a significant distinguishing characteristic in disengagement strategy typologies (Baxter, 1979b, 1982; Cody, 1982; Perras & Lustig, 1982). The typological work in the author's research program (Baxter, 1979a, 1982) has also noted a second underlying dimension, self- or other-orientation; other-oriented strategies display a concern about avoiding hurt for the other party, whereas self-oriented strategies are typically costly for the other party. This dimension may be evident in the disengagement actions identified in the flow-chart model. Cost Escalation and Attributional Conflict may exact costs for the other party, whereas Pseudo-De-escalation (unilateral and bilateral), Negotiated Farewell, and State-of-the-Relationship Talk may be less costly for the other party.

The prevalence of indirect initial disengagement strategies among unilateral as opposed to bilateral resolutions to exit is consistent with previous research (Baxter, 1982; Perras & Lustig, 1982). Unfortunately, indirectness is likely to produce a protracted disengagement period with several "negotiation rounds" before the other party accepts the dissolution. Baxter & Philpott (1980) reported a similar finding in their story completion task. On the assumption that disengagement is anxiety provoking, disengagers would be better served by directness as opposed to indirectness in unilateral resolutions to exit; the former action is more likely than the latter to produce a swift exit. In

asking people to reflect on any regrets they had about a recalled disengagement, Baxter (1979b) in fact found over-reliance on indirectness to be the most frequently mentioned regret.

The findings of this study have some bearing on Altman & Taylor's (1973) hypothesis that dissolving relationships cycle between the extremes of excessive interaction and withdrawal. Although Baxter & Philpott (1980) observed approach/avoidance strategy cycling, these data provide limited support for such cycling at the level of strategy use. Regardless of whether the initial disengagement attempt was direct (approach) or indirect (avoidance) in the unilateral case, second attempts were most likely to be indirect. However, a more relevant level of analysis to Altman & Taylor's hypothesis may rest with relationship-level oscillation between dissolution and repair. One-third of the relationships in this data set oscillated at least once between termination and repair, but the majority of relationships did not undergo such cycling ambivalence. Thus whether at the level of strategy use or at the level of dissolution/repair ambivalence, Altman & Taylor's (1973) posited cycling hypothesis receives limited support. Such cycling may be more likely during Duck's (1982) Intra-psychic stage when the disengager is initially attempting to decide whether to exit the relationship. Once the disengager has made the decision to exit the relationship, regrets and repair action may be less common.

Intriguing research questions follow from this exploratory study of trajectories derived from a flow chart of the dissolution process. One set of issues concerns the relationship problems which precede the decision by at least one of the parties to exit the relationship. The present study noted only whether relationship problems were incremental or sudden and did not analyze the content of these problems. It is possible that different relationship problems may result in different dissolution trajectories. It is also important to realize that this study worked exclusively with retrospective accounts from respondents. The perceived problems which marked the beginning of dissolution may have become apparent to the respondents only with the benefit of hindsight rather than at the time of their occurrence. Subsequent research needs longitudinal data which capture people's perceptions of relational events at the time they occur in order to discern the events which trigger a dissolution decision by one or both relationship parties. Despite their retrospective nature, however, these accounts may shed insight into people's implicit theories of romantic relationships. In accounting for a decision to exit, respondents may reveal their tacit assumptions about how romantic relationships should function (Harré, 1977).

Additional variables should be studied in conjunction with the disengagement trajectories. Dissolution trajectories should be embedded in their respective histories of relationship growth and maintenance to determine possible patterns. In addition, individual-level variables such as sex, age and number of previous relationships should be considered. Finally, dual-perspective data, that is, the perceptions of both relationship parties, should be solicited. As Hill et al. (1976) noted in their study of pre-marital break-ups, there are two sides to a break-up with no necessary agreement between the two accounts as to its timing, its sequence of execution and who initiated it. Although relationship parties may agree in their accounts of the final outcome, they may disagree on their perceptions of bilateralness, directness, repairs and so forth.

This study supports the value of approaching dissolution as a process rather than a static event. Within the parameters of Duck's (1982) Dyadic Phase of dissolution, substantial complexity was found in the negotiation process by which the parties un-bond their relationship.

Baxter's paper suggests that researchers should abandon the search for a simple set of stages by which relationships change and instead should recognize extensive patterns of difference among relationships. Baxter's extremely complex flow chart represents the breakdown of relationships as a sequence of logical, rationalist decisions. How does this model match up to any of your personal experiences of break-up? Do you feel that this flow chart suggests a reasoned rationality in breaking partners that is belied by the to-and-fro discourse of a couple negotiating a break-up? Consider, and perhaps discuss in class, the value of a tidy logical model for something that may be less obviously tidy and logical when we bring communication into it, with all its ins and outs, ambiguities and inherent problematics. On the other hand, tidiness may be what people want to believe: it may be easier for people to accept a tidy account of a messy process because it then becomes a little easier to comprehend it.

Baxter's paper makes things pretty black-and-white and finalized. Perhaps we should look at ways in which people move on after a break-up and not see relationship disengagement as the end of the process. People do, after all, continue to get on with their lives after a significant break-up. As we noted earlier, many formerly romantic partners are forced to continue to interact after a divorce because of the children or other matters to which they are bound in common (e.g., property). In addition a lot of people *want* to stay in contact: some people want to end a romantic or sexual relationship without ceasing to see the other person. Sometimes "Let's just be friends" honestly means just that. Masheter (1997) and others have looked at the ways in which divorced partners maintain contact after their divorce. Other researchers such as Metts, Cupach and Bejlovec (1989), reprinted below, looked at the circumstances that mediated best whether partners in a dissolved relationship would successfully resolve a romantic breakdown into a satisfactory non-romantic relationship.

Metts et al. (1989) were interested in the question of ways in which people redefine their relationship "downwards" from romance and love to some other form of relationship. In particular they are interested in the ways in which "good" and "bad" redefinitions are foreshadowed in the styles that were evident on the set-up of the relationship. In short, do the starting conditions of a relationship set the pathway for any breakdown that may subsequently occur and also set the likely tone of any attempt to reconfigure the relationship after break up? As you read this paper, consider the ways in which people attempt such redefinition, and reflect a little on the process. Are they so different from the processes by which people "redefine" their relationships from "dating" to "serious"? If there are differences, what are they? The study refers to **positive face** and **negative face**. These two concepts refer to people's needs to look good in different ways. **Positive face** refers to people's needs to be seen as the kind of person they "claim" to be in an interaction and to have the attributes that they value in themselves appreciated and approved by their audience. In treating people as accomplished, fun, enjoyable and respected, you address their positive face needs. **Negative face** needs, on the other hand, refer to people's desires to be seen as autonomous individuals with the ability to exercise free choice and not to be imposed upon or taken for granted. When we begin an interaction with a stranger by saying "I'm sorry to bother you but ...", we are recognizing, and appealing to, their negative face needs.

The study uses various techniques we have come across before, such as **Likert scales**, **factor analysis** and **stepwise multiple regression**, but also does a **principal** [note the correct spelling!] **components analysis** and **Varimax rotation**. Other statistics and terms such as alpha scores, main effects, and interaction effects are ones you have met earlier.

Principal components analysis is an attempt to seek deeper structure in a data set and is based on analysis similar to factor analysis, and is drawn from a variety of different measures that all indicate one single underlying factor or component. For example, "tends to laugh at my jokes", "sits close to me", "gazes longingly at me", "listens to all my problems" and "my sense of pleasure increases in the presence of this person" could all be measuring the same underlying component: love. If we postulate the concept of "love" as the factor operating to coordinate responses to these different measures, then we can perhaps explain more of the structure of the data than we can by treating each scale separately. Principal components analysis helps us to discover such underlying structure.

As part of the above procedure, **Varimax rotation** is a technical statistical technique that is used to simplify the data matrix by identifying similarities and interconnections between factors and separating out the ways in which they are intertwined. By manipulating the data in some legitimate statistical ways so that small amounts of loading by a variable on a factor are removed, it is possible to leave the major loading on fewer factors in the foreground. If you like, the method is a way of eliminating "noise" and focusing on "signal".

"I Love You Too Much to Ever Start Liking You": Redefining Romantic Relationships

Sandra Metts, William R. Cupach and Richard A. Bejlovec

The study of relationship disengagement is a rather recent focus for scholars interested in romantic relationships. After a long tradition of attention to determinants of initial attraction and relationship formation, research has recently been directed toward aspects of the disengagement process, including the reasons for disengagement, the communicative strategies by which it is accomplished, and its social and psychological consequences (Duck, 1982). As research findings accumulate, it becomes increasingly clear that relationship disengagement is neither a linear reversal of the formation process, nor an inexorable consequence of relationship breakdown (Duck, 1982). Relationships break down at various levels of connectedness and for various reasons (Duck, 1982). Although breakdown may lead to complete termination of the relationship, it does not necessarily do so (Rusbult, 1987). This paper explores one alternative to termination: redefinition of a romantic relationship such that lovers become friends.

We refer here not to the perfunctory promise "we can still be friends" which is often made during a disengagement episode. Instead we refer to those redefined relationships characterized by a negotiated de-escalation of passion, sexual intimacy, and role expectations which generally attend "romantic" commitments, while at the same time maintaining the scope of psychological intimacy and role expectations which attend "friendship" commitments (Davis & Todd, 1982; Rawlins, 1982). Rather than deny or attempt to eliminate the residual emotions like "attachment"

(Weiss, 1976), couples who are redefining their relationship incorporate residual emotions into the framework of their friendship (Juhasz, 1979). Although the process of redefinition can be difficult, interview data from divorcing couples indicate that it is a constructive and increasingly frequent response to marital dissolution (Ahrons & Wallisch, 1987).

The purpose of this investigation is to explore the correlates of redefinition as it is prefigured in premarital relationships. As Hill et al. (1976) argue, premarital relationships reflect many of the same psychological bonds that characterize marital relationships but because of their relatively less complicated social and economic constraints they are a useful first step in untangling the more complex process of separation in marital relationships. Indeed, much of our current knowledge about relational redefinition is inferred from studies of disengagement in premarital couples. The present investigation extends and refines this work by identifying factors that are potentially relevant to redefinition and assessing their relative contribution. These factors may be divided into two general classes: those associated with the relationship before its initial decline and those associated with the disengagement period.

Characteristics of the relationship before initial decline

Relationships in which the partners were friends before their romantic involvement appear more likely to re-establish that status than relationships which evolve from other origins. Lee (1984) found that college couples who reported a high degree of friendship prior to their romantic involvement were likely to select "scale-down" pattern of disengaging (i.e., attenuate involvement in the relationship) compared to non-friends who were more likely to exhibit a "full-break" pattern (i.e., completely terminate the relationship). Lee proposes that because couples with a history of friendship have a foundation on which to build an intense romantic attachment, their ambivalence toward termination is greater than that of "non-friend" couples. Consequently, they prefer to return to a type of relationship which they remember as secure and to recoup the rewards of friendship rather than to lose contact. Although Lee does not mention a pragmatic dimension, we might surmise also that "friend" couples have a pre-existing script upon which to draw as their relationship once again assumes the properties of friendship. Resuming previous role enactment is therefore perhaps less awkward and effortful than negotiating new roles.

Relationships which are characterized by high levels of emotional and psychological involvement before their decline also appear more likely candidates for redefinition than relationships with low involvement. As Baxter (1983) observes, romantic relationships are generally characterized by two forms of intimacy: sexual and psychological. Sexual intimacy can be abandoned, without necessarily eliminating the psychological closeness. If the psychological closeness is integral to the relationship and highly valued, a couple should be more willing to negotiate a platonic relationship which retains the psychological closeness. Lee (1984) offers some support for this assumption. Factors associated with "scale-down" patterns included stronger commitment and positive feelings for partner and relationship, greater intimacy, socio-emotional involvement, and duration of the relationship.

However, ... Baxter's (1985; 1987) research indicates that disengagers who anticipate future contact with partner and who perceive the relationship to have been very close are more likely to report using direct disengaging strategies (i.e., open statements of their feelings about the state of the relationship) than indirect strategies (i.e., avoidance). Thus, it is possible that socio-emotional involvement motivates the type of disengagement strategy, which in turn becomes the more immediate and salient feature and thus the more powerful predictor of friendship. This interpretation must, of course, be considered in light of other aspects of the disengaging period.

Characteristics associated with the disengagement period

Once a relationship is no longer satisfying to one or both partners, it enters a period of decline. If the relationship cannot be restored to its previous status, it must be endured, terminated, or redefined (Duck, 1982; Rusbult, 1987). The types of communicative strategies employed during this period influence which of the latter two consequences is more likely to result. Banks et al. (1987) found that approximately 17 percent of the variance in staying friends was accounted for by strategy selection. Disengagers who used de-escalation (explicit requests for reduction in intensity and commitment but with some indication that future contact is possible) were significantly more likely to remain friends. Disengagers who used justification (statements expressing reasons for termination) and avoidance (avoiding all contact) were significantly less likely to remain friends. As noted previously, the effect of strategy was so great that no relational variable other than desirability of partner entered the equation.

Obviously, the communicative strategies employed during the disengaging period have a prominent effect on the trajectory of the relationship. However, these strategies do not exist in a vacuum. They enter into a pre-existing and emerging affective context which is subsequently reshaped by their presence (Schwartz & Shaver, 1987). According to Kelley (1984: 107), for example, interpersonal affect is both an appraisal of the outcomes and operative causes in a previous relationship "situation" and an orientation for how we might proceed in subsequent circumstances. Since partners are interdependent, however, one partner's orientation serves to alter the other's, as when an apology serves to mitigate an angry response.

Two emotions in particular have been investigated to determine their role in the disengaging process: anger and guilt. Interest in these emotions arises from the general tenets of equity theory which link anger with perceptions of being underbenefitted (relationship outcomes fall below the level of relationship inputs), and guilt with perceptions of being overbenefitted (relationship outcomes exceed the level of relationship inputs) (Walster et al., 1978). In a reformulation of the relationship between emotions and equity, Schwartz & Shaver (1987: 234) argue that the cognitive calculation implied by the particular definition of unfairness in equity theory, "is far too narrow to form the basis for a general theory of social behavior". Rather, "perceived unfairness" (of which inequity is only one type) is the source of anger and guilt, depending on where the blame is laid for the injustice. Thus, anger, for example, may be induced by a number of situations perceived to be unfair – loss of power, status, or respect, violation of an expectation, judgment that the situation is illegitimate, wrong, or contrary to what ought to be – independently of whether one also feels underbenefitted or not. The Schwartz & Shaver distinction would suggest that efforts to assess the contribution of affective state to the likelihood of redefining a relationship should include both measures of cognitive appraisals of inequity as well as more general measures of emotional states, particularly anger and guilt.

Finally, one other aspect of the disengaging period that should be included in an investigation of redefinition is the sex of the partner who initiates the disengagement. Although no differences appear when sex is considered independently of initiator/ recipient roles (Wilmot et al., 1985), when

considered together, sex and role appear to interact. Hill et al. (1976) found that men seldom reported a continuing friendship with their former partner when she had initiated the breakup. By contrast, 70 percent of the couples remained friends when the man had initiated the breakup and 71 percent remained friends when the breakup was mutual. Hill et al. account for this finding by reference to the relatively greater difficulty men exhibit in letting go of a love relationship when compared to women. This interpretation is supported in the authors' data showing that men fall in love sooner and stay in love longer than their more "pragmatic" female counterparts.

Although Hill et al.'s interpretation is consistent with their data, another interpretation is raised by unpublished interview data (cited in Vaughan, 1986) and studies of divorced couples (Goode, 1956). These data indicate a tendency for dissatisfied husbands to manipulate their wives into actually initiating the divorce, either through neglect or some obvious rule violation. If this is true, only a portion of those men who are left by their partners are distressed and/or resentful. Some may simply not desire further contact with the partner for the same reasons that lead them to orchestrate the breakup. Thus what appears to be isolation from partner based on wounded pride is actually a convenient escape from partner. Others may be aware of their intention to manipulate their partner into breaking up and thereby feel the same kind of guilt that attends the role of initiator. These men may respond like an initiator, making overtures of friendship which are then met with positive responses from their partners.

In summary, the existing research suggests that variables associated with the romantic relationship before its decline and variables associated with the disengaging period contribute in various ways to the likelihood that a post-disengagement friendship will develop. However, a full understanding of the redefinition process is precluded by two limitations in the current literature. First, no previous study has incorporated the range of variables identified here. It is not clear, therefore, which variable or combination of variables is the most salient predictor of relationship redefinition. Second, quantitative studies, especially those of communicative strategies, tend to rely exclusively on data from respondents who initiated the breakup (e.g., Banks et al., 1987; Cody, 1982). Whether factors which influence redefinition for the initiators are comparable to the factors which influence redefinition for their partners has yet to be determined. In order to rectify these limitations and clarify the process of redefinition, we will explore the following questions:

(1)   What is the relative contribution of previous friendship, extent and duration of romantic involvement, disengagement strategy used, affective state during the time of disengagement, and sex of disengager in predicting the redefinition of a romantic relationship to a friendship?
(2)   To what extent does the predictive profile of the initiator of the disengagement differ from that of the recipient?

Method

Students at a large midwestern university served as respondents. A questionnaire was distributed during regular class time to one large section of an introductory course in economics, to an upper division course in psycholinguistics, and to several sections of an introductory course in the fundamentals of communication. Respondents were asked to call to mind a specific romantic relationship which "had changed significantly, either broken up or evolved into a friendship". [Respondents who could not recall such a relationship were directed to complete a separate portion of the questionnaire dealing with terminated friendships. These data were not used in the present analysis.]

Thus, the sample consisted of 347 respondents who could report on a romantic relationship. The average age for this group was 20.7 years, ranging from 17 to 41. The majority were freshmen and sophomores (55 percent). Females constituted 43 percent of the sample and males 57 percent. The average length of the described relationships was 20.6 months and they had ended an average of 22.6 months previously. The number of respondents who considered themselves to be the initiators of relationship change was very similar to the number who considered their partner to be the initiator. Forty-four percent indicated themselves as the initiator and 42 percent indicated their partner. Fourteen percent indicated that the change in the relationship was brought about by both partners.

The first section of the questionnaire contained items measuring (1) the extent of *friendship* before the onset of romantic involvement ("To what extent were you and your partner friends BEFORE the time you started dating?"), (2) the extent of *involvement* in the relationship before its deterioration (including level of commitment, psychological intimacy, love, and respect), and (3) *affective context* during the time of deterioration (including degree of felt anger, happiness, sorrow, guilt, having taken advantage of partner, having been taken advantage of by partner, and degree of support from friends for the relationship). All items were scored on a seven-point Likert-type scale (1 = none or not true; 7 = very much or very true).

Factor analysis was performed on the involvement items and affective state items in order to produce a more parsimonious set of factors. The four involvement items (commitment, love, intimacy, and respect) loaded on a single factor (alpha = .86 for initiator and .84 for recipient). The mean for these items was used in subsequent analyses. The seven affective context items did not load as equity theory would predict: anger did not load with feelings of being underbenefitted and guilt did not load with feelings of being overbenefitted. In fact, more consistent with Schwartz & Shaver's (1987) discussion, no stable factor structure emerged. Therefore, four individual items were selected from the original seven because of their theoretical utility and correlations with the dependent variable. These items measured anger, guilt, feeling overbenefitted (i.e. taking advantage of partner), and feeling underbenefitted (i.e., being taken advantage of by partner).

The second section of the questionnaire contained a list of 35 communication behaviors identified by Baxter (1982) as disengagement strategies. If respondents had identified themselves as initiator or identified the decision as a mutual one, they were asked to rate on a seven-point scale how true each statement was of their behavior during the process of terminating or redefining the relationship. If respondents identified their partner as the initiator, they were asked to rate how true each statement was of their partner's behavior. Because the items were originally constructed by Baxter to reflect an initiator's perspective, some grammatical changes were necessary in these items (e.g., "I stopped doing favors for my partner" became "My partner stopped doing favors for me"). In addition, instructions to non-initiators contained the sentences "Some of the items ask about possible motivation or intentions. Although there are many things about the breakup you may not know, just respond according to your intuitive sense about what your partner might have been thinking or doing during the change process."

Based on the possibility that recipients' perceptions of their partners' strategies are qualitatively different data from initiators' ratings of their own behavior, **factor analyses** were performed separately for initiator and recipient. Data for "mutual decisions" were excluded from analysis at this point. The 35 disengagement strategy items were submitted to **principal components analysis** followed by **Varimax rotation**. Items were required to have a primary loading of at least .50 and secondary loadings not greater than .30 in order to be retained. A minimum of two loading items was necessary to define a factor. Items substantially detracting from internal consistency of a factor were omitted.

Strategies reported by initiators. Four factors were extracted accounting for 43 percent of

the variance. These four factors largely replicate the previous findings of Baxter (1982), thus her labels were applied. Factor one consisted of eight items and was labeled *withdrawal* (e.g., "Kept our conversation brief whenever we talked", "Avoided scheduling future meetings whenever possible", "Disclosed little about my personal activities and interests whenever we talked"). Factor two contained five items reflecting *positive tone* (e.g., "Told my partner that I didn't regret the time we had spent together in the relationship", "Tried to prevent my partner from having any 'hard feelings' about the way the relationship turned out", "Tried to prevent us leaving on a sour note"). The third factor included four items representing *manipulation* ("Asked a third party to break the disengagement news to my partner", "Became unpleasant in the hopes that my partner would make the first move", "Tried to make my partner look selfish in refusing to disengage"). Factor four contained three items which were labeled *directness* ("Openly expressed to my partner my desire to disengage or change the relationship", "Verbally explained to my partner my reasons for desiring the disengagement", "Honestly conveyed my wishes to my partner"). The **alpha reliability coefficients** for each factor were as follows: withdrawal = .85, positive tone = .78, manipulation = .59, and directness = .66. Item scores within each factor were averaged for subsequent data analysis.

Strategies reported by recipient. Four factors were extracted accounting for 42 percent of the variance. The factors were conceptually similar to those found for the initiator. Factor one, *withdrawal*, consisted of ten items (e.g. "Kept our conversation brief whenever we talked", "Avoided contact with me as much as possible", "Avoided scheduling future meetings whenever possible"). Factor two contained five loading items reflecting *positive tone* (e.g., "Told me that he/she didn't regret the time we had spent together in the relationship", "Tried to prevent me from having any 'hard feelings' about the way the relationship turned out". "Tried to prevent us leaving on a sour note"). Factor three contained three items representing *directness*

("Openly expressed to me his/her desire to disengage or change the relationship", "Verbally explained to me his/her reasons for desiring the disengagement", "Honestly conveyed his/her wishes to me"). The fourth factor included two items representing *manipulation* ("Became unpleasant in hopes that I would make the first move", "Intentionally 'leaked' a desire to disengage to someone he/she anticipated would inform me"). Alpha reliability coefficients for each factor were as follows: withdrawal = .87, positive tone = .80, directness = .73, manipulation = .40. Item scores within each factor were averaged for subsequent data analysis. The final section of the questionnaire contained twelve items measuring the dependent variable. These items were similar to those used by Banks et al. (1987) but were written in the present tense for more direct measurement of the current state of the relationship as respondents perceived it. These items assessed both affiliative behaviors toward partner and avoidance behavior. Affiliative items included, for example, "When I have a problem and want to talk it over with someone, I call my ex-partner", "I often include my ex-partner in my social activities", "I have told my ex-partner that I would be there for him/her if I was ever needed", "I consider myself to be friends with my ex-partner", and "I would feel a significant loss in my life if I never had contact with my ex-partner again". Avoidance behaviors included, for example, "I prefer to avoid all contact with my ex-partner", "I would feel awkward if I have social contact with my ex-partner (e.g., ran into him/her at a party)", and "I have changed my plans on occasion to avoid seeing my ex-partner". **Factor analysis** suggested the possibility of a two-factor solution for these items. However, since the factors of affiliation and avoidance appear to be the converse of one another, and since ten of the twelve items exhibited their highest loading on the first unrotated factor, we opted for the more parsimonious unidimensional interpretation. **Alpha reliability** for these items was 0.87 and 0.88 for initiator and recipient respectively.

The questionnaire concluded with demographic questions concerning the length of the relationship, the date of its termination or change, and respondent's age, sex, and year in school.

Results

In order to test the predictors of the current status of the redefined relationship, hierarchical multiple regression was performed. Predictors were entered in blocks in the following order: (1) sex of respondent, (2) length of the previous romantic relationship, (3) previous status of romantic relationship (previous friendship, previous involvement), (4) feelings at the time of the breakup (angry, guilty, underbenefitted, overbenefitted), and (5) strategies used to accomplish disengagement (withdrawal, positive tone, manipulation, directness). Thus, a total of twelve variables were entered in five blocks. Separate analyses were performed for respondents who initiated the breakup (referred to as initiator) and respondents whose partners initiated the breakup (referred to as recipient).

The twelve predictors in the complete model were found to significantly predict current relationship status for initiators ($F = 4.74$, $p < .001$, $R = .54$, $R^2 = .29$, adjusted $R^2 = .23$). Of the twelve variables entered in the equation, only three made significant individual contributions. Being friends before the breakup was positively associated with being friends currently, whereas feeling underbenefitted (taken advantage of) and using withdrawal strategies to disengage were negatively related to being friends currently.

In order to verify the most efficient set of predictors, stepwise multiple regression was conducted. Three variables were found to significantly predict current relationship status: using withdrawal to disengage, being friends before the breakup, and feeling underbenefitted ($F = 17.05$, $p < .001$, $R = .50$, $R^2 = .25$, adjusted $R^2 = .24$). These findings are consistent with the hierarchical analysis.

The twelve variables in the hierarchical model combined to significantly predict current relationship status for the individuals whose partner initiated the breakup ($F = 4.12$, $p < .001$, $R = .52$, $R^2 = .27$, adjusted $R^2 = .20$). Only two variables in the equation made significant contributions. Respondents were more likely to be friends currently if they were friends before the breakup, and if their partners used positive tone strategies to disengage the relationship. Additionally, partner's use of manipulation to disengage the relationship approached significance ($p = .067$).

Follow-up stepwise multiple regression verified the most efficient set of predictors from among the twelve included in the hierarchical analysis. Three variables combined to significantly predict current status of the former romantic relationship ($F = 12.11$, $p < .001$, $R = .45$, $R^2 = .20$, adjusted $R^2 = .19$). Partner's use of positive tone disengagement strategies and being friends before disengagement were positively associated with being friends currently. Partner's use of manipulation strategies to disengage was negatively associated with being friends currently.

It was surprising that sex did not make a significant contribution to predicting current relationship status, even when being entered first in the hierarchical regression analyses. We therefore tested more directly for potential interaction effects between sex and role (i.e., initiator/recipient). An ANOVA was performed with sex and role as independent variables and extent of current friendship as the dependent variable. Neither the main effects nor the interaction were significant.

Discussion

This research offers several insights into the process by which romantic partners redefine their relationships. First, having been friends before being dating partners facilitates post-disengagement friendship. Both those who initiate the disengagement and those who are recipients of their partner's initiative report continued, significant, and voluntary affiliation with their partners. The data analyzed here do not allow us to identify specific reasons why previous friendship is so influential but we offer several possibilities worthy of future examination.

Lee (1984) proposed that when an initial friendship was highly valued and comparatively stable, couples are willing to exert the time and effort necessary to retain that friendship after romantic attachment wanes. While this assumption is probably true, it does not necessarily explain why some attempts to retain the valued friendship are more successful than others. One possibility is that previous friendship promotes a more positive affective context during the disengaging period which may in turn facilitate open communication and the use of prosocial disengaging strategies. Additional research using path analytic models may reveal interesting relationships among previous friendship, events occurring during the disengagement period, and the likelihood of subsequent friendship.

A second possible explanation for the successful negotiation of post-disengagement friendship derives from recent applications of script theory to relationship processes (e.g. Baxter, 1987; Planalp, 1987). This literature suggests at least two possibilities: (1) previously established schemas for relating as friends may facilitate redefinition because uncertainty is relatively low and predictability is relatively high when entering the post-disengagement friendship, and/or (2) partners share in common a **schema** that considers post-disengagement friendship to be a reasonable path for relational trajectories. A variation of the second possibility might also be operative. Presumably, most cross-sex friendships evolve into romantic relationships because of a deepening sense of passionate love. In some cases, however, romantic escalation may result from acting on relational schemas incompatible with ongoing platonic relationships. The belief that romantic involvement "ought" to follow from cross-sex attraction may be held by one or both partners, or may be held by the social network in which the friendship is embedded (Rawlins, 1982). Cross-sex friendships are inherently difficult to manage, and especially so when relevant social networks view platonic involvement as unusual, and when sexual attraction between partners is an unresolved issue (Rawlins, 1982 [Werking, 1997]). Such pressures may propel two friends into a dating relationship when, in fact, friendship was really a more suitable frame for their relationship. In these instances, the dating relationship is the deviation, and the post-disengagement friendship is the continuation of the original state. Future studies of redefinition would profit from exploration of relevant differences in types of pre-romantic friendships and consideration of potential influences of relational schemas (both those of the partners and those of the social network).

A second insight into the redefinition process provided by the present research is that the communication occurring (or not occurring) during the disengaging period contributes a substantial amount of unique variance to the likelihood of becoming friends. The contribution of disengaging strategies to the eventual status of the relationship may reside in the strong association between disengaging strategy and partners' face needs. Baxter (1987) refers to three general classes of disengagement strategies: Relationship Talk, Distance Cueing, and Cost Escalation. Relationship Talk tends to be effortful and stressful for the party desiring disengagement because his/her intentions may be slowed or constrained by partner's displays of anger or hurt feelings. However, Relationship Talk does indicate enough respect for the other party or the relationship to confront the situation openly. Distance Cueing is less effortful for the disengager but indicates a greater concern for his/her negative face (desire to be unrestrained) than for the other party's positive face (desire to be valued). According to Baxter (1987: 207), "The other's **positive face** is threatened under any circumstance, but the threat is

probably greatest with Distance Cueing for it doesn't even show the basic courtesy of a face-to-face accounting". Cost Escalation refers to a variety of tactics used to manipulate the other party into seeking dissolution. Baxter describes cost escalation as a strategy of "last resort" for two reasons. First, it puts the disengager in the less desirable social role as the "broken-up-with". Second, and more importantly, Cost Escalation so adversely implicates the positive face of the other party that it functions simultaneously as a potent form of Distance Cueing.

Our data are remarkably consistent with Baxter's (1987) discussion. For respondents who initiated the disengagement, the use of withdrawal strategies and feeling underbenefitted (taken advantage of in the relationship) were negatively associated with redefinition. This suggests a certain consistency between strategy selection and the cognitive appraisal of one's position vis-à-vis partner. Specifically, it appears that if a person feels underbenefitted, he/she is also more likely to feel justified in attending to his/her own **negative face** at the expense of partner's **positive face** (Distance Cueing). For the respondents who were "broken-up-with", positive tone strategies were positively associated with redefinition and manipulation was negatively associated with redefinition. Not only do positive tone strategies allow for open dialogue (Relationship Talk), they signal to the other party an apparent willingness to endure the discomfort of confrontation for the sake of his/her face needs. Manipulation, measured here by such items as "Partner became unpleasant in hopes that I would make the first move", and "Partner intentionally 'leaked' a desire to disengage to someone he/she anticipated would inform me", is very similar to Baxter's Cost Escalation. The fact that manipulation was a significant predictor of decreased post-disengagement friendship for the recipient whereas withdrawal was not, seems to confirm Baxter's characterization of Cost Escalation as a particularly potent form of termination.

The finding that sex of respondent did not contribute significantly to friendship for either regression analysis nor exhibit a significant interaction effect with initiator role in the

ANOVA is interesting. It is possible that our sample differs in important ways from that of Hill et al.'s (1976) earlier sample. These differences may reflect more general social changes which have moved young men and women closer together in romantic attitudes (Simpson et al., 1986) and thereby reduced differences in attitudes toward post-romantic friendships. An alternative explanation is that retrospective reports are subject to a leveling effect that obscures subtle differences. The interaction between sex and initiator role may be one of these. As Vaughan (1986: 6) notes, "identifying who is the initiator and who is being left behind is not so easy in some cases. Over the course of a long relationship, these roles may be passed back and forth, with one person assuming the role of initiator at one time and the other acting to end the relationship at another". A processual model would more likely detect interaction between sex and role if it does exist.

Several other limitations of the present investigation would be redressed by a processual approach to the study of relational redefinition. Our method, like most used in previous research on disengagement, asked respondents to comment retrospectively on factors which might have influenced the current status of their relationship. This method necessarily focuses respondents' attention on preselected variables which may not exhaust the domain of variables relevant to redefinition.

In addition, retrospective accounts are influenced in undetermined ways by the respondents' post hoc attributions. In the present investigation, for example, respondents who had maintained a friendship with a former romantic partner may recall antecedent events in a positive light, consistent with their current high regard for partner. Whether this recollection inflates the extent of previous friendship and use of positive tone strategies cannot be assessed. Finally, retrospective methods tend to ignore the temporal unfolding of episodes through which relational change is enacted. Multiple strategies are used in various sequences across encounters, influencing and influenced by partner's varying behaviors. Identifying patterns of strategies and related effects is difficult with retrospective accounts. We suggest that scholars interested in redefinition and its kindred states of repair and termination employ longitudinal designs and gather diary data from matched partners.

The redefinition of romantic relationships to friendships is a promising area of study. Our findings indicate that the deterioration of romantic relationships is not necessarily the antecedent of termination. Both factors before the onset of romantic involvement and factors associated with the disengaging period influence the possibility of alternative trajectories. Elaboration of the interplay of these factors deserves systematic investigation.

The Metts et al. study used responses from subjects based on questionnaires and so relies on their ability to recall an event (a negative event) that happened to them in the past. In using retrospective recall, the study is open to any and all of the criticisms that we have leveled against retrospective reports, in Chapter 3, but by most reasonable standards the technique is an acceptable one since we often recall and tell stories about events in the past, whether or not these stories are accurate. The fact that we are recalling something does not necessarily mean that we are recalling the event inaccurately, although of course the careful reader will regard that as a possibility. There are many instances of everyday recall that we do not regard with such skepticism. People may very well have a strong ability to recall what happened to them in such a moment of significant life trauma. The fact that recall may be of distant events does not by any means make it certain that recall is inaccurate. It could well be vividly accurate as are our memories of where we were when we first heard of the events of 11 September 2001. On the other hand, one has a significant personal interest in relationship break-up and so recalling of "the facts" may end up getting colored by our subsequent emotions about the events. Obviously it is human nature to remember hurtful experiences in a way that renders them less wounding, so audiences listening to stories of breakdown may become skeptical about such reports.

The recent research efforts here show the interest that can come from looking at the communication strategies used by people in **PDRs (Post-Dissolution Relationships** – Masuda, 2001). Masuda noted that after the dissolution of a romantic relationship that had reverted to a genuine friendship, partners feel the need to communicate with several different "audiences" about their new situation. Typically, he found, they are aware that outsiders not only will find the PDR relationship "unusual" but also will suspect that they have not been told the whole truth about it. Thus the partners typically construct stories and defenses or counterarguments that clarify for a particular audience (e.g., differently for parents, friends, other outsiders, new partners ...) aspects of the relationship that will be easier for such audiences to accept.

Another intriguing aspect of Masuda's work was the finding that some "audiences" are very protective/jealous of one PDR partner (or of their romantic relationship with that PDR partner) and the PDR partners have to make continuously patient efforts to "correct the audience's prejudice against PDRs in general or their PDR partner, for a while. In many cases, however, such attempts fail and then some PDR partners give up [the attempt to disprove] these audiences' prejudice and choose to avoid talking about the PDRs or talking with these audiences, or sometimes dissolve the relationship with them" (p. 210). In other words, the desire to remove the public and private strains of defining or representing a non-romantic PDR with an "ex" to other people can sometimes in itself lead to a person's preference to dissolve *another* friendship or romantic relationship rather than betray or give up on the "ex" as a friend.

This serves to emphasize the point that after relationship dissolution life *continues* rather than ends and even a relationship with an "ex" can continue to be significant, just as a relationship with a deceased parent or spouse can continue in a person's head in the absence of the person. Some old relationship approaches ended with ending and are guilty of separating relationship incidents from the ongoing lives of the people who reported them. Clearly the ending of a relationship is not, for very many people, the end of their lives; they regroup, rebuild, and move along. The A to E model from Attraction to Ending (Levinger, 1976) is a limited view that focuses on the life of the *relationship* rather than on the *individual* who is having a relationship. Individuals survive break-up – however caused – and they go on to other relationships and to life after break-up. Few models have examined things from this angle but it is necessary to see relationships from the individual point of view rather than vice versa if we are to understand how relationships figure in people's lives.

An early model of relationship breakdown was proposed by Duck (1982) and was widely cited but little researched. The original model has been repeatedly reprinted in major introductory textbooks despite its lack of empirical support and Rollie and Duck (in press) felt encouraged to offer a broad revision of the model that takes account of the rebirth of people after relational ending. It depicts several different stages in the process, not because the stages are supposed to be very different and distinct, but rather like Baxter's flow-chart that we read about earlier in this chapter, it proposes that there are complex interlinkages. The model supposes that dissolution has different emphases at different points in the extended process and these are depicted, along with examples of the concerns and goals of each person at each stage, in Figure A, reproduced from Duck (1982).

BREAKDOWN: Dissatisfaction with relationship

↓

Threshold: I can't stand this any more

↓

INTRA-PSYCHIC PHASE
Personal focus on partner's behavior
Assess adequacy of partner's role performance
Depict and evaluate negative aspects of being in the relationship
Consider costs of withdrawal
Assess positive aspects of alternative relationships
Face the "express/repress dilemma"

↓

Threshold: I'd be justified in withdrawing

↓

DYADIC PHASE
Face "confrontation/avoidance dilemma"
Confront partner
Negotiate in "Our Relationship Talks"
Attempt repair and reconciliation?
Assess joint costs of withdrawal or reduced intimacy

↓

Threshold: I mean it

↓

SOCIAL PHASE
Negotiate post-dissolution state with partner
Initiate gossip/discussion in social network
Create publicly negotiable face-saving/blame-placing stories and accounts
Consider and face up to implied social network effects, if any
Call in intervention teams?

↓

Threshold: It's now inevitable

↓

GRAVE-DRESSING PHASE
"Getting over" activity
Retrospection; reformulative postmortem attribution
Public distribution of own version of break-up story

Figure A   A sketch of the main phases of dissolving personal relationships
Source: Figure 2 from Duck (1982) © Academic Press, reproduced with permission.

Duck assumes that breakdown is not much different from other processes of evaluation and assessment that occur in other parts of life. Indeed he was at pains to argue that any model of relationship breakdown must not start with the assumption that breaking up is fundamentally different from other relationship processes nor that it involves psychological forces different from those that are employed in the regular run of life. It is important, he argued, to see breakdown as stemming from everyday behaviors and running with them. Often people do not know at the start of the process that breakdown really is what they are doing. It becomes clear only later in the process. To separate breakdown from other relational processes makes the mistake of assuming that partners are aware of what they are doing from the very beginning. It fails to recognize that a lot of the processes in relationship breakdown can in fact lead to relationship repair and change rather than to ending. Furthermore, many of the things that people do in breakdown are done precisely because at that point people do NOT believe that the relationship is ending. In fact, it would be a good idea for us all (especially researchers) to think of relationship *disturbance* rather than dissolution, because – at least from the point of view of people doing it at the time – the outcome is by no means a foregone conclusion, in the way that "relationship dissolution" might imply.

Duck's (1982) model was based on the idea of process but it stopped short at the end of the relationship though it did focus on processes of self-adjustment in so far as the Grave-Dressing phase deals with that. It is preferable to accept the Grave-Dressing phase as a place where the relationship is buried but the person is reborn. The person arises from the burial of the former relationship in ways that create future possibilities for further relationships. Rollie and Duck (in press) label that phase as the Resurrection Process and we suppose that it is one where the person rebuilds a new persona to project into future relationships.

Rollie and Duck (in press) note that an important aspect of relationship dissolution is "where people go next". The previous experiences of ending affect a person's future relationship performances and expectations in unknown ways. For most people the end of a relationship is not the end of their whole social life and most people who break up one relationship eventually move on to others. Some theories, however, assume that some people will be more hurt or dented by relational endings than will others. For example, Attachment Theory will predict that those who are Secure (i.e., pretty comfortable with most of their relationships) will tend to be less affected by break-up than will other folks. All the same, if the broken relationship was a deep and serious one, then the rebound to resurrection is likely to be a significant adjustment for everyone and one that some older people may choose never to make, regarding loyalty to their deceased lifelong partner as meaning that new partners should not be sought or countenanced.

In understanding the processes of relationship breakdown therefore we should be ever alert to the ways in which people cope AFTER the breakdown of a significant relationship and build on the early research that looked at the processes from breakdown themselves in order to explore the impact of such breakdowns in the subsequent lives of the ex-partners. One immediate consequence of break-up, bereavement or relational loss can be loneliness, to which we next turn. However loneliness is not the only possible outcome of a broken relationship.

11   Loneliness

"How can you ask me how have I been?
I think you should know well the shape that I'm in
   You tell me you wonder if I was okay
   Well that's a damn fool thing to say."

Lee Ann Womack – *Lonely Too*

The complexity and interrelatedness of personal relationships is startling. Take for example the multifaceted emotion of loneliness. It is difficult to exhaustively list all the aspects of loneliness one should keep in mind when embarking on a research project. For example, we should consider both social loneliness (e.g., insufficient social network) and emotional loneliness (e.g., absence of an intense relationship) but also take into account both the negative and positive aspects of each experience. We need to account for demographic and contextual factors and how they influence our expectations about our social relationships. But, we must also consider how the evaluations of others and the dynamics of social exchanges affect our self-image and expectations for other social interactions. As you can see, the number of variables to consider is daunting in length and not nearly complete. In this chapter we will attempt to take a narrow issue within this larger set of literature and examine how two different research programs address common research questions.

We will begin our discussion of loneliness with Spitzberg and Canary's (1985) careful consideration of both long- and short-term loneliness. One may assume that long-term loneliness may be related to a dispositional explanation and short term more situation or context specific. However, Spitzberg and Canary take an attributional approach in explaining loneliness, emphasizing contextual factors rather than factors such as shyness, anxiety or self-esteem. The second article in this chapter (Tornstam, 1992) however, addresses dispositional factors more directly but generally attempts to integrate them along with contextual factors when explaining their results.

Spitzberg and Canary (1985) propose that the interpersonal styles of chronically lonely people are flawed and their social awkwardness may lead them to have negative social exchanges with others. In addition, these interactions should produce negative evaluations from their conversational partners. These assessments may be consistent with the expectations of lonely people and may further cement their loneliness by making them more avoidant of future social contacts. Spitzberg and Canary argue this cycle should be more prevalent for those individuals who make stable, internal and uncontrollable attributions. Therefore, individuals who make situational/contextual attributions about their loneliness should be less avoidant, possess fewer negative expectations about social interactions, and experience more positive social interactions than the chronically lonely. Appropriately, the authors measure short-term/situational loneliness as well as long-term loneliness. In addition, two types of relational competence (self-rated, other-rated) are assessed for each participant. This approach enables them to obtain the complete set of cognitions from both sides of the conversational dyad. Finally, you may wish to consider the authors' approach to "context-specific" relational competence and the implications it has for understanding loneliness. Is loneliness best conceptualized as a disposition or a response to situational constraints? Also, consider the extent to which loneliness results from (or is the cause of) poor social experiences.

As with previous chapters, we ask you to attend to methodological and statistical issues as you read this article. For example, the statistic **eta (η)** will be introduced in this chapter. It is a measure of the relationship between an independent variable and a dependent variable and is useful in describing how much of the dependent variable can be explained by the independent variables when it is squared (η^2). This may sound similar to another statistic (R^2) you encountered in Chapter 6 when read about multiple regression. Eta is used most often in conjunction with ANOVA to determine the effect size of an independent variable; however, it is basically identical to R^2 in this context (Hayes, 1988). In addition to eta, you may want to pay particular attention to Spitzberg and Canary's efforts to validate the loneliness scale they create in this article. It may serve as a model for assessing the psychometric properties of scales you may choose to construct in the future.

Loneliness and Relationally Competent Communication

Brian H. Spitzberg and Daniel J. Canary

Communication is a fallible method of initiating and sustaining human contact. While communication functions effectively for most people most of the time in providing satisfactory relationships, for many others communication processes are flawed and disappointing. Once the single means of human contact is disparaged, isolation and accompanying loneliness are perpetuated.

The purpose of this study is to examine the connection between the experience of loneliness and relationally competent communication. We find it helpful to define that connection from an attributional orientation.

Hence, after brief discussion of loneliness, **attribution theory** and relational competence, three hypotheses are presented and tested.

Loneliness has been defined as a state of dissatisfaction with achieved, versus desired, relational intimacy (Spitzberg, 1981). Such dissatisfaction exists to the degree that social networks are perceived to be somehow insufficient (Peplau & Perlman, 1979). Self-reported loneliness has been associated with social failure (Horowitz & French, 1979), psychological maladjustment (Putney & Putney, 1964), depression (Beck & Young,

1978), drug abuse, suicide and premature mortality (Sermat, 1980). Loneliness has also been found to be related positively to shyness (Cheek & Busch, 1981), communication apprehension (Spitzberg, 1981), submissiveness or hostility (Moore, 1974), discrepancy between perceived and reflected self-concept (Moore, 1976), and difficulty in being amiable (Horowitz & French, 1979). Inverse relationships have been found to exist between loneliness and positive attributes, including social assertiveness (Sermat, 1980), self-disclosure intimacy (Solano et al., 1982), and supportiveness (Wood, 1979).

Collectively these studies evidence a possible reciprocal cycle that perpetuates loneliness. Shyness and depression may act materially to isolate lonely individuals from the very relationships that could diminish their loneliness. It seems plausible that avoidance and fear of interaction would, over time, lead to the atrophy of important social skills, such as expressiveness and interaction management. Young (1979a), for example, identifies "common behavioral blocks" among clients who were lonely. These blocks include anxiety in social settings, awkwardness, lack of assertiveness, as well as choice of inappropriate partners. Deficient communicative skills, in turn (when finally utilized), may result in negative social experiences and deeper loneliness. Jones et al. (1982), found that lonely individuals appeared to converse with "less awareness of or concern for others, with less responsiveness, and in a more self-focused or self-absorbed manner" (p. 685). Thus, for the lonely person, perceptual and communicative processes act to perpetuate the very state they wish to escape.

Despite the theoretical appeal of this depiction, research directly linking loneliness and perceived social communicative skills is inconsistent. After four studies regarding interpersonal consequences of loneliness, Jones et al. (1981) could find only piecemeal support for their hypothesis that lonely subjects would be perceived as socially unskilled. Their most consistent finding was that lonely subjects evaluated *themselves* as lower in social skills and

attractiveness than either their conversational partners or third-party raters did. Sloan and Solano (1984) found that lonely subjects talked less than non-lonely subjects but were not particularly self-focused or less self-disclosive than non-lonely subjects. In a similar vein, Chelune et al. (1980) found no relationship between loneliness, self-disclosure, flexibility, and either self-rating or other-ratings or social skills.

It is possible that these studies failed to find relationships between loneliness and communication because of imprecise conceptualization and operationalization of loneliness. These studies viewed loneliness as a molar level state of perceived discrepancy between actual and desired interpersonal intimacy. It is our contention that loneliness is a phenomenon integrally affected by people's explanations for their successes and failures in social and intimate relationships. Failure to take into account people's explanations of loneliness made the predictions of these studies overly simplistic.

Attribution theory is concerned primarily with the ways in which humans perceive, label and act upon causes of social events. One useful attributional approach to studying loneliness has been elaborated by Peplau and colleagues (e.g., Peplau & Perlman, 1979). Essentially attributions of loneliness are arrayed along three causal dimensions: internality, stability and controllability. Accordingly a person can attribute loneliness to internal causes (e.g., lack of social skills) or external causes (e.g., restrictive situation). At the same time loneliness can be attributed to stable factors (e.g., inability to meet people) or unstable ones (e.g., being new in the neighbourhood). Finally, loneliness can be attributed to controllable causes (e.g., lack of effort in meeting people) or relatively uncontrollable ones (e.g., job transfer).

An attributional approach provides several insights into loneliness. Persons who attribute loneliness to unstable, external and controllable causes are more likely to take steps to remedy their loneliness (e.g., to expend effort to meet people and establish relationships) than are those who attribute loneliness to stable, internal and uncontrollable causes. Furthermore, chronically lonely people are much more likely than situationally lonely people to attribute their loneliness to stable, uncontrollable causes. Loneliness that endures over time regardless of, or despite, efforts to establish satisfying relationships, is likely to be perceived as resistant to change. One probable result of such perceptions is a frustration and dissatisfaction associated with social interaction generally. Since it fails to change things, social interaction is viewed as useless or negatively reinforcing, or both. A person may blame self (internal attribution; e.g., "I'm so socially inept") or the context (external attribution; e.g., "It's just too hard to meet people around here"). Either way, social interaction is devalued. Negative attitudes towards interaction may result in anxiety and social-skill deficits in communicative encounters either from skill atrophy, amotivation or repeated negative reinforcement in social episodes. Spitzberg (1981), for example, found that chronically lonely subjects reported significantly higher communication apprehension than did situationally lonely subjects. Gerson and Perlman (1979) found that situationally lonely subjects were rated as significantly more communicatively expressive than chronically lonely subjects. These findings suggest that the duration of loneliness and communicative skill are related, but the precise nature of this relationship is not clear.

A variety of findings support the view that as the experience of loneliness endures over time, attributions of causes to stable, uncontrollable factors increase; and these causal attributions lead to diminished self-perceived and other-perceived social skills in the view of self and others. Yet, before we can establish our hypotheses based on this approach, the general construct of social skills needs to be recast within a framework specifically tied to interpersonal interaction. In order to better understand the effects of loneliness from an interpersonal perspective, the notion of relational competence should be delineated.

Competence is typically a synonym for ability. When speaking of "social" competence, theorists are usually referring to the ability to engage in normal or appropriate interaction across a variety of social situations. This general ability, in turn, is thought to depend upon a favourable developmental history and the learning of certain social skills (Argyle, 1980). For example, many researchers view assertiveness as a crucial social skill because it involves achieving or defending one's rights while simultaneously preserving appropriate norms of social interaction. Similarly, many researchers identify empathy, role-taking and the ability to take others' or generalized societal perspectives as central social skills. These skills allow interactants to adapt their behaviour to social expectations, thereby increasing the likelihood of ongoing social reinforcement and goal attainment. Still others have cast social competence as a general cognitive ability to think analytically and to solve problems (chapters in Wine & Smye, 1981). However, despite the variety of approaches to competence, few studies have directly examined the role of such skills in creating the impression of being a good interactant, that is, a competent communicator. Instead, these researchers generally examine the relationship of social skills to psychological health or to other psychological traits. When social skills are examined in actual interaction episodes, the criterion most frequently used is simply a gross level, one-item judgement of "socially skilled or socially unskilled".

Communicative competence has also been conceptualized in many diverse ways. Communicative competence is often viewed and measured as a set of interrelated skills such as self-disclosure, behavioural flexibility, interaction management and relaxation (e.g., Duran, 1983). Still others choose to view communicative competence as an ability to manage meaning (e.g., Pearce & Cronen, 1980) and communicate ideas accurately (Powers & Lowery, 1980). While these perspectives differ considerably in many respects, they all share two common threads: (1) competence is seen as an attribute of an individual and (2) most instruments that have been developed to operationalize these constructs measure it as a trait or generalizable attribute.

In contrast, Spitzberg and Cupach (1984a) have developed the notion of relational competence, conceptualized as the extent to which objectives functionally related to communication are fulfilled through interaction appropriate to the interpersonal context. This definition contains two components of competence – effectiveness and appropriateness. Thus, to be competent, a person's communication needs to be both effective in achieving personal objectives and appropriate to the relationship and social context.

At the dyadic level of analysis, relational competence can be assessed by referencing each interactant's self-rated competence and other-rated competence. In a conversation between persons A and B, A's self-rated competence is A's perception of his or her own competence in this particular conversational episode. A's other-rated competence, on the other hand, is B's assessment of A's competence in the same conversation. A's self-rated competence has been found to be related significantly to A's ratings of B's competence and both measures have been found to be related substantially and positively to A's communication satisfaction, perceived confirmation and perceptions of conversational appropriateness and effectiveness (Spitzberg & Cupach, 1983). Relational competence represents a context-specific, interpersonal conversational construct. It assesses each actor's self-perceptions and allows each to be a participant-observer of the other person's communicative skill as well.

According to the attributional framework of loneliness, several predictions can be made which are relevant to relationally competent communication. Given that stability of loneliness is likely to engender perceptions of self-incompetence, it is expected that: *H1: Loneliness chronicity is negatively related to self-rated competence.* Furthermore, stable attributions of loneliness are presumed to result in attributions of uncontrollability, which, in turn, impair communicative motivation and skills. Thus A's loneliness chronicity should

be negatively related to B's rating of A's communicative competence in a given conversation. More generally, we hypothesize: *H2: Loneliness chronicity is negatively related to other-rated competence.* It appears likely that the increasing hopelessness, despair and depression accompanying stable attributions of loneliness develop with negative views of self *and* others. For chronically lonely persons who perceive stable and uncontrollable causes of their loneliness, interaction becomes an effort in futility since interaction with another person cannot change things. Because the interaction itself has little reward value, the partner is also perceived negatively. The prediction suggested by this line of reasoning is that loneliness chronicity is inversely related to perceptions of competence for one's partner in a conversation. Given the consistent research findings indicating that loneliness is related to negative evaluations of others, it seems reasonable to make such a prediction even controlling for the other person's loneliness. Hence, we expect to find that: *H3: A's loneliness chronicity is related negatively to A's rating of B's competence even when B's loneliness is controlled for.*

Method

Participants were 188 students in communication classes at two private western universities. Samples were combined for statistical analyses. Sixty-three percent of the sample was female, and the ethnic distribution was 70 percent white, 12 percent black, 8 percent Asian and 7 percent Hispanic.

Competence was assessed by four self-report **Likert-type instruments**. Self-Rated Competence is a twenty-eight-item instrument assessing context-specific impressions of self's interaction management, other-orientation, expressiveness and anxiety in a conversation.

Rating of Alter-Competence is a twenty-seven-item measure assessing context specific impressions of one's partner's interaction management, other-orientation and expressiveness.

Both scales have been found to be unaffected by **social desirability biases** [tendency to represent oneself in an overly positive light on surveys], and strongly and positively related to such relevant criteria as communication satisfaction, perceived confirmation, perceived appropriateness and effectiveness and positive affect in a particular conversation (Spitzberg & Cupach, 1983). The scales have also been found to be related to impressions of skills based upon discrete behaviours such as eye contact, vocal variety, topic maintenance and body lean (e.g., Spitzberg & Cupach, 1984b).

Measures of appropriateness and effectiveness were developed specifically for this study. These measures are exploratory in nature, given that the sample size does not permit extreme confidence in factor analytic procedures. Basically "appropriateness" refers to perceptions of other's behaviours that violate self's expectations or sense of propriety, and "effectiveness" to self's sense of reward attainment and dominance in the conversation.

Loneliness was assessed by an instrument developed by Young (1979b). His loneliness inventory consists of seventeen items, each of which is represented by a graduated sequence of four loneliness stability and intensity "stem" descriptions. For example, Item 10 reads as follows:

(1) I don't miss anyone in particular right now.
(2) I miss someone who isn't here now.
(3) I often think about a particular person I was close to.
(4) I cannot stop thinking about someone I lost.

When the seventeen items are summed, the measure represents a dimension of situational (short-term) versus chronic (long-term) loneliness. The higher the score on the measure, the more it reflects chronic loneliness. Young (1979b) found that his instrument correlated positively with depression ($r = .43$ to $.50$), and anxiety ($r = .24$ to $.36$).

As a validity check on loneliness stability, two forms of the Abbreviated Loneliness Scale (ABLS) developed by Ellison and Paloutzian (1979) were included. The ABLS is a six-item Likert-type measure that is negatively associated with self-reported social skill ($r = -.55$) and self-esteem ($r = -.57$). The two forms used were akin to the operationalization used by Spitzberg (1981) in his study of situational and chronic loneliness. Specifically the six items were repeated – but the instructions for the first set required the subject to refer to the previous two weeks, whereas the second set referred to the respondent's lifetime. In this manner, the subject's current and ongoing loneliness was assessed. It was expected that when combined, these measures would be positively correlated with the loneliness inventory.

Student volunteers were solicited in classrooms to participate in a study of "conversations and interpersonal relationships." In no instance did a student refuse to participate, although some provided insufficient information on their questionnaires and were excluded from those analyses. Students were paired, and each group was orally instructed to engage in a get-acquainted conversation. This get-acquainted exercise has been used successfully in previous competence research and it was considered particularly relevant to the study of loneliness, since loneliness is perpetuated by the incompetent management of such relationally initiative conversations (Spitzberg & Cupach, 1983). Many (44 percent) labeled their partners as acquaintances, 27 percent rated their relationship as friends, 15 percent considered themselves as colleagues, 4 percent defined themselves as lovers and 9 percent rated the relationship as "other."

Overall, the induction appears to have been successful in producing conversations that were moderately involving, fairly normal and relatively typical of other conversations experienced by these subjects. Because the intent of this study is to observe the effect of loneliness on "normal" conversations, and because the get-acquainted conversation is particularly relevant to the maintenance of loneliness, the induction used in this study appears to possess acceptable internal and external validity. In other words, subjects appeared to utilize their normal repertoire of conversational skills. Indeed, the mean self-ratings of competence was high (Mean = 119.25, scale range = 28.14, scale mid-point = 84), implying that subjects were motivated sufficiently to call forth their impression management skills to produce what they perceived to be competent performances.

Following 15 minutes of interaction, the participants were asked to stop conversing and complete a questionnaire concerning their reactions to the preceding interaction and general perceptions regarding interpersonal relationships. The questionnaire took about 15 minutes to complete.

Results

The Loneliness Chronicity Scale (LCS) did correlate positively with Two-Week Loneliness ($r = .75$, $p < .01$) and Lifetime Loneliness ($r = .53$, $p < .01$). The higher [correlation] for Two-Week Loneliness was not expected since the Lifetime Loneliness Scale was intended as a closer approximation of chronic loneliness. A possible methodological reason for this result is that the LCS may be measuring an "intensity" dimension of loneliness more than a duration dimension. The LCS items contain features of both dimensions, but subjects may be responding more to the intensity of their loneliness than to its duration or frequency. Thus subjects may be reporting on how they feel currently rather than how they have felt in the past. For example, the stem "I am often disturbed about how unsatisfactory my relationships now are compared with other times in my life" may cue subjects to respond more on the nature of the affect involved and less on the time element involved (e.g., "often" versus "for several years"). The result would be a closer relationship between currently felt loneliness (i.e., two-week loneliness) and the LCS. A compatible, but potentially more troublesome, interpretation is that loneliness is not an experience that is easily or accurately remembered. People may be acutely aware of their current feelings of loneliness and only vaguely aware of how often or how long they have been lonely in the past. This would act to make current or recent reports of loneliness more reliable indicators in comparison to reports of past loneliness. Unfortunately, available research cannot resolve this anomaly. Some studies have found current loneliness to be related to reported frequency and duration of loneliness, while other studies have found no relationship (Schultz & Moore, 1984). Clearly, to resolve this issue, more reliable measures of loneliness duration and frequency need to be developed which do not confound these factors with intensity of loneliness.

As expected the appropriateness and effectiveness measures were related positively to the competence measures. Appropriateness correlated more strongly with Rating of Alter-Competence ($r = .69$) than with Self-Rated Competence ($r = .51$); whereas the inverse is true of Effectiveness, which correlated higher with Self-Rated Competence ($r = .62$) than with Rating of Alter-Competence ($r = .54$).

Hypothesis 1 predicted that loneliness would be related inversely to Self-Rated Competence. This hypothesis is supported, with the Loneliness Chronicity Scale related significantly and negatively to Self-Rated Competence ($r = -.31$, $p < .01$). It is apparent, however, that this is a modest effect size indicating a relatively minor contribution to the impression of Self-Rated Competence.

When exploring relationships such as this, it is desirable to examine "where" the effect is most pronounced. For example, it may be that moderately chronically lonely people vary randomly in their communicative competence, whereas very chronically lonely people clearly experience communication skill deficits. To explore this possibility further, scores on the LCS were divided into three groups representing high, medium and low loneliness subjects, based on cut-off points one standard deviation above (>31) and below (<20) the mean. A one-way analysis of variance was then performed with Self-Rated Competence as the dependent measure. The analysis of variance was highly significant ($F = 9.72$, $p > .0001$, $\eta^2 = .0970$), with post hoc Scheffe contrasts indicating that high lonely subjects differ significantly ($p < .05$) from low and medium lonely subjects.

Hypothesis 2 predicted that loneliness chronicity would be related inversely to other-rated competence. This correlation is $-.16$ ($p < .05$). Thus, while supported, the small amount of **shared variance** [amount of other-rated competence uniquely attributable to loneliness chronicity] again indicates that caution should accompany interpretation of the association between loneliness and other-competence. Utilizing the procedure previously mentioned, a post hoc one-way analysis of variance was performed with other-competence as the dependent measure. The results were highly significant ($F = 7.51$, $p < .001$, $\eta^2 = .1057$) with high lonely individuals differ, as predicted ($p < .05$) from low and moderately lonely subjects when rated by their partners.

Hypothesis 3 predicted that A's loneliness would be related inversely to A's rating of B's competence, controlling for B's loneliness. This hypothesis was not supported. The partial correlation between loneliness and Rating of Alter-Competence, controlling for other's loneliness is non-significant ($r = -.09$). These results are not surprising given the non-significant zero-order relationship between loneliness and Rating of Alter-Competence ($r = -.08$).

Finally, a post hoc analysis of variance reveals a significant difference among high, moderate and low loneliness groups ($F = 4.58$, $p < .01$, $\eta^2 = .0486$), with high lonely subjects rating their partners significantly ($p < .05$) lower in competence than low or moderately lonely subjects, *not* controlling for other's loneliness. Hence B's loneliness

does not make an appreciable effect on A's perception of B's competence when A's loneliness is the predictor. It appears, rather, that lonely subjects tend to rate all others as relatively more incompetent in their communication.

Discussion

In this study we examined the effects of loneliness and relational competence from an attributional perspective. There are at least four points that merit discussion at this juncture.

First, the hypotheses were generally supported, lending credence to the attributional framework from which they were derived. The only surprise in terms of our predictions is the finding that lonely, relative to non-lonely, subjects rate all others as more incompetent, not further discriminating against lonely others on the competence measures. Thus we find a picture of a chronically lonely person as someone who devalues both self and others' communicative competence and generally is perceived by conversational partners as relationally incompetent. It appears that the stability of chronic loneliness impairs the very tool needed to achieve relational satisfaction.

The forming pattern of results suggests a self-fulfilling prophecy model of loneliness maintenance. Results from this study and others consistently support the conclusion that lonely individuals tend to perceive themselves and others negatively (e.g., Jones et al., 1982). With the onset of loneliness may come such devaluing affects as depression and lowered self-esteem (e.g., Schultz & Moore, 1984). Such affective states may "filter" the person's view of the social world. Interaction with others loses some of its value since it has not prevented the onset of loneliness. If loneliness continues, interaction becomes discounted as a viable coping response. In the process, lonely people tend to be less involved

(Sloan & Solano, 1984), expressive (Gerson & Perlman, 1979), and motivated (Spitzberg, 1981) in interaction. If interactional partners perceive lonely persons as uninvolved and less competent, relationships are less likely to be initiated and maintained. Interaction will in fact become less positively reinforcing. Lonely people will be further isolated, both by self and by others, from the social networks needed to break the cycle. In essence, if lonely people believe and act as if interaction cannot solve their problems, it will not solve their problems. Obviously such a processual cycle is difficult to confirm through standard measurement techniques. It nevertheless poses important concerns for both therapy and research in the future.

Second, although the hypotheses were supported, the overall effect sizes of the loneliness measures were low. There are three apparent reasons for the low correlations. First, and simply, loneliness does not account for all the variance in communicative competence. To be sure, other variables moderate the loneliness–competence link (e.g., non-verbal immediacy, anxiety, self-concept, relationship status, etc.). These relationships need to be explored further. Second, the measures may not be able to identify the transitory nature of loneliness. Although loneliness is a common experience, it is a time-bound and frequently transitory one (e.g., Schultz & Moore, 1984). Participants who identified themselves as lonely may have been in a transitional state to or from a more satisfying one. Such transitions could have moderated the effects of loneliness beyond efforts to account for chronicity. The supplementary analyses support this explanation insofar as the high and low loneliness difference scores produced more impressive results. The high, medium and low classifications may have adjusted for many of the peripheral or transitional cases. Third, the correlations may have been restricted by measurement problems, such as the moderate reliability of the LCS (alpha = .81). Although the LCS is related to

duration and intensity of loneliness, the validity of the scale is by no means proven. The development of valid measures of loneliness chronicity is an important research pursuit for the future.

Third, problems emerged with the instruments used to validate the Loneliness Chronicity Scale. An unexpected finding was that the LCS correlated higher with two-week ($r = .75$) than with lifetime loneliness ($r = .53$). There is no obvious reason why the two-week measure provides the stronger correlation, given that the LCS is designed to account for both long- and short-term loneliness. It may be that those who are situationally lonely make meaningful responses on the two-week measure because they are focused on the present, but find themselves less able to focus cognitively on their past experience of loneliness. Of course, the chronically lonely can respond more accurately to the two-week and lifetime measures, for what is reported on one's lifetime should hold for the past two weeks as well.

Finally, the results of this study suggest that loneliness manifests both behavioural and cognitive characteristics. That is, lonely people devalue communication and are perceived as less competent communicators. Efforts to develop approaches to clinical intervention should be sensitive to both the social skill deficits involved in loneliness and the attributional processes that may be operating to affect perceptions of the social milieu. A situational versus chronic distinction provides a way of adapting the best therapy to the subject. For example, situationally lonely persons may respond best to cognitive inoculation, in which they would be forewarned of the perceptions likely to result from prolonged experience of loneliness and instructed to discount their validity. Chronically lonely persons are more likely to need both cognitive restructuring and social skills training to reinforce productive communicative behaviour. These speculations appear to be useful directions for clinical research.

Did Spitzberg and Canary find support for their hypotheses? Examining the simple correlations, the authors suggest they only provide modest support for their hypotheses. Why might they claim only modest support? Correlations of .30 explain only 9 percent of the variance out of a total possible 100 percent (if you square a correlation you will get the percentage of variance accounted for by that relationship) and several key correlations were lower than this benchmark. However, the authors' secondary analysis, which categorized participants as possessing high, moderate or low loneliness, yielded stronger results. Not only did very lonely people rate their own relational competence as low, their conversational partners also gave them low marks in relational competence. Of particular interest, however, is the finding that very lonely participants rated their conversation partner as having low relational competence. The authors suggest that devaluing "self" and "other" social competence reduces the desire for social interactions and these cognitions perpetuate and solidify chronic loneliness. Finally, the authors of this article take a decidedly cognitive approach but assume that chronic loneliness will be expressed in a variety of situations and will be long-term. Does this suggest that loneliness is a "trait" or a more context-dependent "state?" Or, is it better to consider that loneliness is multifaceted and although it may be acute, it may be temporary and situation specific. This latter approach adds the interesting possibility that people can be lonely in some social situations but not others because they are less confident in their social skills in these situations. For example, a person may feel confident in structured social situations at work (and not lonely) but that same person may lack confidence in his/her social skills in less structured situations (such as a party) and experience loneliness in this context.

Spitzberg and Canary present a frank appraisal of the limitations of their study. Of the issues presented, which do you think is the most cogent? Can their discussion be a valuable asset for future research as they suggest, providing interested parties a guide to expanding and clarifying findings reported in this article? Finally, one additional methodological issue to consider in this and in other articles you will read involves **regression to the mean**. First, let us consider the meaning of this term. When one attempts to measure a variable (e.g., Loneliness) our instrument will not be perfectly reliable (i.e., each time you fill out a questionnaire your loneliness score will vary a bit). The greater the unreliability in the loneliness questionnaire, the greater your loneliness score will change from one time you take the survey to the next time due to a variety of reasons (e.g., ambiguous questions, being ill, feeling happier). It also seems reasonable to assume that the greater the length of time between filling out a questionnaire from time 1 to time 2 the more your score will change. So, if we know loneliness scores *will* change over time, and we select as one of our research groups a set of people who score at one extreme end of a loneliness scale (e.g., highly lonely), which direction will their scores change over time? Will their scores become more extreme (even more lonely), or perhaps less extreme, and move closer to the mean of the entire group? Chances are that if the survey is not 100 percent reliable then the scores of the highly lonely group (extreme group) will change/**regress toward the mean** (middle) of the distribution (reflecting less loneliness) if they are tested at a later date. Why? A score at the 95th percentile has very little room to get more extreme (95 → 100), but much more room to become less extreme (95 → 0). Remember that Spitzberg and Canary reported only *modest* correlations when using the full range of loneliness scores, but found *larger* effects when comparisons were made between more *extreme* groups. Since their measure of loneliness was not perfectly reliable (and no measure can ever be perfectly reliable) it is possible that larger differences reported in the secondary analysis may weaken as subjects' loneliness scores *regress* to the moderate range over time. You may want to keep "regression to the mean" on your checklist as you critically read future articles and assess the explanations offered by authors for their research findings.

A final issue to consider before moving on to the last article in this chapter involves the issue of sampling. We would assume that loneliness is universally experienced since it has been described in roughly similar ways across time and in most cultures. However, does this broader experience of loneliness vary based on the social role limitations and our understanding of these roles? For example, do the roles that students play (and the social context they live within) affect their understanding and experience of loneliness? How might this differ for older or married individuals? Is the intensity of a single lifelong partner enough to ward off loneliness in married individuals or perhaps a number of more superficial relationships are adequate? Might these experiences differ for men and women? The next article in this chapter will address these questions by examining loneliness within marriage.

Some definitions of loneliness do not include as a major component the experience of loneliness within a marriage or other committed long-term relationships since one may assume the presence of a partner. Married samples often serve as comparison groups for those assumed to be lonely (i.e., without a long-term or committed partner). Tornstam, as well as several other scholars, believe that the experience of loneliness within long-term relationships is a significant topic in its own right.

Why might someone be lonely within marriage? Absence of a partner due to work, excessive childcare responsibilities, inability to maintain a social network larger than one's immediate family, and unfulfilled expectations may contribute to the experience of loneliness. In addition, Tornstam considers whether men and women carry different expectations into committed relationships and how they might affect the experience of loneliness. The body of previous work suggests women's lower self-esteem and greater expectations for intimacy may lead them to experience more loneliness than their husbands. However, Tornstam reports that sex differences appear inconsistently across the previous literature and he suggests that this lack of consistency may be the result of using special or narrow samples, such as college students, who experience different role expectations than the larger population. Indeed, few college students are married, thus women may not experience loneliness related to sex role differences until they enter into a long-term committed relationship. You may wish to consider how broad a sample would be necessary for Tornstam to be confident he has a good mix of distinctly different role expectations. Finally, as you read Tornstam's thoughtful consideration of his results you will notice he systematically rules out the most probable explanations for the effects he reported. You may want to consider which alternative explanations are left for his findings.

Loneliness in Marriage

Lars Tornstam

As Peplau and Perlman (1982) noted in their sourcebook of theory and research, there are several reasons for the growing interest in loneliness research. A first reason is that experiences of loneliness are quite common. Several studies show that a considerable proportion of adult individuals in Western societies do, from time to time, suffer from feelings of loneliness. Secondly, it has been found that feelings of loneliness are not only unpleasant, but also correlate with suicide, alcohol abuse and deteriorated health. A third reason is that the study of loneliness focuses on the condition of the social institutions of today's society. A surprisingly high proportion of married people experience loneliness. Fourth, studies of loneliness offer a new pathway to the study of value patterns which are central in Western society. Love and friendship are important values in society, and the loneliness studies offer an alternative theoretical approach to these phenomena.

The definition of loneliness has been discussed at length by others and will not be repeated here (e.g., Peplau & Perlman [1982] discuss twelve different definitions). Only some basic distinctions will be mentioned. First, loneliness sometimes refers to a state of social isolation, e.g., the lack of social contacts, and sometimes to subjective feelings of loneliness. Several studies have shown the correlation between these two aspects of loneliness to be far from perfect (e.g., Conner et al., 1979).

In studies of the aetiology of loneliness, correlations have been found with the size and the quality of the social network (e.g., Perlman et al., 1978), with losses, but also with developmental experiences. Tornstam (1988, 1990) found developmental experiences, such as having an insecure childhood and difficulties in making friends during childhood, to have an explanatory power as high as deficiencies in the present social network.

Not surprisingly, earlier studies have found loneliness to be more prevalent among never married, divorced and widowed individuals, in comparison with married ones (e.g., de Jong-Gierveld & Raadschelders, 1982). The proportion of "lonely" respondents differs in different studies due to differences in the phrasing of the questions and to differences in the way of categorizing the response alternatives, as well as to differences in samples, but the general pattern is the same. The divorced, the widowed and those who have never married are more lonely. More or less self-evident explanations have been offered to explain the loneliness among non-married respondents. What has been ignored is the surprisingly high proportion of married individuals reporting loneliness. As will be reported below, in the present study 40 percent of the married respondents feel lonely often or sometimes, 16 percent feel lonely together with other people and 7 percent feel lonely "right now."

When it comes to sex differences in loneliness, earlier studies have produced contradictory results. In a review of various studies, where the sex differences in loneliness were targeted, Borys and Perlman (1985) found that twenty-four out of twenty-eight studies using the UCLA Loneliness Scale show no sex differences in loneliness. When differences are found, males typically have higher loneliness scores. But, as Borys and Perlman (1985) also noted, the UCLA scale does not explicitly ask people whether they feel lonely, but rather assesses this indirectly. If people are directly asked if they feel lonely, studies tend to show women being more lonely than men. This has also been the usual finding in Scandinavian studies (e.g., Tornstam, 1988).

Borys and Perlman (1985) offer four possible explanations of the fact that women report higher degrees of loneliness in such studies. The first possible explanation is that women have lower self-esteem, which causes a higher degree of feelings of loneliness. The second explanation is offered in terms of sex roles, where it is supposed to be easier for women than for men to express various kinds of difficulties. The third explanation is that women consider interpersonal relations more important than men do, which causes women to feel deficiencies in their social relationships to be more unpleasant and noteworthy. The final explanation would be in terms of genetic, hormonal or physiological factors. Borys and Perlman (1985) found by experiment that the second explanation is more probable. Women are more apt to acknowledge their loneliness than men.

There are a couple of important drawbacks in the above studies, which make them less suited to answer the questions about sex differences in loneliness. One such drawback is that many of the studies are based on rather small and special samples. For instance, the experiment undertaken by Borys and Perlman (1985) was done on 117 psychology students. Furthermore, almost all studies where no sex differences are found or where men show higher loneliness scores are based on samples of students, while almost all studies where women show higher loneliness scores are larger population studies.

Another drawback is that the earlier studies do not sufficiently elaborate the question of sex differences in loneliness. Men and women are compared as to the degree of loneliness, without distinguishing between, for example, men and women of different ages, not married vs married, with large or restricted social networks, etc. Neither do the earlier studies take into account the variables connected with the above explanations mentioned by Borys and Perlman (1985).

What is needed to elaborate the question of sex differences in loneliness is a large representative population study, where several of these variables are controlled for at the same time. The present study is a step in that direction. In addition to offering some answers to old questions, this study also adds two new dimensions to the study of sex differences in loneliness. One of these questions is related to how men and women themselves attribute the causes to their feelings of loneliness. The other question is related to the differences in coping behaviour.

The questions to be answered in this study can now be formulated as follows: 1). Is there a sex difference in loneliness, and if so, 2). Is that sex difference the same in all age groups and among married and non-married? 3). Is there support for the conclusion by Borys and Perlman (1985), that women are more apt to acknowledge their loneliness than men? This shall be called *the acknowledgement hypothesis*. 4). Could a sex difference in loneliness (with women reporting higher degrees of loneliness) be explained by the fact that women consider interpersonal relationships more important than men do, or that they expect more intimacy in a relationship? This shall be called *the intimacy hypothesis*. 5). Could a sex difference in loneliness (with women reporting higher degrees of loneliness) be explained by lower self-esteem in women? This shall be called *the self-esteem hypothesis*. 6). Could a sex difference in loneliness (with women reporting higher degrees of loneliness) be explained by other traits or variables which correlate with loneliness, such as the size of the social network, access to intimate friends or experiences during childhood and adolescence? This shall be called *the confounding variables hypothesis*. 7). Are there any differences in the ways in which men and women themselves attribute the causes of loneliness? 8). Are there any differences in the ways in which men and women cope with loneliness?

Method

The present study was based on a simple random sample of all Swedish inhabitants 15–80 years of age. In Sweden all inhabitants are registered in a population file, from which representative samples can be drawn by computer. This facility was used for this study. A mail questionnaire, focusing on various aspects of loneliness, was sent to the 4179 subjects in the sample.

The dropout rate of the total sample was 34 percent, leaving 2795 as the remaining number of subjects. A close analysis of the respondent group has shown it to be representative of the whole Swedish population in the corresponding age groups as to the distribution of age, sex and marital status (Tornstam, 1988).

Measures

Loneliness. Respondents' feelings of loneliness were assessed through a series of eleven questions, which is a mix of items used by others and items developed by the author. It was stressed that the questions referred to feelings of loneliness only, not to whether one was isolated or not. The answers to the eleven questions were analysed with a factor analysis that separated three dimensions of loneliness. The first dimension includes indicators related to the quantity or intensity of the loneliness, which a previous analysis (Tornstam, 1988) has shown to be mainly connected with situational aspects of the social network. The second dimension is qualitative, as it describes the constant feeling of loneliness in a lonely personality type. This loneliness dimension is related to developmental experiences. The third dimension singles out an indicator meant to

tap the positive kind of loneliness, namely, solitude.

In the present study I used only the first dimension of the loneliness scale, since it is the dimension which is primarily related to the social network and the changes in the network. Personality traits and developmental experiences, which are related to the second loneliness dimension, do not contribute to the explanation of the differences to be described below.

The specific questions behind the loneliness dimension analysed in the present study were answered by the use of four to six response alternatives (e.g., "Do you occasionally feel lonely" ["Yes, often" (8 percent) to "No, never"] factor loading .86). The extreme is shown in parentheses, and the percentage of all the respondents using the most "negative" response alternative is shown along with the factor loading. The **Cronbach's alpha** for the five items is .84, which is satisfactory (Bohrnstedt & Knoke, 1982).

From the distribution of the responses over the response alternatives it can be concluded that the major pattern in this sample is not a pattern of extreme loneliness, at least not on the basis of the proportion of respondents using the most "lonely" response alternatives. However, in this article I am not interested in establishing any description of an absolute level of loneliness in the population or its subgroups. Instead, my aim is to explore differences in loneliness between men and women, and in particular to describe the determinants of certain differences. To do this I utilize an index of loneliness. It should be mentioned that when I use such procedures I gain in accuracy and stability of the measures, but cannot pinpoint any absolute level of loneliness. When working with indexes, the cutting point decided for "lonely" and "not lonely" is totally arbitrary.

Expectations for relationship. In order to tap expectations for relationships, the respondents in this study were asked to state how important various aspects of a relationship are for the creation of a close and intimate relationship. A factor analysis showed the expectations to form two different dimensions of expectation. The first of these two dimensions was labeled expectation for intimacy, the second expectation of solidarity. In this context I omit the second dimension from the discussion, since men and women do not differ in this kind of expectation. For both sexes the expectation of solidarity is, however, higher for each consecutive older age group ($p < .001$, eta (men) = .32, eta (women) = .26). The eta coefficient (measures the degree of association between membership in a group (e.g., male or female) and a dependent variable). It ranges between 0 and 1 and as a measure of association, (you can square eta and determine the percent of the variance attributed to group membership, similar to R^2.)

Regarding the expectation for intimacy, a **Likert scale** index was constructed on the basis of the responses from items (e.g., "You should be able to trust each other completely"). Responses were given on a 4-point scale ranging from "unimportant" to "very important." The Cronbach's alpha for the five items is .71, which is just above what is acceptable.

Self-esteem, or the lack of the same, was measured by five items with four response alternatives ranging from fully agree to not agreeing at all (e.g., "Do you have a feeling that people understand and respect you?"). These five items do not correlate strongly enough to form a unidimensional index. Because of this they are used individually in the analysis.

Attributed causes of loneliness. Following Rubenstein and Shaver (1982), I included a series of items where the respondents themselves were given the opportunity to state the causes to which they attribute their feelings of loneliness. These questions were addressed to the respondents who had experienced loneliness at least occasionally during the last 5 years. The respondents could check as few or as many as they wanted of twenty-four different "causes" derived from qualitative research by

Rubenstein and Shaver (1982) (e.g., "moved often").

Coping behaviour. In this study the respondents were also asked what they do when feeling lonely. The respondents could check as many as they wanted of twenty-one different alternative behaviours, ranging from emotional reactions such as crying to active coping by, for example, visiting or calling somebody.

The social network. In this study the social network was measured in several different ways. The respondents were asked how many persons they regularly met outside school or work and how often they met them. The corresponding question was also asked specifically regarding neighbours, relatives and other friends.

To get closer to the qualitative aspect of the social network the respondents were asked how many persons they have with whom they really can share their joys and sorrows. We also asked the respondents to indicate the person who is closest to the respondent in the sense that they can talk openly about everything – both joys and sorrows.

Results

The distribution of loneliness

In both theoretical discussion and common belief there are some subgroups in which loneliness is thought to be more prevalent. As already mentioned above, the non-married constitute such a subgroup. Another subgroup where loneliness is commonly believed to be especially prevalent is the elderly. Quite reasonable theoretical discussions of role loss, loss of spouse, etc., predict such a pattern. Several studies have, however, falsified this assumption (e.g., Rubenstein et al., 1979). Longitudinal studies and studies including respondents in advanced age, however, do show an increase in loneliness in elderly groups (e.g., Mullins et al., 1988).

In the present **cross-sectional** study we find another, more complicated, age-related pattern, when we distinguish between married and unmarried men and women. First, for married men we find no statistically significant correlation between age and loneliness at all, even if there is a tendency for a decline in loneliness with age. For married women we find a significant and almost linear decline in loneliness with age. For both the unmarried women and men we find a pattern with a peak in the age group 30–39, a following decline and a slight increase in the age group 70–80 years. These patterns should, however, be interpreted with some caution, since this study is a cross-sectional one. The differences could be a result of a **cohort effect** (apparent age differences are confounded with shared social experiences among people (cohort) born at about the same time, e.g., baby-boomers). In this study, for example, younger generations of married women may be more vulnerable to feelings of loneliness than older generations. An ongoing analysis of a qualitative study of elderly people's life histories seems, however, to support the quantitative data. Changing views of life, together with coping mechanisms, seem to counterbalance the negative effects of aging.

There is also of course the possibility that there are cohort differences in the willingness to identify and admit to feelings of loneliness. This is, however, less likely, since we should in that case find a more consistent age-related pattern in loneliness rather than different patterns for the married and unmarried.

Returning to the first two questions to be answered in this analysis: whether there is a sex difference in loneliness and whether this difference is the same in all age groups and among married and non-married. There certainly is a sex difference in loneliness, but this difference is found only among married respondents. Relying on the statistical analysis, we must further restrict this difference to married respondents in the age groups 20–49 years of age. It is only in this age group that we find a statistically

significant difference in the loneliness experienced by men and women. Among the unmarried respondents, who of course experience higher degrees of loneliness than the married ones, there are no differences in the degree of loneliness between men and women.

This pattern may explain some of the confusion in results described by Borys and Perlman (1985). If young unmarried students are used as the study population, we can expect to find no sex differences in loneliness. If, on the other hand, married respondents between 20 and 49 years of age are included in the study, we can expect to find sex differences in loneliness. This might also be the reason why population studies more often than not show sex differences in loneliness.

The observation that the sex difference in loneliness is restricted to married people of the ages 20–49 of course raises the question why. The following analysis might shed some light on that question, even if we at this stage are unable to give a full and complete answer.

The acknowledgement hypothesis assumes that women more willingly admit their feelings of loneliness. Rather than there being a real sex difference in loneliness, this explanation is in terms of an omission error with regard to the male responses. This explanation is less likely to be right because the difference in reported loneliness between men and women is restricted to married respondents in a certain age group. If the explanation were to be accepted, we should find a *general* difference in the reported loneliness between men and women. Instead, the age-related loneliness pattern among the unmarried is identical for men and women. The conclusion is that the difference in reported loneliness between married men and women is real, and has to be explained in a way other than an assumed omission error in the male responses or a higher tendency among women to acknowledge their feelings of loneliness.

The intimacy hypothesis assumes that women have higher expectations for a relationship.

In particular the expectation for intimacy is supposed to be higher. This, at the same time, produces a higher probability of being disappointed with regard to the expectation for intimacy, resulting in feelings of loneliness.

Our data confirm some of the assumptions in the intimacy hypothesis. In the younger age groups there is a considerable difference in the expectation for intimacy between men and women. For every consecutive age group, however, this difference decreases. This is due to the fact that the expectation for intimacy declines with age for women ($p < .001$, eta = .21). For men there is no statistically significant difference across the age groups. An example of the differences in the answers to the specific questions is that among women between 15 and 39 years of age, 52 percent say it is very important for a relationship that the partners are really interested in each other's problems. The corresponding percentage among men in the same age group is 38 percent. The immediate interpretation of the pattern is that women, being socialized with a romantic view on relationships, start out with high expectations for intimacy, but are taught by real-life experiences to reduce these expectations during the life course. This interpretation, however, cannot be accepted without some caution. Since the data are cross-sectional, there could be a cohort effect involved. The pattern would also appear if every younger cohort of women had higher expectations for intimacy than the next older one.

Although interesting in itself, the difference in the expectations for intimacy does not explain the differences in loneliness in married men and women aged 20–49. There is no correlation between loneliness and the expectation for intimacy. Subsequent analysis shows that the difference in loneliness is not reduced when controlling for the differences in expectation for intimacy.

The self-esteem hypothesis as proposed by Borys and Perlman (1985), as well as by Perlman and Peplau (1981), argues that self-esteem might be associated with loneliness. If women are lower in self-esteem, this might explain the sex difference.

Only in two of the indicators of self-esteem did we find a sex difference. More of the women answer affirmatively to the question "Do you worry about how to manage things?" Among the married women, 20–49 years of age, 61 percent fully or partly answered the question affirmatively, as compared to 46 percent among the men ($p < .001$, eta =. 17). On the other hand, a larger proportion of the men answered affirmatively to the question "Has life taught you to be careful not to believe in people's promises?" Among the married men, 20–49 years of age, 76 percent partly or fully agree that it has, while the corresponding proportion among the women is 65 percent ($p < .001$, eta = .18).

The correlations between the loneliness measure and the indicators of self-esteem are, however, quite strong. Worries about how to manage things and feeling downhearted about the future are especially associated with loneliness. Additional analysis, where the five indicators of self-esteem, together with the sex variable, were used as determinants (independent variables) and the loneliness index as the dependent variable, shows that the explanatory power of the sex variable is only slightly reduced when the indicators of self-esteem are controlled for. This means that self-esteem, as we have measured it, cannot explain away the initial sex difference in loneliness.

The confounding variables hypothesis. An alternative way to explain the observed sex difference in loneliness would be the assumption that married men and women differ with regard to other traits or variables, which correlate with loneliness. From an earlier analysis (Tornstam, 1988), we know that the degree of loneliness correlates with a number of variables such as, for example, lack of warmth and security during childhood, difficulties in making friends during childhood, difficulties with the opposite sex during adolescence, the size of the social network, the number of intimate friends and losses of significant others. The only one of these variables where married women and men aged 20–49 differ is regarding the number of intimate friends. Women have a larger number of intimates in comparison with men. The analysis shows that the difference in loneliness between the married men and women in fact slightly increases if the difference in the number of intimates is controlled for. Consequently, the difference in loneliness between married men and women aged 20–49 cannot be wiped out by controlling for the above-mentioned type of variables.

Another hypothesis was that married women with small children become isolated at home, and thereby come to experience more loneliness. Controlling for whether the married women in the target group had babies, small children, school children, teenagers or whether they are employed inside or outside the home, we found the difference in loneliness between the married men and women aged 20–49 to remain the same. No part of the original difference is explained by controlling for these variables.

Even if neither the size of the social network nor the number of intimate friends could explain away the initial sex difference in loneliness, there are some overlooked aspects of the quality of the social network that might add to the understanding of the observed sex difference in loneliness. As shown above, women have higher expectations of intimacy in a relationship in comparison with men. Lowenthal and Haven (1968) have shown that access to at least one real intimate is more important for life satisfaction than is the size of the social network. However, it might be important to discover just who this intimate person is.

In this study I did ask the respondents who the person was who was most close to the respondent in the sense that they could talk openly about everything – both joys and sorrows. I found a general pattern of married men naming their wives as the closest person, to a higher degree than married women naming their husbands as the closest person. On the other hand, married women name children, parents or other friends as closest person to a larger extent

than married men do. Among married men in general, 89 percent name their wife as closest person, while only 77 percent of the married women name their husband as closest person ($p < .001$, eta = .15). Almost identical differences were found in Finland by Øberg et al. (1987) and in Norway by Thorsen (1990). The difference between married men who name their wife as closest person and married women naming their husbands as closest person is statistically significant in all age groups except the youngest and the oldest ones.

Generally, as in our target groups (married men and women 20–49 years of age), there is a correlation between the degree of experienced loneliness and whether respondents name their spouse as closest person or not ($p < .001$, eta = .22). The degree of loneliness is higher among respondents who do not name their spouse as closest person. Since this proportion is higher among women, the difference in loneliness between married men and women 20–49 years of age might be affected when controlling for whether the respondent has or has not named the spouse as closest person. We do find a specified correlation, where the statistically significant difference disappears among respondents not naming the spouse as closest person ($p = .323$, eta =.13), but remains among respondents who name the spouse as closest person ($p < .001$, eta = .14). But this disappearance of the statistical difference is primarily due to the fact that the group which does not name the spouse as closest person is relatively small. The eta coefficients are almost the same in both groups, which means that we cannot explain away the initial sex difference in loneliness by controlling for whether the spouse is the closest person or not.

Attributed causes of loneliness

Among the married men and women 20–49 years of age, there are statistically significant differences in the degree to which six of the earlier described twenty-four "causes" were used to account for the respondents' feelings of loneliness.

Women are much higher on "causes" like "being misunderstood," "not needed" and "being an uninteresting person," while men are higher on "travel often" and "being far from home." The women are, with one exception, higher on relational causes whereas the men are higher on situational "causes," the exception being "new job," where women are higher than men.

Where the attributed cause "being misunderstood" is related to ages ranging from 20 to 80, there is an age-related pattern in the differences between men and women. The difference is highly significant in the ages 20–49, but nonexistent in ages 50+. The same age-related pattern is found in the attributed cause "not needed." A similar pattern, but with the men higher than the women is found in the attributed causes "travel too often" and "being far from home." Here the men are significantly higher than the women, but only in the age groups 20–49.

Since such striking differences in the attributed causes of loneliness are found in the ages between 20 and 49, a plausible hypothesis would be that some of the difference in the degree of loneliness among married men and women 20–49 years of age, could be due to these differences. This assumption is, however, not confirmed by our analysis. When the above-mentioned causes of loneliness and the sex variable are used as predictors, the difference in experienced loneliness between married men and women still remains.

Coping behaviour

In general, the most prevalent behaviour related to loneliness is watching TV. Of the respondents who have experienced loneliness at least occasionally during the last 5 years, 46 percent say watching TV is one of the things they do. Other common activities are calling somebody (43 percent), thinking (45 percent), reading (38 percent) and listening to music (36 percent). Women do, to a

higher extent than men, react to feelings of loneliness by crying, but also by being more active in contacting other people. Men, on the other hand, turn more than women to activities such as watching TV, movies, exercising, work and drinking alcohol.

Basically, this pattern is the same among the married men and women 20–49 years of age. There are, however, certain differences in the coping patterns, depending on whether the respondents do or do not name the spouse as their closest intimate in life. The married women who do not name their spouse as the closest person in life tend to visit others more than do the married women who do name their spouse as closest person in life. The percentage of "visitors" is 34 and 25 percent in these two groups, respectively.

The married men who do not name the spouse as closest person in life are, in comparison with the married men who do name their spouse as closest person in life, higher on thinking (62/42 percent) and drinking alcohol (18/8 percent). Coping with loneliness seems to be more passive, inward and flight oriented among married men who do not name the spouse as closest person. Married women who do not name the spouse as closest friend tend to be more active and externally oriented in their coping with loneliness. Interestingly enough, this difference is not reflected in the degree to which the coping behaviour used by married men and women helps to counteract the loneliness. Among both married men and women in the ages between 20 and 49, who have felt lonely at least occasionally during the last 5 years, the proportion stating their coping behaviour to be very or quite effective is 81 percent. Seemingly quite different coping behaviours in men and women are equally effective – according to the respondents' own judgements, that is.

Discussion

The first question to be answered by this study was whether there is a sex difference in loneliness or not. Previous studies have produced very confusing results. In this study, however, it is quite clear that there is a sex difference in loneliness. But, as an answer to the second question for this analysis, this difference is restricted to married subjects between 20 and 49 years of age. This might, at the same time, be the reason why earlier studies have produced confusing results. If the pattern in this study is a general one, we would, for example, expect to find no sex differences in studies where young unmarried students are the subjects of study.

A new question is, of course, why the sex difference in loneliness is restricted to married men and women between 20 and 49 years of age. There are several possible explanations for this.

One explanation might be that this is a result of a cohort effect in the sense that only the younger cohorts are sensitive to the subtle factors causing differences in loneliness between wife and husband. The older cohorts might have had their marriages filled with a simple struggle for existence, which left no room for the exclusive feelings of loneliness. Such an interpretation is in concordance with the reasoning of Inglehart (1977), when, based on the theory of Maslow (1954), he attempts to explain the differences in value patterns between countries and cohorts. He finds that the value patterns are different in countries with different standards of living, as well as between cohorts within the countries. In countries with a lower standard of living, as well as in older cohorts, the value pattern is more "materialistic", while in countries with higher standards of living, as well as in younger cohorts, the stress is on post-material values, where questions about, for example, self-actualization come to the fore. If, during your childhood and adolescence you experience a simple struggle for existence, you carry this experience with you in your value system throughout life. The fulfillment of basic material needs becomes more important in your value system. If, on the other hand, you started your life on a high material

level, the questions about self-actualization and self-fulfillment come to the fore from the very beginning. The same type of reasoning could be used to explain why relatively younger married individuals are sensitive to loneliness, while older ones are not. However, since this is a cross-sectional study, this possibility cannot be tested. The observed age differences could just as well be explained as a process of change within the life course, in terms of, for example, an increased ability to cope with loneliness.

Another possible explanation of the observed pattern could be that many "bad" marriages have ended before the respondents reach the age of 50, leaving a larger proportion of non-lonely married respondents in the analysis after that age. The slope of the loneliness curves for married men and women is consistent with such an explanation. So is another interpretation, assuming a process of coping and adaptation within marriage. Individuals learn to overcome differences and unrealistic expectations in marriage, thereby reducing the feelings of loneliness. Given a measure of the duration of the marriage, we would have been able to disentangle some of the problem, but not all of it. Finding, for example, that individuals in marriages of long duration are less lonely, would still not answer the question whether this is a result of an adaptation process or a result of loss of those marriages that began with high initial differences in expectations, thus leaving only those marriages that started well to grow into long-lasting ones. In order to disentangle these possible explanations for the observed pattern, a longitudinal study is needed.

The third question to be answered in this analysis was whether there is support for the assumption that the sex difference in loneliness can be explained by women's higher willingness to acknowledge their loneliness. If this explanation were true, we would expect to find a general sex difference in loneliness. Since the observed sex difference is restricted to married individuals between 20 and 49 years of age, this explanation cannot be accepted.

The fourth question was whether a sex difference in loneliness could be explained by the fact that women have higher expectations of a relationship than men. In this study we certainly find that younger women have higher expectations of intimacy than men do. But, according to our analysis, this does not explain away the sex differences in loneliness. This might of course be due to the fact that our measure of the expectations of the relationship was inadequate. Theoretical as well as empirical evidence certainly does predict that such differences in expectations would produce higher degrees of loneliness in married women, in comparison with married men. But, according to our analysis, this does not explain away the sex differences in loneliness. Thorsen (1988) describes a series of investigations showing men's relationships to be less open and intimate and, instead, more marked by competition. Women's relationships are, on the other hand, more marked by intimacy and emotions. These differences should, from a theoretical point of view, produce a higher degree of loneliness in married women. It is recommended that future research on sex differences in loneliness try to elaborate the expectations for the relationship more thoroughly than I have been able to do in this study.

The fifth question in this analysis was whether sex differences in loneliness could be explained by lower self-esteem in women. Even if the results show some correlations between sex and self-esteem and substantial correlations between self-esteem and loneliness, the differences in self-esteem between men and women do not explain away the observed sex difference in loneliness.

In relation to the sixth question, a series of correlates of loneliness were tested in order to see if they could explain the observed sex difference. Among these correlates are lack of warmth and security during childhood, difficulties in making friends during childhood, difficulties with the opposite sex during adolescence, the size of the social network, the number of intimate friends and losses of significant others. None of these factors could explain away the observed sex differences in loneliness.

Even after answering the seventh and eighth questions for this analysis, where men and women are shown to attribute their loneliness to somewhat different causes, and also cope with loneliness differently, we have a remaining sex difference in loneliness.

This fact yields itself to two different interpretations. The first and perhaps most plausible one is that some of the measures were not elaborated enough. I have pointed to the possibility that a further exploration into the expectations for a relationship might be fruitful. Another interpretation is that the explanation of the observed sex difference is to be found on quite another theoretical level. Borys and Perlman (1985) offer a last possibility, that sex differences might be explained in terms of genetic, hormonal or physiological factors. The results of this study can certainly not give any evidence for this, but, on the other hand, nothing in this study can rule this possibility out.

After reading this article you should have two clear impressions of loneliness. First, non-married people in this sample were lonelier than married people. This result is well supported by a host of studies and across a number of cultures (e.g., Stack, 1998). Second, women experienced greater loneliness than men within marriage, and although this sex difference occurred only for married couples between the ages 20 and 49, older women still reported greater loneliness than men in every age group. Tornstam considers the multifaceted nature of loneliness and critically evaluates a large number of possible explanations for his results. However, he is unable to rule out a number of possible explanations, leaving his conclusions a little unsettled.

He even considers genetic, hormonal or physiological factors as possibly being behind the reported sex differences (even though he did not measure any of these in the study). Perhaps separating the non-married adults into widowed, divorced and never married while assessing the impact of adult children (i.e., Pinquart, 2003) would add greater clarity to these results. In addition, longitudinal studies that avoid cohort effects may add a different perspective on some of the issues of loneliness, especially with regard to dispositional factors. Additional perspectives may be added by using experimental designs such as the person perception design (i.e., Sprecher, McKinney, & Orbuch, 1987) since the results of Spitzberg and Canary (1985) and others suggest that lonely individuals may not accurately perceive themselves and others in social exchanges.

12 The Importance of Social Networks

Most of the chapters up to here have presented a decidedly dyadic view of relationships – that is to say, they have focused on the couple or a dyad as the target relationship and have not attended to the influence of outsiders. Yet even when we regard our relationships as "personal" and "private", they are still subject to the oversight of other people. For example, although sex can be a loving expression of marital intimacy in a marriage – the sort of relationships typically encouraged and praised by society – it is banned from occurring in public and other people may call the police if a married couple tested the rule. Also think for a moment how many of your friends, dates, partners, you met through third parties, either by direct introduction or as an indirect consequence of you knowing the third party. Finally, think about the people with whom you discuss relationships and relational problems: these people are usually quite content to offer advice about what YOU should do, even though you know that your intimate relationships are "personal" and "private". Even if you decide not to take the offered advice, you are sure to think carefully about it before you continue to conduct the [personal!] relationship.

Until quite recently, when sociologists began to bring forward some interesting ideas connecting "networks" to "the personal", there has been insufficient attention given to the role of outsiders on the internal dynamics of relationships. Starting with the "Person is social" article from Milardo and Wellman, this chapter will go on to explore some of the ways in which network influences can be measured and observed in the behaviors that we primarily think of as being "private and personal".

As you will see, the papers here develop a sophisticated view of the nature of external influences on relationships and together they serve to make us more aware of the fact that personal relationships are not *just* personal. For example, we have many more relationships with people who are NOT intimate (e.g., neighbors, work-mates, classmates, teachers, shop assistants, even some family members whom we see only rarely and who are not personally close to us) than we do with close friends. All the same we are often significantly affected by those relationships (for example, we usually feel more embarrassment in front of strangers than in front of people we know intimately; we may be more concerned about the judgments of strangers than of intimates who "accept us for what we are").

The first paper by Milardo and Wellman (1992) was originally a paper introducing a special issue of the *Journal of Social and Personal Relationships* devoted specifically to this matter. In their distinction – and then ultimate reconciliation – of the social and the personal, Milardo and Wellman make some very important points that we should understand not only in their own right but also in terms of their likelihood of adding something to previous chapters and to our overall understanding of relationships. In particular, they point out that most of our relationships simply are not intimate and that many of them exist not for the pure pleasure of their enactment but for their social utility. That is to say, they are *useful* to us. A "connection" can put in a good word for us to a potential employer or might even be able to get a parking ticket cancelled or look after our interests in the "office politics" while we are on vacation. Even friendship itself is not completely a matter of individual choice but is patterned and structured by social conventions and practices. For example, most of your friends are probably from the same nationality, ethnicity, religious background, socioeconomic and educational history and relatively similar scholastic attainments. How interesting that you "freely" chose them in such a way, isn't it!!! Some of the papers here note that such connections and practices often have roots in the social and economic circumstances of the people concerned and cannot be dismissed as the result of chance, but rather should be recognized as the results of organizing large-scale social structural principles of whose impact we are all too often unaware.

The article below by Milardo and Wellman introduces us to some of these issues, pointing out that the "hot tub" of intimate relationships is not necessarily the most influential factor in the way we conduct our lives. They introduce the concept of **"weak ties"**, that is the connections that are not based on close intimacy and which are nevertheless important influences on our lives.

The Personal is Social

Robert M. Milardo and Barry Wellman

Contributors to this journal have largely emphasized the personal – even though social comes first in the title. The field has become myopic, with most papers focusing on emotionally supportive close relationships: friends, spouses, and lovers. Analyses have often wrenched such ties out of the networks in which they are embedded and the social contexts that structure and constrain them. To make matters worse, a high proportion of research has used a narrow selection of respondents: materially comfortable members of the Western world, white, heterosexual, and living in privatized social worlds. This atypical population has often served as the basis of would-be universal generalizations.

... We have tried to broaden the ways in which [the social nature of personal relationships] is used and the contexts in which it is studied. Five principal criteria guided our work:

1. Variety of relationships: There are more relationships worth studying in heaven and earth than love, marriage, and friendship. People work together, are neighborly, fight, plot, and just talk. Network members form factions that can support and inflame custody battles between divorcing couples. Friends occasionally forsake one another.

In a world where people have many hundreds of ties, we often need to extend analysis to more than a few close relationships. Recent estimates of the total size of personal networks suggest that North Americans have over one thousand informal relationships (see Milardo, 1992, pp. 447–61) [*reprinted as the next article in this chapter*]. Ties of acquaintanceship far outnumber a person's twenty or so active ties of intimacy, support, companionship, or routine contact. Such **weak ties** are more than pale imitations of close ties. They are quantitatively important because there are so many of them. They are the basis for many of the allies or enemies people have when things get complicated. They form potential outlets for changing lives when people change jobs, spouses, neighborhoods, or political systems. They lend familiarity and a sense of community to daily routines. The number and variety of **weak ties** suggest the impossibility of using close ties to study all personal relationships. Moreover, Milardo's review shows that it is also not possible to talk about 'the social network' as a single entity. Significant other, exchange, and interactional networks are not only conceptually unique; their memberships often differ widely. For example, frequently-seen network members seldom are intimates.

2. Contents of relationships: The emphasis that personal relationship analysts place on emotional closeness reflects the preoccupations of the affluent, secure Western world with getting people to like one another. Yet there is more to life than a hot tub. Relationships often have social utility as well as being ends in themselves, for people depend on their ties for physical, social, and political survival. Even in the closest relationships, partners may be intimate without liking or freely choosing each other.

Relationships are often based on complementary (or competing) interests rather than on mutual interest. For example, Hungarians have complex systems of interpersonal exchanges for building homes in a cash-poor society. If one's cousin does 10 hours of

electrical work then one may be obligated to provide an aunt with 25 hours of cement-mixing (Sik, 1988). In comfortable Toronto, women neighbors often work together minding children even though they dislike each other (Wellman & Wellman, 1992). Torontonians receive a variety of supportive resources from such neighbors as well as from spouses and other network members.

3. Relationships function in networks: Pair relationships do not function in isolation but as parts of networks. A social network is not a pile of straw where each tie exists independently. Even Romeo and Juliet found this out – the hard way. The course of their true love ran smoothly until the war between their networks destroyed them. Every relationship between two people is conditioned by their separate and mutual relationships with others. Densely knit cliques mobilize social support and social control. For example, subordinate chickens sometimes form a coalition to overcome the dominant bird in a pecking order (Chase, 1974). A social network is not a metaphor. It is an analytically defined phenomenon with measurable properties of size, composition, structure, and contents.

People who need help may be more concerned about getting it than about which tie supplies it. Thus, most Toronto men have several emotionally supportive relationships even though men tend to be less emotionally supportive than women … [C]ouples organize their separate and shared ties with network members and … their networks are linked to personal and relational outcomes. Their results suggest that the marital structures that spouses create constrain behavior, and that the influence of networks can vary according to the balance of household and social domains.

4. Social contexts affect the nature of ties: Some personal relationship analysts have become so preoccupied with why some undergraduates blush when they stumble into each other's arms that they have forgotten to wonder about the circumstances that put people into contact and the larger consequences of their couplings. Consider those ethnographic film accounts of American small colleges, *Animal House* and *School Daze*. Race, class, life-style, and sex strongly determine who goes with whom – sexually or fraternally. Filmmakers John Landis and Spike Lee are more socially aware than scholars who do not ask how the nature of the societies affects who relates to whom, what are the issues with which people must contend, and what resources people need and have to offer.

The very nature of social support varies between societies. van Tilburg (1992) examines how a major life transition, retirement, affects supportive relationships in the Netherlands. Wellman & Wellman (1992) argue that the kin-dominated households of England are quite different from the household-centered networks of Toronto. Werner et al. (1992) compare the social contexts of domestic relations in Taiwanese and Welsh communities. They discuss the influence of social and environmental factors on relationships between partners and on the partners' obligations to their families and communities – influences that frame courtships, weddings, placemakings and future lives.

5. Marital and community affairs are diversified: ... [Marital] and community ties are not singular classes of relations but are richly diversified. As relational pairs organize their lives, they create a variety of understandings that have consequences for how they relate to each other and to others. As intrusive observers, we have only small clues on which to base our analyses, the fruits of a few queries taken in a brief moment of a relationship's career.

For the future, ... it is time for personal relationship analysts to re-examine the world of work and expand it beyond the managerialist preoccupations of organizational behavior analysts ... It is time to analyze the interplay between relationships and politics. It is time to document how personal relations implement the workings of interlocking corporate networks that channel huge amounts of money and goods. In short, it is time for personal relationship analysts to leave self-imposed ghettoes, burst out into the world, and use our skills and lore ...

As you were reading this article you may have seen important criticisms that could have been leveled against some of the previous papers that you have read here. The authors are certainly right that most of the papers in the personal relationships field are about young, relatively well-off, Westerners whose linkages to relationships of utility and support are quite poorly explored. The very form of those relationships themselves (freely chosen "hot tubs" of intimacy and support-seeking aimed at "personal satisfactions") is to some extent determined by the economic and material circumstances in which those people are happily situated. Members of subsistence-economic tribes in the Sudan are more likely to search collectively for food than for intimacy or personal growth.

A fuller understanding of the roles of the network in our relational lives is created by a fuller understanding of the sorts of networks to which we can belong. Milardo's paper, below, looks at this in terms of the larger numbers of network relationships in which we are embedded. For *each* person with whom we are really intimate there are probably twenty or more with whom we interact freely but are not close. These non-close, weak ties are extremely influential in forming our experiences of life. Milardo's article takes us beneath the surface to look at how they work. Milardo expounds on the notion of the social network and identifies four types to which we all belong. One interesting question is the degree to which these networks do and do not overlap (for example the question of whether we get our information from the same network as we get our significant intimacies).

In each case, if the particular network is "real" for people then it will be quite stable and perhaps even consistent across time and so Milardo reports on some ways of checking that the measures are getting at something real and lasting. One method for doing this is to measure **test–retest reliability** and you might already have worked out that this means that a particular thing is measured/tested on one occasion and then retested on another occasion. If the thing itself has real stability, then, the scores on test one and on test two should be pretty close to identical. For example we would expect test–retest reliability to be high for underlying and lasting traits or abilities such as intelligence, musical ability, swimming skill or vocabulary size.

Milardo discusses **convergent and discriminant validity**. Convergent validity assesses whether a measure is valid because it is associated with another measure of the same construct (for example, a measure of "people I like" should be associated with a person's choices of "close intimate network members"). Discriminant validity does the reverse and shows that your measure is not highly associated with something that it shouldn't highly predict (for example, a measure of teenage tobacco use might be tainted if it correlates too highly with a measure of "school problems". Though school problems are connected with teenage tobacco use, the two ideas of "tobacco" and "school problems" are distinct). Together, the two forms of validity, convergent (correlates with what it is supposed to correlate with) and discriminant (not correlated with what it is not supposed to be correlated with), are useful in convincing readers of the value of a particular measure. Since Milardo is considering different types of networks, it is very important that they are in reality different types and not simply badly measured in a way that makes them *appear to be* different when they are not in fact.

The boundaries within which we can be most reasonably confident that we have included the meaningful range of subjective experience are defined by **95% confidence intervals**. Thus the 95% confidence intervals about the mean include all the data that we can reasonably assume (with 95% confidence) are fully representative of the group we are studying.

Conflict-habituated ties are relationships where people are quite used to conflict, such that a particular occasion of it does not disturb them terribly much.

Comparative Methods for Delineating Social Networks

Robert M. Milardo

Four basic types of personal networks can be identified. The network of *significant others*, sometimes referred to as a network of intimates, includes those people whom respondents believe to be important. Parents, close friends, and kin typify members of this network. *Exchange networks* refer to collectives of people who provide, or are thought to provide, material or symbolic support. In addition to supportive ties, exchange networks include people who are critical or who directly refuse to provide aid. *Interactive networks* include those with whom interactions typically occur, and as I demonstrate, the membership of interactive networks need not substantially overlap with significant other or exchange networks. Finally, we can usefully conceptualize a global network, composed of all those people known by a respondent. For practical reasons, *global networks* are limited to those individuals who are living (although ancestors can be important purveyors of support and interference), those individuals who are known by name (so they can be listed) and only those individuals who would also recognize the respondent. This latter requirement means eliminating people recognized by the respondent but who do not reciprocate that recognition, and consequently with whom interaction is unlikely (e.g., political figures, entertainers).

These four prototypes capture much of what we mean by an individual's "social network" and in large part how a network is typically operationalized. Each of the four types, and the methodologies associated with their measurement, can best be thought of as proxies for a particular sector of interest or for the entire global network. We can then question how well each of these measures perform as proxies, in terms of their reliability, stability over time and the extent of their **convergent and discriminant validity**.

Surprisingly little attention has been given to detailing just what it is that personal networks represent conceptually or how a network delimited in terms of the people considered significant differs from other name-eliciting procedures. Barnes (1954: 42) defined networks as a "set of points, some of which are joined by lines. The points of the image are people ... and the lines indicate which people interact with each other". This and other early attempts at defining social networks were attractive because of their simplicity, but they are utterly abstract and largely metaphorical. In a very real sense, the development of different methods for

delineating networks created a conceptual vacuum. Just as the invention of the microscope allowed new observations, which then required a reconceptualization of what was being observed, substantial and consistent variations in significant other, exchange, and interactive networks suggest several refinements in the overall conceptualization of personal networks.

Networks of significant others

The delineation of networks of people considered important or close to respondents with a single name-eliciting question is indisputably the most commonly used procedure. Surra and I view significant others as representative of an individual's psychological network. That is, those "people to whom [Person] P is committed emotionally and psychologically, who provide P with a concept of self, and who can sustain or alter [P's] self-definition through communication" (Surra & Milardo, 1991: 12). People become members through a history of significant personal communications, or because they are significant to other people considered important (e.g., a parent of a fiancé), but, once established, such a relationship need not require frequent, recent, or long interaction. As I detail at a later point, my own empirical work and that of others bear out this lack of association between the degree of contemporary face-to-face interaction and membership in the significant other network.

The relative advantages and disadvantages of this method for enumerating a network have been detailed elsewhere (Milardo, 1988) where it is argued that the method is useful because of its directness and simplicity, but also is limited because of the wide array of personal associates that it typically omits. Nonetheless, the size of this network and its composition are surprisingly consistent across a [selection] of research. Table 1 depicts the findings of several studies, each of which employed a somewhat different

Milardo, Table I   *Networks of significant others*

Citation	Name-eliciting Q	Sample	n	Mean	SD	Kin %
Bernard et al. (1990)	"With whom can you discuss important matters?"	Adult volunteers, mean age 37, Jacksonville, FL	98	6.88	4.89	50
		Adult volunteers, mean age 33, Mexico City	99	2.95	2.66	67
Johnson & Milardo (1984)	"Those people whose opinions of your personal life are important to you."	Simple random, college students	434	5.8	1.4	52
Marsden (1987)	"… discussed important matters within the past 6 months."	US national probability sample	1531	3.01	1.77	55
van Sonderen et al. (1990)	"… persons who mean a lot to you and without whom life would be difficult."	Dutch adult volunteers in transition, ranging from early 20s to the elderly	304	5.18	NA	NA
Wellman et al. (1988)	"all persons with whom [respondents] were significantly 'in touch'"?	Adult volunteers, median age 44, Toronto	33	5	2.5	48
Wellman (1979)	"the persons outside your home that you feel closest to" (Maximum of 6)	Random sample, adults, Toronto	845	4.7	NA	50

name-eliciting question as well as widely different samples.

Networks of significant others average about 5 members with some consistent exceptions … [and] … are composed largely of immediate kin, about 50 percent, and perhaps partially as a consequence are fairly stable … Rapkin & Stein (1989) report relatively high **test–retest reliabilities** of .72 overall and .83 for kin only, when comparing overall sizes of the networks identified at two points in time, rather than comparing actual similarity of membership.

Exchange networks

Unlike the network of significant others, which focuses largely on sentimental ties, exchange networks are conceptualized in terms of the people "who provide material and emotional assistance" (Fischer, 1982: 35). The intention is to identify people with whom the probability of rewarding, or unrewarding, social exchanges is high. The enumeration of exchange networks is based on a set of name-eliciting questions, typically ten to twelve, that elicit a broad spectrum of network members drawn from a variety of social settings. Prototypes include recreational companions, and people who are valued for their judgments or support. The use of multiple name-eliciting questions rests on the assumption that sampling across a variety of social exchanges and settings that typify the lives of many produces a more representative sample of a network constituency than simply examining one specific class of close relationships, and it

Milardo, Table 2   *Exchange networks*

Citation	Number of Name-eliciting Qs	Sample	n	Mean	SD	Kin %
Fischer (1982)	11	Random sample, adults, Northern California	1050	18.5	Range 2–65	42
Bernard et al. (1990)	11	Adult volunteers, Jacksonville, FL	98	21.8	16.66	40
		Adult volunteers, Mexico City	99	10.05	6.5	46
Milardo (1989)	12	Adult volunteers, mean age 33	50	22.8	7.8	37
Rands (1988)	6	Adult volunteers	40			
		Pre-marital separation		20.75	NA	48
		Post-marital separation		17.95	NA	39
van Sonderen et al. (1990)	20	Dutch adults	304	20.7	6.9	NA
Ulin & Milardo (1992)	11	Lesbian couples	116	20.5	6.6	19

improves generalizations about other features of network structure.

Across the six studies summarized in Table 2, exchange networks average approximately 20 members with the exception of the Mexico City sample. This consistency is surprising because the samples are fairly heterogeneous and vary substantially in terms of age, marital status, and sexual preference, if not in terms of race and class. Relative to the network of significant others, exchange networks include a lower proportion of kin, approximately 40 percent, and not unexpectedly a wider array of friends, neighbors, and co-workers. The lesbian couples reported on by Ulin & Milardo (1992) are distinct in that their networks include far fewer kin, a condition that reflects either selective closeting, with the sexual orientation of these women hidden from kin, or the outright rejection of their lifestyle by kin. One impact of this fracturing of their networks is a lower proportion of kin and a limitation on the exchange of resources that typically reinforce and strengthen heterosexual couples, while simultaneously increasing the degree of criticism and interference.

Lesbian couples are unique as a group and comparatively homogeneous in that they have violated strong heterosexual norms, a violation that appears to influence the composition of their networks, but not their overall size. We could expect similar effects for heterosexual partners who challenge the status quo, for instance by violating religious boundaries in the selection of a mate or traditions regarding childcare, the division of household labor and so on, all with potentially negative outcomes.

[Differences] within each sample are considerable. For instance, placing **95 percent confidence intervals** about the means suggests networks will range from approximately 6 to 34 members for most individuals ...

With some exceptions the enumeration of exchange networks, and each of the other types, omits people with whom interaction is characterized by conflict and hostility, and yet such ties are common and consequential. Milardo (1988) included a question concerning the people with whom spouses routinely experienced conflict (modeled after Barrera, 1981). One or more **conflict-habituated ties** were nominated by 79 percent of the spouses and the majority of these ties (57 percent) were unmentioned in response to the other eleven name-eliciting questions. Contrary to popular belief, in-laws were far less likely to be nominated as people with whom conflict typically occurs relative to either blood kin or co-workers.

The consequences of conflictive ties with network members are undoubtedly significant. For example, Bolger et al. (1989) examined the daily stress reported by spouses over a 6-week period. Interpersonal conflicts had the greatest consequences for emotional health accounting for nearly 80 percent of the variation in spouses' moods. As in the case of marital interaction where negative interchanges can outstrip the effects of positive exchanges, negative interactions often have stronger and longer lasting effects than positive exchanges (Rook, 1992).

Equally important is the relative balance of support and interference in even the closest most highly valued ties. Positive support as well as interference and criticism are apt to be characteristic of close relationships, particularly those with kin ...

Interactive networks

Systematic enumeration of the people with whom interactions occur is rare largely because of the implicit assumption that mass survey techniques, such as the enumeration of exchange networks, are sufficient proxies for estimating social participation, an assumption that is unsupported empirically. In typical survey research, respondents are required to indicate with whom they have interacted over some period of time (the precise time-frame may or may not be specified) or how often they interact with specific groups such as kin. Responses to queries of this sort are both retrospective and respondent aggregated in the sense that respondents must recall the identity of interactants, while simultaneously providing aggregated composites of the frequency of interaction. In contrast, contemporary measures of social participation, which are based on diaries or

personal interviews completed daily, narrow the period between the occurrence of a social episode and its documentation. Respondents identify the people with whom they interact as those interactions occur, thus minimizing errors in recall and the need for complex aggregations ...

The identification of interactive networks has been based on structured diaries completed daily. Milardo et al. (1983) required student volunteers to record all interactions that were over 10 minutes in length and voluntary. These latter requirements were designed to simplify the procedure and eliminate brief encounters as well as interactions that involved formal contacts with others (e.g., teachers, business associates). Each day for 2 weeks respondents maintained records on each interaction, including who was present, their relationship, and other information on the interaction's content. The 89 respondents in the first wave of this longitudinal study reported on well over 4000 social episodes, or about 4.6 per day, and in so doing identified an average of 26 network members ...

One disadvantage of this technique is the requirement that respondents monitor and record their own interactions daily. A potentially more reliable procedure involves the use of daily phone interviews. Milardo (1989) interviewed spouses on each of 7 nonconsecutive days and gathered data on each social episode that occurred over the previous 24 hours. Spouses reported an average of 2.4 voluntary interactions per day and they identified an average of nearly 16 network members ...

Yet another surprising finding derived from the work on spouses' interactive networks is the lack of overlap between this network and the exchange network. By gathering data on the exchange networks of spouses via face-to-face interviews and interactive networks via daily phone interviews, a direct comparison of their memberships was possible (Milardo, 1989). The measure of convergence or overlap in the exchange and interactive network represents the proportion of members who were identified in both networks relative to the total number of different people identified in either network. The degree of overlap averages slightly less than 25 percent. In short, there is little convergence between the methods. Exchange and interactive networks produce distinctly different constituencies. In fact, there is little relationship between the size of each. Individuals with large exchange networks do not have correspondingly large interactive networks and the frequency of interaction with members of the interactive network is uncorrelated with the size of the exchange network. The size of exchange networks simply fails to predict the degree of social participation.

Exchange networks seem to represent beliefs about one's life space and the availability of social opportunity, companionship and support – a kind of psychological network. Whereas interactive networks represent day-to-day social experience. Although both networks are undoubtedly important, they are apt to function in different ways, the former influencing one's psychological sense of community and the latter actual day-to-day exchange. Personal well-being may be influenced by a sense of integration or by the belief that support will be forthcoming should the need arise. On the other hand, the actual availability and exchange of support are requisite for the disadvantaged single parent who struggles to feed, clothe and shelter children.

Global networks

A portrait, in terms of overall size or composition, of all people known to an individual has engendered little interest on the part of relationship scholars, although describing global networks is as essential to the science of personal relationships as charting the movement of heavenly bodies was to Newtonian physics. Fortunately, a few social scientists have begun such an effort, describing the contours of a network that can be usefully depicted as the population from which all other personal networks are derived.

Two intriguing methods for sampling global networks have been developed. Of course, the most straightforward approach would be to simply have respondents list all of the people they know, a potentially formidable task in both time and mental acuity. In order to provide some structure to the enumeration of this network, Killworth et al. (1984) developed a **"reverse small world" procedure**. Essentially respondents are provided with a dossier on each of 500 targets. The dossiers are fictitious, but realistic, and include a name and location, in addition to information on age, sex, occupation, organizational affiliations, and hobbies. The task for participants is to get a message to each target. To do so, participants are asked to nominate someone they know who might know the target or at least be able to pass the message along to another who might know the target …

The reverse small world procedure elicits network members who may serve as a conduit for information to people outside the respondent's network of acquaintances, and as such captures a limited part of the global network. The nomination of others is after all based on a single task and potentially omits people who would be judged incapable or inappropriate as messengers (Freeman & Thompson, 1989).

A second procedure is based on the premise that if we had a list of all the world's people, we could then generate a random list of names, ask respondents to identify the people whom they know and who would know them, and eventually estimate a network's size. With the possible exception of records kept by intelligence agencies, no such list is available. However there is "Ma Bell". Based on a method first developed by Pool & Kochen (1989), Killworth et al. (1990) generated a random list of names taken from a phone directory. Respondents are asked to review the list and identify all the people they know with identical family names. Because the size of the sample is known, and the number of family names in the phone directory can be estimated (i.e., an estimate of population size), each respondent's list of network members can be scaled up based on the population estimate. Doing so yields an average global network of approximately 1700 individuals (±400) for North Americans, and much smaller networks for adults in Mexico City, approximately 570 (±460).

These estimates of global networks are based on several assumptions: for example that the family names of network members are represented in a phone directory, that the distribution of names does not substantially vary between sufficiently large directories and that this distribution adequately represents the distribution of names in a respondent's network. Nonetheless, the estimates for North Americans are similar to those reported by Freeman & Thompson (1989) ($M = 2025$), and by Johnsen (cited in Bernard et al., 1990, $M = 1520$).

Several conclusions can be drawn from this work. First, networks are large – and, incidentally, respondents are unable to guess accurately their size, else the sophisticated methods would be unnecessary. The correlations of respondents' guesses of the numbers of others known never account for more than 18 percent of the variance in the observed size of their networks. Secondly, because Killworth, Bernard and their colleagues collected data on significant others, exchange and global networks, direct comparisons are possible. Perhaps most importantly the size of any one network fails to predict the size of any other. Intercorrelations never account for more than 28 percent of the variance.

In comparing the question of whether the network types overlap, significant others are typically included in exchange networks as noted earlier. However, when taken together the significant other and exchange network identify a tiny portion of the global network, in fact less than 50 percent of all kin, 50 percent of all friends and a substantial minority of other personal associates. On average, this translates to an omission of 10–15 kin and 30–40 friends.

Conclusions

The name-eliciting strategies reviewed yield surprisingly different portraits of personal

networks. Significant other and exchange networks, rather than characterizing day-to-day social activity, provide information about people's psychological sense of community. They differ conceptually in terms of the kind and function of relations that typify each network, and in terms of the actual composition of their memberships. Interactive networks provide a view of daily, and often quite ordinary, social exchange. The members of this network are distinct and essentially non-overlapping with the members of the exchange network, nor are the sizes of these networks correlated. Presumably significant other and interactive networks will demonstrate a similar level of divergence but such a direct comparison has yet to be accomplished. Global networks present another view and one which is as yet unknown in its consequences. The overwhelming size and variation in global networks suggests they are important in understanding access to influence and scarce resources. Although several additional procedures have been developed to enumerate personal networks, such methods typically either lack a clear conceptual foundation, or in fact are hybrids of the types detailed herein (for a review see Marsden, 1990).

Additionally, we may question the correlations of structural features – like size, composition or interconnectedness – across types. For instance, can the size or interconnectedness of an exchange network serve as a reliable and accurate estimate of similar features of any other type? This is an important issue because it makes little sense to speak of network structure and its linkage to relationship outcomes without qualification, if structural features vary widely across the networks of any one individual. Just as networks differ in size, composition or connectedness between individuals, and as a result have differential effects, intra-individual variations in network types are apt to have differential effects. A clearer portrait of variations across network types in their key structural properties will permit important theoretical refinements.

Milardo points out the different ways in which our active daily lives presume not only intimacy but also information, utilitarian exchange, and interaction. These observations are important for two reasons: first they note that our emotional lives depend on more than intimate associations; second they note that there is a connection between our psychological lives and our material circumstances – the places, people and sorts of exchange in which we can participate. The circumstances influence our psychological well-being, are derived from a sense of integration into a community or by the belief that support will be forthcoming, should the need arise, but that support/exchange networks do not predict the degree of social participation.

An issue not covered by the above articles is whether and how the network experiences of different folks might also be connected to their social or economic circumstances. Some people can presume the ability to purchase support whenever necessary because they are wealthy; others may have to acquire it through various forms of exchange that do not involve money (for example, providing service of one kind – say baby-sitting – to a friend who can provide service of another kind back – say construction work). In the next paper, by Graham Allan, the case is presented for the need to attend to socioeconomic circumstances in order to fully understand network and friendship patterns.

Once we step outside of the world of affluent Westernism – the world of the "hot-tub" identified by Milardo and Wellman – or when we are able to see as analysts that such a world is not all there is, then a number of interesting issues arise. For example, what about the fact that most research looks at the relatively well off? What sorts of relationships do poorer folks have? To broaden the question more extensively, what are the influences of material circumstances, like poverty, on the nature of friendships? Graham Allan, an English sociologist, has considered these kinds of questions in relation to friendship in two major books and has also written the following article that questions the source of the structural and circumstantial underpinnings of relationships and the things that limit or constrain not only our choices of friendship but also our performance of it.

Friendship, Sociology and Social Structure

Graham Allan

The study of personal relationships has developed enormously over the last 20 years. In part, this has involved ... a paradigmatic shift in focus away from an over-riding concern with the characteristics and properties of individuals to one in which relationships are viewed as emergent. That is, they are understood as interactional, as being constructed contextually and as having their distinct "natural histories", which impinge on their future pathways, though not in a determinate fashion (Duck, 1993) ...

... While relationship research has moved very clearly from the individual to the dyad, and focused more on both process and context in analyzing relationship behavior, the integration of a sociological perspective (i.e., one concerned with structural and cultural characteristics rather than personal ones) within these developing frames of knowledge has been slow ... However, this [paper's] ... focus is explicitly on friendships rather than personal relationships more generally. Within this, its purpose is to explore what sociological perspectives have to offer the general analysis of friendship as a form of personal tie, and in the process highlight why studying friendships (and other equivalent informal relationships) is more central to dominant sociological concerns than is usually recognized ...

The social construction of friendship

One of the chief concerns of recent sociological approaches to friendship has been to demonstrate that ties of friendship are inherently social rather than just personal (Milardo & Wellman, 1992 ...). That is, rather than being simply a matter determined by the individuals concerned, friendship is patterned according to social conventions whose roots lie in the broader social and economic milieus in which the individuals involved are located. Inherent in this is the notion that friendship is a variable relationship, with the particular form it takes being influenced by the specific context in which it develops (Duck, 1994b; Duck et al., 1997). Thus, while friendships are rightly seen as being constructed through the actions of individuals, these actions are not in some sense "free-floating" but are inevitably bound to the social and economic environment in which they are being enacted. Within this environment, modes of "doing friendship" – and sociability more generally – ... are consonant with the other sets of relationships in which the individuals in question are embedded.

However, while it can be argued that locating friendship within its broader context is the sine qua non of a sociological understanding of the tie, specifying what this entails is more complex. Adams & Allan (1998) distinguish four broad levels of context that influence the particular form which friendship takes: the personal environment level, the network level, the community level, and the societal level, which form a continuum of contextual influence, each in turn being further removed from the individual's immediate sphere of influence. Thus, whereas the personal environment level is concerned with such features of a person's life as economic circumstances, domestic responsibilities and employment commitments, the societal level focuses on the characteristics of the economic and social structures that dominate the social formation at a given time. Just as family and household relationships can be recognized as taking different forms as, for example, industrialization and urbanization develop with modernity, so too other informal relationships, including friendship, also alter as new conditions alter existing patterns of solidarity ...

One of the most interesting analyses of these processes is provided by Silver (1990) in his examination of the impact that the growth of commercial society had on the development of friendship. Contrary to others who had argued that the emergence of market-driven, rational economic organization undermined the social significance of informal solidarities of friendship, Silver suggests that a new form of friendship – one concerned with expressivity rather than instrumentality – was able to blossom under these new conditions. Precisely because the framework of commercial society fostered a separation of economic and personal life, informal ties were no longer contaminated by self-interest or instrumental considerations. In effect the emerging division of labor insulated different modes of activity in novel ways, so that friendships could be formed with sympathetic others based on compatibility rather than calculation of interest ...

Other historical researchers have also examined in detail how the social and economic conditions of people's lives shaped the character of their friendship ties. Oliker (1998), for example, has demonstrated how, amongst the middle class in North America, married women's friendships altered with the onset of industrialization. The separation of industrial and domestic economies, and the control that men exercised over this process, resulted in ideologies of domesticity coming to the fore, which largely limited these women's social and economic participation to the domestic realm. However, Oliker argues that this situation enabled these women to develop intimate friendships with others in a similar position, which became the more important because of the constrained character of their social worlds. As their familial and domestic situation framed their social identities, so ties of friendship provided both an avenue for disclosure and a validation of their worth …

In a quite different way, Wellman (Wellman et al., 1988; Wellman & Wortley, 1990) has illustrated how the changed conditions of the present era have resulted in more geographically dispersed friendship networks than was the case previously. Broadly, developments in transport and communications have led to localities being of reduced salience in social life. Whereas in earlier periods of industrial development, the majority of people was quite fully embedded in local social and economic relationships, now only a minority – typically those with least resources – are in this situation to any great extent. Most people construct social worlds in which neighborhood and locality play only a small part; in particular, their networks of friends and kin tend to be geographically dispersed rather than concentrated in particular places …

[In short,] it is inappropriate to conceptualize friendship as a "natural" or "pure" relationship, that is, as one based solely upon individual choice, feelings and commitment. Rather its form and content are inevitably influenced by the circumstances – or

contexts – under which it is constructed. [C]ontext operates at different levels. Overall, it is the constellation of different contextual features, themselves emergent and therefore changing, which shape both the dominant pattern of friendship and the specific form that individual ties take …

[A]spects of social and economic location, such as class and sex, do not of themselves determine friendship forms and consequently can only be used in a simple fashion to characterize common patterns … For example, there is no pre-determined female or male way of managing friendship, nor can there be a fixed working-, middle- or upper-class pattern. Such an essentialist treatment of these features cannot work, in part because other elements of location and context also influence both the opportunities available for, and the organization of, friendship …

Yet importantly even these claims are historically – that is, contextually – specific. Even if, say, class position is held to influence in a strong fashion the kind of informal solidarities that develop in a particular society at a given time, it does not follow that such patterns will remain constant across time or be similar in other societies with a similar pattern of stratification. Certainly cultural patterns have a level of stability. But equally culture is dynamic … What was once routine cultural practice gives way to new practices as the social formation overall alters or as the material circumstances and social obligations of the group in question change. Transformations in the dominant patterns of sociability in working-class communities in Britain provide an illustration of these processes.

Working-class male sociability: an illustration

In the 1950s and early 1960s a good deal of research was conducted on kinship and community ties in Britain. Informed by concerns that family and neighborhood solidarities were breaking down, these studies investigated patterns of informal support and sociability, particularly within working-class localities. These were of special interest because of the impact that housing regeneration and geographical mobility were thought to be having on "traditional" ways of life. Although their main focus was usually on kinship ties, their community orientation resulted in many of these studies containing a good deal of material pertinent to friendship ... From these studies it was possible to identify a style of working-class non-kin sociability, especially amongst men, which was quite different from the dominant mode of middle-class friendship.

In essence, working-class male non-kin sociability was heavily framed by interactional settings. That is, the relationships tended to be restricted to the particular contexts in which people met, with little attempt being made to extend the boundary of the ties by incorporating them into other settings. Whereas middle-class sociability typically entailed developing friendships by involving people in a number of activities, this was largely absent in working-class sociability. Thus, for example, within middle-class circles, compatible people who met at work would often arrange to go to the theatre or to a concert together, or they might be invited home to a dinner party or a barbecue. Their mode of friendship was to reveal wider aspects of the self by incorporating friends into a range of shared activities, often including couple- or family-oriented ones. Such a broadening of the activities and settings seen as relevant for friendship was *un*common within working-class patterns of sociability. These ties were generally kept quite tightly framed around specific activities and places – a bar, a particular hobby, a sports club – with little effort being made to broaden them in the way the middle class routinely did. Their emphasis was on sociability within that setting rather than a broader revelation of the self through a gradual extension of the relationship's situational boundaries. Importantly within this, the home was rarely used as a means of developing or strengthening friendships.

More commonly, the home was implicitly defined as a "private" arena, one reserved for "family" – however defined – and not taken to be an appropriate site for socializing with non-kin.

As a result of these factors, working-class men frequently claimed to have few, if any, friends. What they had were "mates" ["buddies"], people whom they saw more or less frequently and with whom they enjoyed interacting. But because these relationships tended to be situationally defined, they did not fit easily into the culturally dominant (middle-class) model of what "friendship", as such, entailed. Some researchers took this to indicate that working-class respondents generally lacked the necessary social skills to develop friendships (Klein, 1965). However, it seems more likely that different modes for organizing sociability were dominant in working- and middle-class culture. Middle-class patterns, with their emphasis on individual relationships over specific settings, matched cultural criteria of friendship in a way that working-class sociability, with its prioritizing of setting, did not. (For a fuller discussion of these different modes of sociability, see Allan, 1979; 1989.)

But why was working-class sociability framed as it was? What was it about people's circumstances that fostered this way of managing informalities and, in effect, discouraged the adoption of the middle-class models. The most compelling factor was material deprivation. Particularly in the type of locality most frequently studied, households were dependent on relatively poorly paid and insecure employment, with few having much income above that required for weekly survival. The management of resources was a matter of significant concern. As a consequence, while there might be money for some sociability and leisure – generally unequally distributed between husband and wife – there was a need to keep control over expenditure. One way of doing this was not to become involved in series of open-ended exchanges in which money was spent. Yet to some degree this is what middle-class friendship patterns encouraged.

The underlying basis of most friendships is an equality of exchange; what one friend does now is reciprocated in some equivalent form by the other later. In an economy of poverty and insecurity, avoidance of such obligation can be important if not for particular individuals, then at least collectively within the culture. The dominant mode of working-class sociability facilitated this. By prioritizing setting over relationships, people were able to control their commitment more readily. They were freer to enter and leave a particular arena of sociability without incurring expense than they would have been if the relationship itself was prioritized, as was the case in the middle-class model.

... Other material and social conditions also shape the patterns that emerge. In particular the poverty of people's housing was important. In many of the localities studied, people were living in inadequate housing that lacked basic amenities, even by the standard of the times. Many, for example, still had outside toilets, lacked fixed baths and even shared cooking facilities as well as being overcrowded. In these circumstances, the home was often reserved for family. Especially for those who valued respectability, maintaining some degree of privacy around the domestic sphere was important particularly as inadequate housing (combined with close-knit social networks) made the control of gossip difficult. In this environment it is hardly surprising that the home was not defined as an appropriate arena for entertaining others or as a site for developing friendships. Effectively keeping non-kin ties out of the home again gave people a level of control over the reciprocities in which they were involved.

In addition, though, there was another domestic consideration that influenced friendship patterns: the dominant form of marital relationship. Generally marital roles were highly segregated; there was a marked division of labor, and to quite a large degree husbands and wives led separate lives, rarely being involved in shared sociability outside of kinship. In this regard, men's relationships tended to be removed from the domestic sphere and to be independent of their wives, thereby consolidating the perspective that the home was an inappropriate arena for male sociability. Thus, in the context of limited resources, these comparatively segregated marital roles also helped foster the differences that existed between working-class and middle-class modes of ordering ties of friendship and sociability.

But what happens as social and material conditions alter, as they have been doing over the last 40 years? While some households continue to be in poverty, in particular those who through lack of employment are dependent on state benefits, standards of living have risen for the majority of working-class couples. Changes in married women's labor market participation mean that domestic economies are increasingly built around two incomes, albeit one often significantly smaller than the other. Linked in with this, there have been major changes in housing circumstances. Not only have rates of owner-occupation almost tripled since 1945, but more importantly, average standards of comfort and amenity are far higher than they were. Despite the continuing inequalities and inadequacies that exist in the housing market, for men, especially, improvements in domestic ambience have fostered greater commitment to the home as an arena for leisure and sociable activity.

Although it is easy to romanticize, redefinitions of what constitutes an acceptable marriage or partnership have also been significant here. Within current marital "blueprints" (Cancian, 1987), there is a greater emphasis than previously on notions of "partnership", emotional fulfillment and intimate disclosure (Duncombe & Marsden, 1993; Hawkes, 1996). Encapsulated in this are ideas that wives and husbands should value spending time together. Increasingly, from a cultural viewpoint, a marriage in which the spouses do not want to be together sociably is perceived – rightly or wrongly – as a marriage "in difficulty", in a way that would have little resonance among couples two generations earlier (Mansfield & Collard, 1988).

These changes have had an impact on dominant modes of male, working-class sociability. Although the number of pertinent studies conducted recently is limited compared with the range of family, occupational and community studies from the mid-century period, the sociable relationships that working-class men now sustain do appear to be ordered differently from then. In part, this has involved elements of privatization: a shift in the focus of social activities from neighborhood and community to the private sphere of the home. Yet what has happened is more complex than simply a move from community participation to a life centered predominantly on domestic and familial concerns (Allan & Crow, 1991). First, while there has been a loss of local involvement, this has not meant that sociability itself has necessarily declined. Instead, congruent with Wellman's (Wellman et al., 1988; Wellman & Wortley, 1990) analysis of changing networks in North America, sociable ties are now more geographically dispersed than they were.

Second, the shift from "the public" to "the private" has modified understandings of the nature of the domestic sphere and the role of the home in men's lives. As a result, working-class men are more likely to use the home as a site for sociability. That is, whereas previously ties of sociability were typically framed by specific activities and took place in public settings now it is more likely that the home will play a part in the development and servicing of these ties. For most, some interaction continues to take place in public settings but this will not be exclusively the case. Whether or not such ties become couple friendships, the boundaries constructed around them are more permeable than in the past. They are not defined by setting in the way they were; changes in material resources, domestic ambience and marital ideologies have resulted in the home being more "open" for non-kin sociability.

The point here is not that working-class men's ties are becoming more like traditional middle-class friendships, though this does appear to be happening to a degree. Rather the point is to demonstrate how the material and social environments in which informal relationships develop have an impact on the construction of these relationships. The patterns that were dominant for male, working-class sociability in mid-century are no longer so typical [now that] the circumstances that framed them have altered. The material and ideological shifts that have been outlined briefly here are such as to make change likely. In particular, the altered need to manage reciprocity as poverty reduces, the changed home ambience, and emerging ideologies of partnership and marriage make for different ways of ordering sociable ties. Patterns rooted in previous social and economic environments become modified as new conditions emerge offering different opportunities and constraints.

Status and identity

At a different level, changes in people's personal environments also affect friendship patterns, as can be seen from research that focuses on status and identity. One of the key characteristics of friendship is that it is, broadly speaking, a tie of equality. That is, there is an expectation of reciprocity within the relationship, though the time frame for this and the measurement of equivalence of exchange [differ] across relationships. Equally it is generally important within constructions of friendship that those who are friends treat one another as equal, even if they recognize differences between them. As a consequence of these factors, friends typically occupy similar social and economic locations to one another, and have a broadly similar social status ...

Because of this characteristic of equality, friendship plays a significant role in shaping people's social identities. Through building affinities with others who occupy a similar social and economic location, individuals affirm their own position, cement their status and give substance to their identities (Duck et al., 1997). This is more than simply providing support for the more formal positions people occupy in the social structure. It entails processes by which the individuality of those involved is recognized, while at the same time typically helping them to define themselves …

One of the best examples is Jerrome's (1984) study of a small group of middle-aged, middle-class women in Britain. [S]he indicates how the network of friendships these women sustained with one another contributed to their sense of self through their involvement in valued relationships, which occurred independently of the women's role positions, especially those tied to structural location. In their interactions, the women expressed their individuality, demonstrated their varied qualities and competences, and signified their distinct identities as people. In part, this was achieved by a distancing of themselves from activities in which their individuality was submerged, and especially from their roles as wives. While in many regards their social identities were framed by their class and gender location (wives of successful, middle-class men, in addition to their own economic achievements), within their friendships they were able to be critical of their husbands and marriages in ways that highlighted their own uniqueness.

Yet, most interestingly, the ways through which this was achieved actually reflected aspects of the very structural positions from which distance was being generated. Precisely because of their identity as affluent, later-middle-aged women, their styles of interaction were built upon the valued symbols of this identity. Thus, in particular, the women expressed their sense of self through specific dress and appearance codes and through forms of entertaining, which in many ways epitomized the subcultural standards of women in this social location. Similarly, as with Oliker's (1989) respondents, the women effectively supported the continuation of each other's marriage, despite (or indeed by) providing an outlet for their critical deconstruction. Thus what these friendships involved was the incorporation of a particular mode of femininity as a means of expressing and

authenticating an identity built upon a given structural location …

In a study of younger middle-class wives with dependent children, Harrison (1998) demonstrates [how] … her respondents also valued their friendships for the confirmation of self they provided, particularly as they acted as a counterbalance to their marital and domestic experiences. Although ideologically their husbands were supposed to be akin to "best friends", their failure to share or prioritize their wives' interests, activities and commitments meant that their wives frequently turned to their friends for sociability, practical support and self-validation. Thus with their friends they "let their hair down", discussed events that mattered to them, appraised their lifestyles and relationships, and in other ways revealed their "inner selves". Importantly though, … the manner in which all these things were done revolved around a form of femininity that was entirely consonant with these women's structural location. Being comparatively affluent, the range of cultural and social activities they engaged in with their friends – for example, extensive socializing, shopping in quality stores, going to the theatre or cinema or visiting health clubs – endorsed their status and identity positions. In being themselves they were also cementing their identity as individuals within a broader structural formation.

The link between friendship, identity and status (or stratification more generally) becomes the more intriguing when changes in people's social location are considered (Duck et al., 1997). This happens for a variety of reasons. Amongst the more important are life-course transitions – obtaining employment, leaving (the parental) home, marrying, having children, divorcing. Comparatively, this latter transition has been well-studied by relationship researchers. The research findings show quite clearly that people's informal social networks alter significantly as their marriage ends (Feld & Carter, 1998; Milardo, 1987). The processes involved in this are numerous. To begin with, divorce sometimes involves a "fresh start" – this might entail a change of locality, or sometimes a change in job. Often there is a deliberate attempt to create a different social life, engaging in new activities and establishing fresh routines. Not infrequently, both during the break-up as well as afterwards, there may be periods of self-doubt or reactive depression while the individual comes to terms with the different emotions that marital failure induces. At such time, people may isolate themselves, effectively hiding from friends so as to cope emotionally rather than turning to them for support. There may also be significant financial changes following separation, which make it difficult to engage in previous activities. Other more subtle processes also operate. In particular, relationships with couple friends become more difficult to manage. The taken-for-granted reciprocities and balances inherent in these relationships become more problematic. There is a level of reflexivity in their ordering that was not there before. Moreover, people may ... feel stigmatized by the concern of their friends. Not wanting to be pitied, or in any other way viewed as different, they may opt instead to reduce contact.

Generally the end result of these various processes is that friendship networks alter significantly with marital disruption. Gradually previous friendships fade, to be replaced by new ties that are more congruent with current economic and social status. For instance, separated mothers with dependent children come to spend more time with other single mothers. Having been there themselves, these women often understand the trauma and costs of separation and, as importantly, have developed strategies for coping with the difficulties that arise. Moreover, routine reciprocities develop, based on an equality of position, which generate fewer dilemmas of unbalanced exchange, be these emotional or practical in character. Thus, in general, servicing such new ties is less problematic than servicing some of the friendships established when circumstances were different. As a consequence, over time, friendships established in earlier periods are allowed to fade, while new ties,

more similar in current position, replace them through being given increasing attention.

Yet, what is involved here is not solely a process of friendship networks altering. What is also happening – as it does more generally with any significant status change – is that the emergent ties are helping to create and establish a new identity, in this instance that of "single" or "divorced mother" ... That is, the changing network of friends provides support pertinent to the new circumstances, and in the process, through discussion and other common activities, consolidates the shift in self-definition and self-identity ... Indeed, as the new identity is accepted and possibly embraced, so it is likely that further friendships that develop will also be with people in similar circumstances, further establishing the relevance, validity and authenticity of that identity. The particular status transition involved in this, of course, influences the "content" of the new friendships, but the underlying processes of new friendships fostering such identity reconstruction arise irrespective of the specifics of a given transition.

Friendship and identity in late modernity

It was noted above that the patterns of friendship that emerge within a given social formation are shaped by the character of economic and social relationships within that formation. In turn, there is an articulation between the social location individuals occupy and the identity that their friends help them construct and sustain. The issue for this final section of the paper is how the transformations currently occurring in social structure influence friendship patterns and their significance in identity construction. These transformations – reflected in terms such as postmodernity or late modernity (Giddens, 1991) – are typically held to entail new forms of solidarity with an emphasis on individual fulfillment rather than collective commitment or constraint. With changes in the economic sphere, including rapid technological development, globalization of markets, high levels of job change, and new constellations within the division of labor, old patterns and old certainties no longer apply so securely to the world that people experience.

For example, with changes in the division of labor and job security, traditional aspects of class structure come to be questioned. The idea of careers as ordered progression is no longer so firmly grounded as it was. Obtaining craft training holds no guarantee that technological change will not render the developed skills redundant. Competition from countries with more modern practices or lower levels of pay can lead to the restructuring of local labor markets in ways over which local, or even national, agencies have little control. Patterns of occupational and geographical mobility fragment the solidarities that previously informed social life. While the radicalness of these shifts can be overestimated they do all tend to foster a greater degree of uncertainty and a reduction in the control that people feel they have over the course their life will take. No longer can [people] so readily predict or so sensibly plan for what will happen. In a world of rapid technological and economic change, new social divisions and cohesions emerge, which themselves are likely to be temporary ...

As writers such as Beck (1992) and Giddens (1991; 1992) have theorized, these changes have an impact on the ordering of personal relationships. This is most apparent in terms of partnership, family and household constructions where there is far more diversity now than there was even a generation ago. In Britain this is most evident in terms of household demography where increases in divorce, cohabitation, births to unmarried mothers and step-families have been dramatic since the mid-1970s. At the same time, age at first marriage has increased while the number of people marrying has been in significant decline. For example, in 1991, less than three-quarters of the female population had married by the time they were 30 compared with over

90 percent in 1971. Similarly the number of households in which there are openly gay partnerships has been increasing (Allan & Crow, 1999; Haskey, 1996).

Overall these household arrangements represent a change in the character of commitment in personal and sexual relationships. We are witnessing a strong social endorsement of more flexible and less permanent relationships. Even though many people still believe in life-long heterosexual marriage as an ideal, there is now not only more tolerance of alternatives, but also an acceptance that diversity is inevitable given the character of present-day life-styles ... Compared with mid-twentieth-century there is now a much deeper cultural acceptance that adults should not be bound to each other in relationships that are no longer providing satisfaction or fulfillment ...

The question to be posed here is what happens to other informal relationships, such as friendship, given the kinds of social and economic shifts outlined above. With increased flexibility in personal life and the actual or potential growth of alliances based around life-style interests, does friendship become any more or less important socially? Contrary to some theories of privatization, which have suggested that individuals will become increasingly detached from non-domestic ties of sociability, it is likely under the developing social formation of late modernity that the significance of informal ties will, if anything, be heightened (O'Connor, 1998) ...

The issue of identity is among the most interesting here. In considering the work of Jerrome (1984) and Harrison (1998) above, the role of informal ties in supporting and sustaining identity was highlighted. In a world in which structural "certainties" are no longer as certain as they were and where individuals have to respond to changes that appear to be the result of nebulous and quite abstract forces (most noticeably "market forces") rather than any known agency, establishing a sense of identity and self is likely to be increasingly consequent on informal networks. Part of this ... will be based around "family" ties ... But equally, self-identity will also be constituted through other types of informal relationship, especially friendships ... That is, relationships with friends will continue to be one of the main arenas in which we express ourselves as the people we are. Friends know "the real self" and not just a self that is being portrayed in a particular way for instrumental purposes. Of course, different friends may perceive that "reality" differently, but each, by the nature of their friendship, is thought to have a privileged gaze at the other's character. Indeed because of the types of social and economic transformation that late modernity heralds, friendship may increasingly hold together the "centre" of self. Thus, far from being peripheral, the sphere of personal relationships may become of increasing significance. This is where we "find" ourselves, where we celebrate most clearly who we are, where indeed we become who we are. With the possibility of greater levels of diversity in people's experiences and a heightened emphasis on lifestyle issues, friendships may be recognized increasingly as one of the main sites of activity giving life meaning ...

Conclusion

The principal argument of this essay has been that friendships are framed by the social and economic formations in which they occur. Recent research has shown that they are not freestanding, but are patterned by the contexts within which people's lives are constructed. As these contexts alter, as

the material and social relationships in which individuals are embedded change, so to differing degrees will the character of their friendships. At the same time, friendships (and other equivalent ties) can play a significant part in informing people's identities. Precisely because they appear free-floating and independent of structural location, they can signify the people we "really" are. Yet, because of the equality inherent in friendship, they do this through their articulation with social and economic location. Here the role of friendship in mapping and sustaining social status is clearly of importance, though often neglected outside of community studies. [Indeed] ... recent understandings of late modernity see the personal realm as one of increasing rather than decreasing importance ... The principal theme of [this] article has been that context matters ... Clearly though, context is a complex and somewhat slippery concept carrying different meanings to scholars socialized into different academic traditions. In particular, what counts as "context" is not easily defined. It includes all those elements that are taken to "surround" a relationship and seen as pertinent to its development, maintenance and dissolution (Adams & Allan, 1998). However what is defined as "core" and what as "surround" what as "intrinsic" to the tie and what as "extrinsic", depends upon the questions being posed and the perspectives and models adopted. Nonetheless the concept of "context" is one that offers a path towards the integration of different approaches to personal relationships ...

Allan carefully evaluates the case for seeing the social and economic circumstances of individual lives as influences on their relationships and he points to some other forces that strongly affect – and even create – relational activity (which we might previously have thought of as based on "pure choice"). Note how Allan exposes the different emphasis on the home and other public places as suited for the performance of friendship in his analysis and how he connects those emphases to the economic circumstances of the partners involved. Although you may not have thought before much about the significance of the place where friendship is typically conducted, you may now have an increased understanding of the ways in which economic circumstances can affect usages of place and how place can be a resource for the conduct of relationships. The argument – which would be a good one to discuss in class – is that friendship is affected by place, environment and socioeconomic circumstances. In other words, our emotional life can be limited or expanded by the material circumstances in which we exist.

How did you feel about Allan's claims that it is a relatively new idea for marriage to be based on an expectation that spouses want to spend time together socially? It might have come as a bit of a shock, given our prevailing customary beliefs, to realize that before our great grandparents' time, love was not a necessary component of marriage, at least not as we understand the term in connection with enjoyment of one another's company, and so forth. What other material contexts (other than economic ones) might affect experiences of friendship and relationships in general? For example, consider the material circumstances of your body shape. Do you think that your physical appearance or your sex affects your relational experience? How do you suppose that people with different physical attractiveness levels or disabilities experience relationships? Your class should discuss such ways in which our physical appearance offers a context for our relational experiences (e.g., how our race, sex, age, physical attractiveness set contexts for our relationships).

13   Cyber Relationships

Throughout the previous chapters you have read and considered personal relationships that were formed and maintained in face-to-face interactions. However, in the new millennium the internet has created a new class of relationships and unique ways to augment the normative face-to-face relationships we typically consider. The literature on personal relationships over the past decades has also created a language that we use to explore and understand the lifecycle and dynamics of relationships. However, this language is incomplete because of the unique nature of cyber relationships. For example, we need to consider that communication on the internet can be **synchronous** (occur in real time in a chat room, *AOL Instant Messenger*) or **asynchronous** (messages left to be read at a later time such as emails, and messages on electronic bulletin boards or newsgroups). Another consideration is that the content of these messages may be text, a graphic or a photograph. Although on-line video streaming is a possibility for some individuals it is not for most Internet users. Without real-time face-to-face interactions some information we typically use to understand and convey emotion is lost, so people have adopted several conventions to add symbols that help represent and clarify communication such as a smiley face ☺ to indicate happiness. Although there are many other distinctions that we can draw between cyber and face-to-face relationships, the last one we will consider here is distance, both psychological and geographic. For some individuals, internet communication can close the psychological distance when geographically separated from loved ones. The medium of the internet clearly augments an ongoing face-to-face relationship in these instances. However, some have argued (Kraut, Patterson, Lundmark, Keisler, Mukopadhyuay, & Scherlis, 1998) that rather than supplement face-to-face relationships, computer use actually interferes with seeking out face-to-face interactions with others in close geographic proximity. Perhaps, computer use and cyber relationships are not as evil nor as universally positive as some have painted it, and it remains a tool in relationships and communication much like a phone, that can be used in multiple ways. For a fuller discussion of the issues surrounding personal relationships and the internet see McKenna and Bargh (2000) and Merkle and Richardson (2000).

In this chapter you will read two articles that consider the impact of the internet to be positive on personal relationships. The first article is by Parks and Floyd (1996) and examines relationship development in individuals participating in on-line newsgroups. Using traditional theories created for face-to-face relationship as a gold standard, they evaluate the adequacy of on-line relationships. This is one of the earliest empirical research studies documenting the variety and use of on-line communication in relationships. The second article, also by Parks (Parks & Roberts, 1998), examines the use and impact of a particular type of synchronous on-line communication (MOOs).

Parks and Floyd (1996) begin their discussion of on-line relationship development by presenting two extreme attitudes about on-line relationships (they are a great opportunity – they are deficient). The authors then present a realistic analysis of the potential benefits and risks of developing a relationship on-line. In this discussion you will be introduced to some new ways of thinking about relationships because the medium of the Internet presents limitations (e.g., reduced channel capacity in communications), advantages (e.g., closing geographic distance), and some characteristics that have both costs and benefits (e.g., anonymity) that are different from face-to-face relationships.

Other than laying the groundwork for understanding how the medium affects relationships, Parks and Floyd take several classic theories of relationship development and apply them to on-line relationships. More specifically, they make predictions about the quality of newsgroup relationships based on **Social Penetration Theory**, **Social Presence Theory** and **Social Context Theory**. The evaluation of on-line relationships is based on seven criteria (e.g., commitment, interdependence) from classic theories of relationship development.

One question to consider while reading the article concerns how the criteria are operationalized. In other words, are the measures of the seven criteria consistent with the theories? A second question concerns the applicability of these criteria for relationships that stay on-line versus ones that migrate to face-to-face relationships. More specifically, are evaluations about the quality of relationships, which are exclusively on-line relationships, always deficient compared to those that migrate because the criteria used in the evaluation presuppose face-to-face interactions? A couple of questions to consider concern comparison groups. What exactly is the proper comparison group for newsgroup relationships? Should only face-to-face relationships that do not take advantage of any technology be used, or perhaps those that just avoid computer technology, or maybe just "real relationships" that started in a non-traditional manner is the appropriate comparison group?

Making Friends in Cyberspace

Malcolm R. Parks and Kory Floyd

From its birth as a way of linking a few university and defense laboratories in the late 1960s, the Internet has grown into a global network connecting between millions of people. Social linkages in the form of E-mail and discussion groups appeared in the first days of the Internet and have grown explosively ever since. Today there are over 5,000 Internet discussion groups (Hahn & Stout, 1994). Aside from its sheer size, this new social milieu commands scholarly attention because it is one of the new "collaborative mass media forms" in which messages come from a wide variety of participants with little or no centralized control (Rafaeli & LaRose, 1993). It therefore blurs the traditional boundaries between interpersonal and mass communication phenomena and raises new opportunities and risks for the way individuals relate to one another (e.g., Lea & Spears, 1995).

The purpose of this study was to examine the relational world actually being created through Internet discussion groups (usually called newsgroups). Because the development of personal relationships is a pivotal issue in the larger debate about human relations in cyberspace, this study explores four basic questions: How often do personal relationships form in Internet newsgroups, who has them, how close or developed do they become, and do relationships started on line migrate to other settings?

We begin by examining two conflicting visions that have dominated popular and scholarly debate. On one side are those who view on-line relationships as shallow, impersonal, and often hostile. They assert that only the illusion of community can be created in cyberspace (e.g., Beninger, 1987). On the other side are those who argue that computer-mediated communication liberates interpersonal relations from the confines of physical locality and thus creates opportunities for new, but genuine, personal relationships and communities (e.g., Rheingold, 1993). One vision is of relationships lost, while the other is of relationships liberated and found.

These conflicting visions are not, of course, unique to debates about computer-mediated communication. Instead they reflect long-running, historical debates about the nature of modernity and the social effects of changes in communication and transportation technology (e.g., Marvin, 1987). More specific versions of these debates can be found in the literature on the effects of the reduction in communicative cues associated with computer-mediated communication. They are also reflected in the sharply differing applications of personal relationship theories to on-line settings.

Most of the early research on computer-mediated communication involved laboratory studies in which small groups worked on structured problems for limited periods of time (Garton & Wellman, 1995). Groups that communicated by means of computer (CMC) were compared to groups that communicated face-to-face (FtF). Findings from this line of research have generally emphasized the social disadvantages of computer-mediated communication, therefore implying that highly developed, positive personal relationships should occur infrequently in on-line settings. Computer-mediated groups, for example, have greater difficulty recognizing and moving toward shared points of view (Kiesler & Sproull, 1992). People in CMC groups also engage in more verbal aggression, blunt disclosure, and nonconforming behavior than people in FtF groups (e.g., Dubrovsky, Kiesler, & Sethna, 1991). Such behavior is usually called "flaming," and it has been observed both in laboratory settings and in a variety of business, governmental, educational, and public networks (e.g., Lea, O'Shea, Fung, & Spears, 1992). Such findings may reflect the comparative anonymity afforded by CMC or local norms that make the overt expression of hostility more acceptable in on-line settings (e.g., Lea et al., 1992).

These differences are most often explained by observing that social cues are filtered out in on-line settings (Culnan & Markus, 1987). Relational cues emanating from the physical context are missing, as are nonverbal cues regarding vocal qualities, bodily movement, facial expressions, and physical appearance. CMC is thus judged to have a narrower bandwidth and less information richness than FtF communication (e.g., Daft & Lengel, 1984). According to both **social presence theory** (e.g., Rice, 1987) and **social context cues theory** (Sproull & Kiesler, 1991), this reduction in contextual, visual, and aural cues should cause communication in on-line settings to be more impersonal and nonconforming than communication in face-to-face settings. Both theories predict that participants' awareness of and sensitivity to others will be related to the number of channels or codes available for linking them. Face-to-face communication should breed greater awareness and sensitivity because of its multiplicity of channels, while on-line communication should be more impersonal, less inhibited, and less adaptive. This is not to say that positive personal relationships are impossible. Indeed Sproull and

Kiesler (1991) note that electronic settings sometimes provide more opportunities for social relationships and less evaluation apprehensions than face-to-face settings. Nonetheless, theories of computer-mediated communication that are based on the reduced-cues perspective generally predict that positive personal relationships should occur infrequently rather than frequently.

Claims that computer-mediated communication is characterized by impersonality, hostility, and nonsocial orientation, however, have been challenged repeatedly. The empirical support for some claims is less robust than researchers first suggested, and critics note that the causal antecedent to some effects may have been identified incorrectly. Because people need to manage uncertainty and develop rapport, they will adapt the textual cues to meet their needs when faced with a channel that does not carry visual and aural cues (e.g., Walther, 1992). Time is the key element in this adaptation. While the multiple channels and cues available in FtF interaction speed the exchange of task and relational information, the process is slowed by the "reduced bandwidth" of CMC, that is, the inability of CMC to carry aural and visual cues. The important point, however, is not that CMC is unable to convey relational and personal information, but rather that it may take longer to do so. In a meta-analysis of CMC studies, Walther and his colleagues found that the proportion of socioemotional content was higher when interaction time was not restricted (Walther et al., 1994). Thus, the negative effects attributed to the computer as a medium may have instead been the result of the stringent time restrictions placed on interaction.

As research on CMC moved from the laboratory to the field, it also became apparent that people related to one another in many more ways than had been envisioned by the reduced-cues perspective. Studies of E-mail in the workplace have consistently shown the interpersonal side of CMC. Users commonly report that they socialize, maintain relationships, play games, and receive emotional support via E-mail (e.g., Finholt & Sproull, 1990).

Further evidence that personal relationships are forming on line can be found in a variety of sources, including popular cyberspace travelogues (Rheingold, 1993), the popular press (e.g., Bock, 1994), and a handful of scholarly reports on specific on-line communities (e.g., Brennan, Moore, & Smyth, 1992). These accounts make it clear that on-line relationships are genuine personal relationships in the eyes of the participants. One person who played a **MUD**, for instance, commented that his on-line friendships were "much deeper and have better quality" than his real-life friendships (Bruckman, 1992, p. 23). Another person who had been active in a computer network for church workers said, "I know some of these people better than some of my oldest and best friends" (Wilkins, 1991, p. 56). In some cases, on-line relationships have blossomed into romance and marriage (Bruckman, 1992).

These reports also illustrate how people overcome the technical limitations of CMC. In addition to the well-known use of keyboard characters, or "smileys," to imitate facial expressions and paralinguistic features of conversation (e.g., typing ":-)" to indicate a smile), users frequently express emotion and metacommunicative intent by embedding words in text (Wilkins, 1991). The person who wishes a message to be taken as friendly teasing, for example, may embed a word or phrase like "grin" or "just kidding" in text.

Another way people overcome the technical limitations of CMC is simply to supplement CMC with additional channels of communication. There are several reports of mail, telephone, and face-to-face contact as supplements to CMC (e.g., Ogan, 1993). In some cases, participants in on-line groups have organized social events so that they might meet in person (e.g., Bruckman, 1992).

Popular attention has often fixated on the more manipulative and deceptive aspects of on-line relationships. Cases of gender switching (e.g., men pretending to be women) command particular attention (e.g., Bruckman, 1992). CMC obviously provides rich opportunities for self-presentation and identity manipulation (e.g., Lea & Spears, 1995). However, these opportunities also have a positive side. Cyberspace creates an "identity workshop" in which people learn and test social skills (Bruckman, 1992). Some participants, for example, report that their on-line identities allow them to overcome the shyness they feel in face-to-face interaction (Myers, 1987). People who are isolated or disabled can develop social relationships (e.g., Bock, 1994). Whereas the possibility of abuse always exists, CMC also provides ways for people to transcend the limitations they experience in face-to-face settings (Walther, 1995).

Personal relationship theories visited and revisited

Conflicting predictions regarding on-line relationships can also be obtained from theories of interpersonal communication and relationship development. The relative lack of social cues and the potential for feedback delays, for example, should lead both to higher uncertainty and more difficulty in reducing uncertainty about how to behave, how the partner will behave, and how to explain the partner's behavior. According to uncertainty reduction theory (e.g., Berger & Calabrese, 1975), the inability to reduce uncertainty should prevent, or at least retard, the development of personal relationships.

Existing theories of relational development pose several other challenges for on-line relationships, as Lea and Spears (1995) observe. For example, most theories assume both physical proximity and frequent interaction between prospective partners (e.g., Altman & Taylor, 1973). Existing theories also underscore the importance of physical appearance and physical attraction, especially in the development of romantic relationships (e.g., Berscheid & Walster, 1978). Yet information regarding physical

appearance is usually unavailable in on-line settings.

On-line communicators, therefore, are generally assumed to lack many of the things emphasized in traditional discussions of relationship development: physical proximity, frequent interaction, information about physical appearance, cues about group membership, and information about the broader social context (Lea & Spears, 1995). However, a more optimistic assessment of the potential for personal relationships emerges when we re-examine the assumptions about on-line communication. If Walther's (e.g., 1992) information processing perspective is correct, for instance, people in on-line settings may simply take longer to reduce their uncertainty about one another. The lack of proximity and of visual information might be overcome by arranging meetings or by exchanging photographs either electronically or by mail. Information about membership in social groups can be exchanged easily. Thus, many supposed limitations of CMC may be overdrawn.

More important, however, is the question of whether these conditions are really necessary for the development of relationships. The emphasis placed on factors like physical appearance or proximity may reflect less of a theoretic necessity than a consequence of the fact that most theories of relational development predate the current explosion in computer-mediated communication technology. In **social penetration theory**, for example, the driving force behind relational development is the forecast of a positive reward: cost ratio (Altman & Taylor, 1973). Other exchange-based theories make similar assumptions about what drives development (e.g., Huston & Burgess, 1979). In uncertainty-reduction theory the driving force is the progressive reduction of uncertainty about the partner and the relationship (e.g., Berger, 1988). None of these theories requires physical proximity and frequent interaction as necessary conditions for relational development. These conditions may be helpful, but they are not necessary to arrive at predictions of how rewarding future interactions might be, how one might feel about another person, or how one might be treated by that person.

Whereas studies of face-to-face relationships emphasize the reward and information value of physical appearance and physical attractiveness (e.g., Berscheid & Walster, 1978), no theory of relational development explicitly requires this information as a necessary precondition. Information about physical appearance may serve as a reward or promote inferences about other qualities, but it is not the only source of rewards or of the information used to make inferences. Visions of relationships lost may, therefore, not acknowledge either the capabilities of on-line communication or the necessary conditions in theories of relationship development.

In short, both popular and scholarly accounts present sharply contrasting, often dramatized, views of the possibilities for on-line relationships. What is missing is a systematic research effort to map the prevalence of personal relationships in on-line settings, the basic demographics of relational participants, the levels of development achieved in on-line relationships, and their links to off-line or real-life settings.

How often do personal relationships form in Internet newsgroups?

Our first task was to determine just how common personal relationships were in on-line settings. To do this, as well as to address our other research questions, Internet newsgroups and their contributors were selected through a two-stage sampling procedure. In the first stage, 24 newsgroups were randomly selected from published lists of groups (Hahn & Stout, 1994) in each of four major Usenet newsgroup hierarchies: "comp," "soc," "rec," and "alt." In the second stage, 22 people were randomly chosen from lists of those who had posted messages to these groups over a several-day period. Surveys were then sent to prospective participants by direct E-mail. Responses were received from 176 of the 528 (33.3%) people contacted in this manner. Respondents ranged in age from 15 to 57 years. The typical respondent was 32 years old, more likely to be male than female, and more likely to be single than married. Respondents had typically been involved with newsgroups for approximately two years and contributed to an average of five groups on a monthly basis.

Our primary finding was that personal relationships were common. When we asked if our respondents had formed any new acquaintances, friendships, or other personal relationships as a result of participating in newsgroups, nearly two thirds (60.7%) reported that they had indeed formed a personal relationship with someone they had "met" for the first time via an Internet newsgroup. Further, the likelihood of developing a personal relationship did not differ across the newsgroup hierarchies or groupings we examined. That is, personal relationships seemed equally likely to develop in all sectors we examined. They were not restricted to just a few types of newsgroups. The fact that personal relationships developed for so many of our respondents and across so many different types of newsgroups suggests that criticisms of on-line interaction as being impersonal and hostile are overdrawn. These findings lend more credence to images of relationships liberated than to images of relationships lost.

These findings obviously raise questions about the types of relationships that our respondents were forming. Additional analyses revealed that opposite-sex relationships (55.1%) were slightly more common than same-sex relationships (44.9%), but this difference was not statistically significant. Only a few (7.9%) were romantic. Relationships ranged in duration from less than a month to six years, but most relationships (69.6%) were less than a year old ($Mdn = 5.00$ months, $M = 9.62$ months, $SD = 12.21$). Participants communicated regularly with their on-line partners. Nearly a third (29.7%) reported that they communicated with their partners at least three or four times a week, and over half (55.4%) communicated with their partners on a weekly basis.

Who has on-line personal relationships?

Women were significantly more likely than men to have formed a personal relationship on line. While 72.2% of women had formed a personal relationship, only 54.5% of men had ($\chi^2 = 4.80$, $df = 1$, $p < .05$). Additional research will be needed to distinguish potential explanations for this difference. It may stem from motivational factors. It may simply be that a greater proportion of women are looking for friends. There may be sex differences in the willingness to label an on-line relationship as such. Or, women may simply be more sought after in a medium where more users are male.

Age did not appear to be related to the likelihood of developing a personal relationship on line, nor did marital status. Married, never married, and divorced respondents were equally likely to have personal relationships that started in newsgroups.

The best predictors of whether an individual had developed a personal relationship were the duration and frequency of their participation in newsgroups. People who formed personal relationships on line contributed to significantly more newsgroups ($M = 5.90$ groups, $SD = 6.81$) than did those who had not ($M = 3.62$, $SD = 2.88$), $t(147) = 3.00$, $p < .01$. The two groups did not differ, however, in terms of the number of newsgroups they read. Nor did the two groups differ significantly in terms of either the length of time they had been reading newsgroups in general or the length of time they had been posting to newsgroups in general. Significant differences, however, did emerge when we examined the duration of participation in the particular newsgroup we sampled. Those who had formed on-line relationships had been reading their particular newsgroup longer ($M = 13.34$ months,

$SD = 16.76$) than those who had not ($M = 8.03$ months, $SD = 10.36$), $t(164) = 2.52$, $p < .05$. Moreover, those with a relationship had been posting to their particular newsgroup longer ($M = 12.04$ months, $SD = 16.37$) than those without one ($M = 6.94$ months, $SD = 8.83$), $t(158) = 2.59$, $p < .01$.

The overall frequency of participation in newsgroups also distinguished people who had developed on-line personal relationships from those who had not. Although the two groups did not differ in terms of how frequently they read their favorite newsgroups, they did differ in terms of how often they posted messages to their favorite newsgroups, $t(164) = 3.09$, $p < .005$. Those with on-line relationships contributed more often ($M = 4.01$, $SD = 1.81$) than those without ($M = 3.17$, $SD = 1.54$). Those who had formed a personal relationship also used direct E-mail to respond to a greater number of newsgroup contributors each month ($M = 10.25$, $SD = 15.97$) than those who had not ($M = 4.75$, $SD = 4.30$), $t(121) = 3.28$, $p = .001$.

How developed do on-line personal relationships typically become?

Interpersonal relationships of all types are usually conceptualized as developing from the impersonal to the personal along a series of relatively specific dimensions: increases in interdependence, in the breadth and depth of interaction, in interpersonal predictability and understanding, in the change toward more personalized ways of communicating, in commitment, and in the convergence of the participants' social networks. Respondents who reported having an on-line personal relationship rated its level of development by responding to items designed to measure each of these dimensions. These items were based on previous theoretic discussions and measures of the relationship development process (e.g., Altman & Taylor, 1973). Because there was no comparison sample against which to evaluate levels of development, we used the theoretic midpoint of each scale as a reference point. Although admittedly arbitrary, this procedure allowed us to determine if the majority of responses fell below the midpoint, thus indicating a comparatively low level of development, or above it, thus indicating a comparatively high level of development.

In its most general sense, a relationship develops as its participants come to depend on each other more deeply and in more complex ways (e.g., Kelley, 1979). The personal relationships observed in this sample varied widely in terms of their reported levels of interdependence. The seven items making up the interdependence scale yielded totals that were normally distributed and whose overall mean of 26.60 (*SD* = 8.93) fell close to the theoretic midpoint of the scale. Approximately half (50.5%) of the relationships were above this midpoint, while half (49.5%) were below it. Thus, moderate levels of interdependence typified the sample as a whole.

As relationships develop, the breadth and depth of interaction increases (e.g., Altman & Taylor, 1973). The variety of topics, activities, and communication channels increases. People reveal more important, risky, and personal information. Our respondents generally reported moderate to high levels of breadth and depth in their on-line personal relationships. The observed mean on the breadth scale was 21.12 (*SD* = 4.70) and fell just above the theoretic midpoint of 20. Over half (57.0%) of the subjects recorded breadth scores in the upper half of the scale range. The depth dimension of relational development was assessed using items designed to measure intimacy and self-disclosure. Totals for the items assessing depth produced a mean of 35.45 (*SD* = 11.24), nearly four points higher than the theoretic midpoint of the scale. Almost two thirds (61.2%) of the respondents recorded depth scores in the upper half of the scale range.

Development is also characterized by communicative code change. The participants evolve specialized ways of communicating, such as personal idioms, that allow them to express themselves in more efficient ways and that reinforce their relational identity (e.g., Bell & Healey, 1992). We measured this dimension with a six-item scale whose observed mean was 18.77 (*SD* = 7.20), nearly six points below the theoretic midpoint. Only 21.4% of subjects scored at or above the theoretic midpoint of this scale, suggesting that most of the personal relationships had not developed highly specialized communication patterns.

Perceptions of predictability and understanding are important aspects of development in several theories, especially uncertainty reduction theory (e.g., Berger & Calabrese, 1975). We examined these perceptions using a five-item scale, which yielded a mean of 19.93 (*SD* = 6.23), falling slightly below the theoretic midpoint of 21. Most subjects (59.2%), however, reported that the predictability and understanding in their relationship was in the upper half of the scale range.

Commitment is the expectation that the relationship will continue into the future. It is usually conceptualized as a desire to continue the relationship and the belief that it should and must continue (e.g., Johnson, 1991). The observed mean of our five-item commitment scale was 20.07 (*SD* = 6.57) and fell almost exactly on the theoretic midpoint of the scale. Just under half of the subjects (49.0%) reported commitment levels at or above this midpoint, suggesting moderate levels of commitment in the sample as a whole.

Finally, as relationships develop, network convergence occurs as the participants introduce one another to each other's friends and family and develop a common social circle (e.g., Parks & Eggert, 1991). In on-line relationships, network convergence would imply not only that participants were introduced to one another's on-line contacts, but also to people in their real-life social networks. The seven items used to measure this dimension yielded a mean of 22.95 (*SD* = 9.61), well below the theoretic midpoint of the scale. Only 31.3% of the relationships were rated in the upper half of the scale range. These results indicate that network convergence was not extensive in most of the personal relationships we examined. Inspection of the individual scale items revealed that relational partners believed that there was considerably more convergence among their on-line contacts than between their on-line contacts and their contacts outside of the Internet.

If the relationships-lost view were correct, we should have found very few relationships that scored highly on these seven dimensions. In fact we found many. Depending on the particular dimension, half or more of the relationships registered above the midpoint of the measurement scale. Across the total sample, then, approximately 40% of the respondents had no on-line personal relationships, about 30% had a less developed personal relationship, and about 30% had what might legitimately be considered a highly developed personal relationship.

Do on-line relationships migrate to other settings?

Relationships that began in Internet newsgroups often broadened to include interaction in other channels or settings. Although nearly all respondents used direct E-mail (98.0%) in addition to newsgroup postings, a surprising number also supplemented computer-mediated communication with other forms of contact. About a third had used the telephone (35.3%), the postal service (28.4%), or face-to-face communication (33.3%) to contact their on-line friends. The average number of channels used was 2.68 ($SD = 1.23$), and nearly two thirds (63.7%) of our respondents with personal relationships had used communication channels other than the computer.

These findings imply that relationships that begin on line rarely stay there. Although this expansion in the number of contexts where interaction occurs is typical of the relational development process in general (Parks, 1997), it is particularly noteworthy in on-line relationships. For one thing, it

represents a way in which relational partners can overcome the limitations of computer-mediated channels. Vocal and visual information are added as participants move into other channels. In addition the broadening of communication indicates that people may not draw such a clear line between their on-line and off-line activities.

The new challenges of cyberspace

Our primary finding was that personal relationships were common in [one large on-line] environment: just over 60% of the people in our random sample reported that they had formed a personal relationship of some kind with someone they had first contacted through a newsgroup. Personal relationships were not limited to any one type of newsgroup, but were spread rather evenly across a variety of newsgroups and Usenet hierarchies. Contrary to the relationships-lost perspective, we found that personal relationships are commonplace and evolve naturally as a function of time and experience in the on-line environment of newsgroups. Newsgroups, of course, are not the only on-line venues. A more definitive picture will be gained by extending our observations to other CMC settings (e.g., MUDs and **MOOs**).

The fact that personal relationships in on-line settings are so commonplace poses challenges and opportunities for contemporary approaches to interpersonal communication and relationship development. How participants manage uncertainty, forecast rewards and costs, and obtain rewards is less clear in on-line settings. Because these factors represent central explanatory forces in theories of relationship development, further research is necessary to understand how they function in on-line settings. Future research should also focus on the development of on-line relationships in special populations. The fact that a large proportion of users actually develop personal relationships suggests new opportunities for those who are isolated or disabled in ways that restrict or stigmatize them in face-to-face interaction (e.g., Bock, 1994).

The results of this study also have implications for previous approaches to computer-mediated communication. Personal relationships were found far more often and at a far higher level of development in this study than can be accounted for by the reduced-cues perspective. The finding that those who posted more often and who had been posting for a longer time were more likely to have developed a personal relationship on line is consistent with Walther's (1992) social information-processing perspective. However, the additional finding that nearly two thirds of those whose personal relationships began on line chose to use additional communication channels challenges the belief that participants are denied vocal and visual information. Indeed, no current theory of CMC seems to account for this expansion in channel use. Even within the Internet itself, the information available to relational participants continues to expand as more people use the World Wide Web to exchange pictures, sound, and video. The reduced-cues perspective may simply become a theoretic antique, given the continuing advances in network technology.

The fact that relationships that begin on line rarely stay there raises even more profound questions about our understanding of cyberspace. From the beginning, discussions of cyberspace have almost invariably emphasized its more exotic qualities. Yet for most of our respondents, cyberspace is simply another place to meet. Just like people who meet in other locales, those who meet in cyberspace frequently move their relationships into settings beyond the one in which they met originally. They do not appear to draw a sharp boundary between relationships in cyberspace and those in real life. Furthermore, if cyberspace is becoming just another place to meet, we must rethink our image of the relationships formed there as being somehow removed and exotic.

Parks and Floyd (1996) concluded that on-line relationships are common, perhaps more so for women, and these relationships do not have the negative and hostile qualities characterized by the medium's harshest critics. Although it is unclear exactly why women are more likely to report having participated in on-line relationships, the authors provide four plausible explanations for this effect. Another finding that may run counter to expectations about on-line relationships portrayed by the mass media is that only a small proportion of them were romantic (8 percent). One might be tempted to generalize this finding and assume there are few on-line romantic relationships under development. However, this conclusion may be artifact of a narrow band of possible on-line relationships examined in the study (only newsgroup relationships were studied). It is possible that a higher number of romantic relationships would be found in other on-line mediums (e.g., chat rooms, MOOs) or of course at web sites dedicated to introducing potential dating partners. There has been an explosion of dating web sites since Parks and Floyd's article was published in 1996.

Two questions we asked you to consider while reading the article concerned the adequacy of the criteria and the applicability of criteria based on face-to-face relationship development. Although there are many places where these questions could be applied, a representative criterion is "network convergence," that is to say of the seven items that make up the criterion, three concern on-line convergence, three ask about off-line convergence, and one is ambiguous and could apply to either category (i.e., This person and I do not know any of the same people). The "network convergence" criterion can be compared to the "breadth" and "depth" criteria in which none of the 13 questions exclusively concerns face-to-face interactions. The authors report that on-line relationships have moderate to high levels of breadth and depth, but low network convergence. Perhaps the lack of "network convergence" is a result of the inclusion of a face-to-face standard in operationally defining the criterion and the higher values for "breadth" and "depth" are the result of criteria operationally defined only within the on-line medium. For methodological consistency, should all the criteria be defined within a single medium (i.e., on-line) or should all criteria be a mix of on-line and off-line questions? In addition to these methodological issues there is also a theoretical one. If we attempt to assess the adequacy of on-line relationships using criteria that were developed for face-to-face relationships, should face-to-face components be equally represented in each criterion (e.g., network convergence) or should the questions be based solely on network relationships (e.g., breadth and depth)? A related question involves whether or not a standard of evaluation for on-line relationships should be that on-line relationships migrate to off-line relationships. One might argue that the adequacy of on-line relationships should be evaluated on the basis of solely what happens on-line. If comparisons need to be made to off-line relationships then perhaps this evaluation should be compared to an assessment of off-line relationships evaluated on the same criteria (**operationally defined** for off-line relationships). Finding the appropriate comparison group is replete with sampling issues that we do not have space here to consider, but you may want to list as many as you think of and follow these issues into your reading of the second article in this chapter, Parks and Roberts (1998).

In the previous article, the authors examined newsgroup relationships. You may remember that newsgroups involve **asynchronous** communication where one leaves messages to be picked up or viewed at a later time. Parks and Floyd (1996) found a moderate amount of relationship development in on-line newsgroup relationships using criteria derived from traditional theories of face-to-face relationship development. In the next article, however, Parks and Roberts (1998) examine **MOOs**, which are **synchronous** (real-time) text-based environments that permit fluid and multileveled social communication. The authors provide an excellent description of this virtual environment where people interact with others as their actual selves or create characters that either partially represent themselves or identities that are complete fabrications. People interact within this environment in rooms that are based on the reality created by the participants and these parameters can change based on the input of the characters. It is possible the real-time environment and multifaceted nature of the communication in MOOs will contribute to relationship development on-line. For example, the authors note Walther's (1996) arguments that on-line communications possess structural characteristics that replicate the "stranger on the plane phenomenon" and might lead to strong feelings of intimacy in on-line relationships.

We left you wondering about possible comparison groups at the end of the last article. Parks and Roberts (1998) also considered this issue and found three levels of comparison in this study. First, they used a within-subjects design, asking MOOs users to describe their on-line and off-line relationships. So the same subjects served in the on-line group and the off-line comparison group, providing heightened control for individual differences (although people who never had an on-line relationship are not represented in the data analysis due to the low number of responses). They also used the results of Parks and Floyd (1996) for a third comparison group providing an assessment of on-line relationships created in a different virtual environment (e.g., asynchronous).

As you read Parks and Roberts (1998) you should also consider two issues that carry over from the previous article: the adequacy of the criteria used to evaluate on-line relationships and the appropriateness of using face-to-face-based relational theory to evaluate on-line relationships. To this end, note while you are reading this article that the median number of MOOs characters reported for a subject is four. In other words, MOOs participants may be managing four different versions of themselves. You may want to consider the implications of maintaining four different personas and the issues this situation raises for evaluating the quality of relationship development.

'Making MOOsic': The Development of Personal Relationships On Line and a Comparison to their Off-line Counterparts

Malcolm R. Parks and Lynne D. Roberts

Throughout the early 1990s the Internet doubled in size every 12–15 months and by mid-1997 had grown to involve over 50 million users worldwide (Intelliquest, 1997). Although claims about Internet popularity are often exaggerated, recent surveys indicate that more than 20 million adults in the United States now view the Internet as an indispensable part of their lives (Miller & Clemente, 1997). Whatever else it may be, the Internet is a fundamentally social medium in the broad sense. The Internet was used for personal email almost immediately upon its inception in the early 1970s (Zakon, 1996). Since then a variety of social venues has evolved – chats, newsgroups, mailing lists, interactive World Wide Web sites, and text-based virtual environments known as **MUDs (Multi-User Dimensions or Dungeons)** and **MOOs (MUDs, Object Oriented)**. These social vehicles are also rapidly being integrated into those parts of the Internet that are less obviously social. On-line business sites, information services and magazines regularly provide email chats, newsgroups and other ways for their visitors to interact.

These settings call for research, not only because of the phenomenal growth of the Internet, but also because the social venues of the Internet create new opportunities and risks for the development of interpersonal relationships (Parks & Floyd, 1996). In addition, the social dynamics of cyberspace create new, often challenging, opportunities to test existing theories of interpersonal communication (Lea & Spears, 1995). The purpose of the present study was to map the relational topography of one of the major social venues on the Internet: Multi-User Dimensions, Object Orientated (MOOs). We begin by describing the nature of this popular Internet venue. We then explore a series of research questions that must be addressed if we are to understand the interpersonal dynamics of MOOs and their relatives.

MOOs are "worlds in words" (Marvin, 1995) that allow for synchronous or "real time" discussion between geographically dispersed participants. The initial attraction of MOOing is the opportunity to interact with others from around the world in a social environment. Over time, the motivation changes in order to maintain relationships that have been formed on the MOO (Roberts et al., 1996a).

MOOs are related to a number of other virtual environments including, "chat [room]s" and MUDs. Interactions on MUDs (Multi-User Dimensions or Dungeons) tend to be oriented toward competitive role-playing games, while interactions on most MOOs are less competitive and more social. MOOs differ from chats and other Internet venues because they use text to create and describe characters, virtual places and objects. Each individual creates a character description using simple commands and text. The character is the representation of the individual on the MOO. It is created and controlled by the individual and used to interact with other characters. During the research, for example, we created a character named "Surveyor" to field respondents' questions and comments. A character may be an accurate representation of the individual, a fantasy creation, or something in between. Others, however, routinely view even fantasy descriptions as informative about the real person who stands behind them.

In addition to creating a character, participants may create "rooms" or other virtual places. For example, a participant may contribute to the construction of public spaces, open to all, or to more private virtual spaces such as rooms within his or her virtual "home". Some descriptions are simple, while others represent elaborate attempts to convey their owners' tastes and to create a mood. Participants may also program new virtual objects using object-oriented

language. Using this programming, for example, participants may create furnishings for rooms, a pet that follows them around, or a game that others can play. Thus each participant is potentially the co-creator of a virtual world (Curtis, 1992).

MOOers can "talk" to one another by typing messages using the "say" command. Unlike chat rooms and other real time programs, MOO programs also allow players to "emote" with textual descriptions of actions and emotions, simple preprogrammed scripts, or pictures drawn with standard keyboard characters. For example, to express suspicion of a character named X, Surveyor could type: *emote eyes you warily*. X and others in the same virtual room would then see this on their screen: *Surveyor eyes you warily*.

Using a preprogrammed script, Surveyor might type *eye* X to achieve the same result more quickly. In addition, these programs allow participants to engage in back channel communication by sending messages to a particular character in the group without others seeing them, or paging messages to a character who is not in the same MOO location (Jacobson, 1996). All these features combine to support fluid, multi-layered social interaction.

The number of MOOs now runs into the hundreds and the number of participants world-wide probably runs to the tens of thousands (Schiano, 1997). MOOs figure prominently in larger popular discussions of the Internet (e.g., Turkle, 1995). Although they are often thought to epitomize the best and worst that the Internet revolution may hold for interpersonal relations, there is almost no systematic research describing them. Our goal is to provide a broad empirical description of the actual relational world of MOOs. In the following paragraphs we outline a series of research questions regarding the prevalence, types and development of personal relationships on line.

[The remaining portion of the introduction has been heavily edited]

The primary [research] question (RQ1), of course, is: "What proportion of MOO users have formed personal relationships on line?". [However], there [also] is little in the previous research to suggest what types of personal relationships might be most common among MOO participants. In order to map the interpersonal world of MOOs, we asked (RQ2): "What types of personal relationships do people form on line?".

We know relatively little about the individual or demographic characteristics of people who develop personal relationships on line. As far as we know, this issue has been addressed in only one of the various social venues on line [newsgroups (Parks & Floyd, 1996)]. Sex was the only demographic that emerged as a predictor. Our goal in the present study was to replicate these analyses in a structurally different on-line venue. Our guiding research question (RQ3) was: "Among those who use MOOs, what factors differentiate people who have started personal relationships on line from those who have not?".

Some view on-line relationships as intrinsically shallow illusions of real personal relationships (e.g., Slouka, 1995). Others testify that their on-line relationships are as close or perhaps even closer than their off-line relationships. These conflicting views call for more systematic assessments of the level of development typically achieved in on-line relationships.

A relationship becomes more personal, more developed when: (i) its participants become more interdependent, (ii) interaction increases in depth or intimacy, (iii) interaction increases in breadth or variety, (iv) participants become more committed to maintaining the relationship, (v) participants feel better understood and interaction is more predictable, (vi) personalized ways of communicating emerge, and (vii) the participants' social networks converge. This particular conceptualization of the developmental process was recently advanced by Parks (1997), but draws on long recognized themes in the literature on relational development (e.g., Altman & Taylor, 1973).

These dimensions were used to address two related research questions. One view of relational development emerges when we ask (RQ4): "How do participants rate their MOO relationships along the seven developmental dimensions?". In the present study, however, we also compared relationships started on MOOs to relationships of the same type that the participants had started in face-to-face settings. We asked (RQ5): "How do on-line and off-line relationships compare in terms of their development?".

The Internet is composed of several distinctly different types of media. MOOs, for example, allow real-time, synchronous interaction, while Internet newsgroups are limited to asynchronous interaction. MOOs go beyond newsgroups by allowing private communication and back-channels. We must actively compare relational patterns in the various Internet venues in order to determine whether these technical differences are associated with differences in social and relational characteristics. Although there are a number of differences in the specifics of instrumentation, the measures used in the previous study of newsgroups (Parks & Floyd, 1996) can be compared, at least in part, to the measures used in this study. This allowed us to ask (RQ6): "How does the level of development in relationships started in Internet newsgroups compare with that for relationships started on MOOs?".

One of the least explored aspects of on-line communication is its relationship to life off line. Some commentators portray computer-mediated communication as a doorway into a brave new world that is almost divorced from off-line norms and relationships (e.g., Slouka, 1995). [Parks & Floyd (1996) found that a] third of those who had started a relationship in a newsgroup went on to meet the other person face-to-face. In order to examine the generality of this finding, we first asked (RQ7): "Do relationships started on MOOs migrate to other settings?"; and, if so (RQ8): "Is there any regular pattern of channel choices that people make when moving a relationship from a MOO to face-to-face interaction?".

Method

A total of 235 (51.7% male, 48.3% female) current users of MOOs participated. They ranged in age between 13 and 74 years, but 50 percent were between the ages of 17 and 26 ($M = 27.18$, $SD = 10.26$). The sample was international, representing 14 different countries on all continents except Antarctica, but most respondents were from the United States (78.9%), Canada (8.6%) or Australia (3.4%). Most (63.3%) had never been married, although a sizable minority (29.7%) were married or cohabiting. Relatively few (7%) were separated or divorced. Respondents had completed an average of nearly 15 years of schooling ($M = 14.84$, $SD = 2.92$).

Respondents varied widely in their Internet history and current use of MOOs. The amount of time since they had first started using the Internet ranged from 3 months to 10 years (median and mode = 2.0 years). The amount of time since they had first visited a MOO ranged from the current month to 5 years ($M = 20.94$ months, $SD = 11.96$ months). People are often active on more than one MOO, sometimes maintaining several different characters as a result. Reports of the number of MOOs and characters were positively skewed, but the median number of MOOs and characters was four. Most respondents reported visiting MOOs between 3 and 18 hours per week (median = 12.0, mode = 10.0).

Two surveys were developed. The first contained demographic items, measures of Internet and MOO use, and, for respondents who reported having one, items that assessed the nature and development of a personal relationship that had been initiated on a MOO. Respondents were asked to think of people with whom they had personal relationships on the MOO and then to select from these the one person with whom they had communicated most recently. Several aspects of these relationships were assessed including the type and duration, the amount of communication, and the communication channels used. Respondents also completed a shortened form of a measure of relational development (Parks & Floyd, 1996). Items assessed interdependence, breadth, depth, code change, predictability/understanding, commitment and network convergence of on-line relationships.

In the second survey, respondents were asked to report on an off-line "physical life" or "real-life" relationship that was of the same type as the on-line relationships they had described in the first survey. [The language used to compare on-line and off-line relationships is in a state of flux. The older reference to off-line relationships as "real-life" is giving way to a new designation of them as "physical-life" relationships, no doubt reflecting the reality that people increasingly attribute to on-line social relationships.] For example, respondents who described their on-line relationship as a close friendship in the first survey were asked to describe an off-line close friendship in the second survey. Respondents who did not have an off-line relationship of the same type as their on-line relationship were instructed to think of their most comparable off-line relationship. Within a given type, respondents were instructed to select the person to whom they had talked most recently. In two cases, respondents used the same relationship for both surveys. These respondents were dropped from the study. Items in the second survey paralleled those in the first with some small modifications in wording to better match the off-line context.

A two-stage sampling procedure was used to randomly select MOO users from a range of public-access MOOs. A total of seven different MOOs was selected in the first stage. The largest social MOO (LambdaMOO with 5979 registered members as of September, 1997) and the largest educational MOO (Diversity University with 4612 registered members as of September, 1997) were selected on a priori grounds. Five additional MOOs were randomly selected from a list of MOOs available on the World Wide Web. Several lists of MOOs and MUDs are available on line. We used "Gurk's MOO page" (http://www4. ncsu.edu/unity/users/a/asdamick/www/moo.html). The MOOs included in the final sample were LambdaMOO, RiverMOO, BayMOO, IdMOO, Sprawl, Meridian and Diversity University. A MOO character named "Surveyor" was set up as a research character on each of the selected MOOs to facilitate answering questions from potential respondents.

In the second stage, 1200 individuals were randomly selected from those who had connected to the MOOs within the previous 14 days. The MOOs' internal email systems were used to send letters to these MOO users inviting them to participate in a survey on communication patterns on MOOs. The survey could be completed on the World Wide Web site or by email. Upon completion of the first survey on MOO relationships, respondents were invited to participate in a second survey of off-line relationships.

A total of 235 MOO relationships surveys were completed, to provide a response rate of 20 percent. Two-thirds ($n = 155$) of those who completed the first also completed the second survey on off-line relationships.

Results

Nearly all the respondents (93.6%) reported that they had formed at least one ongoing personal relationship during their interactions on MOOs. Respondents reported an average of 7.27 hours communication per week ($SD = 9.41$) with their relational partners. The typical relationship had a duration of just over a year ($M = 13.31$ months, $SD = 9.03$). The vast majority of respondents had formed several new personal relationships as a result of their MOO experience. The number of new relationships reported varied widely and was positively skewed, but the middle 50 percent of the sample reported having initiated between four and 15 new personal relationships (median = 6.0, mode = 5.0).

Several different types of personal relationships were identified, but the majority were classified by the respondents as close friendships (40.6%), friendships (26.3%) or romantic relationships (26.3%). Because of the small number of work/school associates and acquaintances reported, however, further comparisons of relationship types focused only on friendships, close friendships and romances.

Friendships, close friendships and romances started in MOOs did not differ in terms of their duration (using a stringent critical alpha, .01). There was, however, a significant difference in hours of contact per week by relationship type, $F(2, 187) = 24.05$, $p < .01$. MOO romantic partners spend more time together than MOO close friends, who in turn spend more time together than MOO friends. There was also a significant difference in the frequency of communication among the three relationship types, ($F(2, 141) = 18.33$, $p < .001$). MOO romantic partners met almost daily, while close friends met three to four times per week, and friends met once or twice a week on average. Post-hoc tests indicated that all of these differences were significant.

We also explored whether individuals who reported different types of relationships could be distinguished in terms of their off-line or MOO demographics. The individuals reporting on friendships, close friendships and romances did not significantly differ in terms of age, sex, marital status or education level; or in terms of their history of Internet or MOO use, or number of characters used in MOOs. However, individuals reporting on the three types of relationships did differ in current MOO usage. Individuals reporting on MOO romances used more MOOs ($M = 9.33$, $SD = 14.59$) than those reporting on close friendships ($M = 6.00$, $SD = 3.99$) and friendships ($M = 3.84$, $SD = 2.59$), $F(2, 199) = 6.37$, $p < .01$. They also spent more hours MOOing per week ($M = 24.56$, $SD = 19.01$) than those reporting on close friendships ($M = 16.02$, $SD = 11.98$) and friendships ($M = 9.83$, $SD = 9.33$), $F(2, 198) = 16.51$, $p < .01$.

The vast majority (83.6%) of MOO relationships reported was with members of the opposite sex. Respondents were significantly more likely to report on a MOO relationship with a member of the opposite sex than of the same sex, $\chi^2(1, n = 214) = 97.51$, $p < .001$. Opposite-sex relationships constituted the majority among friends (74%), close friends (90%) and romantic relationships (84%).

We had hoped to compare MOO users who had started personal relationships on line with those who had not. However, because the group that had not formed personal relationships was so small (6.7%), comparisons were not possible and this group was not included in further analyses.

Respondents did differ, as we observed above, in the number of personal relationships they had formed on line. However, the number of relationships reported was not strongly correlated ($rs < .15$) with age, education, Internet history, MOOing history, the number of MOOs and characters used, or the number of hours spent on MOOs per week. There was no significant difference in the number of personal relationships formed by males and females.

We assessed the level of development of personal relationships initiated on MOOs in terms of a series of seven dimensions: interdependence, breadth, depth, code change, predictability/understanding, commitment and network convergence of both on-line and off-line relationships.

The absolute level of relational development was assessed by comparing the observed means for the developmental dimensions with the theoretical midpoints of the scales using single sample t-tests. The interdependence scale, for example, had a theoretical midpoint of 16.00 (i.e., four items, scaled 1–7, yielding a scale range of four to 28.00). A single-sample t-test was used to determine if the observed mean of 17.78 was significantly greater than the theoretic mean of 16.00 (one-tailed test). In this case the test result was significant ($t = 4.29$, $df = 212$, $p < .001$).

These comparisons indicated that the majority of the respondents rated their on-line relationships above the midpoint of nearly every scale measuring relational development. The only exception was the measure that assessed the degree to which the on-line relational partner was introduced to members of the respondent's off-line social network. The observed mean for this scale was significantly below the midpoint of the scale and only 40.8 percent of the sample scored above it. For the remaining seven scales of relational development, however, the observed means were significantly above the theoretical midpoints. Approximately

60–90 percent of the respondents rated their relationships above the midpoints of these scales. This suggested that MOO relationships as a whole showed moderate to high levels of development.

An additional research question (RQ5) focused on how the level of development observed in on-line relationships compared with that in off-line relationships. Participants were asked to select and report on an off-line relationship that was comparable to the on-line relationship they had described. Off-line relationships were of greater durations and respondents spent significantly more hours per week with their off-line relational partners than they did with their MOO counterparts. The off-line relationships showed greater interdependence, predictability/understanding, commitment and off-line network convergence. Although these differences were significant, they were not large in an absolute sense. MOO relationships displayed more convergence of the participants' on-line social networks than did off-line relationships. Moreover, the off-line and MOO relationships reported in this survey did not differ in breadth, depth and code-change dimensions. Although the off-line relationships as a group were clearly more developed, it was notable that the differences were not large and that there were no differences in breadth and depth of interaction.

Next we explored potential differences in the relationships developed in one on-line social venue and another by comparing the means for items of the OnLine Relationships Scales that were shared by this study and Parks and Floyd's (1996) study on newsgroup relationships. In each case, the mean score for newsgroup relationships was lower than the mean scores for MOO relationships and off-line relationships. This held true across all 27 common items. Newsgroup relationships, as a group, were less developed than either MOO or off-line relationships.

Nearly all respondents who had started a personal relationship on a MOO (92.7%) had gone on to use other communication channels in addition to the MOO. The most popular channels were email (80%), telephone (66.8%), cards and letters (54.5%), and photographs exchanged by mail (40.5%). Respondents used an average of almost four additional communication channels ($M = 3.39$, median $= 4.0$, $SD = 1.75$).

A sizable number of respondents who had started personal relationships on line had gone on to meet their relational partners face-to-face (37.7%). The probability of meeting differed according to relational type. Those in romantic relationships were more likely to meet (57.9%) than close friends (35.2%) or friends (22.8%), $\chi^2(2, n = 202) = 15.43$, $p < .001$.

Face-to-face meetings usually occurred only after the relational partners had already used several other communication channels. Only 8.4 percent of respondents who had started an on-line relationship reported moving directly from the MOO to face-to-face contact. Most (66.3%) reported using three or more channels before meeting in person ($M = 3.02$, mode $= 4.00$, $SD = 1.51$). These channels usually augmented the text-only media of MOOs and email with vocal and visual information. Almost two-thirds (61.4%) had both spoken by telephone and obtained pictures on line or by mail before meeting their relational partners for the first time face-to-face. This, too, varied by relational type. Although approximately half of the friends (53.8%) and close friends (48.4%) had exchanged both vocal and visual information before meeting in person, 78.8 percent of the romantic partners had done so, $\chi^2(2, n = 77) = 6.77$, $p < .05$.

Discussion

Our primary finding was that almost all MOO users (93.6%) who responded to our survey had formed a personal relationship of some kind there. In fact, respondents typically had initiated five or six new personal respondents as a result of their MOO experience. Participants had acquaintances, colleagues, friends, close friends,

and romantic partners in the on-line world of MOOs. Close friendships were the most frequently reported relationships in this study, followed by romances and friendships.

Developing personal relationships was so common among those who responded to our survey that it was not possible to identify the factors that differentiated people who had started personal relationships on line from those who had not. Indeed the formation of personal relationships on MOOs can be seen as the norm rather than the exception among those who responded to our survey. Nevertheless, our findings may also reflect a bias in who responded to the survey. Randomly selected MOOers who were not involved in MOO relationships may have chosen not to participate in disproportionate numbers.

The majority of on-line relationships reported on in this study were with members of the opposite sex. This was a consistent finding across all ages, types of relationships and irrespective of marital status. This is in direct contrast to "real-life" where same-sex friendships are more common across the life-span (e.g., Booth & Hess, 1974). Nor is our finding an artifact created by the large number of unmarried adolescents and young adults in our sample. Married respondents were as likely to report opposite-sex as same-sex relationships. It may be that cross-sex friendships are increasingly common in Western society, but recent research by Parker and de Vries (1993) found that even among undergraduate students, the "norm of homosociality" continues, with both males and females reporting almost twice as many same-sex as cross-sex friendships.

A more likely explanation is that MOOs break down the structural and normative constraints on cross-sex friendships off line. The structural constraints include the lack of opportunities for men and women to meet and interact on an ongoing basis, and the status differences between men and women in places (such as the workplace) where they do interact (Booth & Hess, 1974). MOOs provide a social environment where men and women can interact on an ongoing basis. Status differentials, such as age, race, education, employment and social class, are not readily apparent and therefore do not inhibit initial contact between MOOers. Off-line cross-sex relationships are normatively constrained by the social disapproval of intimate cross-sex relationships for married individuals (Booth & Hess, 1974). Friends, romantic partners and other associates often challenge cross-sex friendships in off-line settings (e.g., Werking, 1997). The finding that on-line relationships were not well integrated with participants' off-line relationships suggests the reduction or absence of social censure, as friends and family may be unaware of the existence, extent or importance of on-line cross-sex relationships that an individual may have.

MOOs provide users with the perception of a safe environment for social interaction in which individuals can explore all types of relationships without fear of repercussions in their physical lives (Roberts et al., 1996a). MOO cross-sex relationships develop in a setting where the individuals involved have control over the information about themselves (including name, address and phone number) revealed. The text-only nature of MOOs, the physical distance between MOOers, and the anonymity provided by having a MOO character reduce the perception of risk associated with cross-sex relationships in the physical world (e.g., unwanted physical sexual advances and social censure). However, when relationships transfer from virtual environments to off-line settings, the participants risk finding themselves engaged in relationships that they might otherwise avoid. Thus the apparently fertile environment for cross-sex friendships created by MOOs raises both new opportunities and risks for interpersonal relationships.

The high incidence of cross-sex relationships reported in our research is also in contrast to a previous study of relationships initiated in on-line newsgroups in which opposite-sex relationships did not occur significantly more often than same-sex relationships (Parks & Floyd, 1996). The "real-time" give and take of a synchronous channel, along with the greater communicative subtlety possible on MOOs (e.g., the ability to "emote" actions and emotions), may make it easier and more interesting for men and women to engage in dialogue – thus perhaps accounting for the greater proportion of cross-sex relationships in MOOs than in newsgroups.

Relationships initiated on MOOs typically reached moderate to high levels of relational development. MOO relationships were rated significantly above the midpoints of scales measuring interdependence, depth and breadth of interaction, commitment, predictability and understanding, personalized ways of communicating, and the convergence of social networks on line. Our measure of network convergence between on-line and off-line relationships was the only one whose mean fell before the midpoint of the scale. While MOO partners introduced each other to their on-line contacts, they were less likely to introduce each other to their off-line contacts. This may be partially accounted for by geographical distance between MOOers and the difficulty in introducing on-line relational partners to off-line family and friends if the latter do not have Internet access.

We also compared on-line and off-line relationships in terms of their development. The off-line relationships reported were of longer duration and involved more hours of contact than MOO relationships. Although off-line relationships were generally more developed overall, the differences were substantively small on several dimensions. Most important, perhaps, off-line and on-line relationships did not differ in terms of the levels of breadth and depth they achieved. This is consistent with previous findings where MOO relationships were characterized as intense and involving high rates of self-disclosure (Roberts et al., 1996a). It is also consistent with theoretical predictions of "hyperpersonal" effects in computer-mediated communication (Walther, 1996). Finally, given the generally high levels of development in on-line relationships overall, these findings may suggest that the relative ease of disclosure on-line "pulls" perceptions of development in other dimensions. People may be more likely to attribute commitment and understanding to their relationship when they observe (as the screen makes it easy to do) their own and others' high levels of disclosure across a broad range of topics.

Because the Internet contains several distinct types of social settings, we compared the relational dynamics of MOOs with the relational dynamics described in a previous survey of Internet newsgroup users (Parks & Floyd, 1996). These comparisons indicated that MOOs were an even more active breeding ground for personal relationships than were Internet newsgroups. A much higher proportion of MOOers (93.6%) than newsgroup users (60.7%) formed ongoing personal relationships. The median duration of MOO relationships was over twice as long as the median duration of newsgroup relationships. MOO relational partners contacted each other more frequently than newsgroup relational partners. MOO relationships were more developed than newsgroup relationships on all items of the OnLine Relationships Scales. In addition, MOO relationships are more likely than newsgroup relationships to be cross-sex relationships, and more likely to be romantic in nature.

MOOs and newsgroups vary in a number of ways that may account for these differences in findings. Newsgroups have a specific topic (although this may not be adhered to), while the majority of MOOs are social in nature with no set topic for discussion. Communication in newsgroups is asynchronous, while MOOs are synchronous environments offering "real-time" interaction. In addition, MOOs provide an extensible and dynamic social environment in contrast to the static environment provided by newsgroups – the MOOs themselves are continually growing and changing as members create new virtual places and objects. Finally, MOOs provide for rich, multilayered social interaction through the capacity to emote, direct speech and engage in multiple conversations simultaneously. These factors combine to increase the user's experience of telepresence (the experience of "being there" in a virtual environment) and may contribute to the perceived "reality" of interaction between users (Roberts et al., 1996b).

[A large section of the discussion section has been edited out at this point]

The relationships initiated on MOOs, like those initiated in newsgroups, typically "migrated" to other communication channels. Over 90 percent of those who had started a personal relationship on line had used channels in addition to the MOO. Many of these channels were not computer-mediated: letters, card, telephone, etc. Indeed, over a third had met their relational partners face-to-face. Nearly 60 percent of those who had started a romantic relationship on a MOO went on to meet face-to-face. Our analyses also suggested that people were relatively cautious about the shift from mediated to face-to-face contact and that there were some more or less standard ways of managing the transition. The most common was to make use of the telephone and to exchange pictures and obtain both vocal and visual contact with the other before meeting in person for the first time.

The results of this study, combined with those of the previous study of newsgroups, also shatter the image that "cyberspace" and "real-life" are unrelated. The vast majority of relationships formed on MOOs involved the use of additional communication channels. Many ultimately culminated in face-to-face meetings. Some of our respondents noted that their on-line relationships have resulted in engagements, moving in together, and marriages. One respondent confided: "For a year, my 'significant other' and I communicated via the net, then other means – we began to live together after she came here, about 2 months ago – knowing so much more about each other than is normally possible through a conventional relationship."

Parks and Roberts (1998) report moderate to high levels of relationship development for on-line MOOs relationships. The exception was the "networking" criterion where the integration of on-line relationships into participants' off-line worlds was limited and significantly lower compared to other relationships that began in an off-line setting. The authors suggested several potential reasons for the lack of networking to off-line relationships. For example, the Internet spans great geographic distances and it might be impractical to make attempts for off-line integration over great distances. One also could argue that a stigma might be attached to representing these on-line relationships as "real" in their off-line lives and this potential conflict would lead to the lower network scores. It may also be the case that the multiple personas that participants use in the MOOs environment (a median of 4) would make off-line social integration awkward. Given the potential stigma and difficulty of presenting multiple versions of oneself, perhaps a more appropriate analysis of network convergence would involve introductions of MOOs friends to other on-line friends. Parks and Roberts (1998) found a mean net-to-net networking score of 4.22 (out of seven) that was higher than the net-to-off-line networking score of 3.86. This small increase suggests greater social integration net-to-net and may be a more theoretically consistent measure of networking than one which assumes relationship development must move from an on-line environment to an off-line environment (note not off-to-on-line). Why were these values not higher? It is interesting to note that the net-to-net introductions ($M = 4.22$) for relationships that began on-line were less frequent than face-to-face introductions ($M = 6.26$) for relationships that started off-line. Since these values are from the same subjects they may indicate that maintaining multiple personas on-line may inhibit network convergence on-line as compared to real life where these same people may manage a more integrated single persona.

Another difference between this study and the previous study is the sex composition of the relationships reported in MOOs. Remember that Parks and Floyd (1996) found same-sex friendships were equally likely to occur in a newsgroup as were opposite-sex friendships. In the MOOs environment, however, Parks and Roberts (1998) found that opposite-sex relationships dominated the friendship, close friendship and romantic relationship categories. The authors consider many possible explanations for this result; however, one appears to be more likely than the rest: male–female friendships are not broadly accepted in most societies. However, the Internet and the MOOs environment break down structural and normative constraints, permitting users to explore and enjoy these relationships without the worry of social sanction. Although it is possible that fear of social sanction may cause people to resist integrating cross-sex friends into their off-line lives, participants in the Parks and Roberts (1998) study described these relationships as "satisfactory and important" and therefore the participants may have experienced some growth in their self-identity as a result of time spent on-line.

We began this chapter with questions regarding the nature of cyber relationships and whether they hindered or supplemented real-life relationships. The articles presented in this chapter offer the view that Internet participation can have positive benefits for some individuals and these results suggest that cyberspace may provide a continuing resource for relationship study in the coming years. It is also important to consider that the current parameters placed on relationships and relationship development by the Internet are not static and that any benefit (or hindrance) we can identify today may change with the growth of technology and our comfortableness with the medium.

Glossary

Note: Fuller details of any text in **bold type** may be found under its own heading.

95% confidence intervals: The 95% confidence intervals about the mean include all the data that we can reasonably (with 95% confidence) assume are fully representative of the group we are studying.

Absolute value: A numeric value without a plus or minus sign.

Affect: Emotion.

Alpha coefficients: *See* **Cronbach's alpha.**

Analysis of Covariance (ANCOVA): A type of **ANOVA** where the effect of one or more variables is held constant so that the unique effect of the **independent variables** on the **dependent variable** can be determined.

Analysis of Variance (ANOVA): A statistical technique that indicates the amount of change in the behavior of research participants (**dependent variable**) that is due to the variables manipulated or selected by the researcher (**independent variables**). The unique effect of a single independent variable is referred to as the **main effect** of that variable, while the joint or combined effect of two or more independent variables is called an **interaction effect**.

Asynchronous communication: Communication between two or more people where there is a time delay between each response (e.g., leaving written messages for someone left to be read at a later time, emails, and messages on electronic bulletin boards or newsgroups).

Attractors: In chaos theory patterns of stability or patterns toward which phenomena seem to be drawn are called attractors. For instance, the attractor for a bowl of water sitting peacefully on a table is one of calmness. After being disturbed in some fashion (e.g., stirred or rocked), it is drawn to return to calmness, its attractor.

Attribution Theory: A way of assigning causes to the events that happen to oneself and others. Let's say a person finds it hard to get dates. Attributions can be internal/dispositional (e.g., It's just my personality) or external/situational (e.g., I live in a town where everyone is too old or too young to date). Other aspects to consider about attributions are whether they are stable (I'll never get any dates) and how much control we might have in the situation (If I change my behavior I will get dates).

Basis of power: A foundational source of power in relationships. Individuals may have different sources of power and the appropriateness of a given type may be defined by what the society deems appropriate for that sort of person (e.g., physical attractiveness for males versus females).

Best fitting model/goodness of fit using a chi-square: The **chi-square** statistics test how closely the "actual observations" recorded by the researcher match the "expected observations" which are derived from the null hypothesis.

Between-subjects design: Different individuals in a study are assigned to each condition of an experiment (compare and contrast to "**within-subjects design**").

Between-subjects random assignment: *See* **Random assignment of participants/subjects.**

Bifurcation point: The point at which the previously stable phase becomes unstable and the system shifts to another phase is called a bifurcation point (marks changes in a pattern of behavior).

Bonferroni *p* correction: When multiple statistical tests are performed on a single data set, the probability value used for significance should be lower than .05, making it more difficult to claim that any one hypothesis is supported. The Bonferroni *p* correction is a commonly accepted method that takes into account the total number of statistical tests to be performed on a data set and adjusts the value based on this number.

Butterfly effect: Seemingly insignificant changes that occur at one point in time can result in significant differences in behavior patterns later.

Capitalizing on chance: Repeated tests on a single data set will eventually produce a significant effect, but the effect may be due to chance. For example, with $p = .05$, five times out of 100 we will get a significant effect but it will be due to chance. Therefore, the number of all significance tests (e.g., *t*-test, ANOVAs, correlations) performed on a single data set should be considered when determining whether a research study has fallen prey to this problem (see **Bonferroni *p* correction**).

Categorical scale: A rating scale where participants use discrete or dichotomous alternatives when responding to questions (e.g., My spouse is a demanding person, Yes or No?). *See also* **Continuous scale**.

Causal relationships/direction of causality: Due to the use of appropriate controls an experiment can tell us that one thing/variable (A) causes a second thing/variable (B) to change and not the other way around.

Chi-square and other related statistics: A set of statistics that allow a researcher to test a hypothesis or assess the degree of association between two variables using **nominal data** (e.g., yes/no, presence/absence).

Classical conditioning: A procedure where an individual will begin to make a reflex response to a neutral stimulus simply because it has occurred at roughly the same time as another stimulus that previously had produced the reflex response. *See also* **conditioned response** and **conditioned stimulus**.

Closed-ended questions: Survey or interview questions that have predetermined answers such as "Yes", "No", "Five" or "I did". An example of closed-ended questions is **Confirmatory factor analysis**. *See also* **Exploratory factor analysis**.

Cluster analysis: A statistical technique that groups things based on common or shared characteristics. Initial steps in the analysis may organize items into a cluster based upon single characteristics while later steps attempt to organize the initial clusters into a hierarchy based upon shared features.

Cohen's kappa: A measure of the agreement between coders. This technique essentially assesses the extent to which coders of the same data reach the same conclusions about the manner in which it should be classified. A high kappa indicates good solid agreement between different coders. *Also see* **inter-rater agreement/reliability**.

Cohort effect: An apparent age difference is confounded with the shared social experiences among people, a cohort, who were born at about the same time. This is a particular problem in **cross-sectional designs**.

Comparison level (CL): Part of **exchange theory** that represents the expectation a person has for an acceptable balance of rewards and costs.

Comparison level for alternatives (CL$_{alt}$): Part of **exchange theory** that represents the belief a person has that a different relationship might lead to better outcomes.

Conditioned response: A reflex response to the **conditioned stimulus** without the presence of the **unconditioned stimulus** (e.g., salivation to a bell without the presence of food powder).

Conditioned stimulus: A stimulus that previously did not produce a reflex response but does so later after being repeatedly paired close together in time with an **unconditioned stimulus** (e.g., bell paired with food powder).

Confirmatory factor analysis: A special kind of **factor analysis** where the investigator has working ideas about the structure of the data and sets out to confirm that these hypotheses are good representations.

Conflict-habituated ties: Relationships where people are quite used to conflict, such that a particular occasion of it does not disturb them terribly much.

Construct validity: The degree a test or scale measures what it purports to measure. For example, a basic math test should contain questions that representatively sample the domain of skills required to do basic math and should not contain those that do not fit this domain (for example, it should not measure athletic skill).

Continuous scale: A rating scale where participants use a numeric continuum when responding to questions (e.g., How demanding was the spouse on a five-point scale?). *See also* **Categorical scale**.

Control parameters: Thresholds in a dynamic system that may promote change in the system when crossed (e.g., Gottman's 5-to-1 negativity/positivity ratio).

Controlling for the effects of [a variable]: The scientific method of taking a situation and holding everything constant except one thing, the thing you are interested in testing.

Convenience sample: A group of research participants that are selected based upon their convenient availability to the researcher even if they may not be representative of any larger population.

Convergent validity: Assesses whether a measure is valid because it is associated with another measure of the same construct (for example, a measure of "people I like" should be associated with a person's choices of "close intimate network members").

Correlational study/correlational relationship/*r*-scores: An assessment of the strength of association between two things/variables, represented by the letter 'r' (e.g., $r = 0.86$). Caution must be used when interpreting a correlation because even with a very strong correlation there is no sure way of determining which of two variables (X, Y) causes the other to change.

Counterbalanced design: Half of the research participants are asked question A and then question B, whereas the other half are asked in the order B – A. This procedure is intended to balance or control for any effects of the order in which questions are asked.

Covariance: Two variables are associated in such a way that as one changes the other changes in some predictable fashion.

Cronbach's alpha coefficients/scores: Measures of consistency and agreement between the different subscales of an overall measure. The higher the Cronbach's alpha (α), the more the subscales can be relied upon as measuring the same central underlying concept.

Cross-sectional designs/studies: The researcher picks different populations to represent the groups that the researcher wishes to compare. A researcher might select a sample of 20-year-olds and a sample of 40-year-olds and compare their answers, making the assumption that any differences found in the data are due to the effects of age. A weakness of this design is that any differences found between groups cannot be certainly attributed to age differences, as opposed to **cohort effects**.

Degrees of freedom *df*: At times df is described as the functional number of subjects involved in a statistical analysis and is calculated as the sample size minus 1 ($N - 1$). In **ANOVA**, df are calculated for each **main effect** and **interaction effect** and involve different calculations to determine their exact number.

Demand/withdrawal pattern: Distressed couples often display a demand/withdrawal communication pattern that hinders the ability of the couple to resolve conflicts effectively (e.g., Wife demands a change but husband withdraws from interaction and so avoids further discussion).

Dendrogram: A dendrogram (Greek: "Written as a tree") depicts the relationships between the clusters created during a cluster analysis as the branches of a tree.

Dependent variable: Some aspect of the research participant's thoughts, feelings or behavior expected to change as a result of an experimenter's manipulation of an **independent variable**.

Deterministic change: Predictable change in a system. This type of change is possible if one understands the key factors influencing variability in the system.

Directional (hypothesis): Refers to the ability of a hypothesis to indicate which of a number of groups will exceed or outperform others on some attribute measured in a research study.

Discriminant validity: Indicates whether a measure is not highly associated with something that it shouldn't highly predict (for example, a measure of teenage tobacco use might be tainted if it correlates too highly with a measure of "school problems" and so fails to differentiate other social problems from tobacco use).

Distal causes: An ultimate cause of a behavior that must be inferred through other variables. In evolutionary theory this would be the original environmental conditions that a particular trait is effective at overcoming and results in this trait being more available in the genetic pool of a species because these individuals survive. For example, children act aggressively at their preschool because they are born with a predisposition to act aggressively. The predisposition exists because our genetic ancestors who were aggressive survived long enough to pass their genes into future generations (including the tendency to be aggressive). *See also* **Proximal causes**.

Effect: As a verb it means "to cause" or, as a noun, it means "a consequence".

Effect size: The size of an effect refers to the proportion of the **variance** (variability) in the **dependent variable** attributable to an independent or predictor variable. For example, if the value of a correlation was .52, squaring the correlation will yield a measure of effect size (.27 or 27% of the variability).

Eta (η): A measure of the relationship between an **independent variable** and a **dependent variable** and is useful in describing how much of the dependent variable can be explained by the independent variables when it is squared (η^2). Eta is used most often in conjunction with **ANOVA** to determine the effect size of an independent variable; however, it is basically identical to R^2 in this context (Hayes, 1988).

Evolutionary psychology: An approach to explaining behavior that employs and expands upon the basic tenets of Darwin's theory of evolution. For example, it is believed a main goal of human existence is maximizing one's reproductive fitness (i.e., evolutionary success in passing on one's genes) and that this non-conscious process has shaped somewhat different romantic strategies for women and men.

Exchange theory/interdependence theory: Based on the economics of reciprocity, the basic assumption is that people in relationships seek to maximize their rewards and minimize their costs. This ratio is evaluated in light of the ratios in other known relationships and the probability of forming a relationship with a new partner. Predictions about relationship satisfaction can be made from theory.

Experiential Gestalt: A wholeness of a sensation or experience that is difficult to pick apart and analyze in its parts. For example, we experience a general experiential Gestalt of being in love, when we feel good, but sometimes sad, and know that the other person is the source of this general sense of pleasure and fulfillment, and occasionally also of sadness.

Exploratory factor analysis: A special kind of **factor analysis** where the researcher has no particular assumptions about how things will fall out and is simply exploring the data to see if a structure will emerge. *See also* **Confirmatory factor analysis**.

External validity: An experimental study is said to have external validity if the procedures adopted in the experiment accurately represent the phenomena in the real world that they intend to represent. *See also* **Internal validity**.

Face management: Adopting an appearance or "face" that we are nice people rather than openly and honestly declaring all our deeply held attitudes about controversial topics.

Factor analysis: A statistical technique that takes the different scores that people produce to different items on a test and looks for underlying patterns that can be attributed to specific factors. For example if you score highly on "I like to punch people", "I am often angry", "I take offence easily", "If someone insults me then I usually hit them", then an investigator might find that all of these scores are explained by the same underlying factor, say, Belligerence.

Factor loadings of an item: These are numeric values that are a statistical indication of the extent to which a particular item ("I like to punch people", say) is a good fit with an underlying factor of Belligerence. The higher the loading, the greater the parallelism between the item and factor as a whole.

Factor score: A numeric value that represents how much of a certain underlying trait they possess (identified by a **factor analysis**).

Field of availables: All those people who are available as a possible date or romantic partner (i.e., irrespective of age or anything else, all those people who are "out there" as potential partners).

Field of desirables: Those people whom the person actually desires as a partner.

Field of eligibles: All those people whom a person regards as eligible as a partner (by reason of age, social class, religion, or whatever other criteria the person regards as necessary to be met before any kind of partnership would be sought).

Goodness-of-fit: This is a technique that is used to test whether a sample of data came from a population with a specific hypothesized distribution or, in other words, how well the data fit a particular hypothesis about how it should really look in an ideal world. The general procedure consists of statistically measuring the distance between the hypothesis and the data and then calculating the probability of obtaining data that have a still larger value than the value observed, assuming the hypothesis is true.

Hierarchical cluster analysis: A form of **cluster analysis** that attempts to discover a hierarchy of relatedness among more basic clusters of items identified in earlier analyses.

Hierarchical log-linear logit models: A sophisticated type of regression analysis that uses **nominal data** and is able to examine complex relationships between more than two variables at a time.

Hierarchical regression equation: The order of the **predictor variables** ($X_1 \ldots n$) to be entered into the **multiple regression analyses** (as determined by the researcher).

Hypothesis: A research question that specifies an expected outcome derived from theory or previous research findings.

Hysteresis: Although there are several meanings for this term (e.g., magnetic fields, metallurgy), in the context of personal relationships it refers to the fact that it takes time for the effects of a given cause to be felt. For example, a politician attempting to "kick start" an ailing economy may adopt a policy that does not begin to have its desired effect for many months.

Independent variable: A variable that is manipulated in some fashion by an experimenter with the expectation that the manipulations will cause a predictable change in the research participants' thoughts, feelings, or behavior.

Inductive analysis: A qualitative research technique which involves reading data (e.g., responses to **open-ended questions**) and sorting it into groups so that tentative categories can be set up. Subsequently the validity and usefulness of these first tentative categories are tested against other elements of the data and adjusted as necessary until a category system remains that can satisfactorily incorporate and explain all the data.

Interaction effects (two-way): The joint or combined effect of two **independent variables** on a **dependent variable**. Higher-order interactions are possible by combining more than two independent variables (e.g., three-way interaction).

Interdependence theory: *See* **Exchange theory**.

Internal validity: A research study is said to be internally valid if it is free of confounding factors or employs procedural controls that allow the researcher to rule out alternative explanations for the results of the study (cf. **external validity**).

Inter-rater agreement/reliability: When ratings or interpretations of participants' behavior are subjective, researchers will often have two trained judges rate or evaluate the data independently using a set of scoring criteria. The amount of agreement between judges should be high and is usually reported as the percentage of agreement or a correlation between the judges' ratings.

Introspective units (RCCUs): Behaviors and symbols that reflect the presence of commitment to the relationship during the time period two partners are apart.

Lack of variability: Most statistical analyses presuppose that a set of scores will have a moderate amount of variation around its mean, roughly reflecting a **normal distribution**. Therefore, when a statistic is used on a set of data that has a small amount of variance around its mean (for any of a number of reasons) this violates the assumption that the statistic is based upon and the analysis will produce inaccurate results.

Likert scales: These scales are 1 to *N* (usually 1–7 or 1–5) report scales where a person is presented with a range of possible answers (e.g., Very much agree, Agree, Unsure, Disagree, Very much disagree). The scales are usually numbered rather than given as words, or the words may be translated into numbers (e.g., 1 could be assigned to "Very much agree" and 5 would be assigned to "Very much disagree").

Log-linear analysis: *See* **Hierarchical log-linear logit models**.

Main effect: The effect of a single independent variable on a single dependent variable (see **ANOVA**).

MANOVA (Multivariate Analysis of Variance): Similar to **ANOVA** but the variables may be related or correlated. In ANOVA it is assumed that variables are independent from one another.

Mean: The average of a set of scores calculated by taking the sum of the values and dividing by the total number of scores.

Measurement error: Variation in the data set that has nothing to do with the underlying variables you are observing; instead it is merely an *appearance* of variety that is solely created by errors in recording the observations (e.g., wrong data recorded or incorrectly written down, wrong thing observed).

Metaphors: Oftentimes we will use expressions that contain a high degree of imagery to help us think about or describe things that are really difficult for us to understand. For example, love might be described metaphorically as "a burning fire", not because it is an accurate description but because it is useful to help us think about the intense and dynamic nature of love.

MOOs (Multi-User Dimensions, Object-Orientated): A computer social world that allows synchronous (real-time) text-based discussion over the internet. The participants create a social world/environment with its own unique rules/norms that govern the form and type of social interaction. Norms may be loose or strict as decided by the users. Participants create an on-line character that may or may not accurately represent their real self.

MUDs (Multi-User Dimensions or Dungeons): A computer social world (similar to a **MOO**) that tends to be competitive and involve role-playing games.

Multidimensional scaling (MDS) analysis: This statistical method captures the way people organize items or events and tries to describe the organization using the fewest number of dimensions. The data collection procedure is simple (but the statistical analysis is not); subjects are asked to say how different or similar the items are in a set of things. For example, if the question involved a set of twenty universities, people might be asked "Is the University of Iowa more similar to the University of Minnesota or to Cornell University?" Participants would complete an exhaustive list of comparisons and the statistical analysis would reveal the participants' underlying organization using the fewest number of factors or dimensions possible (e.g., two).

Multiple optimal regression: A form of multiple regression used when the variables do not conform to the assumption of either an increasing or decreasing linear function. *See also* **Multiple regression analysis**.

Multiple regression analysis: A statistical analysis that allows a researcher to examine the unique impact of multiple **independent variables** ($X_1 \ldots n$) on a single **dependent variable** (Y). The analysis produces **regression weights** for each variable so that one can predict the person's score (Y) if the values of X are known.

Negative face: Negative face refers to people's desires to be seen as autonomous individuals with the ability to exercise free choice and not to be imposed upon or taken for granted. *See also* **Positive face**.

Negative predictor: In a **regression analysis** when a **regression weight** has a negative value for a **predictor/independent variable**, the value of the predictor score increases as the value of the dependent variable decreases (e.g., as the amount of self-disclosure increases, the amount of uncertainty in a relationship decreases).

Nominal data: Data in the form of categories that are not ordered or numbered in any way. For example, sex is a nominal variable and people are "male" or "female".

Normal distribution: A statistical term that describes the way in which scores for many variables are to be found in the real world, usually graphed as a bell-shaped curve. It indicates that there are about as many scores above the mean as below it, and that the mean score is the most common, with extreme scores being rare. "Height" is normally distributed in a population, since most people are about average height and both giants and dwarves are rare. "Age at death" is not normally distributed (since the likelihood of death progressively increases with increasing age).

Open-ended questions: Survey or interview questions that do not have a predetermined answer and therefore allow the research participant to create a unique answer (e.g., "How do you maintain a relationship?", "What was going through your mind at that point?").

Operational definition/operationalized: Taking a theoretical variable and creating a way to actually measure or manipulate the variable in research study. This operationalized variable that is used in a study may or may not completely embody all aspects of the theoretical concept and therefore could be deficient in some way.

***p* < 0.05 level**: A shorthand way of saying the results of a study would have happened less than five times out of 100 times by pure chance (the results have a chance probability of less than 0.05, which is 5/100). This probability level is regarded as sufficient grounds for believing the hypothesis has been supported in many scientific disciplines.

Pair-wise comparisons: When *t*-test comparisons are made between scores on two different measures from the same subjects they are called pair-wise comparisons or matched sample *t*-tests.

Parameter estimates: Numeric values produced by a statistical analysis that reflect the relationship between a dependent variable and a set of independent variables.

Partial correlations: A researcher will employ a partial correlation procedure when a third variable (*Z*) is correlated with both variables of interest (*X* and *Y*) and prevents clear assessment of the association between *X* and *Y*. Therefore, the partial correlation procedure produces a measure of the association between *X* and *Y* without the influence of *Z*.

PDR (post-dissolution relationships): A romantic relationship that has come to an end and has reverted back to a friendship.

Pearson correlations: *See* **Correlational study**.

Phase shift: The process by which a system changes from one steady state to a different state because it is unable to resist the pressure.

Positive face: Positive face refers to people's needs to be seen as the kind of person they "claim" to be in an interaction and to have the attributes that they value in themselves appreciated and approved by their audience (for example, being treated as being polite and nice).

Potentially reactive nature: *See* **Reactive**.

Predictor variables: The variables that have a predictable effect on a dependent variable.

Principal components analysis: A statistical procedure that seeks a deeper structure in a data set and is based on an analysis similar to **factor analysis**, and is drawn from a variety of different measures that all indicate one single underlying factor or component. Although similar to **cluster analysis**, the purpose of this analysis is not necessarily to link clusters in a hierarchical tree with a super-cluster at the top; it is to find those things that go together into classes that are separable from other classes found in the data. For example, loose change and writing instruments are separate classes of data but not hierarchically related to one another.

Principle of least interest: The partner who contributes the least resources has the greater power in a relationship.

Probability: Used to assess how likely it is that the results of a study would happen just by pure coincidence or else because of predicted variables. A significant result is one that happens very rarely just by chance alone. For example, if a result would be expected only five times in a 100 by pure chance, then you might be persuaded that the study has supported its prediction.

Prospective units (RCCUs): Behaviors and statements made before a separation that establish the duration of the absence and when the couple will be reunited.

Proximal causes: An explanation that may be directly assessed in the current environment. For example, a child strikes another child to get a toy because he/she saw violence was effective for another child. *See also* **Distal causes**.

Random assignment of participants/subjects: In a **between-subjects** experimental design participants receive only one level of an **independent variable**. Any such procedure of assigning participants must be a random procedure to minimize potential systematic biases in the data.

Random change: A system changes unpredictably regardless of how much we know about the factors involved in the system, no matter how much we know about the initial conditions.

Randomly selected (sample): Use of procedures that employ chance in selecting participants for a study, thereby eliminating any systematic bias in the selection process.

Reactive: When research participants are made keenly aware that their responses or behavior are being assessed by a researcher, the data collection procedure can be said to be reactive. Reactivity may lead participants to respond to questions or situations in ways that are unrepresentative of their normal behavior.

Regression analysis (stepwise): A statistical technique that looks at the overall results and tries to see if a better explanation of them is provided by temporarily ignoring one of the variables or "controlling for" its effects.

Regression to the mean: If the survey is not 100% reliable then the scores of an extreme group (e.g., a highly lonely group) will change/regress toward the mean (middle) of the distribution (reflecting less loneliness) if they are tested at a later date.

Regression weight/beta weight: A positive or negative value produced for each **predictor/independent variable** in a **regression analysis**. Beta weights can be used to predict future outcomes. For example, if a person's score was known for each predictor variable (X_1 … n) then one could use these scores (along with the beta weights) to predict their score on the **dependent variable** (e.g., High School GPA, scores on college entrance exams used to predict college GPA).

Relational Continuity Constructional Units (RCCUs): Behaviors that partners exhibit during an absence to maintain stability in the relationship.

Relational maintenance: Any behaviors performed by couples to keep their relationship in a steady or stable state.

Reliability: *See* **Cronbach's alpha.**

Repeated measures design: A research study where participants complete the same measure at least twice.

Repeated measures MANCOVA (Multivariate Analysis of Covariance): Analysis of several related variables at once, some of which had been assessed more than once.

Representative (sample): A non-systematic way of selecting participants for a research study. There are several methods to achieve the desired representativeness in a sample (*see* **random sample**).

Research Question (RQ): A general research question that does not contain a specific prediction about the anticipated outcome.

Resource-based dependency: Dependency of one partner on another because the other person is providing a desirable resources one needs (e.g., money).

Retrospective accounts: A research method where participants report on something that happened to them some time ago.

Retrospective longitudinal designs/studies: In a retrospective study, one population is studied looking back over a period of time. This is usually accomplished by means of asking participants to reminisce or recall specific events that are of interest to the researcher. A weakness of a retrospective technique is the risk of participants falsely remembering their feelings such a long time ago, so that any reports they give are either systematically biased or unsystematically biased toward the person's current opinion.

Retrospective units (RCCUs): Behaviors and statements made following the separation of a couple that serve to re-establish the stability of the relationship.

Reverse coding: A survey technique where some questions require participants to alter the scale they are using to complete the survey in an effort to maintain a high degree of attention and involvement while completing the research instrument. For example, a "shyness scale" might have some questions where a Yes or strongly agree response indicates a high degree of shyness while other questions are worded in such a way that Yes or strongly agree indicates boldness in social situations. This technique is particularly useful with long surveys.

Root metaphors: Hidden threads to the metaphors that we tend to use about relationships, mostly to do with work, journeys of discovery or irresistible forces. These basic underlying organizing threads provide specific frameworks for metaphors.

Sample: The group of people used in a research study believed to be representative of a larger population.

Schema: A constellation of factual information and personal memories about an individual or thing. Schemata shape our accesses to stored memories and new experiences. For example, information stored in our general schema for police officers affects how we approach and interact with a specific police officer.

Self-selection bias: A group of research participants that are not randomly selected may actually share a systematic bias or characteristic that leads them to respond in ways that are similar in an experimental situation, but their data are unrepresentative of a larger population. For example, if all the participants in a study on pain were volunteers (self-selected) they may share an attraction to or tolerance of pain that is unrepresentative of the attitudes of the general population.

Semantic Differential Scale: A means of measuring the underlying meaning of a topic, idea or object to a person. It consists of a number of bi-polar scales (such as good–bad, pleasant–unpleasant, etc.) on which the person can rate a topic.

Sexual script theory: An extension of social learning theory used to explain patterns of sexual behavior. Men who follow traditional scripts are socialized to desire and engage in frequent casual sexual activity with multiple partners, whereas women are encouraged to limit their sexual experiences to encounters within committed, monogamous relationships (Sprecher et al., 1997).

Shared variance: The degree two or more predictor variables overlap and explain the same effect in a dependent variable (difficult to determine the unique contribution of each variable).

Small-world procedure (reversed): Asks research participants to identify network members who can serve as messengers to people outside their immediate network of information to people outside the respondent's network of confidants.

Social Context Theories: An approach to explaining behavior that relies on the social environment around individuals to provide cues about manner and content of their behaviors and verbal responses (e.g., social roles or scripts).

Social Learning Theory: An approach to explaining behavior that is based on the principles of operant conditioning and the presence and absence of rewards. For example, it is believed that aggressive behavior in adults occurs because individuals have been rewarded for similar behavior in the past and/or individuals have observed others being rewarded for such behavior.

Social Penetration Theory: Usually thought of in the context of self-disclosure, the theory assumes that people will become more self-revealing over time with another individual if the relationship starts with a mutual sharing of a variety of superficial topics and gradually moves to sharing more intimate information.

Social Presence Theory: People receive and send messages in a social interaction as a function of how involved they feel in the communication process. It is assumed that face-to-face interactions would have greater social presence than computer/text-based interactions.

Socially desirable responses: Answering questions in a way that makes an individual look good rather than being otherwise honest answers: their answers are ones that are socially preferred, even "politically correct".

Standard deviation: A measure of how widely a set of scores are scattered around its **mean**. A larger number indicates a greater amount of scatter.

Standardized values: *See Z-values/scores*.

Stochastic change: Predictions about change in the short term are possible; it is more difficult to make long-term predictions.

Stratified random sample: A sample that is selected randomly with the exception that the investigator makes sure that a particularly desired feature is present in the sample. For example, if you want to make sure that you have equal numbers of men and women (say, 50 of each) then you carry out the sampling entirely randomly until one group, say the women, reaches a total of 50 and from that point on you sample randomly only men (i.e., you sample men, randomly, rather than the whole population randomly) until you end up with 50 men as well. The result is a stratified random sample, stratified, in this case, by sex.

Survey research methods: Any of a number of designs that employ questionnaires or other types of self-report instruments to collect data from research participants.

Synchronous communication: Communication between two or more people that occurs in real time (e.g., face-to-face interactions, in a chat room, AOL Instant Messenger). *See also* **Asynchronous communication**.

t-test/paired t-test: The *t*-test, of which the paired *t*-test is one form, essentially measures the amount of difference that is found between the means of scores derived from two samples. In the paired *t*-test the "two samples" are data from two separate groups that are, in theory, "matched" in some way (for example, we might measure men's and women's performance on the same test). In other forms of the *t*-test, the "two samples" are scores from the same person under two separate sets of conditions.

Tenor and vehicle: **Metaphors** involve a tenor and a vehicle: when we suffer the slings and arrows of outrageous fortune or fall in love, the tenor is the thing cited (slings, arrows, falling) and the vehicle is the associated metaphorical image (slings and arrows are weapons of assault; falling occurs when we lose control of ourselves).

Test–retest reliability: A scale or measure is given at two different times to the same group of people and the consistency of their responses is assessed using a correlational analysis.

Unconditioned response: A reflex response (e.g., salivation).

Unconditioned stimulus: An environmental event that always produces a particular reflexive response (e.g., food powder produces salivation).

Variables: An attribute, characteristic, behavior, property or quality measured or manipulated in a research study.

Variance: The natural tendency of any set of scores to vary when measured across people. The researcher's job is to determine how much of the variance is due to chance or "error" and how much the change is because of something more interesting, such as a variable manipulated by researcher.

Percent of variance accounted for: A measure of how well an independent variable can predict/explain changes/variability in the dependent variable.

Varimax rotation: A technical statistical technique (part of a **principal components analysis**) that is used to simplify the data matrix by identifying similarities and interconnections between factors and separating out the ways in which they are intertwined.

Weak ties: Connections to others in our social network that are not based on close intimacy but which are nevertheless important influences on our lives.

Within-subjects design: Each person in a study is exposed to two or more experimental conditions during the experiment (compare to **between-subjects design**).

Z-values/scores: Z-scores are standardized in such a way that the original scores are converted and mapped onto a **normal distribution**. Once this is done, those scores having absolute values greater than 1.96 indicate significant deviation from the mean, at the 0.05 level.

References

Note: Internet addresses for the materials below may change without notification

Acitelli, L.K. (1988). When spouses talk to each other about their relationship. *Journal of Social and Personal Relationships, 5*, 185–99.

Acitelli, L.K. (1992). Sex differences in relationship awareness and marital satisfaction among young married couples. *Personality and Social Psychology Bulletin, 18*, 102–10.

Acitelli, L.K., & Antonucci, T.C. (1990, November). Reciprocity of social support in older married couples. Paper presented to the 43rd Annual Convention of the Gerontological Society of America, Boston, MA.

Acitelli, L.K., Douvan, E., & Veroff, J. (1997). The changing influence of interpersonal perceptions on marital well-being among black and white couples. *Journal of Social and Personal Relationships, 14*, 291–304.

Acker, M., & Davis, M. (1992). Intimacy, passion, and commitment in adult romantic relationships: a test of the triangular theory of love. *Journal of Social and Personal Relationships, 9*, 21–50.

Adams, R., & Allan, G. (Eds.) (1998). *Placing friendship in context*. Cambridge, UK: Cambridge University Press.

Ahrons, C.R., & Wallisch, L.S. (1987). The relationship between former spouses. In D. Perlman & S.W. Duck (Eds.), *Intimate relationships: development, dynamics, and deterioration*. Beverly Hills: Sage.

Ainsworth, M.D.S., Blehar, M.C., Waters, E., & Wall, S. (1978). *Patterns of attachment*. Hillsdale, NJ: Erlbaum.

Aldendenfer, M., & Blashfield, R. (1984). *Cluster analysis*. Newbury Park, CA: Sage.

Allan, G. (1979). *A sociology of friendship and kinship*. London: Allen & Unwin.

Allan, G. (1989). *Friendship: developing sociological perspectives*. Hemel Hempstead, UK: Harvester Wheatsheaf.

Allan, G., & Crow, G. (1991). Privatization, home-centredness and leisure. *Leisure Studies, 10*, 19–32.

Allan, G., & Crow, G. (1999). *Families, households and society*. London: Macmillan.

Allen, A., & Thompson, T. (1984). Agreement, understanding, realization, and feeling understood as predictors of communicative satisfaction in marital dyads. *Journal of Marriage and the Family, 46*, 915–21.

Allgeier, A.R., Byrne, D., Brooks, B., & Revnes, D. (1979). The waffle phenomenon: negative evaluation of those who shift attitudinally. *Journal of Applied Social Psychology, 9*, 170–82.

Altman, I., Vinsel, A., & Brown, B. (1981). Dialectic conceptions in social psychology: an application to social penetration and privacy regulation. In L. Berkowitz (Ed.), *Advances in Experimental Social Psychology: Vol. 14*. London & New York: Academic Press.

Altman, I., & Taylor, D.A. (1973). *Social penetration: the development of interpersonal relationships*. New York: Holt, Rinehart & Winston.

Argyle, M. (1980). Interaction skills and social competence. In P. Feldman and J. Orford (Eds.), *Psychological problems: the social context*. New York: Wiley.

Aron, A., & Aron, E.N. (1991). Love and sexuality. In K. McKinney & S. Sprecher (Eds.), *Sexuality in close relationships* (pp. 25–48). Hillsdale, NJ: Erlbaum.

Aron, A., Dutton, D.G., Aron, E.N., & Iverson, A. (1989). Experiences of falling in love. *Journal of Social and Personal Relationships*, *6*, 243–57.

Aronson, E., & Worchel, P. (1966). Similarity versus liking as determinants of interpersonal attractiveness. *Psychonomic Science*, *5*, 157–8.

Ayres, J. (1983). Strategies to maintain relationships: their identification and perceived usage. *Communication Quarterly*, *3*, 62–7.

Baker, G.L., & Gollub, J.P. (1990). *Chaotic dynamics: an introduction*. Cambridge. MA: Cambridge University Press.

Baker, R.R., & Bellis, M.A. (1995). *Sperm competition: copulation, masturbation, and infidelity*. London: Chapman & Hall.

Banks, S.P., Altendorf, S.M., Greene, J.O., & Cody, M.J. (1987). An examination of relationship disengagement: perceptions, breakup strategies and outcomes. *Western Journal of Speech Communication*, *51*, 19–41.

Barnes, J.A. (1954). Class and committees in a Norwegian island parish. *Human Relations*, *7*, 39–58.

Baron, R.M., Amazeen, P.G., & Beck, P.J. (1994). Local and global dynamics of social relations. In R.R. Vallacher & A. Nowak (Eds.), *Dynamical systems in social psychology* (pp. 111–38). San Diego, CA: Academic Press.

Barrera, J.M. (1981). Social support in the adjustment of pregnant adolescents. In B.H. Gottleib (Ed.), *Social networks and social support* (pp. 69–96). Newbury Park, CA: Sage.

Bartholomew, K. (1990). Avoidance of intimacy: an attachment perspective. *Journal of Social and Personal Relationships*, *7*, 147–78.

Bartholomew, K., & Horowitz, L.M. (1991). Attachment styles among young adults: a test of a four category model. *Journal of Personality and Social Psychology*, *61*, 226–44.

Barton, S. (1994). Chaos, self-organization, and psychology. *American Psychologist*, *49*, 5–14.

Baucom, D.H., & Epstein, N. (1989). The role of cognitive variables in the assessment and treatment of marital discord. In M. Hersen & R.M. Eisler (Eds.), *Progress in behavior modification* (pp. 223–51). Thousand Oaks, CA: Sage.

Baumeister, R.F., & Leary, M.R. (1995). The need to belong: desire for interpersonal attachments as a fundamental human motivation. *Psychological Bulletin*, *117*, 497–529.

Baxter, L.A. (1979a). Self-disclosure as a relationship disengagement strategy: an exploratory investigation. *Human Communication Research*, *5*, 215–22.

Baxter, L.A. (1979b). Self-reported disengagement strategies in friendship relationships. Paper presented to the WSCA Convention.

Baxter, L.A. (1982). Strategies for ending relationships: two studies. *Western Journal of Speech Communication*, *46*, 233–42.

Baxter, L.A. (1983). Relationship disengagement: an examination of the reversal hypothesis. *Western Journal of Speech Communication*, *47*, 85–9.

Baxter, L.A. (1985). Accomplishing relationship disengagement. In S.W. Duck & D. Perlman (Eds.), *Understanding personal relationships*. London: Sage.

Baxter, L.A. (1986). Sex differences in the heterosexual relationship rules embedded in breakup accounts. *Journal of Social and Personal Relationships*, *3*, 289–306.

Baxter, L.A. (1987). Cognition and communication in the relationship process. In R. Burnett, P. McGhee & D. Dark (Eds.), *Accounting for relationships*: *explanation, representation and knowledge*. London: Methuen.

Baxter, L.A. (1994). A dialogic approach to relationship maintenance. In D.J. Canary & L. Stafford (Eds.), *Communication and relational maintenance* (pp. 233–54). San Diego, CA: Academic Press.

Baxter, L.A., & Bullis, C. (1986). Turning points in developing romantic relationships. *Human Communication Research*, *12*, 469–93.

Baxter, L.A., & Dindia, K. (1990). Marital partners' perceptions of marital maintenance strategies. *Journal of Social and Personal Relationships*, *7*, 187–208.

Baxter, L.A., & Montgomery, B.M. (1997). Rethinking communication in personal relationships from a dialectic perspective. In S. Duck (Ed.), *Handbook of personal relationships* (2nd edn, pp. 325–49). New York: Wiley.

Baxter, L.A., & Philpott, J. (1980, November). Relationship disengagement: a process view. Paper presented at the SCA Convention, Chicago.

Baxter, L.A., & Philpott, J. (1982). Attribution-based strategies for initiating and terminating relationships. *Communication Quarterly, 30*, 217–24.

Baxter, L.A., & Wilmot, W. (1982, July). A longitudinal study of communication in same-sex and opposite-sex relationships. Paper presented at the First International Conference on Personal Relationships, Madison.

Baxter, L.A., & Wilmot, W. (1985). Interaction characteristics of disengaging, stable, and growing relationships. In R. Gilmour & S.W. Duck (Eds.), *The emerging field of personal relationships*. Hillsdale, NJ: Erlbaum.

Beck, A.T., & Young, J.E. (1978). College blues. *Psychology Today, 12*, 80–97.

Beck, U. (1992). *Risk society: towards a new modernity*. London: Sage.

Bell, R.A., & Healey, J.G. (1992). Idiomatic communication and interpersonal solidarity in friends' relational cultures. *Human Communication Research, 18*, 307–35.

Belsky, J., & Kelly, J. (1994). *The transition to parenthood: how a first child changes a marriage*. London: Vermilion.

Beninger, J.R. (1987). Personalization of mass media and the growth of pseudo-community. *Communication Research, 14*, 352–71.

Bentler, P.M. (1989). *EQS: structural equations program manual*. Los Angeles, CA: BMDP Statistical Software.

Berger, C.R. (1988). Uncertainty and information exchange in developing relationships. In S.W. Duck (Ed.), *Handbook of personal relationships* (pp. 239–55). London: Wiley.

Berger, C.R., & Calabrese, R.J. (1975). Some explorations in initial interaction and beyond: toward a developmental theory of interpersonal communication. *Human Communication Research, 1*, 99–112.

Berger, P., & Kellner. H. (1964). Marriage and the construction of social reality. *Diogenes, 46*, 1–24.

Berlyne, D.E. (1963). Motivation problems raised by exploratory and epistemic behavior. In S. Koch (Ed.), *Psychology: a study of science, Vol. 5*. New York: McGraw-Hill.

Bernard, H.R., Johnsen, E.G., Killworth, P.D., McCarty, C., Shelley, G.A. & Robinson, S. (1990). Comparing four different methods for measuring personal social networks. *Social Networks, 12*, 179–215.

Bernard, J. (1972). *The future of marriage*. New York: Bantam.

Bernard, J. (1981). *The female world*. New York: Free Press.

Berscheid, E. (1986). Mea culpas and lamentations: Sir Francis, Sir Isaac and the "slow progress of soft psychology". In R. Gilmore & S.W. Duck (Eds.), *The emerging field of personal relationships* (pp. 267–86). Hillsdale, NJ: Erlbaum.

Berscheid, E., & Fei, J. (1977). Romantic love and jealousy. In G. Clanton & L.G. Smith (Eds.), *Jealousy*. Englewood Cliffs, NJ: Prentice-Hall.

Berscheid, E., & Walster, E. (1974). A little bit about love. In T.L. Huston (Ed.), *Foundations of interpersonal attraction* (pp. 355–81). New York: Academic Press.

Berscheid, E., & Walster, E.H. (1978). *Interpersonal attraction*. Reading, MA: Addison-Wesley.

Black, M. (1962). *Models and metaphors. Studies in language and philosophy*. Ithaca, NY: Cornell University Press.

Blankenship, V., Hnat, S.M., Hess, T.G., & Brown, D.R. (1984). Reciprocal interaction and similarity of personality attributes. *Journal of Social and Personal Relationships, 1*, 415–32.

Blood, R.O., & Wolfe, D.M. (1960). *Husbands and wives*. New York: Free Press.

Blumstein, P., & Schwartz, P. (1983). *American couples*. New York: Morrow.

Bochner, A.P. (1982). On the efficacy of openness in close relationships. In M. Burgoon (Ed.), *Communication yearbook 5*. New Brunswick, NJ: Transaction Books.

Bochner, A.P. (1984). The functions of human communication in interpersonal bonding. In C. Arnold and J. Bowers (Eds.), *Handbook of rhetorical and communication theory* (pp. 544–621). Boston, MA: Allyn & Bacon.

Bochner, A.P., Krueger, D.L., & Chmielewski, T.L. (1982). Interpersonal perceptions and marital adjustment. *Journal of Communication, 32,* 135–47.

Bock, P. (1994, 21 February). He's not disabled in cyberspace. *Seattle Times,* pp. A1-2.

Bohrnstedt, G.W., & Knoke, D. (1982). *Statistics for social data analysis.* Itasca, IL: F.E. Peacock.

Bolger, N., DeLongis, A., Kessler, R., & Schilling, E. (1989). Effects of daily stress on negative mood. *Journal of Personality and Social Psychology, 57,* 808–18.

Booth, A., & Hess, E. (1974). Cross-sex friendship. *Journal of Marriage and the Family, 36,* 38–47.

Borys, S., & Perlman, D. (1985). Sex differences in loneliness. *Personality and Social Psychology Bulletin, 11,* 63–74.

Bower, G.H. (1981). Mood and memory. *American Psychologist, 36,* 129–48.

Bowlby, J. (1969). *Attachment and loss. Vol. 1: Attachment.* New York: Basic Books.

Bradbury, T.N., & Fincham, F.D. (1987). Affect and cognition in close relationships: toward an integrative model. *Cognition and Emotion, 1,* 59–87.

Bradford, L. (1980). The death of a dyad. In B. Morse & L. Phelps (Eds.), *Interpersonal communication: a relational perspective.* Minneapolis: Burgess.

Braiker, H., & Kelley, H.H. (1979). Conflict in the development of close relationships. In R. Burgess & T. Huston (Eds.), *Social exchange in developing relationships.* New York: Academic Press.

Brennan, P.F., Moore, S.M., & Smyth, K.A. (1992). Alzheimer's disease caregivers' uses of a computer network. *Western Journal of Nursing Research, 14,* 662–73.

Bringle, R.G., & Buunk, A.P. (1985). Jealousy and social behavior: a review of personal, relationship and situational determinants. In P. Shaver (Ed.), *Review of personality and social psychology* (Vol. 2, pp. 241–64). Beverly Hills, CA: Sage.

Broverman, I.K., Vogel, S.R., Broverman, D.M., Clarkson, F.E. & Rosenkrantz, P. (1972). Sex role stereotypes: A current appraisal. *Journal of Social Issues, 48,* 59–78.

Bruckman, A. (1992). *Identity workshop: emergent social and psychological phenomena in text-based virtual reality.* Unpublished manuscript. MIT Media Laboratory, Cambridge, MA. [On-line]. Available via anonymous ftp:media.mit.edu in pub/MediaMOO/Papers/identity-workshop.ps.

Bruess, C.J.S., & Pearson, J. (1995, November). Like sands through the hour glass: rituals in day-to-day marriage. Paper presented at the Annual Meeting of the Speech Communication Association, San Antonio, TX.

Bullis, C., Clark, C., & Stine, R. (1993). From passion to commitment: turning points in romantic relationships. In P. Kalbfleisch (Ed.), *Interpersonal communication: evolving interpersonal relationships* (pp. 213–36). Hillsdale, NJ: Erlbaum.

Bulmer, M. (1979). Concepts in the analysis of qualitative data. *Sociological Review, 27,* 651–77.

Buss, D.M. (1989). Sex differences in human mate preferences: evolutionary hypotheses tested in 37 cultures. *Behavioral and Brain Sciences, 12,* 1–49.

Buss, D.M. (1999). *Evolutionary psychology: the new science of the mind.* Boston, MA: Allyn & Bacon.

Buss, D.M., Larsen, R.J., Westen, D., & Semmelroth, J. (1992). Sex differences in jealousy: evolution, physiology, and psychology. *Psychological Science, 3,* 251–55.

Buunk, A.P. (1995). Sex, self-esteem, and extradyadic sexual experience as related to jealousy responses. *Journal of Social and Personal Relationships, 12,* 147–53.

Buunk, A.P., & Dijkstra, P. (2000). Extradyadic relationships and jealousy. In C. Hendrick & S.S. Hendrick (Eds.), *Close relationships: a sourcebook* (pp. 317–29). Thousand Oaks, CA: Sage.

Buunk, A.P., & van Driel, B. (1989). *Variant lifestyles and relationships.* Newbury Park, CA: Sage.

Byrne, D. (1961). Interpersonal attraction and attitude similarity. *Journal of Abnormal and Social Psychology, 62,* 713–15.

Byrne, D. (1962). Response to attitude similarity as a junction of affiliation need. *Journal of Personality*, *30*, 164–77.

Byrne, D. (1965). Authoritarianism and response to attitude similarity–dissimilarity. *Journal of Social Psychology*, *66*, 251–6.

Byrne, D. (1971). *The attraction paradigm*. New York: Academic Press.

Byrne, D. (1978). Separation, integration, or parallel play? *Personality and Social Psychology Bulletin*, *4*, 498–9.

Byrne, D. (1979). This week's citation classic. *Current Contents*, 12 February, p.16.

Byrne, D. (1982). Predicting human sexual behavior. *G. Stanley Hall Lecture Series*, *2*, 207–54.

Byrne, D. (1992). The transition from controlled laboratory experimentation to less controlled settings: surprise! Additional variables are operative. *Communication Monographs*, *59*, 190–8.

Byrne, D. (1997a). Why would anyone conduct research on sexual behavior? In G.G. Brannigan, E.R. Allgeier & A.R. Allgeier (Eds.), *The sex scientists*. New York: McGraw-Hill.

Byrne, D. (1997b). An overview (and underview) of research and theory within the attraction paradigm. *Journal of Social and Personal Relationships*, *14*, 417–31.

Byrne, D., & Blaylock, B. (1963). Similarity and assumed similarity of attitudes among husbands and wives. *Journal of Abnormal and Social Psychology*, *67*, 636–40.

Byrne, D., & Buehler, J.A. (1955). A note on the influence of propinquity upon acquaintanceships. *Journal of Abnormal and Social Psychology*, *51*, 147–8.

Byrne, D., & Clore, G.L. (1966). Predicting interpersonal attraction toward strangers presented in three different stimulus modes. *Psychonomic Science*, *4*, 239–40.

Byrne, D., & Clore, G.L. (1967). Effectance arousal and attraction. *Journal of Personality and Social Psychology*, *6*(4), (Whole No. 638).

Byrne, D., & Clore, G.L. (1970). A reinforcement model of evaluative responses. *Personality: An international Journal*, *1*, 103–28.

Byrne, D., & Fisher, W.A. (Eds) (1983). *Adolescents, sex, and contraception*. Hillsdale, NJ: Erlbaum.

Byrne, D., & Griffitt, W. (1966). A developmental investigation of the law of attraction. *Journal of Personality and Social Psychology*, *4*, 699–702.

Byrne, D., & Kelley, K. (1981). *An introduction to personality* (3rd edn). Englewood Cliffs, NJ: Prentice-Hall.

Byrne, D., & Lamberth, J. (1971). Cognitive and reinforcement theories as complementary approaches to the study of attraction. In B.I. Murstein (Ed.), *Theories of attraction and love* (pp. 59–84). New York: Springer.

Byrne, D., & Nelson, D. (1964). Attraction as a function of attitude similarity–dissimilarity: the effect of topic importance. *Psychonomic Science*, *1*, 93–4.

Byrne, D., & Nelson, D. (1965). Attraction as a linear function of proportion of positive reinforcements. *Journal of Personality and Social Psychology*, *1*, 659–63.

Byrne, D., & Rhamey, R. (1965). Magnitude of positive and negative reinforcements as a determinant of attraction. *Journal of Personality and Social Psychology*, *2*, 884–9.

Byrne, D., & Schulte, L. (1990). Personality dispositions as mediators of sexual responses. *Annual Review of Sex Research*, *1*, 93–117.

Byrne, D., & Wong, T.J. (1962). Racial prejudice, interpersonal attraction and assumed dissimilarity of attitudes. *Journal of Abnormal and Social Psychology*, *65*, 246–53.

Byrne, D., Baskett, G.D., & Hodges, L. (1971). Behavioral indicators of interpersonal attraction. *Journal of Applied Social Psychology*, *1*, 137–49.

Byrne, D., Ervin, C.E., & Lamberth, J. (1970). Continuity between the experimental study of attraction and real-life computer dating. *Journal of Personality and Social Psychology*, *16*, 157–65.

Byrne, D., Gouaux, C., Griffitt, W., Lamberth, J., Murakawa, N., Prasad, A. & Ramirez, M. III (1971). The ubiquitous relationship: attitude similarity and attraction. A cross-cultural study. *Human Relations*, *24*, 201–7.

Byrne, D., Griffitt, W., & Stefaniak, D. (1967). Attraction and similarity of personality characteristics. *Journal of Personality and Social Psychology*, *5*, 82–90.

Byrne, D., Griffitt, W., Hudgins, W., & Reeves, K. (1969a). Attitude similarity–dissimilarity and attraction: generality beyond the college sophomore. *Journal of Social Psychology, 79*, 155–61.

Byrne, D., Lamberth, J., Palmer, J., & London, O. (1969b). Sequential effects as a function of explicit and implicit interpolated attraction responses. *Journal of Personality and Social Psychology, 13*, 70–8.

Byrne, D., Nelson, D., & Reeves, K. (1966b). Effects of consensual validation and invalidation on attraction as a function of verifiability. *Journal of Experimental Social Psychology, 2*, 98–107.

Byrne, D., Clore, G.L. & Worchel, P. (1966a). The effect of economic similarity-dissimilarity on interpersonal attraction. *Journal of Personality and Social Psychology, 4*, 220–4.

Cams, D.E. (1973). Talking about sex: notes on first coitus and the double sexual standard. *Journal of Marriage and the Family, 35*, 677–89.

Canary, D.J., & Stafford, L. (1992). Relational maintenance strategies and equity in marriage. *Communication Monographs, 59*, 243–67.

Canary, D.J., & Zelley, E.D. (2000). Current research programs on relational maintenance behaviors. In M.E. Roloff (Ed.), *Communication yearbook 23* (pp. 304–39). Newbury Park, CA: Sage.

Canary, D.J., Cupach, W.R., & Messman, S.J. (1995). *Relationship conflict: conflict in parent–child, friendship, and romantic relationships*. Thousand Oaks, CA: Sage.

Cancian, F. (1987). *Love in America: gender and self-development*. Cambridge, UK: Cambridge University Press.

Cate, R.M., Koval, J., Lloyd, S.A., & Wilson, G. (1995). Assessment of relationship thinking in dating relationships. *Personal Relationships, 2*, 77–95.

Cere, D. (2001). *Courtship today: The view from academia*. [On-line]. Available: http://www.thepublicinterest.com/archives/2001spring/article2.html.

Chase, I. (1974). Models of hierarchy formation in animal societies. *Behavioral Science, 19*, 374–82.

Cheek, J.M., & Busch, C.M. (1981). Influence of shyness on loneliness in a new situation. *Personality and Social Psychology Bulletin, 7*, 573–7.

Chelune, G.J., Sultan, F.E., & Williams, C.L. (1980). Loneliness, self-disclosure and interpersonal effectiveness. *Journal of Consulting and Clinical Psychology, 27*, 462–8.

Christensen, A. (1987). Detection of conflict patterns in couples. In K. Hahlweg & M.J. Goldstein (Eds.), *Understanding major mental disorders: the contribution of family interaction research* (pp. 250–65). New York: Family Process Press.

Christensen, A. (1988). Dysfunctional interaction patterns in couples. In P. Noller & M.A. Fitzpatrick (Eds.), *Perspectives on marital interaction* (pp. 31–52). Clevedon, UK: Multilingual Matters.

Christensen, A., & Heavey, C.L. (1990). Sex and social structure in the demand/withdraw pattern of marital interaction. *Journal of Personality and Social Psychology, 59*, 73–81.

Christensen, A., & Shenk, J.L. (1991). Communication, conflict, and psychological distance in nondistressed, clinic, and divorcing couples. *Journal of Consulting and Clinical Psychology, 59*, 458–63.

Clore, G.L., & Byrne, D. (1974). A reinforcement-affect model of attraction. In T.L. Huston (Ed.), *Foundations of interpersonal attraction* (pp. 143–70). New York: Academic Press.

Clore, G.L., & Gormly, J.B. (1974). Knowing, feeling, and liking: a psycho physiological study of attraction. *Journal of Research in Personality, 8*, 218–30.

Cody, M. (1982). A typology of disengagement strategies and an examination of the role intimacy, reactions to inequity, and relational problems play in strategy selection. *Communication Monographs, 49*, 148–70.

Cohen, J. (1960). A coefficient of agreement for nominal scales. *Educational and Psychological Measurement, 20*, 37–48.

Conner, K.A., Powers, E.A., & Bultena, G.L. (1979). Social interaction and life satisfaction: an empirical assessment of latelife patterns. *Journal of Gerontology, 34*, 116–21.

Conville, R. (1988). Relational transitions: an inquiry into their structure and functions. *Journal of Social and Personal Relationships*, *5*, 423–37.

Cook, K.S., & Emerson, R.M. (1978). Power, equity, commitment in exchange networks. *American Sociological Review*, *43*, 721–39.

Cook, M., & Wilson, G. (Eds.), (1979). *Love & attraction: an international conference*. Oxford: Pergamon Press.

Coombs, R.H., & Kendell, W.F. (1966). Sex differences in dating aspirations and satisfaction with computer-selected partners. *Journal of Marriage and the Family*, *28*, 62–6.

Corsini, R. (1956). Understanding and similarity in marriage. *Journal of Abnormal and Social Psychology*, *52*, 327–32.

Crohan, S. (1992). Marital happiness and spousal consensus on beliefs about marital conflict. *Journal of Social and Personal Relationships*, *9*, 89–102.

Crohan, S., & Veroff, J. (1989). Dimensions of marital well-being in black and white newly-weds. *Journal of Marriage and the Family*, *51*, 379–83.

Cuber, J., & Harroff, P. (1965). *The significant Americans*. New York: Appleton-Century.

Culnan, M.J., & Markus, M.L. (1987). Information technologies. In F. Jablin, L.L. Putnam, K. Roberts, & I. Porter (Eds.), *Handbook of organizational communication* (pp. 420–43). Newbury Park, CA: Sage.

Cunningham, J.D., & Antill, J.K. (1981). Love in developing romantic relationships. In S.W. Duck & R. Gilmour (Eds.), *Personal relationships 2: developing personal relationships*. New York: Academic Press.

Cupach, W.R., & Canary, D.J. (1995). Managing conflict and anger: investigating the sex stereotype hypothesis. In P.J. Kalbfleisch & M.J. Cody (Eds.), *Sex, power, and communication in human relationships* (pp. 233–52). Hillsdale, NJ: Erlbaum.

Cupach, W.R., & Comstock, J. (1990). Satisfaction with sexual communication in marriage: links to sexual satisfaction and dyadic adjustment. *Journal of Social and Personal Relationships*, *7*, 179–86.

Curran, J.P., & Lippold, S. (1975). Effects of physical attraction and attitude similarity on attraction in dating dyads. *Journal of Personality*, *43*, 528–39.

Curtis, P. (1992). MUDding: social phenomenon in text-based virtual realities. *Intertrek*, *3*(3), 26–34.

Daft, R.L., & Lengel, R.H. (1984). Information richness: a new approach to managerial behavior and organizational design. *Research in Organizational Behavior*, *6*, 191–233.

Dainton, M. (1995, November). Interaction in maintained marriages: a description of type, relative routineness, and perceived importance. Paper presented at the Annual Meeting of the Speech Communication Association, San Antonio, TX.

Dainton, M., & Stafford, L. (1993). Routine maintenance behaviors: a comparison of relationship type, partner similarity, and sex differences. *Journal of Social and Personal Relationships*, *10*, 255–71.

Dainton, M., Stafford, L., & Canary, D.J. (1994). Maintenance strategies and physical affection as predictors of love, liking, and satisfaction in marriage. *Communication Reports*, *7*, 88–98.

Daly, M., & Wilson, M. (1988). *Homicide*. New York: Aldine de Gruyter.

Daly, M., Wilson, M., & Weghorst, S.J. (1982). Male sexual jealousy. *Ethology and Sociobiology*, *3*, 11–27.

Davis, K. (1948). *Human society*. New York: Macmillan.

Davis, K.E., & Todd, M.J. (1982). Friendship and love relationships. In K.E. Davis & T.O. Mitchell (Eds.), *Advances in descriptive psychology*, *Vol. 2*. Greenwich, CT: JAI Press.

Davis, M.S. (1973). *Intimate relations*. New York: Free Press.

de Jong-Gierveld, J., & Raadschelders, I. (1982). Types of loneliness. In L.A. Peplau and D. Perlman (Eds.), *Loneliness, a sourcebook of current theory, research and therapy*. New York: Wiley.

Deaux, K., & Lafrance, M. (1998). Sex. In D.T. Gilbert & S.T. Fiske (Eds.), *The handbook of social psychology* (pp. 788–827). New York: McGraw-Hill.

Delamater, J. (1989). The social control of human sexuality. In K. McKinney & S. Sprecher (Eds.), *Human sexuality: The societal and interpersonal context* (pp. 30–62). Norwood, NJ: Ablex.

Delamater, J., & MacCorquodale, P. (1979). *Premarital: attitudes, relationships, behavior*. Madison, WI: University of Wisconsin Press.

Derlega, V.J., & Winstead, B.A. (1986). *Friendship and social interaction*. New York: Springer.

Derlega, V.J., Winstead, B.A., Wong, P.T.P., & Hunter, S. (1985). Gender effects in an initial encounter: a case where men exceed women in disclosure. *Journal of Social and Personal Relationships*, *2*, 25–44.

Dindia, K. (1994). A multiphasic view of relationship maintenance strategies. In D. Canary & L. Stafford (Eds.), *Communication and relational maintenance* (pp. 91–110). San Diego, CA: Academic Press.

Dindia, K., & Baxter, L.A. (1987). Strategies for maintaining and repairing marital relationships. *Journal of Social and Personal Relationships*, *4*, 143–58.

Dindia, K., & Canary, D.J (1993). Definitions and theoretical perspectives on maintenance of relationships. *Journal of Social and Personal Relationships*, *10*, 163–73.

Dindia, K., & Emery, D. (1982). Strategies for maintaining and repairing marital relationships. Paper presented to the first International Conference on Personal Relationships, Madison, WI.

Dindia, K., Fitzpatrick, M.A., & Kenny, D.A. (1989, May). Self-disclosure in spouse and stranger interaction: a social relations analysis. Paper presented at the meeting of the International Communication Association, New Orleans.

Douglas, W. (1987). Affinity-testing initial interactions. *Journal of Social and Personal Relationships*, *4*, 3–15.

Driscoll, R., Davis, K.E., & Lipetz, M.E. (1972). Parental interference and romantic love: the Romeo and Juliet effect. *Journal of Personality and Social Psychology*, *24*, 1–10.

Dubrovsky, V.J., Kiesler, S.B., & Sethna, B.N. (1991). The equalization phenomenon: status effects in computer-mediated and face-to-face decision-making groups. *Human–Computer Interaction*, *6*, 119–46.

Duck, S.W. (1976). Interpersonal communication in developing acquaintance. In G.R. Miller (Ed.), *Explorations in interpersonal communication* (pp.127–47). Beverly Hills, CA: Sage**.**

Duck, S.W. (1982). A topography of relationship disengagement and dissolution. In S.W. Duck (Ed.), *Personal relationships 4: Dissolving personal relationships* (pp. 1–30). New York: Academic Press.

Duck, S.W. (1984a). A perspective on the repair of personal relationships. In S.W. Duck (Ed.), *Personal Relationships 5: Repairing Personal Relationships*. New York: Academic Press.

Duck, S.W. (1984b). A rose is a rose (is a tadpole is a freeway is a film) is a rose. *Journal of Social and Personal Relationships*, *1*, 507–10.

Duck, S.W. (1985). Social and personal relationships. In M.L. Knapp & G.R. Miller (Eds.), *Handbook of interpersonal communication* (pp. 655–86). Beverly Hills, CA: Sage.

Duck, S.W. (1987). Adding apples and oranges: investigators' implicit theories about personal relationships. In R. Burnett, P. McGhee & D. Clarke (Eds.), *Accounting for relationships: explanation, representation and knowledge*. London: Methuen.

Duck, S.W. (1988). *Relating to others*. Milton Keynes: Open University Press/Brooks-Cole.

Duck, S.W. (1991, May). New lamps for old: a new theory of relationships and a fresh look at some old research. Paper presented at the meeting of the International Network on Personal Relationships, Normal/Bloomington, IL.

Duck, S.W. (Ed.) (1993). *Social context and relationships*. London: Sage.

Duck, S.W. (1994a). Steady as (s)he goes: relational maintenance as a shared meaning system. In D.J. Canary & L. Stafford (Eds.), *Communication and relational maintenance* (pp. 45–60). New York: Academic Press.

Duck, S.W. (1994b). *Meaningful relationships: talking, sense, and relating*. Thousand Oaks, CA: Sage.

Duck, S.W., & Lea, M. (1982). Breakdown of relationships as a threat to personal identity. In G.M. Breakwell (Ed.). *Threatened identities*. London: Wiley.

Duck, S.W., & Pond, K. (1989). Friends, Romans, countrymen, lend me your retrospective data: rhetoric and reality in personal relationships. *Review of Personality and Social Psychology*, *10*, 3–27.

Duck, S.W., & VanderVoort, L.A. (2002). Scarlet letters and whited sepulchres: the social marking of relationships as "inappropriate". In R. Goodwin & D. Cramer (Eds.), *Inappropriate relationships: the unconventional, the disapproved, and the forbidden* (pp. 3–24). Mahwah, NJ: Erlbaum.

Duck, S.W., & Wood, J.T. (1995). *Confronting relationship challenges (understanding relationship processes 5)*. Newbury Park, CA: Sage.

Duck, S.W., Rutt, D.J., Hurst, M. & Strejc, H. (1991). Some evident truths about conversations in everyday relationships: all communication is not created equal. *Human Communication Research*, *18*, 228–67.

Duck, S.W., West, L., & Acitelli, L.K. (1997). Sewing the field: the tapestry of relationships in life and research. In S.W. Duck, K. Dindia, W. Ickes, R. Milardo, R. Mills, & B. Sarason (Eds.), *Handbook of personal relationships* (2nd edn). Chichester: Wiley.

Duke, M.P. (1994). Chaos theory and psychology: seven propositions. *Genetic, Social, & General Psychology Monographs*, *120*, 267–86.

Duncombe, J., & Marsden, D. (1993). Love and intimacy: the gender division of emotion and "Emotion Work". *Sociology*, *27*, 221–41.

Duran, R.L. (1983). Communicative adaptability: a measure of social communicative competence. *Communication Quarterly*, *31*, 320–6.

Eagly, A.H., & Wood, W. (1999). The origins of sex differences in human behavior: evolved dispositions versus social roles. *American Psychologist*, *54*, 408–23.

Edwards, J., & Saunders, J. (1981). Coming apart: a model of the marital dissolution decision. *Journal of Marriage and the Family*, *43*, 379–89.

Ehrmann, W. (1959). *Premarital dating behavior*. New York: Henry Holt & Co.

Ellison, C.W., & Paloutzian, R.F. (1979). Developing an abbreviated loneliness scale. Paper presented at the UCLA Conference on Loneliness, Los Angeles.

Erwin, H.R. (1996). The application of topological models to social system dynamics. In W. Sullis & A. Combs (Eds.), *Nonlinear dynamics in human behavior* (pp. 207–32). New York: World Scientific.

Fainsilber, L., & Ortony, A. (1987). Metaphorical uses of language in the expression of emotions. *Metaphor and Symbolic Activity*, *2*, 239–50.

Falbo, T. (1977). The multidimensional scaling of power strategies. *Journal of Personality and Social Psychology*, *35*, 537–48.

Fehr, B. (1993). How do I love thee? … Let me consult my prototype. In S.W. Duck (Ed.), *Individuals in relationships [Understanding relationship processes 1]* (pp. 87–120). Newbury Park, CA: Sage.

Feingold, A. (1990). Gender differences in effects of physical attractiveness on romantic attraction: a comparison across five research paradigms. *Journal of Personality and Social Psychology*, *59*, 981–93.

Feingold, A. (1991). Sex differences in the effects of similarity and physical attractiveness on opposite-sex attraction. *Basic and Applied Social Psychology*, *12*, 357–67.

Feld, S., & Carter, W. (1998). Foci of activity as changing contexts for friendship. In R. Adams & G. Allan (Eds.), *Placing friendship in context*. Cambridge, UK: Cambridge University Press.

Ferrell, M.Z., Tolone, W.L., & Walsh, R.H. (1977). Maturational and societal changes in the double standard: a panel analysis (1967–71; 1970–74). *Journal of Marriage and the Family*, *39*, 255–71.

Fincham, F.D., & Bradbury, T.N. (1987). The assessment of marital quality: a reevaluation. *Journal of Marriage and the Family*, *49*, 797–809.

Finholt, T., & Sproull, L.S. (1990). Electronic groups at work. *Organization Science, 1,* 41–64.

Fischer, C.S. (1982). *To dwell among friends*. Chicago: University of Chicago Press.

Fisher, J.D., & Byrne, D. (1975). Too close for comfort: sex differences in response to invasions of personal space. *Journal of Personality and Social Psychology, 32,* 15–21.

Fitzpatrick, M.A. (1988). *Between husbands and wives: communication in marriage*. Newbury Park, CA: Sage.

Francis, J.L. (1977). Towards the management of heterosexual jealousy. *Journal of Marriage and Family Counseling, 3,* 61–9.

Frank, R.H. (1988). *Passions within reason: the strategic role of the emotions*. New York: Norton.

Frayser, S. (1985). *Varieties of sexual experience: an anthropological perspective*. New Haven, CT: HRAF Press.

Frazier, P.A., & Esterly, E. (1990). Correlates of relationship beliefs: gender, relationship experience and relationship satisfaction. *Journal of Social and Personal Relationships, 7,* 331–52.

Freeman, L.C., & Thompson, C.R. (1989). Estimating acquaintanceship volume. In M. Kochen (Ed.), *The small world* (pp. 147–58). Norwood, NJ: Ablex.

French, J.R.P., & Raven, B.H. (1959). The bases of social power. In D. Cartwright (Ed.), *Studies in social power*. Ann Arbor, MI: University of Michigan Press.

Fuller, D.K. (1982). *Love attitudes and personality style among heterosexual couples*. Unpublished PhD thesis. University of Miami.

Gaelick, L., Bodenhausen. G.V., & Wyer, R.S. (1985). Emotional communication in close relationships. *Journal of Personality and Social Psychology, 49,* 1246–65.

Gagnon, J.H., & Simon, W. (1973). *Sexual conduct: the social sources of human sexuality*. Chicago: Aldine.

Garcia, L.T. (1983). Sexual stereotypes and attributions about sexual arousal. *Journal of Sex Research, 19,* 366–75.

Garton, L., & Wellman, B. (1995). Social impacts of electronic mail in organizations: a review of the research literature. In B. Burleson (Ed.), *Communication yearbook 18* (pp. 434–53). Newbury Park, CA: Sage.

Gerson, A.C., & Perlman, D. (1979). Loneliness and expressive communication. *Journal of Abnormal Psychology, 88,* 258–61.

Giblin, P., Sprenkle, D. & Sheehan, R. (1985). Enrichment outcome research: a meta-analysis of premarital, marital, and family interventions. *Journal of Marital and Family Therapy, 11,* 257–71.

Giddens, A. (1991). *Modernity and self-identity*. Cambridge, UK: Polity.

Giddens, A. (1992). *The transformation of intimacy: sexuality, love and eroticism in modern societies*. Cambridge, UK: Polity.

Gilligan, C. (1982). *In a Different Voice*. Cambridge, MA: Harvard University Press.

Gillispie, D.L. (1971). Who has the power? The marital struggle. *Journal of Marriage and Family Living, 33,* 445–58.

Gleick, J. (1987). *Chaos: making a new science*. New York: Viking Penguin.

Glick, P.C. (1979). *The future of the American Family*. In US Bureau of the Census. Current population reports. Washington D.C.: Government Printing Office. Series P-23. No.78.

Goldstein, J. (1996). Causality and emergence in chaos and complexity theories. In W. Sullis & A. Combs (Eds.), *Nonlinear dynamics in human behavior* (pp. 161–90). New York: World Scientific.

Golightly, C., & Byrne, D. (1964). Attitude statements as positive and negative reinforcements. *Science, 146,* 798–9.

Goodchilds, J.D., Quadrado, C., & Raven, B.H. (1975). Getting one's way: self-report influence strategies. Paper presented at the meeting of the Western Psychological Association, Sacramento, CA.

Goode, W.J. (1956). *After divorce*. Glencoe, IL: Free Press.

Gottman, J.M. (1979). *Marital interaction: experimental investigations*. New York: Academic Press.

Gottman, J.M. (1991). Chaos and regulated change in families: a metaphor for the study of transitions. In P.A. Cowan & E.M. Hetherington (Eds.), *Family traditions* (pp. 247–72). Hillsdale, NJ: Erlbaum.

Gottman, J.M. (1994). *Why marriages succeed or fail*. New York: Simon & Schuster.

Gottman, J.M., & Krokoff, L.J. (1989). Marital interaction and satisfaction: a longitudinal view. *Journal of Consulting and Clinical Psychology, 57*, 47–52.

Gottman, J.M., & Levenson, R.W. (1992). Marital processes predictive of later dissolution: behavior, physiology, and health. *Journal of Personality and Social Psychology, 63*, 221–33.

Gottman, J.M., Swanson, C., & Murray, J. (1999). The mathematics of marital conflict: dynamic mathematical nonlinear modeling of newlywed marital interaction. *Journal of Family Psychology, 13*, 3–19.

Gragnani, A., Rinaldi, S., & Feichtinger, G. (1997). Cyclic dynamics in romantic relationships. *International Journal of Bifurcation and Chaos, 7*, 2611–19.

Graham, E.E. (1997). Turning points and commitment in post-divorce relationships. *Communication Monographs, 64*, 350–68.

Grauerholz, E. (1988). Altruistic-other orientation in intimate relationships. *Social Behavior and Personality, 16*, 127–31.

Griffin, D.W., & Bartholomew, K. (1994a). The metaphysics of measurement: the case of adult attachment. In K. Bartholomew & D. Perlman (Eds.), *Advances in personal relationships. Vol. 5: Attachment processes in adulthood* (pp. 17–52). London: Kingsley.

Griffin, D.W., & Bartholomew, K. (1994b). Models of the self and other: fundamental dimensions underlying measures of adult attachment. *Journal of Personality and Social Psychology, 67*, 430–45.

Griffitt, W. (1970). Environmental effects on interpersonal affective behavior; ambient effective temperature and attraction. *Journal of Personality and Social Psychology, 15*, 240–4.

Griffitt, W., & Byrne, D. (1970). Procedures in the paradigmatic study of attitude similarity and attraction. *Representative Research in Social Psychology, 1*, 33–48.

Griffitt, W., & Kaiser, D.L. (1978). Affect, sex guilt, gender, and the rewarding–punishing effects of erotic stimuli. *Journal of Personality and Social Psychology, 36*, 850–8.

Griffitt, W., & Veitch, R. (1974). Pre-acquaintance attitude similarity and attraction revisited: ten days in a fall-out shelter. *Sociometry, 37*, 163–73.

Grote, N.K. (1993). *Love in the afternoon: perceptions of love before and after marriage in middle-aged men and women*. Unpublished doctoral dissertation, University of Pittsburgh.

Grote, N.K., & Frieze, I.H. (1994). The measurement of friendship-based love in intimate relationships. *Personal Relationships, 1*, 275–300.

Guerrero, L.K., & Andersen, P.A. (1998). The dark side of jealousy and envy: desire, delusion, desperation, and destructive communication. In B.H. Spitzberg & W.R. Cupach (Eds.), *The dark side of close relationships* (pp. 33–70). Mahwah, NJ: Erlbaum.

Guerrero, L.K., Eloy, S.V., & Wabnik, A.I. (1993). Linking maintenance strategies to relationship development and disengagement: a reconceptualization. *Journal of Social and Personal Relationships, 10*, 273–83.

Hahn, H., & Stout, R. (1994). *The internet complete reference*. Berkeley, CA: Osborne McGraw-Hill.

Hansen, G.L. (1987). Extra dyadic relations during courtship. *Journal of Sex Research, 23*, 382–90.

Harré, R. (1977). The ethogenic approach: theory and practice. In L. Berkowitz (Ed.), *Advances in experimental social psychology. Vol. 10*. New York: Academic Press.

Harrison, K. (1998). Rich friendships, affluent friends: middle-class practices of friendship. In R. Adams & G. Allan (Eds.), *Placing friendship in context*. Cambridge, UK: Cambridge University Press.

Harry, J. (1984). *Gay couples*. New York: Praeger.

Harvey, J.H., Agostinelli, G., & Weber, A.L. (1989). Account-making and the formation of expectations about close relationships. In C. Hendrick (Ed.), *Close relationships* (pp. 39–62). Newbury Park, CA: Sage.

Haskey, J. (1996). Population review: (6) families and households in Great Britain. *Population Trends*, *85*, 7–24.

Hatchett, S., Verhoff, J., & Douvan, E. (1995). Factors influencing marital instability among black and white couples. In B. Tucker and C. Mitchell-Kerman (Eds.), *The decline of black marriages*. Newbury Park, CA: Sage.

Hatfield (Walster), E. (1971). Passionate love. In B.I. Murstein (Ed.), *Theories of attraction and love* (pp. 85–99). New York: Springer.

Hatfield, E., & Walster, G. (1978). *A new look at love*. Lantham, MA: University Press of America.

Hatkoff, S., & Lasswell, T.E. (1979). Male–female similarities and differences in conceptualizing love. In M. Cook & G. Wilson (Eds.), *Love & attraction: an international conference*. Oxford: Pergamon Press.

Hawkes, G. (1996). *A sociology of sex and sexuality*. Buckingham, UK: Open University Press.

Hayes, W.L. (1988). *Statistics* (4th edition). New York: Holt, Rinehart and Winston.

Hays, R. (1985). A longitudinal study of friendship development. *Journal of Personality and Social Psychology*, *48*, 909–24.

Heaton, T.B., & Call, V.R.A. (1995). Modeling family dynamics with event history techniques. *Journal of Marriage and the Family*, *57*, 1078–90.

Heavey, C.L., Christensen, A., & Malamuth, N.M. (1995). The longitudinal impact of demand and withdrawal during marital conflict. *Journal of Consulting and Clinical Psychology*, *63*, 797–801.

Heavey, C.L., Layne, C., & Christensen, A. (1993). Sex and conflict structure in marital interaction: a replication and extension. *Journal of Consulting and Clinical Psychology*, *61*, 16–27.

Heiby, E.M. (1995). Chaos theory, nonlinear dynamical models, and psychological assessment. *Psychological Assessment*, *7*, 5–9.

Heider, F. (1958). *The psychology of interpersonal relations*. New York: Wiley.

Hendrick, C., & Hendrick, S.S. (1986). A theory and method of love. *Journal of Personality and Social Psychology*, *50*, 392–402.

Hendrick, C., & Hendrick, S.S. (1988). Lovers wear rose colored glasses. *Journal of Social and Personal Relationships*, *5*, 392–402.

Hendrick, C., & Hendrick, S.S. (1990). A relationship-specific version of the Love Attitudes Scale. *Journal of Social Behavior and Personality*, *5*, 239–54.

Hendrick, C., Hendrick, S.S., Foote, F., & Slapion-Foote, M. (1984). Do men and women love differently? *Journal of Social and Personal Relationships*, *1*, 177–96.

Hendrick, S.S. (1988). A generic measure of relationship satisfaction. *Journal of Marriage and the Family*, *50*, 93–8.

Hendrick, S.S., & Hendrick, C. (1995). Gender differences and similarities in sex and love. *Personal Relationships*, *2*, 55–65.

Hendrick, S.S., Dicke, A., & Hendrick, C. (1998). The Relationship Assessment Scale. *Journal of Social and Personal Relationships*, *15*, 137–42.

Hendrick, S.S., Hendrick, C., & Adler, N.L. (1988). Romantic relationships: love, satisfaction, and staying together. *Journal of Personality and Social Psychology*, *54*, 980–8.

Henley, N. (1975). Power, sex and nonverbal communication. In B. Thorne & N. Henley (Eds.), *Language and sex: difference and dominance*. Rowley, MA: Newbury House.

Herold, E.S., & Mewhinney, D.K. (1993). Gender differences in casual sex and AIDS prevention: a survey of dating bars. *Journal of Sex Research*, *30*, 36–42.

Hill, C.T., Rubin, Z., & Peplau, L.A. (1976). Breakups before marriage: the end of 103 affairs. *Journal of Social Issues*, *32*, 147–68.

Hofstede, G. (1994). *Culture's consequences: international differences in work-related values.* Beverly Hills, CA: Sage.

Hogben, M., Byrne, D., & Hamburger, M.E. (1996). Coercive heterosexual sexuality in dating relationships of college students: implications of differential male–female experiences. *Journal of Psychology and Human Sexuality, 8,* 69–78.

Holtzworth-Munroe, A., Smutzler, N., Bates, L., & Vogel, D.L. (1995, November). Withdraw-demand communication behaviors: Comparing two observational coding systems. Paper presented at the annual meeting of the Association for the Advancement of Behavior Therapy, Washington, DC.

Honeycutt, J.M., Cantrill, J.G., & Greene, R.W. (1989). Memory structures for relational escalation: a cognitive test of the sequencing of relational actions and stages. *Human Communication Research, 16,* 62–90.

Honeycutt, J.M., Woods, B.L., & Fontenot, K. (1993). The endorsement of communication conflict rules as a function of engagement, marriage and marital ideology. *Journal of Social and Personal Relationships, 10,* 285–304.

Horowitz, L.M., & French, R.D.S. (1979). Interpersonal problems of people who describe themselves as lonely. *Journal of Consulting and Clinical Psychology, 47,* 762–4.

Hunter, J. (1980). Factor analysis. In P. Monge & J. Cappella (Eds.), *Multivariate techniques in human communication research* (pp. 229–58). New York: Academic Press.

Hupka, R.B., & Ryan, J.M. (1990). The cultural contribution to jealousy: cross-cultural aggression in sexual jealousy situations. *Behavioral Science Research, 24,* 51–71.

Huston, T.L., & Burgess, R.L. (1979). Social exchange in developing relationships: an overview. In R.L. Burgess & T.L. Huston (Eds.), *Social exchange in developing relationships* (pp. 3–28). New York: Academic Press.

Inglehart, R. (1977). *The silent revolution. Changing values and political styles among Western publics.* Princeton, NJ: Princeton University Press.

Insko, C.A., & Wilson, M. (1977). Interpersonal attraction as a function of social interaction. *Journal of Personality and Social Psychology, 35,* 903–11.

IntelliQuest (1997, 4 September). Latest IntelliQuest survey counts 51 million American adults on the internet/online services in the second quarter 1997. [On-line]. Available: http://www.intelliquest.com/about/release32.htm.

Istvan, J., & Griffitt, W. (1980). Effects of sexual experience on dating desirability and marriage desirability: an experimental study. *Journal of Marriage and the Family, 42,* 377–85.

Jacobson, D. (1996). Contexts and cues in cyberspace: the pragmatics of naming in text-based virtual realities. *Journal of Anthropological Research, 52,* 461–79.

Jacoby, A.P., & Williams, J.D. (1985). Effects of premarital sexual standards and behavior on dating and marriage desirability. *Journal of Marriage and the Family, 47,* 1059–65.

Jerrome, D. (1984). Good company: The sociological implications of friendship. *Sociological Review, 32,* 696–718.

Johnson, D.J., & Rusbult, C.E. (1989). Resisting temptation: devaluation of alternative partners as a means of maintaining commitment in close relationships. *Journal of Personality and Social Psychology, 75,* 967–80.

Johnson, E.M., & Huston, T.L. (1998). The perils of love, or why wives adapt to husbands during the transition to parenthood. *Journal of Marriage and the Family, 60,* 195–204.

Johnson, M.P. (1991). Commitment to personal relationships. In W.H. Jones & D.W. Perlman (Eds.), *Advances in personal relationships* (Vol. 3: pp. 117–43). London: Jessica Kingsley.

Johnson, M.P., & Milardo, R. (1984). Network interference in pair relationships. *Journal of Marriage and the Family, 46,* 893–9.

Johnson, P. (1976). Women and power: Towards a theory of effectiveness. *Journal of Social Issues, 32,* 99–110.

Johnson, P. (1978). Women and interpersonal power. In I.H. Frieze, J.E. Parsons, P. Johnson, D. Ruble, & G. Zellman (Eds.), *Women and sex roles: a social psychological perspective.* New York: Norton.

Jones, W.H., Hobbs, S.A., & Hockenbury, D. (1982). Loneliness and social skill deficits. *Journal of Personality and Social Psychology*, *42*, 682–9.

Jones, W.H., Freemon, J.E., & Goswick, R.A. (1981). The persistence of loneliness: self and other determinants. *Journal of Personality*, *49*, 27–48.

Juhasz, A.M. (1979). A concept of divorce: not busted bond but severed strand. *Alternative Lifestyles*, *2*, 471–82.

Kaats, G.R., & Davis, K.E. (1970). The dynamics of sexual behavior of college students. *Journal of marriage and family*, *32*, 390–99.

Katriel, T., & Philipsen, G. (1981). What we need is communication: "communication" as a cultural category in some American speech. *Communication Monographs*, *48*, 301–17.

Kauffman, S.A. (1991). Antichaos and adaptation. *Scientific American*, *265*, 78–84.

Kelley, D.L. (1999). Relational expectancy fulfillment as an explanatory variable for distinguishing couple types. *Human Communication Research*, *25*, 420–42.

Kelley, H.H. (1979). *Personal relationships: their structure and processes*. New York: Wiley.

Kelley, H.H. (1983). Love and commitment. In H.H. Kelley, E. Berscheid, A. Christensen, J.H. Harvey, T.L. Huston, G. Levinger, E. McClintock, L.A. Peplau, & D.R. Peterson (Eds.), *Close relationships*. San Francisco: Freeman.

Kelley, H.H. (1984). Affect in interpersonal relations. In P. Shaver (Ed.), *Review of personality and social psychology: emotions, relationships, and health*. Beverly Hills, CA: Sage.

Kenny, D.A. (1991, June). Does understanding your partner lead to better outcomes? Paper presented at the Third Annual Convention of American Psychological Society, Washington, DC.

Kiesler, S., & Sproull, L. (1992). Group decision making and communication technology. *Organization Behavior and Human Decision Processes*, *52*, 96–123.

Kilbourne, B.S., Howell, F., & England, P. (1990). A measurement model for subjective marital solidarity: invariance across time, gender, and life cycle stage. *Social Science Research*, *19*, 62–81.

Killworth, P.D., Bernard, H.R., & McCarty, C. (1984). Measuring patterns of acquaintanceship. *Current Anthropology*, *23*, 318–97.

Killworth, P.D., Johnsen, E.G., Bernard, H.R., Shelley, G.A., & McCarty, C. (1990). Estimating the size of personal networks. *Social Networks*, *12*, 289–312.

Kincanon, E., & Powel, W. (1995). Chaotic analysis in psychology and psychoanalysis. *Journal of Psychology*, *129*, 495–505.

Kingston, P.W., & Nock, S.L. (1987). Time together among dual-earner couples. *American Sociological Review*, *52*, 391–400.

Kipnis, D. (1976). *The powerholders*. Chicago: University of Chicago Press.

Klein, J. (1965). *Samples from English cultures. Vol. 1*. London: Routledge & Kegan Paul.

Klinetob, N.A., & Smith, D.A. (1995). Demand–withdraw communication in marital interaction: tests of interspousal contingency and sex role hypothesis. *Journal of Marriage and the Family*, *58*, 945–57.

Kluwer, E.S., Heesink, J.A.M., & Vliert, E.V.D. (2000). The division of labor in close relationships: an asymmetrical conflict issue. *Personal Relationships*, *7*, 263–82.

Knapp, M.L. (1978). *Social intercourse: from greeting to goodbye*. Boston, MA: Allyn & Bacon.

Knapp, M.L. (1984). *Interpersonal communication and human relationships*. Boston, MA: Allyn & Bacon.

Knox, D.H., & Sporakowski, M.J. (1968). Attitudes of college students towards love. *Journal of Marriage and the Family*, *30*, 638–42.

Koch, S., & Deetz, S. (1981). Metaphor analysis of social reality in organizations. *Journal of Applied Communication Research*, *9*, 1–15.

Kovecses, Z. (1988). *The language of love: the semantics of passion in conversational English*. London: Associated University Presses.

Kraut, R., Patterson, M., Lundmark, V., Keisler, S., Mukopadhyuay, T., & Scherlis, W. (1998). Internet paradox: A social technology that reduces social involvement and psychological well-being? *American Psychologist*, *53*, 1017–31.

Kressel, K., Jaffee, N., Tuchman, B., Watson, C., & Deutsch, M. (1980). A typology of divorcing couples: implications for mediation and the divorce process. *Family Process*, *19*, 101–16.

Laing, R.D., Phillipson, H., & Lee, A.R. (1966). *Interpersonal perception: a theory and a method of research*. New York: Springer.

Lakoff, G. (1986). A figure of thought. *Metaphor and Symbolic Activity*, *1*, 215–25.

Lakoff, G., & Johnson, M. (1980). *Metaphors we live by*. Chicago: University of Chicago Press.

Laner, M.R., Laner, R.H., & Palmer, C.E. (1978). Permissive attitudes toward sexual behaviors: a clarification of theoretical explanations. *Journal of Sex Research*, *14*, 137–44.

Lasswell, M., & Lobsenz, N.M. (1980). *Styles of loving*. Garden City, NY: Doubleday.

Lasswell, T.E., & Lasswell, M.E. (1976). I love you, but I'm not in love with you. *Journal of Marriage and Family Counseling*, *38*, 211–24.

Laumann, E.O., Gagnon, J.H., Michael, R.T., & Michaels, S. (1994). *The social organization of sexuality: sexual practices in the United States*. Chicago: University of Chicago Press.

Lea, M., & Spears, R. (1995). Love at first byte? Building personal relationships over computer networks. In J.T. Wood & S.W. Duck (Eds.), *Understudied relationships: off the beaten track* (pp. 197–233). Newbury Park, CA: Sage.

Lea, M., O'Shea, T., Fung, P., & Spears, R. (1992). "Flaming" in computer-mediated communication: observations, explanations and implications. In M. Lea (Ed.), *Contexts of computer-mediated communication* (pp. 89–112). London: Harvester-Wheatsheaf.

Lee, J.A. (1973). *The colors of love: an exploration of the ways of loving*. Don Mills, Ontario: New Press.

Lee, J.A. (1977). A typology of styles of loving. *Personality and Social Psychology Bulletin*, *3*, 173–82.

Lee, L. (1984). Sequences in separation: a framework for investigating endings of the personal (romantic) relationship. *Journal of Social and Personal Relationships*, *1*, 49–74.

Lester, M., & Doherty, W. (1983). Couples' long-term evaluations of their marital encounter experience. *Journal of Marital and Family Therapy*, *9*, 183–8.

Levine, T., & McCroskey, J. (1990). Measuring trait communication apprehension: a test of rival measurement models of the PRCA-24. *Communication Monographs*, *57*, 62–72.

Levinger, G. (1976). A social psychological perspective on marital dissolution. *Journal of Social Studies*, *32*, 21–47.

Levinger, G. (1980). Toward the analysis of close relationships. *Journal of Experimental Social Psychology*, *16*, 510–44.

Levinger, G. (1983). Development and change. In H.H. Kelley et al. (Eds.), *Close Relationships*. San Francisco: W.H. Freeman & Co.

Levinger, G., & Breedlove, J. (1966). Interpersonal attraction and agreement. *Journal of Personality and Social Psychology*, *4*, 367–72.

Lindzey, G., & Byrne, D. (1968). Measurement of social choice and interpersonal attractiveness. In G. Lindzey & E. Aronson (Eds.), *Handbook of Social Psychology*. Vol. 2 (pp. 452–525). Reading, MA: Addison-Wesley.

Lloyd, S.A., Cate, R.M., & Henton, J.M. (1984). Predicting premarital relationship stability: a methodological refinement. *Journal of Marriage and the Family*, *46*, 71–6.

Locke, H.J., & Wallace, K.M. (1959). Short marital adjustment and prediction test: their reliability and validity. *Marriage and Family Living*, *21*, 251–5.

Lorenz, E. (1979). On the prevalence of aperiodicity in simple systems. In J. Mgrmela & J. Marsden (Eds.), *Global analysis* (pp. 53–75). New York: Springer.

Lowenthal, M F., & Haven, C. (1968). Interaction and adaptation: intimacy as a critical variable. *American Sociological Review*, *1*, 20–30.

Luckey, E.B., & Nass, G.D. (1969). A comparison of sexual attitudes and behavior in an international sample. *Journal of Marriage and the Family*, *31*, 364–79.

Lund, M. (1985). The development of investment and commitment scales for predicting continuity of personal relationships. *Journal of Social and Personal Relationships*, *2*, 3–23.

Malinowski, B. (1932). *The sexual life of savages*. Boston, MA: Beacon.

Mannion, K. (1976). Female homosexuality: a comprehensive review of theory and research. *JSAS Catalog of Selected Documents in Psychology, 6*, 44 (Ms. No. 1247).

Mansfield, P., & Collard, J. (1988). *The beginning of the rest of your life? A portrait of newly-wed marriage*. London: Macmillan.

Mark, M.M., & Miller, M.L. (1986). The effects of sexual permissiveness, target gender, subject gender, and attitude toward women on social perception: in search of the double standard. *Sex Roles, 15*, 311–22.

Markman, H.J., & Kraft, S. (1989). Men and women in marriage: dealing with sex differences in marital therapy. *Behavior Therapist, 12*, 51–6.

Markman, H.J., Floyd, F., & Dickson-Markman, F. (1982). Towards a model for the prediction and primary prevention of marital and family distress and dissolution. In S.W. Duck (Ed.), *Personal relationships 4: dissolving personal relationships*. New York: Academic Press.

Markman, H.J., Silvern, L., Clements, M., & Kraft-Hanak, S. (1993). Men and women dealing with conflict in heterosexual relationships. *Journal of Social Issues, 49*, 107–25.

Marsden, P.V. (1987). Core discussion networks of Americans. *American Sociological Review, 52*, 122–31.

Marsden, P.V. (1990). Network data and measurement. *Annual Review of Sociology, 16*, 435–63.

Marvin, C. (1987). *When old technologies were new: thinking about electric communications in the late nineteenth century*. New York: Oxford University Press.

Marvin, L.E. (1995). Spoof, spam, lurk and lag: the aesthetics of text-based virtual realities. *Journal of Computer-Mediated Communication, 1*(2). [On-line]. Available: http://jcmc.huji. ac.il/vol1/issue2/vol1no2.html.

Masheter, C. (1997). Healthy and unhealthy friendship and hostility between ex-spouses. *Journal of Marriage and the Family, 59*, 463–75.

Maslow, A.H. (1954). *Motivation and personality*. New York: Harper & Row.

Masuda, M. (2001). Accounting for post-dissolution relationships. *Communication Studies*. Iowa city, IA, University of Iowa: 277.

Matsumoto, D. (1994). *Cultural influences on research methods and statistics*. Pacific Grove, CA: Brooks-Cole.

McCall, G. (1982). Becoming unrelated: the management of bond dissolution. In S.W. Duck (Ed.), *Personal relationships Dissolving Personal Relationships* 4: New York: Academic Press.

McCormick, N.B. (1994). *Sexual salvation: affirming women's sexual rights and pleasures*. Westport, CT: Praeger.

McCubbin, H.I., McCubbin, M.A., & Thompson, A.I. (1993). Resiliency in families: the role of family schema and appraisal in family adaptation to crises. In T.H. Brubaker (Ed.), *Family relations: challenges for the future* (pp. 153–77). Newbury Park, CA: Sage.

McDonald, G.W. (1977). Family power: reflection and direction. *Pacific Sociological Review, 20*, 607–21.

McDonald, G.W. (1980). Family power: the assessment of a decade of theory and research, 1970–1979. *Journal of Marriage and the Family, 42*, 941–54.

McDonald, R.D. (1962). The effect of reward–punishment and affiliation need on interpersonal attraction. Unpublished PhD thesis, University of Texas.

McFarland, C., & Miller, D.T. (1990). Judgements of self-other similarity: just like other people, only more so. *Personality and Social Psychology Bulletin, 16*, 475–84.

McKenna, K.Y.A., & Bargh, J.A. (2000). Plan 9 from cyberspace: the implications of the internet for personality and social psychology. *Personality and Social Psychology Review, 4*, 57–75.

Mechanic, D. (1978). *Medical sociology* (2nd edn). New York: Free Press.

Medora, N., & Woodward, J.C. (1982). Premarital sexual opinions of undergraduate students at a Midwestern university. *Adolescence, 17*, 213–24.

Mellen, S.L.W. (1981). *The evolution of love*. San Francisco: Freeman.

Mercer, G.W., & Kohn, P.M. (1979). Gender differences in the integration of conservatism, sex urge, and sexual behaviors among college students. *Journal of Sex Research, 15*, 129–42.

Merkle, E.R., & Richardson, R.A. (2000). Digital dating and virtual relating: conceptual computer mediated romantic relationships. *Family Relations, 49*, 187–92.

Michaels, J.W., Edwards, J.N., & Acock, A.C. (1984). Satisfaction in intimate relationships as a function of inequality, inequity, and outcomes. *Social Psychology Quarterly, 47*, 347–57.

Michener, H.A., & Suchner, R. (1972). Tactical use of social power. In J. Tedeschi (Ed.), *The social influence processes* (pp. 239–70). Chicago: Aldine.

Milardo, R. (1987). Changes in social networks of women and men following divorce: a review. *Journal of Family Issues, 8*, 78–96.

Milardo, R. (1988). Families and social networks: an overview of theory and methodology. In R. Milardo (Ed.), *Families and social networks* (pp. 13–47). Newbury Park, CA: Sage.

Milardo, R. (1989). Theoretical and methodological issues in the identification of the social networks of spouses. *Journal of Marriage and the Family, 51*, 165–74.

Milardo, R.M. (1992). Comparative methods for deliniating social networks. *Journal of Social and Personal Relationships, 9*, 447–461.

Milardo, R., & Wellman, B. (1992). The personal is social. *Journal of Social and Personal Relationships, 9*, 339–42.

Milardo, R., Johnson, M.P., & Huston, T. (1983). Developing close relationships. *Journal of Personality and Social Psychology, 44*, 964–76.

Miller, G.R., & Parks, M. (1982). Communication in dissolving relationships. In S.W. Duck (Ed.), *Personal relationships 4: dissolving personal relationships*. New York: Academic Press.

Miller, L.D., Berg, J.H., & Archer, R.L. (1983). Openers: individuals who elicit intimate self-disclosure. *Journal of Personality and Social Psychology, 44*, 1234–44.

Miller, T.E., & Clemente, P.C. (1997). *The 1997 American Internet User Survey: realities beyond the hype*. New York: Find/Svp, Inc. [On-line]. Available: http://www.findsvp.com/.

Montgomery, B.M. (1988). Quality communication in personal relationships. In S.W. Duck, D.F. Hay, S.E. Hobfoll, W. Ickes, & B. Montgomery (Eds.), *Handbook of personal relationships* (pp. 343–62). Chichester, UK: Wiley.

Moore, J.A. (1974). Relationship between loneliness and interpersonal relationships. *Canadian Counsellor, 8*, 84–9.

Moore, J.A. (1976). Loneliness: self-discrepancy and sociological variables. *Canadian Counsellor, 10*, 133–5.

Morin, S.F. (1977). Heterosexual bias in psychological research on lesbianism and male homosexuality. *American Psychologist, 32*, 629–38.

Morrow, G.D., & O'Sullivan, C. (1998). Romantic ideals as comparison levels: implications for satisfaction and commitment in romantic involvements. In V.C. deMunck (Ed.), *Romantic love and sexual behavior: perspectives from the social sciences* (pp. 171–99). Westport, CT: Praeger.

Morrow, G., Clark, E., & Brock, K. (1995). Individual and partner love styles: implications for the quality of romantic involvements. *Journal of Social and Personal Relationships, 12*, 363–87.

Mullins, L.C., Sheppard, H.L., & Andersson, L. (1988). A study of loneliness among a national sample of Swedish elderly. *Comprehensive Gerontology, 2*, 36–43.

Munro, B., & Adams, G.R. (1978). Love American style: a test of role structure theory on changes in attitudes toward love. *Human Relations, 31*, 215–28.

Murray, S.L., Holmes, J.G., & Griffin, D.W. (1996). The self-fulfilling nature of positive illusions in romantic relationships: love is not blind but prescient. *Journal of Personality and Social Psychology, 71*, 1155–80.

Myers, D. (1987). "Anonymity is part of the magic": individual manipulation of computer-mediated communication contexts. *Qualitative Sociology, 10*, 251–66.

Najera, E. (2000). *Attitudes and beliefs about love and sex in marriage*. Unpublished manuscript, Texas Tech University, Lubbock, TX.

Newcomb, T.M. (1956). The prediction of interpersonal attraction. *American Psychologist, 11*, 575–86.

Newcomb, T.M. (1961). *The acquaintance process*. New York: Holt, Rinehart & Winston.

Nisbett, R., & Ross, L. (1980). *Human inference: strategies and shortcomings of social judgment*. Englewood Cliffs, NJ: Prentice-Hall.

Noller, P., Feeney, J.A., Bonnell, D., & Callan, V.J. (1994). A longitudinal study of conflict in early marriage. *Journal of Social and Personal Relationships, 11*, 233–52.

Norton, R. (1983). Measuring marital quality: a critical look at the dependent variable. *Journal of Marriage and the Family, 45*, 141–51.

Nowak, A., & Lewenstein, M. (1994). Dynamical systems: a tool for social psychology? In R.R. Vallacher & A. Nowak (Eds.), *Dynamical systems in social psychology* (pp. 17–53). San Diego, CA: Academic Press.

Nowak, A., & Vallacher, R.R. (1998). *Dynamical social psychology*. New York: Guilford Press.

Øberg, P., Ruth, J.E., & Tornstam, L. (1987). Ensamhetsupplevelser hos de äldre. I: sociala förhållanden. *Gerontologia, 2*, 44–55.

O'Connor, P. (1998). Women's friendships in a post-modern world. In R. Adams & G. Allan (Eds.), *Placing friendship in context*. Cambridge, UK: Cambridge University Press.

Ogan, C. (1993). Listserver communication during the Gulf War: what kind of medium is the electronic bulletin board? *Journal of Broadcasting and Electronic Media, 37*, 177–96.

Oliker, S. (1989). *Best friends and marriage: exchange among women*. Berkeley, CA: University of California Press.

Oliker, S. (1998). The modernization of friendship: individualism, intimacy and gender in the nineteenth century. In R. Adams & G. Allan (Eds.), *Placing friendship in context*. Cambridge, UK: Cambridge University Press.

Oliver, M.B., & Sedikides, C. (1992). Effects of sexual permissiveness or desirability of partner as a function of low and high commitment to relationship. *Social Psychology Quarterly, 55*, 321–33.

Oliver, M.B., & Shibley Hyde, J. (1993). Gender differences in sexuality: a meta-analysis. *Psychological Bulletin, 114*, 29–51.

Ortony, A. (Ed.) (1979). *Metaphor and thought*. New York: Cambridge University Press.

Osgood, C.E., Suci, G.J., & Tannenbaum, P.H. (1957). *The measurement of meaning*. Urbana, IL: University of Illinois Press.

O'Sullivan, L.F. (1995). Less is more: the effects of sexual experience or judgements of men's and women's personality characteristics and relationship desirability. *Sex Roles, 33*, 159–81.

Owen, W. (1984). Interpretive themes in relational communication. *Quarterly Journal of Speech, 70*, 274–87.

Owen, W. (1985). Thematic metaphors in relational communication: a conceptual framework. *Western Journal of Speech Communication, 49*, 1–13.

Owen, W. (1990). Delimiting relational metaphors. *Communication Studies, 41*, 35–53.

Parker, S., & de Vries, B. (1993). Patterns of friendship for women and men in same- and cross-sex relationships. *Journal of Social and Personal Relationships, 10*, 617–26.

Parks, M.R. (1997). Communication networks and relationship life cycles. In S.W. Duck et al. (Eds.), *Handbook of personal relationships* (2nd edn, pp. 351–72). Chichester, UK: Wiley.

Parks, M.R., & Eggert, L.L. (1991). The role of social context in the dynamics of personal relationships. In W.H. Jones & D.W. Perlman (Eds.), *Advances in personal relationships* (Vol. 2, pp. 1–34). London: Kingsley.

Parks, M.R., & Floyd, K. (1996). Making friends in cyberspace. *Journal of Communication, 46*, 80–97.

Pearce, W.B., & Cronen, V.E. (1980). *Communication, action and meaning*. New York: Praeger.

Peplau, L.A. (1979). Power in dating relationships. In J. Freeman (Ed.), *Women: a feminist perspective* (2nd edn, pp. 106–21). Palo Alto, CA: Mayfield.

Peplau, L.A., & Perlman, D. (1979). Blueprint for a social psychological theory of loneliness. In M. Cook and G. Wilson (Eds.), *Love and attraction: proceedings of an international conference*. Oxford: Pergamon.

Peplau, L.A., & Perlman, D. (1982). Perspectives on loneliness. In L.A. Peplau and D. Perlman (Eds.), *Loneliness, a sourcebook of current theory, research and therapy*. New York: Wiley.

Peplau, L.A., Cochran, S., Rook, K., & Padesky, C. (1978). Women in love: attachment and autonomy in lesbian relationships. *Journal of Social Issues, 34(3)*, 7–27.

Pepper, S.C. (1942). *World hypotheses*. Berkeley, CA: University of California Press.

Perlman, D., & Peplau, L.A. (1981). Toward a social psychology of loneliness. In S.W. Duck & R. Gilmore (Eds.), *Personal relationships in disorder. Vol. 3: Personal relationships*. London: Academic Press.

Perlman, D., Gerson, A.C., & Spinner, B. (1978). Loneliness among senior citizens: an empirical report. *Essence, 2*, 239–48.

Perras, M., & Lustig, M. (1982, February). The effects of intimacy level and intent to disengage on the selection of relationship disengagement strategies. Paper presented to WSCA Convention.

Perrin, F.A.C. (1921). Physical attractiveness and repulsions. *Journal of Experimental Psychology, 4*, 203–17.

Pfeiffer, S.M., & Wong, P.T.P. (1989). Multidimensional jealousy. *Journal of Social and Personal Relationships, 6*, 181–96.

Pinquart, M. (2003). Loneliness in married, widowed, divorced, and never-married older adults. *Journal of Personal and Social Relationships, 20*, 31–53.

Planalp, S.K. (1987). Interplay between relational knowledge and events. In R. Burnett, P. McGhee, & D. Clark (Eds.), *Accounting for relationships: explanation, representation and knowledge*. London: Methuen.

Planalp, S.K., & Benson, A. (1992). Friends' and acquaintances' conversations 1: perceived differences. *Journal of Social and Personal Relationships, 9*, 483–506.

Pool, I., & Kochen, M. (1989). Contacts and Influence. In M. Kochen (Ed.), *The small world* (pp. 3–51). Norwood, NJ: Ablex.

Powers, W.G., & Lowery, D.N. (1980). Basic communication fidelity: a fundamental approach. In R.N. Bostrom (Ed.), *Competence in communication: a multidisciplinary approach*. Beverly Hills, CA: Sage.

Putney, S., & Putney, G.J. (1964). *The adjusted American*. New York: Harper & Row.

Quinn, N. (1987). Convergent evidence for a cultural model of American marriage. In D. Holland & N. Quinn (Eds.), *Cultural models in language & thought*. New York: Cambridge University Press.

Rafaeli, S., & LaRose, R.J. (1993). Electronic bulletin boards and "public goods" explanations of collaborative mass media. *Communication Research, 20*, 277–97.

Rands, M. (1988). Changes in social networks following marital separation and divorce. In R. Milardo (Ed.), *Families and Social Networks* (pp. 127–46). Newbury Park, CA: Sage.

Rapkin, B.D., & Stein, C.H. (1989). Defining personal networks. *American Journal of Community Psychology, 17*, 259–67.

Rawlins, W.K. (1982). Cross-sex friendship and the communicative management of sex-role expectations. *Communication Quarterly, 30*, 343–52.

Regan, P.C., & Berscheid, E. (1996). Beliefs about the state, goals, and objects of sexual desire. *Journal of Sexual and Marital Therapy, 22*, 110–20.

Reik, T. (1944). *A psychologist looks at love*. New York: Farrar & Rinehart.

Reis, H.T., & Shaver, P.R. (1988). Intimacy as an interpersonal process. In S.W. Duck, D.F. Hay, S.E. Hobfoll, W. Ickes, & B. Montgomery (Eds.), *Handbook of personal relationships* (pp. 367–90). Chichester, UK: Wiley.

Reis, H.T., Wheeler, L., Spiegel, N., Kernis, M.H., Nezlek, J., & Perri, M. (1982). Physical attractiveness in social interaction: II. Why does appearance affect social experience? *Journal of Personality and Social Psychology, 43*, 979–96.

Reiss, I.L. (1960). *Premarital sexual standards in America*. New York: Free Press.

Reiss, I.L. (1967). *The social context of premarital sexual permissiveness*. New York: Holt, Rinehart & Winston.

Rheingold, H. (1993). *The virtual community: homesteading on the electronic frontier.* Reading, MA: Addison-Wesley.

Rice, R.E. (1987). Computer-mediated communication and organizational innovation. *Journal of Communication, 37,* 65–94.

Roberts, L.D., Smith, L.M., & Pollock, C. (1996a, October). *Social interaction in MOOs: constraints and opportunities of a text-based virtual environment for interpersonal communication.* Paper presented at Virtual Informational Digital Workshop, The Centre for Research in Culture and Communication, Murdoch University, Perth, Western Australia.

Roberts, L.D., Smith, L.M., & Pollock, C. (1996b, November). Exploring virtuality: tele-presence in text-based virtual environments. Paper presented at the Cybermind Conference, Curtin University of Technology, Perth, Western Australia. [On-line]. Available: http://psych.curtin.edu.au/people/Roberts/Telep.htm.

Robins, E. (1989, November). Predictors of personal commitment in college women's dating relationships. Paper presented at the annual meeting of the National Council on Family Relations, New Orleans.

Robinson, L.C., & Blanton, P.W. (1993). Marital strengths in enduring marriages. *Family Relations, 42,* 38–45.

Rollie, S., & Duck, S.W. (in press). Stage theories of marital breakdown. *Handbook of divorce and dissolution of romantic relationships.* J.H. Harvey & M. Fine (Eds.), Mahwah, NJ: Lawrence Erlbaum.

Roloff, M.E., & Colvin, D.H. (1994). When partners transgress: maintaining violated relationships. In D.J. Canary & L. Stafford (Eds.), *Communication and relational maintenance* (pp. 23–43). San Diego, CA: Academic Press.

Rook, K.S. (1992). Detrimental aspects of social relationships. In H.O. Veiel & U. Baumann (Eds.), *The meaning and measurement of social support* (pp. 157–69). New York: Hemisphere.

Rosenbaum, M.E. (1986). On the nondevelopment of relationships. *Journal of Personality and Social Psychology, 51,* 1156–66.

Ross, L., Greene, D., & House, P. (1977). The false consensus effect: an egocentric bias in social perception and attribution processes. *Journal of Experimental Social Psychology, 13,* 279–301.

Rubenstein, C.H., & Shaver, P. (1982). The experience of loneliness. In L.A. Peplau and D. Perlman (Eds.), *Loneliness, a sourcebook of current theory, research and therapy.* New York: Wiley.

Rubenstein, C.H., Shaver, P., & Peplau, L.A. (1979). Loneliness. *Human Nature, 2,* 59–65.

Rubin, Z., Hill, C.T., Peplau, L.A., & Dunkel-Schetter, C. (1980). Self-disclosure in dating couples: sex roles and the ethic of openness. *Journal of Marriage and the Family, 42,* 305–17.

Rubin, Z., Peplau, L.A., & Hill, C.T. (1981). Loving and leaving: sex differences in romantic attachments. *Sex Roles, 7,* 821–35.

Rusbult, C.E. (1983). A longitudinal test of the investment model: the development (and deterioration) of satisfaction and commitment in heterosexual involvement. *Journal of Personality and Social Psychology, 45,* 101–17.

Rusbult, C.E. (1987). Responses to dissatisfaction in close relationships: the exit–voice–loyalty–neglect model. In D. Perlman & S.W. Duck (Eds.), *Intimate relationships: development, dynamics and deterioration.* Beverly Hills, CA: Sage.

Rusbult, C.E., Drigotas, S.M., & Verette, J. (1994). The investment model: an interdependence analysis of commitment processes and relationship maintenance phenomena. In D.J. Canary & L. Stafford (Eds.), *Communication and relational maintenance* (pp. 115–40). San Diego, CA: Academic Press.

Rusbult, C.E., Johnson, D.J., & Morrow, G.D. (1986). Predicting satisfaction and commitment in adult romantic relationships: an assessment of the generalizability of the investment model. *Social Psychology Quarterly, 49,* 81–89.

Rusbult, C.E., Onizuka, R.K., & Lipkus, I. (1993). What do we really want? Mental models of ideal romantic involvement explored through multidimensional scaling. *Journal of Experimental Social Psychology, 29*, 493–527.

Ruvolo, A.P., & Veroff, J. (1997). For better or for worse: real-ideal discrepancies and the marital well-being of newlyweds. *Journal of Social and Personal Relationships, 14*, 223–42.

Sabatelli, R.M., & Cecil-Pigo, E.F. (1985). Relational interdependence and commitment in marriage. *Journal of Marriage and the Family, 47*, 931–7.

Safilios-Rothschild, C. (1970). The study of family power structure: a review 1960–1969. *Journal of Marriage and the Family, 32*, 539–52.

Safilios-Rothschild, C. (1977). *Love, sex, and sex roles*. Englewood Cliffs, NJ: Prentice-Hall.

Saghir, M.T., & Robins, E. (1973). *Male and female homosexuality*. Baltimore: Williams & Wilkins.

Sagrestano, L.M. (1992). Power strategies in interpersonal relationships: the effects of expertise and sex. *Psychology of Women Quarterly, 16*, 481–95.

Sagrestano, L.M., Heavey, C.L., & Christensen, A. (1998). Theoretical approaches to understanding sex differences and similarities in conflict behavior. In D.J. Canary & K. Dindia (Eds.), *Sex differences and similarities in communication: critical essays and empirical investigations of sex and sex in interaction* (pp. 287–302). Mahwah, NJ: Erlbaum.

Salovey, P. (Ed.). (1991). *The psychology of jealousy and envy*. New York: Guilford Press.

Schachter, S. (1951). Deviation, rejection, and communication. *Journal of Abnormal and Social Psychology, 46*, 190–207.

Schachter, S., & Singer, J.E. (1962). Cognitive, social and physiological determinants of emotional states. *Psychological Review, 69*, 379–99.

Schiano, D.J. (1997). Convergent methodologies in cyber-psychology: a case study. *Behavior Research Methods, Instruments and Computers, 29*, 270–3.

Schultz, N.R., Jr, & Moore, D. (1984). Loneliness: correlates, attributions, and coping among older adults. *Personality and Social Psychology Bulletin, 10*, 67–77.

Schwartz, J.C., & Shaver, P. (1987). Emotions and emotion knowledge in interpersonal relations. In W.H. Jones & D. Perlman (Eds.), *Advances in personal relationships*. Greenwich, CT: JAI Press.

Sermat, V. (1980). Some situational and personality correlates of loneliness. In J. Hartog, J.R. Andy, & Y.A. Cohen (Eds.), *The anatomy of loneliness*. New York: IUP.

Shaver, P.R., & Hazan, C. (1994). Attachment. In A.L. Weber & J.H. Harvey (Eds.), *Perspectives on close relationships* (pp. 110–30). Boston, MA: Allyn & Bacon.

Sheets, V.L., & Wolfe, M.D. (2001). Sexual jealousy in heterosexuals, lesbians, and gays. *Sex Roles: A Journal of Research, 44*, 255–76.

Shimonoff, S.B. (1980). *Communication rules: theory and research*. Beverly Hills, CA: Sage.

Sigman, S.J. (1991). Handling the discontinuous aspects of continuing social relationships: toward research of the persistence of social forms. *Communication Theory, 1*, 106–27.

Sik, E. (1988). Reciprocal exchange of labour in Hungary. In R. Pahl (Ed.), *On work* (pp. 527–47). Oxford: Blackwell.

Sillars, A.L. (1985). Interpersonal perception in relationships. In W. Ickes (Ed.), *Compatible and incompatible relationships*. New York: Springer.

Sillars, A.L. (1991). Behavioral observation. In B.M. Montgomery & S.W. Duck (Eds.), *Studying interpersonal interaction* (pp. 197–218). New York: Guilford Press.

Sillars, A.L., & Scott, M.D. (1983). Interpersonal perception between intimates: an integrative review. *Human Communication Research, 10*, 153–76.

Silver, A. (1990). Friendship in commercial society: eighteenth century social theory and modern sociology. *American Journal of Sociology, 95*, 1474–504.

Simpson, J.A., Campbell, G., & Berscheid, E. (1986). The association between romantic love and marriage: Kephart (1967) twice revisited. *Personality and Social Psychology Bulletin, 12*, 363–72.

Sloan, W.W., Jr, & Solano, C.H. (1984). The conversational styles of lonely males with strangers and roommates. *Personality and Social Psychology Bulletin, 10*, 293–301.

Slouka, M. (1995). *War of the worlds: cyberspace and the high-tech assault on reality.* New York: Basic Books.

Smeaton, G., Byrne, D., & Murnen, S.K. (1989). The Revulsion hypothesis revisited: similarity irrelevance or dissimilarity bias? *Journal of Personality and Social Psychology, 56*, 54–9.

Smith, A.J. (1957). Similarity of values and its relation to acceptance and the projection of similarity. *Journal of Psychology, 43*, 251–60.

Smith, A.J. (1958). Perceived similarity and the projection of similarity: the influence of valence. *Journal of Abnormal and Social Psychology, 57*, 376–9.

Smith, D.A., Vivian. D., & O'Leary, K.D. (1991). The misnomer proposition: a critical reappraisal of the longitudinal status of "negativity" in marital communication. *Behavioral Assessment, 13*, 7–24.

Smith, E.R., Byrne, D., Becker, M.A., & Przybyla, D.P.J. (1993). Sexual attitudes of males and females as predictors of interpersonal attraction and marital compatibility. *Journal of Applied Social Psychology, 23*, 1011–34.

Solano, C.H., Batten, P.G., & Parish, E.A. (1982). Loneliness and patterns of self-disclosure. *Journal of Personality and Social Psychology, 43*, 524–31.

Spanier, G., & Lewis, R. (1980) Marital quality: a review of research in the seventies. *Journal of Marriage and the Family, 42*, 825–39.

Spence, K.W. (1944). The nature of theory construction in contemporary psychology. *Psychological Review, 51*, 47–68.

Spitzberg, B.H. (1981). Loneliness and communication apprehension. Paper presented at the Western Speech Communication Association Conference, San Jose, CA.

Spitzberg, B.H., & Cupach, W.R. (1983). The relational competence construct: development and validation. Paper presented at the Speech Communication Association Conference, Washington, DC.

Spitzberg, B.H., & Cupach, W.R. (1984a). *Interpersonal communication competence.* Beverly Hills, CA: Sage.

Spitzberg, B.H., & Cupach, W. R. (1984b). Conversational skills and locus of perception. Paper presented at the Speech Communication Association Conference, Chicago.

Spitzberg, B.H., & Cupach, W.R. (1998). *The dark side of close relationships.* Mahwah, NJ: Erlbaum.

Spreadbury, C.L. (1982). The "permissiveness with affection" norm and the labeling of deviants. *Personnel and Guidance Journal, 60*, 280–2.

Sprecher, S. (1989). Premarital sexual standards for different categories of individuals. *Journal of Sex Research, 26*, 232–49.

Sprecher, S., & Duck, S.W. (1993). Sweet talk: the role of communication in consolidating relationship. *Personality and Social Psychology Bulletin, 20*, 391–400.

Sprecher, S., & McKinney, K. (1987). Barriers in the initiation of intimate heterosexual relationships and strategies for intervention. *Journal of Social Work and Human Sexuality, 5*, 97–110.

Sprecher, S., & McKinney, K. (1993). *Sexuality.* Newbury Park, CA: Sage.

Sprecher, S., & Metts, S. (1989). Development of the "Romantic Beliefs Scale" and examination of the effects of gender and gender-role orientation. *Journal of Social and Personal Relationships, 6*, 387–411.

Sprecher, S., McKinney, K., & Orbuch, T.L. (1987). Has the double standard disappeared? An experimental test. *Social Psychology Quarterly, 50*, 24–31.

Sprecher, S., McKinney, K., & Orbuch, T.L. (1991). The effects of current sexual behavior on friendship, dating, and marriage desirability. *Journal of Sex Research, 28*, 387–408.

Sprecher, S., Regan, P.C., McKinney, K., Maxwell, K., & Wazienski, R. (1997). Preferred level of sexual experience in a date or mate: the merger of two methodologies. *Journal of Sex Research, 34*, 327–37.

Sproull, L., & Kiesler, S. (1991). *Connections: new ways of working in the networked organization*. Cambridge, MA: MIT Press.

Stack, S. (1998). Marriage, family, and loneliness: a cross-national study. *Sociological Perspectives, 41*, 415–32.

Stafford, L., & Canary, D.J. (1991). Maintenance strategies and romantic relationship type, gender, and relational characteristics. *Journal of Social and Personal Relationships, 8*, 217–42.

Stafford, L., & Dainton, M. (1994). The dark side of "normal" family interaction. In W.R. Cupach & B.H. Spitzberg (Eds.), *The dark side of interpersonal communication* (pp. 259–80). Hillsdale, NJ: Erlbaum.

Stamp, G. (1994). The appropriation of the parental role through communication during the transition to parenthood. *Communication Monographs, 61*, 89–112.

Sternberg, R.J. (1986). The triangular theory of love. *Psychological Review, 8*, 119–35.

Sternberg, R.J., & Barnes, M.L. (1985). Real and ideal others in romantic relationships: is four a crowd? *Journal of Personality and Social Psychology, 49*, 1586–608.

Sunnafrank, M. (1984). A communication-based perspective on attitude similarity and interpersonal attraction in early acquaintance. *Communication Monographs, 51*, 372–80.

Sunnafrank, M. (1992). On debunking the attitude similarity myth. *Communication Monographs, 59*, 164–79.

Sunnafrank, M., & Miller, G.R. (1981). The role of initial conversations in determining attraction to similar and dissimilar strangers. *Human Communication Research, 8*, 16–25.

Surra, C.A. (1990). Research and theory on mate selection and premarital relationships in the 1980s. *Journal of Marriage and the Family, 52*, 844–65.

Surra, C.A., & Hughes, D.K. (1997). Commitment processes in accounts of the development of premarital relationships. *Journal of Marriage and the Family, 59*, 5–21.

Surra, C.A., & Milardo, R. (1991). The social psychological context of developing relationships. In W.H. Jones & D. Perlman (Eds.), *Advances in Personal Relationships* (Vol. 3, pp. 1–36). London: Kingsley.

Surra, C.A., Arizzi, P., & Asmussen, L. (1988). The association between reasons for commitment and the development and outcome of marital relationships. *Journal of Social and Personal Relationships, 5*, 47–63.

Symons, D. (1979). *The evolution of human sexuality*. New York: Oxford University Press.

Tannen, D. (1995). *You just don't understand: women and men in conversation*. New York: Ballantine.

Tennov, D. (1979). *Love and limerance*. New York: Stein and Day.

Tesser, A., & Achee, J. (1994). Aggression, love, conformity, and other social psychological catastrophes. In R.R. Vallacher & A. Nowak (Eds.), *Dynamical systems in social psychology* (pp. 95–109). San Diego, CA: Academic Press.

Thelen, E. (1990). Dynamical systems and the generation of individual differences. In J. Colombo & J. Fagen (Eds.), *Individual differences in infancy: reliability, stability, prediction* (pp. 19–43). Hillsdale, NJ: Erlbaum.

Thelen, E., & Ulrich, B.D. (1991). Hidden skills: a dynamic systems analysis of treadmill stepping during the first year. *Monographs of the Society for Research in Child Development*, Serial No. 223, Vol. 56.

Thibaut, J.W., & Kelley, H.H. (1959). *The Social Psychology of Groups*. New York: Wiley.

Thompson, L., & Spanier, G. (1983). The end of marriage and acceptance of marital termination. *Journal of Marriage and the Family, 45*, 103–13.

Thorsen, K. (1988). *Ensomhet som opplevelse og utfordring. En studie av ensomhet blant eldre*. Oslo: Norsk Gerontologisk Institutt.

Thorsen, K. (1990). *Alene og ensom, sammen og lykkelig? Ensomhet i ulike aldersgrupper*. Oslo: Norsk Gerontologisk Institutt.

Tinsley, H.E., & Weiss, D.J. (1975). Interrater reliability and agreement of subjective judgments. *Journal of Counseling Psychology, 22*, 358–76.

Tolhuizen, J.H. (1989). Communication strategies for intensifying dating relationships: identification, use and structure. *Journal of Social and Personal Relationships, 6,* 413–34.

Tornstam, L. (1988). *Ensamhetens ansikten: En studie av ensamhetsupplevelser hos svenskar 1580 ar.* Uppsala: Sociologiska institutionen.

Tornstam, L. (1990). Dimensions of loneliness. *Aging: Clinical and Experimental Research, 2,* 259–65.

Trickett, E.J., & Buchanan, R.M. (1997). The role of personal relationships in transitions: contributions of an ecological perspective. In S.W. Duck (Ed.), *Handbook of personal relationships* (2nd edn, pp. 575–93). New York: Wiley.

Trivers, R.L. (1972). Parental investment and sexual selection. In B. Campbell (Ed.), *Sexual selection and the descent of man* (pp. 136–79). Chicago: Aldine.

Trivers, R.L. (1985). *Social evolution.* Menlo Park, CA: Benjamin/Cummings.

Turkle, S. (1995). *Life on the screen: identity in the age of the internet.* New York: Simon & Schuster.

Ulin, M., & Milardo, R. (1992, July). Network interdependence and lesbian relationships. Paper presented at the VIth International Conference on Personal Relationships, Orono, ME.

van Sonderen, E., Ormel, J., Brilman, E., & van den Heuvell, C. (1990). Personal network delineation. In C.P.M. Knipscheer & T.C. Antonucci (Eds.), *Social network research* (pp. 101–20). Amsterdam: Swets' Zeitlinger.

VanderVoort, L.A., & Duck, S.W. (2004). In appropriate relationships and out of them: the social paradoxes of normative and non-normative relational forms. In. G.A. Allan, J. Duncombe, K. Harrison, & D. Marsden (Eds.), *The State of Affairs.* Mahwah, NJ: Erlbaum.

Vangelisti, A.L., & Banski, M.A. (1993). Couples' debriefing conversations: the impact of gender, occupation, and demographic characteristics. *Family Relations, 42,* 149–57.

van Tilburg, T. (1992). Support networks before and after retirement. *Journal of Personal and Social Relationships, 9,* 385–409.

Vaughan, D. (1986). *Uncoupling: turning points in intimate relationships.* New York: Oxford University Press.

Veroff, J., Douvan, E., & Hatchett. S. (1985). *The early stages of marriage.* NIMH grant proposal, MH 41253-01.

Veroff, J., Young, A.M., & Coon, H.M. (1997). The early years of marriage. In S.W. Duck (Ed.), *Handbook of personal relationships* (2nd edn, pp. 431–50). New York: Wiley.

Vogel, D.L., Wester, S.R., Heesacker, M., & Madon, S. (2003). Confirming sex stereotypes: a social role perspective. *Sex Roles, 48,* 519–28.

Vogel, D.L., Wester, S.R., & Heesacker, M. (1999). Dating relationships and the demand/withdraw pattern of communication. *Sex Roles, 41,* 297–306.

Waller, W.W. (1937). The rating and dating complex. *American Sociological Review, 2,* 727–34.

Waller, W.W., & Hill, R. (1951). *The family, a dynamic interpretation.* New York: Dryden Press.

Walsh, R., Ganza, W., & Finefield, T. (1983). A fifteen year study about sexual permissiveness. Paper presented at the Midwest Sociological Society, April.

Walster [Hatfield], E., Walster, G.W., & Berscheid, E. (1978). *Equity: theory and research.* Boston, MA: Allyn & Bacon.

Walster, E., Aronson, V., Abrahams, D., & Rottmann, L. (1966). The importance of physical attractiveness in dating behavior. *Journal of Personality and Social Psychology, 4,* 508–516.

Walther, J.B. (1992). Interpersonal effects in computer-mediated interaction: a relational perspective. *Communication Research, 19,* 52–90.

Walther, J.B. (1995, 25–29 May). Computer-mediated communication: Impersonal, interpersonal, and hyperpersonal interaction. Paper presented at the annual convention of the International Communication Association, Albuquerque, NM.

Walther, J.B. (1996). Computer-mediated communication: impersonal, interpersonal and hyperpersonal interaction. *Communication Research, 23,* 3–43.

Walther, J.B., Anderson, J.F., & Park, D.W. (1994). Interpersonal effects in computer-mediated interaction: a meta-analysis of social and antisocial communication. *Communication Research, 21,* 460–87.

Wampler, K., & Sprenkle, D. (1980). The Minnesota couple communication program: a follow-up study. *Journal of Marriage and the Family*, *25*, 577–84.

Ward, M. (1995). Butterflies and bifurcations: can chaos theory contribute to our understanding of family systems? *Journal of Marriage and the Family*, *57*, 629–38.

Weiderman, M.W. (1993). Evolved gender differences in mate preferences: evidence from personal advertisements. *Ethology and Sociobiology*, *14*, 331–52.

Weigel, D.J., & Ballard-Reisch, D.D. (1999). All marriages are not maintained equally: marital type, marital quality, and the use of maintenance behaviors. *Personal Relationships*, *6*, 291–303.

Weinberg, M.S., Lottes, I.L., & Shaver, F.M. (1995). Swedish or American heterosexual youth: who is more permissive? *Archives of Sexual Behavior*, *26*, 409–37.

Weis, D.L., Slosnerick, M., Cate, R., & Sollie, D.L. (1986). A survey instrument for assessing the cognitive association of sex, love, and marriage. *Journal of Sex Research*, *32*, 206–20.

Weiss, R.S. (1976). The emotional impact of marital separation. *Journal of Social Issues*, *2*, 135–45.

Wellman, B. (1979). The community question: the intimate networks of East Yorkers. *American Journal of Sociology*, *84*, 1201–31.

Wellman, B., Carrington, P., & Hall, A. (1988). Networks as personal communities. In B. Wellman & S. Berkowitz (Eds.), *Social structures: a network approach* (pp. 130–84). Cambridge, UK: Cambridge University Press.

Wellman, B., & Wellman, B. (1992). Domestic affairs and network relations. *Journal of Social and Personal Relationships*, *9*, 433–46.

Wellman, B., & Wortley, S. (1990). Different strokes by different folks: community ties and social support. *American Journal of Sociology*, *93*, 558–88.

Werking, K.J. (1997). Cross-sex friendship research as ideological practice. In S.W. Duck (Ed.), *Handbook of personal relationships* (2nd edn, pp. 391–410). Chichester, UK: Wiley.

Werner, C., Brown, B., Altman, I., & Staples, B. (1992). Close relationships in their physical and social context: A transactional perspective. *Journal of Social and Personal Relationships*, *9*, 411–31.

Wheeler, L., & Nezlek, J. (1977). Sex difference in social participation. *Journal of Personality and Social Psychology*, *35*, 742–54.

White, G.L. (1977). Inequality of emotional involvement, power, and jealousy in romantic couples. Paper presented at the 85th Annual Convention of the American Psychological Association.

White, J. (1985). Perceived similarity and understanding in married couples. *Journal of Social and Personal Relationships*, *2*, 45–57.

White, L.K. (1983). Determinants of spousal interaction: marital structure of marital happiness. *Journal of Marriage and the Family*, *45*, 511–19.

Wiederman, M.W., & Allgeier, E.R. (1993). Gender differences in sexual jealousy: adaptationist or social learning explanation? *Ethology and Sociobiology*, *14*, 115–40.

Wilkins, H. (1991). Computer talk: long-distance conversations by computer. *Written Communication*, *8*, 56–78.

Wilmot, W.W., & Carbaugh D. (1983). Long-distance lovers: predicting the dissolution of their relationships. Unpublished.

Wilmot, W.W., Carbaugh, D.A. & Baxter, L.A. (1985). Communicative strategies used to terminate romantic relationships. *Western Journal of Speech Communication*, *49*, 204–16.

Wine, J.D., & Smye, M.D. (1981). *Social competence*. New York: Guilford Press.

Winter, D.G. (1973). *The power motive*. New York: Free Press.

Wood, J.T. (1982). Communication and relational culture: bases for the study of human relationships. *Communication Quarterly*, *30*, 75–85.

Wood, J.T. (1995). *Relational Communication: Continuity and Change in Personal Relationships*. Belmont, CA: Wadsworth.

Wood, J.T. (1997). *Gendered lives: communication, gender, and culture.* Belmont, CA: Wadsworth.

Wood, L.A. (1979). Social–psychological correlates of loneliness: a preliminary report. Paper presented at the UCLA Conference on Loneliness, Los Angeles.

Wright, P.H. (1988). Interpreting research on gender differences in friendships: a case for moderation and a plea for caution. *Journal of Social and Personal Relationships, 5,* 367–73.

Wynne, L.C. (1984). The epigenesis of relational systems: a model for understanding family development. *Family Process, 23,* 297–318.

Yerby, J., Buerkel-Rothfuss, N., & Bochner, A.P. (1995). *Understanding family communication.* Scottsdale, AZ: Gorsuch Scarisbrick.

Young, J. (1979a). A cognitive–behavioral approach to the treatment of loneliness. Paper presented at the UCLA Conference on Loneliness, Los Angeles.

Young, J. (1979b). An instrument for measuring loneliness. Paper presented at the American Psychological Association Conference.

Young, T.R. (1991). Chaos theory and symbolic interaction theory: poetics for the postmodern sociologist. *Symbolic Interaction, 14,* 321–34.

Zakon, R.H. (1996). *Hobbes' internet timeline.* [On-line]. Available: http://info.isoc.org/guest/zakon/Internet/History/HIT.html.

Zelnik, M., & Kanter, J.F. (1980). Sexual activity, contraceptive use, and pregnancy among metropolitan teenagers: 1971–1979. *Family Planning Perspectives, 12,* 230–8.

Index of First and Second Authors

Subject Index